45.00

D0934100

Observing Bioethics

Middlesex County College
Library
Edison. NJ 08818

OBSERVING BIOETHICS

RENÉE C. FOX and JUDITH P. SWAZEY

with the assistance of Judith C. Watkins

OXFORD
UNIVERSITY PRESS

2008

OXFORD
UNIVERSITY PRESS

Oxford University Press, Inc., publishes works that further
Oxford University's objective of excellence
in research, scholarship, and education.

Oxford   New York
Auckland   Cape Town   Dar es Salaam   Hong Kong   Karachi
Kuala Lumpur   Madrid   Melbourne   Mexico City   Nairobi
New Delhi   Shanghai   Taipei   Toronto

With offices in
Argentina   Austria   Brazil   Chile   Czech Republic   France   Greece
Guatemala   Hungary   Italy   Japan   Poland   Portugal   Singapore
South Korea   Switzerland   Thailand   Turkey   Ukraine   Vietnam

Copyright © 2008 by Oxford University Press, Inc.

Published by Oxford University Press, Inc.
198 Madison Avenue, New York, New York 10016

www.oup.com

Oxford is a registered trademark of Oxford University Press

All rights reserved. No part of this publication may be reproduced,
stored in a retrieval system, or transmitted, in any form or by any means,
electronic, mechanical, photocopying, recording, or otherwise,
without the prior permission of Oxford University Press.

Library of Congress Cataloging-in-Publication Data
Fox, Renée C. (Renée Claire), 1928–
Observing bioethics / Renée C. Fox and Judith P. Swazey.
p.cm.
Includes bibliographical references and index.
ISBN 978-0-19-536555-9
1. Medical ethics—United States—History.   2. Bioethics—United States—History.
I. Swazey, Judith P.   II. Title.
[DNLM: 1. Bioethics—history—United States. 2. History, 20th Century—United States.
3. Sociology—United States. WB 60 F793o 2008]
R724.F62 2008
174.2—dc22   2007042347

1 3 5 7 9 8 6 4 2

Printed in the United States of America
on acid-free paper

In memory of Willy, who understood and encouraged our work and who still accompanies us, and to Beth, Woody, and Jeff for their caring support of "the team of two"

Acknowledgments

Throughout the course of researching and writing this book, and the years of our involvement in bioethics that preceded it, we have received invaluable help from many sources. We extend our thanks to all those whom we interviewed, and to the members of our advisory committee, for our conversations with them, for the various primary and secondary source documents they shared with us, and for their encouragement of our project.

Among the many people whose assistance and encouragement helped us to complete our work, we are especially indebted to the following individuals: Rachelle Hollander, our program officer at the National Science Foundation; Simone Bateman and also Isabelle Baszanger for their many contributions to chapter 9, "Studying Bioethics in France," including the references and documents that they provided, their insightful observations about French society, and their several, detailed reviews of the chapter; Farhat Moazam and Aamir Jaffrey of the Centre for Bioethics and Culture in Karachi, Pakistan, for the materials they sent us on the history, cultural context, and evolution of bioethics and their Centre in Pakistan, and for Dr. Moazam's careful reviews of the drafts of chapter 10, "The Development of Bioethics in the Islamic Republic of Pakistan"; Daniel Callahan and Leon Kass for their thoughtful reviews and comments on chapter 11, "The Coming of the Culture Wars to American Bioethics"; LeRoy Walters, for arranging to have our interviews deposited at the National Reference Center for Bioethics Literature/Kennedy Institute of Ethics Library, along with Doris Goldstein,

director of library and information services at the Kennedy Institute, and Anita
Nolan, systems librarian and archivist, for their work in the deposition process
and for information they provided about the history of the Institute; and anthro-
pologist/bioethicist Pamela Sankar, who resolved our struggle to find a title for
our book by suggesting *Observing Bioethics.*

We are indebted to The Acadia Institute project staff for their many contributions: to Carla M. Messikomer, the project's senior associate, who participated
in the interviews and in the initial discussions of the study's themes; Judith C.
Watkins, our research associate, for her research and analysis of media coverage
of "Dolly," her examination of the research with human subjects literature for a
chapter that we later decided not to include in the book, her maintenance of the
project bibliography, her scrupulous review of the manuscript for citations and
references, her work on obtaining permissions for quotations, and for undertaking
the book's index; Vicki (Leeman) Hall, our administrative assistant par excellence; and Liane N. Peach, Acadia's business manager, for dealing with the financial aspects of project funding.

A substantial portion of our research and the initial phase of our writing were
made possible by grants from the National Science Foundation's Program on
Societal Dimensions of Engineering, Science, and Technology (SBR–9710570)
for The Acadia Institute Project on Bioethics in American Society, the Greenwall
Foundation, and the National Library of Medicine (RO1 LM 06893). Additionally, travel support was partially defrayed for two trips made by JPS to work on
the book with RCF in Philadelphia by funds from the latter's Andrew W. Mellon
Emeritus Fellowship. The opinions in this book are the authors', and do not reflect
any views of the funders.

Finally, we gratefully acknowledge permission to quote materials from the following sources:

Personal communications to the authors from Simone Bateman, Isabelle
Baszanger, Solomon R. Benatar, Daniel Callahan, Eric Goemare, James Gustafson,
Aamir Jafarey, Leon Kass, Ruth Macklin, Farhat Moazam, William LaFleur, and
Daniel Wikler.

British Medical Journal, for R. Macklin. 2003. Dignity is a useless concept
[editorial]. *British Medical Journal* 237 (Dec. 20): 1419–1420.

Cambridge University Press, for D. Callahan. 2005. Bioethics and the culture
wars. *Cambridge Quarterly of Healthcare Ethics* 4 (4): 424–431. Reprinted with
the permission of Cambridge University Press.

Center for American Progress, for Is there an ethicist in the house? Challenges
for a progressive bioethics, Oct. 3, 2005, symposium transcript; Bioethics and
politics: Past, present, and future, Apr. 21, 2006, symposium transcript.

J. R. Davis, R. De Vries, J. Evans. 2005. The intersection of sociology and bioethics, *Footnotes* (The American Sociological Association) May/June: 21; copyright by the authors.

The Hastings Center, for the following articles in *The Hastings Center Report*:

D. Callahan. 1984. Autonomy: A moral good, not a moral obsession 14 (5): 40–42.
D. Callahan. 1996. Bioethics, our crowd, and ideology 26 (6): 3–4.
J. Katz. 1993. Ethics and clinical research revisited 23 (5): 31–39.
R. Macklin. 2006. The new conservatives in bioethics: Who they are and what do they seek? 36 (1): 34–43.

The Johns Hopkins University Press, for permission to reprint material from the following papers in the *Kennedy Institute of Ethics Journal*, © The Johns Hopkins University Press:

T. Beauchamp. 2003. A defense of the common morality 13 (3): 259–274.
L. Kass. 2005. Reflections on public bioethics: A view from the trenches 15 (3): 221–250.
R. Macklin. 1998. Ethical relativism in a multicultural society 8 (1): 1–22.
W. Reich. 1999. The "wider view": André Hellegers' passionate, integrating intellect and the creation of bioethics 9 (1): 25–51.

Medical Humanities Review, for T. Chambers. 1998. Retrodiction and the histories of bioethics. *Medical Humanities Review* 12 (1): 9–22.

University of Chicago Press, for C. Geertz. 1965. The impact of the concept of culture on the conception of man. In *New views of the nature of man*, ed. J. R. Platt, 93–118. Chicago and London: University of Chicago Press (reprinted in C. Geertz, 1973. *The interpretation of cultures: Selected essays*. New York: Basic Books).

Contents

Observing Bioethics

Introduction
The "Team of Two": Observing Bioethics

This book is written from the perspective of two social scientists—one a sociologist (RCF), the other an historian[1] (JPS)—whose research, writing, and teaching have been focused primarily on health, illness, medicine, and medical research throughout our respective careers, and who have been close collaborators since 1968, when we undertook our first joint study of organ transplantation, chronic hemodialysis, and the development and implantation of an artificial heart (Fox and Swazey 1974). The "team of two" is a sobriquet that was bestowed on us at First Central Hospital in Tianjin, China, where we were doing a mini-ethnographic study in summer 1981 under the auspices of the American Association for the Advancement of Science and the China Association of Science and Technology (Fox and Swazey 1982, 1984). China was still in the throes of recovering from the personal, social, and cultural ravages of Mao Zedong and the "Gang of Four's" Cultural Revolution,[2] and as the nurses and physicians at First Central Hospital became comfortable with our presence, and observed the collaborative way in which we did our research, they began referring to us admiringly, and with ironic wit, as "the Team of Two, not the Gang of Four."

About the Authors and Their "Pre-Bioethics" Links to Bioethics

Considerably before we met and began to work together in 1968, and before the field of bioethics had crystallized sufficiently to become a widely identified

3

entity, questions associated with values and beliefs, and issues that entailed moral dilemmas were central to our sociology and contemporary history of medicine interests, and to the inquiries in which we were engaged.

In 1959, Fox had published *Experiment Perilous*, a participant observation-based study of a metabolic research ward—Ward F-Second (R. C. Fox 1959). Out of their common predicament of confrontation with chronic and terminal illness, high medical uncertainty and risk, severe therapeutic limitations, and constant closeness to death, the physician-investigators of F-Second, and their gravely ill patients who were also their research subjects, fashioned a tragicomic hospital community in which they were collegially committed to medical research. Central to Fox's work was the descriptive analysis of the lived experiences of the patients and physicians of F-Second in the face of the stresses and conflicts that their mutual involvement in advancing the knowledge and therapeutic powers of medicine through clinical research entailed, and of the collective ways that they developed for dealing with these psychological, social, and ethical challenges.

Fox had also conducted firsthand research on the education, training, and professional socialization of medical students during the 1950s, which had bearing on the relationship between certain attributes intrinsic to the role of a physician, and some of the ethical obligations, strains, and dilemmas that are concomitants of this role. Most pertinent in this regard were two essays based on her field experiences: "Training for Uncertainty," in which she identified three basic types of medical uncertainty that are inherent to the physicianhood for which medical students are being prepared (R. C. Fox 1957), and "The Autopsy: Its Place in the Attitude-Learning of Second-Year Students," which focused on the impact that their participation in an autopsy had on students' training in "detached concern," "management of time," and "medical morality," as well as on their training for uncertainty (R. C. Fox 1988).[3]

Both Fox's immersion in the worlds of "experiment perilous" and of the medical school involved her in observing, pondering, and writing about attitudinal, ethical, and existential issues related to death, on the threshold of the time when a surge of concerned medical and public interest in so-called "death and dying" was beginning to occur on the American scene. This period antedated by more than a decade the advent of bioethics, and its preoccupation with the "definition of death," the humane care of the dying, and the foregoing or cessation of life-sustaining treatment.[4]

Swazey, in turn, became interested in value questions and social and policy issues attending developments in science and technology through graduate school courses at Harvard in the area then called "science and society," and, with respect to biology and medicine more specifically, through reading the "pre-bioethics" professional and popular literature that was being published in the 1950s to mid-1960s. Her attention to social and ethical implications of current and prospective advances in biology and medicine was deepened when, at the request of biology majors at Hood College, where she had a one-year teaching appointment while finishing her doctoral dissertation, she gave a semester-long, noncredit seminar on these topics in 1965–1966. Returning to Harvard in 1966, Swazey became a member of a new research group established by the Harvard Program on Technology and Society to examine social, ethical, and policy implications of various advances in biomedical science and technology. As part of that work, she and a colleague, Stanley J. Reiser, a physician and historian, interviewed a number of leading scientists and physicians across the country about issues that might be posed by developments in various areas, including organ replacement (Mendelsohn, Swazey, Taviss 1971).

It was in 1968, at the Harvard program with which Fox also became associated, that Swazey and Fox met, and began their collaborative, Program-supported study of issues posed by scientific and clinical developments in organ replacement. Contributing to our mutual decision to concentrate our joint research in this area was the work that Swazey had been engaged in with the Program, and the prior opportunity that Fox's study of Ward F-Second had given her to observe the path-making clinical trials with the artificial kidney and heart surgery that were being conducted in the 1950s at the Peter Bent Brigham Hospital in Boston, where F-Second was located, and to be on-site in that hospital in 1954, when the world's first successful human kidney transplant was performed there.[5] Organ transplantation and chronic dialysis (and later, the implantation of an artificial heart), we agreed, offered the likelihood of conducting fruitful case studies of therapeutic innovation. They were sufficiently advanced in their development to permit in-depth empirical study through fieldwork and the analysis of primary and secondary sources, which fit our professional interests and research styles; and during the 1960s, when we began our research, what was being described as "the replacement of various body parts by human and man-made substitutes," and "the growing ability to 'rebuild people'" was attracting increasing medical and public attention (Fox and Swazey 1992b: xiv). In addition, even before we set foot in the field, we were both intrigued by the literal and symbolic significance of the extraordinary "gift" of self and life that organ transplantation constituted, and by its potentially exalting and oppressive implications.

By the time that we published our first coauthored book, *The Courage to Fail: A Social View of Organ Transplants and Dialysis*, in 1974, the first two American bioethics centers had been launched: the freestanding Institute of Society, Ethics, and the Life Sciences (the Hastings Center) in 1969, and in 1971, the Joseph and Rose Kennedy Institute for the Study of Human Reproduction and Bioethics (the Kennedy Institute of Ethics) at Georgetown University. But even then, the definition of what was beginning to be called "bioethics" was so nebulous that one of its founders, philosopher Daniel Callahan, described it as a "field" that "[m]ost of its practitioners…wandered into from somewhere else," and that they were "more or less inventing" as they went along. "Its vague and problematic status in philosophy and theology," he commented, "is matched by its even more shaky standing in the life sciences" (Callahan 1973: 68). And its staying power was uncertain at best. In an essay that Fox published at this point in time, she characterized bioethics as "a tentative field" that was one of a number of "new institutional forms…being summoned forth" by the "ethical and existential developments" taking place in "contemporaneous American medicine" (R. C. Fox 1974).

In ways that we did not actively seek or anticipate, we were drawn into the inauguration of U.S. bioethics. Fox was one of two social scientists invited to be a "founder" of the Hastings Center, a term that designated persons involved in developing the Center prior to its formal incorporation in 1969, and she subsequently became a member of its first board. In addition, in 1972, she was named to an editorial advisory board by theologian Warren T. Reich (who was associated with the Kennedy Institute of Ethics), which he formed "to test the feasibility" of producing an *Encyclopedia of Bioethics*, and to "recommend topics, organizational ideas, and personnel" for it (Reich 1978: 1:xii).[6] Swazey was among Hastings's first group of fellows appointed in 1970, and was a member of one of the Center's first research groups (on behavior control). She also began her career-long work on research involving human subjects when she was appointed to the Human Subjects Committee of Boston's Beth Israel Hospital in 1972.

The publication of *The Courage to Fail*, and our "frontlines" knowledge of issues associated with organ replacement from which it originated, also contributed to our being connected with the emerging field of bioethics, since organ transplantation and artificial organs quickly became one of the sets of advances in biology and medicine on which the field of bioethics has consistently focused its attention. Quite unexpectedly, not only were we among the relatively few social scientists who participated in these early phases of bioethics' unfolding, but by virtue of our continuing relationship to the field, we attained longevity within it.

Our Perspective on Bioethics

Our prolonged relationship to bioethics is complex. We do not consider ourselves to be bioethicists, to be engaged in bioethical research, or to be bioethical practitioners. As we have discovered through the interviews that we conducted with a cross-section of first- and second-generation figures in the development of American bioethics, we share this attitude with many persons working in this multi-disciplinary field, who emphatically prefer to be identified by the discipline or the profession in which they were originally trained—whether it is philosophy, theology, religion, medicine, nursing, the law, social science, or literature.

What perhaps distinguishes our somewhat inadvertent relationship to bioethics from that of others associated with the field is that for us, since its inception, bioethics has never been "just bioethics." In our view, "using biology and medicine as a metaphorical language and a symbolic medium, bioethics deals in public spheres and in more private domains with nothing less than beliefs, values, and norms that are basic to our society, its cultural tradition, and its collective conscience" (Fox and Swazey 1984: 336, 360). While recognizing the basic interconnection of bioethics to advances in modern biology, medicine, and biotechnology, we have always been impressed by the degree to which "the value and belief questions with which [the field] has been preoccupied have run parallel to those with which the society has been grappling more broadly," and by their wider "moral, social, and religious connotations" (Fox 1989: 224).

Observing the prominent place that bioethics, the issues with which it is concerned, and the debates that have swirled around them have occupied in the public square of American society since the inception of the field has reinforced our supposition that bioethics has a deep-structure relationship to what philosopher-bioethicist Daniel Callahan has called "the larger moral struggles of our society" (Callahan 1996: 3). One of the most remarkable and resounding features of this field is the extent to which the matters with which it deals have spread beyond the spheres of the contributing intellectual disciplines of which it is composed, and the professional milieus in which their members usually operate, to pervade the public domain. Not only are bioethical questions, cases, and personages constantly, saliently, and often dramatically covered by the print and electronic media, but in addition, in a variety of ways, the executive, legislative, and judicial branches of the government, at every level of the society, have been continually involved with them. This has become increasingly evident in the course of the past decade, as bioethical debate—particularly around issues that pertain to embryonic and stem cell research and end-of-life treatment, and to the roles of religion and government in relationship to them—has taken on some of the characteristics of the "culture wars" between "conservatives" and "liberals" that have erupted in the United States.

Our perspective on the contours of bioethics in the United States is cultural and cross-cultural—that is, we view it both from inside and outside of American society. We are sharply aware of the characteristically Western, and distinctively American attributes of the predominant ethos of U.S. bioethics—its cognitive framework, major concepts and principles, mode of reasoning, and the values and virtues that it has emphasized and de-emphasized. We do not, however, consider the fact that it is imprinted with "Americanness" in certain regards either surprising, or necessarily problematic. Particularly because we do not understand it to be an Olympian intellectual field that is abstracted from and lifted above the society in which it developed, we would not expect it to be a totally acultural or transcultural entity. Nevertheless, we are concerned about—and also critical of—what we regard as the "systematic inattentiveness to the social and cultural sources and implications of its own thought" (Fox and Swazey 1984: 337–338) that many American bioethicists display. One of the origins of this lack of attention is the powerful commitment of analytic philosopher-bioethicists (who are the major architects of the reigning conceptual framework of American bioethics) to a conception of moral universalism that they term "the common morality." The idea of a "common morality" is not unique to philosophy and philosophers. It has roots in the cultural tradition of the West. In the post-World War II years, it found expression in the United Nations Declaration of Human Rights, which both assumed and promoted the notion of a common morality. In bioethics, the notion is often expressed as *the* (not *a*) common morality, which involves principles, philosophers Tom Beauchamp and James Childress affirm, that "all morally serious people," in all places, societies, and cultures, should, and actually do, espouse and share (Beauchamp and Childress 2001: 3–5). This view of common morality is accompanied by a diffuse cautiousness about attaching weight to social and cultural particularities and differences, because of the "slippery-slope" danger that it could lead to so-called "ethical and cultural relativism." In our view, the consequences of these impediments to recognizing the ways in which American bioethical thought is embedded in the society from which it issues have become more significant and far-reaching as bioethics has progressively spread to numerous other societies throughout the world. For although the paradigmatic form in which it has been "exported" has been globally influential, some of its key attributes do not "fit" the cultural traditions, worldviews, historical circumstances, or institutional structures of the societies to which it has traveled. Partly for this reason, there is not only a largely unintentional hegemonic thrust to the way that U.S. bioethics has been exported to other countries but also an important sense in which the field has not yet become as international and multicultural in outlook as it is now appropriate for it to be.

How We and Our Perspective Are Viewed by U.S. Bioethicists

These are some of the key features of the perspective that we have brought to bear on bioethics throughout the years of our relationship to it, and that we have articulated in our publications,[7] teaching, and lecturing, on bioethics-relevant boards and committees in which we have participated, at bioethics meetings that we have attended, and, in the case of Fox, as a member of the President's Commission for the Study of Ethical Problems in Medicine and Biomedicine and Behavioral Research (1979–1981), and, for Swazey, as a member of the Core Group for the National Commission for the Protection of Human Subjects Special Scholarly Study (1976–1977) and the congressionally established Commission on Research Integrity (1994–1995). Our angle of vision originates from our social science training, and our many years of conducting culturally oriented, ethnographic and documentary research in a number of societies,[8] as a sociologist, principally of medicine, and a historian.

Our four decades of experience as observing participants and participant observers both in and of bioethics is recognized and generally respected by other persons active in the field. However, many of the ideas and perspectives about bioethics that we have set forth have been received with considerable ambivalence. There have even been interludes when what we have written has been so irksome to certain bioethicists that they have accused us of being "bioethics bashers" in print, referred to us in more scurrilous terms in private, and for a time consigned us to a persona non grata status. In addition, it has been recurrently intimated that our criticism of bioethics is impelled by a covert desire to demote philosophy from its standing as the foundational discipline of bioethics, and "supplant" it with sociology or some other social science. We consider such reactions to our commentary on bioethics over the years to be personalized projections of the problems of thinking socially and culturally in, and about, American bioethics specifically, and bioethics more generally, which have persistently characterized the field. Describing and analyzing these problems will be two of the foci of this book.

The Genesis of Our Book and Its Database

For a number of years, we had periodically discussed the possibility of writing a book about the social history and sociological import of bioethics in the United States. Such an undertaking began to take shape in 1996, when we developed a proposal for the National Science Foundation's program on Societal Dimensions of Engineering, Science, and Technology to study "the development, roles, and significance of bioethics in American society." The NSF funded the proposal, which was submitted in January 1997, and we began the initial phase of the project that October.[9]

The major primary data that we collected with the support of this grant were 44 face-to-face, semi-structured interviews, ranging in length from two to more than eight hours, which we conducted over the period 1997 to 2000. All but two of the interviewees were first- and second-generation figures in the development of American bioethics, whose baseline disciplines included philosophy, law, religious studies and theology, medicine, and social science.[10] Our own previous and ongoing observations in a variety of bioethical settings, meetings, conferences, discussions, and working groups—principally in the United States, but also in Belgium, France, China, Pakistan, and South Africa—comprised another set of primary data. These data assumed greater importance for us as our conception of the book that we would write evolved. In addition, we amassed a large corpus of both primary and secondary source materials, including a veritable library of published books and articles written about bioethics or bioethical topics, pertinent medical and scientific papers, legal briefs, and court decisions, reports of bioethics commissions and committees, documents concerning the founding, missions, activities, and programs of bioethics centers in the United States and other countries, and copious media materials about bioethics, bioethicists, and bioethical issues. In August 2006, we decided that we needed to cease collecting and using such materials, but did accrue a few more especially pertinent publications until we firmly agreed to stop such additions in spring 2007.

The Book's Evolution

As we assessed and did running analyses of the data we were gathering, we became more unsettled about what kind of book these materials might enable us to write. We had never intended to produce a conventional intellectual or institutional history of bioethics, and we would have found it difficult to deal in that form with some of the more anomalous characteristics of the field—such as the disinclination of persons working in it to think of themselves as bioethicists, or the continuous presence of bioethics in the public square. In any case, while we proceeded with the collection and contemplation of our data, a succession of monographic histories of various aspects of bioethics (containing disparate interpretations of the field) were published (Jonsen 1998; Stevens 2000; Evans 2002; Walter and Klein 2003). In our view, adding still another work to this series would have been superfluous, especially since the life history of bioethics spans only a few decades.

Nor did it seem satisfactory (although we seriously considered it) to build the book around a rather standard sociological analysis of the origins of bioethics in the United States; the biomedical developments, issues, and themes around which it has crystallized; its ethos; its progressive institutionalization and professionalization; its relationship to each of the fields that make up its multidisciplinary matrix (especially philosophy, theology and religious thought, medicine, the law, and the social sciences); and its public policy implications. As competent and comprehensive as this approach might seem to be, we felt that it failed to capture or account for what kind of historical and sociological phenomenon bioethics is; what its social and cultural characteristics are; why it began in the United States, and has achieved public as well as academic prominence here; the extent to which it has spread in a social movement-like way to many other countries in the world; the commanding influence that American bioethics and bioethicists have had on purportedly "international bioethics"; or what the wellsprings, salient features, and significance of bioethics are in some of the societies other than the United States in which it now exists.

As we sifted through the voluminous amount of data we had gathered, we were increasingly impressed and also disappointed by the dearth of information and insights about these aspects of bioethics that they contained. Even our extensive interviews with the American bioethicists who brought the field into being, and were key figures in its shaping and development, were not especially enlightening in this regard.[11] The interviewees were eloquently informative about some of the social and historical factors that they thought had contributed to the "birth" of bioethics; the personal, intellectual, and professional components of their own biographies that had drawn them into the field; the stages through which they had observed bioethics pass; and the roles that they had assumed within it. They were also forthcoming about what they considered to be some of the problems and shortcomings of the field, its continuing ascent on the American scene and elsewhere notwithstanding. By and large, however (with a few exceptions), they had relatively little to say about the ethos of U.S. bioethics—its distinguishing cultural traits, value-commitments, and "moral and aesthetic style and mood" (Geertz 1973: 127)[12]—its societal significance, or about its relationship to bioethics in other countries and regions of the world. Our failure to probe sufficiently into these areas in conducting the interviews might have been partly responsible for the lacunae. But what we found striking was the contrast between the paucity of observations and reflections on the culture of bioethics expressed by our bioethicist interviewees, and the keen awareness of their "courage to fail"[13] ethos that the transplant surgeons we came to know through our earlier research on organ replacement displayed in our ongoing conversations with them. This has proved to be even more true of the members of the international medical humanitarian organization Médecins Sans Frontières/Doctors Without Borders, whom Fox has interviewed in the context of her current research on the moral dilemmas that they encounter in conducting their medical, humanitarian, and human rights witnessing action. They speak vividly and perceptively, without prodding, for example, about what they refer to as their "culture of debate."

What the Book Became

Something akin to a breakthrough occurred when we decided that, in more than the usual authorial sense, we ourselves should become part of the book we were planning. As we came to envisage it, the book would be written primarily from our vantage point as culturally oriented and ethnographically inclined social scientists, who have been both participants in U.S. bioethics and observers of it since the field's emergence in the 1960s, and who also have a lively interest in and some firsthand exposure to bioethics in several other societies. Drawing both explicitly and implicitly on our own experiences in various bioethical settings would be one of the ways in which we would enhance the social and cultural orientation of our overarching framework. Our purview would extend beyond the microcosm of bioethics to explore its relationship to larger societal, national, and international factors and developments. While appreciative of the interesting and important phenomenon that bioethics comprises, the book would also be critical of what we regard as the field's deficiencies and blind spots, especially with respect to matters that, in our opinion, call for deeper social and cultural knowledge, understanding, and analysis.

The structure and style of exposition that would best suit our conception of the book, we decided, would be a series of clustered chapters of varying lengths, including a few short, ethnographically based narratives about bioethics-relevant incidents and events in which we have been directly or indirectly involved over the years. Whenever it was appropriate, we would write in the first person, as "I" or "we." The book would not be evenhandedly comprehensive, fastidiously following the entire trajectory of bioethics, for example, or including within it the widest possible gamut of relevant subtopics. Historically, it would focus primarily on the origins and emergence of bioethics in American society, its early intellectual, professional, and organizational development, and on its global diffusion. Sociologically, its main intent would be to portray and decipher the social, cultural, and cross-cultural nature of the intricate entity that has come to be called bioethics, and to consider and appraise how the field understands, regards, and handles these dimensions of its existence. This is the book that we have written.

The Book's Contents

The five chapters in part 1 examine various ways in which bioethics took root in the American landscape. In chapter 1, we explore the sources, starting points, and early manifestations of American bioethics, and the intriguingly diverse accounts and interpretations of its wellsprings, debut, and initial characteristics contained in the bioethical literature. After noting the existence of an unusual amount of preoccupation with the historical beginnings of such a young field, and some of the "myths of origin" components of this interest, we present our perspective on "the coming of bioethics," drawn from a combination of relevant published works, and our own observations of its early unfolding. Chapter 2 examines the patterns involved in "the coming of bioethicists," drawing on the autobiographical accounts of their entry into the field and their early involvement in it related to us by bioethicists whom we interviewed. Chapter 3 is a vignette that describes the gala inauguration of the Kennedy Institute of Ethics in 1971, recounted by one of us (Fox) who participated in that glittering event, which launched the second center in the United States devoted to bioethics. The symposium that was the centerpiece of this occasion gave voice to some of the "collective conscience" issues with which American bioethics has been concerned from its outset, and made apparent their relationship to the public domain and to the polity, as well as to biology and medicine.

Chapter 4, in turn, is a detailed, content analysis-based case study of the spectacular media coverage of an event that assumed theatrical proportions in the sphere of bioethics: the announcement, in 1997, of the creation and birth of the cloned sheep, Dolly. As such, "Dolly" constitutes a magnified example of the growing attention given to bioethical happenings and issues by the American media; of the media's increasing reliance on a cadre of bioethicists for expert, quotable opinions on these matters; and of some of the implications of these patterns. This case also opens onto one of the most contentious set of questions with which bioethics has been called upon to deal in its public policy role: the prospect of human reproductive cloning, and the use of embryonic stem cells for therapeutic research. The final chapter in part 1 (chapter 5) concentrates on two of the numerous events organized and staged by American bioethicists, or with their collaboration, in recognition of certain anniversaries of some of the prominent U.S. bioethics centers, of what are considered to be foundational documents in the field, and of individuals regarded as bioethics personages. The two celebratory events we focus on are the "Birth of Bioethics" conference held in 1992 to recognize what its organizer identified as the 30th anniversary of the field's inception, and the "Belmont Revisited" conference that took place in 1999, on the twentieth anniversary of the issuance of the principles that came to be considered the bases of ethically conducted research on human subjects. The intellectual content of these meetings, the roster of their invited participants, and their rhetoric and atmosphere are revelatory of the image and conception of themselves and their field that American bioethicists had collectively formed after several decades of bioethics' existence, and of the professional rituals they have developed.

Part 2 could be considered the sociological core of the book, because it is here that we deal extensively (chapter 6) with what we identify as the problems of thinking socially and culturally in American bioethics that have existed since its inception. We associate these problems with certain characteristics of Western philosophical thought—especially those of Anglo-American analytic philosophy in its principlist form, which has had a shaping influence on the predominant conceptual framework of U.S. bioethics; with some distinctive attributes of American values and beliefs, and of American medicine and law; with the historical era and the public contexts in which the genesis and evolution of the field has been embedded; and with the societal mood by which it has been surrounded. The chief deterrents to the integration of social and cultural knowledge, reflection, and analysis into the dominant paradigm of bioethical thought that the chapter explores are the privileged place that American bioethics accords to the precepts of autonomous individualism, individual rights, and rationality; the lesser weight that it attaches to a consideration of the interrelatedness of individuals, community, and common good, to responsibilities, and to feelings; and its strong emphasis on a monistic conception of ethical universalism, which is coupled with a tendency to disregard context, a distrust of particularism, and an aversion to ethical relativism. Impediments to a fuller incorporation of social and cultural variables and reflection into the body of bioethical thought that stem from what philosopher Onora O'Neill has termed the "tenuous interdisciplinarity" of the field (O'Neill 2002b: 2335), and from differences in the methodology and ethos of philosophy and the social sciences, are also examined in this chapter. It is followed, in chapter 7, by a short, anecdotal account of some of the experiences we have had individually, and as a "team of two," in our roles as social scientists, observing and participating in the ongoing of American bioethics.

Part 3 of the book, "Migrations," is concerned with the international development of bioethics, organizationally and through its emergence in a wide array of societies and world regions. In chapter 8, we highlight the major influence that American bioethics and bioethicists have had on the field's global spread. But this American influence, we point out, has not only fostered the diffusion of bioethics; in certain respects it has also curtailed the scope and depth of its internationalization. It is our contention that too little is known—especially by U.S. bioethicists—about how bioethics is configured in the numerous societies in which it now exists. In this connection, in chapters 9 and 10, we present two illustrations of the kinds of historical, social, and cultural factors that are integral to knowledgeable understanding of bioethics in different societies. Bioethics in France, a Western European society with a (now secularized) Christian-Catholic religious tradition, and bioethics in Pakistan, an Islamic, South Asian society, are our case examples. We arrive at the conclusion that the forging of a bioethics that is truly global will require the development of an overarching conceptual framework that is more responsive to social and cultural context and diversity than the American paradigm that presently prevails.

Finally, in part 4 of the book, we take stock of the current state of bioethics in the United States. The culture wars in American bioethics provide one of the vantage points from which we view the field (chapter 11). The other, more international perspective is contained in our concluding afterword, which draws on some of the observations that Renée Fox has made in the context of her ongoing study of Médecins Sans Frontières/Doctors Without Borders. While we recognize and respect the intellectual, moral, and sociological importance of American bioethics, in this concluding section of the book we are particularly concerned with the challenging problems that this intriguing, *sui generis* field faces.

Renée C. Fox and Judith P. Swazey
Philadelphia, Pennsylvania, and Bar Harbor, Maine
Summer 2007

Notes

1. Depending in part on the country and educational setting in which it is taught, history may be classified as a social science discipline, or a discipline in the humanities.
2. Under Chairman Mao Zedong, the Great Proletarian Cultural Revolution engulfed China during the decade of 1966–1976. Soon after Mao's death in September 1976, his wife, Jiang Qing, and her three main associates, who composed the radical group most closely linked to Mao and the Cultural Revolution, were arrested, and denounced as "the Gang of Four."

3. The research on which both of these essays was based was conducted under the aegis of the Bureau of Applied Social Research of Columbia University, within the framework of the long-term studies in the sociology of medical education that it launched in 1952 with support by the Commonwealth Fund. The principal investigators for these studies were sociologists Robert K. Merton and Patricia L. Kendall, and physician George Reader. Although the essay "Training for Uncertainty" was published in a timely fashion, in 1957, as part of the coedited volume by Merton, Reader, and Kendall entitled *The Student-Physician*, for reasons that had to do with the complex dynamics of the Columbia medical education project, the essay on the autopsy was not published until 1988. However, it had circulated widely within both medical and sociological circles before it finally appeared in print.

4. Integral to the complex social and cultural phenomena associated with what historian Michel Vovelle termed "the rediscovery of death" that began to take place at the end of the 1950s and the beginning of the 1960s (Vovelle 1980) were the ramifying effects of nurse-social worker-physician Dame Cicely Saunders's pioneering work in palliative care, and her founding of the hospice movement; and the major impact of psychiatrist Elizabeth Kübler Ross's book *On Death and Dying*, with its delineation of five psychological stages through which a dying person supposedly evolves, and its evocative case materials drawn from her intensive work with incurably ill and dying patients (Kübler-Ross 1969).

   In a personal letter that she wrote to Fox on January 19, 1996, Saunders referred to *Experiment Perilous*, and to the fact that she had often cited and quoted from it, and observed that it appeared in the same year as Herman Feifel's *The Meaning of Death* and her own series in *Nursing Times* on the "Care of the Dying." She concluded that "Something was definitely happening in 1959!" This letter was published in Clark 2002: 359.

5. The kidney transplant, which took place between two identical twin brothers (the Herricks), was performed by Dr. Joseph Murray, for which he later received a Nobel Prize in Physiology or Medicine.

6. The editorial advisory board consisted of 60 members. Twenty-two of them were assembled for face-to-face meetings to formulate initial plans for the *Encyclopedia*. The composition of the entire advisory board consisted of 12 philosophers, 10 theologians, 12 professorial members of medical school faculties, 7 biologists, 3 professors of law, 3 psychiatrists, 3 rabbis, 3 sociologists (including Fox), 2 science and medicine writers, 1 anthropologist, 1 demographer, 1 medical historian, 1 health consultant, and 1 member of the British Parliament. Many of these persons were highly distinguished in their field; some of them were famous. A number of them occupied positions that were as relevant to why they were selected to be members of the board as was their profession (for example, the directors of the Hastings Center and of the Kennedy Institute of Ethics, and the former editor of the *Encyclopedia of the Social Sciences*). The board included persons from Canada, England, France, Greece, Italy, Japan, the Netherlands, Scotland, and Sweden, as well as from the United States. The *Encyclopedia* was published in 1978. Its editor in chief was Warren T. Reich, who was then senior research scholar at the Kennedy Institute's Center for Bioethics, and associate professor of bioethics at the Georgetown University School of Medicine. Georgetown provided some financial assistance for carrying out the project, which was principally funded by the National Endowment for the Humanities Program of Science, Technology and Human Values. One of the most distinctive and, in a way, peculiar features of this encyclopedia is that it was brought into existence before the field of bioethics was firmly established and recognized. As Reich wrote in its introduction, it was "unusual, perhaps unprecedented, for a special encyclopedia to be produced almost simultaneously

with the emergence of its field" (Reich 1978: 1:xvi). It played a significant role in defining and legitimizing bioethics as a field, and in its institutionalization. A second, revised and updated edition of the *Encyclopedia* was published in 1995, under the editorship of Reich; and in 2004, a third, revised and updated edition was published, edited by Stephen G. Post.

7. These publications include R. C. Fox 1974, 1976, 1989, 1990, 1994, 1998,1999; and Fox and Swazey 1984, 2005. The fact that we see bioethics as a social and cultural happening of more than medical and ethical import has led us to encourage sociologists in some of our publications to be "present and active" in the field, "not only as conceptual, empirical, and policy contributors to it, but also as analysts of the social and cultural phenomenon that it represents." Fox coined the concept of a "sociology of bioethics" in this connection (Fox 1989: 224–276; see also Fox 1985).

8. Principal among these societies Belgium, France, the Democratic Republic of Congo, China, and South Africa, as well as the United States.

9. Our project, titled "Bioethics in American Society," was conducted under the aegis of the Acadia Institute, located in Bar Harbor, Maine, of which Swazey was the founding president and Fox a senior scholar and member of the board. Swazey was the principal investigator and Fox the co-principal investigator of the study, which was funded for a 42-month period through August 2000 by the National Science Foundation's Program on Societal Dimensions of Engineering, Science, and Technology. Modifications in our original proposal to the National Science Foundation were made, as suggested by reviewers, in order to "downsize" its scope in relation to available funding for personnel and travel. Additional grants for support of the study were made by the Greenwall Foundation and the National Library of Medicine.

10. The interviews were done by various combinations of the study's three researchers: Swazey, Fox, and Carla M. Messikomer, PhD, who was a senior associate for the project. Swazey conducted the majority of the interviews, and others were conducted by her and Messikomer or Fox, or by Fox and Messikomer.

   Prior to the interviews, those with whom we talked received letters explaining the nature of the study and purposes of the interviews, and a consent form that they were asked to return to us along with a copy of their CV. With two exceptions, due to malfunctions of our recording equipment, the interviews were taped and transcribed, in addition to our taking detailed notes during each session. Full accounts of the two interviews that were not recorded were written based on our notes. As was stipulated in the consent form, each interviewee received a copy of his or her transcript to review and edit.

   In addition to the interviews, the meeting that was held with our project advisory group on September 8, 2000, also was recorded and transcribed, and sent to the attendees for their review.

   Through the intermediary of Dr. LeRoy Walters, then director of the Kennedy Institute of Ethics, transcripts of the interviews and the advisory committee meeting have been deposited in the Institute's archival collection. (See the appendix for lists of the interviewees and members of the advisory committee.)

11. In almost all cases, our interlocutors participated enthusiastically in animated interviews, relating to us as colleagues with whom they were familiar through our long association with the field of bioethics. Many of them expressed appreciation for the opportunity to think out loud about bioethics and their involvement in it that our interviewing provided.

12. Anthropologist Clifford Geertz used this phrase in his essay "Ethos, World View, and the Analysis of Sacred Symbols" (Geertz 1973: 126–141).

13. We are not the inventors of this descriptive phrase that we have used to portray the culture of transplant surgeons. It was coined, and stated with great fervor, by a pioneering heart transplant surgeon in the course of a quite emotional interview that he granted us.

TAKING ROOT IN THE
AMERICAN LANDSCAPE

1

The Coming of Bioethics

In common with efforts to trace, analyze, and interpret the history of most endeavors, there is no single view of the origins and development of the field of bioethics that is accepted as *the* definitive, agreed upon account. Perhaps the most widely accepted aspect of the field's contemporary history is what Spanish historian of medicine and bioethicist Diego Gracia characterizes as "the fact" that "bioethics had its first development in the US,"[1] and subsequently began to spread to countries around the globe (Gracia 2001: 44, 45; see chapter 8, "Bioethics Circles the Globe").

There are many frameworks within which one can describe and analyze the beginnings of bioethics in the United States, which is the subject matter of this first chapter in our book. To us, it is striking that despite its relatively short life span, a number of differing versions exist of when and why bioethics developed in the United States, the great majority of which have been written by persons deeply involved in field. We also find the degree to which American bioethicists have been concerned with identifying and chronicling the field's beginnings, as well as the number and variety of anniversary and other celebratory activities they have held (see chapter 5), intriguing, and somewhat perplexing.

The many and varied accounts of the field's beginning in the United States suggest both the complexity of the phenomenon called bioethics, and the preoccupation of some of its most active participants with the ways that it is understood both within and without the bioethics community. It seems, further, to be associated with a collective search to define, legitimate, and establish a new intellectual field whose characteristics, trajectory, and significance differ markedly in a number of ways from those of other newly emerging disciplines. To begin with, the configuration of bioethics is intricately and to some extent problematically *multi*disciplinary. There were (and still are) tensions between some of the disciplines involved in the emergence of bioethics (e.g., religion and philosophy) about their roles and relationship to this new field, which are manifest in some of the origin stories. That is, to an important degree, the disciplinary backgrounds of those working in this field, their institutional connections to it, and the roles that they (including ourselves) have played within it have influenced their explanatory conceptions of the genesis of bioethics, and their narratives about its evolution.

Moreover, bioethics is not just an intellectual happening. It had a social movement dimension when it appeared on the national scene at a time of social and cultural ferment in the country's history, and was integrally connected with the struggles to affirm and better fulfill fundamental American values, beliefs, and civil rights that were occurring during the 1960s and 1970s. In addition, the development of bioethics was propelled by the immediacy with which its biomedical and ethical preoccupations generated political interest in the legislative and executive branches of the government, and attracted prominent, widespread media attention. Additionally, the salutary opportunities that bioethics offered for the reinvigoration of U.S. philosophy were partly attributable to the fact that the Anglo-American analytic framework of thought that its practitioners applied to bioethical issues made it possible to deal with religiously resonant, basic American values in a rational, secularized way in the public square as well as in academia. And finally, we speculate that implicitly and sometimes explicitly, as they ponder and debate when bioethics began and what this field is, bioethicists are also grappling with moral, quasi-religious, and quasi-political questions. A related thesis has been advanced by medical humanities scholar and bioethicist Tod Chambers. Based on his analysis of the types of histories of the field that have been developed by bioethicists, Chambers holds that

the battle over the historical origins of bioethics is, in the final analysis, a battle over various proposed ends to our present moral problems.... The historical narratives of the rise of the bioethics movement make the ethicist's chosen paradigm appear self-evident, but we must understand this historical reflection as retrodictive rather than causal.... If there is anything that connects all of the histories of the discipline presented in [this] essay, it is the extraordinary certitude the authors seem to possess concerning their particular "take" on the true nature of our moral ills. I believe that the ability to be aware of the rhetoric of one's arguments in turn promotes a hermeneutics of self-doubt, which in turn will foster sounder arguments in the field. (Chambers 1998: 20–21)

In looking at "the coming of bioethics," we begin by considering a sampler of views about when and why the field emerged in the United States.[2] These accounts include, first, the equivalent of a "big bang" moment of creation, which regards the field's emergence, variously, as a response to specific advances in biomedical technologies, to particular sets of issues, or to certain pivotal events. Second, and more often, chroniclers of bioethics' history depict it as emerging more gradually, and for various reasons, in different time frames that include the postwar years of the 1940s or, more commonly, during the mid-1960s to early 1970s or the late 1960s to mid-1970s. These different historical accounts, as we next discuss, have been grouped by some analysts into typologies that provide useful guideposts for sorting out the various "stories" about bioethics' origins. Then, drawing on our involvement in and study of bioethics over the years, we present our perspective on the field's emergence and the initial phase of its institutionalization. While our view is not a unique one, it does see the field's beginnings as a more intricate affair than do most other accounts, attributable to the weaving of a complex tapestry during the 1950s into the mid-1970s that was composed of intertwined social, cultural, medical, and political threads.

Origin Stories

A Technologically Driven Genesis

A number of "moment of creation" accounts have focused on technologically based advances in biomedicine, a view that, as Ezekiel Emanuel critically observes, "has been so widely accepted...that it has attained the status of...the technological axiom of medical ethics" (Emanuel 1991: 9). Religious ethicist Marc Gellman for example, dates the era of contemporary bioethics to the issuance of the Harvard Ad Hoc Committee's report on the definition of brain death in 1968 (Gellman 1991: 115n1). The Committee's proposed use of irreversible coma as the criterion for determining whether and when a person has died was generated primarily by two technological advances: cardiopulmonary life support systems, and organ transplants using cadaveric donors (A definition of irreversible coma 1968).

Another frequently cited technological advance is long-term (chronic) renal dialysis, ushered in by Belding Scribner's invention of the cannula shunt at the University of Washington in 1960, a development that brought with it socially, ethically, and medically anguishing issues about which patients should receive this scarce, potentially life-saving treatment (Fox and Swazey 1974: chaps. 7–9; Swazey 1975). As we discuss more fully in chapter 5, Albert Jonsen, a prominent bioethicist and chronicler of the field's development, chose the November 1962 publication of Shana Alexander's story in *Life* magazine about Seattle's artificial kidney patient selection committee as the event around which he convened a 30th anniversary conference in September 1992, featuring talks by many of those he identified as bioethical "pioneers" who were invited to celebrate the field's "birth" and "review its history and project its future" (Jonsen 1993: S1).[3] Although he portrayed the events in Seattle as marking the start of bioethics in the United States, Jonsen acknowledged in a post-conference letter to the speakers that his identification of a specific birth date in part had the "chauvinistic goal" of linking "the events at [the] University of Washington with the beginnings of the field."[4]

Issues as the Catalyst for Bioethics' Emergence

Others who have delved into the history of contemporary bioethics have linked its emergence on the American scene to constellations of particular issues, some of which in turn were associated with technological developments. Robert Veatch, for example, has pointed to the seminal importance of issues connected with death and dying, which involved both medicine's new armamentarium of life-sustaining technologies and the changes in medical decision making wrought by the rights movements of the 1960s (Veatch 1976; 1993: S7–8; Veatch, interview, 1999: see appendix).

A very different and infrequently noted set of critical issues has been identified by theologian-bioethicist Warren Reich, one the first two members of the Kennedy Institute for Ethics staff. In his account of André Hellegers's work and his "vision for bioethics" in relation to Hellegers's role as a founder and first director of the Kennedy Institute for Ethics, Reich argued that

fertility control was the major issue that spawned bioethics, more than any other single issue—certainly more than any high-technology-related issue in medicine.... [It] was the topic of extensive debates over a period of at least three decades prior to the rise of bioethics—not only by specialists but by the general public as well. The debates were interdisciplinary, involving ethical, religious, legal, and social controversy on the levels of social policy as well as personal ethics and ecclesiastical authority. The theologians, who were the first ethicists working in bioethics, cut their teeth on contraception/sterilization and abortion debates; and in a very real sense, much of the great energy that was turned toward bioethics around 1970/71 was energy that was diverted from the then-increasingly futile church debates on fertility control. (Reich 1999: 37)

Reich's emphasis on fertility control can be attributed, in part, to his great admiration for and close professional relationship with Hellegers, who, growing out of his training and work in physiology and medicine, particularly fetal physiology and obstetrics, and his activities as a prominent, European-schooled Roman Catholic, was deeply involved in fertility control issues. He served, for example, as deputy director of the Pontifical Commission for the Study of Population, Family and Birth (1964–1966) and director of its medical committee,[5] and as a member of President Lyndon Johnson's Committee on Population and Family Planning (1968–1973). His identification with Hellegers notwithstanding, however, and whether or not one agrees with his historical perspective, Reich asks an important question about bioethics' origin stories: "Why is it that the key role played by fertility control debates is overlooked as crucial to the rise of bioethics?" He offers several hypotheses in response to his question:

Perhaps it is because the issue is principally a low-tech problem, regarded as relatively unimportant on those grounds. Perhaps it is because fertility problems typically dealt with ordinary women leading ordinary lives, and that has not been judged important enough to attract major attention. Perhaps it is because it entailed religious controversy, and somehow moral struggles and debates based at least partly on religious concerns are judged not to be the proper object of ethical inquiry. (Reich 1999: 37–38)

The question "becomes a different one," Reich goes on to aver, "when regarded biographically." In his opinion, "[f]ertility control issues, particularly in a Roman Catholic context, constituted the major context that catapulted André Hellegers, Daniel Callahan…and a number of other pioneering figures to the then-new field of bioethics" (Reich 1999: 38; see Callahan 1999a).

Generated by Events: The Nazi Doctors' Trial and the Nuremberg Code

Among significant events that have been viewed as contenders for generating bio-ethics, a special place in history belongs to the medical experiments conducted on prisoners in Nazi concentration camps during World War II, the subsequent trial of the Nazi physicians at Nuremberg, and the promulgation of the Nuremberg Code of human experimentation in 1947 by the tribunal's American judges. Health law-yer and bioethicist George Annas and bioethicist Albert Jonsen are among those who identify these intertwined events as of cardinal importance in the emergence of bioethics in the United States.

In his book-length account of the birth of bioethics, Jonsen pinpointed 1947 as beginning a 40-year era "during which bioethics emerged as a distinct discipline and discourse." The conviction of 23 physicians for war crimes by the Nuremberg Tribunal in 1947 and the issuance of the Nuremberg Code, he explained, "opens my history because it initiated an examination by professional persons in science, medicine, and law of one of modern medicine's central features: scientific research" (Jonsen 1998: xii). George Annas, who has extensively analyzed the history, scope, and implications of the Nuremberg Code in relation to human experimentation and human rights, maintains that "[b]oth American bioethics and international human rights were born from World War II, the Holocaust, and the Nuremberg Tribunals" (Annas 2004: 658; see also Annas 2005b; Annas and Grodin 1992). He views American bioethics as being rooted in the Nazi concentration camps for two principal reasons. First, "the response of the [Tribunal's] American judges to the horror of the Nazi doctors was to articulate, in the first precept of the Nuremberg Code, the doctrine of informed consent." Second, he points to the pro-found influence of the war on some of bioethics' most notable intellectual found-ers, such as psychoanalyst and law professor Jay Katz, and philosopher Hans Jonas. "Both were born in Germany," Annas writes, "and had family members killed in the Holocaust, and the bioethics-related writings of both grew out of their reflections on the war and the concentration camps" (Annas 2004: 660, 661n9; Katz 1993: 32; The Legacy of Hans Jonas 1995).

The Nuremberg Code has been rightly honored, in Katz's words, as "a remarkable document," for "[n]ever before in the history of human experimentation, and never since, has any code or regulation of research declared in such relentless and uncompromising a fashion that the psychological integrity of research subjects must be protected absolutely" (Katz 1992: 327). At the same time, however, the view that the Code, and the Nazi experiments and doctors' trial that led to its formulation, marks the beginning of bioethics in terms of their actual effects in the postwar years is one that some analysts find historically questionable. As we will note, there were some events in the United States during the 1950s that were catalyzed by awareness of Nuremberg, but, by and large, the Nazi medical experiments and the Code drew little attention. David J. Rothman, for example, has pointed out that the Nazi doctors' trial "received very little press coverage" in the United States, and "before the 1970s, the code itself was infrequently cited or discussed in medical journals. American researchers and physicians apparently found Nuremberg irrelevant to their own work" (Rothman 1987: 1198). Those who were aware of the concentration camp experiments—both medical professionals and laypersons—generally saw them as so monstrously barbaric that they had little relevance to American medical research.[6] With respect to the Code itself, Jay Katz, a towering figure in the area of the ethics of research with human subjects, who has long championed the primacy of informed consent for such research, holds that it "was relegated to history almost as soon as it was born."[7] In the United States, as he and others have observed, a major reason why the Code was largely ignored or met with resistance was not only because it was seen as directed toward the types of horrific experiments conducted by the Nazis but also because it ran counter to the medical profession's strong conviction that it had both the right and ability to self-govern its work, and was in the best position to safeguard the welfare of its human research subjects.[8]

Bioethicist Jonathan Moreno also holds that the Nuremberg Code's "immediate influence on American medicine... was, to put it mildly, minimal" (Moreno 2004: 201). Based on his extensive study of the "national security state" that emerged in the postwar years, he argues for a different series of events, albeit related to the Code, as being central to the coming of bioethics in the United States:

The burden of my argument has been that bioethics (including especially human research standards and the modern informed consent doctrine) should be conceptualized as inextricably associated with national security issues, both in its origins and in its attention to contemporary origins, rather than limited to the standard story of the birth of bioethics in scholarly circles in the late 1960s. (Moreno 2004: 198–199)

Although the American medical professional seems to have taken little notice of the Code, Moreno writes, in the wake of the postwar "efforts to confront the emerging challenge of Soviet power," "government officials were sensitive to both [the Code's] legal and political implications" for the human experimentation conducted by national security agencies such as the newly established Atomic Energy Commission and the Department of Defense (Moreno 2004: 201; Moreno and Lederer 1996). Although at the time, they were largely invisible outside of a restricted governmental circle, Moreno has found that the research with human subjects planned and conducted in the name of national defense needs involved "the emergence of the first federal policies in this area," including—with several exceptions—the adoption of informed consent requirements (Moreno 2004: 198, 199).[9]

Organizational and Linguistic Moments of Creation

Others have identified the establishment of two of bioethics' major institutional seedbeds as being synonymous with the field's birth. Tina Stevens, in her controversial account of the "origins and cultural politics" of bioethics in America, equates the start of the Hastings Center in 1969 with the field's appearance, which she sees as part of a more widespread sociocultural pattern of post–atomic bomb ambivalence toward technology. According to her interpretation, Hastings, and hence, in her view, bioethics, was a response to concerns about advances in medicine and its technologies, but, as exemplified by the legal recognition of brain death and the right to die, only fostered an illusion of lay oversight while actually operating to serve the often ethically questionable needs and actions of physicians and researchers (Stevens 2000; Caplan 2002; Stevens and Baker 2002).

Daniel Callahan and Willard Gaylin, the cofounders of the Hastings Center, have not claimed that their center's establishment marked the field's genesis. The creators of the second major bioethics organization, the Joseph and Rose Kennedy Institute for the Study of Human Reproduction and Bioethics at Georgetown University, however, did see their 1971 initiative as being " 'unique in combining ethics and science...and pioneering in developing a new field of joint research' " (Reich 1996). To Reich, one of the Institute's first staff members and the generator and editor of the 1978 landmark first edition of the *Encyclopedia of Bioethics*, the name coined for this new field of joint research, "bioethics," marked the start of the field.

The word *bioethics*, as Reich has documented, had what he terms a bi-located creation. It was a neologism used first in 1970 by biochemist and research oncologist Van Rensselaer Potter at the University of Wisconsin to designate what he envisaged as a new discipline that would integrate knowledge of biology and of human value systems in order to "help humankind toward a rational but cautious participation in the processes of biological and cultural evolution" (quoted in Reich 1993: S7; Potter 1970, 1971).[10] Independently, André Hellegers and Sargent Shriver at Georgetown also coined *bioethics* to refer to the new field of joint research into the ethics of medicine and the biological sciences that would be undertaken at the Kennedy Institute (Reich 1994, 1995). Reich equates the field of bioethics' beginning with the word's Georgetown origins because the term is "so suggestive and powerful; it suggests a new focus, a new bringing together of disciplines in a new way with a new forum that tended to neutralize the ideologic slant that people associated with the word *ethics*" (Reich 1993: S7).

A Multiyear, Multicausal Gestation

While differing in varying degrees and ways about the "why" and "when," most of those who have dealt with the field's contemporary origins agree that bioethics did not have a specific date of conception or birth, a "big bang" moment of creation. LeRoy Walters, somewhat whimsically, once compiled a list of "the top 206 events related to the birth of bioethics, 1925–1975."[11] Depending on the explanations that they favor for its development, however, most chroniclers have defined a shorter time frame than Walters' half-century, holding that bioethics emerged during the mid-1960s to early 1970s, or the late 1960s to mid-1970s. Those favoring a time frame beginning in the mid-1960s are exemplified by Rothman's scholarly history *Strangers at the Bedside*. He identifies the years from 1966 to 1976, beginning with Dr. Henry Beecher's exposé of abuses in human experimentation and ending with the New Jersey Supreme Court's decision in the case of Karen Ann Quinlan, as "the critical period of change" in "both the style and substance of medical decision making." Those transformative changes, Rothman holds, involved a growing "commitment to collective, as against individual, decision making" by physician-colleagues and laypeople, and by policies and procedures governing medical research and treatment (Rothman 1991: 8).

Jonsen—in addition to the two specific dates that he has linked, for different reasons, with the "birth of bioethics" (the 1962 publication of Shana Alexander's story about Seattle's artificial kidney patient selection committee, and the issuance of the Nuremberg Code in 1947)—also has identified a period of time that, in his view, marks bioethics' true emergence as an institutionalized and professionalized field. That time frame begins in the late 1970s: bioethics' "growth into a scholarly field," he has written, "did not begin until a decade [after the establishment of Seattle's dialysis selection committee in 1960] when the Hastings Center and the Kennedy Institute were established, a few individuals were appointed to medical faculties, a literature in scholarly and professional journals sprouted, and conferences began to convene" (Jonsen 1994: ix).

Like Rothman and others, Jonsen attributes those developments, in the first instance, to the moral problems linked with technological advances, which were supported predominantly with public funding, and to the resistance of most physicians and scientists to heed calls for accountability by the funders and others. In this context, as Robert Baker points out, "Jonsen…rais[es] a pivotal question:

'Why did patients and the public attempt to control the medical-scientific elite by turning to *ethics*, that is to philosophers and theologians…rather than to lawyers and the law?' " (Baker 2002: 65). The elements of Jonsen's answer to this question are similar to those given by Robert Veatch. Entrants into the new bioethical enterprise came chiefly from political liberals, engaged by the civil rights and antiwar movements, who were questioning authority on many fronts. "The American public and public agencies, in turn," Baker goes on to observe in his summary of Jonsen's account of the field's origins, "were responsive to this discourse of ethical critique because of an entrenched moralizing tradition inherited from America's Puritan past, because American liberalism is melioristic and reformist, and because the critique evoked such precepts as 'autonomy,' which appeal to the spirit of individualism that lies at the heart of the American moral tradition" (Baker 2002: 65; Jonsen 1998: esp. part 1).

Robert Veatch also locates the beginning of "the new generation of biomedical ethics" in the late 1960s/early 1970s. "In the end," he holds, "the ethic of this generation is an ethic of the lay person in the medical role," an ethic "that in Western society necessarily means an ethic rooted in both the Judeo-Christian tradition and in secular liberal political philosophy" (Veatch 2002: 350). For Veatch, the seminal time was "January 1, 1970—plus or minus 2–3 years." A "remarkable series of events" took place in that period, he writes. Those events involved the rights movements of the 1960s, which challenged "authority and all figures in dominating roles," and what Lewis Thomas (1974) called the "halfway technologies" developed to address the "newly modal" medical problems of chronic, slowly progressive diseases rather than the paradigm of acute infectious diseases. "Perhaps because I finished my own graduate studies that year," Veatch commented, "I see 1970 as the symbolic transition to a pervasive set of changes that I identify with new, systematic efforts to exhume medical ethics from its professionally controlled Hippocratic crypt" (Veatch 2002: 346).

Typologies of Bioethics' Origins

As indicated by the foregoing sampler, there is a variety of what philosopher-bioethicist Eric Juengst calls "origin stories" and anthropologists term "myths of origin" about when, and the reasons for which, the modern field of bioethics took shape. Several scholars, including Juengst, historian Daniel Fox, and medical humanities scholar Tod Chambers, have analyzed these origin stories in terms of the historical models or typologies that they embody. For teaching purposes, Juengst outlined five types of historical accounts, each with several main variants and proponents that he placed into three categories. The first category views bioethics as a "reactive" development, starting (1) "as a response to biomedicine's technological explosion," or (2) "as a response to a radical cultural pluralism," which assumed that because "arguments from first principles no longer work (in biomedical contexts)…[w]e should focus on finding new ways to make shared decisions….” Under the second category, “bioethics as proactive,” he includes (3) its start as a “proactive social movement within the health care system,” and (4) as a “proactive attempt to anticipate the social future.” The third category sees “bioethics as a continuous development,” a field that (5) “really started with Hippocrates,” with “clinical moral traditions” that remain “robust enough to handle our [contemporary] issues.[12]

The assignment of one of the participants in Jonsen’s 1992 “birth of bioethics” conference was to “sketch the…models of history…invoked” by the various accounts that were given of the field’s beginnings. Daniel Fox identified six explanatory models in the presentations, a number of which are the same as Juengst’s five “myths of origin.” The first model is that bioethics “has been the soft side of the golden age of medicine, of the expansion of medical power…the conscience, the sensitive side…. Within [the] broad medicalization of American society, bioethics embraced and brought to bear on medicine the great traditions of moral philosophy, the immediate pressures of civil rights, and concern for minorities of all kinds.” Model two sees bioethics “as a response to technology,” with two variants: “technology is a source of problems to be either anticipated or managed,” or it “exemplifies the need for a counterreformation in medical thinking or for a restoration to an earlier time.” The third explanation “draws heavily on the tradition of the political economy in our thought,” which “tries to look at the history of bioethics in terms of supply and demand—supply of what bioethicists could do and a demand for it.” The fourth, familiar model is that of “great people and great events,” while the fifth is that “the history of bioethics is an assertion of a great cultural tradition during a time of grave and deepening moral crisis for our society.” His sixth model, Fox reported wryly, is one that some of the presenters “drifted toward [but] would probably not identify as a model,” yet it “is the one that most of us really secretly believe, [which] says that history is one damned thing after another” (D. M. Fox 1993).

A third type of analysis showing how bioethicists have accounted for their field’s origins, which focuses on the *why* of the types of histories they have formulated, has been developed by Tod Chambers (1998). Many bioethicists, he points out, “have constructed historical narratives to explain the emergence of their discipline, [a] historical framing [which] is a formal and common feature of the rhetoric of bioethics” (Chambers 1998: 10). Drawing in part on Martin’s work on narrative ethics, Chambers holds that the frames bioethicists construct involve the use of retrodiction, a reversal of cause-effect relations found in history, biography, and fiction, in which “ ‘[i]t is the end of the temporal series–how things eventually turned out–that determines which event began it…. Knowing an effect, we go back in time to find its cause’ ” (Chambers 1998: 11, quoting Martin 1986: 74). According to the tenets of retrodiction, bioethicists “have attempted to construct a particular concept of causality” that explains the emergence of their discipline in relation to the "new moral paradigm" they are proposing. "Because bioethicists believe themselves to be at a point of transition in medical ethics," he continues, "they have traditionally constructed their historical narratives *in medias res*, that is, in the midst of things. Their histories are in a prophetic mode, which not only sees the relation of the past to the present but also envisions a future resolution that will come about because of this new paradigm" (Chambers 1998: 10, 11).

Chambers presents his case for the retrodictive nature of accounts of bioethics' origins by examining the substantially different historical frames presented in connection with the moral paradigms advanced by several prominent bioethicists. Tristram Engelhardt, in *The Foundations of Bioethics* (1986, 1996), views the bioethics movement as one result of the gradual loss of the Christian world view's "unitary moral vision" that provided a "'content-full' way to resolve moral dilemmas." For him, the replacement of that vision by a secular, pluralistic ethic in which the Enlightenment's primary credo, rationality, is the driving force, was the wellspring of bioethics (Chambers 1998: 12). Albert Jonsen and Stephen Toulmin's *The Abuse of Casuistry* (1988), in turn, was written as a "general 'history of moral reasoning,'" but one strongly influenced by the authors' work in bioethics, particularly their experience on the National Commission for the Protection of Human Subjects and the "new casuistry" that the commissioners employed to reach their conclusions and recommendations. According to their narrative, Chambers writes, bioethics' emergence had less to do with technological advances than with a "transformation in the social climate" during the 1960s that involved "challenges to authority and expertise...in many...areas of life" (Chambers 1998: 15; Jonsen and Toulmin 1998: chap. 16). This "ethos of rebellion," in turn, "extended...into the norms of philosophy" as well as those of physician authority, with a "renewed interest by philosophers in moral questions" in which "the older 'fact/value dichotomy' was openly challenged, and a new concreteness and particularity entered moral philosophy" (Jonsen and Toulmin 1998: 305; see also Toulmin 1982).

In his analysis of Ezekiel Emanuel's *The Ends of Human Life* (1991), Chambers holds that the author's "argument for a particular form of communitarianism rests on rewriting [the] historical narrative...that bioethics has arisen due to advances in technology." While technological advances can "'affect' bioethical issues," in what Chambers calls Emanuel's "plot," "this is not the same as arguing that they have *created* these...issues." Rather, Emanuel "contends that the history of bioethics is in actuality the history of political liberalism...[and] thus must be seen within the context of political changes and not in terms of technological progress" (Chambers 1998: 16).

Chambers's fourth example of retrodiction is Edmund Pellegrino and David Thomasma's *The Virtues in Medical Practice* (1993), which "also den[ies] the technological axiom in [the authors'] historical frame." For them, "medicine is at heart a moral community," Chambers states, with historical antecedents dating from the Hippocratic era, but "this idea of medicine as a moral enterprise" threatens to be corroded by social forces that "increasingly treat medicine as a commodity, a political bauble, an investment opportunity, or a bureaucratic power play." According to their narrative, these social forces, which "reinforce self-interest" in place of the profession as a moral community, account for the rise of contemporary medical ethics. As reflected in the title of their book, Pellegrino and Thomasma argue that the medical profession can triumph over self-interest by "reinstating virtue as its foundational value" (Chambers 1998: 18–19).

Our Perspective on the Coming of Bioethics

In common with some other chroniclers, we do not attribute the emergence of contemporary bioethics to the "big bang" thesis of a particular biomedical development or an event at a specific time. Rather, we see the field's emergence and initial shaping as a more complex and lengthier process that encompassed a number of converging social, cultural, and political phenomena and events, and medical and scientific developments. To the extent that other accounts, such as those by Rothman, Jonsen, and Veatch, also have described bioethics' genesis as a multiyear and multicausal occurrence, our perspective is not a unique one, but it does have some differences in terms of its time frame and in the constellation of factors that came together to constitute the phenomenon of bioethics. That time frames can vary in relation to the emphases of a historical account is indicated by the fact that at various other points in this book we refer to the 1960s as marking the beginnings of bioethics in the United States, which we see as the period when the field began to become institutionalized and professionalized. From a broader historical compass, however, we view the emergence of bioethics as occurring during several phases or stages that occurred from the 1950s through the mid-1970s, which, as we sketch in the remainder of this chapter, had various temporal overlaps and ongoing, evolving components.

Phase one, in our historically and sociologically based account, was in the 1950s, when a number of substantive medical-ethical issues were "in the air." The issues concerning medical research and health care that were being addressed by an expanding group of physicians, scientists, theologians, and legal scholars were ones that have continued to be areas of bioethical attention, such as patients' rights, assisted reproduction, euthanasia, and, preeminently, human experimentation. The attention accorded to these subjects gave rise to publications and conferences. They also fostered the establishment of several institutions during the late 1950s and early 1960s that, although they largely would be outside the orbit of what would become "mainstream bioethics," were committed to providing a base for continuing scholarly and educational work. The start of some of these entities highlights an important facet of bioethics' development over the years: the role of private foundations and federal agencies in funding the field's organizations, educational programs, research, and various other activities.

The 1960s constituted the second phase of bioethics' initial development, with several substages during that decade, some of which merged into events during the early to mid-1970s. Viewing the 1960s overall, it was a time of social, cultural, and religious unrest and turbulence in the United States that had a deep influence on the shaping of bioethics and its practitioners. The decade also saw a surge of professional and popular interest in and attention to current or prospective advances in biomedical research and technology and their ethical implications, and to the rights and welfare of human research subjects, which, among other effects, led to bioethics' appearance on the political and polity stage in Washington.

During the early to mid-1960s, bioethics began to acquire more clearly defined contours as scholars from several fields, most notably moral theology and religious studies, as well as medicine, biology, and law, became increasingly involved in medical-ethical issues. In terms of the field's institutionalization, a second subphase occurred in the mid-1960s, when several multiyear working groups were formed to work on research with human subjects and the social and ethical implications of new biomedical technologies. Finally, the end of the decade and the beginning of the 1970s saw the establishment of the first permanent bioethics centers, and the coining of the term *bioethics* itself to describe this emerging area.

Phase three of the field's initial development took place in the early to mid-1970s, with some overlaps from the end of the 1960s. There were numerous signs that bioethics had "arrived." One was the burgeoning corpus of scholarly publications and the start of the first bioethics journals, a literature that had attained enough volume to warrant the first edition of the *Bibliography of Bioethics* in 1975. Another was the entrance of bioethics and the medical humanities in medical school curricula and teaching hospitals, beginning in the late 1960s and early 1970s. By the mid-1970s, both the overlapping (and often conflictual) fields of medical humanities and bioethics saw the need to begin training individuals for their new educational and scholarly roles. One of these programs, the 1974 Haverford Summer Institute, marked the "advent" of philosophers—primarily trained in the Anglo-American analytic school—in bioethics, and, to some, the "real" beginnings of the field. What we see as the final significant development during the late 1960s to the mid-1970s was the arrival of bioethics in the national political and public policy arena in Washington, where it has remained ever since. Beginning with Senator Walter Mondale's first efforts to create a National Commission on Health, Science and Society in 1968, and culminating in the passage in 1974 of legislation mandating the establishment of the National Commission for the Protection of Human Subjects in Biomedical and Behavioral Research, bioethics had become firmly rooted in the public sphere of the American landscape.

Before providing a somewhat fuller but by no means all-inclusive account of these phases and the developments within them, we feel it is important to bear in mind Chambers's caveats about histories of bioethics: We recognize that our view about the field's origins and development has been shaped by our training in history (JPS) and sociology (RCF), and by our more than 40 years as participants in and observers of bioethics in the United States and other countries.

The 1950s: Bioethical Issues in the Air

From our perspective, the "origin story" of what became known as bioethics begins in the 1950s. Jonsen characterizes these years as a period of "medical ethics before bioethics" (Jonsen 1998: chap. 1), predating the events during the 1960s and early to mid-1970s that marked the beginnings of what Veatch calls the "new generation of medical ethics." However, we view the 1950s as a time when issues and activities that eventually would be called "bioethical" were "in the air," being formulated, addressed, and shaped. A number of topics that became foci of bioethical discourse were being addressed by a constellation of physicians, scientists, theologians, and legal scholars, generating papers and books, conferences and conference proceedings, and the beginning of several organizations concerned with religious, ethical, and legal aspects of medical research and health care. The often controversial Joseph Fletcher, for example, "who many would say was the pathbreaker in the 1950s" (Marty 1992: 71), was one of a cluster of Protestant and Catholic moral theologians who were actively engaged with medical-ethical issues and bioethics' institutional beginnings during the 1960s. Well before those years, however, Fletcher, then professor of pastoral theology and Christian ethics at Episcopal Theological School in Cambridge, Massachusetts, was invited to deliver the prestigious Lowell Lectures at Harvard in 1949, which were published as a bellwether text, *Morals and Medicine*, in 1954. His subject matter—the "patient's right to know the truth," contraception, artificial insemination, and euthanasia—Fletcher declared, represented "a field of ethical inquiry [about issues in medical care] clamoring for attention" and "too long neglected" except by Roman Catholic theologians (Fletcher 1954).[13]

Human Experimentation. The bulk of the ethical issues addressed in the United States during the postwar years of the 1950s involved human experimentation,[14] which has continued to be an enduring focus of public policy and academic bioethical attention, crosscutting many of the field's other topical areas.

Foreshadowing the profusion of conferences, publications, and policy activities in the 1960s, an important symposium on "The Problem of Experimentation on Human Beings" was organized by a distinguished professor of medicine, Otto Guttentag, at the University of California School of Medicine, San Francisco (UCSF) in 1951, reaching a far wider audience when the lectures were published in the journal *Science* in 1953 (Guttentag 1953). While the symposium and the publication of its proceedings partly were stimulated by the Nuremberg Trials and Code, they also reflected Guttentag's longer-standing, deep-seated concerns about human experimentation; he believed strongly that "problems" transcending the horrors of the Nazi experiments did exist and should be addressed in public forums and in medical education.

Other important activities during the 1950s included the PHS's first set of principles and procedures for intramural research involving human subjects, issued in connection with the opening of the NIH Clinical Center in 1953, and the Center's use of normal volunteers as well as patient-subjects[15] (Curran 1970; Swazey 1978). As the decade drew to a close, Henry K. Beecher, Dorr Professor of Research in Anesthesia at Harvard Medical School, published a monograph entitled *Experimentation in Man* (1959b), with a paper by the same title appearing in the *Journal of the American Medical Association* the same year (1959a). Beecher's 1966 paper in the *New England Journal of Medicine*, "Ethics and Clinical Research," presenting 22 actual cases of unethical human experimentation (Beecher 1966), is considered to be the bioethics publication that "accelerated the movement that brought human experimentation under rigorous federal and institutional control" (Rothman 1987: 1195). His less frequently cited 1959 book and paper, however, also eloquently expressed his concerns about what he viewed as inadvertently unethical behavior by physician-researchers, as well as his conviction that the best protection from abuses lay not in codes or rules but in the conscientiousness and integrity of the informed researcher.[16]

In 1959, the same year that Beecher published *Experimentation in Man*, a public and professional furor erupted when two researchers published their first paper on studies they had begun in 1956 to develop a vaccine against infectious hepatitis in children. (Rothman and Rothman 1984). Drs. Saul Krugman and Joan P. Giles's research, which became example 16 in Beecher's 1966 "Ethics and Clinical Research" paper, involved infecting a cohort of retarded children, newly institutionalized at New York's Willowbrook State School, with hepatitis, and observing the natural history of the disease. Since the children were incapable of giving their consent, the researchers, who believed that their work was ethically justifiable because hepatitis was endemic in institutionalized populations, and in children usually was a mild, flu-like illness, were vilified by some as Nazis and staunchly supported by others (Jonsen 1998: 154, 164n105). Willowbrook became one of the infamous cases that played an important role in the creation of the National Commission for the Protection of Human Subjects in 1974, the Commission's 1977 report on research involving children, and the subsequent issuance of federal regulations providing "additional protections" for children as a special research population (Levine 1986: chap. 10).

Organizational Developments. Although none of them has been considered to be part of what became known as "mainstream bioethics"—at least by most mainstream bioethicists—the beginnings of several institutions in the 1950s dealing with religious, ethical, and human values, and with legal aspects of medicine also reflected the burgeoning interest in and concern about the ramifications of medicine.

At the University of Texas Medical Center in Houston, the Institute of Religion was founded in 1955 as an interfaith ecumenical organization "to bring a spiritual presence to health care delivery," including educational programs for religious and medical caregivers.[17] In 1968, in the wake of the first human heart transplant by Dr. Christiaan Barnard, the Institute acted on a suggestion by the Medical Center's eminent cardiac surgeon, Dr. Michael DeBakey, to sponsor a major conference on Ethics in Medicine and Technology, with speakers including religionists such as Robert Drinan, SJ, Joseph Fletcher, Paul Ramsey, and Helmut Thielicke (Vaux 1970).[18]

At Boston University, the interdisciplinary Law-Medicine Research Institute began in 1958, and from its inception under the direction of William J. Curran was involved with ethical as well as legal issues.[19] In 1960, the Institute received a grant from the U.S. Public Health Service to study "actual practices" in clinical investigation regarding various legal, moral, and ethical issues. The study was prompted in part by sessions on human experimentation, which focused on developing a response to the Nuremberg Code, at a 1958 National Conference on the Legal Environment of Medical Sciences, cosponsored by the National Society for Medical Research and the University of Chicago (*National Society...1959*). The Law-Medicine Institute study's principal investigator, Irving Ladimer, had worked at the NIH and as secretary of the 1958 National Conference before joining the new Institute's faculty. In addition to conducting the study of clinical investigation, Ladimer and his associates prepared an anthology and bibliography, *Clinical Investigation in Medicine: Legal, Ethical, and Moral Aspects* (1963), one of the first such compilations and, as we remember clearly, an invaluable resource for scholars working on these topics.

A third institution, the Society for Health and Human Values, traces its origins to the end of the 1950s, although it did not emerge as a formal organization for another decade. One of its main generators was Otto Guttentag, who had led the University of California at San Francisco's (UCSF) 1951 conference on human experimentation, and is an often underappreciated figure in the development of medical ethics and the broader area of health and human values, and their roles in medical education. As a prominent United Church of Christ layman as well as physician, Guttentag was part of an ecumenical group of Protestant pastors, theologians, and religiously active physicians at UCSF that formed under the leadership of Ronald McNeur[20] when he became university pastor in 1959. The group's initial activities included a series of "informal conversations in the Student Union on human problems in relation to medicine," started by Guttentag and Paul Sanazaro a professor of clinical medicine and a Presbyterian elder who later became the Association of American Medical College's director of research in medical education (Barker 1987: 2). Those conversations generated various programs and projects that began in the summer of 1961,[21] which in turn led to the development of programs in medical humanities at a number of medical schools, and the formation of the Society for Health and Human Values in 1969.[22]

The 1960s to Mid-1970s

As described in the various accounts of bioethics' origins mentioned above, and in other writings such as Renée Fox's sociological analyses, the 1960s to the mid-1970s were the years during which bioethics became a visible part of the American landscape, growing from the seeds that had been planted in the 1950s. The field's development during the 1960s and early 1970s, from our perspective and that of some other analysts, was generated by a number of converging factors. Among these were the social and cultural unrest and changes in the United States seen in the civil rights and other rights and social protest movements of the time, and the religious turbulence in Roman Catholic and Protestant churches, both of which we discuss in chapter 2 in relation to the backgrounds of early entrants into bioethics. Other prominent factors included the increasing attention given to the ramifications of current or prospective advances in biomedical research and technology,[23] and the growing awareness of and concern about abuses of the rights and welfare of human research subjects.

Religion and Bioethics. As bioethics gained a more clearly defined shape during the early to mid-1960s, scholars from various disciplines that had also been engaged with medical-ethical concerns in the 1950s—most notably moral theology, religious studies, medicine, biology, and law, but not yet, with rare exceptions such as Danner Clouser, from mainstream academic philosophy—began to "wander into the field from somewhere else, more or less inventing it as they [went]" (Callahan 1973). Among the first and, at the time, best-known wanderers into bioethics were Protestant and Catholic theologians such as Joseph Fletcher, James Gustafson, Richard McCormick, and Paul Ramsey, and metaphysically oriented thinkers like philosopher Hans Jonas.[24] They were prominent and esteemed writers, teachers, mentors, and active participants in the beginnings of the Hastings Center and the Kennedy Institute. Nonetheless, the role of American and European theologians[25] and of figures such as Jonas in the emergence of bioethics during the 1960s, and their subsequent influence in relation to the ascendancy and domination of secular philosophers, are a particularly complex aspect of the field's history. One of the prevailing "myths of origin" has been that moral theology, religious thinkers, and their perspectives and themes "played an important role—perhaps even the principal role—in the field's renaissance..." (Walters 1985: 3). Recalling the founding of the Hastings Center, Callahan has written that "when I first became interested in bioethics in the mid-1960's, the only resources were theological or those drawn from within the traditions of medicine, themselves heavily shaped by religion" (Callahan 1990: 2).

In this historical view, moral theology and religious voices became muted and marginalized as bioethics became involved in clinical and public policy settings, and analytic philosophers and their secular concepts, methods, and language gained dominion.[26] However, scholars such as Martin Marty and Stephen Lammers, who have examined the interrelationships between religion and bioethics, argue that it is a fallacy to hold that "there was once a 'golden age' in which religious voices were somehow normative in bioethical discussion" (Lammers 1996: 23). Based on our participation in the early days of bioethics and our analyses of its development, this assessment is compatible with our own. As we have written, "There is a sense in which the most esteemed religiously trained and oriented figures in the early history of bioethics were regarded more as sages than as clear and clarifying thinkers. To the extent that they are remembered today, it is as much for their moral stature as for their intellectual contributions" (Messikomer, Fox, and Swazey 2001: 490).

Beginning the Field's Institutionalization. Preceding the establishment of permanent bioethics centers, a number of multiyear working groups were formed in the 1960s. Among these were the one created in 1966 by legal scholar Paul Freund, a Harvard professor of law and president of the American Academy of Arts and Sciences from 1964–1967, to conduct a "continuing seminar" on issues concerning experimentation with human subjects, and the research group formed in 1966 by the Harvard Program on Technology and Society to examine social and ethical implications of new biomedical technologies (Freund 1970; Mendelsohn, Swazey, and Taviss 1971).[27]

As the turbulent decade of the 1960s ended and a new decade began, there were several indicators that bioethics was achieving a more permanent presence in the United States. Two of what proved to be the field's premier centers were established in 1969 and 1971, respectively: the freestanding Institute for Society, Ethics and the Life Sciences (later renamed the Hastings Center), and the Kennedy Institute for Ethics at Georgetown University. As we have noted, what soon became the field's most commonly used name, "bioethics," was invented in 1970/1971 by Potter in Wisconsin and by Hellegers and Shriver in Washington. A year after the Kennedy Institute was inaugurated a third bioethics center was chartered in St. Louis: the Pope John XXIII Medical-Moral Research and Education Center. The Center, now also known as The National Catholic Bioethics Center, was begun in 1972 with the endorsement of John Cardinal Carberry and the assistance of The Catholic Health Association (then the Catholic Hospital Association); theologian and scientist in the field of pharmacology Fr. Albert Moraczewski, O.P., was named its first president.[28]

A Bioethics Literature. Another indicator that bioethics had arrived and was beginning to become institutionalized in the early to mid-1970s was a growing body of scholarly publications, such as Paul Ramsey's *The Patient as Person* (1970b) and Jay Katz's magisterial work *Experimentation with Human Beings* (1972). As part of its "research and education mission," the Institute for Society, Ethics and the Life Sciences launched its, and the field's, first journal in 1971, *The Hastings Center Report*.[29] A second, shorter-lived scholarly publication, *The Hastings Center Studies*, was first published in 1973. Its inaugural issue included a foundational essay by Daniel Callahan, "Bioethics as a Discipline," which was cited the next year on the authority card for the new subject heading, "bioethics," created by the Library of Congress (Callahan 1973; Reich 1993: S7).

The year 1975 bore witness to the fact that there was a growing body of literature dealing with bioethical matters: the first annual volume of one of the field's major reference works, *The Bibliography of Bioethics*, was developed and edited by the Kennedy Institute for Ethics' director, LeRoy Walters, and was published by the Institute. Another seminal scholarly work also was being prepared at the Kennedy Institute: under the aegis of its originator and editor, Warren Reich, the monumental *Encyclopedia of Bioethics* was published in 1978.

Bioethics, Medical Humanities, and Medical Education. What was variously called bioethics or medical ethics also was entering the academic world of medical schools and teaching hospitals. With what Callahan described as "mixed success," for example, staff from the Hastings Center began to introduce medical ethics into the curriculum at Columbia University's College of Physicians and Surgeons in 1971. Although that effort soon ended after they "came a political cropper," the Center went on to hold an important educational conference in 1972 on the teaching of ethics in medical school (Callahan 1999a: 60–61; Veatch and Gaylin 1972; Veatch, Gaylin, and Morgan 1973). Despite the fact that "bioethics" was a new word, whose meaning and scope were just in the process of definition, an academic title bearing that name was created in 1972, when Albert Jonsen, who was still a Jesuit priest at that time, was appointed adjunct associate professor of bioethics at the University of California, San Francisco (Jonsen 1998: xi). With funding from the Kennedy Foundation, Harvard's School of Public Health began a small program in medical ethics in 1972, with a course co-taught by William Curran, Arthur Dyck, and Stanley Reiser. The next year, in 1973, the first full-fledged medical school program in medical ethics began at the University of Wisconsin, directed by pediatrician Norman Fost. Health lawyer John Robertson also joined the program in 1973, and a third faculty member, philosopher Daniel Wikler, was hired in 1975 with funding for the position provided by a development grant from the Kennedy Foundation (Fost, interview, 2000: see appendix).

In a path that has largely been separate from bioethics, although the two at times have intersected both harmoniously and antagonistically, the field of medical humanities also was making substantial inroads into medical education and the training of faculty who would teach in this multidisciplinary field. Two vital contributions to the development of medical humanities were the financial support of the National Endowment for the Humanities (NEH), which had been established by the U.S. Congress in 1965, and the work of the Society for Health and Human Values (SHHV). NEH grants helped to fund the initiation of some of the first programs in the humanities/medical humanities at several new, innovative medical schools, including the University of Florida at Gainesville, Penn State at Hershey, and the University of Texas Medical Branch at Galveston. Dan (K. Danner) Clouser became the first philosopher appointed to a modern medical school faculty in 1968, when he joined the Department of Humanities at Hershey, which admitted its first class in 1967. Two major figures in the development of the SHHV were involved in establishing the Penn State humanities program and in Clouser's recruitment: E. A. (Al) Vastyan, chair of the Humanities Department, and Hershey's first dean, George Harrell, who had begun the humanities program at the University of Florida School of Medicine in Gainesville before moving to Pennsylvania (Clouser, interview, 1998: see appendix).

By 1976, the SHHV had fostered the development of programs in medical humanities/health and human values at 29 medical schools, and, according to annual data on medical education compiled by the American Medical Association, a total of 63 schools had introduced some type of human values teaching program in its curriculum (Barker 1987: 69). The Society's work in this area, including sending teams of consultants to schools to assist in developing new programs or expanding existing programs, was done largely through its Institute on Human Values in Medicine (IHVM), a major program that began in 1971 and was funded through 1981 primarily by a series of grants from the NEH.[30]

Training Faculty

The Institute on Human Values in Medicine. Complementing its work on establishing health and human values programs in medical schools, the Society for Health and Human Values Institute, again with NEH funds, embarked on a program of conferences and fellowships to train faculty from a range of humanities disciplines and medicine for their new teaching roles. From 1973–1978, 75 fellowships were awarded for periods of study ranging from three months to one year, from a pool of 253 student and faculty applicants at 118 medical schools and universities. In their account of the IHVM's development and work, T. K. McElhinney and Edmund Pellegrino explained that the fellowship "allowed time for doing research, learning about teaching methods and examining the possibility of a personal career change dedicated to integrating humanities, ethics and human values into medical studies and patient care" (McElhinney and Pellegrino 2001: 300). These fellowships proved to be crucial learning and networking experiences for a number of young scholars, including Ronald Carson, Larry Churchill, Loretta Kopelman, Mark Siegler, and David Thomasma, who would become prominent figures in bioethics and clinical ethics as well as the medical humanities. During the 1970s, the Institute's programs and other SHHV activities, such as its annual meeting, served an important function for bioethics as well as for the medical humanities.[31] Although the SHHV focused "not only on ethical issues in health care" but also on "the broader questions of human values that can be addressed through literature and art as well as from theology and philosophy," Jonsen points out that "by bringing together many of the persons who were devoting themselves to teaching ethics in medical schools, SHHV created a community in which common interests were recognized and fostered....The Society was the meeting place for those otherwise lonely figures, the bioethics professors" (Jonsen 1998: 25).

A second Institute program, "Dialogues Between the Disciplines," inaugurated in 1974, functioned both as a training ground and as a vehicle for developing teaching in the humanities and medicine. Four areas were identified as being "crucial to the development of interdisciplinary human values teaching: literature and medicine, history and medicine, religion and medicine, and the social sciences and medicine" (McElhinney and Pellegrino 2001: 308). Interdisciplinary groups of about 10 members each, consisting of physicians and other health professionals and "humanist scholars" were formed for each of these areas, meeting over a two-year period and preparing written reports that, with one exception, were published by university presses.

The Haverford Summer Institute and the Advent of Philosophers. Another key educational program was launched in 1974 at Haverford College in Pennsylvania. The six-week Haverford summer institute, developed by philosopher Samuel Gorovitz, was a watershed event in the composition of the bioethics community and how it approached medical-ethical problems. It was a marker for the entry, and coming domination, of philosophers in bioethics, particularly those schooled in Anglo-American analytic philosophy. Gorovitz, trained in logical positivism and the philosophy of science at the University of California at Los Angeles, ventured into the terrain of medical ethics in the mid-1960s, as an assistant professor of philosophy at Western Reserve University and Case Institute of Technology (subsequently merged as Case Western Reserve University). Pursuing ideas about the need for centers that would engage in a more systematic study of medical ethics that he set forth in a short 1966 paper, "Ethics and the Allocation of Medical Resources," Gorovitz started a project called Moral Problems in Medicine at Case Western's medical school in 1970, with funding from the NEH—its first medical ethics grant—and the Exxon Educational Foundation. Gorovitz gathered a small group of his philosopher-colleagues to work on the project with him, including Ruth Macklin, a young analytic philosopher who had received her PhD at Case in 1968, and became project director when Gorovitz moved to the University of Maryland in 1973. The grant's purpose, Macklin recalled, was to develop a teaching curriculum, and when the group started an undergraduate course, "what we had to do was to find some readings for students...and found...[that there were] precious few that could be used in...a philosophy department course." The readings they did identify were compiled as an anthology, *Moral Problems in Medicine*

(Gorovitz et al. 1976), which "was essentially the first real [systematic] anthology in medical ethics or bioethics" (Macklin, interview, 1999: see appendix).

The prevailing absence of philosophers in bioethics at the time, or even their awareness that such a field existed, is evident in Macklin's recollection of her reply when Gorovitz asked people in the department if they were interested in developing a program in medical ethics. "I, at least, said 'What kind of ethics? Medical what?' I didn't know it was a field, or a growing field.... The Hastings Center had been established in 1969, but it was a very small thing that was not necessarily known by philosophers.... Dan Callahan's background [was] in philosophy although he never taught it and didn't like [academic philosophy]. [T]here were a very few [other philosophers] at the beginning [of Hastings] who were involved...[but they, like Hans Jonas and Robert Neville,] were from the Continental school—from the non-analytic school" (Macklin, interview, 1999: see appendix).

The summer institute at Haverford in 1974, Macklin continued, was a "pivotal" event "in the field [of bioethics] becoming overrun with philosophers." Gorovitz, by then at the University of Maryland, obtained funding from the Rockefeller Brothers Foundation to support a new venture under the auspices of the American Philosophical Association, which he named the Council for Philosophical Studies Institute on Moral Problems in Medicine. Growing out of his Case Western project, the summer institute's purpose was to train philosophers, along with some academic physicians and other faculty, to teach medical ethics from a philosophical perspective. Gorovitz assembled a faculty for the summer institute that included a number of leading philosophers such as William Frankena, Robert Nozick, Judith Jarvis Thomson, and Bernard Williams, as well as three medical ethicists from the Hastings Center: Daniel Callahan, Willard Gaylin, and Robert Veatch. The attendees, in turn, included a number of young scholars such as Natalie Abrams, Tom Beauchamp,[32] Ronald Carson, Tristram Engelhardt, William Ruddick, and Stuart Spicker, who would become important figures in bioethics and the medical humanities, and several of whom also had received fellowships from the SHHV's Institute on Human Values in Medicine.

As suggested by Macklin's comments about the absence of philosophers in the early days of the Hastings Center, and in bioethics more generally, some of the leading philosopher-bioethicists, among them Dan Clouser and Stephen Toulmin, viewed the arrival of academic philosophers, especially those trained in analytic philosophy, as marking the "real" beginnings of bioethics and the assumption of its role in the public square (Clouser 1993, 1978; interview, 1998: see appendix; Toulmin 1982). As he explained in his now classic 1982 paper, Toulmin regarded the entry of moral philosophers into what he termed medical ethics as a mutually beneficial occurrence. It not only brought a needed rational, analytic rigor to the field, he claimed; it virtually "saved the life of ethics." It did this by refocusing philosophers from their preoccupation with abstract metaethics to "the concrete and particular issues that arise in actual practice, whether in medicine or elsewhere…[giving] back to ethics a seriousness and human relevance which it had seemed—at least in the writings of the interwar years—to have lost for good" (Toulmin 1982: 749–750).

Clouser, who wrote the article "Bioethics" for the first edition of the *Encyclopedia of Bioethics* (Clouser 1978), felt strongly that bioethics "[was] not entirely philosophy," for "many disciplines [had] morally relevant insights into [biomedical] activities, as well as organizing concepts." Nonetheless, he said at the 1992 "Birth of Bioethics" conference, "Remember that twenty-five to thirty years ago, medical ethics…was a mixture of religion, whimsy, exhortation, legal precedents, various traditions, philosophies of life, miscellaneous moral rules, and epithets (uttered either by wise or witty physicians). I believe that philosophy provided the push toward systematization, consistency, and clarity, as progress within medicine increasingly erupted into moral dilemmas" (Clouser 1993: S10). Callahan, in "The Hastings Center and the Early Years of Bioethics," expressed comparable thoughts about the difference that philosophers made in bioethics, especially from the perspective of the Center's philosopher-fellows. Before 1974, he observed, "the major figures from ethics tended to have a religious and theological background. The entrance of the philosophers radically tilted the field in a secular direction." "Most of the philosophers," he continued, "were not religious, but more tellingly…they had little use for the theologians and their style of ethical discourse, which they labeled vague, fuzzy, and latently sectarian, not up to the rigorous standards of a more public role for bioethics. After the mid-1970s, I had a constant struggle (which never really ended) to get the philosophers among our fellows even to tolerate theologians at our project meetings: 'what's the point?' they said" (Callahan 1999a: 61).

Funding Bioethics. As bioethics took shape from the 1950s into the early 1970s, there was no dearth of intertwined social, ethical, and human value concerns calling for thoughtful reflection and analysis, or of people from various disciplines interested in such a pursuit. It is highly likely, however, that bioethics would have been stillborn without the funding from private foundations and federal agencies that made possible the various study groups, programs, and centers that marked the new field's emergence. Grants from the NIH supported the Boston University Law-Medicine Institute's study of ethical and legal issues in clinical investigation, and the American Academy of Arts and Science's working party on human experimentation. Harvard's Program on Technology and Society, and the work of its biomedical sciences group, was supported by funds from I.B.M. The Kennedy Foundation provided support for the establishment of the Kennedy Institute for Human Reproduction and Bioethics at Georgetown, the ethics program at the Harvard School of Public Health, and the Program in Medical Ethics at the University of Wisconsin School of Medicine. The development of the Society for Health and Human Values was supported by the United Ministries for Higher Education and the Danforth Foundation, and the Society's Institute on Human Values in Medicine and its fellowship program were funded by NEH.

The NEH proved to be a major supporter of bioethics in its early years. Along with funds from the Exxon Education Foundation, for example, an NEH grant to Case Western launched Gorovitz's project on moral problems in medicine, and the agency also was among the supporters of the Hastings Center in its early years.[33] The Rockefeller Brothers Foundation provided a grant enabling Gorovitz to set up the Council on Philosophical Studies' Institute on Moral Problems in Medicine—more familiarly known as the Haverford Summer Institute—and grants from the Brothers Fund and the Rockefeller Foundation provided major underpinnings for Hastings. The fledgling center also benefited from the financial support of one of its "first benefactors," John D. Rockefeller III, and from his advice to Callahan and Gaylin when they were organizing Hastings that "we would be foolish to become part of a university and to take on all of the problems that doing so would entail" (Callahan 1999a: 57).

A thorough analysis of the funding of bioethics would be an informative part the field's history, providing insights into the types of work that various foundations and federal agencies judged worthy of support over the years, and, if records are available and accessible, why and by whom those judgments were made.[34] Our sense is that there have been alterations in the sources of funding since the 1970s, and in the types of work that have been supported. And, as funding for bioethics, like many areas of biomedicine, becomes harder to secure from federal agencies and private foundations, bioethics centers and individual bioethicists have turned increasingly to corporate sources of support, a move that has generated controversy from within and without the field about the ethics of bioethics.

Bioethics Goes to Washington

In our view, the mid-1970s saw the completion of the first stage of bioethics' presence in the United States. The final major development in this stage was the arrival of bioethical issues, and bioethicists, in Washington. The keystone event in what Rothman (1991: chap. 9) aptly calls "commissioning ethics" was the legislative mandate to establish a National Commission for the Protection of Human Subjects in Biomedical and Behavioral Research in Title II of the 1974 National Research Act (Public Law 93–348).[35] The creation of the National Commission, and the array of reports, recommendations, studies, and papers it produced from 1975–1978, was the culmination of a series of congressional bills and hearings that began in 1968, when Senator Walter Mondale (D-MN) introduced Senate Joint Resolution (S) 145 to establish a National Commission on Health Science and Society.[36] During hearings on his resolution before the Senate Committee on Government Operations' Subcommittee on Government Research in

March, Mondale explained that the bill embodied his conviction that "[r]ecent medical advances raise grave and fundamental ethical and legal concerns for our society." A commission, he believed, would provide an urgently needed forum to study and deliberate the implications of work underway in areas such as genetic engineering, organ transplantation, and behavior control, and the related topics of the use of human subjects and the financing of research (U.S. Senate Subcommittee 1968: 1, 3).

Mondale had expected that many scientists and physicians, as well as the general public, shared his concerns, but the testimony delivered during the hearings spelled the death knell for his bill, which failed to reach the Senate floor. Most of those who spoke or delivered written commentary believed that the ethical and legal issues were being greatly exaggerated, and were sharply critical of the proposed Commission as an unneeded and unwarranted intrusion into medical research. Mondale had encountered the strong prevailing conviction of physicians and researchers that they could and should regulate themselves, which as we have noted, in part accounted for the lack of attention paid to the Nuremberg Code. The folkloric words of one of the country's most eminent surgeons, Dr. Owen Wangensteen, epitomized the deeply held belief in self-governance shared by other noted physicians such as Dr. Henry Beecher: "[T]he fellow who holds the apple can peel it best" (U.S. Senate Subcommittee 1968: 100).

Though surprised and disappointed by the reaction to his concerns and the proposed commission, Mondale was not dissuaded. He reintroduced his legislation (S 71) in 1971—the year in which the Kennedy Institute of Ethics was established—but it again was rebuffed. This time, the most effective opposition came from the Department of Health, Education and Welfare. In his testimony, the assistant secretary for health declared that, in light of activities such as NIH's work on the protection of human subjects and the Hastings Center-NIH Fogarty Center conference on genetics, the administration was "taking the position at this time that legislation is not necessary." Mondale's rejoinder showed that he clearly was frustrated and exasperated by the opposition he was encountering from scientists, physicians, and the government. "'All we are proposing here,'" the senator declared, "'is to create a measly little study commission to look at some very profound issues. I sense an almost psychopathic objection to the public process, a fear that if the public gets involved, it is going to be anti-science, hostile and unsupportive'" (quoted in Jonsen 1998: 94).

In March 1973, an undeterred, determined Mondale successfully reintroduced S 71, to establish an Advisory Commission on Health, Science and Society that would conduct "a comprehensive study of the ethical, social and legal implications of advances in biomedical research and technology." By this point in time, compared with Mondale's unsuccessful efforts in 1968 and 1971, legislators in both the House and Senate were responding to a wave of public concerns, and greater professional awareness, about ethical, social, and legal issues that were emanating from various revelations about cases of human experimentation that violated the rights and/or welfare of subjects, and about a number of biomedical advances.

The Tuskegee Syphilis Study. The most publicized and influential case that raised nationwide awareness about human experimentation issues was the Public Health Service's (PHS) "Study of Untreated Syphilis in the Negro Male," begun in 1932. Based on the lack of knowledge at the time about the pathogenesis of syphilis, it was a designed as a prospective study, putatively in order to document the natural history of the disease as a basis for establishing a "more knowledgeable...control program."[37] The study involved 600 poor, uneducated African American men—399 with syphilis and 201 "controls" without the disease—living in Macon County, Alabama, an area that had one of the highest rates of syphilis in the United States. According to records of the study, those who agreed to take part in it were told they were going to be examined and treated for "bad blood"—a local catchall term for ailments including anemia, fatigue, and syphilis—and in return would receive free medical exams and meals and burial insurance. There was no convincing evidence, however, that the men had ever been adequately informed about the nature and purpose of the study, nor were they offered the then available treatment regimen of arsenic and heavy metal.

The intended length of the study when it was designed and initiated is unclear,[38] but it was still ongoing 40 years later, when, on July 26, 1972, *The New York Times* revealed details about it in a front-page story[39] (Heller 1972). Tuskegee had not been a clandestine project: its existence was known to many within the PHS and its Center for Disease Control (CDC), papers reporting its findings had been published in professional journals since 1936, and the CDC had reviewed it periodically and, as late as 1969, had, with at least one strong vote of dissent, supported its continuation.

There was not a widespread awareness about the existence and exact nature of the study, however, until the *New York Times* story, which unleashed extensive media coverage and a public outcry. Within a month, the Department of Health, Education and Welfare's (DHEW) assistant secretary for health appointed a nine-member Tuskegee Syphilis Study Ad Hoc Advisory Panel, chaired by a respected African American educator, Dr. Broadus Butler, and numbering Dr. Jay Katz among its nine members. At that time, the Panel learned that an estimated 125 of the Tuskegee subjects, including 50 of the controls, were still alive, but their current health status was unknown.

The Panel had three specific charges. First, to "determine whether the study was justified in 1932 and whether it should have been continued when penicillin became generally available."[40] Second, to "recommend whether the study should be continued..., and if not, how it should be terminated in a way consistent with the rights and health needs of its remaining participants." The third, more sweeping charge was to "determine whether existing policies to protect the rights of patients participating in health research conducted or supported by the [DHEW] are adequate and effective and to recommend improvements in these policies, if needed" (U.S. DHEW 1973: charter 1).

After an intensive period of work, the Advisory Panel, which was divided into three subcommittees, each responsible for examining and making recommendations about its assigned charge, sent its initial recommendations to the assistant secretary in late October 1972, and issued its final report on April 28, 1973. It is a document that should be read in full by anyone concerned with human subjects research. With respect to its first charge, the Panel found that undertaking the longitudinal study "was ethically unjustified in 1932," for two principal reasons. First, because, "as initially reported in 1936 and through the years," its "conduct is judged to be scientifically unsound and its results are disproportionately meager compared with the known risks to the human subjects involved." Second, because "there was no evidence that...consent was obtained from the participants" which met "the fundamental ethical rule...that a person should not be subjected to avoidable risk of death or physical harm unless he freely and intelligently consents." With regard to the other half of its first charge, the Panel declared that "[p]enicillin therapy should have been made available to the participants...not later than 1953." Responding to Charge II, the Panel recommended unequivocally that "the study of *untreated* syphilis in Black males...should be terminated immediately. With this most basic recommendation, the participants...are to be given the care now required to treat any disabilities resulting from their participation" (italics by Subcommittee).

The subcommittee that worked on the Panel's third charge, concerning the adequacy and effectiveness of DHEW policies to protect the rights of human research subjects, was chaired by Jay Katz. His profound knowledge about experimentation with human beings (his landmark book with that title was published in 1972, the year the Panel was convened), and his passionate convictions about the primacy of informed, voluntary consent are evident in the Panel's conclusions and recommendations.[41] The report on Charge III emphasized that the Panel's recommendations were not generated only by the Tuskegee Study. Rather, it stated, "[t]he protection of human research subjects is a current and widespread problem," which "should not be surprising, especially in light of the recent Congressional hearings and bills" and the media coverage of a number of ethically problematic experiments over the past decade. Following from this conclusion, the Subcommittee specified what it considered to be five seriously problematic aspects of the DHEW policies, and five policy recommendations to remedy those deficits.

Those familiar with the reports concerning research involving human subjects issued by the first two federal bioethics commissions, the National Commission and the President's Commission, will recognize the extent to which the Advisory Panel's evaluation and recommendations influenced the work of those bodies and

resultant modifications in the federal regulations for the protection of human subjects. The Panel's first policy recommendation, however, has never been adopted,
although, as discussed below, it was part of a 1973 bill introduced by Senator
Edward Kennedy (D-MA) to establish a national commission, and has been
championed by Katz and others for many years. "Congress," the Panel wrote,
"should establish a permanent body with the authority to regulate *at least* all Federally supported research involving human subjects.... This body could be called
the National Human Investigation Board. The Board should be independent of
DHEW, for we do not believe that the agency which both conducts a great deal
of research itself and supports much of the research that is carried on elsewhere
is in a position to carry out dispassionately the functions we have in mind" (U.S.
DHEW 1973: 23–24; italics by Subcommittee).

In November 1972, a month after the Advisory Panel had submitted its initial recommendations to the assistant secretary, DHEW terminated the Tuskegee
Study. To Jay Katz's mounting frustration, however, which he expressed at hearings
held by Sen. Kennedy in March 1973, the agency was slow to act on the Panel's
other recommendations about Tuskegee. Then, in summer 1973, in the settlement
of a class-action lawsuit filed by the National Association for the Advancement
of Colored People after Kennedy's hearings, the survivors were awarded over
$9 million and, as the Advisory Panel had recommended, the government pledged
to provide them with free medical care and burial services.[42,43]

Sixty-five years after the Tuskegee Study was initiated, and 25 years after the
report of the Ad Hoc Advisory Panel, President William J. Clinton issued a public
apology on behalf of the nation for the study.[44] He spoke in the East Room of the
White House, before an invited assemblage that included some of the eight survivors and their families, other family representatives, and members of Congress
and the Cabinet. "The United States government," the president said, "did something that was wrong—deeply, profoundly, morally wrong. It was an outrage to
our commitment to integrity and equality for all our citizens." "You did nothing
wrong," he said to the survivors, "but you were grievously wronged. I apologize,
and I am sorry that this apology had been so long in coming."[45] At the end of his
remarks, Mr. Clinton announced "several steps" to "rebuild [the] broken trust"
that has been a legacy of the Tuskegee Study. These steps included building a
"lasting memorial at Tuskegee," making a commitment "to strengthen researchers' training in bioethics," and by an executive order issued that day, extending the
charter of his National Bioethics Advisory Commission to October 1999 (Clinton
1997c).

Congress and the National Commission. The first months of 1973 saw an
unprecedented amount of attention accorded to bioethical issues in Washington.
Responding to the wave of concerns evoked by Tuskegee and other human experimentation cases that had come to light, and by burgeoning awareness about the

ethical and social implications of new biomedical advances, the Senate and the House of Representatives held hearings to discuss and debate about an explosion of proposed congressional legislation. In the House, Representative Paul Rogers (D-FL), chairman of the Subcommittee on Health and the Environment of the Committee on Interstate and Foreign Commerce, scheduled hearings on some 15 bills, whose sponsors variously proposed, among other things, the creation of a National Human Experimentation Standards Board, a National Commission on Transplantation and Artificial Organs, a Psychosurgery Commission, and a Commission on Medical Technology and the Dignity of Dying (Jonsen 1998: 97). Although none of these bills was reported out of committee, the types of concerns they addressed were recognized when the Rogers committee drafted the House's National Research Act legislation authorizing federal support of medical research (House Resolution [HR] 7724), which included a provision for establishing a national bioethics commission.

In the Senate, as we have noted, Mondale's previously rebuffed bill to establish an Advisory Commission on Health Science and Society now gained passage. Center stage, however, was taken by Sen. Kennedy, chair of the Labor and Public Welfare Committee's Subcommittee on Health, who convened a series of hearings on a range of medical-ethical, social policy, and legal issues similar to those being considered by Rogers's House committee (U.S. Senate Subcommittee on Health 1973). The senator already was engaged with bioethical issues: with his sister and brother-in-law, Eunice Kennedy and Sargent Shriver, he had been instrumental in starting the Kennedy Institute in 1971, and in supporting the new venture with a substantial grant from the Kennedy Foundation, of which the senator was president (Auerbach 1971a; Auerbach 1971b; Reich 1996). Echoing the concerns evoked by the title of Rosenfeld's 1969 book, *The Second Genesis: The Coming Control of Life*, Kennedy began his first hearing on "Quality of Care—Human Experimentation" by declaring that "[s]cientists may stand on the threshold of being able to recreate man." This prospect, he said, can be seen in developments such as neurological and pharmacological behavior modification, transplantation, and the possibilities of genetic engineering opened by James Watson and Francis Crick's deciphering of the genetic code. The Committee's senior Republican member, New York's Jacob Javits, supported the need for hearings, particularly in connection with two bills he had filed: one mandating NIH to establish review committees for extramural research involving human subjects and to require informed consent procedures for such research; the other to fund grants to improve the teaching of medical ethics in medical schools (Jonsen 1998: 95–96).

Kennedy was a skilled politician, and "more artfully than Mondale earlier, structured his hearings to demonstrate the need for outside intervention" in governing both research involving human subjects and medical care (Rothman 1991:184). Sessions were held in February, March, and April 1973 dealing with particular biomedical advances and their ethical ramifications, and with human experimentation, including a meeting in April devoted specifically to the Tuskegee Syphilis Study. Charles McCarthy, who at the time was working in the NIH's Division of Legislative Analysis and who wrote much of the testimony that DHEW officials gave for both the House and Senate hearings, attended most of Kennedy's sessions. Presaging the amount of attention that bioethical issues would receive in the media, McCarthy is still struck by the extensive publicity the national press and television gave to the hearings, including live TV coverage of the Tuskegee session. "As far as I recall," he said, "the only Congressional hearings that had been televised prior to the Kennedy hearings were the Senator Joe McCarthy Un-American activities hearings" (McCarthy, interview, 1999: see appendix).

In June, the Senate subcommittee considered two bills filed by Kennedy: S 2071, parallel to Rogers's HR 7724, dealt with authorization for federal research funding and health manpower, while S 2072 focused on the protection of human subjects. The latter bill included the requirements for NIH-funded extramural research sought by Javits, and Kennedy's provisions for establishing a National Commission for the Protection of Human Subjects. Paul Rogers, in his House legislation, proposed a commission with a limited life span. Kennedy, in contrast, favored the sort of permanent body that the Tuskegee Syphilis Study Advisory Panel had recommended—the standing national human investigation board advocated by Jay Katz. The senator, Charles McCarthy related, "used the Securities and Exchange Commission as a model for the National Commission.... [He] proposed a separate federal agency that would have had authority to regulate human subjects research to make sure that it was ethical" (McCarthy, interview, 1999: see appendix).

Kennedy's bills were approved by the Labor and Public Welfare Committee, with his proposal for a National Commission becoming Title II of the National Research Act legislation. The Senate-House conference committee that worked on reconciling the bills from Kennedy and Rogers endorsed a temporary three-year commission located within NIH, rather than the permanent separate agency that Kennedy, following Katz's lead, had advocated. Katz has suggested, in strong language, that the reason his and Kennedy's proposed permanent commission was not adopted in 1973 (or thereafter)

may have been the Senate's reluctance to expose to public view the value conflicts inherent in the conduct of research. Had the Senate seriously debated the bill, it would have been forced to consider when, if ever, inadequately informed subjects can serve as a means to society's and science's ends. I believed then, as I do now, that the rejection of an NHIB [National Human Investigation Board] was not just a mistake but a subterfuge to avoid giving greater public visibility to the decisions made in the conduct of human experimentation. (Katz 1993: 37–38)

The National Research Act was signed into law by President Richard Nixon on July 12, 1974, as Public Law 93–348, establishing the National Commission for the Protection of Human Subjects in Biomedical and Behavioral Research for a four-year period. Although Mondale's Advisory Commission, in the form that he had envisaged it, had not come to pass, the "comprehensive study" his legislation had called for was incorporated in the mandate to the Commission as section 203 of the National Research Act, as an addition to the group's primary charge of examining and making recommendations about the protection of human subjects in federally funded research. The "special study" subsequently done by the Commission to meet this mandate had three components: a study using the then in vogue Delphi methodology, with a panel of 125 respondents; a public opinion poll; and a "scholarly adjunct" to the special study. The scholarly adjunct was developed to "draw on the experience of a more limited number of leading scholars and scientists to focus on the issues raised in the special study mandate." Stephen Toulmin, then the Commission's staff philosopher, directed the special study. Six faculty from Boston University and Harvard were selected as the "core group" for the scholarly adjunct; their work, and the report they prepared, incorporated the results of a larger discussion group of 25 participants that met in late June 1976. One of us (JPS) was a member of the "core group," and has in her files what is probably a rare copy of the Scholarly Adjunct report, dated December 1976; other than very occasional mentions in the bioethics literature, the Special Study, like so many other reports prepared for or by the government, quietly and quickly fell into oblivion.

The legislation establishing the Commission contained two unusual mandates for federal advisory bodies. First, and in contrast to its successor federal bioethics commissions, it *required* the DHEW secretary to respond to the Commission's recommendations concerning federally funded human subjects research within a specific time frame and in one of two ways: by issuing proposed regulations, or by justifying a decision not to do so. Second, and even more uniquely, the bill mandated the Commission to identify "the basic ethical principles that should underlie the conduct of biomedical and behavioral research involving human subjects and to develop guidelines which should be followed to assure that such research is conducted in accordance with those principles" (*The Belmont Report* 1978: 2). This part of the Commission's charge, LeRoy Walters has related,[46] was written by Charles McCarthy, who subsequently played a principal role in translating the National Commission's recommendations into the Federal policies and regulations for the protection of human subjects.

In response to its second mandate, the Commission first recruited several ethicists to prepare background papers dealing both with general and research-related moral principles,[47] which Toulmin synthesized and analyzed for the commissioners. Armed with these materials, a group of the commissioners, staff, and advisors repaired to a conference center in Maryland, Belmont House, for four days in February 1976 to begin their work. As several participants in the report's preparation recalled at a 1999 conference, "Belmont Revisited," their task proved to be a difficult, time-consuming, and at times contentious one. With final "polishing" done by Tom Beauchamp, Toulmin's successor as staff philosopher, *The Belmont Report* was approved by the full Commission in June 1978, and transmitted to the secretary of DHEW for the Department's response. DHEW published the *Report* in 1978, and it was issued as a notice for public comment in the *Federal Register* in April 1979 (*The Belmont Report* 1978; U.S. DHEW. Office of the Secretary 1979). The short, sparse report sets forth three now well-known principles to "serve as a basic justification for the many practical ethical prescriptions and evaluations of human actions": respect for persons, beneficence, and justice, and then briefly discusses how the "application of the general principles to the conduct of research leads to consideration of [three] requirements: informed consent, risk/benefit assessment, and the selection of research subjects." As we recount in chapter 5, this product of the National Commission has become an iconic document, nationally and internationally, both in the area of research with human subjects and bioethics more generally.

The establishment of the National Commission was a strong sign of the moral and political importance that the panoply of ethical issues involved in research with human subjects and in a variety of biomedical developments had attained among high-ranking members of Congress, both Democratic and Republican, and in the executive branch of the Federal government. Bioethics had come to Washington, and has remained a part of American governance in the form of a series of topically wide-ranging congressionally and presidentially established commissions and a variety of subject-specific advisory bodies.

Viewing bioethics in the United States as a field that has evolved through several stages since the 1950s, the mid-1970s is a reasonable time, historically and sociologically, to date the end of its "emergence" and the beginning of its next phase, that of its progressive institutionalization and professionalization. By the mid-1970s, bioethics was becoming rooted as a multidisciplinary presence in the United States. Although some of its early practitioners were uncertain about the field's long-term prospects, bioethics had gained roles in various scholarly, educational, and policy domains; was providing increasing opportunities for the part-time and full-time employment of a new specialist, the bioethicist; and was well on its way to becoming what James Gustafson later characterized as a "growth industry" (Gustafson 1991).

In the next two chapters, we round out our account of the field's emergence. Chapter 2 explores "the coming of bioethicists" through autobiographical accounts of how persons we interviewed became involved in medical ethics/bioethics during the 1960s to the mid-1970s, and how they thought about the nascent field at that time. Then, in chapter 3, we return to the beginning of the Kennedy Institute of Ethics in 1971, in the form of a personal recollection by one of us (RCF) who participated in the Institute's inaugural event.

Notes

1. In his examination of the field's history, Gracia takes strong exception to what he calls the "extremely parochial and ethnocentric" view that he attributes to a number of Americans that, because bioethics was "born in the US," it is a "a specific product of the American culture...[that] can be spread out, applied, and particularised" in other countries but "cannot be enriched in its essence" (Gracia 2001: 44, 45).

2. Although it is beyond the scope of our study, it is important to note that, as a number of scholars have documented, the contemporary field termed bioethics, medical ethics, or biomedical ethics was preceded by a centuries-long history of attention to moral or ethical dimensions of medicine and biology by moral theologians, primarily those in the Roman Catholic Church, and by physicians and philosophers. Analysts of these historical antecedents also have pointed out the distinctions between the forms and substance of the "old" medical ethics and the "new" bioethics (Baker 1995; Baker, Porter, and Porter 1993, 1995; Numbers and Amundsen 1986).

3. Jonsen defined approximately 60 people as "pioneers of bioethics"—those "whose names had appeared in the first edition of the *Bibliography of Bioethics* (1975) and who had continued to work in this field" (Jonsen 1993: S1).

4. Albert Jonsen, letter to "The Birth of Bioethics" conference faculty, Nov. 9, 1992. This letter was dated 30 years to the day after Alexander's story appeared in *Life* magazine.

5. As Reich observes, events related to the Pontifical Commission, the Second Vatican Council that was convoked by Pope John XXIII from 1962–1965, and the contentious debates generated by the Pope Paul VI's 1968 Encyclical, *Humanae Vitae*, which, despite his Commission's conclusions, upheld the Church's prohibition of all birth control methods except rhythm, "constituted a major watershed for modern ethics in religious context, but with vast ramifications for secular ethics as well.... The debates, documentary conclusions, and lay reactions to papal and episcopal authority in connection with fertility control constituted a turning point in religious moral authority unlike any other in the past 500 years" (Reich 1999: 38).

6. Information about the Nazi medical experiments was available to physicians and others through publications such as Leo Alexander's 1949 paper in the *New England Journal of Medicine*, "Medical Science under Dictatorship" (L. Alexander 1949). Alexander, a psychiatrist, had been a consultant to the secretary of war, working with the Office of the Chief of Counsel for War Crimes. One set of reasons why papers such as Alexander's drew so little attention is proposed in a paper by historian Robert N. Proctor. Analyzing "some myths and misconceptions" about Nazi science and Nazi medical ethics, Proctor writes that what he terms the "myth of Nazi science"—that it was, variously, pseudo-science, shoddy science, or science out of control—"served to reassure *the American public* (author's italics) that abuses like those of the Nazi era could never occur in a liberal democracy" like the United States, where "science was genuine science, secure within democratic institutions, obedient to the rule of law. Post-war ethical codes of conduct could even be dismissed as unnecessary—after all, weren't they designed to prevent abuses that could only occur in a totalitarian society?" (Proctor 2000: 336).

7. Katz goes on to assert, however, that the Code's "bold assertion about the primacy of consent could not be completely denied. The power of its appeal to respect for persons was too strong and survived, however diluted, in subsequent codifications and regulations" (Katz 1992: 228).

8. Based on his extensive experience, Katz views the belief of many researchers in their authority to govern themselves with respect to protecting the rights and welfare of their subjects as a problem that has persisted over the years since Nuremberg. "In countless discussions with research scientists," he related in a paper for Annas and Grodin's book, *The Nazi Doctors and the Nuremberg Code*, "I have learned about their tampering with the principle of voluntary consent in order to get research underway, advance science, and obtain research grants for the sake of protecting their laboratories and professional advancement. All this is done in the belief that physician-scientists can be trusted to safeguard the physical integrity of their research subjects" (Katz 1992: 231).

9. Moreno's research has shown that the Nuremberg Code became the Pentagon's official policy in February 1953, via a top secret memorandum from the secretary of defense to the Army, Navy, and Air Force secretaries. Moreno's analysis indicates, to him, that the "strengthened consent standards…can be seen as an attempt by the postwar national state to protect itself from critics of expanded governmental power" (Moreno 2004: 199; see also Moreno and Lederer 1996; President's Advisory Committee 1996; Proctor 2000).

10. According to Jonsen, the word *bioethics* first appeared in the mass media in the April 19, 1971 issue of *Time*, in which Potter's 1971 book, *Bioethics: Bridge to the Future*, was cited in a story called "Man into Superman: The Promise and Peril of the New Genetics" (Jonsen 1998: 27).

11. Handout at the American Society of Bioethics and Humanities' Bioethics Summer Retreat, Cape Cod, Mass., June 1998.

12. Eric Juengst, class handout, given to Judith Swazey during interview on Sept. 16, 1998.

13. Joseph Fletcher later became best known as a fervent and, in his words, "de-Christian-ized" proponent of what he termed "situation ethics" (Fletcher 1966). Judging from the criticism he has received from many philosophers and bioethicists for what they view as his ethical relativism, philosopher Stephen Toulmin wrote, "You might think that [Fletcher] was the spokesman for laxity and amorality." However, Toulmin, a proponent of casuistry, sees Fletcher as "belong[ing], in fact, to a very respectable line of Protestant (specifically Episcopalian) moral theologians." These theologians included Bishop Kenneth Kirk, "a main influence on [Fletcher] in his youth…[who employed] the 'case method' more usually associated with the Catholic casuists.… So, in retrospect, Joseph Fletcher's introduction of the phrase 'situation ethics' can be viewed as one further chapter in a history of the 'ethics of *cases*,' as contrasted with the 'ethics of *rules and principles*' " (Toulmin 1982: 740).

14. The attention to ethical issues concerning human experimentation, including the development of various guidelines and policies, antedate World War II and its sequelae. For an informative history of human experimentation in the United States from 1890 to 1940, see Lederer 1995.

15. In 1953, in connection with the opening of the Clinical Center by the NIH National Institutes of Health (NIH), the Public Health Service (PHS) issued its first set of principles and procedures for *intramural* clinical research involving human subjects. Congruent with the principles of academic freedom at the time, however, NIH vested extramural grantees and their institutions with the responsibility for protecting human subjects. The first PHS Policy and Procedure Order for *extramural* human subjects research was issued in 1966; that order required peer-committee review only for research that a principal investigator judged to present a physical risk to subjects.

16. In his introduction to *Experimentation in Man*, Beecher wrote that "[t]he breaches of ethical conduct which have come to [my] personal attention are [due to] ignorance or thoughtlessness. They were not willful or unscrupulous in origin. It is hoped that the material included here will help those who would do so to protect themselves from the errors of inexperience" (Beecher 1959b: 4). For discussions of Beecher's work concerning human experimentation, see Katz 1993 and Rothman 1987, 1991.

17. Texas Medical Center Institutions. The Institute of Religion [description], http://www.tmc.edu/institutions/irel.htm (accessed Jan. 10, 2004).

18. In 1993, the Institute held a conference to celebrate the 25th anniversary of its 1968 conference on medicine and technology; the conference's title and theme was "Religion and Medical Ethics: Looking Back, Looking Forward" (Verhey 1996).

19. The Institute's name was shortened to the Law-Medicine Institute, and then in 1970, after Curran moved to Harvard, it became the Center for Law and Health Sciences, with lawyer George Annas as its director and the prominent jurist David Bazelon as chair of its board.

20. In his history of the Health and Human Values Program of the United Ministries in Education, V. L. Barker credits Ronald W. McNeur with being "the catalyst for the formation and development of [the] new exploration in ministry and medical education" that gave rise to the Society for Health and Human Values. McNeur's career was a fascinating one: after earning his master's degree in the philosophical field of pure mathematics, he was a meteorologist during World War II, and then began doctoral studies in theology. In the 1950s, while serving as a pastor in California, his scholarly work concentrated on "reinterpret[ing] the Christian faith for the scientific age," leading to a book: *Space, Time, God*. In 1959, he was appointed director of the Westminister Foundation for the Bay Area and university pastor of the University of California Medical School, San Francisco, where he began his discussions and work with Otto Guttentag, Paul Sanazaro, and others that led to their work on health and human values programs in medical education (Barker 1987: 1–3).

21. The first work project and study, on "Medicine and Meaning," was for second- and third-year medical students at UCSF, who engaged in summer workshops, biblical study, and theological inquiry focused on topics including the identity of the doctor, nonmedical factors in the doctor's practice, the religious dimensions in health and illness, and medical care in a changing society (Barker 1987: 3).

22. The role of ecumenical religious groups in initiating teaching in medical ethics and medical humanities, as did Guttentag and his associates at UCSF and then the programs fostered by the Society for Health and Human Values, also is illustrated by the initiation of clinical ethics teaching in Britain by the London Medical Group (LMG). The LMG began in 1963, as a result of a study commissioned by the ecumenical Student Christian Movement concerning medical educational needs in Britain. That study led to the creation of the LMG, which, through its council of medical students and a consultative council of senior faculty, began a series of interdisciplinary symposia dealing with clinical medical ethics topics. The religious influence at work in the LMG's early programs is evidenced by its first lecture lists, which state that the organization's purpose is " 'to create in the medical schools a dialogue between belief and non-belief.' " As the LMG evolved, it became independent of the Student Christian Movement in 1974, and joined the Society for the Study of Medical Ethics (SSME), a group that had been developed by former LMG students. The next year, in 1975, both the LMG and the SSME formed the still active Institute of Medical Ethics, which that spring began publishing the *Journal of Medical Ethics* (Whong-Barr 2003).

23. Many laypersons, including in this instance policymakers, as well as many physicians and scientists, learned about these biomedical developments and some of their attendant issues through graphically titled newsmagazine articles and books such as G. Taylor's *The Biological Time Bomb* (1968) and A. Rosenfeld's *The Second Genesis: The Coming Control of Life* (1969).

24. There were also a few contributors to bioethics, including Rabbis J. David Bleich, David Feldman, Immanuel Jakobovits, and Seymour Siegel, who spoke and wrote out of Jewish religious tradition.

    Judaism has a long history of teachings based on scripture and rabbinic commentary about moral aspects of medicine. Although these teachings, written in Hebrew, became more available to religious scholars of other faiths with the publications of Jakobovits's *Jewish Medical Ethics* in 1959, Jewish bioethics has been oriented primarily toward its own faith communities (Dorff 1998; Jakobovits 1959).

25. As we discuss in chapter 2, a number of the theologians and religionists became involved in the early years of bioethics not only as direct participants but also, as personified by James Gustafson, as teachers and mentors of individuals who subsequently entered the new field. Other religiously trained persons who began working on bioethical topics as the field developed include, among Protestants, James Childress, Arthur Dyck, John Fletcher, Stanley Hauerwas, Karen Lebacqz, William May, and Ralph Potter Jr. Catholic figures include theologians Charles Curran, Germain Grisez, and Bernard Häring, laicized priests Albert Jonsen and Warren Reich, and prominent Catholic laypersons such as Daniel Callahan and Edmund Pellegrino.

    One of the interesting differences between the emergence of bioethics and of the medical humanities, as seen in the development of the Society for Health and Human Values and the work of the United Ministries in Education, is that the latter primarily drew Protestant pastors, rather than academic theologians, into its membership and programs. This is not to suggest, however, that the clergy who became involved in the United Ministries work in medical education did not have excellent theological training that prepared them for their work in health and human values. For, as Barker points out, "these were people trained in the thought of the Niebuhrs, Bonhoeffer, and Tillich. They were trained in the thought of the existentialists, and knew of the anxiety of the secular person. They had studied Karl Barth" (Barker 1987: 13).

26. For various perspectives on the interrelationships between religion and bioethics, see Callahan and Campbell 1990; Davis and Zoloth 1999; Kass 1990; Lammers 1996; Marty 1992; Messikomer, Fox, and Swazey 2001; Smith 1996; Verhey 1996. In his 1992 paper, Marty synthesizes the themes of nine papers previously published in *Second Opinion* that examine the relationships between theology and medical ethics in the writings of nine important individuals (James Childress, Germain Grisez, James Gustafson, Bernard Häring, Stanley Hauerwas, Immanuel Jakobovits, William May, Richard McCormick, and Paul Ramsey).

27. The Harvard Program on Technology and Society also provided funding for our research on transplantation and dialysis that resulted in our book *The Courage to Fail* (Fox and Swazey 1974).

28. In 1976, the Center began publishing *Ethics & Medics*, a monthly commentary "to keep health care professionals and other concerned individuals abreast of current trends in bioethics from a Catholic perspective." The Center moved its national office from St. Louis to Boston in 1985, where its offices currently are located at St. Elizabeth's Medical Center, which also is the headquarters of Caritas Christi, a Catholic health care system. For further information about the Center and its activities, see www.ncbcenter.org.

29. Another important journal that was launched in 1971 is *Philosophy & Public Affairs*, which over the years has been a venue for bioethically oriented papers. The first issue included a paper called "The Relevance of Nuremberg" by Richard Wasserstrom; an oft-discussed and cited paper by Judith Jarvis Thomson, "A Defense of Abortion"; and a paper by Roger Wertheimer, "Understanding the Abortion Argument."

30. In 1969, Dr. Lorraine Hunt, then in the English Department at the University of Maryland and a member of the SHHV's council, received an NEH grant to study the role of the humanities in medical education. Dr. Hunt's report, in turn, led to SHHV funding by the NEH for a project to advance the involvement of the humanities in medical education. Dr. Hunt became the first director of the project, which was called the Institute on Human Values in Medicine, and Dr. Edmund Pellegrino was appointed chairman of the Institute's advisory committee, which subsequently became its board of directors (Barker 1987: 59–61).

31. The SHHV also engaged in several major publishing activities as part of its scholarly and educational programs. With a grant from the Upjohn Company, for example, it launched and sponsored for five years the *Journal of Medicine and Philosophy*, edited by Edmund Pellegrino (Barker 1987: 85).

32. In the interview that we conducted with him on March 10, 2000, Beauchamp related that he attended the Haverford program as a friend and neighbor of Gorovitz's, not as a "student."

33. During the 1980s, NEH grants also supported the work of individual scholars, such as David Rothman for the research leading to *Strangers at the Bedside* (1991), and Al Jonsen and Stephen Toulmin for their 1988 book, *The Abuse of Casuistry*.

34. To our knowledge, there are no research-based data that would permit a comparative analysis of the sources of, and shifts in, funding for bioethics over the course of its history in the United States, or of the bioethically relevant areas that have been supported. The sources that need to be studied are federal agencies, primarily the National Institutes of Health, broken down into its constituent parts; the National Library of Medicine; the National Science Foundation; private foundations; and, in more recent years, corporations, particularly those involved in areas such as pharmaceuticals, medical devices, and genetic engineering.

    One piece of datum in our files was a 1999 listing from the Foundation Center of grants in the area of bioethics (including medical ethics and science ethics as search terms) by the leading 1,000 foundations in the United States, ranked by endowment, for the four-year period 1995–1998. Roughly 5 percent of these foundations made bioethics grants during this period, and of these, only a few made multiple grants. The top three foundations based on number of grants funded were the Greenwall Foundation (which has been the only foundation with bioethics as a specific program area), the Ford Foundation (predominantly in the areas of reproductive health and technologies), and the Robert Wood Johnson Foundation. Most grants fell into the area of program development, with support for conferences and seminars a distant second. The fewest awards were made for research. (When "research" is cited as the major type of support, however, it often is not clear how it is being defined.)

    A foundation official with whom we talked in 1999 hypothesized that there were several reasons why foundations generally had not been supportive of funding bioethics. One reason, he speculated, was "concern about the sensitive nature of projects" (e.g., those involving controversial areas such as assisted suicide, neonatology, and nonbeating heart organ donors) that might "cause problems" if a foundation's support for work on such topics attracted media attention. Although this individual did not think that bioethics per se would become more fundable in the near future, he did express his opinion that there was a growing interest in policy aspects of biomedicine and health care that might result in a greater readiness to consider ethics as a project component.

Information such as the foregoing, while of some interest, highlights the need for more in-depth data that would permit a thorough analysis of funding patterns over time.

35. Presaging the formation of federal bioethics advisory groups and commissions, the NIH's National Heart and Lung Institute created the Artificial Heart Assessment Panel in 1972, as part of its Artificial Heart Program. The Panel's task was to attempt "to forsee and to come to grips with the legal, social, ethical, medical, economic and psychological implications" of a totally implantable artificial heart. Given its broad scope, the Panel was not an ethics body per se, although its 10 members did include one bioethicist, Albert Jonsen (NHLI 1973).

36. For accounts of the intertwined bioethical, political, and policy developments leading to the creation of the National Commission, and the Commission's work, see Gray 1995; Jonsen 1998: chap. 4; and Rothman 1991: chap. 9.

The Commission produced an extensive number of reports, recommendations, and background papers by consultants, dealing with research involving the fetus (1975), prisoners (1976), children (1977), and those institutionalized as mentally infirm (1978); psychosurgery (1977); the disclosure of research information (1977); institutional review boards (1978); the delivery of health services (1978); the Special Study (1978); and the *Belmont Report* (1978). Under an NIH contract, papers were prepared for the Commission by attorneys George Annas, Leonard Glantz, and Barbara Katz on the origins of the law of informed consent to human experimentation, the current status of the law, and on research with children, prisoners, and the institutionalized mentally infirm; these papers comprised the first five chapters of their important 1977 book *Informed Consent to Human Experimentation: The Subject's Dilemma* (Annas, Glantz, Katz 1977).

37. Before the study began, the Tuskegee Ad Hoc Advisory Panel reported in its October 25, 1972, initial recommendation: "There was common medical knowledge...that untreated syphilitic infection produces disability and premature morbidity." "To date," the Panel went on to comment with what we read as implicit sarcasm, "this study has confirmed that untreated syphilitic infection produces disability and premature morbidity" (U.S. DHEW 1973: 12).

38. With respect to the study's 40-year duration, the Tuskegee Ad Hoc Advisory Panel stated in its final report that "[b]ecause of the paucity of information available today on the manner in which the study was conceived, designed, and sustained, scientific justification for a short-term demonstration study in 1932 cannot be ruled out" (U.S. DHEW 1973: 12).

39. The *New York Times* story was generated through a classic instance of whistle-blowing by persons unable to get a response to their concerns within their organization. Information about the study was provided to the press by a PHS employee, Peter Buxtun, who, after he learned of the study, had for several years vainly tried to persuade the PHS Center for Disease Control to seriously examine the morality of the research, and in one of his final letters to the agency linked its continuance with racial politics. This letter led the CDC to convene a technical and medical advisory panel, which, while conceding the study needed scientific upgrading, recommended that it should continue. After this decision was made, Buxton talked with an Associated Press reporter,

who in turned relayed his information to *New York Times* reporter Jean Heller (Jonsen 1998: 147).

40. Penicillin was recognized as the treatment of choice for syphilis in 1945, and the PHS established its Rapid Treatment Centers for syphilis in 1947. The drug had become widely available by 1953, leading the Advisory Panel to conclude that the therapy "should have been made available to the participants in the study not later than 1953" (U.S. DHEW 1973: 12).

41. Katz's strong convictions about the vital importance of informed consent was expressed in his minority report addendum to the Panel Report on Charge I: "There is ample evidence in the records available to us," he wrote, "that the consent to participation was not obtained from the … Study subjects, but that instead they were exploited, manipulated, and deceived. They were treated…as objects of research. [This is] the most fundamental reason for condemning the Tuskegee Study at its inception and throughout its continuation." (U.S. DHEW 1973: 14). In a similar vein, writing 20 years later about the disregard of the Nuremberg Code's significance in relation to some of the major cases involving abuse of the rights and welfare of human subjects, Katz declared: "Consider the Tuskegee Syphilis Study, begun in 1932, years prior to the concentration camp experiments, continued during the Holocaust, and not terminated until 1972.… [U]nless [the] requirement [of voluntary consent] is clearly asserted (and any exception clearly specified), the slippery slope of engineering consent stretches out before us, leading inexorably to Tuskegee, the Jewish Chronic Disease Hospital in Brooklyn, LSD experiments in Manhattan, DES experiments in Chicago" (Katz 1992: 230–231).

42. There are extensive archival resources, documents, papers, and books about the Tuskegee Study that can be located through a search engine such as Google. Among book-length assessments, see Jones 1981 and Reverby 2000; papers include a set published in *The Hastings Center Report* in 1992, 20 years after the *New York Times* story and the Ad Hoc Advisory Panel's creation.

43. The Tuskegee Syphilis Study continues to be powerfully symbolic to this day, especially to many African Americans, among whom it has contributed to a diffuse, lingering distrust concerning their relationship to White physicians. Awareness of the study, and its documented and alleged abuses of the rights and welfare of research subjects, has been kept alive by a number of books and other venues, among which James H. Jones's *Bad Blood* (1981) has had a particularly strong impact.

44. President Clinton himself had created the precedent of a public apology by the president regarding human experimentation. In a White House ceremony in October 1995, Mr. Clinton received the extensive report of the Advisory Committee on Human Radiation Experiments that he had appointed in 1993, after disclosures about secret government experiments conducted at several major teaching hospitals in 1945 to determine the excretion rates of plutonium in connection with the safety of radiation workers. In accepting the report, which documented some 4,000 radiation experiments between 1944–1974, the president stated that "the United States of America offers a sincere apology to those of our citizens who were subjected to these experiments, to their families and to their communities." "When the government does wrong," he declared, "we have a moral responsibility to admit it" (Hebert 1995; see Mastroianni and Kahn 1996 [a special issue of the Kennedy Institute of Ethics Journal on the Advisory Committee on Human Radiation Experiments], and President's Advisory Committee on Human Radiation Experiments 1996 ([the Committee's final report]).

45. A list, with summaries, of news coverage of Clinton's apology is on Tuskegee University's Web site, Tuskegee University, news coverage [undated].
46. Walters related this at the Medical College of Wisconsin's symposium honoring the 25th anniversary of the *Belmont Report*, held on May 14, 2004; see chapter 5, which examines the 20th and 25th Belmont anniversary meetings.
47. The ethicists commissioned to prepare the background essays were Kurt Baier, James Childress, Tristram Engelhardt, Alasdair MacIntyre, and LeRoy Walters. The one other commissioned paper, by clinical epidemiologist Alvin Feinstein, dealt with research design.

2

The Coming of Bioethicists

The early entrants into bioethics with whom we conversed—those who migrated into the nascent field during the 1960s and early to mid-1970s,[1] and helped to define and shape it—came from different disciplines (principally philosophy, religion, law, and medicine), and from diverse geographic, community, familial, and social backgrounds. Nevertheless, there were some strikingly common patterns[2] in their accounts of the aspects of their biographies that propelled them toward involving themselves in this ambiguous new entity.

Three sets of commonalities predominated: the role that religion had played in their lives; their histories of social activism, especially their participation in various of the American rights movements, the antiwar protests, and the religious ferment during the 1960s; and the influence of certain educational institutions, teachers, and mentors.

The Roles of Religion

One of the most striking patterns among the early entrants, as well as among our other interviewees,[3] was the complex role that religion had played for many of them in their intertwined upbringing, education, and relationship to bioethics and its issues. By and large, we found that whether they were religiously or secularly oriented, they "had more than a casual relationship to religion.... [None of them] seemed to be indifferent to religion or inclined to trivialize it, even if they described themselves as highly secularized persons who had 'left the church,' or in a few instances, as atheists" (Messikomer, Fox, and Swazey 2001: 487).

The faith traditions to which most early entrants belonged were Roman Catholicism and an array of Protestant denominations. A small number were Jewish in origin. Among those with a Jewish heritage, only one person portrayed himself as having been "quite religious"; but, he added, after his adolescence, he gradually abandoned his religious beliefs. The other Jewish interviewees told us that they grew up in families that they variously described in terms such as "nonreligious," composed of "secular Jews," "Jewish by nationality and culture, not by religious practice," "secularly and culturally Jewish," and as a family comprised of "Jewish atheists," who had a "Jewish identity," but rejected "theology," and "the supernatural." "My parents were Holocaust survivors," one interviewee told us, and they kept a kosher home. "We were sort of religiously Jewish, but primarily culturally Jewish," is the way that she characterized her family. The strongest connection with being Jewish that her family communicated to her, she testified, was as "a way to make the world better," and through "identifying with the oppressed, the violated, and the abused." Similarly, another future bioethicist who depicted the Jewish family in which he was raised as "stridently secular" and "very far left" ("my mother and her...siblings all became Socialists," he recounted) also associated their relationship to Judaism with a commitment to furthering justice. "It was the classical story of the secularization of prophetic Judaism," he explained, "and the belief that somehow in socialism lay the solution to the problem of justice in which the Jewish tradition had [always] been so interested."

In contrast to the incipient bioethicists who, on the whole, came from secularized Jewish backgrounds, those who had roots in Protestantism and Catholicism were inclined to depict their family upbringing as devoutly and traditionally religious.[4] "My parents took their religion seriously," said one interviewee who grew up in the American Baptist Church. "I went to church every Sunday...participated in the youth programs, and went to church camp...in [my] early formative years." One of our Catholic interviewees who decided to become a seminarian after one year of law school declared that thinking about becoming a priest "was just like the air you breathed" in his family and in the parochial schools he attended. By and large, even those who later disaffiliated themselves from the organized religion in which they were raised did not become totally disaffected from it. "I was never one of those angry disbelievers who thought that the Church had ruined his life," asserted a philosopher-bioethicist who "left" Roman Catholicism. "I got a lot out of that tradition.... It's at least as good a tradition as the hard-line, secular tradition—more interesting and richer, in fact."

A number of our Protestant and Catholic interviewees (Tom Beauchamp, Ronald Carson, James Childress, K. Danner Clouser, John Fletcher, James Gustafson, Albert Jonsen, Charles McCarthy, Warren Reich, Robert Veatch, LeRoy Walters) elected to pursue religious studies for an undergraduate bachelor of divinity (termed a BD or BDiv) degree. The majority of these individuals (Carson, Childress, Fletcher, Gustafson, Jonsen, Reich, Walters) went on to receive doctoral-level degrees in religious studies, theology, or Christian ethics, bringing their religiously grounded convictions and moral concerns and training into the new field of bioethics. Some of these individuals became ordained clergymen, and served for various lengths of time as ministers or priests before they elected to follow other pursuits, primarily teaching, involving their religious training or, in the case of a Protestant minister and the Roman Catholic priests in our group, until they made the decision to become laicized.

Three other BD recipients (Beauchamp, Clouser, McCarthy), after deliberating about the career path they wanted to follow, or, in the case of a priest, at the direction of his Order, continued their graduate education in philosophy. A fourth BD recipient (Veatch) was allowed to create his own interdisciplinary doctoral coursework in Harvard's Religion and Society Program, becoming the first person thereby to receive a PhD in medical ethics.

In addition to studying for undergraduate or graduate degrees, there were other ways in which some of the first entrants into bioethics expressed their strongly held religious values and beliefs. One interviewee, who decided to become a physician, attended a Jesuit secondary school and university. As a college undergraduate, in addition to his premedical classes, he took four years of theology and philosophy courses. He explained to us that this was because he "felt called upon to do medicine as a moral enterprise." His being a physician and his Catholicism, he affirmed, "are not separable," and for him both are inextricably related to his involvement in human values in medicine and in bioethics.

Social Activism

For a number of the early entrants, the influences and events that shaped their movement into bioethics and the convictions and foci they brought to their work included their social activism during the turbulent era of the 1960s, while they were attending college, graduate school, and/or professional school. This was a time of social protest in American society, spearheaded by the civil rights and antiwar movements and the rise of a new women's movement, which embodied antipaternalism and distrust of the authority and power wielded by powerful groups and institutions, and emphasized individual rights and choice as fundamental bases of freedom, equality, justice, and dignity. This also was also a period of upheavals in Catholicism and Protestantism. It was a time when the Second Vatican Council took place (1962–1965), whose intent, in the words of Pope John XXIII, was to "throw open the windows of the Church so that we can see out and the people can see in"; when the controversial encyclical *Humanae Vitae* ("Of Human Life: On the Regulation of Birth"), written by Pope Paul VI, was promulgated (1968), which upheld the Catholic Church's traditional prohibition of all forms of contraception and of abortion; and when within Protestantism, various radical and secular movements developed, such as the "Death of God," that fostered a deep questioning about the relationship of the moral authority of organized religion and religious institutions to individual decision making.

Several of our interviewees were militantly involved in the civil rights movement in a frontline, hands-on way. They took part in sit-ins, protest marches, and picketing in their local communities, and at sites of national symbolic and political significance, such as Selma, Alabama, and Washington, D.C. In two cases, they spent time working in impoverished areas in Mississippi under the aegis of the Medical Committee for Human Rights and the Law Students' Civil Rights Research Council.

A lawyer-bioethicist whom we interviewed reminisced about all the time in college, starting with his freshman year, that he spent in jail because of his involvement in civil rights demonstrations. His engagement with civil rights issues, he told us, grew in depth and scope through his locally based activism, and through participation in larger, landmark events such as the Selma march after his school's political action committee became an affiliate of Students for a Democratic Society (SDS). Part of his "inspiration" for his civil rights activities, he continued, came from being exposed to the work being done by a law school professor in various civil rights groups, including the SDS. His decision to go to law school, he related, grew directly out of his civil rights activities, and his "realization that lawyers played a very important role [in this sphere]." During this period in his life, he thought he would work for a civil rights organization after graduating from Yale Law School, which he chose primarily because "the Yale tradition at the time [was one of] social activism."

"The galvanizing civil rights experience for me," recalled another interviewee, took place in the small city, largely "a comfortable middle-class community," where he was attending a divinity school. "Somebody got wind about the experience of a black woman, a recent master's degree graduate, who had been evicted from her apartment on dubious grounds. The seminarians discussed with their teachers in and outside of their classes "what our responsibility [was] in this concrete situation":

Our decision was to commit an act of civil disobedience. For me, the rationale for breaking the law was that there are unjust laws and higher laws, and there are times when law-abiding people have to break the law for a higher purpose.... So we chained ourselves, black and white together, across [a busy boulevard], at 4:45 on a Friday evening, when rush hour would be at its height.... We sat down in the street and sang "We Shall Overcome." We were arrested, booked, [and] got great press coverage, which exposed the injustice.

"It was an event that politicized and radicalized me," he went on to say. He and one other seminarian in his class "decided that we would not become ordained":

Part of being politicized, I think, was wanting to see ideas acted upon, beliefs acted upon.... [To me], mainline Protestantism, with rare and notable exceptions...was not deeply, morally engaged in the civil rights struggle. I wasn't sure I wanted to be part of [a setting] where hard questions don't get asked and injustice gets blinked at.... When the decision time came, late in my divinity school years, about what to do next, [I opted for]...graduate work.

Another interviewee described the ideological connections between the feminist and civil rights movements and the anti-Vietnam War movement, in which he was involved as a volunteer draft counselor during his college years in Boston. At the heart of the "social upheavals" of that time, he contended, were convictions and questions about individual rights:

The idea that women had rights, for example, and should be treated as equally as everybody else [was one that raised] the question of where rights come from and what equality meant.... Women couldn't [legally] have abortions and birth control was an issue in Boston.... It was a time in which the idea of people having rights, the civil rights movement, was flourishing. People were still trying to figure out what to do about the *Brown v. Board of Education* decision in the 1950s outlawing segregated schools, and bussing issues in Boston made that very relevant. We had the war in Vietnam, draft dodgers, the question of disobedience to authority, and the question of right and wrong.

What he called these "issues of individual motivation and responsibility," which he also considered to be "larger issues of society...and morality," later drew him to participate in bioethics.

The upheavals in the 1960s that took place in Roman Catholicism had profound effects on our three interviewees who at the time were ordained priests (Jonsen, McCarthy, and Reich), which contributed both to their decisions to leave the priesthood, and to their attraction to bioethics. From his historical perspective, Reich has written, events related to the reforms of the Second Vatican Council, the 1966 Pontifical Commission on Birth Control formed by Pope Paul VI, and the subsequent issuance of his *Humanae Vitae* encyclical which, despite the Commission's recommendations, upheld the Church's prohibition of all birth control except the rhythm method, "constituted a major watershed for modern ethics in religious context, but with vast ramifications for secular ethics as well" (Reich 1999: 38).

The decisions of Jonsen, McCarthy, and Reich to leave the priesthood involved a number of factors, but each told us that his greatest religious doubts about whether he could continue to accept and be obedient to the moral authority of the Church was generated by *Humanae Vitae*. Albert Jonsen, who had entered the Jesuit order as a novice in 1949 at the age of 18, and was ordained in 1962, was teaching moral theology and philosophical ethics at the University of San Francisco (USF), a Jesuit Catholic University, when *Humanae Vitae* was promulgated by the Vatican. "I felt that I couldn't be a teacher of Catholic moral theology, given that position," Jonsen averred. To me, "to be a teacher of Catholic moral theology with that kind of [papal] restriction was unconscionable.... Also, the Catholic position on abortion was unacceptable to me. I thought it was untrue to its own historical roots."

"There was some relief," he went on to say, when he became president of USF in 1969, because in that position he did not have to teach. But in 1972, at the end of his term as president, he resumed teaching as an adjunct associate professor at the University of California, San Francisco School of Medicine—this time in the area of medical ethics and bioethics, in which he had become increasingly interested. Although his sense of a priestly vocation had diminished, he said, he remained "an active priest" until 1975, when he asked and was given permission to be released from his Jesuit vows and the Roman Catholic priesthood.

Charles McCarthy had been ordained by the Paulist Fathers in 1956, and under their aegis obtained masters and doctoral degrees in philosophy at the University of Toronto, taking courses that combined his interests in philosophy and normative political theory. During the period 1961–1971 he consecutively taught political theory and other subjects at St. Paul's College (the Paulist seminary in Washington, D.C.), George Washington University, and The Catholic University of America. When he was laicized in 1971, he began his career in bioethics and federal policy making, accepting a position as a legislative analyst at the National Institutes of Health, and the next year, chaired the committee that drafted the Department of Health, Education and Welfare's regulations to protect human research subjects, which were published as proposed regulations in 1973 and became final regulations as 45CFR46 in 1974.

McCarthy related how incensed he was with the bishops for their "misuse of authority" in connection with the firing of two faculty members—moral theologians Charles Curran and Daniel Maguire—at The Catholic University of America because of their critical stance toward papal doctrines, and also how angry he felt "at the way the principles of Vatican II were ignored." However, he told us, his decision to leave the priesthood was initiated primarily by the pope's encyclical "against contraception":

Despite the fact that most respected theologians in the world had informed the pope, "Do not try to ban contraception," the pope [did so].... I joined the group that was demonstrating in Washington, D.C. against the encyclical and the bishops who supported it. After more time passed I finally decided: "I cannot continue to wear the Roman collar, although I am a loyal Catholic. I believe that what I stand for is more in line with the best Catholic traditions than the current leadership in the church." However, if you wear the collar, you are in effect saying publicly, "I stand for everything that the official church stands for."... I didn't and couldn't support *Humanae Vitae*...[and] I felt I had to leave the active priesthood. It took me several years to act that out.

The third former priest who became a bioethicist, Warren Reich, was ordained in 1958 in what he described as "a small American order whose short title is Trinity Missions," and then assigned to study for an STD (doctorate in sacred theology) degree in moral theology. After receiving his degree at the Gregorian University in Rome, Reich returned to the United States, and taught at the Trinity seminary and at The Catholic University of America, which, as a pontifical university, has had a special relationship to the Vatican since its founding in 1887 by the U.S. bishops with the approval of Pope Leo XIII. Reich said:

The turning point [for me] began…when the Catholic University of America tried to fire… Charles Curran, based on complaints that he published and taught some things on birth control in disagreement with the Church's teaching. They simply dismissed him…without giving adequate explanation…. The entire faculty…walked out…. The mobilization of the entire university against high-handed ecclesiastical authority was unheard of, because blind loyalty to authority was the standard.

The board of trustees, Reich commented, "was furious over the strike, but…had to negotiate," and Curran was reinstated.

On the heels of the Curran controversy, Reich continued, the pope issued *Humanae Vitae*, "rejecting the findings of the Papal Commission that had recommended the opposite." Reich, vacationing in Europe, "got word from Charlie [Curran], signed a statement of dissent, and helped organize the dissent network [in Europe]…. The board of trustees of the university tried to fire all 20 of us who had signed this statement." A yearlong academic hearing ensued, which "was very much like a trial, with charges that made the stakes very high; defense testimony from all of us; and four powerful law firms." In the end, the hearing board "found in our favor…[that we had not] acted irresponsibly as academic professors of theology, even though we were teaching in a pontifical university." Soon, however, with a new university administration in charge, Reich and almost all of the other dissent document signers, were "eased out, one way or another." "By this time," Reich stated, "I had a great aversion, a deeply uncomfortable feel, about the ecclesiastical environment, [and] I ended up leaving the priesthood within a year or two." Then, "out of the blue, when things looked very desperate" for him with regard to finding a new job, André Hellegers, the founder of the Kennedy Institute of Ethics at Georgetown University, invited Reich to join the initial staff as a senior research scholar.

During the social and cultural upheavals of the 1960s, the strongly held values and beliefs about individualism and individual rights, and challenges to the moral authority of both secular and religious institutions, that were championed by many of our interviewees, and by other members of the first cohorts of bioethicists as well, had significant consequences for the foci, atmosphere, and ethos of the emerging field of bioethics. The initial bioethicists carried their beliefs about individual rights, antipaternalism, and antiauthority into the new field. This exerted a strong influence on "the very earliest aspect of bioethics," one of the interviewees maintained. Bioethics "took on what seemed to be the first major offense of medicine of the time, which [was] its incredible paternalism. And that means we latched onto the principle of autonomy and we affirmed the right of individual patients to make choices."

Educational and Training Trajectories

The educational paths that led to our interviewees' decisions to venture into bioethics involved their undergraduate and graduate-level training and experiences,
the institutions from which they received their academic degrees, and the programs in which they were enrolled that explicitly introduced them to bioethics
and to the medical humanities. The highest academic degrees awarded to these
bioethicists-in-becoming were clustered in four principal fields. Nine individuals
received doctoral degrees in philosophy, seven in religious studies/theology, six
earned medical degrees (two of whom also earned PhDs in philosophy, and one a
PhD in biochemistry), and five persons, a JD or LLB law degree.[5,6] This distribution of degrees and fields was proportionately representative of the composition
of bioethics more generally.

The institutions at which these 27 early bioethicists did their graduate and professional training were led by Harvard and Yale (seven and six individuals, respectively). Those who matriculated at Harvard included three persons who pursued
doctoral studies in philosophy, two in law, one in biochemistry, and one in medical ethics. Four of those who attended Yale engaged in doctoral studies in religion
and moral theology, one pursued a law degree, and one his MD.[7] In contrast to
these clusters at Harvard and Yale, the other 14 individuals whom we interviewed
studied at 14 different schools dispersed throughout the U.S. and in several cases,
abroad.

A number of bioethically important linkages, centered at Yale and Harvard, were
formed during the early 1960s. The members of what James Gustafson described
as an "informal network" included himself and Frederick (Fritz) Redlich, professor and chairman of psychiatry at Yale Medical School, who became dean in 1967;
anesthesiologist Henry Beecher at Harvard Medical School; professor of social
ethics Ralph Potter at Harvard Divinity School; health lawyer Irving Ladimer at
Boston University's Law-Medicine Institute; moral theologian Paul Ramsey at
Princeton; Rabbi Seymour Siegel at New York's Jewish Theological Seminary;
and Richard McCormick, SJ, then based at a Jesuit seminary in Indiana. As we
discussed in chapter 1, social and intellectual networking among both faculty and
students drawn to bioethical issues also took place through contacts and mem-
berships in organizations such as the Hastings Center, the Kennedy Institute, the
Society for Health and Human Values, and the Society of Christian Ethics, and
through participation in early training programs, such as the Harvard School of
Public Health's MPH Program in medical ethics, the Institute on Human Values in
Medicine fellowship program, and the Haverford Summer Institute. These interconnections fostered interest in bioethics, spread knowledge of it, helped to shape
the contours and contents of the emerging new field, and provided social and
professional support for those who became affiliated with it at this still-tentative
stage in its development.

The learning, stimuli, and networking opportunities provided by interactions with senior figures through attending conferences is illustrated by Howard Brody. As a college student, a science professor introduced him to *The Hastings Center Report*, and then, at the end of Brody's first year in medical school in 1972, he learned from this same professor that Hastings was sponsoring the First International Conference on Teaching Medical Ethics. Brody attended the conference, with financial support from the medical school. "I got to meet...basically all the leaders in the field," people like Dan Callahan, Ed Pellegrino, Bob Veatch, and Henry Beecher, he reminisced, adding "of course, at that time, you could get almost everyone in the U.S. who was seriously interested in bioethics in one room [and] it didn't have to be a large room. It was a phenomenal experience for a medical student." When he came back from that meeting, he continued, "I wrote up a proposal on how you could teach medical ethics in the medical school at Michigan State University, and...I dusted off my idea of...doing a joint degree [in medicine and philosophy]."

Influential Teachers

Within this mesh of relationships, certain figures stood out as especially influential teachers and mentors. Two of the persons most frequently and admiringly mentioned in this regard were theologian and religious ethicist James Gustafson, and psychiatrist/psychoanalyst Jay Katz.[8]

James Gustafson. After James Gustafson received his PhD from Yale Divinity School in 1955, he became a member of its faculty,[9] and also of Yale's Department of Religious Studies when it was formed in 1963. He began giving occasional lectures on bioethical topics in 1961, became involved in discussions about medical ethics at the medical school, was a member of the Hastings Center's Founders group, and over time published materials examining the relationships between theology and medical ethics (see, e.g., Gustafson 1970, 1975, 1978, 1990, 1995, 1996). However, he told us, rather than being interested in medical ethics or bioethics per se, he viewed them within a general, overarching framework of theology and ethics.

Among the students at Yale on whom he had an enduring influence were a number who eventually became prominent bioethicists—including James Childress, Albert Jonsen, and LeRoy Walters.[10] "He was the best teacher [of graduate students] I've ever encountered," James Childress testified. "[F]or me [he] is a model of the great teacher who is not interested in a master-disciple relationship but rather in empowering and enabling students to go their own directions by attending to major texts, figures, and traditions." Albert Jonsen described Gustafson as a teacher who was "really magisterial in the best sense.... He never lecture[d] his graduate students.... [I]t was always how he could draw their minds into the problematic of the author that we were reading. He insisted over and over again that we [not] overlay somebody else's thought with our own.... The two-year seminar that all the graduate students did with him was beautiful in that respect.... That was a tremendous experience."

When he moved to the University of Chicago in 1972 to become the Divinity School's University Professor of Theological Ethics and a member of the Committee on Social Thought, Gustafson continued to be an important teacher of future bioethicists, and also served as an informal teacher and mentor for individuals such as physician and clinical ethicist Mark Siegler. Siegler had been interested and involved in medical-ethical issues during his medical school and residency training at Chicago, and then as a new faculty member directing the hospital's small medical intensive care unit. The primary person who "introduced [me] to the literature and language of medical ethics," Siegler asserted, was James Gustafson. "Every week or two we would meet in Jim's...wonderful book-lined office at the divinity school.... Many weeks I'd come over with a case that was troubling me and my students, often from the medical ICU.... We would talk about my case and Jim would direct me to readings on ethics and the new literature of bioethics. [He] was a wonderful teacher, gentle, Socratic, and very insightful." Through Gustafson, Siegler met what he characterized as an "unbelievable" group of "philosophers, theologians, and social philosophers" in and around the Chicago campus, who also became his informal medical ethics teachers. These included Richard McCormick, Leon Kass, and Stephen Toulmin, who had served as the National Commission's first staff philosopher, and with whom Siegler met regularly for some three years beginning in the late 1970s, as he had with Gustafson in the early 1970s.

Jay Katz. Early in the 1960s, prior to the crystallization and formal emergence of bioethics, Jay Katz became seriously interested in issues of human experimentation. His interest had emotional and moral as well as intellectual roots in his personal history, as an individual born in Nazi Germany from which he had escaped to the United States with his parents just before the German army invaded Poland. After he had completed his training in medicine and psychiatry at Harvard, Katz joined the Yale Law School faculty where his special fields were psychoanalysis and law, family law, and law and medicine. In this context, he began to study the medical experiments that had been carried out on prisoners in the Nazi concentration camp of Auschwitz. This launched him on what was to become his lifelong work as a major thinker in the sphere of the ethics of human experimentation, who has made a major contribution to the definition and development of the doctrine of informed consent. Katz not only considered the informed consent of medical investigators' subjects to be legally, ethically, and interpersonally essential to any permissible human research but also to all doctor-patient relationships in therapeutic settings. In his view, the joint decision making that the implementation of this precept requires has the powerful potential of breaking through what Katz has termed the "silence" that too often prevails between physicians and their patients. It is a silence that he believes is conducive to nondisclosure and paternalistically authoritarian behavior on the part of doctors, and mutual distrust between them and their patients, especially in situations of medical uncertainty when physicians are faced with the limits of their knowledge and efficacy (Katz 1984). It is out of this background, multiprofessional and interdisciplinary competence, and set of convictions that Katz made a stirring, long-lasting impression as a teacher on a gamut of evolving bioethicists, which was not confined to those with whom he had contact in the classrooms of Yale.

When he was a medical student at Yale, physician-bioethicist Norman Fost told us, there were several "seminal events...that got me headed down [the bioethics] track." One of these, which he described as a "transforming event," was taking a fourth-year elective seminar on psychiatry and the law with Katz. The seminar, Fost still remembered vividly, "consisted of four cases...involving patients [Katz] had had in therapy, that raised profound ethical dilemmas.... [T]hey were just riveting...."

Ruth Faden never had a conventional teacher-student relationship with Jay Katz; nor did she do any of her studies at Yale. But she continues to marvel over the fact that when Albert Jonsen, who was a member of her PhD dissertation committee, called and told him about her work, Katz offered to meet with her and read her dissertation. "I was amazed," she said, and to this day she is grateful to him for how "incredibly encouraging" he was about her "working on a psychological model or theory of informed consent."

Lawyer/bioethicist George Annas wistfully remarked that he had "always wished" he "had had [Jay Katz] as a mentor" at the inception of his career. Nevertheless, since the mid-1980s, Annas has regarded Katz as his mentor—a "very, very supportive, terrific" one—in matters concerning the ethical conduct of research with human subjects, on which he, like Katz, has centered a great deal of his professional attention. It is not only Katz's intellect and his teacherly qualities that Annas admires, but morally, he has "always thought of him as a hero," because of the role that Katz played in making what has come to be known as "research ethics" a cause.

It is lawyer-bioethicist Alexander Capron who has had one of the longest, most continuous, and significant relationships to Katz, since his days as a Yale law school student, when he enrolled in Katz's law and psychiatry course. Without reservation, he has declared, in "the substance of what I've done, Jay [Katz] is my major intellectual mentor."

After receiving his LLB degree in 1969, Capron returned to Yale from 1970–1972 as a lecturer, and as a research associate working with Katz [along with Eleanor Swift (Glass), a student research assistant] on *Experimentation with Human Beings* (Katz 1972), a volume that came to be regarded as a groundbreaking, monumental casebook in the field. "That was…a huge education for me," Capron said, "because I hadn't taken the human experimentation course [in law school]… [and] I was more of a sounding board for him at first." However, Capron's contribution quickly transcended this role, and when the book was published, it listed Katz as the author, "[w]ith the assistance of Alexander Capron and Eleanor Swift Glass." Even before *Experimentation with Human Beings* was completed, Katz and Capron had begun working on a second book, which this time they coauthored. It was entitled *Catastrophic Diseases: Who Decides What?* and as its subtitle indicates, it was built around a "psychosocial and legal analysis of the problems posed by hemodialysis and organ transplantation" (Katz and Capron 1975).

"My early years" working with Jay Katz, Capron said, were determining experiences in "basically cast[ing] me as a person who was going to be involved in these [law and medicine and bioethical] issues." For Capron, more decisive than the encouragement that he received from Katz to work in what he deemed this "valuable field," was the influence that Katz had on his thinking. In part, he mused, "[it's] the kinds of questions that he instilled":

Jay is very much committed to the notion of people being enabled to make decisions and doctors communicating to them.… For Jay, it's a human, not an abstract, philosophical activity. And hence, it is full of all the problems of communication, of transference, of unconscious drives and impulses, and all the barriers that…make the perfection that you can write out as a lawyer or as a philosopher all but unachievable, but nevertheless worth thinking about, [and] trying to do something about.… And that, I suppose, was what changed my perspective.

In various combinations, the sets of influences and events discussed in the preceding sections eventuated in our interviewees' decisions to work in the sphere of bioethics. Among the settings in which they began to engage in bioethical research, teaching, and writing were ones that are still major and greatly expanded loci of bioethical activity today: in university-based and free standing centers and programs, and in academic departments, most notably of philosophy, theology, and religious studies; in medical schools and teaching hospitals; in certain federal government agencies such as the National Institutes of Health; and in advisory bodies to the government such as bioethics commissions and the National Academy of Sciences.[11]

As they talked about the wellsprings of the early commitment they had made to the amorphous new enterprise of bioethics, only a few of our interviewees mentioned having experienced any regrets about their decisions, even though in some cases they had been confronted by senior professors who cautioned them about the risks they were taking. In a particularly dramatic instance, one of our interlocutors was vehemently admonished by a major teacher for "betraying" his training in philosophy and "throwing away a promising career" by opting to enter "whatever the hell this field [is]."

Although by and large they were resolute about the decisions they had made, a number of these venturesome first bioethicists referred to the uncertainty they had felt about the field's prognosis about how durable it would be, and how long-lasting the careers within it on which they had set forth would be. "I felt sure that this whole field would probably collapse," one of our interlocutors candidly admitted. "Even though I'd given up my [philosophy] job [to develop a new department of medical humanities and ethics], I thought it was just a fad [that might last for] 10 years [at the most]."

This prediction has not been borne out. Bioethics is now in its fourth decade in the United States, where it has grown and become more familiar and institutionalized in academia, in the media, and in the polity. It has also spread and developed internationally, as we discuss in chapters 8–10. There are prominent bioethicists who contend that it has achieved a position of power in American society. Nevertheless, some members of the field's founding group maintain a wary, evanescent view of the field's future—likening it in one case to a bubble that may some day burst. In this connection, they are particularly concerned about what they consider to be the insufficient scholarly intellectual recognition that bioethics has attained; the diminution of the field's proactive, critical stance that its greater "routinization" has brought in its wake; and most recently (as will be seen in chapter 11), about the potentially self-destructive effects of the penetration of American bioethics by the U.S. "culture wars."

Notes

1. Out of our total of 45 in-depth interviews, we classified 27 individuals as "early entrants" based on their becoming involved in bioethics during the 1960s and early to mid-1970s. These 27 are: George Annas, Tom Beauchamp, Howard Brody, Daniel Callahan, Arthur Caplan, Alexander Capron, Ronald Carson, James Childress, Danner Clouser, Norman Daniels, Tristram Engelhardt, Ruth Faden, John Fletcher, Norman Fost, Leonard Glantz, James Gustafson, Albert Jonsen, Leon Kass, Patricia King, Ruth Macklin, Charles McCarthy, Barbara Mishkin, Edmund Pellegrino, Warren Reich, Mark Siegler, Robert Veatch, and LeRoy Walters. Unless otherwise noted, the quotations used in this chapter are drawn from the interviews we conducted with them. See the appendix for the dates on which the interviews were conducted.

   There were a number of important figures in the development of bioethics whom we were unable to interview for various reasons, such as their medical problems during the course of our study, their deaths before we began our project, problems in contacting them to schedule an interview, and budgetary constraints that limited the number of interviews we could conduct. Among these figures were Henry Beecher, Willard Gaylin, Samuel Gorovitz, André Hellegers, Hans Jonas, Jay Katz, William May, Stephen Toulmin, and Paul Ramsey.

2. The term "common patterns" does not mean that all of our interviewees shared these aspects of their personal biographies that led them to become bioethicists. Rather, it means that many, rather than all of them, did so in various combinations.

3. The role of religion among our early entrants should be seen in the context of the fact that a number of distinguished theologians, mainly Protestant and Catholic, were among the first cohorts of bioethicists. In addition to those whom we interviewed, these figures included Protestant theologians Joseph Fletcher and Paul Ramsey, and Catholic theologian Richard McCormick, SJ. Religiously attuned inputs into the emerging field also were made by prominent Catholic laymen such as physician André Hellegers, as well as by the metaphysically oriented philosopher Hans Jonas. For a fuller discussion of the much-debated role of religion in American bioethics, see Messikomer, Fox, and Swazey 2001.

4. One exception to this pattern was a philosopher-bioethicist who commented that he was "raised as a secular Roman Catholic."

5. In the United States, the LLB degree has been replaced by the JD degree, with Yale University, where Alexander Capron studied law and received an LLB, being one of the last to convert. Both the former LLB and the JD are a "first professional degree" in law. Many law schools also have a one-year master's degree program for an LLM degree, which is primarily for JD graduates who are interested in teaching law. There are no PhD degree programs in law.

6. The recipients who received degrees in these fields were as follows. Philosophy: Tom Beauchamp, Howard Brody, Daniel Callahan, Arthur Caplan, Dan Clouser, Norman Daniels, Tristram Engelhardt, Ruth Macklin, Charles McCarthy. Religious studies/ theology: Ronald Carson, James Childress, John Fletcher, James Gustafson, Albert Jonsen, Warren Reich, LeRoy Walters. Medicine: Howard Brody, Tristram Engelhardt, Norman Fost, Leon Kass, Edmund Pellegrino, Mark Siegler; of these six, Brody and Engelhardt also earned PhDs in philosophy, and Kass a PhD in biochemistry. Law: George Annas, Alexander Capron, Leonard Glantz, Patricia King, Barbara Mishkin. Only two of the early entrants received degrees outside of these four fields: Ruth Faden earned her PhD degree in an Attitudes and Behavior Program at Berkeley, and Robert Veatch fashioned his own doctoral degree studies in Harvard's Religion and Society Program at Harvard, earning a degree in medical ethics.

7. Harvard, known at the time for its training in analytic philosophy, was the institution selected by three future philosopher-bioethicists (Callahan, Clouser, Daniels). Two other individuals (Annas, King) received their law degrees from Harvard, one (Kass) earned a PhD in biochemistry, and one (Veatch) his PhD in medical ethics. Yale had an important cluster of four of those who received doctoral degrees in religion/moral theology (Childress, Gustafson, Jonsen, Walters), one LLB recipient (Capron), and one MD (Fost). The other 14 individuals whom we interviewed studied at 14 different schools in the U.S. and abroad.

8. A number of other individuals were cited by our early entrants as having influenced, in various ways, their work and pursuit of a career in bioethics. These include, in alphabetical order: David Bazelon, chief justice of the United States Courts of Appeals for the District of Columbia Circuit; Alexander Capron, law and medicine/bioethics; Roderick Firth, philosopher; Joseph Fletcher, theologian; Renée Fox, sociologist of medicine; Willard Gaylin, psychiatrist and cofounder of the Hastings Center; Stanley Hauerwas, theologian; André Hellegers, physician and founder of the Kennedy Institute of Ethics; Hans Jonas, philosopher; Albert Jonsen, bioethicist; Leon Kass, physician/bioethicist; Richard McCormick, theologian; and Paul Ramsey, theologian.

9. Gustafson's mentor at Yale Divinity School, he told us, was an eminent figure in Protestant theological ethics, H. Richard Niebuhr (brother of another important academic theologian, Reinhold Niebuhr). When H. Richard Niebuhr retired as the chaired professor of Christian Ethics, Gustafson succeeded him in that position, and he and his

colleague David Little had primary responsibility for teaching religious ethics in the Niebuhrian tradition. In addition to his work and teaching in theology and religious ethics, another important area of Gustafson's teaching consisted of courses in the sociology of religion, which he gave from 1955 to 1966. He had majored in sociology as an undergraduate at Northwestern University, where he received a BS degree in 1948. His sociology of religion teaching at Yale, he told us, drew on classical sociological works, especially the writings of Émile Durkheim and Max Weber, and on the empirical research of certain sociologists, such as Joseph Fichter, SJ, and his studies of urban Catholic parishes. The range of Gustafson's teaching also is exemplified by courses he taught on subjects such as law and the gospel, and on the social teachings of 20th-century Christian churches including Roman Catholic and Eastern Orthodox, as well as Protestant churches.

10. We did not interview a number of Gustafson's Yale students who subsequently became involved in bioethics. These included Stanley Hauerwas, Paul Menzel, Gene Outka, and Allen Verhey. Additionally, during 1962–1963, when Gustafson filled in for a former Yale colleague who had moved to Harvard Divinity School, he supervised the dissertation of two other early bioethicists: Arthur Dyck and Ralph Potter.
11. The locales at which our early entrants initiated their full-time or part-time work in bioethics were the following, with individuals at each locale listed alphabetically:

Institutes and Centers

The Hastings Center: Daniel Callahan (cofounder), Arthur Caplan, Robert Veatch as full-time bioethicists.

The Kennedy Institute of Ethics: Tom Beauchamp, Warren Reich, LeRoy Walters (the first director) as full-time bioethicists (Beauchamp began working on bioethical issues in both the philosophy department and the Kennedy Institute at Georgetown before moving full time to the Institute). Two other individuals whose early work in bioethics included an affiliation with the Institute were Leon Kass, who was a research professor in bioethics from 1974–1976, and Ruth Faden, who became a senior research fellow in 1978.

Boston University Center for Law and Health Sciences: George Annas and Leonard Glantz.

Academic Departments

Case Western, Department of Philosophy: Ruth Macklin
Johns Hopkins School of Public Health: Ruth Faden
New College (Sarasota, Fla.), [No departments]: assistant professor of religion, Ronald Carson
Tufts University, Department of Philosophy: Norman Daniels
University of Virginia, Department of Religious Studies: James Childress
Yale University, Divinity School: James Gustafson
Yale University, Law School: Alexander Capron

Medical Schools/Teaching Hospitals

Michigan State University: Howard Brody
Pennsylvania State University Hershey: Danner Clouser

University of California, San Francisco: Albert Jonsen

University of Chicago: Mark Siegler

University of Tennessee: Edmund Pellegrino

University of Texas Medical Branch at Galveston, Institute for Medical Humanities: Tristram Engelhardt

University of Wisconsin School of Medicine Program in Medical Ethics: Norman Fost

Federal Government Agencies and Advisory Bodies

National Academy of Sciences, Committee on the Life Sciences and Social Policy: Leon Kass

NIH Clinical Center Bioethics Program: John Fletcher

NIH Division of Legislative Analysis: Charles McCarthy

National Institute of Child Health and Human Development: Barbara Mishkin (special assistant for bioethics to the scientific director)

National Commission for the Protection of Human Subjects: Patricia King (commissioner)

3

"Choices on Our Conscience"

The Inauguration of the Kennedy Institute of Ethics

It was a gala, star-studded event—exciting beyond belief. The issues had hardly ever been discussed anywhere in a public place, and they did it right. It was at the Kennedy Center—a huge crowd, many panels and lectures, with many glitterati, including leading figures in academic disciplines, but also superstars from the media. The panels were moderated by the top media people. And scholars who weren't previously noted for their involvement with bioethics.... It was a...fascinating, stimulating [day]. It was wonderful. (Fost, interview, 2000: see appendix)

This was the exuberant way in which pediatrician-bioethicist Norman Fost described the international symposium that took place under the auspices of the Joseph P. Kennedy Jr. Foundation on October 16, 1971, at the John F. Kennedy Center for the Performing Arts, in Washington, D.C. Entitled "Choices on Our Conscience," the symposium, in which RCF was invited to participate, was a multifaceted inaugural event. It was billed as "a symposium on human rights, retardation, and research," with the larger intention of considering "the ethical problems raised by dramatic advances in technology and science, particularly the fields of biology, genetics, and medicine." The meeting was explicitly designed to galvanize a process through which the public, members of the polity, the media, and educators, as well as biological and medical scientists, physicians, philosophers, theologians, jurists, and behavioral and social scientists would be involved in a "concerted inquiry" into the significance of these advances and the development of a "body of informed discourse" about their implications for "human life and human good" (Choices on our Conscience 1971: 52–53). It was also a staged public announcement of the launching of the Joseph and Rose Kennedy Institute for the Study of Human Reproduction and Bioethics at Georgetown University, initially funded by a grant from the Joseph P. Kennedy Jr. Foundation (of which Senator Edward M. Kennedy was president, and Eunice Kennedy Shriver, executive secretary). Media stories about the founding of the Kennedy Institute were published just before the symposium took place, such as the one that appeared in *The Washington Post* on October 2, 1971: "Institute for 'Bioethics': GU to Study Medicine's Life and Death Decisions" (Auerbach 1971b). In addition, the symposium was the first programmed affair to occur at the newly constructed John F. Kennedy Center for the Performing Arts.

In all these regards, it was a Kennedy family-organized happening. The prominence and range of their public life, their political influence, their symbolic importance, and their collective charisma enabled them to summon a dazzling array of persons of unusually diverse disciplinary and professional backgrounds, from Belgium, England, France, and Switzerland, and as far away as India, as well as from various parts of the United States. Most of the participants, guests, and attendees paid their own way to be present.

The opening plenary session and three of the panels that followed were moderated by individuals who were media personages at the time: Roger Mudd, John Chancellor, Frank McGee, and Norman Podhoretz. The distinguished moderators for the other four panel sessions were the Right Reverend Paul Moore Jr., Bishop Coadjustor of New York; William McElroy, director of the National Science Foundation; Columbia University Professor of Philosophy Charles Frankel; and Philip Handler, president of the National Academy of Sciences. The galaxy of "essayists" and "respondents" on the program included four Nobel laureates in medically relevant scientific fields: Sir John Eccles, Joshua Lederberg, Jacques Monod, and James Watson. Other prominent medical scientists and physicians included geneticist Jerome LeJeune, pediatrician Robert E. Cooke, obstetrician-gynecologist André Hellegers, Patrick Steptoe (renowned for his pioneering of in vitro human fertilization), neurophysiologist and psychiatrist José M. R. Delgado, and John Knowles, director of the Massachusetts General Hospital and president-elect of the Rockefeller Foundation. There were eminent theologians, religionists, and clergymen: John Fletcher, James Gustafson, Michael Hamilton (canon of the Washington National Cathedral), Ivan Illich, Richard McCormick, and Paul Ramsey. The roster of participants also included towering scholars of the stature of Leszek Kolakowski of Oxford University, and distinguished academics in fields that spanned education, ethics, health economics, law, legal medicine, physiology, public health, psychiatry, psychology, and sociology. There were social critics, such as Germaine Greer and Michael Harrington; leaders of nongovernmental voluntary organizations, including Renée Sylvie Portray, secretary general of the Association Nationale pour l'Aide aux Enfants Retardés (in Brussels); Yvonne Posternak, president of the International League of Societies for the Mentally

Retarded (Geneva); and Andrew Young, chairman of the Atlanta Community Relations Committee; journalists of note included Claudine Escoffier-Lambotte, medical editor of *Le Monde*, and Anatole Shub, European editor of *Harper's Magazine* and the Moscow and Paris correspondent for *The Washington Post*. And, adding a special aura to the gathering, there were the luminous, prophetic, and spiritual figures of Elie Wiesel and Mother Teresa of Calcutta.

The launching pad and centerpiece of the symposium was a 30-minute documentary film made by Guggenheim Productions, whose head, Charles Guggenheim, had been in charge of public relations for John F. Kennedy's presidential campaign. The film portrayed the history of a baby born with Down syndrome and duodenal atresia. The latter condition involved an intestinal block that was potentially correctable through surgery, without which the infant could not be fed, and consequently would die. The baby's parents chose not to have the surgery performed. The mother, a nurse, recalled cases she had seen of children with Down syndrome who were both severely mentally retarded, and suffered from serious physical health problems. And both parents expressed concern about whether it would be "fair" to their two "normal" children to have a sibling afflicted in this way. The hospital where the infant was receiving care sought the counsel of a judge, and was advised it was unlikely that a court would overturn the parents' decision. Subsequently, the baby was placed in a side room of the hospital nursery where, after 11 days, he/she died from starvation. In the film, the hospital staff was depicted as profoundly upset by watching the day-by-day demise of the infant, and by their powerlessness to do anything either to prevent the baby's death or to hasten it.

The case was extrapolated from one that had occurred at Johns Hopkins Hospital, on the pediatric service where Dr. Norman Fost was chief resident at the time. It had "occupied an enormous amount of our time and interest," he recalled, and "led to the formation of a group that met regularly in the evening to discuss that case and what else we should be doing about ethics at our institution." "While this child was in the hospital and still alive," he added, "I went to the medical records room and found other cases of children with Down syndrome and duodenal atresia who had been allowed to starve to death at Hopkins. Many of the doctors who cared for them were there, and I remember talking with them about this" (Fost, interview, 2000: see appendix).

The film was made with actors rather than with the parents, physicians, and nurses who had actually been involved—although Fost was in three of its frames ("a well-kept secret," he told us, with a tinge of pride). The initiator of the idea of producing the film was Robert E. Cooke, pediatrician-in-chief at Johns Hopkins Hospital—in Fost's view, "a legendary figure in American pediatrics"—who was also chairman of the Kennedy Foundation Advisory Board. Cooke shared with the Kennedy family their deep interest in mental retardation that had its inception in the fact that one of Joseph and Rose Kennedy's children, Kathleen, had been severely mentally retarded from birth. Two of Robert Cooke's own children were also profoundly retarded. Cooke, along with Dr. André Hellegers, was instrumental in encouraging the Kennedys to start putting some of the money they had allocated for biological research on retardation into bioethics, and persuading them to establish the Kennedy Institute for Bioethics at Georgetown.

About a year before the film was produced, I (RCF) received a phone call from Dr. Cooke during which he described the case around which it would turn, and the part that it would play in the Kennedy symposium that was being planned. He explained that the film would include a small-group discussion about the ethical issues that the case raised, and he implied that I was a potential candidate for the cast of discussants. He went on to ask me how I would approach the case. To the best of my recollection, I responded by telling him that despite the fatal consequences of the tragic choice the parents had made, and its devastating impact on the medical and nursing staff, I could appreciate how anguishing the situation was for this mother and father, and also the painful complexity of the medical, social, and moral questions it raised. Although Dr. Cooke listened to what I said respectfully, and intimated that I might hear from him again as the film developed, I had the impression that my perspective on the case did not coincide with his inclination to regard the parents' decision to forego surgery as unequivocally—perhaps even inexcusably—wrong.

Many months later, however, I received a second call from Dr. Cooke—this time to inform me that the group discussion part of the documentary was about to be filmed, and that he was concerned that the participants under consideration did not represent a broad enough range of perspectives on the case. I ventured the opinion that I was not surprised to hear this, because in my previous conversation with him I had the impression that the response that was expected, if not sought, was tipped in the direction of profound moral disapproval of the decision that the parents had made, and of their reasons for doing so. Cooke neither affirmed nor denied this, but he did invite me to become one of the filmed discussants along with psychologist, author, columnist, and mother Sidney Callahan (who was also the wife of Daniel Callahan); William Curran, professor of legal medicine at the Harvard University School of Public Health and member of the Kennedy Inter-Faculty Program in Medical Ethics at Harvard; Reverend John Fletcher, then director of the Intermet Theological Institute in Washington, D.C.; and Cooke himself.

The film that Guggenheim produced not only served its original purpose as the opening event that articulated and humanized the central issues of "conscience" around which the Kennedy symposium turned; it also became a widely used and appreciated teaching tool in colleges, universities, medical schools, and medical centers. "I have not seen anything better from the standpoint of getting a class of students, or residents, or doctors...to start thinking and talking about issues of limiting treatment based on handicaps," Fost, now director of the Program in Medical Ethics at the University of Wisconsin-Madison, has testified (Fost, interview, 2000: see appendix). But as a participant in it, I felt that the film was tipped in the direction of passing harsh moral judgment on the inhumanity of the parents who allowed their baby to starve to death in the sequestered corner of a hospital nursery, and that it portrayed the anger and the angst of the house staff and nurses more sympathetically than it did the feelings of the parents. My impression was reinforced by the way that the discussion section of the film was edited. Comments that I had made about the deep dilemmas that this case epitomized were excised from it.

At 9 A.M., on October 16, 1971, in the Eisenhower Theatre of the Kennedy Center, the symposium was opened by welcoming remarks delivered by Sargent Shriver, and by a plenary session called "Who Should Survive: Is Survival a Right?" The session, moderated by Roger Mudd, then a news commentator in Washington, D.C., for CBS, began with a showing of the film, followed by a live discussion of the case it depicted by the panelists in the film, along with the so-called essayists—jurist Paul Freund; theologian James Gustafson; social critic Michael Harrington; Sidney Callahan, who had also been one of the film's panelists; U.S. Senator Walter Mondale; and Renée Sylvie Portray, secretary general of the Association Nationale pour l'Aide aux Enfants Retardés and mother of a retarded child, who had written commentaries on the legal, moral and ethical, social, psychological, familial, and public policy aspects of the issues the case in the film raised.

I was particulary struck and also moved and disturbed by the image of a child with Down syndrome that cumulatively emerged from the plenary session, to which Renée Sylvie Portray was an especially eloquent contributor. She told the assemblage that her 20-year-old son, with an IQ of 40, held a job and had hobbies. He is "a useful member of the community and a happy member of the family," she declared. In their concerted effort to destigmatize Down syndrome (that was colloquially referred to as "mongolism" by both medical professionals and laypersons at that time, because the characteristics accompanying this chromosomally based condition may include a flat face with a short nose and an upward slant of the eyes), and to play down the gravity of mental retardation, the participants in the session painted a picture of an essentially healthy youngster, who in all respects was "normal" except for a mild degree of mental retardation, and who had the endearing quality of being more than usually affectionate. As I listened to their discussion, in my mind's eye I could see a smiling, beloved child, watched over by happy, caring parents, riding his/her little tricycle into the sunset. The possibility that such a child might be born with major heart defects, severe mental deficiencies, grave intestinal difficulties, and/or underdeveloped reproductive organs, with the suffering, quality of life questions, and the need for continuous, in some cases, lifelong familial or institutional as well as medical care, was scarcely mentioned. With as much sensitivity as possible, I ventured to raise these issues. Roger Mudd gave me more opportunity to do so than I had been accorded in the case history-based film.

Following the morning-long plenary session, the symposium moved to the Shoreham Hotel where, throughout the afternoon, a series of seven panels were held (some of which overlapped). Five of these began with a case study, and concerned phenomena and ethical issues associated with procreation and mental retardation: "Who Should Be Born? Is Procreation a Right?"; "The Human Rights of the Retarded: An Inquiry into the Personal Freedom of the Retarded in Sexual, Educational, Social and Political Activities"; "Fabricated Babies: The Ethics of the New Technologies in Beginning Life"; "The Use and Misuse of Labeling: The Ethics of Testing, Tracking, and Filing" (this dealt with the practice and consequences of labeling a child in our society as "retarded," "handicapped," or "culturally deprived"); and "The Modification of Human Behavior: The Ethics of Human Control" (which began with a case study of the use of operant conditioning in the control of the behavior of retarded people). The last two panels—"Why Should People Care?" and "How Should People Care?: The Ethics of Medical Services"—were organized around discussions of the "dimension of moral, philosophical, and religious questions" that had been "implicit throughout the panels of the day," including questions of why and how we should care about and for our "fellow human beings," especially those who are sick, handicapped, or poor, within and beyond our health care system and society. (I was one of the respondents for the "How Should People Care?" panel.)

The hospitality surrounding the symposium had the attributes of a Washington, D.C. extravaganza. In my capacity as a participant in the film and the plenary session that initiated the symposium, and on one of the subsequent panels, I was invited to two of the dinners that were planned around the symposium. The first of these took place at the home of Eunice Kennedy and Sargent Shriver the evening before the symposium. Their spacious house not only overflowed with all the symposium participants, and a variety of Washington notables, but also with a flock of children and young people who were members of the Kennedy family. I was seated at what I presumed was one of the head tables, because its occupants included Dr. Cooke and Senator Edward Kennedy (who sat in the chair right next to me, on my left). Quite unintentionally, I raised a small stir at the table at one point in the course of the conversation by wondering out loud if informed voluntary consent had been obtained from the "real" parents of the baby born with Down syndrome who was featured in the film, for their "story" to be depicted in this way. My query triggered a worried consultation between Senator Kennedy and his sister Eunice Kennedy Shriver about whether this was a matter that should be taken up with their lawyer.

The second dinner that I attended took place the next day. It was a much smaller affair, held in Georgetown, in the elegant townhouse of former governor Averill

Harriman, and his wife, Pamela, who at that time reigned as the doyenne of Washington hostesses. The guests, who were seated around a beautifully appointed table, included Elie Weisel on my left, Governor Harriman on my right, and Jacques Monod, directly across from me.

There was a sense in which the climactic pièce de résistance of the entire symposium was the award ceremony that brought it to a close. Certain individuals were honored for their exceptional scientific, humanitarian, or existential contributions to care and caring in the sphere of health and illness. In grateful recognition, each recipient was presented with a piece of crystal sculpture on which was embossed the logo of the symposium—an angel holding a baby in her arms—and a check. Numerous members of the Kennedy family were mobilized for these presentations. Joan Kennedy played an accompanying solo piece on the piano, and it was a group of Kennedy youngsters who presented one of the awards to Dr. John Enders, in recognition of all the children's lives he had saved throughout the world, they said, through his development of a vaccine for measles.

A hush fell over the entire audience when Mother Teresa of Calcutta, clad in a blue-bordered white sari and head covering—the garb of the Missionaries of Charity that she founded—made her way onto the stage on sandaled feet to wordlessly accept her award. The aura of her serene and silent presence, and the care of the desperately ill, destitute, and dying persons that she incarnated, purged the assemblage of Washington, D.C. glitter and ballyhoo. We should have all paid our way to travel to Calcutta for this symposium, said Elie Weisel, who was sitting next to me. I agreed.

Although the Kennedy Symposium could hardly be called a prototypical bioethics conference or event, it had initiatory significance in the history of the field. It ushered in the second major center devoted to bioethics in the United States, two years after the founding of the Institute for Society, Ethics, and the Life Sciences, later known as the Hastings Center. The agenda of the meeting was more concentrated on mental retardation, Down syndrome, the social predicament and rights of children born with these conditions, and the giving of care and its wellsprings, than the issues on which American bioethics has centered its attention. But its preoccupation with the beginning of life, death at life's inception, new technologies of procreation, and genetically based disease and disability were consonant with what became some of the enduring foci of bioethical concern.

One of the most significant characteristics of the symposium was the theatrically arranged statement that it made about the *public* importance of the bioethical questions that the "advances in biological, genetic, and medical science" are raising, and "the choices" with which they confront "individuals and society"(Choices on our Conscience 1971: 52). In a "call to action" document issued two months after the symposium, 21 of its participants exhorted "the various publics of which this country is comprised...[to] register their concern for these issues...so laden with potential for human welfare or woe, for human decency or human callousness...through their political representatives." It proposed numerous concrete steps focused on education and communication to foster public discussion and awareness of these matters. The steps included greater assistance to the media in their coverage; more support for "the training of reporters and public commentators on the social and ethical implications of scientific developments"; and public forums, adult education programs, and open interchanges among "scientists, lawyers, physicians, clergymen, public officials, and educators on the concrete moral pressures each is under as they confront the decisions they must take."

Other recommendations involved allowing open access to public institutions, "especially those which deal with the sick, the mentally ill, the retarded, and the handicapped," in order to heighten "public sensitivity to the daily dilemmas faced by institutional administrators and staff"; making these ethical issues "an integral part of the educational process," in the curricula of primary and secondary schools, colleges, universities, and professional schools; initiating the examination by professional bodies of their codes of conduct "in the light of new social needs and ethical dilemmas"; and developing more effective means of open communication between legislators, scientific experts, and the public. The signatories also called for scrutinizing existing legal structures to "ascertain whether, under the conditions established by the new technologies, some persons especially among the powerless and the helpless, such as infants, the sick, the retarded, and the elderly, have rights that stand in need of defense"; and allocating funds by Congress for research on "the social and ethical consequences of scientific decision" (Choices on our Conscience 1971: 54–56).

Only some of these recommendations for action have been implemented as U.S. bioethics has evolved. But the way that the Kennedy Symposium brought bioethics to Washington in 1971, and the repercussions that it had, dramatize the fact that from its inception, the emergence of American bioethics constituted something more than the coming into being of a new intellectual discipline. In fact, U.S. bioethics was—and it continues to be—a happening that deeply involves the public domain and the polity, as well as the collective conscience of American society.

4

"Hello, Dolly"
Bioethics in the Media

The announcement of her birth was stunning news for scientists and policy makers as well as the general public. The placid-looking visage of Dolly, a lamb born seven months earlier at the Roslin Institute in Edinburgh, Scotland, first gazed out at the world from the front pages of newspapers on Sunday, February 23, 1997. She was a healthy-looking, plump young sheep, named for the singer Dolly Parton. But she was far from an ordinary sheep, for Dolly was the first mammal successfully cloned from an adult cell, produced by Dr. Ian Wilmut and his colleagues using a technique called somatic cell nuclear transfer. Four days later, on February 27, the scientific report on the Roslin team's work was published in the prestigious British journal, *Nature* (Wilmut et al. 1997). The cover of that issue of the usually staid journal was sky blue; in its center was an aquamarine-colored petri dish with a picture of a lamb superimposed on the dish. Underneath was an inscription in white letters, "A flock of clones." The title of the report from Wilmut et al. ("Viable Offspring Derived from Fetal and Adult Mammalian Cells") made no mention of cloning, nor did the paper itself, written "in the stylized form of scientific writing that is as rigid as a haiku" (Kolata 1998: 31), venture into the ethically and socially laden implications of their feat.

The revelation of Dolly's creation unleashed a worldwide torrent of print and electronic media coverage, with a profusion of commentaries from assorted experts in fields including ethics, religion, law, biomedical science, and medicine. From the outset, for the journalists and the sources they called upon, and for a fascinated public, the cardinal, explosive issue raised by Dolly's birth was that this technique could, in principle, be used to clone people. In the opinion of bioethicist Arthur Caplan, "No event in the past thirty years in biomedical research has commanded so much public interest and policy attention on both sides of the Atlantic" as did Dolly's creation (Caplan 2004a).

This was not the first time that the intertwined subjects of human reproductive cloning[1] and genetic engineering had attracted the attention of the lay public, or of professionals delving into ethical, religious, and social issues posed by advances in biology and medicine. Aldous Huxley's *Brave New World* (1932), a biting social commentary about a society that employed genetic engineering and the routine production of clones at the Central London Hatchery, is still a powerful, widely read and often cited book, and a number of fictional works about cloning appeared in the late 1960s and 1970s.[2] The depiction of the cloning of Hitlerian dictators in Ira Levin's *The Boys from Brazil* (1976) and its 1978 film adaptation served as a widely used worst-case scenario in discussions about what Dolly might lead to.[3]

During the 1970s, as bioethicist Daniel Callahan noted post-Dolly, cloning was discussed both in its own right and as "one of the symbolic issues of what was, at that time, called 'the new biology'" (Callahan 1998: 141).[4] In one of the first major stories about Dolly, he commented to reporter Gina Kolata that although "'[e]thicists mulled over the frightening implications... scientists dismissed these discussions as idle speculation about impossible things...and urged ethicists not to dwell on the topic. A lot of scientists got upset. They said that this is exactly the sort of thing that brings science into bad repute and you people should stop talking about it'" (Kolata 1997g: A15). A somewhat different explanation of why ethical deliberations were not pursued too extensively after the flurry of papers in the 1970s was offered by biologist and ethicist Ed Berger, when he commented on the need for widespread public debate in the wake of Dolly: "'[T]he moral and ethical questions got postponed partly because they were just too hard....They never took place, we never said, what are the serious ethical arguments against it. And we have to have that debate now'" (Kenen 1997).[5]

With the birth of Dolly, the realization that human cloning had moved into the realm of scientific possibility triggered an almost instantaneous flurry of calls for renewed ethical deliberations and new or expanded laws banning human cloning. In the United States, media attention was increased when, on Monday, February 24, the day after the news of Dolly was first revealed, President Bill Clinton sent a letter to Harold T. Shapiro, chair of the National Bioethics Advisory Commission (NBAC) that the president had established by an executive order in October 1995, directing the Commission to "undertake a thorough review of the legal and ethical issues associated with this new technology," and report back to him within 90 days "with recommendations on possible federal actions to prevent its abuse." NBAC had not held its first full meeting until October 1996, a year after it was established, and when Clinton charged them with the cloning report, the Commission was still in the process of recruiting an executive director and other staff, and dealing with budget uncertainties. After NBAC's first meeting, Shapiro formed two subcommittees to begin working on the two issues that the president had initially mandated it to address: human subjects protections and the management and use of genetic information. Then, in February 1997, the work of the still nascent Commission "was diverted toward an unexpected development": Dolly and the president's request for a report on cloning (National Bioethics Advisory Commission 1998: 12). The president characterized the technique that had produced Dolly as an advance that "could offer potential benefits in such areas as medical research and agriculture," but that "also raises serious ethical questions, particularly with respect to [its] possible use...to clone human embryos" (Clinton 1997a).

Dolly quickly became the scientific icon of 1997, adorning the covers of popular magazines, and of professional journals such as *Science*, which featured her as the "breakthrough of the year," with an article titled "The Lamb That Roared" (Pennisi 1997). We were intrigued by the news of Dolly's creation and ensuing events, which unfolded while we were considering possible case studies that would illustrate bioethics' roles in some of the public domains that it has come to occupy. The coverage of Dolly seemed to us to dramatize the fact that one of the sets of factors that contributed to the development of bioethics was the American public's long-standing interest in scientific and medical advances and the issues that they entail, and the way that they are featured in the print and electronic media.

Discussions about bioethical issues involved in medicine and science in the media, and the role of many bioethicists as national or local commentators on those issues, have become the field's most visible public domain, and can reach and potentially educate or influence a far wider audience than is possible in bioethics' academic, clinical, or public policy roles. To wit, a year after Dolly's birth was announced, a university teacher of philosophy and bioethics, in a paper about media coverage of Dolly and human cloning, observed that "[w]ithout having read a single article, heard a single presentation or taken a single bioethics class, most Americans have already received training in the ethics of cloning" (Hopkins 1998: 6).

Dolly, we decided, would be an informative case study of bioethics in the media for a number of reasons. These included the fact that the lay and professional responses to the import of her cloning not only involved "strictly ethical" issues. Rather, the reactions, both positive and negative, especially to the prospect of cloning human beings, encompassed as many, if not more, religious, sociocultural, and legal dimensions as they did philosophically grounded bioethical issues. A second factor was that Dolly's cloning quickly entered into two intertwined areas of bioethics' public domains: the role of religion in the public square and in public policy, and the role of bioethics commissions in policy formation in American society. Third, we were struck by the volume of the print and electronic media attention to Dolly and the possible implications of her creation, and felt that this extensive coverage would provide a magnified example of the "mediatization" of bioethical issues along with rich data. Still another reason for selecting Dolly was that the prospect of human reproductive cloning raised by her birth, and the question of how that prospect should be dealt with, dramatically illustrated the difficulties of achieving a public, societal consensus through political processes about ultimate questions of values and beliefs, such as "what is a person?" which are evoked by such a scientific development.

We used three sources of information to examine how the media covered Dolly. We first collected a convenience sample of stories in newspapers and in news magazines, and Web site transcripts or summaries of television coverage on news programs.[6] Second, to begin a more comprehensive systematic analysis, we ran a DIALOG search of U.S. newspapers for February and March 1997 that generated over 1,000 entries. Third, from this search we selected 16 major U.S. daily newspapers that are diverse both geographically and in the scope of their coverage for a detailed analyis.[7] Then, using two commercial databases,[8] we searched for articles covering two clusters of events: the announcement of Dolly's cloning and the issues it was perceived to have raised, and the completion of the NBAC report, *Cloning Human Beings*, requested by President Clinton.

Before turning to the results of our media analysis, we want to underscore its principal objective: although the case study takes note of bioethicists who were involved in the media coverage of Dolly, and what they had to say, our focus is on the bioethically, religiously, socially, and policy-relevant issues conveyed to the public, not on bioethicists themselves. With that in mind, we look at the messages and information transmitted to readers by the headlines, content, and themes of the media coverage, and the sources used by the press to provide "expert" perspectives and opinions.

Breaking the Embargo: Patterns in the First Stories

News of Dolly's existence, and the implications of her birth, began to sweep around the world on Sunday, February 23, 1997. Robin Mckie, science editor of a London newspaper, *The Observer*, broke the story in a page-one account headlined "Scientists Clone Adult Sheep," with a photo of the soon-to-be famous offspring, who was not called "Dolly" in his coverage (Mckie 1997). Ian Wilmut and his collaborators had refrained from publishing a report on their research for several months after Dolly was born. They did so at the request of PPL Therapeutics, the biotechnology company that was supporting their work and, once the cloned lamb seemed to be healthy, wanted to file for a patent on the use of the somatic cell nuclear transfer technique. When the researchers got the green light from the company, they submitted a four-page paper to *Nature*, which was accepted on January 10, 1997, and scheduled for publication on Thursday February 27, four days after Mckie's scoop.

Like several other leading journals, *Nature* alerts reporters to publications that they hope will attract media coverage through a "tip sheet," sent by e-mail or fax a week before the journal's publication date, and on request also will send recipients of the press release a prepublication copy of a paper. This is done with the informal normative understanding that any print or broadcast coverage is embargoed until the day the journal is published. Based on the brief press release,[9] a number of scientifically knowledgeable reporters, realizing the significance of the forthcoming paper, began contacting their sources for comments and preparing stories about the cloned lamb for release on February 27, or sooner if, as does happen, the embargo was broken.[10] Mckie's story in *The Observer*, which he later said he had obtained from his own sources rather than from the *Nature* press release, put the embargoed news in the public domain, freeing journalists and their papers to publish their own stories prior to *Nature*'s publication date.

Hot on the heels of Mckie's story, several other newspapers and news agencies (traditionally known as wire services) also reported on Dolly's advent on the same day, February 23.[11] On that first day of coverage, many American readers began to learn about Dolly and the prospects—both positive and alarming—that her cloning raised through front-page stories in *The New York Times*, the *Chicago Tribune*, and the *Los Angeles Times*,[12] and a story from Reuters on page 2 of the *Philadelphia Inquirer* (Kolata 1997 f; Kotulak 1997a; Maugh 1997c; Reuters 1997). The largest audience to learn about Dolly on that Sunday probably were the watchers of CNN evening news, which had an almost five-minute long segment that included comments by Ian Wilmut and geneticist Patrick Dixon on the "significance, potential use, & ethics of the research" that had produced her (Sheep cloning 1997).

Patterns in the Initial Media Coverage

In the first newspaper stories about Dolly, the sorts of headlines, the content and tone of the reportage, the kinds of sources contacted by the journalists, and the nature of the commentators' reactions that were quoted or paraphrased typified many features of the flood of coverage that began the next day, on Monday, February 24.

Dolly Headlines. As readers scan newspapers, their decisions about whether or not to read a story, editorial, or other material often is determined by how interesting or attention catching a headline is.[13] Most of the headlines in our February 23 sample conveyed straight news, such as the Agence France Presse's "Scottish Researchers Produce First Clone from Adult Animal" (Agence France Press 1997). The headline writer for the Reuter's story in the *Philadelphia Inquirer* chose to emphasize the potential benefits of Dolly's creation: "...It Could Lead to Advances in Medicine and the Study of Aging" (Reuters 1997). Others sought to capture readers' attention by featuring what most people would consider to be a more pessimistic or alarming prospec ("First Mammal Is Cloned: Breakthrough

Could Make It Possible to Duplicate Humans" [Kotulak 1997a]) or tried to reassure readers that the new cloning technology would not run amok ("Scientists Pledge: No Production Line Cloning" [Quinn 1997]). And, beginning the word-play that would be used for many later headlines, the Scottish *Sunday Mail* headlined its brief story with "Send in the Clones," a takeoff on "Send in the clowns" from the hit musical *A Little Night Music* (Send in the Clones 1997).

Content Themes. As did Mckie's embargo-breaking story in *The Observer*, most of the first accounts of Dolly conveyed three sets of information and messages: about the cloning technique, its potential beneficial applications, and its potential dangers. The amounts of detail and emphases varied, dependent partly on the stories' length, and on whether the reporters, anticipating that the news would break before *Nature*'s publication date, had contacted people for comments, and had their story ready to go to press. Mckie's 1,041-word story in *The Observer* included a "science explainer" about the nature of the cloning technique used by Wilmut and his team, why it was "a landmark in biological research," and, a point emphasized in Great Britain, "a triumph for UK science" because it "should lead to breakthroughs in work on ageing, genetics, and medicine." He went on to alert readers why this scientific advance "is also likely to cause alarm," because the technique "could be used on humans," drawing parallels with *Brave New World* and *The Boys from Brazil*. After raising these nightmare specters, he reassured readers that human cloning would be illegal in the United Kingdom "under the laws governing fertilisation research," and that, moreover, "[n]o responsible biologist would support such work, say scientists." Nonetheless, after elaborating on the "enormous importance" of the "breakthrough," Mckie ended his story by direly predicting that "it is the prospect of cloning people, creating armies of dictators, that will attract most attention."

The First Commentators. The United Kingdom and news agency reporters, who had a short lead time to file their stories after Mckie's article appeared, drew almost exclusively on British and Scottish contacts for comments on Dolly,[14] as well as on remarks made by Wilmut on a BBC Radio program, "The World This Weekend."[15] The reporters used statements by Wilmut and other scientist-sources to tell readers why the Roslin Institute experiment had been done and what it involved, including the "enormous inefficiency" of the somatic cell nuclear transfer technique, because it took 277 attempts to produce Dolly, and the advances in animal and human genetics applications they hoped it eventually would yield. From day one, however, as seen in Mckie's story, the media's major angle on Dolly was that her creation had taken human cloning from the realm of fiction—scientific and sociopolitical—to the world of scientific possibility.

In addition to Wilmut, who quickly became almost as great a media celebrity as Dolly (Kolata 1997e), the most frequently used commentator was Dr. Patrick

Dixon, a geneticist and author of *The Genetic Revolution*. Other sources included Dr. Ron James, managing director of PPL Therapeutics; Dr. Richard Nicholson, editor of *The Bulletin of Medical Ethics*, who brought the voices of ethicists and religionists into play; Dr. Donald Bruce, director of the Church of Scotland's society, religion, and technology project; and an unnamed "Scottish ethical expert."

The commentators were unanimous in their condemnation of using the somatic cell nuclear transfer technique for human cloning, on ethical, religious, and legal grounds. When asked if his team's cloning technique could be done with humans, Wilmut cautiously replied, "Possibly. We really don't know." But because "there is no clinical reason to do this," he wondered "why you would make another human being?" However, while he called cloning humans "repugnant" and emphasized that he and his Roslin Institute colleagues "would all find it ethically unacceptable and would not do it," he acknowledged that "[w]e are aware that there is potential for misuse, and we have provided information to ethicists and the [British] Human Embryology Authority" (Agence France Presse 1997; Quinn 1997; Ritter 1997).

Speaking, respectively, in secular bioethical and in theologically grounded terms, Nicholson and Bruce expressed their concerns about how cloning might or would affect human individuality and dignity, matters that would become a major argument against cloning in the months ahead. These fears were expressed with respect to cloning even one person, but were magnified by the thought of mass-producing human clones in carbon or photocopy fashion.[16]

The first commentators were divided about whether they thought Dolly would lead to human cloning for various purposes. When interviewed by Joe Quinn of the British Press Association, the managing director of Edinburgh's PPL company, sponsor of the Roslin group's work, "dismissed the idea of production-line cloning of humans" that had been captured in Mckie's carbon copy image of "armies of dictators," "saying this would be both unethical and illegal," and something he doesn't " 'think [is] ever going to happen' " (Quinn 1997). But others were not so sure. The various reactions to Dolly and to the possibility of human cloning attributed to geneticist Patrick Dixon illustrate how journalists' choices about which parts of an interviewee's remarks to use, or not use, can color the messages sent to readers. As quoted by the Agence France Presse, Dixon lauded the Roslin team's work as " 'an historic event…without parallel in genetic advances,' " and expressed his view " 'that this allows us potentially to produce replicas of any living human beings.' " The technique, he also was quoted as noting with no elaboration, " 'will bring with it a huge number of ethical questions' " (Agence France Presse 1997). More dire scenarios were painted by Dixon's statements in the *Sunday Telegraph* and *Press Association* stories. The implications of this advance, he was quoted as saying in the *Telegraph*, are " 'horrendous.… We will probably be able to clone the dead from cells taken from their bodies before they die,' " enabling parents " 'to 'reproduce' a carbon copy of a child who tragically died. This is something that needs to be regulated and outlawed' " (Matthews and Thornton 1997). And in his *Press*

Association story, Quinn presented other predictions by Dixon as to why people might someday want clones: "Showbiz moguls wanting to recreate dead stars[,] Dictators wanting to produce copies of themselves[,] And patients with serious illness like leukaemia wanting a 'twin' for spare part surgery" (Quinn 1997).

Among the U.S. newspapers that carried stories on February 23,[17] the *New York Times's* Gina Kolata, with the approval of the deputy science editor, had begun preparing a "major story" as soon as she received the prepublication copy of the *Nature* paper on February 21, which the paper would be ready to "rush…into print" if the embargo was broken (Kolata 1998: 31–32). Her story was substantially longer than others published that day, and drew upon a more extensive array of commentators (Kolata 1997f). She used five diverse sources to amplify her presentation of the scientific work and its implications for medicine, agriculture, and human cloning. The source she employed most extensively was Ian Wilmut, drawing on a telephone interview with him and on his interview by Quinn for the British Press Association, to describe the experiment and its hoped-for applications for genetic medicine and animal husbandry, and express his opposition to the possibility of using the technique to produce human clones. Her outside commentators were Neal First, a professor of animal biotechnology and reproductive biology who had pioneered a cloning method using embryonic cells;[18] biology professor Lee Silver, author of a soon to be published book on cloning titled *Remaking Eden* (Silver 1997); law professor Lori Andrews, a specialist in reproductive issues; and medical ethicist Ronald Munson. Silver was cited only briefly by Kolata, to convey a scientist's amazement about Dolly's existence and the new vistas it opened—not stating whether those were positive or negative. " 'It's unbelievable,' Dr. Silver said. 'It basically means that there are no limits. It means all of science fiction is true.' " The legal and bioethical experts, in turn, voiced their belief that, irrespective of laws banning human cloning, it could not be stopped if it became technically feasible. " 'I could see it going on surreptitiously,' " Andrews declared. Australia initially banned in vitro fertilization, she pointed out, " '[s]o scientists moved to Singapore' and offered the procedure there. 'I can imagine new crimes.' " Munson expressed a similar conviction: " 'The genie is out of the bottle.… 'This technology is not, in principle, policeable.' "

Dolly and Human Cloning: Ethical, Religious, and Policy Sequelae: Media Coverage, February 24–March 31, 1997

With the embargo broken on February 23, a flood tide of media coverage of Dolly's creation and its implications, primarily for human cloning, began the next day.[19] Commentators promptly weighed in on the prospect of human cloning in the stories that appeared on February 24. Philosopher-bioethicist Arthur Caplan and health lawyer-bioethicist George Annas, for example, respectively decried human cloning as "morally despicable," and cautioned that "the issues have to do with whether it's ethical to create a creature with the same genetic identity and whether this could lead to looking at children as commodities" (Vedantam 1997a).

A few days later, on March 4, President Clinton generated another newsworthy event when he issued a "Memorandum for the heads of executive departments and agencies, Subject: prohibition on federal funding for cloning of human beings" (Clinton 1997b). Although he had banned federal support for creating human embryos for research purposes in 1994, Clinton explained, those rules, and their extension by Congress in the FY96 and FY97 appropriations bills, "do not explicitly cover human embryos created for implantation, and do not cover all federal agencies. I want to make it absolutely clear that no Federal funds will be used for human cloning."[20,21]

In this section, we look at three aspects of the Dolly-related publications in the newspapers that we sampled through March 31, 1997: the types of coverage; the headlines that were written to attract readers' attention; and the "voices" that the reporters quoted or paraphrased, or who spoke through opinion pieces, to impart views about the bioethical, religious, legal, and policy issues posed by Dolly's creation. Then, in the next section, we examine the smaller amount of media coverage from June 1–15, 1997, when NBAC finalized its report and submitted it to Mr. Clinton, and the White House promptly acted on one of the report's key recommendations.

Types of Coverage

The 251 articles identified in our search fell into four categories. The greatest amount of space was devoted to *news stories* (44 percent). Another 10 percent were *science explainers*, dealing with topics such as cloning techniques and genetics, that often accompanied the news stories.[22] The extent of the reactions that Dolly's cloning evoked is indicated by the fact that slightly over one-third of all articles in our media sample consisted of *editorials, opinion pieces* (*Op-Ed essays*), and *letters to the editor*.[23] Editorials included a long "cover editorial" of more than 1,300 words in *Newsday*, headlined "Genesis the Sequel" (1997). Op-Ed pieces presented the views of religious scholars Nancy Duff (1997a, 1997b) and Martin Marty (1997a, 1997b, 1997c), Cardinal Anthony Bevilacqua (1997), bioethicists Daniel Callahan (1997b) and Thomas Murray (1997), health care lawyers/bioethicists George Annas (1997) and Alan Meisel (1997), and science historian Daniel Kevles (1997). A small number of articles appeared in the *business* pages (4 percent of our sample), discussing topics such as the potential payoffs in medicine and animal husbandry that Dolly had created for PPL Therapeutics and other biotechnology companies. Our final category was the ubiquitous *"other,"* into which we placed slightly more than 9.5 percent of the coverage. This included articles in which the search terms "sheep" and "clone" were used as metaphors or other lead-ins for a different topic, such as the "cloning" of a star basketball player, celebrity, or race horse.

Headline Messages

Headline writers can choose various ways to frame a story, editorial, or Op-Ed column, and the type of message conveyed by a headline can strongly influence whether readers decide to read the piece and how they react to what it conveys. To examine headline messages about Dolly, we sorted the 359 headline segments[24] in our sample into 7 categories.[25] Six of these, and the percentages of coverage for which they were used, are:[26]

1. *Straight news*—identifies no underlying message, such as "Scientists Report Cloning an Adult Mammal" (28 percent).
2. *Wordplay*—uses puns, literary allusions, and witticisms about sheep, lamb, wolves, etc. (17 percent).
3. *Alarming or pessimistic messages*—indicate that new ideas can be dangerous and that science and technology create changes faster than we can understand and deal with them (17 percent). For example, "The human race will never be the same in this new scientific wasteland of sexless reproduction."
4. *Optimistic messages*—detail the capacity of science and technology to make life better (13 percent), such as "Don't be too hasty with laws on cloning. Research that aims at cloning humans could end up having benign and practical uses." The "optimistic" headlines tended to stress specific, practical benefits of cloning, and there was often a deliberate attempt to calm and reassure readers who might be alarmed about the breakthrough and to convey concerns about restrictive legislation.
5. *Conflicts about cloning*—alert readers to *conflicts* about cloning (11 percent), particularly to differences of opinion about the ethical, religious, and policy issues it entails. For example, "Theologians Join Scientists in a Widening and Difficult Debate," "Playing God?: Moral Insight Ought to Accompany Science," and "When It Comes to Cloning, for Some, Any Hint of a Limit on Scientific Inquiry Is an Affront Akin to Blasphemy. Where and When Can Lines Be Drawn?"
6. *Historical importance*—pays attention to this significant advance (7 percent). For example, "Big, astounding science!!" and "Genesis the Sequel."[27]

The Commentators

Ethical, religious, social, and policy perspectives on and opinions about Dolly and human cloning were solicited by many reporters in our media sample. Some of the sources were primarily local, whose names might be familiar to a particular newspapers' readers, while others, many of whose names also appeared on Op-Ed pages, were well-known figures in their professional fields and, in some cases, also to the general public who followed popular coverage of bioethical issues. A number of the commentators were involved with NBAC's cloning report (National Bioethics Advisory Commission 1997a; 1997b). These included NBAC commissioners Patricia Backlar, Alexander Capron, Alta Charo, James Childress, and Thomas Murray; law professor Lori Andrews; and several of those whom NBAC had invited to testify at commission meetings: bioethicist Ruth Macklin, health law professor John Robertson, and figures from four major religious traditions—Rabbi Moshe Tendler, Islamic scholar Abdulaziz Sachedina, Protestant theologian Gilbert Meilaender, and Father Albert Moraczewski from the National Conference of Catholic Bishops.

The most frequently quoted or paraphrased commentators on Dolly were George Annas and Arthur Caplan, who probably are the print and electronic media's two most utilized "experts" for comments on a range of news-making ethical issues in biology and medicine. As the frequency with which Annas and Caplan are called upon by the media suggests, many of the sources used by reporters to comment on Dolly are known for their work on bioethical issues and often identified as "bioethicists," although they have other primary fields in which they work such as law, philosophy, medicine, or religion. Significantly, however, it was neither bioethical nor legal/policy issues about which journalists most often contacted their sources. Rather, the largest number of commentators in our sample were asked to address the religious import of human reproductive cloning from the perspectives of various faith traditions, which many people quickly saw as the most deep-seated, profound implication of Dolly's creation.[28] For, as NBAC chairman Harold Shapiro observed, the meta-questions evoked by cloning concern "matters as central as procreation, family, human identity formation and the meaning of life and death," about which "much of what we think and feel springs...from religious or spiritual sources" (Shapiro 1999: 8–9).[29]

The comments that reporters used in their stories, and the views expressed in editorials and Op-Ed pieces, presented a spectrum of perspectives about two central issues raised by Dolly's creation: why human cloning should be opposed or, in limited, specific circumstances, might be morally justified; and how efforts to clone a child could be controlled or prevented.[30]

Human Reproductive Cloning. When asked to discuss human reproductive cloning, almost all commentators expressed their opposition to such a prospect. A few, however, told the press that there were some circumstances in which creating a child by this means might be morally and socially acceptable. Law professor John Robertson, a strong proponent of reproductive rights, for example, reportedly said that he could "envision times when cloning might be understandable," such as in "the case of a couple whose baby was dying and who wanted, literally, to replace the child. Mr. Robertson does not think that would be so reprehensible" (Kolata 1997g: A15). Some religious scholars also voiced a cautious acceptance of cloning human beings. Theology professor Nancy Murphy explained that because she believes that "a person has a single, physical nature, from which all its qualities grow," she has "no qualms about the nature of a clone. 'It'll just be a plain, old human being…like any ordinary person'" (Kloehn and Salopek 1997). Theologian Ted Peters stated that while he had "'not heard any good reasons for cloning humans,'" he "sees no problem religiously or theologically…. [C]loning may appear to be playing God 'because the birth process is mysterious.' But it is more like 'playing human. We should not just leave nature alone without any technological intervention'" (H. T. Gray 1997).

A number of commentators carefully sought to refute the notion, engraved in popular culture through fiction and some media accounts after Dolly's birth, that human clones would be "Xeroxed copies" of their genetic parent.[31] A few sources, however, perpetuated this cloning mythology, with statements such as that by health law professor and NBAC commissioner Lori Andrews that "we may soon be able to 'clone great thinkers, beauties, or athletes without their knowledge or consent…all that would be needed would be some cells'" (Next, really prolific cows 1997).

These and other sources to whom the press turned, however, explained that there were other, far more serious reasons to oppose reproductive cloning. Among the bioethicists whose views were included in stories, some, such as Arthur Caplan, were concerned about the risks to the cloned fetus: "To even justify doing the experiment, you would have to say, 'What will we do if we produce a malformed baby? What is the ethical purpose of even trying?'" (Kendall 1997). For others, human cloning raised deep moral and sociocultural issues about our conceptions of children, parents, and what it means to be a human being. Daniel Callahan, for example, voiced his belief that human cloning epitomized "a profound threat to what might be called the right to our own identity" (Callahan 1997b; see also Callahan 1997a and Monmaney 1997). In a similar vein, bioethicist Eric Parens expressed his belief that "'we make a mistake if what we value most are the sorts of traits that are encoded in our genome. This way of thinking contributes to misconceptions about what it means to be a human being'" (Successful cloning 1997). NBAC commissioner Thomas Murray held that "the possibility of [human cloning] needs to be seen as part of 'a broader cultural debate about the moral significance of parenthood. It's a wake-up call to think about what's really at the heart of what we value about the parent-child relationship'" (Spotts and Marquand 1997; see also Murray 1997). For physician and humanist Leon Kass, who would become embroiled in the contentious debates about human reproductive cloning and stem-cell research as chairman of President George W. Bush's Council on Bioethics (Bush 2001; President's Council on Bioethics 2002, 2004a), the "'revulsion'" that some proponents of a ban on cloning were expressing " 'is not an argument, but repugnance is often the emotional bearer of deep wisdom' " (Vedantam 1997d).[32]

If the positions of the Roman Catholic, Jewish, Protestant, and Islamic religious thinkers cited by the press conveyed any clear message to the public, it was that there is no single religious view, much less a religiously grounded consensus, about cloning human beings. Rather, readers learned, there is a diversity of perspectives within and across major faith traditions, both as to why cloning children could be justifiable under certain circumstances, and why such a reproductive technique always would violate fundamental religious tenets and moral norms.[33] The Islamic scholars cited by reporters came the closest to agreeing that their religious beliefs did not prohibit human cloning, but, at the same time, they issued a number of caveats about its use.[34] Roman Catholic sources pointed to a number of moral concerns raised by the possibility of human cloning. Moreover, the press reported, Dolly had led the Vatican to issue a statement, "Reflections on Cloning," in 1997 that urged an international ban on human reproductive cloning, and strongly opposed therapeutic cloning with stem cells as an "instrumental use of a human being [that] gravely offends human diginity and human kind." The document was described by rector and ethicist Father J. J. McCarthy as a " 'bioethics document' " that taught that " '[l]ife is a gift of the Creator and not a result of human manufacture' " (Hearts of the city 1997). Although the Roman Catholic Church reportedly would view human cloning as an " 'affront to human dignity,' "[35] some Catholic commentators also pointed out that if children eventually were cloned, they would still have a human soul, and that "the Catholic Church would be first in line to defend their rights as full-fledged children of God"[36] (Rodgers-Melnick 1997).

Differing perspectives from Judaism were conveyed by scholars such as rabbis Moshe Tendler and Elliott Dorff. Tendler said that he saw possible good reasons for human cloning, but he also expressed his conviction, as a Jew living in "the historical shadow of the Nazi eugenics program 'the danger of abusing the science is too great to allow its use' " (Rodgers-Melnick 1997). Dorff explained that " '[w]e may not clone ourselves,…for we are not granted permission to live forever…to clone ourselves would be to worship ourselves rather than God, and that is idolatry of the worst kind' " (Hearts of the city 1997).

The Protestant clergy and theologians who expressed either their opposition to reproductive cloning or their cautious acceptance of it also did so for a variety of reasons, deriving in part from their particular denominational beliefs (which often were not identified in the press). Pastor Ellis Robinson, for example, presented the position that ' "once again, science has overstepped its bounds.… God should determine life, not imperfect human beings, he said.… 'We are not responsible enough to handle human cloning' " (H. T. Gray 1997). Ronald Cole-Turner, a professor of theology and ethics, critically observed that " '[c]loning is no short cut to resurrection.…We live once, we die once, we are transformed. We do not live once, then again, and again.' " On the positive side, however, he felt that " 'Dolly…has already accomplished a great miracle. She has inspired an international call for public theology'" (Long 1997b). Another prominent theologian, Langdon Gilkey, told the press that he "see[s] God's contribution to an individual not as a distinct gift of supernatural spirit, but in the workings of genetics and environment." Nonetheless, he worried that a clone "'would not be a full human being. It would be a sort of fleshy robot. I don't know that, but I'm worried.... We're creating something that looks like a human, but is it a person?'" (Kloehn and Salopek 1997).

Several of the Protestant commentators pointed out that they saw the need for churches and religious communities to take an active role in dealing with the moral and social issues posed by cloning—issues that, in the knowledgeable view of theologian James Gustafson, "'have not changed much from '60s and '70s'" (Spotts and Marquand 1997). "The church (along with other religious bodies, governmental agencies, lawyers, and others)," theological ethicist Nancy Duff urged, "must help forge a responsible path for this new technology before it proceeds further" (Duff 1997b), and another theologian, stating that "'we have to try to restrain [cloning],'" expressed his optimism that "'religious communities will be very important in creating...a cultural environment'" that would exercise such restraints (Rodgers-Melnick 1997). Some other theologians, however, were less sanguine about the leadership role that Protestantism could play. "'In this country,'" one observed, "'the Roman Catholic Church continues to have sufficient cohesiveness to be able to address questions like this in ways that their members will at least take seriously. But I don't have a lot of confidence in what you might call mainstream Protestantism'" (Rodgers-Melnick 1997).

As a final example of the religious perspectives conveyed to readers, a well-known religion columnist recalled a critique of ethical discourse by the late Paul Ramsey, a religious ethicist who had been one of the intellectual founders of bioethics. Ramsey, Peter Steinfels wrote, "replied [to Joshua Lederberg's arguments for human cloning three decades ago] with a major address, 'Shall We Clone a Man?' later published in his book, 'Fabricated Man'" (Ramsey 1970a). "As [he] suggested in 'Fabricated Man,' Steinfels continued, "ethical discussion that frets about awesome technical possibilities but from the start is unwilling ever to say 'no' is ultimately frivolous. 'It would perhaps be better not to raise the ethical issues [Ramsey wrote], than not to raise them in earnest'" (Steinfels 1997).

Controlling Human Reproductive Cloning. In addition to presenting concerns about reproductive cloning, some reporters asked their sources how, or whether, such an attempt could be forestalled. A number of bioethicists, health lawyers, and other experts expressed their sense that a legislative ban would be imposed, but that, in the end, laws would not prevent attempts from being made. A *New York Times* Op-Ed piece by science historian Daniel Kevles was representative of this view: "[A]s the technology evolves to invite human experimentation, it would be best to watch and regulate rather than prohibit. Outlaw the exploration of human cloning and it will surely go offshore, only to turn into bootleg science that will find its way back to our borders simply because people want it" (Kevles 1997).[37]

Reactions were mixed to proposed state statutes, and to President Clinton's March 4 executive order banning the use of federal funds for human reproductive cloning research and requesting voluntary compliance from privately funded entities. Commenting on the president's rationale for his executive order, bioethicist Ruth Macklin declared that "'[s]cience fiction is a poor basis for making public policy. Evidence, not surmise, is required to conclude that the psychological harm of cloning someone outweighs the benefits. What constitutes a violation of human dignity, when no one has been harmed and no one's right has been violated?'" (Vedantam 1997f). In contrast to Macklin's position, two other well-known bioethicists, Ruth Faden and Arthur Caplan, expressed support for the president's action. Faden "welcomed the [president's] ban as a necessary 'time out' while scientists decide how far to go," and she "predicted the president 'will get a considerable amount of cooperation from the scientific community, even though the private ban is voluntary and unenforceable'" (Cooke and Maier 1997). Caplan called the ban a "sensible approach to a volatile scientific issue," on somewhat different grounds than Faden. At this time, he told the press, human cloning research "'is too risky, too dangerous to undertake. We're only at the Wright Brothers' stage of development with respect to cloning technology'" (Cimons and Peterson 1997).

Other commentators, such as health law professor Lori Andrews and philosopher James Childress, also voiced their concern that while the president could effectively ban federal funding, a voluntary halt on work by privately funded groups was unenforceable. The ban is "'an important symbolic message,'" Andrews stated, "'but of little practical import.... [E]verybody is suggesting it will come through the private clinics, which are not heavily regulated,...and operate on a philosophy of 'just show me the money'" (Seelye 1997; Cooke and Maier 1997). An additional caution, voiced by bioethicist and religious ethicist Ronald Green, was that any human cloning legislation should be carefully crafted so that it does not "'shut down other related forms of research that could unlock the secrets to disease'" (Ross 1997). And a few sources scathingly criticized any effort to prohibit human cloning, such as the president's order. "'I'm uncomfortable with sanctimonious and ill-thought-out presidential decrees where the president has determined we have created a boundary beyond which humanity dare not go,'" declared sociologist James Hughes. "'Humanity should be in control of its own destiny'" (Vedantam 1997c).

The NBAC Report: *Cloning Human Beings:* Media Coverage, June 1–15, 1997

Coverage and Headline Messages

Compared with the amount of coverage that Dolly's creation evoked, the June 1997 issuance of the NBAC report that President Clinton had requested on

February 24 received relatively scant coverage by the newspapers in our sample. This suggests, to us, that bioethical policy deliberations generated by Dolly were deemed by the papers to be of less interest to their readers than the more dramatic news of her cloning and its implications.[38] Our search identified only 33 stories and one editorial in 12 of the 16 papers in our media sample during the two-week period June 1–15.[39,40] The coverage fell into three groups. The first, from June 1–6, reported on the commissioners' efforts to complete their report and the contentious issues with which they were grappling. The second, on June 8 and 9, gave accounts of NBAC's June 7 meeting during which the report was finalized, and the content of and reasons for its major recommendations. The third cluster was occasioned by the June 9 ceremony at which NBAC chairman Dr. Harold Shapiro formally presented the report to the president, and Clinton announced the legislation he planned to propose. After this event, our search found only two more items: a June 12 editorial in the *Los Angeles Times* expressing support for Clinton's legislative proposal (Balance on the cloning issue 1997), and a lengthy feature story in *The Christian Science Monitor* on June 13, based on interviews with four NBAC commissioners (Spotts 1997).

The majority of the headlines stressed NBAC's and the president's negative reaction to the prospect of human cloning, using terms such as "ban," "prohibit," "limit," and "outlaw." A smaller number of stories, and the single editorial, conveyed a more positive message: NBAC "to offer cloning guidelines," "expected to OK human cloning," "Cloning backed, but not of babies," and "Balance on the cloning issue. Clinton's legislation offers some sensible middle ground." A few headline writers used wordplay to emphasize the controversial nature of human cloning and of NBAC's deliberations, such as "Anatomy of a Decision: Ethics Panel's Wooly Work." After the latter headline, a "highlight" before the body of the story read "Devising a policy on cloning represented a rare clash of science, religion, and medicine" (Spotts 1997).

The Commentators

The reporters who wrote about NBAC's cloning report turned to many of the commissioners (11 of 18) for comments on the document's preparation and contents, giving perspectives from their areas of professional expertise and from their experiences in drafting the report. Alexander Capron and Thomas Murray were the most frequently cited members.[41] The press also called on a number of outside (non-NBAC) sources to provide their readers with an array of views about the report and the president's response to it. These commentators came from bioethics, health law and constitutional law, religion and moral theology, basic biological research and clinical medicine, industry, patient advocacy and pro-life spokespersons, the U.S. Congress, and from concerned citizens who had given public testimony at NBAC meetings.[42]

Reproductive Cloning. As was the case in the February and March stories triggered by Dolly's birth, readers of the NBAC coverage learned that that there was almost unanimous opposition to the idea of cloning human beings on the part of the NBAC's commissioners, President Clinton and Vice President Gore, speakers at NBAC meetings, and the outside commentators contacted by reporters.[43] However, reporters also made it clear that the opposition to human reproductive cloning did not rest on a unified basis; rather, the reasons marshaled against it had proved to be extremely contentious within as well as outside the Commission.

The Commissioners' Work: Complexity and Controversy. Some of the press accounts gave the public a glimpse into the workings of a federal commission such as NBAC, especially the unusually challenging task it faced not only because of its subject matter but also due to the Commission's nascent stage of development and, for such a federal advisory group, the unusually short period of 90 days it had to meet Clinton's directive. As recounted by Spotts in his *Christian Science Monitor* feature story, "Anatomy of a Decision," a few days after he received the president's February 24 letter, NBAC's chairman convened a small group of commissioners "to help chart the committee's course" on its cloning report (Spotts 1997). Some two weeks later, on March 13–14, the full commission gathered for the first of the five open meetings it would hold to formulate and deliberate the issues they would deal with, listen to invited speakers and those who wished to give public testimony, and review drafts of the report. Commissioners such as Alexander Capron and James Childress were veterans at the work of bioethics advisory bodies. For others members, who had never been on a national commission, NBAC's first meeting on March 13–14 "was a jump-in-with-both-feet experience." Molecular biologist Carol Greider found that " 'for me it was a total mystery. Since I had never been on one of these panels, I had no idea how one would put together a set of recommendations and a report in a short time' " (Spotts 1997).

A number of other stories also sought to convey the pressures commissioners felt to complete their report on time. Their efforts were characterized as "frantic" (Weiss 1997), and the pace at which they worked during the week before their final meeting on June 7 as "frenzied" (Kolata 1997d). In an interview five days before that meeting, one harried member, Alta Charo, was quoted as saying that " 'I divide my life into B.D. and A.D.—before Dolly and after Dolly. I'm hoping to move on to A.R.—after report' " (Kolata 1997d). The commissioners' discussions, the press reported, at times were rancorous: Charo characterized one session on ethical issues as a "real bloodbath" (Spotts 1997), and another commissioner recalled members "shouting" at each other during a dinner discussion (Long 1997a). The process of developing the report's findings and recommendations, Capron said after the document was finalized, was like " 'building an airplane while it is in flight,' " and the meeting on June 7 before the commissioners took a final vote on the report's contents was described as involving a "learned and tedious discussion" during which "the group bickered over adjectives and phrases—even commas—as they attempted to define ethical objections to cloning" (Recer 1997b).

Media Themes: Hanging Their Hat on Safety. In their coverage of the commissioners' struggles to craft their conclusions and recommendations, the press concentrated on two major topics: why NBAC was focusing on the safety of human reproductive cloning as the grounds for concluding that such work should not be attempted, and their recommendation about how it should be proscribed. A third important aspect of the commission's decision-making process, which received less media attention, centered on why the group had dealt only with human reproductive cloning, and not also with cloning embryos solely for research purposes. Although some articles presented views both supporting and criticizing the commission for this decision, only one story, by Spotts, explained why this aspect of cloning had not been tackled by NBAC. Given their 90-day time frame, commissioner Thomas Murray explained to Spotts, " 'We had to decide pretty quickly what the scope of the report would be.' The prospect of cloning children 'seemed to be at the core of the public reaction and the novel use of [the technique] with profound moral implications. So we knew we had to address that.' " Murray also offered a second rationale: " 'The president had declared in 1994 that there should be no use of federal funds to create any embryos for research, and whatever else the Dolly technique is, it's the creation of an embryo.' " Beyond Murray's explanations, Spotts related, it had become evident by the time of an NBAC meeting in mid-April that the commissioners would not reach a consensus on cloning embryos for research, and also how controversial any position they might adopt would be. " 'We were getting a better idea of the applications in the biomedical area that would be at risk if we were to recommend something that shut this technology down broadly,' Charo says... 'You immediately get yourself caught in the abortion debates about research on embryos, and you get yourself caught on the worst part of those debates because you're not just using embryos left over from in vitro fertilization procedures. You're making new embryos which you would then not permit to develop into a child' " (Spotts 1997).

The commission's decision not to address embryo cloning for research was greeted positively by commentators such as investigators and biotechnology industry members. But this omission drew sharply worded criticism from others, among them pro-life spokespersons who hold that life begins at conception. John Kavanaugh-O'Keefe, director of the American Life League's American Bioethics Advisory Commission, who gave public testimony at three commission meetings, declared that the proposed legislation " 'would, in essence, be a ban with a wink. It would be okay to clone as long as you kill' " (Weiss 1997). His American Life League colleague, Sheena Talbot, also denounced embryo-cloning research, stating that " '[t]he tinkering of human cloning in the laboratory and in the manipulation of human life in the petri dish is evil in itself' " (Kerr 1997b).

By the time of their May 17 meeting, as the deadline for forwarding a report to the president loomed, the Commission was ready to vote on a working document. The central conclusion reported in the early June stories was that " '[a]t this time, it is morally unacceptable for anyone...to attempt to create a child using the adult [somatic cell] nuclear transfer technique...because of the lack of safety and effectiveness of this method in humans' " (Long 1997a). None of the commissioners or their invited speakers supported the idea of reproductive cloning, for a mix of ethical, religious, and social reasons. Why, then, did they rest their case on safety, and, by stating "at this time," seem to leave the door open to the possibility that producing children by this means might be acceptable in the future? Several members were quoted by reporters explaining why NBAC had adopted this position. They pointed out that Ian Wilmut and his colleagues had stated in their *Nature* paper that Dolly was the 277th embryo the Roslin team had produced; only 29 had survived long enough to be implanted in ewes, and of those 29, only Dolly survived (Vedantam 1997b). Moreover, there were unanswered questions about whether Dolly, or other clones, would be afflicted with problems of premature cell aging or defects from accumulated genetic mutations. " 'The safety concern,' " Murray told reporters, " 'is so preeminent and so unanimously shared that the decision was a slam dunk' " (Long 1997a). " 'It's like a court trying to decide a very complex question,' " he explained in another story, " 'you can do it exhaustively or you can decide on the issue that is the clearest' " (Weiss 1997).

The commissioners wrestled with religious, philosophical, and legal aspects of reproductive cloning, aided in their deliberations by papers they commissioned and the perspectives of invited speakers and those who gave public testimony at meetings.[44] But efforts to achieve consensus on any of these issues proved so elusive that, as commissioner Lawrence Miike said, " 'We have hung our hat on the safety issue. We have not said we favor one side or the another' " (Neikirk 1997). This acknowledgment was echoed by James Childress's statement that " '[b]eyond the safety issue I am not sure we have a consensus' " (Long 1997a).

It seems unlikely that NBAC's commissioners would have reached agreement on many, if any, topics other than safety even if they had had substantially more than 90 days to complete their report, due, in important ways, to the problematic issue of how a federal bioethics commission should handle religious positions. Reporter Karen Long told her *Cleveland Plain Dealer* readers that commissioners Murray and Childress had been assigned the report's section on religious perspectives, and they "worked hard to write a...chapter in which readers would recognize their own convictions and see them treated respectfully." But, Murray told her, " 'They won't see their views declared the winner. We didn't have to, because of the safety concerns' " (Long 1997a). Being able to avoid the difficulties posed by invoking religious positions as a basis for their conclusions and recommendations was a relief to NBAC members. As commissioner Bernard Lo, a physician and bioethicist, told Long, " 'I think the problem in a society that has a separation of church and state is how do we take strongly held religious beliefs which are not universally shared, which are divergent, and include them in the making of public policy.' "[45]

Differing religious views on why human cloning should not be attempted, however, were not the only difficult set of issues that NBAC confronted. As Capron explained to Kolata, cloning " 'is genuinely controversial, unlike some topics in bioethics.' " It divided people within and without NBAC into two extremes, he related:

On the one side are those who stress "scientific and reproductive freedom." They argue that even though some people are repulsed by the idea of creating genetically identical copies of living people, this country has a strong tradition of not preventing scientific research and not intervening in people's right to reproduce. On the other side, Mr. Capron said, are those who emphasize the "sanctity of life and traditional family values." They argue that cloning is fundamentally different from what is normally thought of as reproduction and that it would threaten people's notions of what it means to be human, with a unique identity and with well-defined relationships in a family. (Kolata 1977d; see also Capron 1997)

In the end, then, as the *Washington Post*'s Rick Weiss and other reporters pointed out, the commissioners settled for having sections in their report that cataloged ethical, religious, and legal as well as scientific questions about human cloning it had not fully addressed much less resolved, and which they believed needed to be discussed over time and in depth, "so the national debate can continue to evolve" (Weiss 1997).

Federal versus Private Funding. Having concluded that human cloning is "morally unacceptable" because of potential risks to the developing fetus, the Commission's other major task was to respond to the president's directive to make "recommendations on possible federal actions to prevent [this technology's] abuse" (Clinton 1997a). From accounts of the report's drafting and the final version approved on June 7, readers learned that NBAC had recommended three major policy actions: (1) continue the moratorium Clinton had instituted in March banning the use of federal funding "in support of any attempt to create a child by somatic cell nuclear transfer," (2) issue an immediate request "to private and non-federally funded sectors" to voluntarily comply with the ban, and (3) enact federal legislation to "prohibit anyone from attempting, whether in a research or clinical setting," to use the Dolly technique to create a child. Two significant caveats came with this third recommendation: first, a three- to five-year sunset clause, at which point the scientific status of cloning and its attendant ethical and social issues would be reviewed to determine whether the legislative ban is still needed; second, "any regulatory or legislative actions undertaken to effect the…prohibition…should be carefully written so as not to interfere with other important areas of scientific research," such as cloning human DNA sequences and cell lines or research on cloning animals by somatic cell nuclear transfer (National Bioethics Advisory Commission 1997a, iii–iv).

Among the sources the press called on to provide reactions to the policy recommendations, some conservative legislators, such as Republican Senator Christopher Bond, took exception to the sunset clause provision, stating that " '[the commissioners] are leaving the door wide open to future cloning. I had hoped that the federal ethics commission would not be afraid to make a strong moral statement that human cloning is wrong, period, and should be banned' " (Recer 1997a). Seeking voluntary compliance from researchers or clinicians not using federal funds was a strategy that troubled some commissioners. " 'My concern,' " commissioner Bernard Lo said, " 'is that I think there will be physicians in I.V.F. clinics who will be willing to break a moratorium, especially if they are urged to by infertile couples.' " "If even one clinic actually clones a human being, he said, the floodgates will be opened and 'it will be hard to go back' " (Kolata 1997d). Dissatisfaction with this aspect of the report also was conveyed by another commissioner, who spoke on the condition of anonymity. He characterized the regulations banning the use of federal funds for embryo research and the lack of regulations covering the private sector as " 'the worst of both worlds' " because " '[t]he place you're likely to get all the rules strictly adhered to and research published openly is the federal government…and the place where things will get done shoddily and just done for the money will be the private IVF (fertility) clinics that already have bad reputations for conducting research without proper oversight' " (Weiss 1997).

Once again, reporters called upon Arthur Caplan and George Annas for their comments on the report. Caplan pointed out that by recommending a ban only on somatic cell nuclear transfer, private sector labs could legally attempt human cloning by the embryo splitting method used to clone animals (Neikirk 1997). Annas, in turn, criticized the commission for using possible harm to children as the basis for a legislative ban on cloning, which, in his opinion, "duck[ed] the moral questions." Some medical experts also voiced doubts about whether an "anti-cloning law" was warranted, Kolata reported, since there have been many "experimental, and unsafe, procedures, like transplants with baboon hearts," which have not been prohibited. One of her sources, an infertility specialist, remarked that "cloning is no more unsafe 'than many things we do.' " Another expert she contacted, a developmental biologist, concurred with this judgment. "It seems clear to him," Kolata told her readers, "that in citing safety, the commission members are 'trying to give a biological basis for a moral argument' " (Kolata 1997c).

The President's Proposal. NBAC chairman Harold Shapiro formally presented the Commission's report to President Clinton and Vice President Gore at a ceremony in the White House Rose Garden on June 9. As press accounts had already made clear, Shapiro explained for the public record that reaching the final conclusions and recommendations in *Cloning Human Beings* had been a difficult, often contentious process. The core difficulty, he emphasized, lay in the Commission's recognition of and respect for pluralism in American society. It was a hard task, he stated, " 'in part because conflicting values are at stake; in part because Americans disagree on the implications of this new technology for the social and cultural values they hold dearest; in part because it's difficult to decide if and when our liberties should be restricted' " (Harris 1997).46 It also was hard, Shapiro noted, for the commissioners to decide whether their "moral and ethical reservations about cloning 'were sufficient for us to suggest a legislative solution for the moment [because] we all understand there are moral views that many of us have, which we do not want to translate into law out of respect for those who have totally different views' " (Associated Press 1997a, 1997b).

In the limited coverage of Clinton's speech when he formally received the report, the press related that the president accepted NBAC's position on safety issues, declaring that " 'attempting to clone a human being is unacceptably dangerous to the child and morally unacceptable to our society.' " " 'I believe strongly,' " Clinton stated, " 'that this conclusion reflects a national consensus' " (Harris 1997). Reflecting as well his own moral beliefs, he also averred that attempts to clone a human would jeopardize " 'the sacred family bonds at the very core of our ideals and our society' " (Associated Press 1997b). Accordingly, he announced, he would propose federal legislation to ban cloning " 'for the purposes of creating a child' " for a period of five years, providing time to " 'continue the national dialogue on cloning' " (Harris 1997). With respect to extending the moratorium, however, Clinton also proposed to extend the ban to the private sector, going well beyond NBAC's recommendation for voluntary compliance (National Bioethics Advisory Commission 1997a: iii).47

Given the public testimony by pro-life spokespersons during NBAC meetings, and their comments in the press, neither Clinton nor the NBAC commissioners could have been surprised that antiabortion groups excoriated the Commission for not dealing with research using cloned human embryos, and the president for not including a ban on such research in his proposed legislation, a contentious set of issues that were noted by the press. NBAC, declared the president of the American Life League, " 'rejects the humanity of the cloned embryo, which will eventually be subject to experimentation and will eventually be deprived of his or her life' " (Harris 1997). From Congress, Rep. Vernon Ehlers (R-Mich.), who had introduced legislation to ban human cloning earlier in 1997, declared that his bill would permit research into cloning tissue to go forward, but would not allow embryo research. " 'This is a major controversy in in-vitro fertilization,' " Ehlers was quoted as saying. " 'It's uncharted legal and moral territory. At this point, it would be a mistake to allow the research to go forward in that direction' " (Enda and Vedantam 1997).

In addition, some newspapers readers were alerted to two other controversial matters posed by the NBAC report and the president's proposal. An issue "that promises to be divisive," Knight-Ridder news service reporters wrote, "is how much leeway a ban should give to scientists who are conducting research that stops short of cloning. One of the promises of cloning research is that it could lead to genetic enhancement, to help 'improve' people's genes." A warning against " 'any type of enhancement that would reduce the diversity of the human race whether it comes from gene therapy or cloning' " was elicited from Abbey Myers, president of the National Organization for Rare Disorders. The organization, she told the reporters, " 'believes that manipulating genes to make people conform to social pressure is wrong,' " and " 'we would be entering the world of George Orwell if we did do enhancement" ' (Enda and Vedantam 1997).

The second issue was a legal one: does Congress have the constitutional authority to impose a ban on privately funded cloning research? On the one hand, the press reported, "White House officials said that Congress has the authority to regulate cloning through interstate commerce laws" (Enda and Vedantam 1997). To constitutional law experts Cass Sunstein and Harold Edgar, however, the matter was far less clear-cut. " 'It's very much a gray area,' " Sunstein observed, and expressed his opinion that while Congress does have the power to regulate interstate commerce, if it "was argued that that was sufficient for it to ban cloning, 'the first reaction of most people will be to smile and say, What's the connection?' " Sunstein also raised the question of " 'whether scientific experimentation is protected by the First Amendment.' " Edgar, in turn, pointed out that cloning " 'is an issue of family law much like marriage, divorce, and in-vitro fertilization, which generally are covered by state laws.' " Law professor John Robertson agreed with Edgar's opinion, and added that " '[i]f cloning is considered to be a type of reproduction, then a law banning cloning might be considered an infringement of people's reproductive rights' " (Savage 1997; Kolata 1997c; Enda and Vedantam 1997).

Reflections on the Coverage of Dolly and Human Cloning

Coverage of bioethical issues has become a media staple in the United States, both reflecting and contributing to the public's interest in these topics. The *New York Times*, for example, has created an online Bioethics Forum/Message Board, which, on its October 9, 2004 posting, invited the paper's readers to "discuss stem cell research, cloning and other ethical issues relating to biology."[48] Another online source that illustrates the profusion of bioethics news stories was announced in September 2004 by the University of Pennsylvania's Center for Bioethics: the creation of a new "editors' blog" for *The American Journal of Bioethics* (*AJOB*). The blog was developed because the Center's bioethics.net Web site received 100–300 bioethics news stories daily, but could only post "about four" of them a day. These stories were read by a total of some 10,000 people a week, and "it was obviously time for us to do a better job of sorting and annotating news about, and of relevance to, bioethics" (e-mail to bioethics fellows list from Erin Wieand, administrative and financial officer, Dept. of Medical Ethics/Center for Bioethics, University of Pennsylvania, Sept. 26, 2004. See http://blog.bioethics.net).

Individuals involved in bioethics have mixed feelings about the extent of the media's interest in bioethical issues, and about the nature of the field's involvement with the media. On the one hand, many believe that media coverage plays an important public-educational role. At the same time, there are concerns about the nature of that coverage, and about the role of bioethical commentators. In discussing what he feels some of bioethics' major weaknesses have been, for example, physician and bioethicist Norman Fost cited his belief that "[bioethics] has been captured by the media too much." Newspapers, he continued, "pander to the readership by just putting sound bites and [short] quotes on complex issues, and bioethicists, including myself, get sucked into it." Nonetheless, he added, the media has had some "public education utility—it's better than nothing" (Fost, interview, 2000: see appendix). James Gustafson feels that there is a certain amount of "voyeurism" in the field, focusing on "dramatic things" and "looking at them from the outside" that he characterizes as "gee whiz ethics" (Gustafson, interview, 1999: see appendix). Physician-bioethicist Steven Miles, akin to Gustafson, has decried what he calls the "new media midway" of "human curiosities" and criticized the purportedly educational role that medical ethicist commentators have assumed, which serve to "affirm the newsworthiness and propriety of public voyeurism" of what he terms these "medical docu-soaps." "Ethicists' soundbites," he holds, "are usually ambiguous or self-evident truths and rarely enable viewers to morally engage the issues" (S. H. Miles 2004: 39).

Albeit a circumscribed case study, the coverage of Dolly and human cloning in the materials we analyzed, coupled with other studies of science and medicine in the media,[49] provides some instructive insights into how the media portray the ethical issues generated by a dramatic biomedical development. Based on our study, it is evident that the amount and types of information and the views about the import of Dolly's creation that the public acquired were highly variable, dependent in part on which newspapers they read, how regularly they followed that paper's coverage, and what additional sources, such as television and weekly newsmagazines, they turned to.

Although he was one of the most repeatedly tapped critical commentators on Dolly, Arthur Caplan, while discussing Dolly in an article on stem cell and cloning politics[50] in the German paper, *Die Zeit*, censured "the world's media, governments, and scientific and religious communities" (but not, we note, the bioethics community) for the "shameful way" in which they "responded to her birth." The announcement of her creation, he charged, "was a botched mess for which the media bear the brunt of the blame," with initial—and subsequent—reportage that involved "all manner of misinformation, hype, and rumor" (Caplan 2004b).

As exemplified by the media's extensive coverage in 1997 of the Raelian cult's claims to have produced human clones, there was indeed "misinformation, hype, and rumor" in some of the print and electronic media's coverage of Dolly and her possible import. In July 1997, soon after NBAC's report was presented to President Clinton, the International Raelian Movement, self-described as "the world's largest UFO-related nonprofit organization," announced that it had established a company called Clonaid which, for a fee of $200,000, promised to give "eternal life" through nuclear transfer cloning combined with memory and personality trait transfer (media; advertisements www.clonaid.com). Subsequently, in December 2002 and January 2003, Clonaid claimed that it had successfully produced three cloned babies. Although researchers and clinicians were quick to cast doubt on Clonaid's announcement about the birth of "Baby Eve," unless it could be scientifically proved through verified DNA testing, the media continued to present a barrage of "news" stories and features about the company, its purported clonings, and its parent cult, the Raelians. Caplan was a major source called upon by television, radio, and newspapers to discuss Clonaid's claims, which he vigorously sought to debunk. He reserved his most strenuous criticism, however, for the media. Its "misleading" coverage, he charged, was an irresponsible "fiasco," which left "the American people...confused, scared, and clueless" about human cloning and the serious ethical and policy issues it entails (Caplan 2003). Within the limitations of print media space and television time, however, with some exception such as the reports about the Raelians and Clonaid, we found that there was a considerable amount of sound and thoughtful coverage of the genuine biomedical, religious, ethical, policy, and social and cultural implications, both positive and negative, of the first mammal to be successful cloned from an adult cell.

Our analysis of the commentators in the "Dolly" and "NBAC" coverage, from science and medicine, industry, law, religion, and bioethics, also demonstrates, as have other studies, that the sources reporters turn to for further information or opinions, and the statements by those sources that they include in their write-ups, can strongly influence the content and tone of a news or feature story. The same observation holds for the editorials, headlines, and Op-Ed pieces that a paper chooses to run. Depending on what messages media decided to emphasize, readers were given what Wilkie and Graham term a "discourse of concern" or a "discourse of promise" about Dolly, or a mixture of the two (Wilkie and Graham 1998: 153, 155).[51] Further, with respect to communicating technological risk in event-centered reporting, as sociologist Dorothy Nelkin and others have shown, the media generally does not place competing perspectives in a readily understandable context (Friedman et al. 1996; Nelkin 1989). That is, as we also found for the range of views about the acceptability of human cloning, rather than interpreting or analyzing differences of opinion, reporters often emphasize the conflict between those perspectives.

Laypeople learn about many, probably most, medical, scientific, and techno-logical advances and attendant ethical issues through the mass media, and their level of understanding of those advances and issues thus is heavily dependent on the quality of media coverage.[52] In this respect, journalists, intentionally or not, fold the job of educator into their primary job of news reporters, and journalism becomes the filter for public understanding (Winsten 1985). However, as Wilkie and Graham point out, advances that become major news events, such as Dolly, "[do] not happen in a vacuum. There is already a social, cultural, and scientific context that will color the way in which the news is reported and interpreted" (Wilkie and Graham 1998: 156). The public response to Dolly, as Nelkin and S. Lindee wrote in a paper titled "Cloning in the Popular Imagination," "reflects the futuristic fantasies and Frankenstein fears that have more broadly surrounded research in genetics and especially genetic engineering.... Appearing to promise both amazing new control over nature and terrifying dehumanization, cloning has gripped the popular imagination" (Nelkin and Lindee 1998: 145). Because many people had seen movies, read novels, or followed newspaper stories that had cre-ated a preexisting level of awareness of and interest in cloning before Dolly burst into the news,[53] they were already tuned in to one of the social contexts of her creation: the "worst-case scenarios" such as those depicted in *Brave New World* or *The Boys from Brazil*, which many reporters and commentators invoked, par-ticularly during the early coverage.

In an earlier study, Nelkin and Lindee examined the popular appeal of what they term "genetic essentialism," a "deterministic tendency to reduce...personality and behavior—the very identity of individuals—to their genes" (Nelkin and Lindee 1995; 1998: 145). The responses to Dolly, they subsequently found, "mirrored those...in the popular culture reactions to the Human Genome Project and its mapping of genes." Dolly, like the gene, promptly became a "cultural icon" with an array of both hopeful and fearful symbolic associations.[54]

Our examination of newspaper coverage of Dolly and human cloning sub-stantiates Nelkin and Lindee's statement that "media messages matter." "Dolly," they wrote, "is only a lamb and she is depicted again and again as cuddly and cute.... But as a symbolic site for the exploration of identity, heredity, destiny, and the social meaning of science, she is a spectacular beast" (Nelkin and Lindee 1998:148).

Postmortem

Goodbye, Dolly

Her death on February 14, 2003, occasioned obituaries in print and electronic media around the world. Born on July 5, 1996, she was six years old when she was euthanized at a veterinary school near the Roslin Institute. Accord-ing to Dr. Ian Wilmut, Dolly was suffering from a progressive lung infection, and her veterinarians felt that it "would be more merciful to end her life than to continue treatment." Pastured sheep, Wilmut explained, can live for 11 or 12 years, but those who live indoors, as Dolly had for security reasons, are susceptible to lung infections. After conducting a postmortem to learn if any signs of possible cloning-related premature aging or diseases could be detected, the Roslin group planned to give Dolly to the National Museum of Scotland in Edinburgh, where she would be put on display. Wilmut said there were no plans to try to clone Dolly, but her obituaries noted that she was survived by six lambs, fathered by David, a Welsh mountain ram (Kolata 2003; E. Ross 2003).

After Dolly: Cloning and the Stem Cell Wars

The intensive and extensive attention to cloning generated by Dolly did not fade from public view or from bioethical, religious, and public policy arenas after the completion of NBAC's report and Clinton's recommendations in 1997, or after Dolly's death. Rather, the ferment over cloning has intensified. The principal focus of the post-Dolly maelstrom in the United States and elsewhere has been on the derivation and use of *human embryonic stem cells*,[55] rather than the *adult* sheep's cell from which Dolly was cloned.

It was not until 1998, a year after Dolly's birth was announced, that the successful in vitro isolation and culturing of human embryonic stem cells (ESCs) was announced by Dr. James Thompson at the University of Wisconsin, Madison. Like Dolly in 1997, stem cell research made the cover of *Science* in 1999 as the breakthrough of the year,[56] the research equivalent of being *Time* magazine's "person of the year." And, because of the political, religious, and ethical issues that their production and use entail, embryonic stem cells have been the subject of widespread attention about the morality of the three methods by which human embryonic stem cells can be derived: from "excess" frozen embryos stored in in vitro fertilization (IVF) clinics; from embryos created by IVF with eggs donated solely to produce stem cells; and, still only a potential technique, which some of its opponents believe entails a "slippery slope" leading to reproductive cloning, obtaining stem cells from embryos produced asexually from adult cells by somatic cell nuclear transfer. These means of obtaining embryonic stem cells have been such religiously and politically volatile matters primarily because of the strongly held beliefs and values about when human life begins, and, therefore, whether the deliberate destruction of an embryo during the first days of its existence constitutes the abortion of a human being.[57] As we discuss in chapter 11, the explicit and implicit linkages between the derivation of stem cells and abortion became highly charged aspects of the culture wars in American society during President George W. Bush's presidency.

The use of ESCs for therapeutic research, as well as the prospect of human reproductive cloning, have been the subject of ongoing coverage by lay media, of professional conferences and publications, of legislative debate and legislation in many countries, of efforts to craft international policies through the UN, of attention to embryonic stem cells by President Clinton (National Bioethics Advisory Commission 1999a, 1999b)[58] and to stem cells and human cloning by his successor, George W. Bush (President's Council on Bioethics 2002, 2004a),[59] and of rancorous, highly politicized debates in the U.S. Congress. These debates have focused on two sets of issues: first, whether all human cloning should be banned, or whether only reproductive cloning should be prohibited and cloning for therapeutic research allowed under strict guideline; and, second, whether the strict limitations on the derivation of human stem cells imposed by President Bush should be relaxed.[60,61]

As we will discuss more fully in chapter 11, the means of obtaining embryonic stem cells, and the close linkage of those means with the long-standing and divisive issue of abortion, have become embedded in the socially, ethically, and politically complex "culture wars" that are a prominent feature of the American landscape, as well as that of other countries. In summer 2007, when this chapter was undergoing its final revisions, there were no signs that what has been aptly called "the stem cells wars," unleashed by Dolly's creation, would end or even abate in the foreseeable future.

Notes

1. We use the term "reproductive cloning" to refer to using the somatic cell nuclear transfer technique to clone an embryo and implant it into a woman's uterus with the intent of producing a baby. The other, also much debated, use of the technique is for the development of pluripotent stem cell lines for biomedical research purposes; these stem cells are not developed to a stage where they can be implanted and develop into an embryo. The latter technique is often termed "therapeutic cloning" or "cloning for biomedical research," to distinguish it from "reproductive cloning."
2. A listing of books, stories, and movies about human cloning and genetic engineering can be found at www.magicdragon.com, using the search term "human cloning."
3. Another book, *In His Image: The Cloning of a Man* (1978), was penned by David Rorvik, a respected medical reporter. The book attracted considerable fanfare even before it was issued by an established publisher, J. B. Lippincott, garnering extensive newspaper and television coverage as a purportedly true account of the birth of the first human clone. From the outset, scientists were highly skeptical about Rorvik's claim, given the state-of-the-art of cloning technology in the 1970s, and within months of *In His Image*'s publication, the author and publisher were sued for defamation by a British scientist whose research was cited in the book. When Rorvik failed to provide evidence that the cloned child existed, the court ruled that the book was "a fraud and a hoax," and Lippincott subsequently paid damages to the scientist (Broad 1981, 1982; Hilts 1982; www.museumofhoaxes.com). In a case study, "Rorvik's Baby," in J. Goodfield's book *Reflections on Science and the Media*, she examines the reasons for what she characterized as the media's "initial kid-glove treatment" of Rorvik's claims (Goodfield 1981: 51–67).

4. Discussion and debates about the social implications and ethics of human cloning during the 1960s and 1970s were catalyzed by the cloning of tadpoles in 1962, the first such advance beyond producing cloned plants and vegetables, and by the speculation of eminent scientists like Nobel laureates James D. Watson and Joshua Lederberg that cloning humans might be technically possible (Watson 1971, 1973; Lederberg 1966). Nonfiction books about prospective developments in biology and medicine included discussions about the possibility of human cloning in works such as Gordon Rattray Taylor's *The Biological Time Bomb* (1968) and Lewis Thomas's *The Medusa and the Snail* (Thomas 1979). A number of articles and book chapters by philosophers, moral theologians, and physicians engaged in the emerging field of bioethics also began appearing in the scholarly literature, authored by figures including Hans Jonas (1974), Joseph Fletcher (1971, reprinted in J. Fletcher 1974), Paul Ramsey (1970a; see Vaux 1970 for Ramsey's original presentation of his response to Lederberg, delivered at a 1968 conference held by the Institute of Religion at the Texas Medical Center), Leon Kass (1972), and Leon Eisenberg (1976). See also Verhey 1994 for an analysis of the debate about cloning that took place in the 1960s and 1970s.

5. Discussions about human cloning by bioethicists and moral theologians continued to be published into the mid-1990s, prior to the birth of Dolly. See, for example, Brown 1995; Human cloning and Catholic teaching 1994; McCormick 1993; Verhey 1994. Verhey's paper is one of six articles on embryo cloning by nuclear transplantation and embryo splitting in the *Kennedy Institute of Ethics Journal* 4 (3) (1994).

6. We collected our initial examples of media coverage from newspapers and news magazines to which we subscribed, and transcripts of electronic media coverage available online and from the Vanderbilt University Television News Archive.

7. Seven of the 16 newspapers are self-described as national, while the others are local or regional. The newspapers we used were: *Atlanta Journal & Constitution, Boston Globe, Chicago Tribune, Christian Science Monitor, Denver Post, Houston Chronicle, Kansas City Star, Los Angeles Times, Newsday, New York Times, Philadelphia Inquirer, Pittsburgh Post-Gazette, Cleveland Plain Dealer, Seattle Times, St. Louis Post-Dispatch*, and the *Washington Post*. Of these, the seven papers that are self-described as national are the *Boston Globe, Chicago Tribune, Christian Science Monitor, Los Angeles Times, New York Times, Seattle Times*, and the *Washington Post*.

8. We used the Lexis-Nexis database to search 15 of the 16 papers; DIALOG was used for the *Philadelphia Inquirer*, which is not available on Lexis-Nexis. The "Dolly search" covered five weeks, from the day of the first stories, on February 23, 1997, to March 31, by which time peak coverage had waned. The "NBAC search" covered materials from June 1–15, 1997, when the Commission was preparing and submitting its report to the president, and he responded to its recommendations.

The Dolly search looked for the text words *clone* or *cloned* and *sheep* when indexed as the main topic, defined by Lexis-Nexis as appearing in the headline or lead portion of the article. We realized that by not using the term "human," our sample did not represent all the coverage of cloning in the 16 news outlets we selected. Based on an initial trial search with DIALOG, we estimate that inclusion of the term "human" would have generated about 800 articles during our Dolly search period. For budgetary reasons, however, we needed to work with a manageable number of full-text articles for our analysis, and our major goal was to generate an analytic "window" on how editorial and Op-Ed writers, headline writers, and journalists and their sources were presenting the Dolly story. The NBAC search looked for the words *national*, *bioethics, advisory, commission,* or *NBAC* anywhere in the text of articles in the 16 papers. With the text words we used, the Dolly search yielded 251 articles, including editorials and Op-Ed essays, and the NBAC search yielded a far smaller number of 34 publications. The media analysis in this chapter is based primarily on the publications in our sample of 16 newspapers.

9. In her description of how the news about Dolly broke in the media, Gina Kolata, the veteran *New York Times* science writer, quoted part of the short press release she received in her e-mail on February 20 from *Nature*: " 'The lamb on this week's cover was raised from a single oocyte (egg cell), whose nucleus had been replaced with that from an adult sheep mammary gland cell. It may be the first mammal to have been raised from a cell derived from adult tissue.' " The tip sheet, Kolata went on to write, "concluded, with historic understatement, 'The implications of this work are far-reaching' " (Kolata 1998: 29).

10. For more detailed accounts of how the news about Dolly was broken, see Kolata 1998, and Wilkie and Graham 1998. Both these accounts note that Mckie later said he had obtained the story from his own sources rather than from the *Nature* press release, so that he technically was not violating the embargo norm.

11. This feat was possible, as Wilkie and Graham explained, for two reasons (1998, 153). First, British national newspapers customarily obtain copies of their rivals' first editions, and incorporate any rival's exclusive stories into their own later editions, as did UK papers such as the *London Sunday Telegraph* (Matthews and Thornton 1997) and *Sunday Times (London)* (Norton 1997) and Scotland's *Sunday Mail* (Send in the clones 1997). Second, the *Observer* story was picked up by a number of prominent news agencies, including Agence France Presse (1997), the Associated Press (Ritter 1997), the British Press Association (Quinn 1997), Reuters (1997), and United Press International (1997), which automatically feed the agency's stories to their subscribers. The news agency feeds, coupled with the time difference between Britain and North America, also enabled papers in the United States and Canada to feature the story in their second or late Sunday editions. The rapid global spread of the news about Dolly is illustrated by the three one-sentence summaries carried by China's Xinhua News Agency on February 23 under "major news items in leading british [*sic*] newspapers" and "major news items in leading u.s. [*sic*] newspapers."

12. The February 23 *New York Times* story by Kolata was also carried in slightly shorter form by *The Denver Post* and the *Pittsburgh Post-Gazette* (see, for example, Kolata 1997b), and the *Chicago Tribune* story by Kotulak by the *Seattle Times* on February 23; T. H. Maugh's February 23 story was published the next day by the *Philadelphia Inquirier* (Kolata 1997a, 1997b; Kotulak 1997b; Maugh 1997a).

13. The importance of headlines makes them a specialized area of journalistic expertise, which is taught in editing courses in journalism schools and, on many papers, assigned to seasoned reporters who have "graduated" to the copy desk.

14. Only three of the first stories about Dolly, those in *The Observer*, the *London Sunday Times*, and by United Press International, did not include comments by outside sources. The first Associated Press story was the only one in the initial coverage that used non-UK commentators. One of the "expert sources" was Caird Rexroad Jr., identified as "an animal gene expert" for the U.S. Agricultural Research Service, who, science writer Malcom Ritter said, described the Roslin team's experiment as "historic for showing that whole mammals could be regenerated from mature-body cells other than sperm or egg." The second was Carl Feldbaum, president of the Biotechnology Industry Organization, a trade association for companies and research centers in the

United States and other countries, who said he could " 'think of no ethical reason to apply [Wilmut's technique] to human beings,' " and urged, on behalf of the Organization, that human cloning " 'be prohibited by law' " (Ritter 1997).

15. We did not track down the date and time of the BBC program in relation to the publication of Mckie's *Observer* story, which several writers state was how the news was broken. However, *Chicago Tribune* reporter Ronald Kotulak identified a story by Reuters news agency on Saturday, February 22, "quoting an author of the study [by Wilmut et al.]" as the first media report (Kotulak 1997a).

16. Medical ethicist Richard Nicholson expressed his surprise that the experiment had been approved by the responsible British government agency, the Home Office Animal Procedures Committee. " 'It was a nice technical problem,' " he was quoted as saying, " 'but what is its value if it comes with the enormous risk of some nut trying to clone himself?' " (Matthews and Thornton 1997). In more measured tones, the Church of Scotland's Donald Bruce voiced his theological reservations about the mass cloning of animals: " 'God created the universe with a strong diversity, and such diversity is to be rejoiced in. The idea of making things identical seems to go in the opposite direction. [I]f [cloning] became part of a general production of animals, a lot of Christians would raise ethical concerns.' " Dr. Bruce had even graver reservations about cloning people, because " 'God created people unique, and that would be against the basic dignity of human life' " (Quinn 1997).

17. The opening sentences of the four stories published on February 23 sent different types of messages to their readers. Kolata flagged the story behind the scientific advance in her first sentence: "In a feat that may be the one bit of genetic engineering that has been anticipated and dreaded more than any other..." (1997f). The beginning of the Reuters piece emphasized the benefits that the Roslin group's "breakthrough" could produce. Maugh began his story in the *Los Angeles Times* by describing what the "unprecedented feat" involved, with no mention of the human cloning prospect until the fourth paragraph (Maugh 1997b). Kotulak, in turn, began his report in the *Chicago Tribune* with an alarming message: "Scottish researchers," his readers were told, "have broken one of nature's greatest taboos...[a] remarkable achievement [that] could create an ethical quagmire about its use in humans" (Kotulak 1997a).

18. Kolata used Neal First to explain the "significant revolution" for the livestock industry that the cloning technique could create if it became "highly efficient." An interview with First also was extensively used by Kotulak as the only outside source in his *Chicago Tribune* story. The animal biotechnology expert described, in some detail, the technique's great potential for animal husbandry, and the reporter also presented his appraisal of its application for human cloning. In addition, Kotulak drew on his interview with First to make a further important point, one that was generally ignored in the science-fiction-becomes-reality coverage of human cloning: "a duplicate body does not mean a duplicate person. The clone's brain would be far different from that of the donor, as it must start from scratch and build its own world of experience. A cloned Hitler, for example, might turn out to be a philanthropist."

19. Journalistic and public interest was further fueled by the March 2 announcement that scientists at the Oregon Regional Primary Center had successfully cloned the first primates: two artificially twinned monkeys had been produced by the same type of embryo splitting technique used to reproduce livestock, in contrast to the adult cell method that had been used for Dolly. The press quoted reactions by scientists to the news; it was, they said, an important achievement for experimental work with monkeys,

but, in contrast to Dolly, " 'there is nothing whatever surprising' " about the Oregon work. In the same coverage, however, journalists told their readers the production of cloned monkeys "is a potentially important step toward the much-discussed idea of cloning humans" (Cooke 1997).

20. Law professor Alexander Capron, a member of NBAC and an authority on research with human subjects, pointed out that "cloning embryos to make babies may be an 'experiment,' but that does not make it 'research,' as that term is defined in the federal regulations, since it is not necessarily linked to a search for 'generalizable knowledge' " (Capron 1997: 175).

21. Clinton's March 4 executive order was covered in particular detail and depth by *Newsday*, including reactions by several bioethicists, by a science historian, and by the president of the Bioetchnology Industry Organization (Cooke and Maier 1997).

22. Slightly more than half of the news stories and science explainers were written by staff reporters. The rest were "external pieces" from news agencies, or from other newspapers through syndication. For example, lengthy and substantive articles by well-known science and medicine reporters, Gina Kolata (*New York Times*), Ronald Kotulak (*Chicago Tribune*), Thomas Maugh (*Los Angeles Times*), and Rick Weiss (*Washington Post*), appeared in the *Denver Post*, *Pittsburgh Post-Gazette*, *Cleveland Plain Dealer*, and *Houston Chronicle*—papers that depend heavily on outside sources for national and international news stories.

23. Letters to the editor were not included in our analysis.

24. Headlines often include subheadlines, or are made up of several phrases separated by full stops, that can convey more than one message. For example, "Top Scientists Warn against Cloning Panic; Recreating Humans Would Be Unethical, Experts Say," sends readers two different messages about cloning. Consequently, although our media sample has 251 articles, the headlines were made up of 359 separate phrases or segments.

25. The categories we used were based on concepts used in a study by the Columbia Graduate School of Journalism's Project for Excellence in Journalism (Framing the news 1997). Researchers analyzed all the front-page stories printed in January and February 1999 in three national and four regional papers, as part of a pilot study to identify various narrative frames and underlying messages used by journalists. Although this study did not analyze headlines for their underlying messages, we felt that the discussion of narrative frames and underlying social and cultural messages commonly found in daily journalism had themes that could be applied to our analysis of Dolly headlines.

26. The seventh group of headlines, about 11 percent of our sample, was put into an "*other*" category. An example of this type of headline was "Read Science Fiction to Find Out about the Impact of Cloning."

27. Another way of looking at the types of messages sent via headlines is by the sorts of articles for which they were written. News/science explainer stories, as one would expect, most often carried straight news headlines (45 percent with only 8 percent using wordplay). Headline segments conveying conflict (13 percent) or pessimism (12 percent) about cloning outstripped those with an optimistic message (9 percent). Optimism and wordplay, in turn, characterized the business-story headlines (30 percent each), with only 10 percent taking a pessimistic stance. The headline writers for editorials/opinion pieces favored wordplay, which accounted for 26 percent of these headline segments. For these types of articles, as for news stories, headlines conveying pessimism or conflict about cloning substantially exceeded those with an optimistic message (19 percent, 13 percent, and 9 percent, respectively).

28. In analyzing the commentators used by the press in our sample of "Dolly" coverage from February 24–March 31, 1997, we categorized the sources, in terms of their pri-

mary advanced degree and principal professional affiliation, into four groups: bioethics/ethics, religion/theology, law, and "other." Out of the total of 72 commentators, there were 35 (49 percent) religionists/theologians, 23 (32 percent) bioethicists/ethicists, 7 (10 percent) lawyers (several of whom were variously identified as lawyers and/or ethicists by the press), and 7 (10 percent) in an "other" category. The latter category consisted of a geneticist and obstetrician, an animal biotechnologist, a science historian, a sociologist, a spokesman for the animal rights activist group PETA (People for the Ethical Treatment of Animals), a philosopher, and the director of an academic center for animals and public policy. We did not tally the number of times that individual commentators appeared in press accounts.

29. Although there was no allusion to religious issues in President Clinton's February 24 directive to NBAC to undertake a study of cloning, his March 4 Executive Order prohibiting the use of federal funds for human cloning research stated that like "any discovery that touches upon human creation, [cloning] is not simply a matter of scientific inquiry; it is a matter of morality and spirituality as well" (Clinton 1997b).

30. A third cluster dealt with the pros and cons of animal cloning by somatic cell nuclear transfer. Although the benefits of the somatic cell technique for animal husbandry were being hailed by many, scientific and ethical reservations also were being voiced. Andrew Rowan, director of Tufts University's Center for Animals and Public Policy, cautioned that " '[w]henever you fiddle with nature you always end up with unanticipated problems. That's the one paradigm we can be sure of—that we'll have problems along with the advantages' " (Tye 1997). One such problem that worried philosopher Bernard Rollin, who worked on issues concerning the genetic engineering of animals, was disease resistance: "Herds composed of animals with identical genetic stock are more susceptible to a range of infectious agents, he said, because their genetically determined disease defenses are limited. 'I'm very concerned about untoward effects in these animals' " (Monmaney 1997). Strong ethical objections were voiced by animal rights activist Michael McGraw, who declared that " 'Dolly's cloning is unethical.' It is time 'our society learned to respect our fellows, not exploit them for every fool thing' " (Tye 1997). A more measured ethical concern was expressed by a senior figure in bioethics, LeRoy Walters: " 'In the quest for higher production of say, milk or eggs, one must take into account the welfare of the animals during their lifetime and the quality of their lives' " (Vedantam 1997a).

31. See, for example, the views expressed by Kevin FitzGerald, a Jesuit priest and geneticist (Kolata 1997g) and by bioethicist Dianne Barthels (Kenen 1997), and also by *Newsweek* reporter Sharon Begley in that magazine's cover story, which depicted three infants standing in laboratory beakers and the caption, "Can we clone humans?" (Begley 1997).

32. See Kaye 1998 for an insightful and cautionary sociological analysis of why the prospect of human reproductive cloning has evoked what NBAC dismissively termed "overwhelming public anxiety," "instinctive distrust," and "perceived fear," largely rooted in science fiction and in "gross misunderstanding of human biology and psychology," and what commentators such as bioethicist Ruth Mackin and biologist Richard Lewontin denigrated, respectively, as "panic" and "unthinking disgust," and as "deep cultural prejudice" and the type of genetic determinism "propagated by the press and by vulgarizers of science" (Lewontin 1997: 18, 20–21; Macklin 1997; National Bioethics Advisory Commission 1997a: ii, 3, 63, 69).

33. For an overview of religious positions on human cloning, including cloning-relevant themes that are prominent in major faith traditions, such as the meaning of responsible human dominion over nature, human dignity and destiny, procreation, and family life,

see National Bioethics Advisory Commission 1997a: chap. 3: which draws, in part, on papers and testimony by a number of the religious commentators in the press coverage of Dolly. See also NBAC's commissioned background paper "Religious Perspectives on Human Cloning" (Campbell 1997).

34. " 'Knowledge is given to us by God,' " Imam Tahib Adid stated. " 'The question, for me at least, is not that we should not use this divinely-given creativity, but how.' " (Ribadeneira 1997). Similarly, Islamic scholar Abdulaziz Sachedina pointed out that " '[h]uman beings can actively intervene in the acts of nature, including interfering early in the embryonic stage.' Muslim scholars [share] 'almost a unanimity on the therapeutic uses of cloning, as long as the religious lines of the child remain unblemished' " (Vedantam 1997d). However, other authorities cautioned that because reproductive cloning "confuses relationships within families," it "could affect Islamic laws concerning inheritance, parental obligations, and marriage," and pointed out that " '[a]ccording to Islam, not all that can be done should be done' " (H. T. Gray 1997, Hearts of the city 1997).

35. See, for example, the statements by Cardinal Anthony Bevilacqua (1997) and Fr. Albert Moraczweski, founder of The National Conference of Catholic Bishops (Vedantam 1997e, 1997f).

36. See, for example, the views expressed by Fr. Kevin FitzGerald (Kolata 1997g); Rev. Richard McCormick (H. T. Gray 1997); and Bishop Donald Wuerl (Rodgers-Melnick 1997).

37. See also, for example, health law professors/bioethicists Alan Meisel (1997) and George Annas (Tye 1997; Weiss 1997) and bioethicist Ronald Munson (Kolata 1997f).

38. Despite the relative paucity of press coverage, and unusual for a government document, the NBAC report was reviewed critically and at length in the *New York Times Review of Books* by biologist Richard C. Lewontin (1997).

39. One national and three regional papers in our sample did not cover the NBAC report: the *Boston Globe*, *Atlanta Journal & Constitution*, *Kansas City Star*, and *Philadelphia Inquirer*.

40. In the papers that did report on NBAC's recommendations and the president's response, 16 articles (including one editorial and three brief news summaries) were written by staff reporters, while 14 were provided from a wire service, and four were syndicated from the parent newspaper.

41. Others whose names appeared in stories included the Commission chair, Harold Shapiro, president of Princeton University; physicians and bioethicists Bernard Lo and Ezekiel Emanuel; religion scholar and bioethicist James Childress; physician and lawyer Lawrence Miike; geneticist and pediatrician David Cox; molecular biologist Carol Greider; law professor and bioethicist Alta Charo; and Steven Holtzman, chief business officer of a pharmaceutical company. In a few instances, commissioners also spoke about what they felt were particularly sensitive topics on the condition of anonymity.

42. These individuals included 4 of the 15 people who had been invited by NBAC to give presentations at their meetings: Protestant theologian Gilbert Meilaender Jr.; Jewish scholar and biology professor Rabbi Moshe Tendler; health law professor John Robertson, who specializes in reproductive issues; and molecular biologist Shirley Tilghman. Several people who gave public testimony at NBAC meetings also were sought out by the press. These included pro-life advocates John Cavanaugh-O'Keefe and Sheena Talbot of the American Life League, Virginia attorney Alan Grayson, District of Columbia resident Mary Lyman Jackson, and pro-cloning advocate Randolfe Wicker. Two of the country's most frequently quoted bioethicists, Arthur

Caplan and health lawyer George Annas, were called upon by the *Chicago Tribune* and *New York Times*, respectively. Other sources included constitutional law specialists Cass Sunstein and Harold Edgar, who were asked to comment on the constitutionality of Clinton's proposed legislation to ban reproductive cloning work done with private resources. Critical reactions to the Commission's reliance on safety concerns were elicited from infertility specialist Dr. Mark Sauer and developmental biologist Dr. Davor Solter. Industry reactions affirming the importance of cloning research were obtained from Carl Feldbaum, head of the Biotechnology Industry Organization, and Alan Holmer, president of the politically powerful Pharmaceutical Manufacturers Association. Strong stances against any form of human cloning, including research with embryonic cells, and thus the shortcomings of NBAC's recommendations, were expressed by Cardinal John O'Connor of New York and the president of the American Life League, Judie Brown. Abby Myers, president of the National Organization for Rare Disorders, voiced her group's opposition to cloning research that might lead to genetic enhancement capabilities. Two of the most frequently cited commentators were Republican Congressman Vernon Ehlers and Senator Christopher Bond, who, as strong proponents of federal legislation to prohibit human embryo research utilizing cloning techniques, vigorously objected to the NBAC report and the president's legislative proposal.

43. The one pro-cloning advocate noted by the press (Kerr 1997a) was Randolfe Wicker, a gay activist and founder of the Clone Rights United Front in New York City, who had spoken at NBAC's June 7 meeting and had been mentioned in some earlier press accounts as the human cloning debate unfolded.

44. For lists of invited speakers and those who gave public testimony, see National Bioethics Advisory Commission 1997a; the commissioned papers were published as vol. 2 of the NBAC report (National Bioethics Advisory Commission 1997b).

45. The status and influence of religion in American bioethics, and the relationship between bioethics and religion in the polity, have been controversial and complex matters since the field's beginnings. For discussions of the interplay of bioethics and religion in NBAC's work on human cloning, in addition to the NBAC report itself, see Campbell and Woolfrey 1998; James Childress's paper, "Religion, Morality, and Public Policy: The Controversy about Human Cloning," in which he draws on his role as an NBAC member to reflect on the role of religious beliefs in the development of bioethical public policy in a "liberal, pluralistic democracy" (Childress 1999); and the discussion of NBAC's work on cloning, and the role of religion in American bioethics more broadly, in Messikomer, Fox, and Swazey 2001. For more general examinations of religion and bioethics, see Davis and Zoloth 1999; Verhey 1996; Verhey and Lammers 1993.

46. In a scholarly paper on NBAC's cloning report, Shapiro wrote that "[t]here was little agreement on the relative importance of the various ethical and theological issues raised by this new cloning technique. There was no agreement on which philosophical approach was most relevant or how any particular approach might inform public policy or private action in this particular arena. Indeed, there seemed little convergence on either the right questions or right answers" (Shapiro 1999: 10).

47. In their remarks, Clinton and Gore also took note of the possible benefits that could come from cloning research using cells derived from human embryos, or from animal cloning. "'The cloning of human cells and genes,'" Gore stated, "'does not pose the same ethical questions as cloning an entire human being,'" while the president affirmed that "'there is nothing inherently immoral or wrong with these new

techniques—used for proper purposes.'" Indeed, he declared, "'they hold the promise of revolutionary new medical treatments and life-saving cures… better crops and stronger livestock'" (Harris 1997).

48. See http://forums.nytimes.com/top/readersopinions/forums/science/bioethics/index.

49. See, for example, Nelkin 1984, 1987, 1989; Nelkin and Lindee 1995; Friedman et al. 1996; Goodfield 1981; Winsten 1985. For analyses and commentary specifically of the media's coverage of Dolly, see Hopkins 1998; Nelkin and Lindee 1998; Turner 1997; Wilkie and Graham 1998.

50. Caplan's major thrust in this article was not on Dolly, but, as the translated title of his piece indicates, on the President's Council on Bioethics (see chapter 11), about which he has been a staunch and activist critic: "Power Failure—How the President's Council on Bioethics Lost Its credibility and What This means for the Future of Ethical Debate in America and in Europe about Advances in Biomedicine" (Caplan 2004b).

51. Wilkie and Graham's excellent paper, "Power without Responsibility: Media Portrayals of Dolly and Science," principally analyzes British broadsheet newspaper coverage. It also examines some of the corresponding coverage in U.S. newspapers, and discusses the "striking contrasts" they found that relate to "journalistic practices [and] also to the public status and position of science in the two countries" (1998: 150).

52. In his paper, "Science and the Media: The Boundaries of Truth," J. A. Winsten (1985) analyzes factors that determine whether or not a scientific or medical development becomes news, and constraints on the quality of that news.

53. Looking at a computerized database of British newspaper clippings for 1996, the year before Dolly, Wilkie and Graham found that the words *clone*, *cloned*, *clones*, or *cloning* appeared in 1,140 articles.

54. In another paper on Dolly and human cloning in the media, P. D. Hopkins focused on the characterization of cloning as an ethical problem, with examples drawn primarily from news magazine coverage. His analysis, much like ours and Nelkin and Lindee's, found that "the primary characterization of cloning as an ethical issue centers around three interconnected worries: the loss of human uniqueness and individuality, the pathological motivations of anyone who would want to clone, and the fear of 'out-of-control' science creating a 'brave new world.'" (Hopkins 1998: 6).

55. Stem cells are unspecialized cells that can renew or replicate themselves indefinitely in a cell line culture, which is why they often are called "immortal." They also can differentiate into more mature cells with specialized functions; in humans they can become more than 200 types of cells. When a stem cell can differentiate into multiple tissue types associated with different organs, it is called "multipotent" or "pluripotent." There are three types of stem cells: (1) Adult stem cells can be derived from a number of adult tissues, such as bone marrow. As of 2003, researchers had found that adult stem cells are not as pluripotent as embryonic ones, and thus are not thought to have as much promise for regenerative medicine; (2) Fetal stem cells are primitive cell types in the fetus that gradually develop into the body's various organs. Research with fetal cells thus far has been limited to only a few types, including neural stem cells that have received publicity concerning their use in to-date unsuccessful clinical experiments to alleviate Parkinson's disease; and (3) Embryonic stem cells, which are held by most investigators to be the most promising for regenerative medicine, and the focus of the controversy about stem cell research. These cells are found in the inner cell mass of the blastocyst, an early stage in the developing embryo that exists from about the fourth to seventh day after fertilization. There are some 30 embryonic stem cells in the blastocyst, and if they are successfully removed they can be cultured in vitro, and, in principle, can proliferate indefinitely and retain their multipotency.

The main source of human embryonic stem cells has been from "surplus" or "excess" embryos frozen after in vitro fertilization. In the United States and Great Britain, there is a five-year limit on the length of time that the frozen embryos can be stored, because after that time they may not be biologically suitable for use in another fertilization attempt. After the five-year maximum period, the embryos are discarded. In 2003, there were an estimated 400,000 frozen one- to five-day-old embryos, some therefore at the blastocyst stage, stored in IVF clinics in the United States, and hundreds of thousands in other countries. Clinics vary as to whether they ask a woman, or couple, if they are willing to donate surplus embryos for research, either before or, usually, after they are frozen. On average, only a small fraction of blastocysts, after being in frozen storage, will yield stem cells. For a survey study of the "embryo disposal practices" of American IVF clinics, see Gurmankin, Sisti, and Caplan 2004.

56. Many biomedical researchers and clinicians believe that stem cells, particularly those derived from embryos rather than adults, hold such enormous therapeutic promise that they coined the term "regenerative medicine" to encompass the large number of diseases and disorders that they foresee as being treatable with stem cells (National Research Council and Institute of Medicine 2002). The extensive national and international interest in and work on regenerative medicine is indicated by the establishment of organizations such as the nonprofit Regenerative Medicine Foundation and the International Society for Stem Cell Research, and World Congresses on Regenerative Medicine. A Google search for "regenerative medicine" in July 2007 yielded approximately 1,480,000 entries.

57. Whether or not one believes that human life begins at the moment of conception—which is a religious or philosophical rather than a scientifically grounded belief—most individuals and groups that have addressed embryonic and fetal research, including several federal bioethics advisory bodies, have called for adhering to a principle of respect for embryos and fetuses as forms of human life.

58. In a November 14, 1998 letter to NBAC Chair Harold Shapiro, during the week, as the president phrased it in his letter, that "the creation of an embryonic stem cell that is part human, part cow" was announced, Clinton asked the Commission to conduct a "thorough review" of the issues involved in human stem cell research, "balancing all medical and ethical considerations." The use of somatic cell nuclear transfer was only one facet of NBAC's deliberations on embryonic stem cells, and of the report transmitted to the president in September 1999. Its recommendation on this means of deriving stem cells was brief: "Federal agencies should not fund research involving the derivation or use of human [embryonic stem] cells from embryos made using [somatic cell nuclear transfer] into oocytes" (National Bioethics Advisory Commission 1999a: 7). The reason given for this position was a pragmatic one: federal funding should not be provided "at this time, because other sources are likely to provide the cells needed for preliminary stages of research." Nevertheless, the commissioners added, because "there is significant reason to believe that their use may have therapeutic potential, "the medical utility and scientific progress of this line of research should be monitored closely" (National Bioethics Advisory Commission 1999a: 7; 1999b).

59. Mr. Bush had been under intense pressure from various constituencies to decide whether he would allow federal funding for embryonic stem cell research. Until the terrorist attacks on September 11, 2000, most unusually for a scientific topic, this had been the defining issue and decision of his presidency. For a further discussion of the president's establishment of his Council on Bioethics, see chapter 11. In its report on using embryonic stem cells for human cloning, the Council was unanimous in opposing reproductive cloning, going beyond NBAC's position that it should not be

attempted because of its risks, but also because it is "morally unacceptable." Council members, however, were divided in their ethical and policy positions regarding cloning for biomedical research. A narrow majority recommended a four-year moratorium on the creation of cloned embryos to provide time for full "democratic deliberation," while a minority favored permitting research cloning to proceed "without substantial delay," subject to "the necessary regulatory protections to avoid abuses and misuses of cloned embryos." Despite their differing positions, however, the report pointed out that "we agree that all parties to the debate have concerns vital to defend, vital not only to themselves but to all of us. No human being and no society can afford to be callous to the needs of suffering humanity, or cavalier about the treatment of nascent human life, or indifferent to the social effects of adopting one course of action rather than another" (President's Council on Bioethics 2002: xxi–xxxix). For a thoughtful commentary on the Council's report on *Human Cloning and Human Dignity*, see Childress 2003. See also the Council's subsequent report, "Monitoring Stem Cell Research" (President's Council on Bioethics 2004a).

60. For a compendium of materials on the ethical, religious, and policy issues and positions evoked by Dolly's birth, with contributions and primary source documents from the United States, the United Kingdom, Europe, and Australia, see Ruse and Sheppard 2000.

61. In addition to the ethical, religious, and policy issues surrounding the derivation and use of human stem cells, the field was engulfed in a major, high-profile case of research misconduct at the end of 2005 and early 2006. The case involved widely heralded publications by veterinarian Hwang Woo Suk of Seoul National University, South Korea, dealing with how he and his team had, for the first time, created 11 donor-specific human stem cell lines from cloned human blastocysts. The South Korean team's apparent breakthrough achievement offered the prospect of genetically "customized" disease-specific stem cell transplants for patients, and the South Korean government bestowed the title of "Supreme Scientist" on Hwang and issued a postage stamp in his honor showing a patient stepping out of a wheelchair. However, a university investigation committee, formed to examine allegations that data had been fabricated, found that Hwang, and possibly other of his coauthors, had fabricated data in what had been thought to be their two seminal papers published in *Science* in 2004 and 2005. The journal's editor-in-chief, Donald Kennedy, issued a retraction of the papers in January 2006. In March 2006 Hwang was dismissed from Seoul National University, was banned from working in a public position for five years, and faced criminal charges that included fraudulent use of government funds. The university levied less severe penalties on the coauthors of the 2004 and 2005 papers. The only claim by Hwang that was validated by the investigation was that he and his team had cloned the first dog, which they named "Snuppy" after Seoul National University, an accomplishment that was announced in an August 2005 paper in *Nature* (Kennedy 2006; Oransky 2005; Seoul National University 2006; Vogel 2005; Weiss 2005b, 2006; Wohn 2006).

5

Celebrating Bioethics and Bioethicists

Bioethics in the United States has been noticeably preoccupied with explaining, chronicling, and commemorating its beginnings. It has developed a number of different narrative accounts about how, why, and where it began, some of which resemble what anthropologists term "myths of origin." In addition, the field has organized and been involved in an array of events in ceremonial celebration of its inception, of the anniversaries of some of its prominent bioethics centers, in recognition of what are viewed as foundational documents in the development of bioethics, and in homage to persons who are considered to be seminal figures in its emergence and evolution.

Examples of such events and awards, many of which emanated from the Hastings Center and the Kennedy Institute of Ethics, include:

- The Hasting Center's marking of its 25th anniversary at its annual 1994 meeting, followed by a special issue of *The Hastings Center Report* devoted to the papers that were presented on this occasion (The quest for justice and community in health care 1994).
- A 1996 issue of *The Hastings Center Report* in honor of Daniel Callahan's retirement as president and cofounder of the Center that contained papers presented at this annual meeting, which "reflect[ed] on enduring themes" in Callahan's work that have also "animated both the Center and bioethics as an emerging discipline over the past twenty-seven years" (Crigger 1996: 2).

- The banquet held by the Kennedy Institute of Ethics on March 12, 1996, in celebration of its 25th anniversary, which paid tribute to André E. Hellegers, its founding director, announced the establishment of the LeRoy B. Walters Scholarship, and was addressed by Sargent Shriver.
- The holding of a second 25th anniversary event at the Kennedy Institute in March of the same year in the form of talks delivered at its annual Advanced Bioethics Course by 20 present and former research scholars, on the topic of "Bioethics in the Twenty-First Century," and the subsequent publication of a special issue of the Institute's journal that contained 18 of these presentations.
- The Kennedy Institute's year-long recognition of its 30th anniversary, culminating in a three-day conference in April 2002 on "The State of Bioethics: From Seminal Works to Contemporary Explorations," whose papers were published as a book entitled *The Story of Bioethics: From Seminal Works to Contemporary Exploration* (Walter and Klein 2003).
- The dedication of the Fall 2005 issue of the University of Minnesota's *Bioethics Examiner* "celebrating 20 years" of its Center for Bioethics' "history."
- The creation of a series of awards in recognition of the merit and distinction of particular individuals, and their contributions to the field of bioethics. These have included the Kennedy Institute's LeRoy B. Walters Scholarship, the Henry K. Beecher Award created by the Hastings Center in 1976, and the Lifetime Achievement Award and the Distinguished Service Award created by the American Society for Bioethics and the Humanities in 1998 and 1999, respectively.[1]

What is striking about these occasions is that a field with such a short history of only some four to five decades (depending on when its emergence in the United States is dated) has been motivated to arrange so many ritual events.

This chapter focuses on recollections of two major bioethics fetes that one of us, Judith Swazey, attended: the "Birth of Bioethics" conference convoked in 1992 by Albert (Al) Jonsen, a prominent bioethicist trained in moral philosophy and theology, and the "Belmont Revisited" conference that was held in 1999 to not only commemorate the 20th anniversary of the *Belmont Report*'s issuance but also to reexamine the fundamental ethical principles for research with human subjects that it articulated. Additionally, we present our impressions of two programs that took place in 2004 to celebrate *Belmont*'s 25th anniversary—one held at the Medical College of Wisconsin, and the other arranged by the Federal Office for Human Research Protections.[2] The intent of describing these gatherings is not only to give an account of what they entailed but also to provide a springboard from which to explore the collective meaning of the numerous "cultural performances"[3] of this sort in which American bioethicists have participated.

Celebrating the "Birth of Bioethics" and Its "Pioneers"

In his role as a chronicler of the field's development, Albert Jonsen has attributed the field's beginnings both to a series of events and issues over a number of years, and to a specific event and moment in time (see chapter 1). With respect to the latter historiography, he organized a "30th anniversary" conference in Seattle on September 23–24, 1992, to celebrate the "birth" of bioethics, "review its history, and project its future" (Jonsen 1993: S1). Jonsen, who was then chair of the Department of Medical Ethics and History at the University of Washington, built the conference around the event that he declared had launched the field of bioethics: the November 9, 1962 publication in *Life* magazine of a vivid and poignant story entitled "They Decide Who Lives, Who Dies: Medical Miracle Puts a Moral Burden on a Small Community," written by the distinguished journalist Shana Alexander (Alexander 1962).[4] One of his reasons for selecting the date of Alexander's story as an inaugural benchmark, Jonsen subsequently acknowledged, was so that his university could "claim a birthright" to bioethics (Jonsen 1993: S1).

Alexander's piece centered on the seven-member committee of laypersons that she called the "Life and Death Committee," which had been formed in the wake of the 1960 invention of the shunted cannula by Dr. Belding Scribner, professor of medicine at the University of Washington School of Medicine, which had made chronic, long-term dialysis possible. Because, at that time, the number of patients in end-stage renal disease who were candidates for dialysis exceeded the number of machines that were available for this treatment at the University's small, new Artificial Kidney Center, Scribner's achievement had the painful consequence of making it necessary to select which individuals would receive this scarce, potentially life-saving technology (Fox and Swazey 1974: chaps. 7–8; Swazey 1975).

The individuals whom Jonsen invited to speak at the conference were persons he identified as bioethical "pioneers," those "whose name had appeared in the first edition of the *Bibliography of Bioethics* (1975), and who had continued to work in the field. Some "sixty persons made the cut," Jonsen reported, "and, of those, forty-two came to Seattle" (Jonsen 1993: S1).[5]

The two of us were among those identified as still-active "pioneers" who received invitations to take part in the conference, and were asked to present a 30-minute lecture at the opening session focusing on the advent of chronic dialysis and the work of Seattle's patient selection committee. These were subjects we had studied firsthand, and to which we had devoted three chapters in our book *The Courage to Fail*: " 'To Give Life': A Study of Seattle's Hemodialysis Program," "Patient Selection and the Right to Die: Problems Facing Seattle's Kidney Center," and "Ernie Crowfeather" (Fox and Swazey 1974: chaps. 8–10). Although in the end Fox was unable to attend the conference, Swazey (JPS) accepted the invitation to present a paper on our behalf. Participating in the conference, we felt, would provide us with the opportunity both to offer our perspective on whether Alexander's article did indeed constitute the field's beginning, and to do some participant observation at this "birthday" gathering.

The session began with a showing of excerpts from the NBC documentary *Who Shall Live*, followed by a brief comment by Belding Scribner, and Shana Alexander's talk, listed in the program as "Covering the God Committee." It concluded with JPS delivering our lecture, to which Jonsen had assigned the title "Discovering the Ethical Dilemma."

Thirty years ago, when she was "a young staff writer for *Life* magazine," Alexander recounted, she had spent six months in Seattle "for the most awesome and disturbing story [she had ever] worked on, the one about the life and death committee, the so-called God committee" (S. Alexander 1993: S5). "But we are here to speak about bioethics," she continued after that brief recollection, and for the rest of her presentation she talked about how technology has changed how we die, perhaps even "the nature of death itself,…from an event to a process." Because technological advances have "made possible things that the patient might not want," Alexander said, "[w]hat we're really talking about is who is going to manage the process." Implicitly harking back to the Seattle committee, she told the audience that "certain kinds of sorting" had recently become important to her. "What I want to do is sort out my options for the inevitable, for my own death." She spoke movingly in this connection, about her 75-year-old friend and neighbor, Anna, who was terminally ill with inoperable esophageal cancer, and was "dying the way I want to die, at home, surrounded and lovingly tended by her family."

When JPS followed Shana Alexander to the podium, she told the audience that rather than calling our talk "Discovering the Ethical Dilemma," as it was listed in the program, we had titled it "But Was It Bioethics?" She began her presentation by recalling the first meeting we had had with Belding Scribner—familiarly called "Scrib"—in 1969, and how over time that conversation led to many rich and frank discussions with him and his associates about the complexity of the dilemma-ridden patient selection issues they faced, their painfulness, and the aspects of the difficult decisions and choices they had to make that could not be totally eliminated, even in a more just and equitable allocation system. Through Scrib, we also had the privileged opportunity to observe meetings of the Northwest Kidney Center's Medical Advisory Committee, and its lay Admissions and Policy Committee—the so-called patient selection committee that Shana Alexander had dubbed the "God Committee." Her story in *Life* magazine, JPS noted, had unleashed a storm of public and professional controversy about the lay selection committee for which Scrib and his colleagues, and members of the committee, were—naively, Scrib said in his comments—totally unprepared.

These recollections provided a context for the central thesis of our paper: that the creation of the Kidney Center's patient selection committee, and Alexander's account of it, had occurred in the early phase of the field's emergence, before it was named "bioethics" and began to be an identifiable, organized entity. Historically and sociologically, JPS stated, as she had learned when doing graduate work in the history of science, it is "difficult to determine precisely when a new field, discipline, or subspeciality comes into being. Whatever the emerging sphere of intellectual endeavor,…persons are already working in that area well before it is institutionally recognized as such. Some of these precursors are retrospectively considered to be 'pioneers,' and similarly, certain moments, phenomena, or events are designated in hindsight as marking *the* origin of the field in question" (Swazey 1993: S5). "This is not to say," we affirmed, "that no concentrated or systematic reflection on ethical, social, and religious dimensions of the medical, scientific, and technological progress was taking place in the 1950s and [early to mid-] 1960s." Indeed, during those years, physicians like Belding Scribner and others "did acutely experience and seriously ponder what we currently identify as questions of biomedical ethics" (Swazey 1993: S6).

The tightly scheduled mornings and afternoons covered a wealth of topics related to the development of bioethics in the United States over some three decades: Warren Reich's presentation "How Bioethics Got Its Name"; Daniel Callahan's "Why America Accepted Bioethics"; Harold Vanderpool addressing "What Bioethics Used to Look Like"; and a block of four presentations that dealt with bioethics' contributions to various groups and areas of study—"What Bioethics Brought to the Public" (Arthur Caplan), "What Bioethics Brought to Medicine" (Edmund Pellegrino), "What Bioethics Brought to Philosophy" (Danner Clouser), and "What Bioethics Brought to Law" (Angela Holder); and a panel called "Three Views of the History of Bioethics," with David Rothman, Daniel Fox, and Stanley Reiser. At the conference dinner, a session was devoted to "How Medicine and Theology Learned to Converse" including in its roster of discussants four physicians, a Protestant theologian, and a Dominican Catholic priest.[6]

The sessions also featured panels concerned with a spectrum of major substantive topics on which bioethics had focused throughout its history. The first of these, which built on the opening session's focus on Seattle's dialysis patients, examined the trajectories of "from selection to rationing," followed by panels exploring "from experiment to clinical trials," "from foregoing life support to aid-in-dying," "from abortion to reproductive technology," and "from cloning to genome." Another panel turned to certain intellectual attributes of bioethics: its creation as a discipline, the "principles" and "theory" underlying it, and the place and problem of the notion of "community" within its conceptual framework. The audience then heard three diverse "views of the history of bioethics" in a panel composed of David Rothman, Daniel Fox, and Stanley Reiser. Next came short tributes delivered by theologians Kenneth Vaux and David Smith to two fellow theologians regarded as antithetic foundational thinkers in the annals of bioethics: Joseph Fletcher and Paul Ramsey.[7] The meeting's final two-part session had a discussion about "patients and policies" led by physician-philosopher Howard

Brody, with a panel from the Group Health Cooperative, and a concluding address by Al Jonsen, reflecting on the conference and "The Once and Future Bioethics."

The "Birth of Bioethics" conference validated, and to a degree enhanced, Jonsen's own standing as a pioneer bioethicist. In addition, as he candidly stated in the postconference thank-you letters that he sent to the speakers, he had had a "selfish objective" in organizing this "birthday party": the "chauvinistic goal" of "link[ing] events at the University of Washington in 1963…with the beginning of the field of bioethics." In this letter, he also expressed the hope that it had "stimulated valuable historical [memory and] reflection" that could "create a record of our work over these last decades."[8]

For the conference participants and some of its attendees, the two-day gathering had a *gemeinschaft* sort of significance. In a way that was akin to an alumni reunion, it provided an opportunity for people who might only meet occasionally to reconnect, reminisce, and catch up with one another's activities. It was pervaded by an "our crowd,"[9] "we are bioethicists" feeling, and an intermixed sense of surprise and victory over the fact that the field had not only survived this long, but had attained considerable recognition. Jonsen made several humorous references in the course of the proceedings to the fact that the life span of bioethics was now sufficient for its so-called "pioneers" to be aging, and for a new generation of bioethicists to have come into existence.

Commemorating and Assessing *The Belmont Report*

In the annals of bioethics in the United States, few documents are more widely known in this country (and in many others as well), than the *Belmont Report*.[10] "Just over 5,500 words, this compact report, with its three principles, has been remarkably important and influential" (Childress, Meslin, and Shapiro 2005: xv). It has attained a venerated status as a document of "historical and enduring significance" that not only provides ethical guidelines for research involving human subjects—one of bioethics' original and most long-lasting foci of concern, whose influence also has "extended well beyond [its] initial context into medical practice and health care…and related public policies" (Childress, Meslin, and Shapiro 2005: vii; Childress 2005: 244).

The Belmont Report, as we noted in chapter 1, was drafted by the National Commission for the Protection of Human Subjects, in response to its congressional charge "to identify the basic ethical principles that should underlie the conduct of biomedical and behavioral research involving human subjects and to develop guidelines which should be followed to assure that such research is conducted in accordance with those principles" (U.S. DHEW. Office of the Secretary 1979: 23192). The document is divided into three sections. Part A delineates the boundaries between biomedical and behavioral research and "the practice of accepted therapy." Part B, the core of the report, sets forth "three basic principles" that are "among those generally accepted in our cultural tradition" and that are "particularly relevant to the ethics of research involving human subjects." These are "respect for persons" (which "divides into two separate moral requirements": to "acknowledge autonomy and…to protect those with diminished autonomy"); "beneficence" (which encompasses two "general rules": the obligations to "do no harm," and to "maximize possible benefits, and minimize possible harms"); and the principle of "justice." Part C then states how the application of these general principles to the conduct of research "leads to consideration of the… requirements [of] informed consent, risk/benefit assessment, and the selection of subjects of research."

Although *Belmont* was transmitted by the Commission to the President, Congress, and the Secretary of the Department of Health, Education, and Welfare (DHEW) on September 30, 1978, and published with appendices soon thereafter by DHEW (*The Belmont Report* 1978), the year that is used to mark its anniversary is 1979, when it was published as a Notice of Report for Public Comment in the *Federal Register* on April 18. The *Report* has received commemorative as well as intellectual and ethical attention by the bioethical community, including government officials, clinical investigators, and institutional committees involved with the protection of human research subjects.

In the years since it was issued, the *Report* has been treated as especially noteworthy for at least two reasons. It was produced by the first in a series of federal bioethics commissions established to deliberate on and make policy recommendations about bioethical issues, and to various degrees, *Belmont* and the National Commission's other reports have implicitly and explicitly influenced the work of successor groups. Second, and most important, the "basic ethical principles" and their "applications" enunciated in the *Report* serve as the foundation for the U.S. federal regulations for the protection of human research subjects, and as an exemplar that has been frequently cited and used by groups in other countries. Furthermore, *The Belmont Report* is one of the first documents in which the axes of "principlism"—the chief conceptual and justificatory framework for U.S. bioethics—were articulated. As Tom Beauchamp has reported, the drafting of the *Belmont* principles and of those in the first edition of the canonical bioethics text, *Principles of Biomedical Ethics*, which he coauthored with James Childress, took place at the same time. "The two works were written simultaneously," he has explained, "the one inevitably influencing the other…. I was often simultaneously drafting material on the same principle or topic both for the National Commission and for my colleague Childress, while he was at the same time writing material for me to inspect…. Despite their entirely independent origins," and the differences in "the two schemas of principles" that developed, "these projects grew up and matured together" (Beauchamp 2005a: 15).

The 20th Anniversary: *Belmont* Revisited

In 1998, the National Bioethics Commission's (NBAC) executive director Eric Meslin told us, the Commission's agenda included plans to "revisit the *Belmont Report*, hopefully in time to produce a paper coinciding with the 20th anniversary of the [*Report*'s] publication...next April." This idea, Meslin recalled, was raised during one of NBAC's first meetings, when Commissioner Ezekiel Emanuel brought up what he viewed as the need to add "respect for community" as a fourth *Belmont* principle (Meslin, interview, 1998: see appendix). The "possibility of [NBAC's] developing a 'Belmont Report' of its own—updating, if necessary, the National Commission's work by drafting a set of ethical principles that would be relevant and useful for researchers," Shapiro and Meslin commented in the conclusion to their conference paper, was "revisited during at least two Commission meetings." However, partly because of the Commission's already laden agenda and its limited resources, and uncertainty about when NBAC would cease to exist, this project was not undertaken (Shapiro and Meslin 2005: 73). Instead, chiefly through the collaboration of NBAC's chair, Princeton University president Harold Shapiro, Meslin, and Commissioner James Childress, plans were developed for a "Belmont Revisited" conference to take place on April 16–17, 1999, at a time that would coincide with the 20th anniversary of its publication in the *Federal Register*. It was held at the University of Virginia (Childress's home institution), supported by the University's Center for Biomedical Ethics, its Institute for Practical Ethics, the Virginia Health Policy Institute, Princeton University, and the federal Office of Protection from Research Risks, as well as by NBAC; and it was cochaired by Childress and Shapiro. The conference was designed not only to pay homage to the report but also to recall the context in which it was developed and the complexities involved in its drafting, to discuss its influence, and to consider whether, after two decades, it should be revised.

The conference speakers, Childress related to us, were chosen by him, Shapiro, Meslin, and another NBAC commissioner, physician Eric Cassell. Five groups of people, Childress said, were selected to address the meeting's thematic areas: (1) members of the National Commission and staff who "produced" the *Belmont* principles, and some of their consultants; (2) representatives from groups such as other bioethics commissions and government agencies that implemented or used the report in various ways; (3) individuals to address *Belmont*'s "institutionalization in medicine" and its "institutionalization in ethics"; (4) speakers who could provide "critical perspectives" on and "assessments" of the *Report*'s uses; and (5) discussants about areas of "expansion" of the principles and their application, such as the implications of autonomy for work in human genetics, and of the principles when the "community" rather than the individual is the focus of research.[11,12]

From the contemporary history and sociological perspectives of our study, four aspects of the anniversary conference papers and discussions, and the subsequent publication of the edited proceedings, were particularly interesting. These were the accounts by Tom Beauchamp and Al Jonsen of how and by whom the *Report* was written; discussion of its influence on subsequent federal bioethical commissions and federal regulations for the protection of human research subjects; assessments of both the document's importance and shortcomings over the past two decades; and the evaluation of the conference itself.[13]

Drafting the *Belmont Report*

During the two days of the conference, participants repeatedly described it as "the family reunion," and like most such reunions, this gathering was not always a harmonious one. In fact, the conference opened on a somewhat disputatious note when Al Jonsen and Tom Beauchamp presented their differing accounts of how and by whom the *Report* was written. Jonsen began by stating that when he was a Jesuit seminarian, he had learned to use hermeneutics for scriptural analysis, and he contended that this was a useful tool for analyzing the origins of bioethics. "*Belmont* in a sense is a piece of Holy Scripture," he declared, by which he seemed to mean that "the current text...of *Belmont* [was] what Biblical scholars would call the Ur-text" (Jonsen 2005: 10). With this statement as prelude, he then proceeded to present "the hermeneutics of *Belmont*," identifying six elements involved in such an analysis.

Jonsen's first two analytic elements bore on his historiography of *Belmont*'s writing: marking the date and time of a document's composition, and identifying its author. Dating the report by its April 1979 publication in the *Federal Register*, he said, gives a false impression of "the time of composition," which, more accurately, was "between 1974 (when the National Commission began meeting) and 1979." What is commonly thought of as the *Report*'s place of origin also is misleading, he stated. That place "was not [the]Belmont [House].... It was Belmont only in part.... [It was] "also Washington D.C. and San Francisco." With respect to the latter locale, Jonsen had written in *The Birth of Bioethics* about how a small group—he and commissioners Joseph Brady and Karen Lebacqz, former staff philosopher Stephen Toulmin, and staff director Michael Yesley—had met for two days in his "rooftop study" in September 1977, during a National Commission meeting in his "hometown" of San Francisco. The San Francisco group's goal, Jonsen stated, was "to produce the crisp document that Brady had called for" during the February 1976 deliberations at Belmont House (Jonsen 1998: 103).

Turning to the second element in hermeneutical analysis—authorship—Jonsen declared, "I disagree with Tom Beauchamp," and then quoted from Beauchamp's statement in his paper that when he succeeded Toulmin in December 1976 as the Commission's staff philosopher, "[M]y first assignment and only major assignment [from Yesley] was to write the 'Belmont Paper,' as it was then called."

In rebuttal, Jonsen averred that "many people wrote the Belmont Paper.... The composition of the document [came about] with many minds working in a variety of ways.... [It was] a composite document with the words of many people going into it."

When Beauchamp followed Jonsen to the podium, he read directly from his paper the very statement that Jonsen had challenged: "My first and only major assignment was to write the 'Belmont Paper.'" Continuing with his text, Beauchamp stated that "Yesley told me that he was assigning me full time to this task," adding that "this was Yesley's decision, not the Commission's." During his presentation, Beauchamp charged that "all my colleagues [not just Jonsen] have got it wrong" about how the principles came about and how the report was written, and he enumerated specific examples of what he called "errors in Al Jonsen's book." He reminded Jonsen, for example, that he, not Toulmin, had been at the September 1997 San Francisco work session at Jonsen's home. And he disputed Jonsen's allegation that this meeting had been called to revise the June 1976 draft of the Belmont paper. Rather, he insisted, this draft had been thoroughly recast by that time.

There was also some sparring between Beauchamp and Jonsen about the role that principlist reasoning based on moral principles, and casuist reasoning from particular cases and families of cases, had played in the work of the Commission, and about the relationship between them—with Jonsen being a greater advocate of the virtues of casuistical reasoning than Beauchamp, and Beauchamp insisting more strongly than Jonsen in their exchanges that casuistry and principles were complementary.[14]

The respondent to these first two speakers, Harold Vanderpool, followed (see note 13). His presentation contained a narrative summary of the "fascinating set of contrasts [and] compatibilities" in Jonsen's and Beauchamp's accounts, and an itemized list of differing versions given in Jonsen's *Birth of Bioethics* and Beauchamp's paper. He also provided a "critical review" of the *Belmont Report*, specifying the reasons why and the ways in which he believed that it needed to be revised. What he recommended was "not a wholesale or...extreme revision," but one that nevertheless would consider "add[ing] ethical principles and issues" to it. Childress then invited Jonsen, Beauchamp, and Vanderpool to join him for a discussion (see note 13). During his comments, Vanderpool had remarked that "we need to smoke a peace pipe" with respect to the differences between Jonsen's and Beauchamp's historical accounts. Collegiality prevailed, albeit with some evident tensions, in the remarks that Jonsen and Beauchamp made at this juncture. "The disagreements between us," Jonsen said, "show us how difficult such an exegesis is even when we are separated [from the origin of the report] by only a few decades.... To depend on one's memory is problematic" because that brings with it "difficulty of recall and difficulty of the dates of documents." Beauchamp, in turn, expressed his view that "the huge differences in the body of memory that

I have and Al has come from the fact that Al was on the Commission and I was staff. Staff work each day, [while] the commission works one time each month [on the issues under discussion]."

Belmont, Bioethics Commissions, and the Federal Regulations

In the segment of the program that explored *Belmont*'s influence on successor bioethics commissions and on the federal regulations for the protection of human research subjects, Dr. Gary Ellis, director of NIH's Office for Protection from Research Risks (OPRR, now the Office for Human Research Protections), attested to the report's enduring importance for the work of his office (see note 13). Every few years, he said, OPRR reprints the *Report* in lots of 15,000 copies, "and they invariably all disappear." That statistic, he added, is "becoming anachronistic" because *Belmont* has been posted on OPRR's Web site "and the frequency of its consumption is not readily tracked. With gratitude and respect for the National Commission's scholarship, I say: Not bad for 20 years out.... Today, OPRR, perhaps to a greater extent on a daily basis than any other collection of professionals, uses, discusses, cites, and interprets the *Belmont Report*.... [T]hose 5–1/2 pages are living and breathing in OPRR's hands."

Speakers also assessed the role of *Belmont* in the work of five bioethics commissions that followed the National Commission. In chronological order, those groups, created between 1978 and 1995, were the HEW Secretary's Ethics Advisory Board (1978–1980), the President's Commission for the Study of Ethical Problems in Medicine and Biomedical and Behavioral Research (1978–1983), the National Bioethics Advisory Commission (1995–2001), and two advisory bodies that were established to examine specific bioethically relevant policy issues: the NIH's Recombinant DNA Advisory Committee's (RAC) subcommittee to review human gene therapy protocols, appointed in 1983; and the President's Advisory Committee on the Human Radiation Experiments (1994–1995). The effects of *Belmont* on those bodies, in the speakers' views, were more intricate and nuanced than the direct significance attributed to it by OPRR.

Charles McCarthy, who served as staff director of the HEW Secretary's Ethics Advisory Board (EAB), maintained that the *Belmont* principles were implicitly "embedded" in all four of the reports issued by the EAB "during its brief lifespan from 1978–1980" (see note 13). The National Commission and *Belmont*, he said, had indirect, "inter-personnel" influences on the EAB's work, through for example, the Commission's assistant staff director, Barbara Mishkin, becoming deputy director and then staff director of the EAB, and the linkage provided by LeRoy Walters's work for both the Commission and the Board.

In discussing *Belmont*'s influence on the work of the RAC's oversight of gene therapy research, LeRoy Walters pointed out that assessing the report's effects involved sorting out the influences of "pre-Belmont sources," "direct and indirect literary influences," and "personal connections" among the National Commission, the President's Commission, and the Human Gene Therapy Subcommittee. The RAC subcommittee's 1984 document, "Points to Consider in Human Gene Therapy," Walters maintained, was "based solidly" on *Belmont*, Beauchamp and Childress's *Principles of Biomedical Ethics*, and the President's Commission's *Splicing Life* report (see note 13).

In the introduction to her presentation, Ruth Faden, chair of the Advisory Committee on the Human Radiation Experiments (ACHRE), stated that by the time that the Advisory Committee was convened by President Clinton in January 1994, "the *Belmont Report* had assumed almost constitutional status internationally as the dominant framework for evaluating the ethics of research with human subjects." It was with regard to issues concerning the protection of the rights and interests of human subjects, she said, that the *Report*, with its stress on the moral aspects of human research, had the most meaning for the Advisory Committee's work. However, she attested, the Advisory Committee's ethical framework was not derived from *Belmont*; and it included additional principles and moral themes, with special emphasis on the role of "trust" and "openness" that *Belmont* did not address (Faden et al. 2005: 14).

In their coauthored paper, Harold Shapiro, the chair of NBAC, and its executive director, Eric Meslin, affirmed that the *Belmont Report* and its ethical principles had provided important grounding for NBAC's work. But the degree of *Belmont*'s influence, they went on to say, varied according to the set of questions with which NBAC was dealing. For example, whereas the *Report* and its principles figured significantly in NBAC's reports on research on persons with mental disorders, on human biological materials, and on clinical trials in developing countries, it had little influence on NBAC's report on the use of somatic cell nuclear transfer to clone human beings; and some of the ethical questions with which NBAC had to deal in framing its report on stem cell research had not been addressed by *Belmont* (Shapiro and Meslin 2005).

The appraisal made by Alexander Capron of the impact of the *Report* on the President's Commission, for which he served as executive director, differed dramatically. Drawing on Sherlock Holmes's "curious incident of the dog in the night-time"—curious because the dog "did nothing"—Capron stated at the outset of his talk that the "curious aspect of the *Belmont Report* is that it played virtually no part in the deliberations or conclusions of the President's Commission." Observing that when he first began to do research for his conference paper, he had been surprised and puzzled by this "absence of influence," he proceeded to analyze the factors that might have contributed to this "mystery." Most important, he concluded, was the fact that "our [the President's Commission's] method of analysis was not merely inductive but highly contextual.... [I]t depended upon careful examination of the specifics of the various topics and a search for practical conclusions about them—not abstract philosophy—that made sense in the context of the particular topic" (Capron 2005: 29, 36).

The *Belmont* Principles

A centerpiece of this 20th anniversary conference was the block of sessions focused on a reexamination of the three *Belmont* principles—respect for persons, beneficence, and justice—their import, strengths, limitations, and the unresolved questions surrounding them.

Respect for Persons. The first, and arguably the key principle set forth in *Belmont* is respect for persons, which, the *Report* states, "incorporates at least two ethical convictions: ...that individuals should be treated as autonomous agents, and...that persons with diminished autonomy are entitled to protection." This principle, in turn, has been viewed as the underpinning of the requirement for informed consent in the ethical conduct of research involving human subjects. Because of its paramountcy, and especially because of its emphasis on individual autonomy, respect for persons has been one of the most contentiously debated principles in bioethics both with regard to human subjects research and medical care. Many of the issues that it has evoked were explored in papers delivered by theological ethicist Karen Lebacqz (a former member of the National Commission), and by professor of social medicine/bioethicist Larry Churchill.

Lebacqz charged that after *Belmont*, the power of this "fundamental principle" had been narrowed and diminished when it was reduced to respect for autonomy, and that autonomy, in turn, had been reduced when it was interpreted in terms of John Stuart Mill's notion of "liberty"—a self-determining freedom of individual choice. The focus on respect for autonomy in works such as *Principles of Biomedical Ethics*, she held, "is unfortunate in two ways." First, "the respect due to non-autonomous persons is lost," and, second, it has engendered an "exclusive focus on *autonomy* as defining of persons," in contrast to other perspectives such as the feminist literature's stress on "*relationality* and its implications of connection and commitment," or the traditional Roman Catholic understanding of the "social context" in which persons acquire and express their identity, and the connection between the "flourishing" of the individual and the "common good." Moreover, she continued, the "logical outcome" of reducing respect for persons to autonomy and autonomy to self-determination is "that the broad-ranging *principle* of 'respect for persons' is then truncated into the *rule* of 'informed consent.' The only question we ask is whether one *consented* to medical intervention or use of technologies. Any question as to whether such interventions or technologies are *right* is utterly lost."

These questions, she stated, lead to the issue of whether "the problem lies not with particular principles, but with the use of principles at all." Perhaps, she rhetorically suggested, "[W]e should henceforth eschew principles, and throw out the Belmont Report, seeing it as of historical interest but as of little lasting value." This is a strategy, she then declared, that she rejected, noting that she largely agreed with Beauchamp and Childress's argument in *Principles of Biomedical Ethics* that "[o]nly a faulty conception of the nature and interpretation of principles would lead to the conclusion that principles have no integral role in moral reasoning in concrete circumstances" (Beauchamp and Childress 1994: 107). Rather than rejecting principles as "morally bankrupt," Lebacqz contended, they should be reinterpreted and extended. Thus, she argued, respect for persons needs to encompass "a more communal understanding and tradition than has permeated the 'informed consent' approach"—one that embraces respect for families and communities as well as individuals, and makes recourse to the "Western tradition of *covenant*." With regard to beneficence, she said, if she were writing principles today, she would "draw on the religious traditions that underlie American society and invoke a concern for *compassion* to supplement beneficence." In making this suggestion, she departed from her manuscript to comment that she "wished philosophers would spend as much time reading religious and theological writings as she spent reading philosophy." With regard to justice, too, she continued, "[T]here is an understanding rooted in several of the religious traditions that underlie this country that would broaden our understanding of what justice in research would require." Thus, in addition to treating equals equally, "justice may also be understood as requiring *attention to power differentials* and to *the liberation of the oppressed*." If such a broader understanding of justice was adopted, she pointed out, "it might require some fundamental critique of the research enterprise itself…. The Commission did not raise these types of questions. We accepted the research enterprise as it stood in the U.S. at that time. We asked questions *within* that framework, but did not question the basic framework itself." "Such questions have yet to be raised with seriousness in the dominant bioethical community," she contended, "though they have been the meat of feminist bioethics for some time" (Lebacqz 2005: 106–108, author's emphases).

The sharp critique of *Belmont*'s first principle, respect for persons, which Larry Churchill delivered, emanated from his conviction that the way that it had been interpreted by the Commission constituted a "weak and distorted understanding of self-determination"—an insufficiently strong and a "flawed notion of autonomy" that could be "damaging to the enterprise of research with human subjects."

To remedy the problem, Churchill proposed a twofold reformulation. First, he argued, because respect for persons is "less an ethical principle than an ontological claim," it "should be thought of as a basic or foundational commitment guiding research with human subjects," and as such it "should be removed as the first principle," and presented "as the guiding vision for everything that follows" in the basic ethical principles section of the report. Second, "respect for autonomy" should become the first of *Belmont*'s three ethical principles, which "will provide the more precise focus needed to make sense of the exacting informed consent requirements found elsewhere in Belmont...and in the federal Common Rule" (Churchill 2005: 111, 117–118).

The Role of Community. A catalyst for the 20th anniversary "Belmont Revisited" conference, as we have noted, was the contention made by Commissioner Ezekiel Emanuel at the first NBAC meeting that the three *Belmont* principles did not adequately deal with "community." Emanuel extended this argument further in the presentation that he made at the conference in conjunction with Charles Weijer, a fellow physician-bioethicist, who had served as a consultant to NBAC. The *Report*, they stated, "was written under the grip of an individualist vision," and they proposed that an independent fourth principle of "respect for community," entailing an "obligation to respect the values and interests of the community in research, and, whenever possible, to protect the community from harm," should be added to the established *Belmont* three. They delineated a five-step approach to developing a typology that they claimed would systematically identify and distinguish different communities, and provide a rational basis on which to devise and apply appropriate protections for particular communities (Emanuel and Weijer 2005: 171, 181).[15]

Emanuel's and Weijer's definition of community, and their insistence on a new principle of respect for community, aroused as much animated discussion as the differing accounts of the origins of the *Belmont Report* that were presented by Jonsen and Beauchamp at the beginning of the conference. Several women speakers voiced strong objections to the omission of "women as a community" in Emanuel's and Weijer's conceptual framework. And in a thoughtful commentary on the issues involved in the protection of communities in research, Jonathan Moreno pointed out that *Belmont* had been attentive to the fact that there are certain groups in the population—such as the example of the poor, minimally educated African American men who were the subjects of the infamous Tuskegee Syphilis Study—who are particularly "vulnerable" to coercion and exploitation. Moreno took a stand against the need for a fourth principle to protect such communities and groups. Rather, he argued, their vulnerability both to "wrongful inclusion [and] exclusion" in research could and should be handled under the principle of justice, conceived as "fairness" (see note 13).

Justice. As the framers of *Belmont* observed, the "basic ethical principle" of justice can be formulated in several ways, two of which they saw as particularly relevant to research with human subjects: "justice in the sense of 'fairness in distribution' or 'what is deserved,'" and justice as meaning "that equals ought to be treated equally." The application of these two general conceptions, the *Report* states, "is relevant to the selection of subjects at two levels: the social and the individual." Individual justice requires that researchers exhibit "fairness" in the selection of subjects, while social justice "requires that distinctions be drawn between classes of subjects that ought, and ought not, to participate in any particular kind of research."

Law professor Patricia King, who had been a member of both the National Commission and the President's Commission, delivered the chief paper on justice at the conference. She began by recounting how the National Commission had approached the principle of justice, and preceded to analyze why, in her opinion, it had focused on distributive justice, which pertained to the selection of subjects for research, and on the protection of those among them who were vulnerable to being misused. She was critical of the fact that the National Commission had largely "ignored" other aspects of justice, specifically compensatory and procedural justice, and proceeded to examine what she termed justice "beyond *Belmont*." King highlighted "a striking shift from the emphasis on exclusion of members of vulnerable groups to one of inclusion in research" that had taken place, primarily, in her opinion, through the emergence and spread of the HIV/AIDS epidemic during the 1980s and 1990s, and the struggle to gain access to new, anti-retroviral drugs with their potential therapeutic effects. These developments, she said, had contributed to a generalized change in perspective that now "emphasizes therapeutic rather than non-therapeutic research, access rather than protection, and benefits rather than risks and burdens" of research, and of their fair distribution. Quoting from *Belmont*, she called attention to the fact that "the reasons underlying the vulnerability of certain groups—'social, racial, sexual and cultural biases institutionalized in society'—are the same today as in previous decades." Balancing the protection of vulnerable individuals and groups, she declared, and the "creation of opportunities for [their] inclusion in research" will call for more than distributive justice. It should also include "procedural justice"—for example, the participation of women and members of minority groups in establishing research agendas—and "compensatory justice," in the form of compensation for research-incurred injuries (King 2005: 139–140, 144, 145).

Beneficence. Physician Robert Levine, a special consultant to the National Commission who developed the *Report*'s first section on "Boundaries between Practice and Research," was the spokesperson for the principle of beneficence. Beneficence, he asserted, which is embedded in the "do no harm" tradition of medicine, is as important as the first Belmont principle, "respect for persons." In fact, he stated, the National Commission viewed the three "fundamental" ethical principles that they identified as having, "at least in the abstract, equal moral force." The Commission's conception of beneficence, he went on to say, encompasses both the obligation to do good (beneficence) and the obligation to do no harm (nonmaleficence)—the fourth principle that Beauchamp and Childress added to the *Belmont* trinity in their *Principles of Biomedical Ethics*. Beneficence, in the way that it is interpreted by *Belmont*, Levine held, is an ethical imperative in research involving human subjects because it not only undergirds the obligation to "secure the well-being of the individuals who serve as research subjects" but also the obligation "to develop information that will form the basis of being better able to serve the well-being of similar persons in the future" (Levine 2005: 127, 129).[16]

Dealing with Conflicts among the Principles. The final session of the conference addressed what medical ethicist Robert Veatch, another consultant to the National Commission, defined as "the single most crucial problem with *Belmont*: its failure to make clear what should happen when the [three] principles conflict among themselves"—for example, when in assessing a proposed research protocol, an institutional review board (IRB) faces the predicament of having "one principle [support] one conclusion about [that] protocol while another leads to a different conclusion." Veatch examined several possible resolutions to this problem in his paper: a "single principle" stance, "affirm[ing] one single principle as foundational"; a "simultaneity view," in which "all the principles must be satisfied simultaneously in order for a protocol to be morally acceptable"; a "balancing view," in which "the principles taken together must merely be "satisfied 'on balance' "; and a "ranking view," which "holds that principles can be rank-ordered, and that the highest-ranking principle must be fully satisfied before the next in rank is considered." The "ambiguity in the *Belmont Report*, as well as in other National Commission documents and government regulations, in this regard, Veatch opined, "suggests that there is an urgent need to develop a theory of what should happen" when proposed research involves a conflict among principles (Veatch 2005: 185, 186, 190, 197). In the absence of such a theory, the approach that Veatch articulated seemed to combine simultaneity and ranking views, with limited balancing.

Philosopher Henry Richardson took a stance against relying on the "global" and "conflict-resolution" types of "balancing" used by Gert, Culver, and Clouser in *Bioethics: A Return to Fundamentals* (1997), and by Beauchamp and Childress in *Principles of Biomedical Ethics* (1994). Rather, he argued for the superiority of the model of "specification" for which he is well known (Richardson 1990). "[M]y complaint," Richardson explained, "is that relying on the metaphor of balancing leads one to offer the mere semblance of reason giving, where real reason giving is wanted, and the mere appearance of guiding action, where actual guidance is wanted." For these reasons, which he examined in his paper, he contended that "specification is a more fruitful and explicit way of resolving a concrete issue than is balancing" (Richardson 2005: 205, 206, 218).

Finally, James Childress made a brief response to Richardson's and Veatch's presentations (see note 13). He prefaced it by referring to the earlier presentations and discussion on "respect for community." In his judgment, he said, while it was important to pay more attention to relationships and community, this could be done within the framework of "the three existing [*Belmont*] principles." A "new principle of respect for community" was not needed. He then commented on Veatch's and Richardson's differing approaches to dealing with conflict among these principles. Whereas Veatch's model focused primarily on the "weight, strength, or stringency" of ethical principles and rules, he said, Richardson's mainly addressed their "meaning, range, and scope." He predicted that debate would continue about how to avoid, reduce, or resolve conflicts among principles, and counseled against choosing a single way to deal with them.[17]

The Meaning of "Belmont Revisited"

It should not be taken for granted that an entire conference of several days' duration was devoted to the *Belmont* principles, or that most of the papers prepared for this conference were subsequently published in further developed form, in a 279-page book that included the *Report* as an appendix to the volume (Childress, Meslin, and Shapiro 2005). Although in a number of ways "Belmont Revisited" resembled many other intellectual or academic conferences and their published sequelae, it differed markedly from them in at least two conspicuous respects: the intensity of its concentration on a subject as specific and narrowly hewed as three ethical principles; and, above all, the more than respectful attitude of esteem with which the conference approached the principles. To be sure, it was made explicit by its organizers that "revisiting" *Belmont* meant examining and assessing this set of principles, with the aim of improving the present and future ethical framework and guidelines for research with human subjects, medical practice, and related public policy. Moreover, virtually every participant in the conference who prepared a paper or served as a discussant conscientiously considered how these principles might be reformulated, reinterpreted, modified, sharpened, broadened, enriched, and/or deepened. And yet, underlying and permeating the conference, and the book that grew out of it, was a shared reverential admiration for the historic status, philosophical excellence, conciseness, ramifying import, and lasting significance of the *Belmont* principles and the report in which they were articulated. This collective sentiment was expressed by many of the conference's participants. "If there was ever an example of twenty pages of philosophical ethics that have left an indelible mark on the public," Robert Veatch stated, "it is surely *Belmont*. That it is still cited by philosophers, researchers, institutional review boards (IRBs), and courts as one of the most important, if not the definitive, codifications of the principles of research ethics testifies to its importance" (Veatch 2005: 186). Susan Sherwin commented with admiration on the fact that "[o]ne of the most striking things about the *Belmont Report*, looking back thirty years later, is how incisive and comprehensive it manages to be in so few pages" (Sherwin 2005: 148). Ruth Faden and her coauthors referred to the "almost constitutional status" that the *Report* had "assumed" (Faden et al. 2005: 41). And Albert Jonsen went even further by not only linking Belmont's principles to the U.S. Constitution but also to the Bible: "Just as our Constitution requires a Supreme Court to interpret its majestically open-ended phrases," he wrote, "and, if I may allude to my own Catholic tradition, as the Bible requires a living Magisterium to interpret its mystic and metaphoric message, so does *Belmont*, a much more modest document than the Constitution or Bible, require a constantly moving and creative interpretation and application" (Jonsen 2005: 10). Substantively and symbolically, this sort of testimony associated *Belmont* with what sociologist Robert Bellah has identified as "civil religion" (Bellah 1967). The secular sacralization of the *Belmont* document and what it has come to collectively represent made the "Revisited" meeting more than a conference, a reunion, or an anniversary celebration, though all these elements were integral to it.

The members and staff of the National Commission, and their consultants, who were among the chief participants in the conference, were viewed as persons of high regard, even notables, at this gathering because of their role in producing *Belmont*. The honor accorded to the framers of the *Report* and its principles was a factor that united those attending the conference. At the same time, it also contributed to the disagreement that Jonsen and Beauchamp voiced about the origins and evolution of the document, and the work that went into its drafts and redrafts. The claims that each of them made about the part that he played in this process bore some resemblance to "disputes over priority of discovery" that occur frequently among scientists (Merton 1957).

In the epilogue that he wrote to the volume that grew out of the 20th anniversary conference, James Childress stated that "looking back to the *Belmont* principles is a way to look—and to move—forward. We look back not because we suppose that the *Belmont* principles are adequate for contemporary biomedical research and practice but instead to recognize their historical and contemporary significance by engaging and interrogating them in current conversations about bioethical guidance." The principles "do not exhaust that conversation," he averred. "Only a *Belmont* fundamentalist—and I have never met one—would think otherwise" (Childress 2005: 244, 251). The Belmont Revisited conference constituted an important, serious "conversation" of the sort that Childress envisaged. It entailed discussion and debate about "narrowing [the] range" of the principle of respect for persons, "expanding the meaning, range, and scope" of the principle of justice, and about "revisiting" the three principles "in light of concerns about relationships and community"—including the possibility of adding a "new principle of respect for community" to the triad (Childress 2005: 247, 249). And yet, in the end, the grand conclusion that was reached was that "a broader and richer interpretation of the principles is sufficient" (Childress 2005: 249). Although this judgment may not have resulted from "fundamentalist" thinking, it does suggest that the institutionalized veneration of the *Belmont* principles has created powerful resistances to changing them in any major or deep-structured way.[18] More than cognitive factors underlie the immutability of these principles. They are also supported by strong beliefs in their rightness and goodness that contain elements of ideology.

Silver Anniversary Celebrations of the *Belmont Report*

The Medical College of Wisconsin Symposium. The 25th anniversary of the *Belmont Report* and the 30th anniversary of the establishment of the National Commission were celebrated at a one-day symposium convened by the Medical College of Wisconsin (MCW) in Milwaukee on May 14, 2004.[19] Not surprisingly, the symposium featured many of the same themes and speakers as had the "Belmont Revisited" conference.

The program was an intensive one, which began with a series of welcomes and opening remarks that included the reading of a letter from Senator Edward Kennedy, and a video message from the Secretary of Health and Human Services, Tommy Thompson, who, when his message was introduced, was referred to as "a small-town boy" who had served as the governor of Wisconsin. In his letter, Kennedy referred several times to "the Belmont Commission," and hailed the *Report* for its "outstanding service to the nation and the world community." The keynote address was delivered by Bernard Schwetz, DVM, PhD, interim director of the Office for Human Research Protections. He thanked the Commission and lauded the "lasting impact" of *Belmont* because it had provided an "analytic framework" of basic principles for the resolution of ethical problems arising from research with human subjects at that time and for the future, and spoke briefly about the role of OHRP and what he saw as "the big issues" today, including "the long-term stability" of the research protection "enterprise."

The program continued with a series of panel discussions by Commission members, staff, and consultants, during which they spoke reminiscently about the *Report*'s creation, the involvement of legislators and regulators in research involving human subjects, and the legacy of *Belmont* in "the wide world of contemporary bioethics" (Medical College of Wisconsin 2004). The first groups of panelists—commissioners Joseph Brady, Robert Cooke, and Albert Jonsen, and Commission consultant Robert Levine—spoke about the creation of *Belmont*, which was identified in the program title as the event that had "institute[ed] research ethics in the United States." Next, a panel composed of commissioners Patricia King and Donald Seldin, and Commission consultant James Childress considered the topic "Gaps in the Foundation—Belmont's Shortcomings: How Has Research Been Shortchanged?"

After tributes were paid to the members of the National Commission and its staff and consultants, the six commissioners attending the symposium continued their recollections, in a panel entitled "The National Commission...: Diverse, Opinionated, and Cohesive." They were followed by Stephen Toulmin, the Commission's first staff philosopher. In a brief talk entitled "A Return to Reason:

Ethical Theory and Practice," he spoke about the ways in which, "like others here, my life was changed by working with the National Commission." Through his role with the Commission and subsequent activities, he said, he had learned that academic philosophers "should not confine themselves to a specialty, to being an isolated expert." And with implicit reference to his now classic 1982 paper, "How Medicine Saved the Life of Ethics," Toulmin said, "I would add, 'Ethics saved the soul of medicine.'" The final segment of the symposium consisted of four short talks: a "historical perspective" on "what almost happened to research" by Charles McCarthy, who had played a major role at the NIH in developing legislation, policies, and regulations concerning the protection of human subjects; Commissioner Karen Lebacqz addressing the topic "Gaps in the Foundation— Belmont's Shortcomings"; the Commission's director, Michael Yesley, describing why "Principles are Great, But…a Pragmatic Perspective on Belmont"; and Tom Beauchamp's concluding talk called "The Legacy of Belmont."

As we viewed the videotapes of the MCW symposium, we were not so much struck by its substantive content—much of which was familiar to us from the Belmont Revisited conference—as we were by the atmosphere in which the symposium unfolded. To begin with, the day had a reunion-like ambience, put into words by Al Jonsen, who spoke of the joy of "seeing dear friends again after 25 years" (although many of the persons assembled had worked with one another on various projects since their participation on the National Commission, and had been together only five years earlier at the 20th anniversary Belmont Revisited conference).

One speaker after another described his or her involvement with the Commission exuberantly, as an "exhilarating," "professionally transforming," "intellectually formative" experience that "changed [his or her] life." The day resonated with accolades voiced by the commissioners, staff, and consultants about the caliber of the people (largely themselves), associated with the Commission, and the ways they all had worked together. ("The National Commission…: Diverse, Opinionated, and Cohesive" was the title of one of the symposium panels.) Staff, consultants, and commissioners had lofty praise for one another—for the spirit of "mutual respect," "good humor," "camaraderie," and "respect for differences" with which they had collaborated to draft *Belmont* and the other Commission reports as well. "The strength of the National Commission," one commissioner declared, "lay in the intellect of its members and their obstinancy. There was no 'yes ma'am, yes sir' [during our meetings]." And "we had a terrific staff," said another commissioner. "There was a lot of intellectual machinery." "Whoever chose the Commission," a third commissioner exclaimed, "ought to be given a big plaque." The tributes to the *Belmont Report* that were delivered at the Medical College of Wisconsin symposium surpassed those emanating from Belmont Revisited. Commissioner Joseph Brady, a behavioral biologist, for example, declared that the

Report had been "consecrated" by its impact. There have been "a few single documents that changed the world—*Belmont* was one of them," pediatrician Robert Cooke avowed. Lawyer Patricia King said that she thought of the *Report* "as a document like the Constitution, or the Declaration of Independence"—a document that "incorporates [fundamental] values and principles, in this case those that help us resolve issues in medicine and research." "Like the Constitution," she continued, the *Report* "has to be revisited from time to time and understood in changing times and contexts." And in the closing talk on "the legacy of *Belmont*," given by philosopher Tom Beauchamp, he referred to the "near-canonical role" that the *Report* had played in federal policies for the protection of human subjects, characterizing it further as "the only government document, and one of the few documents generally, that has influenced the entire field of bioethics."

The tributes were not only verbal in nature. In addition, Commissioner Joseph Brady, along with Alison Ryan Glassey, the daughter of the Commission's deceased chairman, obstetrician-gynecologist Kenneth Ryan, presented a plaque in memory of Ryan and the three other members of the Commission who had died: lawyers David Louisell and Robert Turtle, and neurophysiologist and psychologist Elliot Stellar. Glassey spoke about her father, and how he had "lived the three *Belmont* principles"; and she also praised the National Commission as a group. Individual awards were then presented to the commissioner, staff, and consultant "Belmonters" in attendance, by the symposium moderator, Wendy Kaiser, MCW's Clinical Research Education manager, and by the College's Senior Associate Dean for Research and Vice President for Technology, William Hendee.

The OHRP's Commemoration. On November 16, 2004, the members, consultants, and staff of the National Commission were assembled once more, this time to attend a brief, highly ritualized ceremony, organized by the Department of Health and Human Services' Office for Human Research Protections (OHRP, formerly the Office for Protection from Research Risks), in honor of them as "writers of the *Belmont Report*," on the occasion of the *Report*'s 25th anniversary.[20] The ceremony began with the singing of the American national anthem, the "Star-Spangled Banner." Claude Allen, assistant secretary of the Department of Health and Human Services, then welcomed the group and paid tribute to the National Commission members, as video clip images of those who were present flashed behind him on a screen. This was followed by historical reminiscences about the congressional origins of the National Commission by Senator Edward Kennedy and former representative Paul Rogers, who had, respectively, chaired the U.S. Senate and House of Representatives committees involved in the hearings and consequent legislation that established the Commission.[21]

In rapid sequence, former commissioners and staff then went to the podium to offer their "recollections." Several speakers referred to the remarkable collegiality that had characterized the Commission, the "common language" it had developed, and the way it had reached consensus in formulating the *Report*. And physician Donald Seldin, one of the commissioners, said that what had impressed him the most was the fact that in the *Belmont Report*, "moral reflection [had become] official government language."

Following the series of reminiscences, as had been done at the MCW symposium, plaques were presented to the commissioners and staff, including plaques for the deceased chair, Kenneth Ryan, which was accepted by his daughter, and for the three other deceased commissioners. Al Jonsen then ascended the podium once more to offer "some reflections on behalf of the commissioners." The *Report* was "conceived at the Belmont House" in 1976, some 200 years after the drafting of the Declaration of Independence, he declared. It has "made it for 25 years," in contrast to most documents published in the *Federal Register* that "don't [last that long]." *Belmont* has endured, he affirmed, because it captured "a republic of ideals" about the purpose of research—namely, that the benefits of research "must flow to the common good" of future patients, to "the health of the whole human community."

LeRoy Walters next presented parallel "reflections on behalf of the staff and consultants." He spoke about the important roles that had been played by Senator Walter Mondale in his efforts to legislatively establish a national bioethics advisory committee, and by Charles McCarthy, who, over the years, had "translated" the National Commission's recommendations into Federal guidelines. Like those who had testified before him, Walters linked the success of the Commission's work with the "listening and learning" that had occurred between its members and staff, and the "mutual respect" that they had for each other. *Belmont* and its principles, he affirmed in conclusion, was the National Commission's "crowning achievement," as a document that "articulates a vision of how all people, research subjects and patients, should be treated." In the wake of that tribute, the program ended, with a final round of applause "for one last recognition of the commissioners and staff."

The federal government's commemorative program, held under the auspices of the Office for Human Research Protections, had been an occasion at which certain perceived connections between *Belmont*, its principles and framers, the American polity, and some of the solemn values, beliefs, and symbols of American civil religion were more manifestly on display than at the other *Belmont* anniversary events.

Interpreting the Rites of Bioethics

What factors seem to have contributed to the range of ritual events that have occurred with notable frequency over the course of the relatively abbreviated history of bioethics? And what accounts for the fact that the field has paid so much self-conscious attention to the short span of its existence—chronicling it in detail, and celebrating it recurrently in public performance ways? Our examination of this phenomenon—of which the Birth of Bioethics conference and the cluster of Belmont-associated gatherings are illustrative examples—suggests that two seemingly contradictory sets of patterns underlie their occurrence.

The ambiguous nature of exactly what bioethics is, combined with a heritage of uncertainty about its staying power and survival, appear to be one of the basic sources of the kinds of anniversaries, birthdays, testimonies, tributes, and awards that we have identified. A number of the major figures in bioethics' early years whom we interviewed feelingly described both the unsettling nonclarity of the initial definition and content of this de novo entity, which, in Daniel Callahan's words, had to be "made up as we went along," and its nebulous prognosis. Is bioethics a "discipline," an (interdisciplinary) "field," or, as LeRoy Walters phrased it, a conglomerate of "standard methods of analysis from classical fields like theological ethics and philosophical ethics that are use[d] within a particular sphere of human activity"? (Walters, interview, 2000: see appendix). And how long would bioethics last? "When I started working in the field in 1969," David Smith publicly stated at the Birth of Bioethics conference, "senior colleagues advised me against it. 'It's just a fad that will pass' " [they said]. And in our interview with him, LeRoy Walters told us that "there have been moments during the almost 30 years now that I have been at Georgetown when I've had an image of a soap bubble in my mind, and I just wondered when is this bubble going to burst. Because it seem[ed] as if the field started to take off in the '70s and then the question [arose]: Is this a fad? Has this become less important, less interesting, less vibrant? (Walters, interview, 2000: see appendix). "[W]ho would have predicted...when bioethics was first established...that this esoteric field, or seemingly esoteric field...would survive and prosper?" Jonathan Moreno exclaimed at a panel discussion organized around the publication of his book *Is There an Ethicist in the House?*, which took place at the Center for American Progress in October 2005 (Center for American Progress 2005).

In the face of the originally ill-defined conception of bioethics, the improvised aspects of its development, and the predictions that were made about how transitory it might be, the succession of anniversary and celebratory events that have taken place, with their ambience of reunion, constitute a collective statement about the factuality of the field. They represent an ongoing affirmation that it is "real," that it has endured, that it is professional, and that it has a strong sense of intellectual and moral colleagueship. These programmed happenings are related as well to the striving of bioethics to achieve greater legitimacy—to cease to be a "cultural curiosity," to "make it into the higher reaches of academia," to become "a respectable part of the biomedical establishment" without being "an accommodating handmaiden" to it (Callahan 1996: 3), and to be recognized as an influential presence and force in the public square. In this connection, one of the sentiments that some of our interviewees expressed was chagrin that they and the field of bioethics had not been accorded the professional status and honors that more orthodox intellectual disciplines, and those who belong to them, receive. This sort of disappointment may be an ingredient in the "celebration-of-self" dimensions of bioethics' ceremonious conferences, and the conferring of awards on its "own" highly respected members—"founders," "pioneers," individuals who are viewed as moral exemplars, persons who have rendered "distinguished service" to the field, and those who have been singled out for their "lifetime" intellectual achievements (within a field that is still too young to span a lifetime). In addition, they are mediums through which a sense of appreciation for the continuation and development of the field, and the degree of institutionalized solidity and success that it has attained, have been dramaturgically expressed.

There is a second set of patterns that also seems to have contributed to the florescence, themes, and symbols of the bioethics celebrations and ceremonies, which appear to be antitheses of the kinds of insecurities about the field that helped to foster such events. These are the affirmations that are rhetorically and emblematically expressed at such occasions about the moral significance of the thought and the work of bioethics and bioethicists, their relationship to core precepts and concerns of the American cultural tradition and societal community, their ethical universalism, and their influence in the sphere of public policy. They are most pronounced, and also most congratulatory and self-congratulatory, when they are invoked in reference to the constellation of principles that conceptually frame bioethics, particularly in connection with the virtual enshrinement of the *Belmont Report* that has seemingly occurred, and the reification of its trinity of principles. These more triumphal patterns are related to the kind of moral compass that bioethics is conceived, and conceives itself, to be, to the aura of subliminal as well as conscious patriotic pride that surrounds American bioethics, and to its place in the public square. The vying among bioethicists to be recognized as originators or founders of the field, or as chief drafters of its foundational documents that have occasionally erupted at ceremonious bioethics gatherings, appears to have as much to do with these connotations of U.S. bioethics as with its intellectual grounding.[22]

Notes

1. Dr. Henry K. Beecher was the first recipient of the Beecher Award, in 1976. Subsequent recipients have included Sissela Bok, Daniel Callahan, K. Danner Clouser, Hans Jonas, Jay Katz, Richard McCormick, and Edmund Pellegrino. In consecutive order, those accorded the American Association of Bioethics and Humanities' (ASBH) Lifetime Achievement Award were Edmund Pellegrino; Albert R. Jonsen; John Fletcher; Daniel Callahan; Ruth Macklin; Jay Katz; a trio of recipients in 2004, Tom Beauchamp, James F. Childress, and Joanne Trautman Banks; Eric Cassell; two recipients in 2006, Bernard Gert and Ronald Cranford; and Renée Fox. The ASBH's Distinguished Service Awards recipients have included Loretta Kopelman, Robert Arnold, Steven Miles,

Stuart Youngner, David Barnard, Marion Secundy, Tom Tomlinson, Betty Wolder Levin, Les Rothenberg, Mark Kuczewski, Hilda Lindemann Nelson, Thomas H. Murray, and Chester Burns.

2. We viewed a videotape of the Belmont 25th anniversary program held at the Medical College of Wisconsin together, and JPS watched a webcast of the Office for Human Research Protections' meeting.

3. The term "cultural performances" was introduced by anthropologist M. Singer in his article "The Cultural Pattern of Indian Civilization" (1955). It was invoked and cited by anthropologist Clifford Geertz in his essay "Religion As a Cultural System" (Geertz 1973: 113).

4. Shana Alexander, who was the first female staff writer employed by *Life*, died of cancer in June 2005, at age 79. Her obituaries, which appeared in hundreds of papers worldwide, paid tribute to her as a "pioneering journalist" who reported on many of the major news stories of her time, as the author of nonfiction books, and as a "passionate debater" who gained fame in the late 1970s for her "Point-Counterpoint" appearances opposite James Kilpatrick on CBS's *60 Minutes*. (See, for example, M. Fox, "Shana Alexander, 79, Dies; Passionate Debater on TV," *New York Times*, June 25, 2005: A16; Associated Press, "Pioneering Journalist Shana Alexander Dies: Commentator Known for Her Articles, Appearances on 60 Minutes," June 24, 2005, www.msnbc.msn.com/id/8340821).

5. In his remarks at the end of the meeting's opening session, Jonsen noted that "some of the pioneers regret that they could not be present: James Gustafson, Richard McCormick, Sissela Bok, Willard Gaylin, William Curran, Leon Kass, [and] Stephen Toulmin."

6. The four physicians were Eric Cassell, Michael Kaback, Arno Motulsky, and Fred Rosner. The Protestant theologian was Thomas McCormick, a senior lecturer in medical history and ethics, and director of counseling at the University of Washington. Kevin O'Rourke, director of the Center for Health Care Ethics at St. Louis University Medical Center, was the Dominican priest.

7. "In the early days of bioethics," Daniel Callahan has written, "there was an interesting debate between the views of Joseph Fletcher—who never said no…[to] morally controverted scientific research…and those of Paul Ramsey—who usually said no and who argued that the capacity to do so was a test of moral seriousness" (Callahan 1996: 3).

8. A. Jonsen, Letter to "The Birth of Bioethics" conference faculty, November 9, 1992. An abridged selection of the talks was published as a special supplement to *The Hastings Center Report* (Jonsen 1993), and a filmed oral history record was made available for purchase, in the form of a single videotape of "highlights" consisting of excerpts from the conference, and an archival set of 14 videotapes containing the entire program. In addition, the speakers' manuscripts and transcripts of the conference discussions served as one of many sources of data for Jonsen's book, *The Birth of Bioethics*, published six years later (Jonsen 1998).

9. With a touch of irony, Daniel Callahan used the term "our crowd" to refer to the bioethics community in his introductory piece to the issue of *The Hastings Center Report* published in his honor upon his retirement (Callahan 1996).

10. The *Belmont Report* was named for Belmont House, a conference center in the Maryland countryside then owned by the Smithsonian Institution, where members of the National Commission, staff, and consultants held a 4-day retreat in February 1976 to work on the report. The Office for Human Research Protections (OHRP) has created a Belmont Archive Web site, which includes a *Belmont Report* educational

video, a history of the report and the federal regulations, and oral history interviews with members, staff, and consultants of the National Commission: see www.hhs gov/ohrp/belmontArchive.

11. Informal discussion by JPS and Carla Messikomer with James Childress, November 6, 1999, about the Belmont Revisited Conference and its planning process.

12. JPS and our study's senior research associate, sociologist Carla M. Messikomer, were granted permission to attend the conference as observers. The materials about the meeting used in this chapter include their field notes and draft papers and outlines by the speakers that were distributed to attendees, and the published papers (Childress, Meslin, and Shapiro 2005).

13. The book deriving from the conference contained many, but not all, of the edited versions of the papers presented at the conference. Three of the conference papers that we discuss, which were not in *Belmont Revisited*, were those by Gary Ellis, Charles McCarthy, and LeRoy Walters. Additionally, the book did not include the invited commentaries by James Childress, Jonathan Moreno, and Harold Vanderpool, and the discussion sessions held during the conference, portions of which we also quote from and discuss.

14. By the time that the book based on the "Belmont Revisited" conference was published, Beauchamp's and Jonsen's views about the dynamics of principlism and casuistry, and the part that they played in *Belmont* seem to have been reconciled, compared with their conference presentations and discussion. "The National Commission's deliberations and conclusions," Beauchamp wrote in this regard, "are best understood in terms of reasoning in which principles are interpreted and specified by the force of examples and counterexamples that emerge from experience with cases. It is doubtful that Jonsen ever intended to deny this understanding of principles and their roles, despite the widely held view that casuistry dispenses with principles. Jonsen has said that 'casuistic analysis does not deny the relevance of principle and theory'".... [He] goes on to point out that casuistry is 'complementary to principles' and that 'casuistry is not an alternative to principles: No sound casuistry can dispense with principles'" (Beauchamp 2005: 19–20; Jonsen 2005).

15. We cannot resist commenting here on the fact that Emanuel's and Weijer's typology of different kinds of communities, their characteristics, and their moral relevance in biomedical research seems to have been drawn up with virtually no reference to the abundant social science literature on community. In our view, this is a prime example of what philosopher David Benatar has called the "problem of 'disciplinary slip'" that besets the pluridisciplinary field of bioethics—that is, "slip[ping] from working in one's own discipline, in which one is trained, to working in another, in which one is not" (Benatar D 2006: 17). From our perspective, whatever philosophical merits Emmanuel's and Weijer's position might have is compromised by what appears to be their superficial understanding of concepts such as culture, social institutions, social organizations, political authority, and social communication.

16. Given Levine's long-standing conviction about the importance of eliminating what he has viewed as the misleading distinction between "therapeutic" and "nontherapeutic" research, and the efforts he had undertaken with the Commission, and subsequently, to achieve this goal (see, for example, Levine 1986), it was not surprising that he also used this occasion to revisit the issue. The National Commission, he pointed out in his paper had "explicitly repudiated the distinction between therapeutic and nontherapeutic research," replacing it with "a much more rational system." And yet, he commented ruefully, this "illogical" and "distorting" distinction still lingers on.

17. In addition to the "*Belmont* Revisited" papers that we have identified and discussed in the text of this essay, those presented at the conference also included: an account by physician Eric Cassell of how the principles have been applied to clinical medicine; a philosophical/historical commentary on *Belmont* and "the deprofessionalization of medical ethics" by historian Robert Baker; an examination of the *Belmont* principles "through a feminist lens" by philosopher Susan Sherwin, with special attention to issues of "social justice" that affect "oppressed groups"; and a sociological interpretation of principlism from the perspective of Max Weber's ideas about the development of "formal rationality," by sociologist John Evans.

18. Further reflection is needed on why the *Belmont Report* continues to be treated as a relatively immutable document that can be "revisited," but not revised. This is especially puzzling when it is compared, for example, with the Nuremberg Code. Although the Code has greater historic stature and symbolic power in the realm of the ethics and regulation of experimentation with human subjects than *Belmont*, it has not impeded the development and promulgation of other international documents such as the Declaration of Helsinki.

19. The symposium could be seen live on a Web cast, and videotapes of the meeting were later made available for purchase.

20. The edited version of OHRP's 25th anniversary program can be viewed with a free RealPlayer download on the Belmont Archive Web site (www.hhs.gov/ohrp/belmont/Archive). The description of this occasion on the Web site hails the *Report* as "a milestone in Federal responsibility, leadership and commitment"—a statement that seems to pay greater tribute to the government bodies that established the National Commission, mandated the writing of what became the *Report*, and used it as a foundation for instituting federal regulations for the protection of human subjects, than to the *Report* itself, or its drafters.

21. Kennedy's remarks were written in the form of a letter addressed to the Secretary of the Department of Health and Human Services, which was read to the assemblage by the interim director of OHRP. Rogers, who was present at the ceremony, delivered his comments in person.

22. We are not unaware of the fact that despite the repeated testimonial statements about the outstanding and fruitful collaborative relations between bioethicists that were repeatedly made at the conferences and commemorations that we reviewed, both institutional and interpersonal rivalry exists in the field, and controversy, as well—including controversy about the status of principles in bioethical thought, and so-called "principlism." In chapter 11, we will discuss in detail how and why the relative civility that previously existed in bioethical debate has been seriously disrupted in recent years by the "culture wars" occurring inside as well as outside the field.

SOCIETY, CULTURE, AND BIOETHICS

6

Thinking Socially and Culturally in Bioethics

From the inception of American bioethics, and throughout its intellectual evolution, integrating social and cultural insights and facts, analysis and interpretation into the theoretical framework, the methodology, and the substantive knowledge base of the field has been consistently problematic. The reasons for this are not self-obvious or simple. Nor are the issues involved in thinking socially and culturally unique to bioethics, or solely attributable to its distinctive ethos and the institutional forms it has taken. These issues have roots in major concepts, conundrums, and leitmotifs of Western philosophical thought, in the intellectual tradition and value system of American society, in the historical context in which U.S. bioethics has developed, and in the continuous presence of bioethical topics, cases, and quandaries in the public domain. They are also related to some of the intellectual and cultural characteristics of American medicine, of Anglo-American analytic philosophy, and of present-day American social science.

Individualism and Autonomy

Perhaps the greatest deterrent to the incorporation of social and cultural analysis into the matrix of bioethics has been the primacy that the field has accorded to a conception of individualism and individual rights that emphasizes the values of individual autonomy and self-determination—what has come to be known in the terminology of bioethics as the principle of "respect for persons," as well as "respect for autonomy." This accentuated individualism has origins in what

Andrew Delbanco (1999) identifies as one of the "predominant ideas" around which American society and culture have been organized since the beginning of the country's history—a distinctively American conception of the self that has roots in the Protestant Christianity of the seventeenth- and eighteenth-century New England Puritans. In *Democracy in America* by French social philosopher Alexis de Tocqueville, based on his remarkably astute observations and penetrating conversations with Americans during his visit to the United States in the 1830s when the country was still a young nation, he coined the term "individualism" to express what he viewed as a striking "new idea" that was salient in American mores (de Tocqueville 1835). He admired this individualism, and what Ralph Waldo Emerson later celebrated as the spirit of "self-reliance" that underlay it. But de Tocqueville was also concerned about the "danger" that "each man forever thrown back on himself alone...shut up in the solitude of his own heart" might imperil the structure of voluntary association—the civil society—and thereby encourage the development of democratic despotism (Bellah, Madsen, and Sullivan et al. 1985). Paradoxically, some of the origins and consequences of this genre of individualism are social in nature.

The particular historical period in which the field of bioethics developed in the United States was "a time of social ferment and protest in American society, spearheaded by the civil rights and anti-war movements, and the beginning of a new women's movement...with their emphasis on individual rights and choice as fundamental bases of freedom, equality, and justice,... their anti-paternalism, and their distrust of authority" and "establishment" institutions (Messikomer, Fox, and Swazey 2001: 491). As our interviews with first- and second-generation bioethicists revealed, what was then the nascent field of bioethics attracted a sizeable number of persons who had been intensively engaged in these movements during their college, graduate school, and/or professional school years. They carried their militant individualism, antipaternalism, and antiauthority convictions with them into the new field, whose individualism-grounded values and rights language they helped to shape (see chapter 2).

Reflecting in part the legacy of the Nuremberg Code, promulgated by the judges presiding over the trial of the German physicians who conducted horrific medical experiments on concentration camp prisoners during World War II, the first set of issues that the new bioethics tackled concerned experimentation with human subjects (see chapter 1). Special attention was given to the conditions under which ethical human experimentation might take place, with particular emphasis on the moral necessity of obtaining the informed and voluntary consent of persons who participate in such research, both in order to protect them from coercion, abuse, and harm and, in the words of lawyer Paul A. Freund, to serve the "symbolic function [of] recalling the respect for individual integrity that should inform the quest for knowledge" (Freund 1970: xvi). The preoccupation of early bioethics with human experimentation, the rights of human subjects, and the ways in which those rights could be violated by medical researchers, quickly expanded into a more general ethical critique of how physicians related to and treated patients. "That's where the term [autonomy] got its original meaning," philosopher Ruth Macklin asserts. "It was the autonomy of the patient versus the paternalism of physicians...respect for the patient both in the research setting...and in the patient setting." What is more, she contends, in the first years of the 1970s, bioethicists wrote and spoke of autonomy "with regard to rights in the rights movement" (Macklin, Acadia Advisory Committee: see appendix). Robert Veatch, who, like Macklin, belongs to the first generation of American bioethicists, agrees with Macklin. "I think that the spin-off from the civil rights and the women's movement of the 1960s," he opines, "was an acute awareness that patients' rights were being abused":

It was sort of a crisis mentality.... We've got a first problem to clean up. Let's get rights of patients, informed consent, right of refusal.... There's so obviously an abuse taking place, let's fix it the way we're fixing the civil rights problems.... Then we'll go on to the tougher stuff.... If you view early bioethics as evolving from the anti-war movement and the civil rights movement,...the rights language got converted into patients' rights.... The very earliest aspect of bioethics took on what seemed to be the first major offense of medicine at the time, which [was] its incredible paternalism. And that means we latched onto the principle of autonomy, and we affirmed the right of individual patients to make choices in the most individualistic sense. (Veatch, interview, 1999: see appendix; Veatch, Acadia Advisory Committee: see appendix)[1]

The same impetus that by the end of the 1960s helped to establish "a recognized right not to take part in medical research," Daniel Callahan has written, contributed to the development of "a corresponding right to terminate medical treatment" in the 1970s, especially in the case of decision making about foregoing or stopping the life-sustaining treatment of terminally ill patients (Callahan 2000: 40). Something akin to a patient's rights movement arose in the United States during the 1970s, which focused on "what [Western] philosophers sometimes call liberty rights: the right to choose to conduct one's life in one's own way provided it does not infringe on the right of others" (Veatch 1981: 48). The ethical stance of the movement was articulated in *A Patient's Bill of Rights*, issued by the American Hospital Association in 1973. Not only was the fervid autonomy-centered ethos of bioethics compatible with such a "liberty rights" outlook; the dawning influence of bioethics on the American scene helped to reinforce it.

Looking back at this time from the perspective of one of the founders of U.S. bioethics, and the cofounder of the first American bioethics institute—the Hastings Center—Daniel Callahan has affirmed:

The drive for autonomy that was the major moral mark of the 1960s and 1970s in medical ethics was indispensable. It brought patients into a full partnership with physicians in their medical care. There can be no return to those good old days that understood doctors to be good old boys who could work out moral problems among themselves in the locker room. (Callahan 1984: 42)

At the daylong meeting we held with the advisory group for our study in September 2000, we had a chance to discuss with several of the Hastings Center's first staff members what we viewed as the difficulty of reconciling this "drive for autonomy" with paying serious attention to the influence of social and cultural factors on the context in which medical ethical questions occur, and how they are defined and experienced, or to large-scale societal problems like access to health care and the just allocation of scarce resources. Our advisors maintained that neither at the inception of bioethics, nor in the later phases of its development, was "the focus on autonomy…meant to be the autonomy of the individual versus the community" (Macklin), and that from the beginning, the participants in bioethics understood that ethics was not an "abstract" entity, but that it was "rooted in history and culture" (Caplan). Arthur Caplan held that "cultural sensitivity may have…been present at Hastings early, but it has not been part of the mainstream of American bioethics." While participants in the meeting conceded, in Caplan's words, that there had "definitely been an absence of health policy and meta-policy analysis in a lot of bioethics discussion and teaching for a long time," they cautioned that this should not be "mixed up with an indifference to the social and cultural." And they politely but firmly suggested that perhaps we were "underestimating…the social character of bioethics"—diplomatically attributing our mistaken appraisal to the informants we had interviewed for our research who might be "missing a lot…and therefore not giving [us] the signals [we] should be getting," rather than to a deficiency in our own "observational skills" (Veatch).

The inclination of these early bioethicists to play down "individual versus community" tensions in bioethics that result from the paramountcy accorded to autonomy is thrown into question by a recurrent theme of self-criticism that has appeared in the bioethical literature from the mid-1980s to the present. Admonitory statements about the overweening emphasis that some principlist approaches place on "rights talk" and "the dominance of one particular right: autonomy" (Childress 1994: 76; see also Childress 1990) have been repeatedly made by premier bioethical thinkers and spokespersons for the field, who have warned against the danger of autonomy becoming a "moral obsession" rather than a "moral good" (Callahan 1984). Using provocative phrases like "autonomy's temporary triumph" (Veatch 1984: 38–40), "autonomy unbounded," and "self-determination run amok" (Callahan 1992: 55), they have "argued sharply against overextending and overweighing the principle of respect for autonomy in relation to other general moral considerations" (Childress 1994: 76)—particularly those social values that involve moral "obligation to the human community—past, present, and future" (Morison 1984: 43, 48):

But is a society based upon an individualistic search for autonomy, and a cherishing of moral independence, a good community? There is little to suggest that it is. By flying in the face of those goods that have constituted valid communities, we have left nothing with which to build bonds between and among people. Community requires constraints, limits, and taboos, just as it requires shared ideals, common dreams, and a vision of self that is part of a wide collectivity. By bringing into the medical relationship the most sterile and straitened notions of an autonomous self, ethics has borrowed not from the richest portion of the tradition but from the thinnest.... (Callahan 1984: 42)

More recently, while appreciatively acknowledging the "enormous role that conceptions of 'rational autonomy' [presently] play" in bioethics, British philosopher Onora O'Neill has expressed the opinion that there is a "need to understand what is awry in the passion for autonomy and complacency about the rights culture that dominate contemporary bioethics...if we are to move to...robust arguments for alternative views" (O'Neill 2002b: 2335):

By themselves,...conceptions of individual autonomy cannot provide a sufficient and convincing starting point for bioethics, or even for medical ethics. They may encourage ethically questionable forms of individualism and self-expression and may heighten rather than reduce public mistrust in medicine, science and biotechnology.... Even when individual autonomy is coupled with other ethical standards, problems persist. Most often it is combined with a Millian principle of avoiding harm. This is unsatisfactory. If we assume a full Utilitarian account of maximizing happiness, we subordinate and marginalize individual autonomy itself; if we do not, the line between harmful and non-harmful action and policies will often be blurred. The supposed triumph of individual autonomy over other principles in bioethics is, I conclude, an unsustainable illusion. (O'Neill 2002a: 73)

Universalism, Particularism, and Relativism

A second major obstacle to integrating a social and cultural perspective into bioethical thought is associated with the way that the field deals with what both philosophers and social scientists refer to as the concepts of "universalism" and "particularism," the value-orientations that they embody, and the tensions that exist between them.[2] "The central dilemma," Daniel Callahan has stated, is that "[an] overriding effort to devise ethical principles neglects the complexity of individual moral lives and social circumstances, while an indiscriminate immersion in their particularity allows no room for ethical distinctions and prudential judgments" (Callahan 1999b: 290).

The issues surrounding universalism and particularism intersect with those of "contextuality"—that is, the role that social, cultural, and historical factors and "locations" play in shaping values, beliefs, and commitments, conceptions of self and of relationships to others and, more generally, what are regarded and espoused as moral precepts and ethical behavior. Callahan has taken the position that "[n]o decisive choice should be made between universalism and particularism. Each will have its place in different situations and each will ordinarily have to be influenced and informed by the other" (Callahan 2000: 31). For him, this also entails "the balancing of universality and contextuality" (Callahan 2003a: 497). The Dutch physician and philosopher Henk ten Have has expressed his convictions about the inextricable relationship between universalism and particularism, in more European-flavored philosophical language:

> The *universal* human condition of existence as a communal-cultural being can only be realized in *particular* ways; the communitarian self is constituted by particular cultural characteristics. A richer medical ethics can result from taking seriously the basic idea of moral community, and concomitantly, the various narratives about the particularities of people as communal beings. (ten Have and Gordijn 2001: 79; authors' italics)

The contrasting tendency of American bioethical thought has been to dichotomize and polarize the notions of universalism and particularism, and even to view them as antagonistic antitheses. As one of the field's senior figures noted, this is one primary manifestation of the field's propensity to get "trapped in binaries" that are difficult to reconcile (Gustafson, interview, 1999: see appendix). Within this framework, the overall skew of the field is tipped in the direction of an intellectual and moral preference for universalism, in the form of transcendent principles that "rise above" the particularities of historical circumstances and tradition, and of social and cultural context and locale.

U. S. bioethicists' penchant for universalism is rooted in the overarching conceptual framework within which American bioethics has developed. Its regnant paradigm was brought into the field and made prominent within it by philosophers, who rapidly became the most intellectually influential subgroup of bioethicists. Many of them believed that there could be no serious ethics that did not aspire to identify and articulate certain universalistic principles. Most of these philosophers were trained in the Anglo-American tradition of analytic philosophy—the dominant approach of the major American philosophy departments—with its emphasis on theory, methodology, and technique, and its utilitarian, neo-Kantian, and "contractarian" outlooks. They "arrived on the bioethics scene" with "the turn toward normative ethics in their field, and the drive to ground ethics in good theory" that characterized American academic philosophy in the 1960s and 1970s (Callahan 2000: 40). The kind of theory that they sought was a perspective that would enable them to deliberate moral questions, decisions, and actions logically, rationally, and objectively, with rigor, and in a language of moral discourse that would cogently and forcefully express a universal motivating ideal. The universal precepts that they aspired to identify and articulate were what philosophers Tom L. Beauchamp and James F. Childress, in the fifth edition of their *Principles of Biomedical Ethics*, describe as "the set of norms that all morally serious persons share as *the common morality*." "The common morality binds all persons in all places," they state, and "no norms are more basic in the moral life" (Beauchamp and Childress 2001: 3; authors' italics).[3]

Robert Veatch, who considers the emergence of the concept of "common morality" to be "[o]ne of the most exciting and important developments in recent ethical theory—especially bioethical theory," identifies its "core idea" as the claim that "there is some primitive, pretheoretical insight that is shared by all normal, morally serious humans...in all places and cultures" regarding moral requiredness. They "intuit," "see," "or in some other way know that some behaviors are...generally wrong" (most particularly, "lying, stealing, breaking promises, killing a human being, and the like"); that other behaviors are generally right; that some "character traits [virtues] are generally praiseworthy, others [vices] blameworthy" (Veatch 2003: 189–191).[4]

In an interview-conversation with us, Tom Beauchamp, who is perhaps the strongest articulator, proponent, and defender of the idea of "the common morality" among philosopher-bioethicists, vehemently insisted that such standards are "intrinsic to morality itself":

Although very abstract,... [they] are normative, and you can recognize when they are being violated. And when they are being violated, it is unethical conduct, and it is not unethical conduct because this, that, or the other society says it is, or this, that, or the other person says it is. It is unethical conduct because it is unethical conduct by anybody, anywhere, at any time.... [[I]t is not necessarily recognized by those persons as being unethical conduct. They may think it is perfectly ethical conduct; that is a separate question. But it is unethical conduct.... I don't think it is a matter of my ethics or American ethics.... I don't think it is a culturally driven bioethics. It is the boundaries of ethics—the boundaries of morality is what I prefer to think of it as being. And if you reach over those boundaries, then you violate one of these principles and, therefore, you engage in immoral conduct or are unethical. And I think *everybody* knows that who is morally serious. (Beauchamp, interview, 2000: see appendix)

Three years after our conversation with him, with increased ardor and greater stringency, Beauchamp developed these ideas and convictions more formally and fully in a special issue of the *Kennedy Institute of Ethics Journal* concerning the thematic question: "Is There a Common Morality?" "I define the 'common morality,'" Beauchamp wrote, "as the set of norms shared by all persons committed to the objectives of morality. The objectives of morality, I will argue, are those of promoting human flourishing by counteracting conditions that cause the quality of people's lives to worsen":

The common morality is not merely a morality that differs from other moralities. It is applicable to all people in all places, and all human conduct is rightly judged by its standards. Virtually all people in all cultures grow up with an understanding of the basic demands that morality makes upon everyone....

I have defined the common morality in terms of the set of norms shared by all persons committed to the objectives of morality.... I have claimed that amoral people, immoral people, and people driven by ideologies that override moral obligations are not pursuing the objectives of morality, whatever else they may be pursuing....

I am not assuming that all persons in all societies do in fact accept the norms of the common morality.... As noted previously, many amoral, immoral, and selectively moral persons do not embrace various demands of the common morality. Some persons are morally weak, others morally depraved; morality can be misunderstood, rejected, or overridden by other values....

[It] is preposterous to hold that a customary set of norms or a consensus set of norms is justified by the fact of custom or consensus. More preposterous still is the idea that norms qualify for inclusion in the common morality because they are rooted in custom or consensus. The proposition that moral justification derives from custom or consensus is a moral travesty. Any given society's customary or consensus position may be a distorted outlook that functions to block awareness of common morality requirements. Some societies are in the influential grip of leaders who promote religious zealotries or political ideologies that depart profoundly from the common morality. Such persons may be deeply committed to their particular outlook...but these individuals should not be said to be morally committed merely because they are committed to a supremely valued point of view. (Beauchamp 2003: 260, 263, 265, 266)

Beauchamp proposes that his "claim that all persons committed to morality and all well functioning societies adhere to the general standards of action" that he enumerates can, and should be, "empirically tested" (Beauchamp 2003: 263). He also recognizes that "the one universal common morality" is "not necessarily where [it] ought to be," but may stand "in need of improvement" to bring it closer to what it "universally ought to be" (Beauchamp 2003: 272). Nonetheless, he is uncompromising when he avers that "[a] pluralist who repudiates universalist norms is a relativist"—using the term "relativist" in a morally disparaging way (Beauchamp 2003: 262). A theory of common morality that is cross-culturally relative, he insists, and thereby "deprived of its capacity to criticize existing groups or communities whose viewpoints are morally deficient would be an ineffectual theory" (Beauchamp 2003: 272). And in his conversation with us, he declared that what makes him a "universalist" is that he believes that "everything is lost if you are not. Then slavery becomes justifiable, and everything becomes justifiable, whether you try to do it through relativism, or try to do it through something else, that is what is going to happen" (Beauchamp, interview, 2000: see appendix).[5]

A somewhat more nuanced, but no less forceful stance "against relativism" has been taken by Ruth Macklin. Talking with us about her book-length treatment of "cultural diversity and the search for ethical universals in medicine," that she entitled *Against Relativism*, Macklin commented that "I certainly try...to reject the notion of moral absolutes, and as any philosopher would do, you have to make a lot of distinctions (Macklin, interview, 1999: see appendix). She thus attempts to eschew the most extreme positions that have been taken regarding the "long-standing debate [that] surrounds the question whether ethics is relative to time and place":

One side argues that there is no obvious source of universal morality and that ethical rightness and wrongness are products of their cultural and historical setting. Opponents claim that even if a universal set of ethical norms has not yet been articulated or agreed upon, ethical relativism is a pernicious doctrine that must be rejected. The first group replies that the search for universal ethical precepts is a quest for the Holy Grail. The second group responds with the telling charge: If ethics were relative to time, place, and culture, then what the Nazis did was "right" for them, and there is no basis for moral criticism by anyone outside the Nazi society. (Macklin 1999: 4)

Macklin finds a "kernel of truth" in both sides of what she calls this "unsophi ticated version of the debate" (Macklin 1999: 4). Nevertheless, as the title that she chose for her book indicates, the central thrust of her work is based on the supposition that "even if we grant that cultural relativity is an accurate description of the world's diversity," these facts do not "compel the conclusion that what is right or wrong can be determined only by the beliefs and practices within a particular culture or subculture" (Macklin 1999: 4). Quite to the contrary, she writes, "there are universal standards that are (or ought to be) binding on cultural groups or nations despite their ignorance or rejection of those standards." Paramount among these are "human rights," that are "by definition rights that belong to all people, wherever they may dwell and whatever may be the political system or the cultural traditions of their country or region of the world" (Macklin 1999: 243). However, she insists, "[t]o acknowledge the existence of universal ethical principles is not a commitment to moral absolutism. Ethical principles always require interpretation when they are applied to particular social institutions, such as a health care system or the practice of medicine. In the particulars, there is ample room to tolerate cultural diversity" (Macklin 1999: 273–274). In her opinion, this kind of "tolerance" and "flexibility" that avoids "mindless rigidity" does not constitute "a pernicious form of ethical relativism."

And yet, though Macklin acknowledges that in some instances it may be permissible, even appropriate, to take cultural differences into account in applying ethical standards, when she refers to such cases, she describes the "degree of ethical relativism" that is "undeniably present" in them as involving "lower," "less-than-ideal" versions of universal standards (Macklin 1999: 264). In the end, in the final chapter of her book, she ties the idea of "moral progress," and judgment about whether it "exists or has taken place," to what she regards as the ethical universals of "humaneness" and "humanity" that are embedded in the concept of "human rights" (Macklin 1999: 252). And she resoundingly asserts that "our social institutions would still be in the dark ages if we had not progressed to a stage where human rights are recognized and upheld." "Once we uphold and promote human rights," she concludes, "we have taken a stance against relativism" (Mackin 1999: 274).

In her later book, *Double Standards in Medical Research in Developing Countries*, Macklin explores "the ethical controversies [surrounding] the design and conduct of international medical research sponsored by industrialized countries or industry, and carried out in developing countries" (Macklin 2004a: i). In this context, too, she expresses the same vehement espousal of universal ethical standards, while recognizing and deploring the political, economic, and human rights conditions that may deter their full realization:

The purpose of biomedical research is to contribute to scientific knowledge that can be used to provide better clinical care and introduce better public health measures for all people, not just the inhabitants of wealthy countries or the wealthy inhabitants of poor countries. In the service of that goal, the conduct of research should conform to universal ethical principles governing research, despite the political factors that prevent a universal, harmonized set of ethical guidelines. It is ludicrous to hold that there are Western ethical imperatives that apply only to the West, African ethical imperatives that apply only to Africa, and Asian ethical principles that apply only to that part of the world. (Macklin 2004a: 60)

For Macklin, then, making nonuniversalistic concessions to "differences" incurs the grave ethical risk of "accept[ing] and even endors[ing] double standards" (Macklin 2004a: 260).

Reflecting on the significance that a number of prominent American bioethicists attach to their conception of ethical universalism, and the ardor with which they do so, summoned up for us two statements about the interrelationships that can exist between cultural pluralism and universalism, one by UNESCO, and the other by the former president of the Czech Republic, Václav Havel. During the 31st meeting of its General Conference in 2001, UNESCO's 185 member states unanimously adopted what it termed a "Universal Declaration on Cultural Diversity." Approved "in the wake of the events of 11 September 2001," the Declaration was described as "the founding act of a new ethic being promoted by UNESCO at the dawn of the 21st century." This declaration raised the notion of cultural diversity to the level of a universal principle about "the 'common heritage' of humanity, as necessary for humankind as biodiversity is for nature," and made "its defence an ethical imperative indissociable from respect for the dignity of the individual" (UNESCO 2002). There are relatively few signs as yet that the kind of conceptual and moral reconciliation between universalism and particularism, and between individual rights and social and cultural rights that this declaration articulates has significantly influenced the outlook of what is termed international bioethics.

In the address he made when he was awarded the Liberty Medal at Independence Hall in Philadelphia on July 4, 1994, Havel spoke eloquently and passionately about the importance of identifying, affirming, and implementing "the values or basic moral imperatives [that]…the various spheres of civilization, culture, nations, or continents…have in common," and powerfully expressed his conviction that "the central political task…of the century is the creation of a new model of coexistence among the various cultures, peoples, races and religious spheres, within a single interconnected civilization," with an "awareness [that] endows us with the capacity for self-transcendence" (Havel 1994). What we find equally striking about Havel's invocation of universalism is that, in contrast to the outlook that prevails in U.S. bioethics, he does not profess to know precisely and definitively what these common and imperative moral values are. He insists that the "new model of coexistence" must enable us to be "global and at the same time multicultural"—that is, both universalistic and particularistic—and he regards the process of seeking and finding these values, achieving consensus about them, and ensuring their fulfillment to be as complex as it is urgent.

There are a few thinkers in the field of bioethics, such as physician and philosopher H. Tristam Englehardt Jr. who, like Havel, are inclined to use the term "global" to refer to the quest for a universally shared and binding morality, while acknowledging and respecting the importance of cultural pluralism and moral diversity. However, Engelhardt is more skeptical than Havel about whether we can find "procedures" or "strategies" for reconciling the "global" and the "particular" in a way, as he puts it, that will "[a]t the very least," enable us "to live together as moral strangers" (Engelhardt 2006: 17).[6]

Some Implications of Bioethics' Conception of Individualism and Universalism

The rights-oriented notion of rational, autonomous individualism that is pivotal in the framework of bioethical thought has tended to bend it away from values that give weight to responsibilities, duties, and obligations, to human dependency and interdependency, to trust, to a self-surpassing sense of solidarity with known and unknown persons, to community and society, and to qualities of the heart like sympathy, caring, and compassion—especially in response to the suffering of others (R. C. Fox 1994: 53; R. C. Fox 1999: 9). Nor is this form of individualism compatible with the kind of "ethical responsibility across the generations" precept that is core to the cultural traditions of many Asian, South Asian, African, and Middle Eastern societies. In Japan, for example, as historian William LaFleur points out, such an "intergenerational ethic" that "posit[s] ethical responsibility both backwards and forwards in time—to benefit progeny by revering ancestry," is "articulated within Confucianism, Buddhism, and Shinto" (LaFleur 2004).

Bioethics' conception of ethical universality has also inclined the field to devalue social and cultural differences both by minimizing their importance, and by highlighting the association between such differences and health-related cultural beliefs and practices that bioethicists consider morally problematic, or wrong. In this latter regard, American bioethicists have paid considerable attention to practices that they view as emanations of the oppression and discrimination to which women are subject in many "foreign," traditional societies. Among these practices are the ritual of female genital cutting (circumcision) performed in certain countries on the African continent, which they portray as an especially abominable custom that "mutilates" women; the beating of a wife by her husband if she "disobeys" him, which occurs in many households in southern Iraq; and restrictions on women's access to health care in a fundamentalist Islamic regime such as that of the Taliban in Afghanistan. "Bioethics does not well serve society simply by promoting respect for other cultures," Callahan has written. If it "is to be of any value at all, that value will come from its effort to help devise responsible ways of making justifiable moral judgments...[about] which practices and values should be accepted and affirmed, which simply tolerated, and which rejected" (Callahan 2000: 44).

It appears to us that within the context of the rather limited extent to which U.S. bioethics has taken social and cultural diversity seriously into account, it has disproportionately focused on "practices and values" in other societies that it judges to be "morally unacceptable." "As an anthropologist [working in bioethics]," Patricia Marshall reflected, "I'm often put in a position where there is an implicit challenge regarding universalism and relativism.... [My being asked] 'what do you think about female circumcision or genital mutilation?'... is a classic example. It's sensationalized and it's almost a caricature of the issues. It's a way to try to make something complex into something simple" (Marshall, interview, 2000: see appendix). This type of ethical challenge partly reflects what Marshall and her colleague, Barbara A. Koenig, characterize as "a fear of unbridled relativism" (Marshall and Koenig 2004b), which in turn has contributed to the recurrent reference in the bioethical literature to what is viewed as the most horrendous example of where suspending judgment about societal and cultural differences could lead— to the unspeakable moral implications of remaining silent, neutral, or tolerant in the face of the commission of such evil as the Nazi medical war crimes.

Within the sphere of American society, the downplaying of cultural differences to which U.S. bioethicists have been prone has assumed a significant part in the conspicuous degree to which they have been inclined to overlook the exceptional cultural diversity and pluralism of the United States—the very country that most of them inhabit. Among philosophers who are actively engaged in bioethics, Leigh Turner (whose faculty appointment is at McGill University in Canada) is one of the few who has dealt explicitly in his writings with the importance of recognizing "the plural moral traditions that are found in multicultural, multiethnic, multifaith societies such as the United States and Canada," whose citizenry is composed of successive waves of immigrants from all over the world. He gives credence to the existence of a shared "civic culture" or "civic religion" in the United States. Nevertheless, he continues, within this country, and also in Canada, "there are, at present, a host of debates [taking place] concerning...the boundaries of tolerance and intolerance, assimilation and respect for diversity." He goes on to argue that "whatever common morality exists in contemporary American society is an achieved morality, one built and articulated over time through public education; civic strife; the gradual elaboration of policies, codes, and laws; and processes of acculturation for those unfamiliar with its lineaments...[r]ather than being found in the moral beacon of a transhistorical, transcultural, 'common moral sense.'" Furthermore, he continues, "there exist in the U.S. both regions of shared understanding and domains of radical disagreement...zones of consensus and zones of conflict.... Platitudes about common moral intuitions merely obscure the variable visions of moral life to be found in contemporary North America," he concludes (Turner 2003: 192, 209–211, 216).

By and large, it is only occasionally that bioethicists examine or refer to the substantial historical, sociological, and anthropological literature on ethnic, religious, social class, occupational, and other subcultures in American society, which is pertinent to the country's multiculturalism, and has potential bearing on issues surrounding bioethically relevant beliefs and practices in specific American social settings. One exception to this patterned inattention, however, are the implications of Navajo Native American beliefs about the cosmic power of thoughts and words for how it is appropriate to conduct discussions about medical treatment or non-treatment, the risks that they entail, the expected course of a patient's condition, and the prognosis about its outcome in that cultural milieu. There is one article in particular that is cited by both philosophers and social scientists who work in the area of bioethics: "Western Bioethics on the Navajo Reservation: Benefit or Harm?" (Carrese and Rhodes 1995). On the basis of the focused ethnographic inquiry that they carried out on a Navajo Indian reservation in Arizona, the authors conclude that "speaking in a negative way" to Navajo persons about their illness, the hazards it entails, or about any intimations of death can be harmful to them, because of their belief that this can bring to pass the eventualities to which the words, and the thoughts from which they emanate refer. Interestingly, Ruth Macklin, who is one of the philosopher-bioethicists who take the findings reported in this article seriously into consideration, has responded to it by saying that she thinks there is an ethical "solution" to this situation:

The principle of beneficence supports the withholding of information about risks of treat-ment from Navajos who adhere to the traditional belief system, but so, too, does the prin-ciple of respect for autonomy. Navajos holding traditional beliefs can act autonomously only when they are not thinking in a negative way, so physicians who withhold bad news are not being paternalistic in the usual sense (acting in what *they* believe is in the patient's best interest). Instead, they are acting in what the Navajo patients themselves believe is in their own best interest, and that shows respect for autonomy. (Macklin 1999: 264; author's italics)

Heeding "the call for cultural awareness and sensitivity" in this way, she "admits," involves "a degree of ethical relativism," but she regards it as accept-able because "it is still consistent with adherence to" what she steadfastly defines as "more fundamental ethical principles"—namely, autonomy and beneficence (Macklin 1999: 264).[7] While granting that the limited degree of ethical relativ-ism that Carrese and Rhodes describe can be justified, Macklin firmly cautions that universal ethical principles should not, in all cases, give way to the beliefs and practices of differing cultural groups in this country:

The multicultural composition of the United States can pose problems for physicians and patients who come from diverse backgrounds. Although respect for cultural diversity man-dates tolerance of the beliefs and practices of others, in some situations excessive tolerance can produce harms to patients. Careful analysis is needed to determine which values are culturally relative and which rest on underlying universal ethical principles. A conception of justice as equality challenges the notion that it is always necessary to respect all the beliefs and practices of every cultural group. (Macklin 1998: 1)

U. S. bioethicists' moral preference for universalism, their inclination to distrust particularism, and their aversion to relativism have also contributed to the difficulties that they have had in recognizing and acknowledging the ways in which their approach to ethics and their mode of reasoning about moral questions have been influenced by Western, and specifically American, culture patterns. As Henk ten Have wrote in an essay entitled "Principlism. A Western European Appraisal," "the dominant conception of bioethics has been developed within a particular cultural context":

> The fundamental ethos of applied bioethics, its analytical framework, methodology, and language, its concerns and emphases, and its very institutionalization have been shaped by beliefs, values, and modes of thinking grounded in specific social and cultural traditions.... The literature, however, only rarely attends to or reflects upon the sociocultural value system within and through which it operates. Scholars usually assume that its principles, theories, and moral views are transcultural. (ten Have 1994: 106)

In effect, American bioethics has shown a tendency toward what French sociologist Pierre Bourdieu has termed "the imperialism of the universal"—"universalizing its own...particular characteristics by tacitly establishing them in a universal model" (Bourdieu 2001: 3). There are elements of paradox and irony in the way that particularistic Western cultural assumptions have contributed to the importance that bioethics attaches to universalism.

Bioethics has taken a certain position with regard to some of the most important dilemma- and tension-ridden issues with which Western philosophy and its major thinkers have continually grappled. Isaiah Berlin, for example, dealt with these matters within the framework of what he termed "the difficult question of 'human nature.'" The belief in "the idea that all men at all times in all places are endowed with actual or potential knowledge of universal, timeless, unalterable truths," he reflected, "form[s] the heart of central European tradition, from Plato and the Stoics through the Middle Ages, and perhaps the Enlightenment as well—to our own day, indeed." However, he went on to say, Vico and Marx challenged this belief with their contention that "what is called human nature varies and differs from culture to culture, or even within cultures." In Berlin's view, Vico and Marx were "right." "[H]uman beings differ," he stated; "their understanding of the world differs; and some kind of historical or anthropological explanation of why such differences arise is in principle possible, though that explanation itself may to some degree reflect the particular concepts and categories of the particular culture to which these students of their subject belong." Furthermore, Berlin asserted, "I do not think this leads to relativism of any kind." For, he explained, although he did not believe that there is a "fixed human nature," he did believe that there is "a common human nature": that there is enough in common between all the individuals, groups, societies, and cultures continually "going through various modifications"—"certain basic needs" that they share—to make possible the sort of communication between them on which "all thought,...feeling, imagination, [and] action" depend (Berlin 2004: 26).

Berlin's conception of "value pluralism" did not embrace what he regarded as another "fundamental in the Western intellectual tradition"—namely, that "all genuine human values must be combinable in a harmonious whole," and that where such conflicts occur, "there is a single right answer that all reasonable people are bound to accept." Rather, he advanced "as a universal truth" the view that "conflicts of values are real and inescapable, with some of them having no satisfactory solution" (J. Gray 2006: 20).

The polymath philosopher-social scientist Ernest Gellner has described these universalism/particularism issues as emanating from two "distinctive visions of the nature of man...[of] what human beings are really like and what they "ought to be like." On the one hand, he wrote, there is the "atomic-universalist-individualist vision," identified with empiricism, rationalism, and with *Gesellschaft*. On the other, there is the holistic, "organic," "communal-cultural vision," that stresses community connectedness, particularism, participation in a distinctive culture, and *Gemeinschaft*. Gellner held that choosing between these two sets of alternatives is both erroneous and dangerous—intellectually, morally, and socially. He advocated combining elements of each of these polar outlooks, however difficult that might be. What he envisioned and recommended was a "third option," which would recognize that only "shared culture can...endow life with order and meaning." He acknowledged that "the notion of a culture-transcending truth," which he regarded as inseparable from cognitive (especially scientific) development and economic growth, "is not only a central part of our own [Western] culture, but that the possibility of transcending cultural limits" constitutes one of the most important facts about human life (Gellner 1968: in passim).[8]

As already indicated, American bioethics is tipped sharply toward the first pole that Gellner delineated—the one that emphasizes a rational, individualistic, and universalist perspective. Those bioethicists who are professionally well trained in philosophy are especially aware of the larger philosophical theories, viewpoints, and debates to which their orientation is a response. However, partly because bioethics is not strictly academic in nature, but is primarily a multidisciplinary, clinically applicable, and policy-relevant field with a public and a popular as well as a professional audience, the published literature and documents that it has generated do not usually contain extensive analyses and discussions that relate the issues it deliberates to this larger philosophical tradition. As a consequence, the sort of commitment that U.S. bioethics has made to the values of individualism and universalism, and the way that it is expressed in the literature and in public arenas, has the semblance of being as ideologically driven as intellectually impelled.

Daniel Callahan considers this value-set to be an integral part of the ideology of "liberal individualism" that has come to prevail in bioethics. "I call this an ideology rather than a moral theory," he explains, "because it is a set of essentially

political and social values brought into bioethics, not as formal theory but as a
vital background constellation of values. If it does not function as a moral theory
as philosophers have understood that concept, it is clearly present and pervasive
as a litmus test of the acceptability of certain ideas and ways of framing issues"
(Callahan 2003a: 498).

Principlism

The predominant theoretical and methodological framework within which the
autonomous individualism and the nonparticularist universalism of American bioethical thought has been solidified is "principlism"—"the use of moral principles
to address issues and resolve case quandaries" (DuBose, Hamel, and O'Connell
1994: 1). While there have been a number of differing versions of principlism (see,
e.g., Engelhardt 1986; Veatch 1981), the most dominant and influential one, both
in the United States and other countries, has been the four principles approach
formulated by Beauchamp and Childress, which gained such ascendancy in the
young field of bioethics that, as Albert Jonsen put it, bioethics virtually "became
principlist" (Jonsen 1994: ix).

Principles of Biomedical Ethics, coauthored by Tom L. Beauchamp and James F.
Childress, first published in 1979, and republished in four successive editions (1983,
1989, 1994, 2001), was embraced as the canonical text that articulated the framework of moral principles fundamental to bioethics. The authors set forth an ethical
perspective grounded in a spare, "relatively small set of concepts" (Gustafson 1990:
127), derived from what they identified as "considered judgments in the common
morality and medical tradition" that they were attempting to "fit into...a coherent
package" (Beauchamp and Childress 2001: 23). The four prima facie, binding principles around which they structured their text are "(1) *respect for autonomy* (a norm
of respecting the decision-making capacities of autonomous persons), (2) *nonmaleficence* (a norm of avoiding the causation of harm), (3) *beneficence* (a group of
norms for providing benefits and balancing benefits against risks and costs), (4) *justice* (a group of norms for distributing benefits, risks, and costs fairly)" (Beauchamp
and Childress 2001: 12; authors' emphases).

Beauchamp and Childress did not conceive of these abstract principles as
unconditional, "absolute and eternal" (Childress, interview, 1999: see appendix),
or as constituting a general moral theory. In their words, "Our four clusters of
principles...provide only a framework for identifying and reflecting on moral
problems" (Beauchamp and Childress 2001: 15). Nor do they regard the principles as the constituent elements of a program that can or should be formulai-
cally applied to moral decision making, action, and living a moral life. Rather, as
they state in their fifth edition, they consider "rules, rights, virtues,...moral ideals
[and]...moral emotions" to be as important as principles for guiding action, and
for a comprehensive view of the moral life" (Beauchamp and Childress 2001:

13–14). And in their view, it is not only the "principle-based approach…[that] captures[s] an important part of the moral life and moral action," but so do the "casuistical, virtue-based, and care relationship" philosophical approaches—each in its own way. "The difficulty is to determine what that part is, and how important it is," Childress remarked to us (Childress, interview, 1999: see appendix).

When the four principles are deployed by persons as highly trained in philosophical and theological ethics as Beauchamp and Childress to identify, interpret, and analyze ethical problems that occur in concrete situations and cases, they are used with skill, subtlety, and flexibility. Inductive as well as deductive reasoning is employed, norms and rules are "tailored" so that they can guide actions in specific situations, the meaning and strength of different principles are assessed, and conflicting principles are weighed and balanced. Furthermore, throughout their book, they "maintain…that various moral principles can and do conflict in moral life," and that "[on] some occasions, moral dilemmas are so deep that specifying and balancing principles will not determine an overriding *ought*" (authors' emphasis). "Although we generally have ways of reasoning about what we should do," they state, "we may not be able to reach a clear resolution in many cases. In these cases, the dilemma only becomes more difficult and remains unsolved even after the most careful reflection." Explicitly acknowledging such moral dilemmas, they comment, "helps avert unwarranted expectations of moral principles and theories" (Beauchamp and Childress 2001: 11).

Nevertheless, in the burgeoning multidisciplinary field of bioethics, what developed were precisely the over-expectations of principles that Beauchamp and Childress thought should be avoided, and their use in an "overly simplified, reductionistic,… mechanically applied way"—"along the lines of a narrow engineering model," as Childress put it—accompanied by a tendency to think that "if one can repeat those [principles] or use them, then you're a bioethicist" (Childress 1994: 91–92, 96; Childress, interview, 1999: see appendix). This state of affairs was graphically described by philosophers K. Danner Clouser and Bernard Gert with respect to the three *Belmont* principles:

Throughout the land arising from the throngs of converts to bioethics awareness, there can be heard a mantra…"beneficence…autonomy…justice." It is this ritual incantation in the face of biomedical dilemmas that beckons our inquiry.…Brandishing these several principles, adherents to the "principle approach" go forth to confront the quandaries of biomedical ethics. (Clouser and Gert 1990: 219–220)

Biologists, physicians, lawyers, and some public officials and social scientists, with little or no background in philosophical thought, were among those who joined these "throngs," along with a number of philosophers and religionists whose prior education in principles-oriented ethics and experience in utilizing it were meager. "I was introduced, along with legions of students, to medical ethics through…this classic text," wrote South African health lawyer/bioethicist

170 SOCIETY, CULTURE, AND BIOETHICS

Theodore Fleischer in a review of the fifth edition of *Principles of Biomedical Ethics*. "Most health givers, even if they haven't read the entire book, have absorbed the four principles of medical ethics popularized by the authors…—or the 'Georgetown mantra,' to use the code phrase" (Fleischer 2002: 1582). Short, intensive courses designed to introduce initiates to the "basic principles" of bioethics were organized. The best known and most sought after of these have been offered by the Kennedy Institute of Ethics at Georgetown University. It was for this reason that a number of the criticisms of the "tiresome invocation of the applied ethics mantra" in bioethics that surfaced in the 1990s (Arras 1991: 48–49) termed it "the Georgetown mantra."

By the beginning of the 1990s, mounting concerns were being expressed by bioethicists in the United States and other countries about what were viewed as the limitations of principlism, accompanied by calls for the use of other approaches such as casuistry, virtue ethics, phenomenology, and hermeneutics (see, e.g., DuBose, Hamel, and O'Connell 1994). The critics—mainly qualified philosophers who were respected bioethicists—were concerned that "principlism ha[d] distorted bioethics and scholarship in bioethics, by offering some relatively abstract, philosophical categories…that ha[d] tempted some newcomers to philosophical and theological ethics to suppose that they…ha[d] become experts in ethics because they [could] chant the mantra." Principles are "tools in the service of bioethics," critics contended. "Tools imply skillful users and appropriate contexts of use.… We cannot make up for using them poorly by claiming that they have some special status in and of themselves." For whether they are used adroitly or amateurishly, these commentators maintained, "the problem is not principles per se," but the "theoretical hegemony" they have been accorded: the tendency toward an "exhaustive reliance" on them. "Principles have…been asked to do too much work in bioethics" (Churchill 1994: 321–322).

Callahan had this to say:

Ethics…must try to develop general principles and some specific rules; that is not all there is to ethics, but it is an important part of it. It cannot otherwise do its proper work or offer fully helpful moral guidance and insight. Principles, however, should not be understood as moral trump cards. They are at best seen as ways of organizing our moral thought, giving it a shape and formal structure. (Callahan 1999b: 290–291)

The enthusiastic adoption of a stripped-down, monolithic version of principlism by American bioethics, its institutionalization as the primary framework of U.S. bioethical thought, and the fixed form in which it has been utilized—especially by those who have little background in philosophy—have been reinforced by a number of factors. To begin with, it is compatible with the scientific positivism of biomedicine, the primary mode of thought in which the physicians and biologists involved in bioethics have been professionally trained. As Jonsen observed, for example, the principlist "style of normative ethics" that bioethics adopted, along with its substantive focus, "gave [bioethicists] a language to speak with [their] audience [of] doctors, nurses, and others in health care" (Jonsen 1994: xvi).

In addition, principlism mirrors the epistemological split in modern Western medical thinking between what is and is not considered to be "biomedical" and authentically and rigorously scientific. It also reflects the long-standing difficulties of American medicine in integrating its core conceptions of the individual patient and the doctor-patient relationship with recognition of social and cultural influences on health and illness, and commitment to the "common good" in the form of the health of the public. In the opinion of Warren T. Reich, Editor-in-Chief of the first and second editions of *The Encyclopedia of Bioethics,* it is partly through the coming together of the American, principles-based form of analytic philosophy codified in "the Beauchamp-Childress book" and "the biomedical model" that a "narrow...vision" of bioethics came to prevail, rather than the broader, more inclusive conception of the field around which Reich structured the two editions of the *Encyclopedia* (1978 and 1995):

...[B]ioethics became the ethics of biomedicine, meaning taking care of patients...the ethics of the physician-patient relationship,...and research issues,...the relationship between researcher and subject, with a few other issues tacked on [such as] health care distribution.... I believe that in the...mentality of most of the people who call themselves bioethicists this is what the field has generally meant in a dominant way...[even though] there have always been other voices.... (Reich, interview, 2000: see appendix)

There are also significant points of intersection between the principles outlook of bioethics and the ethos of American law that, as lawyer Alexander Capron points out, has had a "pervasive effect on the content and methods of bioethics.... The law has made large contributions to the methodology of bioethics and is the framework within which bioethics-as-public-policy is carried out." He attributes this to the fact that "American institutions and commentators have had a disproportionate influence in shaping the content and methodology of the field, and that influence has tended to emphasize the law and particular legally based values.... Americans have the habit of looking to the courts to resolve contentious moral questions," he goes on to say, "and we expect the courts to implement certain values that are central to our culture" (Capron 1999: 296, 297, 301). When bioethical issues, questions, and dilemmas find their way into the U.S. courts, he believes, they are adjudicated through a legal process that has much in common with the philosophical principlism of the field. It is a largely "acontextual" process that favors clean, abstract, major principles rather than empirical findings and facts; "proceduralism," in preference to "specific normative conclusions;" the language of rights—usually framed in Constitutional terms, but sometimes drawn from natural law or from "broadly stated international covenants"—that places greater emphasis on "one's right to do something" than "what is the right thing to do"; an approach that "reflects a normative commitment to preferring individual choice over other measures of correct action, such as expert judgment, group allegiance, social welfare, or divine command;" and one that is resolutely secular (Capron 1999: 295, 297, 316–318). These attributes of American law, he affirms, have reinforced their counterparts in U.S. bioethics.

Lawyer George Annas and philosopher and physician Carl Elliot go further than Capron in their views about the relationships between law and bioethics. "American law, not philosophy or medicine," Annas forcefully argues, "is primarily responsible for the agenda, development, and current state of American bioethics" (Annas 1993: 3). "American bioethics," he contends, "is more pragmatic than principled. And to the extent that American bioethics has principles, they are mostly drawn from American law, including liberty (autonomy) and justice" (Annas 2005a: xiv). Elliot, in turn, asserts that "[t]he law is the *lingua franca* of bioethics," and that "the law's influence on bioethics has been much deeper and more subtle" than "the language of rights and autonomy." In his critical view, "[Bioethics] has given us a picture of morality as somehow like the law in structure—for example, as a set of rules that govern interactions between strangers. This picture of morality may work adequately as long as we are in fact talking about interactions between strangers, especially strangers whose relationship is adversarial," he concedes. "But it overlooks the kinds of questions that are crucial to morality, and it distorts many others" (Elliot 1999: xxviii).

What is more difficult to explain is the massive influence that principlism, and the Beauchamp and Childress text in all its editions, has had on bioethics in the multitude of countries in which the field has progressively emerged as an area of concern, intellectual reflection, and policy formulation. "The book's influence has crossed global boundaries," Theodore Fleischer declares. "In South Africa, where I teach and practice bioethics, Beauchamp and Childress's principles are finding their way into medical jargon." Fleischer praises the text and the biomedical principles it incarnates as an "indispensable resource" for teachers, clinicians, ethicists, and students, even though he comments on the fact that Beauchamp and Childress do not deal with "problems of achieving justice in health care and health research in the developing world" faced by a society like South Africa, to which he hopes they will pay attention in the book's "next edition" (Fleischer 2002: 1583).

In a number of ways the international diffusion of a principles-based bioethics, and of the four-principles paradigm that Beauchamp and Childress have set forth is cross-culturally problematic. This is especially true of "our modern Western and American outlook on the person," sociologist Willy De Craemer observed, which "tends to be culturally particularistic and inadvertently ethnocentric. To a significant degree, it rests on the implicit assumption that its ideas about personhood are common to many, if not most, other societies and cultures" (De Craemer 1983: 19, 21). Quite to the contrary, he contends, it is not the Western, American conception of the person as an autonomous, self-determining, and self-governing individual that prevails globally. Rather, it is a "contextual, relational" view of personhood, that is "inseparab[le] from social solidarity," and embedded in kinship, group, and community (De Craemer 1983: 32). Drawing on his scholarly and firsthand knowledge of Central African and Japanese societies, De Craemer describes how irrespective of the differences in their cultural traditions and stages of development, "what they have in common is a perspective on the human person that most non-Western societies and cultures in the world share" (De Craemer 1983: 32):

In an African framework [selfhood] is defined, understood, and experienced as part of a living system of social relationships. What is emphasized in this view of the person is social context, namely a group, a category, or both.… [The] relationship of the individual to significant, kinship-and-village-defined others is so constitutive of the self that any serious disruption of these relationships does dangerous, even obliterating damage to the person and is believed to be supernaturally threatening and potentially destructive to the family and community as a whole.…

[In] the Japanese idea of personhood,… preoccupation with, concern about, and sensitivity to social relationships and social interactions with other persons are dominant and pervasive. The Japanese concepts of self and self-identity are reflections of the "social relativism"…that Japanese commentators single out as one of the chief characteristics of their society.… What it means to be a person…in the Japanese sense, cannot be understood without reference to the individual's social ties: the particular…"human nexus" to which he or she belongs, from which one derives identity, and to which one is totally committed.…

In its relational emphasis the Japanese outlook on the person bears some resemblance to the Bantu [Central African] perspective. But in contradistinction, … it is… more this-wordly. The anxiety about relations with significant others is human-sized and human-focused without the supernatural or cosmic connotations that African anxiety carries with it.

[Nevertheless], "belongingness" for Japanese is not confined to a social frame or reference group in the here and now. It also includes one's group and place of origin, and groups and places to which one previously belonged (such as one's birthplace, the house in which one was raised, the school from which one graduated), and also symbolic locations (like the house registry in which one's name is inscribed, and the historical era and generation with which one identifies). Japanese refer to these original, previous, and symbolic forms of filiation as "belonging by memory." (De Craemer 1983: 22–23, 26–27)

Bioethics and Social Science

There are bioethicists who would contend that this portrayal of the ethos of American bioethics does not take into account the fact that from its outset, social scientists—principally anthropologists and sociologists—have been involved in the field, bringing with them their epistemological emphasis on the role of both rational and nonrational social and cultural factors in moral life, their active interest in social and cultural as well as individual differences and diversity, and the importance that they attribute to relatedness and reciprocity, solidarity and community, and to feelings and sentiments. However, compared to philosophers, physicians, and lawyers, social scientist participants in bioethics have been relatively few in number; and their outlook, modes of thought, and bodies of empirical knowledge have had a minimal effect on the conceptual framework, premises, value-orientation, and agenda of bioethics.

This is not to maintain that bioethicists are oblivious to the corpus of published social scientific works that have direct bearing on matters with which the field is preoccupied. Many of them have some knowledgeable awareness of this body of literature (a substantial proportion of which is based on firsthand studies conducted by the authors). These social science-based works are concerned with experimentation with human subjects (particularly phenomena and issues surrounding informed consent, and institutional review boards and ethics committees); clinical research; death and dying; extending or foregoing life-sustaining treatment (in a number of instances in the context of an intensive-care nursery); genetic screening and counseling; organ replacement; medical errors and mistakes; medical uncertainty and risk; the professional socialization of physicians and nurses; resource allocation in the delivery of health care; and the growth of corporate medicine.[9] However, as political philosopher Bruce Jennings has observed, "Most writings in bioethics still draw faintheartedly and unimaginatively, or not at all, on social scientific studies that address the setting, institutional context, and cultural forces relating to the bioethical problem at hand":

All the while, of course, these writings typically make large claims—or worse, assumptions—about setting, context, and culture. These claims, in turn, are not harmless asides, sociological *obiter dicta*; they do affect the normative ethical positions offered in various ways. For one thing, these sociological claims affect the reasonableness of the arguments made, since the reasonableness of an ethical argument that balances conflicting values and weighs benefits and burdens often depends on the context within which this balancing and weighing goes on. Moreover, background claims and assumptions can quietly set the agenda of ethical argument in the first place; they affect the very selection of problems and topics to be discussed. (Jennings 1990: 262)[10]

Sociologist Adam Hedgecoe has commented on the fact that although there has been "a move from within philosophical bioethics, an 'empirical turn' that would seek to combine traditional philosophical medical ethics with empirical research...there seems to be a curious blind spot regarding medical sociology on the part of the supporters of empirical bioethics." For "ethicists interested in incorporating empirical research into their work," he has written, "we do not need a new discipline, 'empirical ethics,' to think empirically about empirical issues. We already have at least one discipline that does that: medical sociology." Accordingly, he holds, "if medical ethicists are interested in the lived experience of the social world of modern medicine, an obvious solution would be to read some medical sociology, rather than look towards developing a new discipline" (Hedgecoe 2007: 168, 174). The forcefulness with which he has expressed this opinion notwithstanding, it is with candid humility that he says that "it is not at all clear what form this engagement" between ethicists and social scientists should take. As he had suggested previously, he noted, he would like to see ethicists "approach work in this area with a view to challenge theory, a reflexive awareness of their own context and with a politely skeptical point of view" (Hedgecoe 2007: 174).

On a more personal level, in the course of an interview with us, one of the most recognized and appreciated social scientists in the field of bioethics (an anthropologist) confided that she "still feel[s] like a player in the backroom of bioethics"—"like someone outside the nexus of authority...in which the dominant voices continue to be those of philosophers, physicians, and lawyers" (Marshall, interview, 2000: see appendix).

A fundamental reason for the restricted influence that the social sciences have had on the core of bioethics is what Onora O'Neill has termed the "tenuous interdisciplinarity" of the field (O'Neill 2002b: 2335). To begin with, in her opinion, bioethics is "not a discipline." Rather, it is "a meeting ground for a number of disciplines, discourses, and organizations concerned with ethical, legal, and social questions raised by advances in medicine, science, and biotechnology" (O'Neill 2002a: 1). Although it is precisely because it is such a "meeting ground" that, as sociologist Raymond De Vries has put it, bioethics regards itself as "famously interdisciplined" (De Vries 2003: 280), in practice, the interchange that takes place between its groups of participants is substantially thin. It does not involve the complexity and depth of what theologian-ethicist James Gustafson regards as a true "intersection of disciplines," the profound challenges of "navigating their intersections," and of the interpenetration of different ways of seeing, thinking, feeling, valuing, and believing that this entails, or confrontation with the fact that such encounters between disciplines can raise as many questions as they answer (Gustafson 2004: esp. 1–17, 18–43, 78–95).

Contrasting dramatically with the constrained interdisciplinarity of bioethics are what sociologist Neil Smelser has described as the "permeability" of sociology, and what anthropologist Clifford Geertz has depicted as the analytic "interplay" that anthropology's "questing" to "find its way to a...viable concept of man" requires:

...[S]ociology's walls are *permeable*.... [I]ts subject matter overlaps with psychology, anthropology, economics, history, law, political science, and more. It shamelessly borrows and lends empirical findings, theoretical orientations, and methodological tools to and from all of these. Sociology leads all other behavioral and social sciences in cross-citations. (Smelser 2003: 7; author's emphases)

We must...descend into detail, past the misleading tags, past the metaphysical types, past the empty similarities to grasp firmly the essential character of not only the various cultures but the various sorts of individuals within each culture, if we wish to encounter humanity face to face. In this area, the road to the general, to the revelatory simplicities of science, lies through a concern with the particular, the circumstantial, the concrete, but a concern organized and directed in terms of...analyses of the sort of theoretical physical evolution, of the functioning of the nervous system, of social organization, of psychological process, of cultural patterning, and so on—and, most especially, in terms of the interplay among them. (Geertz 1965: 117–118)

Entwined with the porousness of sociology, Smelser contends, and "the complex, multi-vision, multi-paradigmatic [characteristics of this often] conflict-ridden field with indistinct boundaries," are its "very self-regarding and

self-evaluating" qualities. Smelser notes that Raymond Aron, a French sociologist, once commented that "sociology seems to be marked by the incessant
quest for itself" (Smelser 2003: 7–8). But in Smelser's view, "sociology has no
monopoly on "self-preoccupation" and "self-evaluation." Among the social sciences, he maintains, contemporary anthropology may be even more self-reflexive.
Geertz poetically expresses his agreement with Smelser: "Bent over his own
chips, stones, and common plants," he writes, "the anthropologist broods, too,
upon the true and insignificant, glimpsing in it, or so he thinks, fleetingly and
insecurely, the disturbing, changeful image of himself" (Geertz 1965: 118).

These characteristics of the intellectual subcultures of anthropology and sociology and their ambience are sufficiently different from those that prevail in bioethics to implicitly complicate their interdisciplinary understanding and appreciation
of each other, and their prospects for collaboration.

A more explicit source of tension between the social sciences and bioethics is the
kind of "cultural relativism" that Marshall and Koenig consider "foundational in the
development of anthropology" (2004b: 220; see also Marshall 1992, Marshall and
Koenig 1996, 2004a). As Geertz explains, this at-once conceptual, epistemological,
methodological, and philosophical perspective is "one in which culture, and the
variability of culture, [is] taken into account rather than written off as caprice and
prejudice, and yet, at the same time, one in which the governing principle of the
field, 'the basic unity of mankind,' [is] not turned into an empty phrase":

[I]t is not that there are no generalizations that can be made about man as man, save that
he is the most various animal, or that the study of culture has nothing to contribute toward
the uncovering of such generalizations. My point is that such generalizations are not to be
discovered through a Baconian search for cultural universals, a kind of public-opinion poll-
ing of the world's peoples in search of a *consensus gentium* that does not in fact exist, and,
further, that the attempt to do so leads to precisely the sort of relativism the whole approach
was expressly designed to avoid....

[T]he notion that the essence of what it means to be human is most clearly revealed in
those features of human culture that are universal rather than in those that are distinctive to
this people or that is a prejudice that we are not necessarily obliged to share. Is it in grasping such general facts—that man has everywhere some sort of "religion"—or in grasping
the richness of this religious phenomenon or that—in Balinese trance or Indian ritualism,
Aztec human sacrifice or Zuñi rain-dancing that we grasp him? Is the fact that marriage is
universal (if it is) as penetrating a comment on what we are as the facts concerning Hima-
layan polyandry, or those fantastic Australian marriage rules, or the elaborate bride-price
systems of Bantu Africa?...

We are, in sum, incomplete or unfinished animals who complete or finish ourselves
through culture—and not through culture in general but through highly particular forms
of it: Dobuan and Javanese, Hopi and Italian, upper-class and lower-class, academic and
commercial....

To be human...is thus not to be Everyman; it is to be a particular kind of man, and of
course men differ.... Within the society, differences are recognized, too—the way a rice
peasant becomes human and Javanese differs from the way that a civil servant does. This
is not a matter of tolerance and ethical relativism, for not all ways of being human are

regarded as being equally admirable by far.... The point is that there are different ways; and to shift to the anthropologist's perspective now, it is in a systematic review and analysis of these—of the Plains Indian's bravura, the Hindu's obsessiveness, the Frenchman's rationalism, the Berber's anarchism, the American's optimism...that we shall find out what it is, or can be, to be a man. (Geertz 1965: 97, 102, 105, 112–113, 117; author's emphases)

This is not the crude or absolutist form of particularism and relativism that bioethicists most fear, and repudiate. Rather, it comes closer to the "anti anti-relativism" position that Geertz takes in a later essay—expressed in a "double negative," he comments, because it "enables one to reject something without thereby committing oneself to what it rejects":

It has not been anthropological theory...that has made our field seem to be a massive argument against absolutism in thought, morals, and esthetic judgment; it has been anthropological data: customs, crania, living floors, and lexicons.... The relativist bent...anthropology induces in those who have much traffic with its materials, is thus in some sense implicit in the field as such; in cultural anthropology perhaps particularly, but in much of archaeology, anthropological linguistics, and physical anthropology as well.... Once this fact is grasped, and "relativism" and "anti-relativism" are seen as general responses to the way in which Kroeber once called the centrifugal impulses of anthropology—distant places, distant times, distant species...distant grammars—affects our sense of things, the whole discussion comes rather into focus....

[W]e were the first to insist that we see the lives of others through lenses of our own grinding and that they look back on ours through ones of their own....

The objection to anti-relativism is not that it rejects an it's-all-how-you-look-at-it approach to knowledge or a when-in-Rome approach to morality, but that it imagines that they can only be defeated by placing morality beyond culture and knowledge beyond both.... If we wanted home truths, we should have stayed at home. (Geertz 2000: 44–45, 65)

The intricate interweaving between the universal and the particular in anthropology's conception of cultural diversity, and its "relativist bent" that derives, as Geertz phrases it, from "the distances" that the field has "established" and "the elsewheres" it has "located," not only challenge the fervid universalism of American bioethics but also its tone of moral certitude, and its inadvertent ethnocentrism. Although this difference in perspective is a source of considerable tension between bioethics and anthropology, Raymond De Vries contends that "anthropology has a less troubled relationship with bioethics than sociology." He attributes this primarily to the fact that sociologists have not only acted as collaborators "*in*" bioethics, "lending their skills to bioethics, [and] using their discipline to help bioethicists deal with the issues that they treat." They have also functioned as sociologists "*of*" bioethics, "stepping back" from involvement in the field to observe, analyze, and critically comment on bioethics as a social and cultural, as well as intellectual happening; on bioethicists as social actors within it; and on the sociocultural factors that influence why certain issues become defined as moral problems, and others not.[11] "To the extent that bioethicists distinguish sociology and anthropology," he comments, "they expect anthropology—which they perceive as the study of 'other,' 'exotic' people—to sort out the proper way to approach these people when they enter the health care system." But bioethicists "do not expect to become the exotic subjects" of sociological research, he quips (De Vries 2003: 280; author's emphases).

We ourselves have functioned both in the role of social scientists "in" and "of" bioethics. And in this latter capacity, we have strongly urged other social scientists "to be more present and active in bioethics, not only as conceptual, empirical, and policy contributors to it, but also as analysts of the social and cultural phenomenon that it represents." For if we have been correct in affirming over the years that "bioethics is not just bioethics," that it is "more than medical," and that it deals with "nothing less than beliefs, values, and norms that are basic to our society, its cultural tradition, and its 'collective conscience,' then it is vital that the best, most insightful, and morally sensitive sociological thinking be integral to it" (R. C. Fox 1989: 266). We can attest to the fact that the most outraged reactions to our publications and professional presentations that we have received from within the bioethics community have occurred in response to our sociology *of* bioethics analyses; however, what is considered to be our sociology *in* bioethics writings has also received its share of less than friendly criticism.

Whatever differences may exist in the way that sociology and anthropology are viewed and received by bioethicists, another set of factors that, from early on, has driven a wedge between bioethics and social scientific approaches more generally, is the distinctions that philosophers make between "descriptive" and "normative" ethics, and the invidious comparison that they are prone to draw between the two. Descriptive ethics refers to the existing world "*as it is*"—to how people actually experience their lives as moral beings—whereas normative ethics pertains to the world, and to people's experiences and behavior within it, as they morally *ought* to be. This is a dichotomous distinction that tends to carry with it the implication that normative thought is not only more important than "mere" description but also intellectually and morally superior to it, and that there is a danger that too much immersion in existing reality may insidiously lead to uncritically accepting "what is" as justified or unalterable. In this perspective, the realm of normative ethical reflection, theoretically "lifted above" and largely dissociated from empirical contexts, is viewed as the province of philosophy and philosophers, and the kind of "factual data" that are characteristically produced by social scientific research are regarded as both secondary and inferior to the insights generated by philosophically based ethical analysis. In the introductory chapter to their coauthored text on *Methods in Medical Ethics*, for example, Jeremy Sugarman and Daniel P. Sulmasy state that "normative ethics seems to be at the core of ethical inquiry.... [T]he other types of ethical inquiry," they go on to say, "are only important, meaningful, and useful because of the normative questions that are at stake":

...As a general rule, one is only interested in knowing what percent of the population thinks something ought to be done in particular circumstances, or how people behave in such circumstances, if it is interesting and important to know how one ought to behave in such circumstances.... A good deal of empirical research in ethics...carefully describ[es] anthropological, sociological, psychological, and epidemiological facts that are of interest. They are of interest because the subject is normative. But the techniques are descriptive and the conclusions have no immediate normative implications. (Sugarman and Sulmasy 2001: 4, 10)

There is dissonance between this kind of contrast between the normative and the descriptive, empirical, and factual that has been transposed from philosophy into bioethics, and some of the basic intellectual and moral premises of the social sciences that underlie the conceptual and empirical work of its practitioners. These premises include the assumption that serious knowledge and understanding of the existing world has value in its own right, and that there is an important normative dimension to lived experience and social reality. Related additional premises hold that it is the "duty" of social scientists to "take cognizance of the real world [and]...to get it straight," because it is prerequisite for morally responsible social reform (Wolf 1998), and that an approach to the study of values "which looks toward the behavior of actual people in actual societies living in terms of actual cultures" would not "replace...moral philosophy by descriptive ethics," but could help to make it more "relevant" (Geertz 1973: 141).

Bioethics, Social Science Research, and Ethnography

The bioethical intellectual community, we have argued, has had an overall propensity to embrace the positivist approach of Anglo-American philosophy, based on rationally justified principles and rules directed at "what *ought* to be the case...[rather than] what *is* the case" (Hoffmaster 1990: 241; author's emphases). This propensity is linked with bioethicists' inclination to conceive of social scientists' empirical research as being restricted to discovering facts, and their wary insistence that whatever bearing social knowledge may have on ethical analysis, "[e]thics must, in the end, be ethics, not social science" (Callahan 1999b: 285). There has been, however, some movement in the direction of using methods of social inquiry to deepen understanding of how physicians, nurses, and other health professionals, medical researchers and research subjects, and patients and their families actually experience and respond to bioethical issues. Foremost among the methods of research being adopted as a way of exploring in-depth the "lived experience" of morality is ethnography. In recent years, something akin to an "ethnography bandwagon" seems to have surged among American bioethicists who have expressed considerable enthusiasm about the value of obtaining "thickly descriptive" (Geertz 1973: 3–30), firsthand accounts of how morally relevant experiences are encountered and dealt with in the everyday reality of the people involved in them. One of its most articulate advocates has been Barry Hoffmaster. In an article that evokes Toulmin's oft-cited paper "How Medicine Saved the Life of Ethics" (1982), Hoffmaster has gone so far as to suggest that ethnography can help to "save the life of medical ethics" from the sterility of confining itself to "top down" analyses based on abstract, general, universal moral principles (Hoffmaster 1992).

Yet by and large, bioethicists have tended to cleave to an untutored, facile conception of what ethnography entails—one that is based on the unspoken assumption that it requires little more than going to the field, digging into it, and simply "doing" ethnography. There is a notable lack of recognition of the cluster of qualitative field methods of research (observation and participant observation, face-to-face in situ interviewing, the discovery and collection of primary and secondary documents), the modes of chronicling and recording data, the microscopic description and analysis and their interpretive application to larger phenomena, and the narrative discourse that are involved. Knowledge of the part that anthropology and sociology have played in developing ethnography, of its century-long history, and of the great corpus of monographic works that have emanated from it (which often include extensive firsthand accounts of the emotional, cultural, and ethical challenges of this form of research) is sparse among bioethicists. Nor is there widespread understanding in the bioethics community of:

- the complex interpersonal and reflexive role of the participant observer, and the evocative journey-into-self as well as into the lives of others that are core to ethnography;
- the skill that it takes to manage, understand, and constantly analyze this role, and the ethical as well as intellectual importance of doing so;
- the capacity not only to listen, but to hear;
- the interwoven inductive and deductive "on the hoof" chains of reasoning from theory, and from observation and interviewing, that ethnographic inquiry calls for;
- the role-conflicts and moral dilemmas that it summons up—especially those associated with the Janus-faced issues of over-involvement with the persons being studied, and of alienation from them, and with the "therapeutic temptation" to actively intervene in situations encountered in the field out of the desire to rectify or change things "for the better";
- the semi-literary genre of ethnographic writing and its intent of transporting readers to the social world where the author has been a participant observer;
- the time and endurance, as well as training and experience, that all these aspects of conducting, producing, and authoring good ethnography take (R. C. Fox 2004).

Among some of the participants in bioethics who are not only enthusiastic about what ethnography could contribute to the field, but who also have a more sophisticated comprehension of what it entails, there is a notable tendency to attribute powers to ethnography that extend far beyond the methodological properties and capacities of this particular form of social science research. Such an inclination is present, for example, in an article by sociologist Eugene B. Gallagher and several nurse-coauthors, who have conducted ethnographic studies of chronic hemodialysis patients and their "disposition toward the possibility of receiving a renal transplant," and of "critical decision-making in neonatal intensive care units." In their exposition about how "clinical or philosophical bioethics" might be "enriched" by the perspective of what they call "social bioethics," the authors identify the latter, and the enhancement of bioethics it could effect, exclusively with "ethnographically-oriented social science," rather than with social science more generally: "Social bioethics links clinical or philosophical bioethics with ethnographically oriented social science," they write (Gallagher et al. 1998: 169).

Bruce Jennings equates ethnography with a critique of the "individualistic and universalistic [American] liberalism" that predominates in "the ideological structure of mainstream autonomy bioethics," and of its propensity to play down, or ignore, what he terms "difference liberalism." He coined the neologisms "bioethnography" and "bioethnographers" to refer to ethnographic research conducted by social scientists that involves firsthand studies of health care delivery and clinical settings and quandaries that have bioethical significance, and he contends that they are inherently critical of bioethics in ways that he feels are greatly needed:

In substantive terms the bioethnnographic critique has a moral point of view of its own (often left implicit) and has to do with the relationship between autonomy and pluralism. It is predicated on the insight…that the ideal of autonomy cannot easily be reconciled with respect for difference, recognizing and validating the identity of others, and tolerance…. According to its critics, an autonomy-centered bioethics emphasizes notions of individual choice and future-oriented planning that are foreign to the lived reality of the poor, the marginalized, and people of color in a multicultural society like the United States.

The bioethnographic critique goes on to make a second important point. By normalizing and universalizing a particular set of cultural assumptions and privileged behaviors and a class-specific conception of rational moral choice, bioethics makes both a practical and ethical mistake. Practically, bioethics is unable to give adequate clinical and public policy guidance to professionals who confront culturally diverse patients and citizens. These people are rendered invisible and voiceless by bioethics, and their special needs are not met. Ethically, bioethics fails to respect persons because it erases their particularity and their culturally constituted identities.

Finally, the bioethnographic critique concludes that mainstream bioethics must become more sensitive to the culture-bound assumptions that lie at the heart of its own conceptual and philosophic framework; it must purge that framework of notions that erase difference or that fail to provide equal respect for the inassimilable "other." (Jennings 1998: 260–261)

Patricia Marshall and Barbara Koenig claim that ethnography is intrinsic to the fact that "[i]ssues of social justice in health care across the world—until recently neglected in traditional bioethics debates focused on individual choices and the dilemmas created by new technologies in research-rich countries"—are being addressed by their fellow anthropologists. "Anthropologists working in bioethics are deeply concerned about global health disparities," they say. And "the need for broadening the boundaries of bioethics beyond the confines of Western medicine and the limited attention to the political economy of social suffering is increasingly recognized by anthropologists engaged in discussions of global medical morality." They regard ethnography, "which unifies the work of anthropologists," as more than a methodological orientation allowing "fine-grained attention to [be paid] to local social and cultural processes." Rather, they insist, "its theoretical foundation requires that the ethnographer draw connections between local suffering and global social and political processes" (Marshall and Koenig 2004b: 219; see also Marshall 1992; Marshall and Koenig 1996, 2004a).

Although there is a heartening connection between this kind of advocacy for ethnography and momentum toward strengthening and broadening social and cultural thinking in bioethics, there are ways in which such "ethnography enthusiasm" is troubling. It implies that ethnography is the only mode of social science research that is suitable for bioethical inquiry, and that its adoption as *the* method par excellence will automatically have a transforming effect on bioethics and on the bioethicists who deploy it. That transformation is seen as one that will make the field more sensitive and responsive to the social and cultural dimensions of morality, globally as well nationally—especially to social and cultural differences, social sources of suffering, structural inequities, and issues of social justice. Ethnography per se does not have these transfiguring capacities. In our view, if bioethicists who are not trained ethnographers engage in this sort of research, and carry such misunderstandings and illusory expectations into the field with them, they might do more harm than good to the prospects of advancing social and cultural thinking in bioethics.

Beyond these methodological concerns and over-expectations, as sociologist Adam Hedgecoe has astutely pointed out, a too zealous, "saving bioethics through ethnography" stance could result in a "version" of the field that reduces the "intellectual space" and the role of philosophy and the philosopher "to a worryingly unspecified level," rather than to the "incorporation" of the "social sciences into bioethics in a more equitable manner" (Hedgecoe 2004: 129).

Developments in the Integration of Social Science into Bioethics and Bioethics into Social Science

As the following three examples suggest, there are some promising signs that the kind of equitable integration of social science and social thought and bioethics that Hedgecoe envisions is beginning to occur. The first example involves the ethnographic fieldwork that Steven Wainwright, Clare Williams, and their collaborators have been conducting among scientists engaged in investigations with human embryonic stem cells, and their therapeutic potential for the treatment of diseases such as diabetes (Wainwright, Williams, Michael et al. 2006). Wainwright and Williams are both sociologists and nurses, with extensive firsthand clinical experience in the fields of intensive care medicine and organ transplantation. Their stem cell project is part of a larger investigational undertaking associated with their mutual interest in the relationship between new biomedical technologies, science—especially genetics—and society; "laboratory life"; "translational" research that entails working from the laboratory bench to the bedside, and from the bedside to the bench; "ethical issues that are part of biomedical science in action"; and how science and technology studies, medical sociology, and the sociology of the "biomedical body" can illumine these phenomena. At the core of their studies of stem-cell research are their participant observation in the laboratories where scientists involved in this area are working, and their interviews with individual scientists in these settings about "what [they] view as ethical sources of human embryos and stem cells"; their "perceptions of embryos, and the ways in which they draw ethical boundaries for the use of embryos and human embryo stem cells in the laboratory"; and how they "perceive regulatory frameworks in stem cell research." Their research constitutes a rare attempt to explore in a firsthand way how scientists think about genetics, discuss it with one another, and practice it within their scientific subculture (Wainwright, Williams, Michael et al. 2006b; 2007 in press).

In the opinion of Wainwright, Williams, and their colleagues, the "scientists' accounts" that they have obtained are "very different from 'narrow' philosophical accounts of bioethics because they do not situate themselves in a position of detached abstract rationality, but rather, are centrally implicated in the substantive ethics of practice." For that reason, they hold that an "empirically informed," "socially embedded" analysis of their accounts not only "provides a more grounded and detailed analysis of perspectives, processes, and practices that may be erased or 'skated over' by purely philosophical analyses." It also has "direct relevance for the traditional aspiration of philosophical bioethics, i.e. for appraising accounts of what is ethically defensible, or what 'ought to be.'... Appraising their coherence, credibility and defensibility means, amongst other things, attending to how institutions and agents...embody and enact ethical work" (Wainwright, Williams, Cribb et al. 2006: 745).

A second example is sociologist Raymond De Vries's book, *A Pleasing Birth: Midwives and Maternity Care in the Netherlands* (2005), and the way that it has been reviewed in the bioethics literature. De Vries's work is based on the field research that he conducted during the 1990s on the preferred "Dutch way" of delivering babies, which is giving birth at home attended by midwives or their own "house doctors" (general practitioners). He describes and analyzes how what the Dutch call "a pleasing birth" in the setting of a family home fits into the larger Dutch value system. He proceeds from this case study to emphasize how culture is involved on the macro- as well as the micro-level of a society in the way that its health care system is organized, and states that any effort to change it must take this into account.

In her review of *A Pleasing Birth* in *The Hastings Center Report*, Nancy Berlinger, the Center's deputy director and associate for religious studies, hailed it as an "important and wonderfully engrossing new book." "Cultural change," she wrote, is crucial to "an understanding of how health care delivery works," of "how health care policy came to be, and why certain improvements have failed to take hold.... [T]o forget about culture, or to fail to take it seriously or dismiss it as soft stuff is...a permanent fatal error." Because in her eyes, De Vries's book meets the highest criteria of serious cultural analysis, she recommends that it "belongs on the shelf of every scholar," and that it "shouldn't [just] sit [there]" (Berlinger 2006).

Our third example is of a different sort. It emanates from a small interdisciplinary group (including three philosophers, three sociologists, two religionists, two anthropologists, a lawyer, and a political scientist) who spent the 2003–2004 academic year together in residence at the School of Social Sciences of Princeton's Institute of Advanced Studies.[12] Their year-long dialogues appear to have resulted in a socially oriented convergence of their disciplinary perspective, which continued to be reflected in their ongoing publications,[13] activities such as organizing conferences, and their plans for collaborative research.[14]

The three sociologists who participated in the Princeton bioethics group (Bosk, Davis, and De Vries) also were members of the program committee headed by sociologist John Evans that organized a two-day "Sociology of Bioethics" conference, which took place in March 2005. The first day's program, held at Georgetown University, included formal presentations, semistructured discussions, and a dinner with a keynote speaker. The second day was a four-session "mini-conference" presented as part of the annual meeting of the Eastern Sociological Society in Washington, D.C. "The conference's organizing premise," Davis, De Vries, and Evans reported, "was that sociology has an important contribution to make to bioethics."

It is little remembered now, but bioethics began as an interdisciplinary conversation that included a number of well-known sociologists.... Over the years, however, as the field developed and was institutionalized, it came to be dominated by philosophers and forms of argumentation drawn from analytic philosophy. Sociologists, along with scholars from other disciplines, moved to the periphery, a move that has impoverished bioethical debates.

Despite marginalization, sociologists have nonetheless made important individual contributions. Conference organizers,...seeking to build upon [these contributions], recognized that sociology has theoretical and methodological tools that can fruitfully deepen and expand the agenda of bioethics. At the same time, they recognized the general lack of communication between scholars who are working on bioethical questions from a sociological perspective.... The conference, then, aimed to press the question of how sociology can effectively and institutionally contribute to the field of bioethics and bring differently situated sociologists into conversation with one another. (Davis, De Vries, and Evans 2005)

In his communication to prospective participants in this conference, Evans used more exuberant language to describe the occasion as "a watershed event in the nascent history of the sociology of bioethics," designed to expand and transform the informal contacts between sociologists working on bioethical topics into a more formally organized group of scholars.[15] Although the incipient professionalization and institutionalization of the sociology of bioethics as a subfield of sociology has the potentiality of strengthening some of the interdisciplinary strands of bioethics, enhancing its social components, and broadening its agenda, it also carries with it the risk of a paradoxical side effect. If it eventuated in the domination of bioethics by a social science, rather than by philosophy, it might contribute to difficulties in achieving more substantial interdisciplinarity comparable to those that bioethics currently faces.

The introduction to a special issue of the journal *Sociology of Health and Illness* devoted to the topic of "social science and bioethics" is reassuring in this regard. Coedited by sociologists Raymond De Vries, Kristina Orfali, and Charles Bosk, and religionist and social ethicist Leigh Turner, it expresses the desire to break through what they characterize as "the often troubled relationship between bioethics and the social sciences," and the "tiresome back and forth critique between them" (De Vries et al. 2006: 666, 677).[16] They hope to do this, in part, by making "awareness of difference [between bioethicists and social scientists] productive," through "put[ting] aside the desire to transform ethicists into empirical social scientists or to make social scientists better philosophers":

Bioethicists need not be social scientists. Social scientists need not be philosophers.... We do need take heed of each the other's objections. Instead of trying to erase differences, we need to understand them and find ways to learn from them. (De Vries et al. 2006: 668)

Social Justice

The presence and status of social scientists among bioethicists, and the impact of social science on the framework of bioethics, are not the only indicators of how socially oriented U.S. bioethics can be said to be. A different sort of measure is the amount of attention it has devoted to issues of social justice. In this regard, physician-bioethicist Steven Miles finds American bioethics seriously remiss. Taking inventory of the distribution of topics dealt with in the bioethical literature, he concludes that:

Bioethics writes a tenth as often on the 45 million Americans who are uninsured as it does on the care of the two million persons who are dying each year. In the last decade Medline lists 300 Bioethics articles on assisted reproduction, 100 on gene therapy and less than a dozen on health care ethics facing two million prisoners in the United States. There is a robust work on gender, but little on the poor, communities of color, or migrants. A handful of articles probe the relationship between bioethics and human rights. There is a large body of work on research ethics in poor countries but much less on such countries' access to biotechnology, health aid, or on economic sanctions that interdict medicines and public health supplies.

In Miles's opinion, "American Bioethics partly reflects a national culture in which a respect for liberty often eclipses a sense of social justice. Bioethicists' substantial focus on issues like genetics or new reproductive technologies over issues like unaffordable health care reflect the culture" (Miles 2002: 2, 5).

Norman Daniels—who, along with Daniel Brock and Alan Buchanan, are the main American philosophers writing about bioethical issues of distributive justice and health care[17]—is reluctant to attribute the paucity of attention that U.S. bioethics has paid to these matters to "an American psyche or culture." However, he has noted that there are a great many more "people in Europe…looking at issues about priorities in health care" accompanied by "a lot of concern about equity" than in the United States; that it is "striking how individualistic our approach is to health care"; and that "population health and its equitable distribution is not the area of health care or health policy that has ever attracted much attention from the [U.S.] bioethics community" (Daniels, interview, 1999: see appendix). Especially in its early decades, Daniels has commented, "bioethics concentrated on problems arising in two important areas: the…largely noninstitutional examination of…the dyadic, very special relationships that hold between doctors and patients and between researchers and subjects, and Promethean challenges—the powers and responsibilities that come with new knowledge and…exotic…technologies in medicine and the life sciences, including those that bear on extending and terminating life" (Daniels 2006: 22). "In the early 1970s," he recalled when we talked with him, "the topics that put bioethics on the map…were not about national health issues…[and] national health insurance reform. I don't even know if anything emerged in the literature.… I remember trying to work on that topic for this course that I put together. I could [only] find [one article] that had any bearing…and I could find nothing on rights to health care.… My sense is that people in the field were picking up on issues that were getting grants.… It seems to me that people in ethics generally don't lead problems; they tail them," he ventured. "They get onto issues when there's already a public policy debate going on about them" (Daniels, interview, 1999: see appendix).

Daniels is a strong advocate of what he terms "a broader bioethics agenda," which contains within its scope larger issues of social and distributive justice. These include "health inequalities between different social groups and the policies needed to reduce them; intergenerational equity in the context of rapid societal aging; and international health inequalities and the institutions and policies that have influence on them.… There are good reasons for pursuing this broader agenda," he has declared:

> The agenda aligns bioethics with the goal of more effectively promoting a fundamental good—namely, improved population health, especially for those who enjoy less of it, domestically and internationally. It focuses bioethics on the pursuit of justice. Justice obliges us to pursue fairness in the promotion of health, but policy needs the guidance of ethics in determining what this means. These population issues provide the relevant institutional context in which we should think about the role of new technologies and the dyadic relationships of health care and medical research. (Daniels 2006: 23)

However, Daniels points out, "for bioethics to play this role, it must draw on—and train its practitioners in—a wider range of philosophical skills and social science disciplines" (Daniels 2006: 23). He believes that one of the major reasons that accounts for the relative inattention by U.S. bioethics to justice in health care is the interdisciplinary challenge that "serious work" in this area poses. When we interviewed him, he gave personal testimony about the ardors of developing such competence:

You have to have a willingness to look at political science and economics. And this takes an enormous…intellectual investment to get up to speed where you really have a good mastery of literature and work in distributive justice…. Dan Brock had a background in economics before becoming a philosopher, and Alan Buchanan and I were political philosophers—he…by training and I…by choice as I started to teach and write…. [T]here were only a handful of us like that…. [T]hat work became very complex as different disciplines began to dig into Rawls' work [on *The Theory of Justice*]—for example, economists, game theorists, and so on. It was fairly technical, and to stay at the cutting edge of work in political philosophy took an enormous investment of intellectual effort. [In addition], if you want to do serious work on justice in health care you don't just look at a special issue or problem, like something within the doctor-patient relationship or a particular technology that's coming along. You have to learn something about the whole design of the health care system—who gets health care, who doesn't, what were the determinants of health care, and so on. This is really a full-time intellectual task, to master a whole body of literature that is much more significant and of vaster scope than most of the background literature on particular problems that you work on in isolation in bioethics. So when I began to do the background work for the seminar at Brown that led to my paper on distributive justice and health care needs [Daniels 1986], I sat down and read health economics textbooks, and I read bunches of books on the sociology of health care, comparative health care systems,… [and] literature on the access to health care in considerable detail. In effect, I would say I did the equivalent of a Ph.D. in health policy just to get to the point where I felt comfortable talking about health care systems. (Daniels, interview, 1999: see appendix)

Physician-anthropologist Paul Farmer also has remarked on the fact that "[t]here have been few attempts to ground medical ethics in political economy, history, anthropology, sociology, and other contextualizing disciplines" (adding rather cynically that "each of these would have no doubt lent its own native silliness"). However, this is not what he regards as the major source of his impression "in attending ethics rounds and reading the now-copious ethics literature…that the problem of poverty and racism, and a lack of national health insurance figure only rarely" in a field "dominated by endless discussions of brain death, organ transplantation, xenotransplantation, and care at the end of life." "Silence reigns," he charges, "[w]hen the end of life comes early—from death in childbirth, say, or from tuberculosis or infantile diarrhea," which he considers to be great ethical "scandal[s]." As Farmer sees it, from the national and international vantage point of a physician "who serves the poor in Haiti, Boston, Peru, and Russia," in the role of an infectious disease specialist and consultant, the "leading ethical question of our time" concerns what he passionately calls the "obscene disparities" that exist globally between "too much care," on the one hand, and "no care at all," on the other. "In the broader social field in which the 'bottom billion' have no access at all to modern medicine," he declares, "the very real dilemmas of those who *do* have access to care have been the focus of most inquiry by medical ethicists." In his opinion, bioethics has "almost nothing" to say about this burning question of social justice, in an era that is characterized by "the persistence of readily treatable maladies and the growth of both science and economic inequality" on a world scale. This is related to what he terms the need to "resocialize the way we see ethical dilemmas in medicine," so that in practice, and not just in rhetoric, health becomes a "human right" for "everybody" that extends to the "poor...disempowered...and marginalized"—the "lot of most of humanity," who bear the heaviest "burden of disease" (Farmer 2003: 196–212; author's emphasis). There is a sense in which Farmer's morally indignant critique and ethical exhortation constitute an indictment of the nonuniversality of the supposed universalism of the predominant paradigm of American bioethics.

Other Sources of a More Socially Oriented Bioethics

We want to make clear that social science and social scientists are not (and, in our opinion, should not be considered to be) the only potential sources of a bioethics that accords greater weight and value to placing moral issues in a social, cultural, and historical context, and that views the issues on which it chooses to center in a socially and culturally appreciative, critical, and self-critical perspective. The development of a feminist approach to bioethics, for one, has strengthened and enriched the social purview of the field through its emphasis on the social embeddedness of persons, their identity and agency in a complex of social factors such as gender, class, ethnicity, and race, and the importance it attaches to relationships involving caring, responsibility, reciprocity, sensitivity, fidelity, and trust (Gudorf 1994; Sherwin 1992; Holmes and Purdy 1992).

Philosopher Daniel Callahan has infused the field, since its inception, with a social perspective that emanates from what he calls his "predilection" for a communitarian outlook that underlies most of his voluminous writings. "I understand communitarianism to include a social rather than individual starting point for ethical analysis," he has stated, that takes seriously the notions of "common good" and "the public interest" as well as the idea of "individual good." This outlook, he continues, also makes "a solid place for substantive reflection and judgment about ends and goals"—in particular, in bioethics, "substantive inquiry into the nature of good and evil in scientific progress and innovation," and their impact on "society as a whole, its values, and its social institutions" (Callahan 2003a: 496, 506–507). In *What Price Better Health? Hazards of the Research Imperative* (2003b), Callahan brings his communitarian perspective to bear on the American research community, exploring in detail and depth many ethical questions associated with modern medical research, and with the societal roles of government, universities, and the pharmaceutical industry in this domain. The provocative critique around which this book turns is grounded in Callahan's conviction that the social value of medical research and of the health care to which it supposedly contributes should not be determined by the economic status of its recipients, or by a pure profit motive. Rather, in his view, it should be guided by more egalitarian values and norms that are conducive to improving the state of health of the entire population, and of making fundamental health care accessible to all. Within this framework, he finds it unjustifiable to be spending billions of dollars for the development of medical, scientific, and technological innovations that are marginally beneficial to health, and that are mainly available to Americans of privileged socioeconomic backgrounds, especially because, he contends, these so-called advances augment the price of health care, and thereby contribute to depriving a growing number of citizens of health insurance coverage. For Callahan this is a flagrant violation of his communitarian belief that we should not succumb to "an overweening research imperative," or allow ourselves to be "at the mercy of biomedical developments that will have their way with us." "It should be the other way around," he declares (Callahan 2003a: 507).

In an astute review of *What Price Better Health?*, economist Uwe Reinhardt characterizes the book (that he considers "a must-read for anyone concerned with medical research and…with health policy at large") as "less a critique of the nation's medical research enterprise—which strikes me as perfectly attuned to American values—than of American culture itself. That theme comes though time and again," Reinhardt observes, "when Callahan refuses to identify individuals for the shortcomings he perceives. Instead, he lets the reader conclude that American health care is part of a larger economic system that sometimes can bring out the worst in otherwise decent human beings" (Reinhardt 2004). For us, too, Callahan's book is an example of a morally resonant macroanalysis and interpretation of certain attributes of American society and culture, based on a thoughtful and critical study by a socially oriented and committed philosopher-bioethicist of the nexus between medical research, health, and health care in the United States.

Another example of a genre of socially and culturally attuned exploration and analysis by a bioethicist who is not a social scientist is the imaginative and illuminating book about the prevalence and meaning of the "enhancement technologies" of American medicine, *Better Than Well: American Medicine Meets the American Dream*, by physician and philosopher Carl Elliott (2003). In an eclectic, interdisciplinary fashion, the book draws on the author's medical, psychiatric, and philosophical training; his participation in a project called "Enhancement Technologies and Human Identity," funded by the Social Sciences and Humanities Research Council of Canada that, as he describes it, functioned "like a traveling salon"; the wide-ranging interviews and conversations that he conducted via e-mail, online discussion groups, and face-to-face encounters with an extensive array of strangers, friends, family members, students, and colleagues "involved with the technologies in question—some as clinicians, some as patients, some as consumers or clients"; and on library, archival, and media research. Although "I am not an anthropologist, a sociologist, or a historian," he states, "I have carpetbagged from all these fields for this book" (Elliott 2003: 333–336).

Elliott uses the relatively new term "enhancement technologies," as bioethicists do, "to designate a variety of drugs and procedures that are employed by doctors not just to control illness, but also to improve human capacities or characteristics." The aim of his book, he states, "is not to make an argument so much as a diagnosis…to try to put my finger on some of the reasons behind the uneasiness that many of us feel about these technologies even as we embrace them," and also "to hazard a guess or two as to why Americans in particular produce and use enhancement technologies in quantities that are often…unprecedented anywhere else in the world." In order to understand both the enthusiasm and the moral qualms they elicit, Elliott holds, "[w]e need to place these technologies in a cultural and historical context":

[W]e need to understand ourselves as inheritors of a cultural tradition in which the significance of life has become deeply bound up with self-fulfillment. We need to understand the complex relationship between self-fulfillment and authenticity, and the paradoxical way in which a person can see an enhancement technology as a way to achieve a more authentic self, even as the technology dramatically alters his or her identity. We need to understand something about the institutional structures in which enhancement technologies are provided, especially the way that our impatience with moral authority has given way to an embrace of technological expertise. We also need to figure out why self-presentation began to assume such importance in American life in the early twentieth century, and how it has been sustained by our particular culture. (Elliott 2003: xx–xxi)

As Elliott's vividly written, richly illustrated narrative describes, in the extravaganza of enhancement drugs and procedures to which Americans make recourse, and the procession of individuals who utilize them, what emerges is a portrait of a society in which many people are driven by a restless and relentless "search for some peculiar kind of American happiness"—an "American Dream" kind of questing "obligation to be happy," that is linked to self-fulfillment, self-realization, and success. From this, Elliott concludes, "you get something of the ethic that motivates the desire for enhancement technologies. Once self-fulfillment is hitched to the success of a human life, it comes perilously close to an obligation—not an obligation to God, country, or family, but an obligation to the self. We are compelled to pursue fulfillment through enhancement technologies not in order to get ahead of others, but to make sure that we have lived our lives to the fullest" (Elliott 2003: 302–304).

Better than Well is a new type of penetrating social and cultural bioethical commentary. At the same time, as Clifford Geertz states in the comment that he wrote for the book jacket, "this observant, offbeat description of…who we are or wish to be...[and] how we live now...that is also a biting critique of it" is "in the grand tradition" of American social scientists such as Thorstein Veblen, David Riesman and Erving Goffman, and literary artists like Walker Percy.

A final example of sources and forms of a more socially oriented bioethics that is emerging from outside the social sciences is what philosopher Jeffrey Blustein and physician Alan R. Fleischman[18] are calling "urban bioethics." This new endeavor was sparked by the dedication of the New York Academy of Medicine to "enhancing the health of the public through research, education, policy analysis, and advocacy, with a particular focus on disadvantaged urban populations" (Whitcomb 2004). In a coauthored article written for a special theme issue of *Academic Medicine* on urban health (edited by Fleischman), Blustein and Fleischman define urban bioethics as "an area of inquiry within the discipline of bioethics that focuses on ethical issues, problems, and conflicts relating to medicine, science, health care, and the environment that typically arise in urban settings." Urban bioethics, they go on to say, "challenges traditional bioethics" in two ways. It calls for an "examination of value concerns in a multicultural context, including issues relating to equity and disparity, and public health concerns that may highlight conflict between individual rights and the common good." And it "also challenges bioethics to broaden its primary focus on individual self-determination and respect for autonomy to include the interests of family, community, and society" (Blustein and Fleischman 2004: 1198).

The philosopher and physician coauthors identify population density, cultural and racial diversity, and disparity in the health status and quality of care among minority populations as "three paradigmatic characteristics of cities." It is in the spheres of these attributes of cities that they situate what they regard as the "work" of urban bioethics—namely, "identifying ethical concerns and value conflicts" in these areas, and "creating interventions to affect population health outcomes." As an example of this work, they cite research on the appropriateness and effectiveness of controversial "harm reduction" programs involving the provision of clean needles to intravenous drug users in the inner city to decrease the transmission of HIV/AIDS and hepatitis C among them. Such research, they state, can be helpful to public health leaders and policymakers in "clarifying and analyzing the...fundamental value conflicts at stake" in "creat[ing] health policy to deal with this... public heath problem in the face of strong disagreement." Urban bioethics, they affirm, can also assist in examining the "role of bias and discrimination in professional decision making and patient outcomes"—especially the way that a health provider's attitudes and beliefs about "age, gender, socioeconomic status, race, ethnicity, or other cultural factors [can] affect objectivity in responding to health complaints and needs" (Blustein and Fleischman 2004: 1200–1201).

In this latter connection, the authors advocate integrating "cultural competency education" into the training of all health professionals, in order to make them more "culturally sensitive" and more capable of the sort of "empathic communication" with patients of diverse backgrounds that has the prospect of improving health outcomes, and of significantly decreasing health disparities in urban populations. Invoking the Institute of Medicine report on *Unequal Treatment* (Institute of Medicine 2002), they aver that social science training is an important component of cultural competency education. In turn, they state, urban bioethics can "contribut[e] to the social science literature in this area, and [help] educators to craft interventions to affect professional attitudes and behavior" (Blustein and Fleischman 2004: 1202).

As Blustein and Fleischman attest, the outlook of urban bioethics on ethical problems associated with medicine and health care is markedly different from the perspective of what they term "traditional bioethics." Their approach emphasizes how crucial it is, both morally and practically, to think socially and culturally about the issues surrounding the health of populations in urban environments— with particular attention paid to public health, cultural diversity, social justice, and the predicament of city inhabitants who are subject to discrimination, poverty, social exclusion, and deprivation. In addition, an integral component of their notion of urban bioethics entails fashioning and implementing "ethically responsible" action that is "aimed at improving the health of urban populations" (Blustein and Fleischman 2004: 1202).

Blustein and Fleischman's call for an urban bioethics, we believe, admirably addresses many of the social and cultural factors associated with health, illness, and care that we have contended in this chapter are inadequately dealt with by "mainstream" U.S. bioethics. At the same time, however, we wonder why and whether the problems of health in cities about which they are deeply concerned, and the way they approach them, should be called "bioethics." In our opinion, all ethical questions connected with health and medicine do not necessarily belong to the domain of bioethics. For this reason, in the final analysis, we do not wholly agree with their conclusion that urban bioethics adds "a new dimension to the discipline of bioethics as traditionally conceived and practiced" (Blustein and Fleischman 2004: 1202). It seems to us that its justification for being, and its merits, do not depend on its donning the mantle of bioethics, although bioethics has much to learn from it.

Overview

What, then, can be said in overview about the current state of "thinking socially and culturally" in U.S. bioethics? Although the principle of individual autonomy has remained salient in bioethical thought, insistence on its supremacy is not as paramount and unequivocal as it was earlier. Principlism is still the "leading theory in the field," Callahan maintains, and its "driving force…in practice is autonomy." But, as he points out, "even among those who espouse 'principlism'…there is a lively awareness of its problems and liabilities." And efforts have been made within the field to broaden its conceptual framework by incorporating other moral theories and methods into its analytic philosophy-dominated perspective—among them feminist ethics, the ethics of virtue and care, pragmatism, and communitarian, contextualist, and casuistical approaches (Callahan 1999b: 278, 283).

In addition, American bioethicists have been manifesting growing appreciation for the importance of moving beyond being locked into their own consciousness by the logic and cogency of their abstract, "experience-distant" thought (Farmer 2003: 204), and for the value of developing and learning from close-up empirical knowledge of "lived" ethical situations. In this connection, they have embraced ethnography (to some extent, as we have shown, with facile assumptions or over-expectations). They are also showing an interest in developing a humanistic, narrative form of ethics in which the "story" of an illness and the effects it has had on the people involved is usually recounted by a patient or a family member.

Nevertheless, the integration of social and cultural reflection and analysis into the body of U.S. bioethical thought is still more tentative than firm—inhibited by the converging impact of multiplex factors. Among these factors, as this chapter has shown, are the enduring power of the concept of respect for autonomy, and the persistent tensions in the field between an individualistic and a communitarian vision, the factual "is" and the moral "ought" of descriptive and normative ethics, and between universalism and particularism. These factors, in turn, have played a role in the subordinate status that bioethics has accorded to social and cultural context and differences, and to pluralism, social suffering, and justice. Additionally, the relatively shallow interdisciplinarity in bioethics has contributed to the problematic aspects of the field's relationship with the social sciences. There are, first, significant disparities between the ethos of the social sciences and that of bioethics. Second, for reasons attributable to both fields, there has been a sparse representation of social scientists among bioethicists. These reasons include the failure of social scientists to recognize the social and cultural import of the phenomenon of bioethics, and, in bioethics, a continuing uneasiness with "the contention that the social sciences…offer a better way forward" for the field—even on the part of those philosopher-bioethicists most convinced that the social sciences provide "forms of knowledge pertinent to ethics and parallel to…necessary ingredients of ethics" (Callahan 1999b: 285). This uneasiness, in turn, has been coupled with expressed apprehension, especially by some philosophers, that the still limited number of social scientists who are at once active and critical participants in the field desire to "supplant philosophy," and locate bioethics within their own discipline (Chambers 2000: 27).

To break through these constraining factors, and make further progress in more deeply embedding social and cultural knowledge and insights, perspectives and modes of thought in the analytic framework of bioethics will require systematic conceptual work that is both resolute and collaborative.

Notes

1. "The issues and themes of the medical ethics that emerged in the 70s," Veatch has stated in less colloquial language, "were largely shaped by the problems bequeathed to us by clinicians and patients of the day...that led us...to see medical ethics as a conflict between the old Hippocratic paternalism (having the physician do what he or she thought was best for the patient) and a principle of autonomy" (Veatch 1984).

2. The concepts of "universalism" and "particularism" were considered by sociologist Talcott Parsons to be basic components of his general theory of social action—one of five concept-pairs that he called the "pattern variables" of social role-definition and of value-orientation. He regarded "universalism" and "particularism" as constituting one of the fundamental axes around which social action is oriented and organized in all social systems, from the microscopic to the macroscopic. The other four pattern-variable pairs that he delineated were: "affectivity" and "affective neutrality," "self-orientation" and "collectivity-orientation," "achievement" and "ascription," and "specificity" and "diffuseness." In his view, each of these sets of variables entailed a crucial set of choices for individuals or groups engaged in social action, which posed a major dilemma of orientation. See especially Parsons 1951: 58–67, 101–112.

3. When we interviewed James Childress in 1999, prior to the publication of the 5th edition of *Principles of Biomedical Ethics* in 2001, he was more equivocal than Beauchamp about the relationship between their four principles and the common morality. When we asked him about whether it made sense to him to conceptually tackle the issue of the cultural specificity within which the four principles has been developed, he replied: "When we're talking about common morality we're not necessarily thinking about it in universal terms, and so we leave that open. I don't think we've resolved whether to tackle that or not" (Childress, interview, 1999: see appendix).

4. In talking with us about the development of a concept of common morality by Beauchamp and also by Bernard Gert, Veatch commented that the belief of both of these philosophers that "they are able to articulate moral theories that have roots in something called a 'common morality'" is "not unlike Catholic moral theologians who believe that reason can produce an understanding of the natural law that is universal" (Veatch, interview, March 26, 1999: see appendix).

5. Although it has come to occupy a prominent place in the ethos of American bioethics, the conception of universal principles rooted in a common morality that should make them binding on all peoples in all societies and cultures has by no means been uncritically accepted by all participants in the field, particularly with respect to the development of an international bioethics (see chapter 8). In the bioethics literature, the *Kennedy Institute of Ethics Journal* has published a number of papers critically examining universalism and a common morality; Robert Baker, for example, has leveled a strong critique of what he terms "moral fundamentalism" (Baker 1998a: 201; see also Baker 1998b). A later issue of the Kennedy Institute journal focused on "common morality," with several articles by philosopher-bioethicists that challenged Beauchamp's ideas, both on empirical and theoretical grounds (Turner 2003; De Grazia 2003; Brand-Ballard 2003). As another example, writing about "bioethics in the third millennium," philosopher and physician Tristram Engelhardt has expounded on his convictions about why the field must "come seriously to terms with moral pluralism" (Engelhardt 1999: 225).

6. Engelhardt's introductory paper is part of a volume that he edited that is concerned with moral diversity and its implications for the possibility of a global morality, "using

bioethics as its heuristic" (Engelhardt 2006: 5). Two papers in this book that we found particularly edifying are Kevin Wilde, S. J.'s "Global and Particular Bioethics," and David Solomion's "Domestic Disarray and Imperial Ambitions: Contemporary Applied Ethics and the Prospect for Global Bioethics" (Solomon 2006; Wildes 2006).

7. Another article that has found its way into the bioethical literature was published in the same 1995 issue of the *Journal of the American Medical Association* in which "Western Bioethics on the Navajo Reservation" appeared. The article throws some light on how the members of four other ethnic groups in the United States (African Americans, European Americans, Korean Americans, and Mexican Americans) tend to make medical decisions. "Ethnicity and Attitudes Toward Patient Autonomy," by physician Leslie Blackhall et al. (1995), which is based on a survey sample of 800 subjects aged 65 years and older (200 persons in each of the four ethnic groups), reports that Korean Americans and Mexican Americans were less likely than African Americans and European Americans to believe that a patient should be told of his/her terminal prognosis, and more likely to believe that this information, and medical decision making in general, should be entrusted to and handled by the patient's family.

8. More recently, philosopher Kwame Anthony Appiah has proposed "cosmopolitanism" as a notion that can help to conceptually and substantively link "universalism" and "particularism." "[C]osmopolitanism is, in a slogan, universality plus difference," he writes. "There are two strands...two ideals...that intertwine in the notion of cosmopolitanism. One...universal concern...is the idea that we have obligations to others...that stretch beyond those to whom we are related by ties of kith and kind, or...the ties of a shared citizenship. The other...respect for legitimate difference...is that we take seriously the value not just of human life but of particular human lives, which means taking an interest in the practices and beliefs that lend them significance. People are different...and there is much to learn from our differences.... [We] neither expect nor desire that every person or every society should converge on a single mode of life."

   Appiah distinguishes between what he terms the "malign universalism" of "fundamentalism," which is "intolerant" of differences and of "conversation between people from different ways of life," and the "benign universalism" of cosmopolitanism, which entails a commitment to "pluralism," to "fallibilism"—"the sense that our knowledge is imperfect, provisional, subject to revision in the face of new evidence"—and to "tolerance"albeit in a form that sets limits on toleration that also "requires a concept of the *in*tolerable" (Appiah 2006: xv, xxi, 144, 151).

9. The following are examples of some of the book-length works by social scientists pertinent to these bioethical topics:

   Clinical Research, Experimentation with Human Subjects: Renée C. Fox, *Experiment Perilous: Physicians and Patients Facing the Unknown* (1959); Bernard Barber, John J. Lally, Julia Loughlin Makarusha, and Daniel Sullivan, *Research on Human Subjects: Problems of Social Control in Medical Experimentation* (1973); Bradford H. Grey, *Human Subjects in Medical Experimentation: A Sociological Study of the Conduct and Regulation of Clinical Research* (1975); Bernard Barber, *Informed Consent in Medical Therapy and Research* (1980); Charles W. Lidz, Alan Meisel, Eviatar Zerubavel, Mary Carter, and Regina M. Sestak, *Informed Consent: A Study of Decision-Making in Psychiatry* (1984).

   Death and Dying: Barney G. Glaser and Anselm Strauss, *Awareness of Dying* (1965); Barney G. Glaser and Anselm L. Strauss, *Anguish: A Case Study of a Dying Trajectory*; David Sudnow, *Passing On: The Social Organization of Dying* (1967); Barney G. Glaser and Anselm Strauss, *Time for Dying* (1968).

Life-Sustaining Treatment; Intensive Care: Diana Crane, *The Sanctity of Social Life: Physicians' Treatment of Critically Ill Patients* (1975); Myra Bluebond-Langner, *The Private Worlds of Dying Children* (1978); Jeanne H. Guillemin and Lynda L. Holstron, *Mixed Blessings: Intensive Care for Newborns* (1986).

Organ Replacement: Renée C. Fox and Judith P. Swazey, *The Courage to Fail: A Social View of Organ Transplants and Dialysis* (1974); Roberta G. Simmons, Susan D. Klein, and Richard L. Simmons, *Gifts of Life: The Social and Psychological Impact of Organ Transplantation* (1977); Renée C. Fox and Judith P. Swazey, *Spare Parts: Organ Replacement in American Society* (1992); Margaret Lock, *Twice Dead: Organ Transplants and the Reinvention of Death* (2002).

Abortion: Kristen Luker, *Abortion and the Politics of Motherhood* (1984); Jonathan B. Imber, *Abortion and the Private Practice of Medicine* (1986); Carol Joffe, *Doctors of Conscience: The Struggle to Provide Abortion before and after* Roe v. Wade (1995).

Medical Errors and Mistakes: Charles L. Bosk, *Forgive and Remember: Managing Medical Failure* (1979).

Growth of Corporate Medicine: Paul Starr, *The Social Transformation of American Medicine* (1982).

10. The bioethicists whom we interviewed had various perspectives on the place of the social sciences in bioethics. Alexander Capron, for example, noted that "in any field there is a tension between those who would like to theorize and those who insist that the more painstaking work of developing observations and data ought to come into the picture.... [The] principlists, as opposed to say the phenomenologists among the philosophers, would be inclined to think that the data are relatively unimportant because the principle leads you to the conclusion. I guess my lawyer side...leaves me thinking that the devil is in the details in a lot of [these bioethical issues], and you've got to study the details" (Capron, interview, 1998: see appendix). Daniel Callahan ascribed some of the paucity of social science input in the bioethics literature to an "intellectual timidity" in many younger bioethicists. "When I started out," he remarked, "most of us were amateurs and we felt in order to do bioethics well we had to learn a little bit of law, a little bit of medicine, and little bit of social science, and we certainly had to know some philosophy and theology.... [W]hat I find now with a lot of the younger people is...[an] intellectual timidity, a nervousness.... [T]hey come into [bioethics] thinking this is a very big field, it's very specialized....They have a picture of this broad, very demanding field that's now broken up into [many] subspecialties, each one of which would require a lifetime of learning" (Callahan, interview, 2000: see appendix).

11. Distinctions drawn between sociology *in* and sociology *of* bioethics have antecedents in distinctions between sociology *in* medicine and *of* medicine.

12. The group consisted of philosopher and physician Carl Elliott (in the status of a visiting faculty member); philosophers Louis Charland and Noam Zohar; sociologists Charles Bosk, Raymond De Vries, and Joseph Davis; anthropologists Philippe Bourgeois and Adriana Petryna; religionists Tod Chambers and Leigh Turner; legal scholar Trudo Lemmens; and political scientist Iris Young (who was more peripherally involved). In addition, the late anthropologist Clifford Geertz was a participant in the bioethics group, in the capacity of a permanent faculty member of the Institute's School of Social Sciences, and its former director.

   A portion of our discussion of the Princeton group and its work, including the relevant endnotes, is adapted from Fox and Swazey 2005: 366.

13. The Fall 2004 issue of *The Hastings Center Report* 35 (4), for example, had several papers that discussed ethical concerns associated with the influence of the pharmaceuti-

cal industry. Three of the four papers were written by members of the Princeton group: T. Lemmens, "Piercing the Veil of Corporate Secrecy about Clinical Trials" (14–18); C. Elliott, "Pharma Goes to the Laundry: Public Relations and the Business of Medical Education" (18–23); and R. De Vries and C. Bosk, "The Bioethics of Business: Rethinking the Relationship between Bioethics Consultants and Corporate Clients" (28–32).

14. Members of the Princeton group drafted a research proposal to study firsthand how international guidelines for the protection of human subjects in the global marketplace are (and are not) implemented in the regulatory systems of a cross-section of different societies, with special attention paid to the needs of multinational corporations and the rights of national citizens in the area of industrialized drug testing. The research team listed in the proposal is composed of De Vries, Petryana, Lemmens, and Bosk from the Princeton group, joined by philosopher-bioethicist Jeffrey Kahn.

15. J. Evans, e-mail to "possible conference participants," Oct. 11, 2004; Fox, as one of the possible participants, received this e-mail.

16. The 2006 special issue of *Sociology of Health and Illness* on the relationship between bioethics and the sciences, edited by De Vries, Turner, Orfali, and Bosk, was published as a book in 2007 by Blackwell.

17. See, for example, Brock 2000, 2001; Daniels 1986; Daniels et al. 1999, 2000; Daniels, Light, and Caplan 1996; Daniels and Sabin 2002; Daniels and Walker 1985.

18. Fleischman is a former vice president for academic affairs at the New York Academy of Medicine, where he continues to be a senior advisor. Both he and Blustein are faculty members at the Albert Einsten College of Medicine in New York City—Fleischman as a clinical professor of pediatrics, epidemiology, and public health, and Blustein as a professor of bioethics in the Department of Epidemiology and Population Health.

7

Reminiscences of
Observing Participants

Along the continuum of our extensive association with bioethics, we have encountered a series of reactions to our manner of approaching and analyzing bioethical phenomena and issues that have personally confronted us with the challenges of thinking socially and culturally in and about the field. Among the earliest of these experiences were those that accompanied the way that one of us (RCF) was viewed in the setting of the early days of the Hastings Center when it was still known as the Institute of Society, Ethics, and the Life Sciences.

As the original name of the Hastings Center indicates, one of the premises on which it was founded was the idea that ethical analysis should be concerned with "society"—with social and "common" good, and the public interest, as well as with individual good. The cofounders of the Institute, philosopher Daniel Callahan and psychiatrist Willard Gaylin, also shared the conviction that there was fundamental value in assembling a broadly interdisciplinary group of intellectuals (including theologians, biologists, physicians, lawyers and jurists, historians, social scientists and a variety of humanists, as well as philosophers) who, from their multiple perspectives, could ponder together the questions around which the nascent field of bioethics was crystallizing. "Two points were essential to that commitment," Daniel Callahan has explained:

One of them was that the issues of the field, whether birth, life, or death, should always be looked at through the prism of every discipline that had something of pertinence to say. A corollary conviction was that no single discipline could claim to have a privileged status in analyzing the ethical issues. (Callahan 1999a: 63)

Because of their emphasis on "society" and interdisciplinarity, Callahan and Gaylin saw fit to include social scientists among the so-called "founding members" or "Founders of the Institute." In March 1969, sociologist Donald P. Warwick, then at Harvard University, and I were the two social scientists invited to become members of this founding group.[1] Subsequently, when nine of the founders were named to the Institute's board, I served as its first and only social scientist member until sociologist Robin Williams was elected to it in 1973. In these rather singular capacities, I had the opportunity to bring my trained sociological perspective to bear on the matters with which the Institute and bioethics dealt in this inaugural phase of their organizational existence.

At that time, and over the course of the years that followed, Callahan responded with some sensitivity to any allusion I made about the field of bioethics not being "enthusiastically welcoming" to social scientists. "That seems to me to very much overstate the case, since I think there has been a good deal of effort to find social scientists," he stated in the otherwise appreciative letter that he wrote to me in March 1976, in response to the draft copy of my article "Advanced Medical Technology—Social and Ethical Implications" (Fox 1976), which I had sent to him. "I would make a subtle distinction here," he went on to say:

I think there has been resistance to a kind of barefoot empiricism—the notion that a mere collection of data will suffice to deal with value questions, or that one cannot even begin thinking about value or ethical problems until one has amassed a great deal of data. I suspect there has been some resistance to that perspective—though that has not really been a characteristic of most of the social scientists involved in our Institute. What I have always looked for are those social scientists who work on a broader, more historical scale.... Your own work, as well as that of Daniel Bell, Robert Nisbet, and some others seems to me to move well beyond empirical work as such. And to the extent that it does so, it becomes a great deal easier to have an ongoing dialogue between social scientists and those in other disciplines. (Callahan, personal communication, Mar. 11, 1976)

Despite the fact that I was a full and, in certain respects, appreciated participant in the effervescent intellectual life that characterized the Institute in its early years, a number of its members from other disciplines were disinclined to associate my ideas and insights with my formation as a social scientist. They were more disposed to attribute what they considered valid or valuable in my reflections to me personally, in an ad feminam way, citing what several of them termed my "intuitive intelligence." Leon Kass, one of the bioethicists we interviewed who was involved in the Institute during this period, clearly remembered that this was the case. Furthermore, he recollected, at that time he thought that I gave too much credit to my mentor, sociological theorist Talcott Parsons, and to the Harvard Department of Social Relations that he had established where I was trained, as major influences in the way that I approached bioethical issues. In any case, Kass said, "[Renée] was an outsider at those early meetings for her insistence on the importance of cultural questions" (Kass, interview, 2000: see appendix).

With some amusement, I also recall the rather ambivalent acknowledgment that I received from a prominent philosopher-founder of the Institute who paid me what he regarded as a humor-tinged compliment: "You are not *really* a sociologist," he declared, "because you write so well!"

Nor has this been the only context in which intuition and expressiveness, rather than professionally shaped observation, reasoning, and interpretation, have been invoked to "explain" the source of my input to a bioethical discussion, or where questions have been raised about the significance that I attached to cultural factors. This occurred, for example, at a conference organized by the principal physicians and academic administrators at the University of Utah Medical Center who had been involved in the implantation of a Jarvik-7 total artificial heart in Dr. Barney Clark, the first person to receive this device as a permanent replacement for his own heart. The conference was held at Alta, Utah, in October 1983, seven months after Dr. Clark had died of circulatory collapse due to multiorgan system failure 112 days after he received his implant. The purpose of the conference was to provide an opportunity for the members of the Utah Artificial Heart Program and Dr. Clark's caregivers, along with a small number of invited outside participants, to reflect on some of the ethical, legal, economic, political, and social issues that the experimental implant had entailed, and what implications they had for the prospect of implanting a Jarvik-7 heart in a second patient. I was one of the "invited experts" who took part in the conference (Shaw 1984). There was general consensus at the meeting that among the "most provocative and controversial" ideas presented at the conference was my "contention that several unique features of the artificial heart experience with Dr. Clark were due to the…influence of the Mormon culture prevalent in the region" of Salt Lake City, Utah (Shaw 1984: 105). One of the underlying premises of the paper that I delivered was that in "largely implicit and unintended ways…Mormon culture and religion" had played a significant role in shaping the Utah artificial heart team's "values, vocabulary, and imagery; its conception of itself; its leadership and organization; and its relationships—to colleagues, to its special patient Barney Clark and his family, to the IRB, to the press and to the American public." "Mormonism in this sense," I stated, "added certain dimensions of meaning and mission to the implantation of the artificial heart in Barney Clark. It also helped to create some of the distinctive phenomena and problems that the heart team developed" (Fox 1984: 85–86). Several members of the implant team who were both startled and disquieted by this aspect of my analysis vocally expressed their disaccord with it. In response to their reaction, my analysis of Mormon influence was defended by a prominent bioethicist-participant in the conference—a moral philosopher-theologian—who publicly advised those assembled to listen carefully to what I had said because, as he put it, although he didn't always know where my ideas came from, he had learned over time that they often were relevantly on target.

Not all the bioethicists who have commented on my mode of thought have been consistent in the allegations that they have made about it. In fact, some have been strikingly contradictory. This is vividly illustrated by the fact that the same bioethicist at the "after Barney Clark" conference who implied that the sources of my insights were enigmatic, claimed at a retreat held by the President's Commission for the Study of Ethical Problems in Medicine and Biomedical and Behavioral Research (of which he and I were members) that my way of thinking was no different from his or, for that matter, from that of the other non-social scientist commissioners. Theologian James Gustafson, who led the retreat, disagreed with this statement. In fact, in a letter dated November 6, 1981, that he wrote after the retreat to Alexander Capron, who was then executive director of the commission, he made explicit reference to the fact that the perspective that I brought to the discussion differed in what he considered important ways from the "highly individualist...understandings of man," and "the claims...to rights" characteristic of other Commission members. Gustafson recommended to Capron that one of the respects in which he felt that the "individualism" premise of the Commission needed to be "qualified" was with regard to its "perception of persons as individuals" rather than as "persons in relations with others." It was in this connection that he referred to the difference in my outlook:

The "persons in relations" is what, in my judgment, lies behind many of Renée Fox's queries, with which I have great sympathy, and more than that—agreement. How we describe the network of interrelatedness within which persons are perceived and considered is critical. It defines both what persons and what institutional factors have to be taken into account in policy and more interpersonal choices.... The discourse between Wasserstrom and Fox shows that in some cases resolution of differences will be difficult, but if that could have been pursued, my hunch is that even if there was not agreement there would have been more concessions to the appropriateness of Fox's concerns. (Gustafson, personal communication to Alexander Capron, Nov. 6, 1981; quoted by permission)

On the President's Commission, I also encountered another kind of difference between my sociological outlook on bioethical questions, and the way that they were approached by some of the commissioners less disposed to view them socially. To a considerable degree, the Commission was given the option of deciding upon the agenda of issues with which it would deal. One topic under consideration was access to health care and inequalities of services in the United States, especially the failure to provide basic health services to more than 40 million people in the country. The prospect of examining and commenting upon this topic proved to be controversial. Virtually all the commissioners said that they were troubled by these characteristics of the American health care system. Nevertheless, a number of them argued, these conditions were not *ethical* issues. Rather, they were emanations of social, economic, and political factors, and therefore fell outside the Commission's mandate. In the discussion that ensued, my rejoinder to this contention was that as a social scientist, I could not accept the dichotomy that was being set forth—namely, that the distinction between the domains of the social and the ethical was so sharp and absolute that social problems did not have ethical components and import, and ethical problems were devoid of social content and significance.

In the end, somewhat reluctantly, the Commission did produce a report entitled *Securing Access to Health Care: The Ethical Implications of Differences in the Availability of Health Services* (President's Commission for the Study of Ethical Problems in Medicine and Biomedical and Behavioral Research. *Securing Access* 1983)—not because its members were persuaded by my declaration, but largely due to the conviction of its executive director, Alexander Capron, that this project should be undertaken.[2] In the Summary of Conclusions section of the Introduction to the Report, a carefully circumscribed statement was made about the ethical "mandate" of the Commission with regard to the problem of differences in people's access to health care:

In this Report, the President's Commission does not propose any new policy, for its mandate lies in ethics not in health policy development. But it has tried to provide a framework within which debates about health policy might take place, and on the basis of which policymakers can ascertain whether some proposals do a better job than others of securing health care on an equitable basis. (President's Commission for the Study of Ethical Problems in Medicine and Biomedical and Behavioral Research. *Securing Access* 1983)

Among the 10 monographs published by the President's Commission during its existence from January 1980 to March 1983, the report on *Securing Access to Health Care* was considered by the members and staffers of the President's Commission to be only a "partial success." In a survey of their assessments of their work and of differences in the effects of the reports they produced, conducted by sociologist Bradford H. Gray, they "praised [*Securing Access*] for the data it brought together on the uninsured and for articulating what became an influential ethical argument about the access issue (stated in terms of societal obligations rather than individual rights). But some were critical of the report, feeling that it had been watered down at the insistence of conservative Reagan-appointed commissioners, and several noted the report's lack of impact on public policy" (B. H. Gray 1995: 289). In their view, it was the report titled *Deciding to Forego Life-Sustaining Treatment* (President's Commission for the Study of Ethical Problems in Medicine and Biomedical and Behavioral Research 1983) that had both the most "critical impact on public policy" and the most "significant impact on bioethics" (B. H. Gray 1995: 286). This appraisal was substantiated by Gray's review of citations to the Commission's reports in court cases, law journals, medical journals, and the media. *Deciding to Forego Life-Sustaining Treatment* was "in a class by itself"—the most frequently cited document in all these contexts (B. H. Gray 1995: 274–276).

As coresearchers and coauthors, the two of us (Fox and Swazey) have been objects of strong criticism in bioethical circles for some of our published social and cultural analyses and interpretations. Indisputably, it was a coauthored article that we published in 1984 that caused the greatest furor. The article was based on the six weeks that we spent during the summer of 1981 in the People's Republic of China doing sociological field research at the Tianjin First Central Hospital, under the joint auspices of the American Association for the Advancement of Science and the China Association of Science and Technology (Fox and Swazey 1984). The hospital that our Chinese colleagues chose as the site for our participant observation was not only known for its leadership in the modernization of medical science, technology, and care that was being ideologically promoted at that time under the banner of "The Four Modernizations," but also for its activity in matters pertaining to medical ethics—what the Chinese termed "medical morality."

Before our departure for China, we read an article written by H. Tristram Engelhardt about a two-week-long trip to China that he and a group of fellow American bioethicists had made in 1979. Entitled "Bioethics in the People's Republic of China," it was published in *The Hastings Center Report* (Engelhardt 1980). As we later wrote, we were struck by the fact that Engelhardt attributed solely to Maoism-Leninism-Marxism what he termed the "moral viewpoint" of the Chinese scientists, professionals, and intellectuals with whom he and his travel companions discussed questions of medical ethics. He made no allusion to possible Confucian, Taoist, or Buddhist influences on how the Chinese approached ethical matters. Furthermore, he expressed puzzlement over what he experienced as the "resistance" of his Chinese interlocutors to "intellectually justifying" their moral outlook within what he defined as a logical philosophical framework. In our view, Engelhardt's account was "inadvertently ethnocentric," both in its failure to discern the origins, patterns, and logic of the Chinese ethical thinking that he encountered, and in its nonrecognition of the extent to which the way that his group reasoned about ethics was "imprinted with Western and American cultural influences." The title of his article ("Bioethics in the People's Republic of China") notwithstanding, we wondered whether what was considered to be bioethics in the United States existed in China, and if so, in what form.

Upon our return to the United States, we wrote an article about the components of what the Chinese called "medical morality," to which we had been introduced through our immersion in the social world of the Tianjin First Central Hospital. It highlighted the "Chinese-ness" of the Taoist, Confucian, Buddhist, and Maoist-Marxist ideas that had been blended into Chinese medical morality, and then proceeded to contrast it with what we characterized as the Western, and specifically American, attributes of U.S. bioethics. Our article began with pointed criticism of the "cultural myopia" displayed by the Engelhardt piece that we had read prior to our trip. "Cultural nearsightedness," we stated, was "not confined to those occasions when American bioethicists venture forth to other lands, but...was pervasively present in [U.S. bioethics'] systematic inattention to the social and cultural sources and implications of its own thought" (Fox and Swazey 1984: 337–338). In effect we invoked what philosopher-classicist Martha Nussbaum, in another connection, has called the lack of "a Socratic knowledge of...their ignorance—both of other world cultures and, to a great extent, of [their] own" (Nussbaum 1996: 147). The article ended with our concerned comments about what we regarded as the "impoverished and skewed expression of our society's cultural tradition" that had been institutionalized in the prevailing ethos of American bioethics. If "bioethics is not just bioethics," we concluded, but in a broader sense is "an indicator of the general state of American ideas, values, and beliefs, of our collective self-knowledge, and our understanding of other societies and cultures—then there is every reason to be worried about who we are, what we have become, what we know, and where we are going in a greatly changed and changing society and world."

We submitted the manuscript of our paper, which we entitled "Medical Morality Is Not Bioethics: Medical Ethics in China and the United States," to *The Hastings Center Report*, which had published Engelhardt's account of his group's trip to China. In due course, we were informed that the journal might be willing to publish the Chinese medical morality section of the paper, without our comparative analysis of American bioethics and our prefatory comments on the Engelhardt article. The mixed message that we received about our critique of American bioethics contained reservations about its validity, while also intimating that it was redundant because leading bioethicists—most particularly Daniel Callahan—had already published articles raising questions about the conceptual framework and worldview of American bioethics that replicated ours. In the end, "Medical Morality Is Not Bioethics" was published in its entirety in *Perspectives in Biology and Medicine* (Fox and Swazey 1984). Our commentary on American bioethics became somewhat of a cause célèbre among bioethicists. The most passionate, published repudiation of the validity of our underlying argument and of the observations on which we based it was written by the distinguished U.S. philosopher-bioethicist Samuel Gorovitz in a paper that he entitled "Baiting Bioethics" (Gorovitz 1986).[3] The overall intent of his article was to "report various criticisms of bioethics...and begin the process of evaluating them as a start toward an account of what is reasonable to expect of the field and what should be urged regarding its future directions." Gorovitz emphatically stated that he did not "consider bioethics immune to responsible criticism, or deny that even...irresponsible attacks [could] prompt constructive reflection." The field "can only benefit from greater attention to systematic assessment of what its critics say," he wrote. "The unexamined discipline invites the philosopher's critical scrutiny no less than the unexamined life" (Gorovitz 1986: 356, 372). In his detailed account and analysis of our paper, and his caustically worded rebuttal to it, Gorovitz not only characterized our conclusion "that medical morality as they observed it in hospitals in China is not the same as bioethics in the writings of American philosophers," as "startlingly unsurprising;" he also alleged that our intention was "to do more than affirm two obviously disparate activities are not the same." "Their article is a broadside attack on bioethics," he contended, "and the news from China simply provides the vehicle for their tendentious polemic." He expressed doubts about whether our "biting attack" on bioethics was based on a systematic study of "contemporary work" in the field, or on "empirical evidence about where [its] center of gravity lies." "[P]erhaps," he suggested, "their description of bioethics reflects a general revulsion at endeavors they see as inadequately like the social sciences or insufficiently respectful of them." He was especially indignant about what he defined as the unjust way in which we had "mischaracteriz[ed]" the "outlook" and influence of "analytic philosophers writing in bioethics." In our critique of bioethics, he maintained, "[t]he analytic philosophers are the villains. Other voices, heard at times, are few and faint; the analytic crowd has captured center stage, and moral and conceptual carnage is the result." And he vehemently challenged what he called the "case" we had made "that individualism and autonomy have an illegitimate hegemony in bio-ethical thought." "[I]t is simply untrue," he categorically stated, "that autonomy has been an unduly emphasized value in bioethics."

Despite the ardor of Gorovitz's refutation of this aspect of our commentary, he admitted to having a "lingering sense" that our "attack on bioethics would not have been so eloquent or impassioned were there not a grain of truth" in what we had said. Furthermore, he stated, he wanted "to be careful to give [us our] due." Criticisms like ours, he conceded, "suggest that writers in bioethics should take greater pains to clarify their positions, and to say more about why autonomy and individualism are of such value and what their relationship is to the phenomena of interpersonal interconnectedness." In the end, he even went so far as to say that "Fox and Swazey perform a useful service in prompting us…to acknowledge more often, more explicitly, and more richly, the moral significance of the social dimensions of our lives" (Gorovitz 1986: 363–368).

At the time, we did not know that our article had also elicited strong albeit silent support from certain members of the bioethics community—including law-yer Patricia King, who had been one of the members of the group of bioethicists who had made the journey to China in 1979 with Engelhardt. In the interview that we conducted with her in 1999, King told us that she had been "dismayed at the behavior of our [bioethics] group" in China:

[T]he reason I was dismayed…was that when we would have meetings with people we were always trying to tell them about the values of autonomy. We never listened to them talk about community; we never listened to them talk about the importance of the whole…. We were so willing to criticize the Chinese and not learn anything from them…. I said, "You know, I am missing everything. And who are we to come to one of the oldest civiliza-tions in the world and tell them that you have it all backwards?"… [S]o when your article came out you made enormous sense to me. (King, interview, 1999: see appendix)

The stir that "Medical Morality Is Not Bioethics" caused was prolonged. But the outrage it initially evoked subsided over time, and even gave way in some instances to affirmations about its continuing significant role in challenging the degree to which American bioethics was intellectually and culturally "sealed into itself." The increasingly positive response to the article resulted in part from the growing internationalization of bioethics that took place during the 1990s and into the early 2000s. Nevertheless, as recently as 2000, religionist-bioethicist Tod Chambers attributed "fable-like" qualities to our account of what he called our "epiphanic journey" to China. "It is as if these sociologists have been strangers in a strange land in the United States medical ethics community," Chambers wrote, "and by coming to China they have found their true homeland, their true family—people who see their approach as natural and common." Furthermore, he alleged, underlying the way that we described medical ethics in China and the United States was "Fox and Swazey's desire to supplant philosophy with sociology" (Chambers 2000: 27). To us, such continuing misconceptions are indicative of the fact that despite the progress that has been made in thinking socially and culturally in bioethics, there is still a considerable distance to go.

Even more recently—in 2004—philosopher Tom Beauchamp referred with vexation in print to "the surprisingly influential thesis of Renée Fox and Judith Swazey (a thesis advanced without evidence or argument) that mainstream ethical theory—based in Anglo-American analytic philosophical thought—has led 'American bioethics' into 'an impoverished and skewed expression of our society's cultural tradition'" (Beauchamp 2004: 211). Although the excerpt that Beauchamp quoted came from our "Medical Morality Is Not Bioethics" essay, he did not cite it directly. Rather, he drew it secondarily from an article by Nicholas A. Christakis, entitled "Ethics Are Local: Engaging Cross-Cultural Variation in the Ethics for Clinical Research" (Christakis 1992), of which Beauchamp was disapproving because he felt that it epitomized the arguments of "critics of universal norms...[who] propose that universalist ethics be replaced in bioethics by pluralism, multiculturalism, postmodernism, or a practice-based account of morals" (Beauchamp 2004: 210). Although Beauchamp referred to him as a critic "who hail[ed] from disciplines other than philosophy" (Beauchamp 2004: 210), he did not specify that Christakis is both a physician and a sociologist. This illustrates the tension between philosophical and social scientific thought that continues to exist inside of bioethics, and of one of the major sets of issues around which it is centered. It is also indicative of the rather deficient sociology of knowledge-based understanding in the field of the intellectual backgrounds and professionally trained outlook of social scientist participants in bioethics, even by philosopher-bioethicists of the highest caliber.

"At least you got to the table," some bioethicists sympathetic to the input of social science to bioethics have told us. "But your voice was definitely marginalized," anthropologist-bioethicist Patricia Marshall has commented, going on to generously say that nonetheless, she and her relatively few anthropologist colleagues in bioethics (such as Barbara Koenig and Betty Levin) are "grateful" to us for the fact that we were among the first to work "in the uncharted territory" linking social science and bioethics. In a frank conversation with philosopher Ruth Macklin, Marshall told us, she referred to "this notion of marginality, or being on the periphery" in bioethics. She reported that Macklin replied, "You're not on the periphery. We all feel that way"—to which Marshall responded: "Ruth, come on, you are not on the periphery; you are front and center. You have the bioethics pedigree that sets you out front. I'm very much on the periphery. I have a totally different tradition than you do." "The voice of social science for the most part has been silenced," Patricia Marshall insisted—at least, "until recently" (Marshall, interview, 2000: see appendix).

Issues of marginality notwithstanding, there is at least one of our coauthored publications that has received what appears to be unqualified approval within the bioethics community. It is the final chapter of our book *Spare Parts: Organ Replacement in American Society* (Fox and Swazey 1992b). In this chapter, which we called "Leaving the Field," we wrote in an intense personal way about our involvement as "journeyers into the field, participant observers, and chroniclers,...in the development of organ transplantation, the artificial kidney, and the artificial heart throughout most of their contemporaneous medical and social history and for many years of our working lives" (Fox and Swazey 1992b:197).

We went on to describe our gradual recognition in ourselves of "the signs and symptoms of what we diagnosed as 'participant-observer burnout'"—symptoms, we stated, that were related to aspects of organ replacement endeavors that we had always found troubling. Foremost among these, we explained, were components of the "courage to fail" outlook and value system that not only characterized transplantation and artificial organ pioneers, but permeated the entire field of organ replacement in the United States. "This ethos," we wrote, "includes a classically American frontier outlook: heroic, pioneering, adventurous, optimistic, and determined. It also involves, however, a bellicose, 'death is the enemy' perspective; a rescue-oriented and often zealous determination to maintain life at any cost; and a relentless, hubris-ridden refusal to accept limits" (Fox and Swazey 1992b: 199). We identified some of the experiences and events that had progressively led us to believe that "the missionary-like ardor about organ replacement that now exists, the overidealization of the quality and duration of life that can ensue, and the seemingly limitless attempts to procure and implant organs that are currently taking place have gotten out of hand" (Fox and Swazey 1992b: 204). We also deplored the fact that, in our opinion, the amount of emotional, scientific, and clinical energy devoted to organ replacement in American society, and of money invested in it helped to "divert attention and human and financial resources away from far more basic and widespread public and individual health care needs in our society"—most notably the inaccessibility of basic health care to millions of inhabitants of this country (Fox and Swazey 1992b: 208). We ended the chapter with the joint declaration that for these various reasons we had decided to take leave of the field of organ replacement—by which we meant that we would no longer conduct firsthand research in this area. "In the final analysis," we concluded, "our departure from the field...is not only impelled by our need and desire to distance ourselves...emotionally. It is also a value statement on our part":

> By our leave-taking we are intentionally separating ourselves from what we believe has become an overly zealous medical and societal commitment to the endless perpetuation of life and to repairing and rebuilding people through organ replacement—and from the human suffering and the social, cultural, and spiritual harm we believe such unexamined excess can, and already has, brought in its wake. (Fox and Swazey 1992b: 210)

In contrast to the ambivalent attitude of *The Hastings Center Report* to our "Medical Morality Is Not Bioethics" paper, and its reluctance to publish the section of it that dealt comparatively and critically with American bioethics, the editors of the *Report* contacted us about their keen interest in reproducing our "Leaving the Field" chapter in the journal.[4] Upon receiving our permission to do so, it was rapidly published in the September–October 1992 issue (Fox and Swazey 1992a).

To our knowledge, no negative comments by bioethicists on the final "leaving the field" chapter in *Spare Parts*, or the article derived from it, have appeared in print. And in our informal exchanges with them, they have been more inclined to commend than to criticize us for the questions about transplantation that we have raised.[5] We do not take this for granted; nor can we easily explain it. For, by and large, bioethicists have paid more attention to problems surrounding the scarcity of donated organs and the establishment and operation of a fair system of access to them, than they have to the questions on which our "leaving the field" testimony centered. And although concern about how audacious, vigorous, and indefatigable medical and surgical interventions should be, especially in the face of end-stage illness, has long been a central consideration on the bioethics agenda—whether, why, when, how, and by whom limits should be set on efforts to sustain and prolong life are not considered a settled matter. They continue to evoke serious bioethical debate. Furthermore (as we shall discuss at length in chapter 11), establishing and accepting limits in medical progress has become one of the most controversial issues in the "culture wars" that currently beset bioethics.

There is one earnest, congratulatory response that we received to our "leaving the field" declaration from a bioethicist that was based on a rather comic misunderstanding. In the open letter of resignation from the American Society of Bioethics and the Humanities (ASBH) that Steven Miles sent to its board and officers on March 31, 2004, he likened the action that he was taking to the departure from the field that he thought we had announced. "I do not share the coyness of some colleagues about being referred to as a medical-, clinical-, or bio-ethicist," he wrote:

> This is what we do for much of our professional lives. It is what society calls us.... I am a medical ethicist. Unlike Renée Fox, I am not "leaving the field" though I agree with her prescient analysis of its shortcomings. I am however leaving the Society because I believe that the life and mission of the field is better embodied and pursued in other professional affiliations.

We felt compelled to set the record straight. And so we wrote Miles an e-mail, praising him for "having the 'courage' to act on [his] convictions," which we told him we felt was "all too rare these days." However, there was one thing that he had said in his letter to the ASBH, we continued, that we wanted to call to his attention, because it misrepresented our own decision to "leave the field." "We did not leave/have not left the field of *bioethics*," we explained. "Rather, the last chapter in *Spare Parts* dealt with our decision to discontinue our long-time ethnographic studies of organ transplantation and artificial organs." In fact, we informed him, we are presently engaged in the process of writing a whole book about bioethics—its development, import, and our relationship to the field.

Notes

1. Judith Swazey became a member of the first group of fellows at the Institute in 1970, and in 1980 was appointed to the largely ceremonious one-year term as vice president.
2. On a number of occasions during my (RCF's) term as a commissioner, Alex Capron asked for my sociological reflections on a topic under discussion. One such instance that I remember occurred in connection with the Commission's report on medical, legal, and ethical issues in the determination of death, entitled *Defining Death*, that was issued in July 1981. While he was working on a draft of this report, Capron wrote me a letter in which said that his "greatest worry" about it at that moment was that "it [did] not convey much about the sociocultural aspects of 'defining' death." "Do you think you could give this point special attention and lend a hand with some textual suggestions?" he asked. "This would be greatly appreciated," he continued, "as I now feel very solitary in my efforts" (Capron, personal communication, Sept. 19, 1980). I responded to his request with a four-page, single-spaced letter, which he respectfully received. But as I reread the *Defining Death* report today, I see virtually no trace of the suggestions that I made for placing it within a larger sociocultural framework. Nevertheless, in ways that were not always visible or audible, as I had found when he and I co-taught a seminar on issues in bioethics in his early years on the law faculty at the University of Pennsylvania, Capron was consistently interested in thinking socially, as well as biomedically, legally, and philosophically, about the questions on which the Commission deliberated.
3. Gorovitz became aware of our paper, "Medical Morality Is Not Bioethics," in 1983, prior to its publication in 1984. In September 1983, he wrote to Renée Fox asking her for information about any of her publications in which she had expressed criticisms about bioethics. This request, he explained, was in connection with a paper he would

be presenting at the April 1984 meeting of the American Philosophical Association dealing with criticisms of the field and his assessment of them. In her reply, Fox told Gorovitz about our forthcoming paper, and suggested that he contact the editor of *Perspectives in Biology and Medicine* about obtaining an advance copy of it, which he subsequently did.

4. In 1973, the *Report* had published another, short piece about our work on organ replacement, "Chronicle of a Cadaver Transplant" (Fox and Swazey 1973).

5. More surprisingly, and more remarkably as well, is the approval that we have received from a transplant surgeon of the stature of Thomas E. Starzl, who has told us: "[Y]ou were that little voice of conscience.... I think in a very real way you were asking, right from the beginning, whether what was being pawned off as treatment might, in a very real sense, be a disease in and of itself. In other words, if the treatment were so morbid, so uncertain, so emotionally destructive and fundamentally so unbiologic that the game was not worth the candle, that the penalties exceeded the gains.... [T]hat questioning was always there, although it was pretty covert in your first book [*The Courage to Fail*], but it was naked in your second book [*Spare Parts*]. And it's a legitimate question because what you were laying out in your writings, actually if it hadn't occurred to *someone* in the darkest moments of night who were [sic] doing these things, then they were not exhibiting any insight" (quoted in Fox 2003: 148–149).

MIGRATIONS

8

Bioethics Circles the Globe

In most countries, the inception and early phases of bioethics have taken place during the 1980s and 1990s, some 20 to 30 years later than the period when bioethics made its formal appearance in the United States. This seeming time lag is partly attributable to the largely undocumented, gradual process through which the emergence of American bioethics, its crystallization, progressive institutionalization, and its professional and public policy impact on medical practice and research have incrementally contributed to the development of bioethics in other countries and regions of the world. It is noteworthy that bioethics now exists in a wide and diverse array of societies;[1] that the same cluster of modern Western biomedical and technological advances around which American bioethical concerns center are among the core foci of bioethics in these different contexts; and that the major conceptual framework within which bioethical issues are addressed and deliberated in the United States has been internationally diffused. This is not to say that the worldwide attention now being paid to bioethical questions can be ascribed solely, or even predominantly, to American sources. But the shaping effects that U.S. bioethics and bioethicists have had on the field's international spread and evolution are striking—including the explicit ways in which the paradigm of American bioethics is now regarded in some societal and cultural milieus as a model *not* to be emulated.

Historically however, according to Daniel Callahan, the global spread of American bioethics did not originate as an effort by bioethicists in the United States to exert a hegemonic influence over the field's development in other countries.

Rather, he remembers that by the end of the 1970s, the Hastings Center and other bioethics programs were "getting a steady stream of requests from other countries to help them get bioethics started in their own countries. In almost every country, there was no field of bioethics and, at best, a very thin old-fashioned medical ethics taught in medical schools. We did not initiate those efforts; they came to us [at Hastings]. They wanted anything and every thing we could send them. So we sent them back issues of the *Report*, gave them free subscriptions, found grant money to hold workshops in their countries, and some fellowship money to bring them to the U.S. And we constantly urged them to integrate the material we sent into their own cultural context" (Callahan, personal communication, July 31, 2006).

The International Influence of American Bioethics and Bioethicists

The Influence of Bioethical Principles

Two sets of ethical principles are constituent elements in the global influence of American bioethics. The first set consists of the three principles—respect for persons, beneficence, and justice—that were enunciated in the *Belmont Report* of the U.S. National Commission for the Protection of Human Subjects of Biomedical Research, issued in 1978. As we have shown in chapter 5, these precepts, which were presented as "basic" to the ethics of research involving human subjects, and to the concomitant requirements of informed consent, a favorable risk/benefit assessment, and fair procedures in the selection of subjects, became the venerated cornerstones of U.S. regulations for the protection of human research subjects. The Belmont principles have been embraced with high respect by many other countries as fundamental to the guidelines and policies for research with human subjects that they have developed, or are in the process of instituting.

The second cluster of principles that has had an extensive and powerful international influence on bioethical thought and practice is the set of purportedly universal, "common morality" norms—the four principles of respect for autonomy, beneficence, nonmaleficence, and justice—articulated by Tom Beauchamp and James Childress, which they present as a basic framework for "identifying and reflecting on moral problems" in their renowned *Principles of Biomedical Ethics* text (see chapter 6). This "four-principles approach" has been so widely disseminated across national boundaries that it has become a kind of bioethical lingua franca.[2]

Founding of International Organizations and Participation in Them

The impact of American bioethicists and their perspective have also been felt internationally through some of the organizations they have helped to found, and their participation in them. In fact, it could be said that Americans have been prime movers in the creation and functioning of such international institutions, and in the establishment of formal and informal interconnections between bioethicists from different societies through the intermediary of these institutions.

Preeminent among them is the International Association of Bioethics (IAB), inaugurated in 1992, whose stated objectives are "to be truly international, linking all those working in bioethics and related fields, facilitating mutual contact, and encouraging the discussion of cross-cultural aspects in bioethics." One of the IAB's major vehicles for accomplishing these aims is convening biennial world congresses of bioethics. As of 2006, eight congresses had been held: in Amsterdam (1992), Buenos Aires (1994), San Francisco (1996), Tokyo (1998), London (2000), Brasilia (2002), Sydney (2004), and Beijing (2006), with a ninth scheduled to convene in Croatia in 2008. Along with the Australian philosopher Peter Singer, now a faculty member at Princeton University, American philosopher Daniel Wikler was a founder of this association, and served successive terms as its first vice president and president. He was subsequently chair of the International Advisory Committee for the 2006 World Congress in Beijing, with the authority to nominate the members of this committee. U. S. legal scholar Alexander Capron was a member of the IAB's original board, and later its vice president (2004–2006). American philosopher Ruth Macklin has been both vice president (1997–1999) and president of the IAB (1999–2001); and she and Margaret Battin, professor of philosophy at the University of Utah, have been board members. Although the IAB was "intended to represent global bioethics," as has been true from its inception, "a majority of its members are from North American and European countries," with the largest number consistently being from the United States, and secondly, from the United Kingdom. In 2001, the most recent date for which IAB membership figures were available when this chapter was written, out of a total of 586 members, 156 (26.6 percent) came from the United States, and 77 (13 percent) from the United Kingdom. No other countries reached double-digit percentages (Macer 2003). The composition of the IAB board in 2002 showed the same skew toward a predominance of U.S. and UK representation: out of its membership of 21 persons, three were from the United States (the Association's constitutional limit for board members from any one country), and five from the United Kingdom (a number augmented by the fact that three of these members had recently migrated to England from elsewhere).[3]

Prominent American bioethicists were also pivotal figures in establishing the Global Summit of National Bioethics Commissions. It developed out of the First International Summit of National Bioethics Advisory Bodies held in San Francisco in November 1996, which was convened by the U.S. National Bioethics Advisory Committee (NBAC), in conjunction with the third World Congress of the IAB that was meeting in San Francisco. Alexander Capron, a member of NBAC, and also the former executive director of the U.S. President's Commission for the Study of

Ethical Problems in Medicine and Biomedical and Behavioral Research (1979–1983), played the primary role in convoking this Summit, whose purpose was to give bioethics commissions in different countries an opportunity to get to know one another. The response was so positive that it led to a second International Summit in Tokyo in 1998, once again with NBAC as its host, and in association with the fourth World Congress of the IAB. This Summit, which was cochaired by the heads of American, French, and Japanese bioethics commissions, was more systematically organized than the first meeting, chiefly by the efforts of U.S. philosopher Eric M. Meslin, at that time the executive director of NBAC, with the assistance of Capron and Wikler.

On November 4, 1988, signatories from 31 countries ratified a document that created the Global Summit of National Bioethics Commissions. The document, titled *"Tokyo Communiqué,"* took note of "the history of international efforts in this century both to promote progress in biology and medicine as a means of improving the human condition, and to safeguard the well-being and respect the worth of all, particularly those made vulnerable by disease." It "recognize[ed] that developments in the life sciences and in the provision of health care and public health services generate ever more complex issues for advisory bodies in all nations" (concerning, for example, "access to health care resources in the face of scarcity, permissible means to reduce suffering in the process of dying, the prospect of creating human beings through cloning, selecting the sex of children, transgenic animals and genetically engineered foods, and molecular therapy for the enhancement of human capacities rather than the treatment of disease"). The *Communiqué* pointed out that many issues have "international ramifications," citing as examples of such issues the need for research that would make drugs and nutritional interventions accessible to the poorest nations, sustainable development, standards for clinical trials of drugs and vaccines in developing societies, the manipulations of the human genome, payment for human organs for transplantation, and ownership of DNA information. The Global Summit was being formed, its founding manifesto stated, out of a common aspiration to "advance the field of bioethics, which attempts to analyze and understand such issues," and a conviction about "the importance of working together to promote education and enlightenment around the world, of increasing the know-how of national commissions in dealing with difficult issues, and of developing the necessary information-gathering and policy-making capabilities, particularly in nations that now lack academic and governmental resources" (www.who.int/entity/ethics/globalsummit_tokyocomm).

American bioethicists have even been centrally involved in helping to organize events such as the first international bioethics conference held in the Arab world: the United Arab Emirates (UAE) International Conference on Healthcare Ethics, which took place in Abu Dhabi in March 2002. The six-person International Program Advisory Committee for this conference included Ruth Macklin and Daniel Wikler. They had coequal status with the four other members of the Committee–

the assistant undersecretary for curative medicine of the United Arab Emirates Ministry of Health, the secretary general of the Islamic Organization for Medical Sciences in Kuwait, the president of the Emirates Medical Association, and the managing director of the Gulf Centre for Excellence in Ethics in the United Arab Emirates. In addition, Macklin and Wikler gave papers at the conference.

Acting as Consultants and Advisors

The influential international roles that American bioethicists have assumed are not confined to organizational initiatives, or to making presentations at the escalating number of "international," "world," or "global" conferences that are being held in a broadening spectrum of cities, countries, and continents. U. S. bioethicists have also filled a variety of roles as invited consultants to governmental and nongovernmental organizations and to medical schools in an array of countries, and as advisors to international bodies such as the Council of International Organizations of Medical Sciences (CIOMS),[4] WHO, UNAIDS, UNESCO, and the Pan American Health Organization (PAHO). It is noteworthy, Ruth Macklin has observed, how frequently American bioethicists are consulted on matters that pertain to research ethics. In her opinion, this is a paramount source of their international influence. "I think that any [American bioethicist] working in the area of research ethics is looked upon as knowledgeable and influential because of the long history of U.S. involvement in research ethics," she contends, "[and] our own long years spent in addressing these issues" (Macklin, personal communication, Aug. 13, 2002). Macklin's book *Double Standards in Medical Research in Developing Countries* (2004a), the first published text on ethical requirements for conducting international collaborative medical research in developing countries, and the controversies and debates about what standards should guide it, is a product of such authoritative knowledge and policy participation in this area of bioethics. In his review of her book, South African physician Solomon Benatar, founder and director of the Centre for Bioethics at the University of Cape Town, characterizes Macklin as "an ideal author for such a text," because of her "active involvement in many of these international deliberations combined with her critical insight and philosophical analysis" (S. R. Benatar 2004: 198).

The issues on which the professional reasoning and expert advice of American bioethicists have been sought also extend into the sphere of medical treatment and the delivery of care. For example, Macklin and Norman Daniels were each commissioned by WHO to write a background paper on "equity" and "fair process" in connection with the WHO and UNAIDS "3 by 5 initiative" to treat three million people living with HIV/AIDS by 2005. Their papers had considerable influence on the formulation of treatment guidelines issued by these international organizations for a public health approach to "scaling up" antiretroviral therapy for HIV/AIDS in resource-limited settings. Macklin and Wikler are especially prominent among the American bioethicists who have repeatedly served in such capacities.

Appointments to Positions in the World Health Organization (WHO)

The recurrence with which Wikler has been called upon to act as a bioethicist consultant/advisor in the international arena has grown partly out of another kind of function that he, and subsequently Alexander Capron, have assumed: term-appointments to WHO. From 1999 to 2001, Wikler was senior staff ethicist at WHO, in the department known as Choosing Interventions: Effectiveness, Quality, Costs, and Ethics (EQC), within the Global Program on Evidence for Health Policy. He was followed by Capron, who occupied the position of director of the Department of Ethics, Trade, Human Rights, and Health Law in the Sustainable Development and Healthy Environments cluster at WHO headquarters in Geneva until 2006, from which post he reported directly to WHO'S director-general.

As his title implies, the scope of Capron's directorship extended considerably beyond the parameters of the ethicist role that Wikler formerly held and that he helped to shape. The Department of Ethics, Trade, Human Rights, and Health Law (ETH) was created by Jong-Wook Lee when he became director general of WHO in July 2003. In the words of ETH's mission statement, it "brings together four distinct but related fields," with the aim of providing "new responses to the new challenges facing WHO and its member states in the 21st century," and ensuring that "human dignity, justice and security in health are incorporated into programs and policies across WHO."[5] Capron's expanded role entailed setting the department and its manifold activities into motion—work that involved collaborating with other departments in the organization's Geneva headquarters, with WHO regional and country offices, and with "partner" experts from outside the organization engaged in specific projects. He informally organized his department's undertakings around four teams as focal points for the examination of issues raised by activities throughout the organization in the spheres of "ethics and health," "health and human rights," "globalization, trade and health," and "health legislation." The "ethics and health" initiative was centered on bioethical questions and dilemmas associated with health care and health care delivery, clinical research, and the development and deployment of diagnostic, therapeutic, and preventive biotechnology, and how they are experienced by patients, research subjects, family members, physicians, health care and public health administrators, and the larger society. These matters of concern cover "a wide range of global bioethical topics," including ethical issues in public health, professional ethics, ethics of human subjects research, biotechnology ethics (global and local issues in genetic databases, organ and tissue transplantation, implications of human stem cell research, ethical and cultural issues in genetics and genomics, human research and reproductive cloning, and GMOs for pharmaceuticals and food), and equity in access to health care resources (especially equitable access to treatment and care for HIV/AIDS, the ethics of long-term care, and the individual, familial, and societal obligations connected with it, and the rationalization and prioritization of services).

The second sphere of activity, health and human rights, pertained to WHO's diffuse efforts to integrate a "human rights-based approach" into its own work, to support governments in incorporating this approach in their health development activities, and to "advance the right to health in international law and international development processes."

The third area, globalization, trade and health, involved WHO's actions to "promote an effective health dimension to economic policies" by working to "achieve greater policy coherence between trade and health policy so that international trade and trade rules maximize health benefits and minimize health risks, especially for poor and vulnerable populations." This program of work was preoccupied with the implications for public health of multilateral World Trade Organization agreements and rules that affect the cross-border spread of infectious diseases, sanitary measures, the environment, health services and trade in services, access to drugs, tobacco control, food safety and food security, trade-related property rights, and traditional medical knowledge.

The fourth area, health and legislation, was principally concerned with the compilation of national and international health legislation, with an emphasis on public health law, which it makes available both electronically and in print, in the form of an *International Digest of Health Legislation*.

Capron's responsibilities, then, entailed integrating bioethical issues with larger medical, and more-than-medical, ethical questions, in a multisocietal and multicultural global framework of committed action. It has linked bioethics with human rights, public health, the economy, and the law, and was dedicated to the fulfillment of the values of justice, equity, safety, and dignity in a way that paid special attention to the health predicaments and needs of populations that are poor and at risk. In a number of respects, there is a striking difference between the perspective that this American lawyer-bioethicist worked to implement in his role as WHO's director of ETH, and what continues to be the preponderant outlook of U.S. bioethics. It is a discrepancy that is characteristic of the relationship of U.S. bioethics to the international arena more generally, which we will discuss toward the end of this chapter.

American Sources of International Training in Bioethics

In a variety of ways, a number of American organizations have been providing educational opportunities, resources, and facilities for training in bioethics on an international scale. One of the most significant of these activities is the involvement of the Fogarty International Center of the U.S. National Institutes of Health in supporting training programs in research ethics. The Fogarty Center is especially interested in helping to build the research ethics capacity in developing countries, where the vulnerability of persons enrolled as human subjects in medical trials, and their exposure to potential exploitation and harm, may be increased by the local economic, political, and social conditions under which they live, and by the fact that many of these trials emanate from medical centers in the "developed" world—often in collaboration with large pharmaceutical companies, whose prestige, power, and finances may allow them to dominate how the research is conducted. Fogarty grants have been made primarily to institutions outside the United States, either independently or in relationship to certain American centers. Fogarty funding has also established programs in research ethics directed by American bioethicists in their home institutions, to which recipients of Fogarty fellowships from other countries come to be trained. Some of these grants make additional provisions for the U.S. bioethicist in charge of the program to travel to the particular country or world area from which the trainees come in order to organize and teach workshops there as well.

Providing training in bioethics in centers located in the United States to individuals who travel to this country from abroad for that purpose is neither confined to Fogarty programs, nor to research ethics. Since the early days of U.S. bioethics, a continuous stream of persons has come to the United States to advance their theoretical and practical knowledge in the field, and their competence in academic and clinical as well as research ethics, by enrolling in workshops, short courses, seminars, and/or master's degree programs. This has enabled them to use American library resources to become more widely acquainted with the bioethics literature, and to spend time at prominent bioethics centers where they have obtained a firsthand view of their activities and established ongoing relations with their members and their projects. The Hastings Center and the Kennedy Institute of Ethics at Georgetown University—the first bioethics centers created in the United States—have received and hosted an especially large number of such foreign visitors, and have offered an array of intellectual events and training opportunities that have attracted them. Courses in principles of biomedical ethics given by the Kennedy Institute, based on Beauchamp and Childress's "four principles," have been especially sought after and appreciated.[6] The cumulative impact of these educational offerings on the procession of persons from different countries who have experienced them in the United States, and of the conception of bioethics that they have carried home with them and relayed to others, comprise one of the most significant long-term influences that American bioethics has had on the international scene.

Genres of International Research

Research concerning the ethical dimensions of health care and biomedicine in other countries, principally in the developing world, constitutes still another type of American involvement in the international domain of bioethics. As illustrated by the following three examples, such work has been conducted through various venues: on a programmatic basis, by bioethicists conducting studies for internationally oriented foundations in an advisory or consultant capacity, and by individually initiated projects.

The Hasting Center's International Programs. Upon his retirement in 1996 as the founding president of the Hastings Center, Daniel Callahan became director of its International Programs. Callahan had had a long-standing interest in international issues, sparked in part by the year he spent working at the Population Council in 1969, when he was creating the Center. As Robert Veatch recalled, "By the mid-1970s, [Hastings] was actively trying to study the ethics of linking international population aid to parochial American values about the way fertility should be controlled." According to Veatch, some 10 countries were involved in the project, "with international participants at every meeting" (Acadia Advisory Committee: see appendix). With a somewhat different historical recall, Callahan remembered that Hastings "started having international programs…in the mid-1980s," when, with a grant from the Soros Foundation, "we began running workshops in different parts of the world" (Acadia Advisory Committee: see appendix).

Under Callahan's leadership, the initial work of Hastings' International Programs focused mainly on health policy in Western and Eastern Europe, centering on his long-established interest in bioethical issues that concern "setting limits" on unbounded expectations of medical progress, on the desperate and marginal use of medical means to "combat" disease and "win out" over death, and on "medical goals in an aging society." By 2001, the topical and geographical emphasis of the program had shifted toward concentration on ethical concerns and exigencies surrounding the HIV/AIDS epidemic in Africa and the Caribbean. In collaboration with Weill Medical College of Cornell University and the Centres Gheskio (a Haitian health services and research institution), the Hastings program engaged in a project that addressed ethical issues associated with the HIV prevention research being conducted in Haiti. Its goals were to "improve dialogue and interaction between investigators and study subjects in Haiti, and between research investigators and local IRBs, and to strengthen present informed consent practices." As part of this undertaking, the Center staff planned three trips to Port-au-Prince, Haiti, to "facilitate conversations and ethics workshops among local medical researchers involved in HIV prevention trials and IRBs" (Hastings Center 2001: 9).

Additionally, in East Africa, in partnership with the Kenya Medical Research Institute in Nairobi, the Hastings International Program initiated a project that dealt with the ethical dilemmas encountered by physicians, nurses, and other health care workers on the front lines of the epidemic. Under the aegis of Angela Wasunna, the Program's associate from Kenya, the ambitious multiple aims of this project included "working toward establishing national and regional pilot forums for dialogue and education among medical practitioners, developing international materials on the major ethical, legal, and human rights challenges faced by health care workers, and developing problem-solving tools to assist health care workers, physicians' associations, patients, policy makers, legislators, and the general public to deal with these challenges" (Hastings Center 2001: 9–10).

Foundation-Consultant Bioethical Research. There is another genre of ethical theory-guided research, combined with the roles of consultant and advisor, in which a relatively small number of American bioethicists have engaged, which has had international repercussions. Foremost among such internationally oriented research undertakings is the Ford Foundation-supported inquiry that Ruth Macklin conducted over the course of 1991–1996 into ethical issues associated with reproductive health and sexuality in developing countries. Within the framework and orbit of this study, as Macklin states, she "sought to combine empirical information about the actual customs and cultural practices of [her] research with an analysis based on ethical theory and widely accepted principles of biomedical ethics." Central to the issues that she addressed were those "related to cultural relativity and ethical relativism": to the "long-standing debate in ethics and public policy…[about] the fact that ethical beliefs and practices may vary from one place to another, giving rise to the question whether there are any overarching universal ethical precepts" (Macklin 1999: v). Her project involved visits to Argentina, Brazil, Chile, Colombia, Peru, and Mexico, to the Philippines, Egypt, Niger, India, Bangladesh, and China.

The information Macklin gathered was obtained from interviews, informal conversations, and meetings that she had with individuals and groups to whom she was introduced by the Ford Foundation's program officers. The persons she met "included physicians, lawyers, social scientists, academic researchers, clergy, personnel in Ministries of Health, other government employees, women's health advocates, representatives of numerous and varied nongovernmental organizations, journalists, and other philosophers and ethicists" (Macklin 1999: vi). Macklin does not claim that she was doing sociological or anthropological research. Although she believes that most of her sources were reliable, she candidly states that the kinds of "anecdotes and personal accounts" she amassed were "no substitute for carefully designed studies by social scientists" (Macklin 1999: x). Her project involved the intertwining of the sort of inquiry she was conducting, with technical assistance and consultancy feedback to Ford Foundation staff and grantees both about ethical questions concerning reproductive health and sexuality, and about doing research on these phenomena and issues. Macklin has given lectures based on this applied bioethics project in numerous countries and at many international meetings. In addition, it provided the contextual background and concrete materials for the at-once highly respected and controversial book that she published in 1999—*Against Relativism: Cultural Diversity and the Search for Ethical Univer-*

sals in Medicine—which, as its title denotes, took a strong and reasoned st against both ethical and cultural relativism (Macklin 1999).[7]

Problematic Aspects of the International Predominance of U.S. Bioethics

U.S. bioethics and bioethicists, then, have played a leading role in erecting the conceptual and organizational scaffolding for what is termed international or global bioethics, in establishing its agenda, and in conveying its analytic perspective and substantive foci. American bioethicists have been primary architects of the international bioethics organizations that have been created, and among the most active and influential participants in them. Furthermore, they have been recurrently called upon by international organizations concerned with health to assume ethics-relevant offices within them, and to provide expert ethical counsel and instruction. One of the patterns that has emerged from our overview of U.S. bioethicists' presence in the international arena is the preponderance of a relatively small, nuclear group of Americans who are continually involved in this sphere, often in prominent intellectual, organizational, and policy capacities.[8]

However, the important part that U.S. bioethics and bioethicists have played in the global diffusion and development of the field has also had a deterring effect on its internationalization. As Japanese historian William LaFleur once remarked to us, "Bioethics has become international without becoming internationalized" (LaFleur, personal communication, June 3, 2007).

To a significant degree, surgeon-bioethicist Farhat Moazam has commented, this is a consequence of the fact that the principles-based paradigm of U.S. bioethics, which is "rooted in Anglo-European and American history and [their] philosophical traditions"—its claims to universality notwithstanding—is "the dominant language and methodology of almost all international discourse in bioethics."[9] The core problem, as South African physician and bioethicist Solomon Benatar has put it, is that "the grand theme of universalism as equal to Americanism is an enormous challenge to overcome" (S. R. Benatar, personal communication, 2007).

The attributes of this framework that have curtailed a deeper and wider internationalization of bioethics are the same characteristics that have inhibited the integration of social and cultural analysis into the body of bioethical thought. They include (1) the small and restricted set of concepts on which it is based, and a reluctance to expand them through the formulation and legitimization of additional principles; (2) the importance given to the precept of autonomous individualism, with an emphasis on individual rights; (3) the attachment of less weight to the connections between self and others, human dependency and interdependency, community, and common good; (4) a commitment to ethical universalism, accompanied by wariness about the ethical relativism that can result from paying too much attention to the particularities of histori-cal circumstances and traditions, and to social and cultural contexts, locales, and differences; and (5) the resolutely secular orientation of this philosophical framework.[10] These features of the model of American bioethical thought are especially problematic for the many societies in the world, especially African, Asian, and Near and Middle Eastern societies, whose social structure, tradi-tion, and collective sense of meaning are historically and culturally embedded in communal values and beliefs that emphasize kinship-connectedness, mutual dependence, responsibility, and a religiously grounded conception of the "gen-eral order of existence" (Geertz 1973: 98–108), to which these relationships and duties are considered integral.

There are stirrings of discontent among some American bioethicists, as well as amid European and non-Western participants in the field, about what they view as the "cultural imperialism" underlying the concepts and concerns of the U.S. ethi-cal framework, the expansionist way in which it has been "exported abroad" ("like Coca Cola," a senior figure in U.S. bioethics whom we interviewed quipped), and about the hegemonic "Americanization" of bioethics that has taken place (Carson, interview, 1999: see appendix; Englehardt, interview, 1999: see appendix; O'Connell, interview, 2000: see appendix). "The next step for American bioethics is to become more international and universal," George Annas has exhorted—"not as an imperialist project, but as a learning project" (Annas 2005a: xvi). In addi-tion, both American and non-American critics, inside and outside of the bioethics fold, associate the strong American influence on the field, emanating from an affluent country, with the relative inattention they feel it has paid to the moral questions and challenges posed by "global health"—most notably, by the state of health and access to care in developing societies where epidemics of infectious diseases are rampant, "deplorable poverty" and a "yawning gap" between the rich and the poor exist, and "pathologies of power" and abuses of human rights and social justice prevail (Farmer and Campos 2004; Farmer 1995, 2003; S. R. Bena-tar 1998, 2005; S. R. Benatar and Fox 2005; Annas 2005b: 3; Fox and Swazey 2005).[11] Bioethics has been faulted for its failure to address infectious disease, and Australian bioethicist Michael Selgelid (2005) has suggested that this deficit may be linked to the field's inattention to poverty and health care in developing coun-tries. There are, however, some indications that American bioethics, belatedly in our view, is beginning to heed issues posed by the global problems of infectious disease. A group of philosopher-bioethicists and physicians at the University of Utah has initiated what they describe as "a long-term project of assessing the significance of infectious disease for bioethics." Their foci are both retrospective and contemporaneous. The project is speculatively considering the question of whether "bioethics would have looked different had the image of quickly mov-ing, possibly deadly contagion been at the forefront...?" And it is examining the implications of today's rampant spread of contagious diseases for key bioethics tenets such as informed consent, confidentiality, and justice, and for such matters as the individualistic patient-centered model of decision making at the end of life (Francis et al. 2006).

There are signs, too, in the words of Dutch physician and philosopher Henk ten Have, of "a growing awareness" in European countries that "the dominant conception [of bioethics]...the analytic principles approach...that originated in the American...context [and] seems to prevail in bioethics debates everywhere in the world," is not sufficiently attentive to "certain fundamental aspects" of "a European perspective" (ten Have and Gordijn 2001: 53). What some of these more "typically European issues and perspectives in present-day bioethics" are is discernable in the textbook that ten Have coedited with Dutch clinical ethicist Bert Gordijn (ten Have and Gordijn 2001), and in the 2002–2003 syllabus for the European master in bioethics program out of which the book developed.[12] Their conceptual emphases include:

- orientation to the "theoretical pluralism, characteristic [of] European philosophical traditions," especially "philosophical and theological theories about man, solidarity, [the] meaning of life and death, care, [the] goals of medicine, [and] the technological imperative," and their "impact on the development of European health care ethics" (European Master in Bioethics Syllabus 2002–2003: 1–2).
- a view of the corporeal, existential, and experiential entwinement of the human person and body in human identity and moral being, as conceived by philosophical anthropology, phenomenology, and hermeneutics.
- recognition of the importance of being aware of the "actual experiences" of physicians, nurses, and patients, and the "particularities" of the "socio-cultural context" and "practical setting" in which "they and others experience their moral lives,...the roles they play, the relationships in which they participate, the expectations they have, and the values they cherish" (ten Have and Gordijn 2001).
- serious consideration to "the basic idea of moral community," "the *universal* human condition of existence as a communal-cultural being," and the *particular* [cultural] ways" in which the "communitarian self" is "constituted" and "realized" (ten Have and Gordijn 2001: 79, authors' italics).
- a comparative historical perspective on ethical issues—one that attaches importance to examining why specific bioethical problems "appear, reappear, and...disappear in medical discourse," and "why certain problems emerge in various health care practices and others do not" (ten Have and Gordijn 2001).

Substantively, the book and the European master in bioethics curriculum focus on topics such as:

- vulnerability, pain and suffering, particularly in connection with dying and death.
- the relationship between religion and bioethics, especially Christian, Jewish, Muslim, Hindu, and Buddhist conceptions of the beginning and end of life.
- ethical issues that pertain to children and elderly persons.
- ethical problems in the sphere of public health and prevention, and the conflicts between the interests of the population and those of the individual that they may involve.
- choices in health care and its organization that summon up issues of access to resources, their allocation, and their limits.
- questions of social justice that encompass the relationship between solidarity and social insurance, and whether there is a duty to make medicine economical.

The field visits that are built into the curriculum not only involve firsthand contacts with a variety of health care institutions, hospitals, and laboratories but also experiences—such as visiting the Hague, lunching with members of (the Dutch) Parliament, and traveling to the Natzweiler Concentration Camp near Strasbourg—that dramatize and personalize the links between bioethics, international human rights law, the polity, the Nazi medical war crimes, and the Holocaust which, from a European vantage point, are felt to be of vital moral as well as historical importance.

The insistent claim by George Annas that "[b]oth American bioethics and international human rights were born from World War II"—the medical experiments conducted in the Nazi concentration camps, the subsequent Doctors' Trial by the International Military Tribunal at Nuremberg, and the Nuremberg Code that the Tribunal enunciated—is considered controversial in some U.S. bioethics circles (Annas 2005a: 161–162; 2005b: 3).[13] But, as the foregoing suggests, in European contexts—above all in the setting of Germany—they are unarguably viewed as being interconnected in this way, and as wellsprings of deeply moral bioethical reflection and decision making. German sociologist Tanja Krones makes this clear in her account of what she terms the "context-sensitive" bioethics debate that has been taking place in Germany since 2000 regarding preimplantation genetic diagnosis, stem cell research, advance directives, and euthanasia. One of the major features that underlies this debate, she writes, is "the horror of Nazi Germany," which is still present. "The continuing awareness of the potential for inhumane outbursts has produced a high level of public sensitivity towards issues having to do with eugenics and possible discrimination toward the disabled." A second underlying attribute of the debate that she identifies is German constitutional law, with its roots in "Kantian universal principles and the right to life of every human being" (Krones 2006: 274). German political scientist Katrin Braun regards the constitution and its Article 1, which secures "human dignity" and gives it "exceptional status" that "cannot be revised or outweighed by other rights, such as freedom of research," as "important features of postwar, democratic, antitotalitarian German identity" (Braun 2005: 44–45).

As we shall discuss in chapter 11 ("The Coming of the Culture Wars to American Bioethics"), the concept of human dignity that Germans regard as the supreme expression of the morality of their post–World War II society—the pillar and the guarantor of the antitotalitarian, democratic nature of their nation-state—is viewed by some American bioethicists as a vague notion, which could properly be subsumed under the principle of autonomy, and lately, one that they associate with an ultraconservative, politicized stance against stem cell research, modes of assisted reproduction, and human cloning—a standpoint to which they polemically object. This is a cogent example of how and why the over-Americanization of so-called international bioethics can run counter to its internationalization.

What Is Needed to "Internationalize" International Bioethics

It is both remarkable and regrettable how little is known about the origins, auspices, contours, and contents of bioethics in the numerous societies in which it now exists. There is, so to speak, no world map of the "geography" of bioethics that identifies the countries in which bioethics has emerged and developed, or that provides cartographic information about its salient features in these various locales. Only occasionally have we chanced upon publications, like the several on which we have drawn in this chapter, that provide knowledge, data, and understanding of the sorts that we think are needed for bioethics to become more than nominally international.

There is a notable absence of organized will to break through the predominant, American-imprinted paradigm of bioethics in systematic ways that would bring it closer to a conceptual framework that is at once global and multicultural. American bioethicists have contributed to this inertia. Even though during and since the 1990s more of them have become intellectually, institutionally, and interpersonally involved in international bioethics, many have entered this arena with a dearth of knowledge of other societies and cultures and, to a considerable extent, of their own. It is a rare U.S. bioethicist who, like Daniel Wikler, has experienced and put into words the critical perspective that he feels he has gained on his unusual, culturally shaped ways of thinking, through his in situ bioethical involvement in another society:

I'm one of a small group of bioethicists working on a resource allocation problem in an Asian country. It's not a theoretical exercise; they have an actual decision to make. In trying to draw from our own work to make useful contributions to their deliberations, I'm learning more about our own work—what might be good, what is questionable, and what is probably useless—than I did in many discussions with like-minded peers at home. (Wikler, personal communication to Farhat Moazam and Aamir Jafarey, May 3, 2005, quoted by permission)

James Childress, the coformulator of the American-born "four-principles" approach to bioethics that has been globally disseminated, has recognized in print that in contrast to "the U.S. ethical framework for addressing research involving human subjects,...evolving European frameworks...identif[y] autonomy, dignity, integrity, and vulnerability within a social justice framework of solidarity and responsibility," and that "human rights, for which, in many documents, human dignity is the foundation," is "[a]nother framework that appears in many international formulations of principles of biomedical research." But he goes no further conceptually than to say that it would be "useful to examine" these differences, and that "[i]n the context of globalization, attention to the human-rights framework is imperative" (Childress 2005: 250).

In our view, what is required are detailed studies in-depth of what are considered to be matters of bioethical concern in a cross-section of societies, how they manifest themselves in different sociocultural settings, and how they are experienced and responded to by individuals in various statuses and roles, and by social groups and institutions confronted with these issues. The insights and knowledge yielded up by such studies, viewed singly and in comparison with one another, would constitute important ingredients for the theoretical and empirical work that needs to be undertaken to fine-tune the conceptual framework of bioethics, so that it responds more readily and perceptively to social and cultural diversity, without succumbing to extreme forms of cultural and ethical relativism. With this need in mind, in the following two chapters, we present sketches of the development of bioethics in two different societies—the one, Western European (France), and the other, South Asian (Pakistan)—in which we highlight features of bioethics in those countries that must be taken into account in any truly global conception of the field.

Notes

1. One of the clearest indications of the extent to which bioethics has developed and become institutionalized around the globe is the number of national, regional, and international bioethics organizations that have been established. The most comprehensive compilation of these organizations we have found is that maintained by the National Reference Center for Bioethics Literature (NRCBL), formerly the Kennedy Institute of Ethics Library, which was awarded a competitive five-year grant from the National Library of Medicine to serve as the National Reference Center, "dedicated to collecting and organizing the burgeoning bioethics literature, and providing reference services. The original grant was extended for three years, and eventually converted to a [continuing] NLM contract" (www.georgetown.edu/nrcbl/nrc/aboutNRCBL [last updated September 2004]).

   The registry includes a variety of associations, centers, institutes, commissions, and councils specific to a given country. Many of these are university-affiliated, while others are units of professional—chiefly, medical—organizations; some are bodies established to deal with issues of health ethics and research within national organizations; and some are dedicated to particular issues, such as reproduction, or research with human subjects. The registry also lists regional groups, according to the country in which they are headquartered. Among these are the Asian Bioethics Association (Japan), Central and East European Association of Bioethics (Hungary), Bioethics Division of the Council of Europe (France), European Association of Centres of Medical Ethics (the Netherlands), European Commission's Group on Ethics in Science and New Technologies (Belgium), the Forum for Ethical Review Committees in the Asian and Western Pacific Region (Thailand), and the Pan American Health Organization/World Health Organization Regional Program on Bioethics and Health (Chile). (Although as will be seen in chapter 10, bioethics organizations have also been established in Pakistan and in the United Arab Emirates, they are not listed in the NRCBL registry because they were founded after 2004.)

In addition, bioethics has given rise to several organizations that are international in their compass. These include two freestanding bodies developed by bioethicists, which hold periodic meetings in various countries: the International Association of Bioethics, and the Global Summit of National Bioethics Committees. Still other bioethics groups have been formed as components of major international organizations, such as UNESCO's International Bioethics Committee, headquartered in Paris, and WHO's Geneva-based Ethics and Health Program.

2. The sales figures that we were able to obtain from the publisher of Beauchamp and Childress's *Principles of Biomedical Ethics* (Oxford University Press, [USA]) are impressive indicators of its extraordinary, far-reaching readership. The book has been published in five successive editions. Figures for the sales of the first edition were no longer in the publisher's system, but as of May 2003, a total of close to 5,000 hardcover copies, and more than 14,200 paperback copies of its second, third, fourth, and fifth editions had been sold. In addition, the fourth edition has been translated into Italian, Polish, Portuguese, and Spanish, and the fifth edition into Japanese. Sales figures for these translations were not available, nor were there records of translations of the first, second, and third editions that may have been published. However impressive they are, these data *under*estimate the number of books that have been purchased. Furthermore, they do not provide information about how many people may have consulted or studied the copies that were bought, or about the range of countries in which the English-language editions of the book have been utilized.

3. Other than the United States and the United Kingdom, the countries from which a few persons were listed as IAB members in 2001 included: China (54 members), Australia (48 members), Brazil (32 members), Canada (32 members), the Netherlands (29 members), Japan (24 members), Argentina (14 members), Italy (14 members), and Israel (14 members). The membership figure for Brazil may have been temporarily augmented by the fact that the IAB World Congress was held in Brasilia in 2001, which was attended by as many as 851 persons from Brazil.

   The 2005 board membership listed on the IAB Web site as of its August 24, 2005 update represented 12 countries and UNESCO-Thailand. Although Alexander Capron was identified as being from Switzerland, where he was based in the WHO post that he then occupied, he is a U.S. citizen. By this reckoning, the United States had four board members, followed by Australia and Brazil with three each, and the United Kingdom with two (www.bioethics-international.org/board [accessed Jan. 23, 2006]).

4. Ruth Macklin has also served as a vice president of CIOMS.

5. All the quoted descriptive phrases about the four fields in which ETH's activities are concentrated are taken from http://www.who.int/eth/en, and its links.

6. The Kennedy Institute of Ethics has also created an International Bioethics Exchange Program (IBEP) to foster "research and education in the developing world by donating multiple volumes of the *Bibliography of Bioethics* [that is published under their auspices] to libraries…in order to encourage the development of bioethics reference sources in those countries." In turn, the program's description notes, "IBEP is eager to collect documents about bioethics from exchange participants," which will be added to the Institute's National Reference Center for Bioethics Literature, and "considered for inclusion" in the *Bibliography of Bioethics* (Walters, Kahn, and Goldstein 2005: 10).

7. See the discussion of Macklin's *Against Relativism* in chapter 6.

8. Ruth Macklin, Daniel Wikler, and Alexander Capron are among the most salient of these American bioethicists.

9. Farhat Moazam made this comment in a talk that she gave in April 2005 in Karachi, Pakistan, at the Center for Biomedical Ethics and Culture (CBEC) that she directs. In chapter 10, we will present an account of the origins and development of CBEC, and of Farhat Moazam's central role in its history, within the larger context of the unfolding of bioethics in the Islamic Republic of Pakistan.

10. These attributes of the conceptual framework of U.S. bioethics are discussed in detail in chapter 6, and in Fox and Swazey 2005.

11. In our view, as we have written elsewhere, the relative inattention of U.S. bioethics to global health and health care issues also stems from the field's "insular and insulated perspective," and from the "concomitant tendency…to define these problems as macroeconomic and macropolitical, rather than moral in nature" (Fox and Swazey 2005: 363).

12. Information about the master of bioethics course can be accessed at www.masterbioethics.org, which lists a variety of sources about the program. An announcement about the program was published in the May 2001 issue of the journal *Medicine, Health Care, and Philosophy* (4 [2]: 258), which is published by Springer Netherlands.

13. Nevertheless, along with Annas, philosopher Hans Jonas and psychiatrist Jay Katz (both of whom were born in Germany and had relatives who were incarcerated and died in Nazi concentration camps), Alexander Capron, and Arthur Caplan are among the members of the U.S. bioethics community who regard it of capital moral as well as historical importance to acknowledge and remember these connections (see chapter 1).

9

Studying Bioethics in France

This chapter addresses the question of what factors would need to be considered in a study of bioethics in France, if its orientation, development, contents, and meaning were viewed in the context of the social institutions and cultural traditions of French society. Our primary purpose is not to explore the "French-ness" of French bioethics for its own sake. Nor do we want to unduly emphasize its distinctive characteristics. Rather, our goal is to present a case-illustration of the sorts of variables that are pertinent to a better understanding of the ways in which bioethics is configured in different societies, and of why we think that this kind of informed understanding is crucial for the greater empirical, conceptual, and attitudinal internationalization of bioethics.

We recognize that we are not qualified to write a comprehensive historical account of bioethics in France, or to systematically examine its relationship to French society and culture. But with the collaborative help of French sociologist Simone Bateman (who holds dual American citizenship), we have been able to identify and reflect on some of the components of such an analysis in a way that we hope suggests how the kind of study of French bioethics that is needed might be framed.[1] After describing the formal beginning of bioethics in France, we turn to certain aspects of the field that have caught our attention, and that we believe warrant further empirical investigation. These include the professional and public authority of French physicians; the scope of what are considered to be bioethical issues; the connections among bioethics, the polity, and the law; the proliferation of a variety of training programs in bioethics; the prolonged unwillingness of the

French Parliament, and even France's National Consultative Ethics Committee on Life Sciences and Health, to consider end-of-life issues, and the events that eventually led them to do so; and finally, some of the values around which French bioethics is structured.

The Formal Inception of Bioethics: The National Consultative Ethics Committee

The formal debut of bioethics in France occurred at the beginning of the 1980s. Its development in this societal setting occurred very slowly, in part due to the resistance of many who considered bioethics a "phenomenon that was too associated with American culture to be 'importable'" (Bateman Novaes 1998: 12).[2]

The pivotal event that marked the "institutional birth" of bioethics in France (Minot 2000: 426) was the installation of the National Consultative Ethics Committee on Life Sciences and Health (Comité Consultatif National d'Éthique pour les Sciences de la Vie et de la Santé) on February 23, 1983, by a decree of then-President of the Republic François Mitterand. Its precursor was the Medical Ethics Committee (Comité de l'éthique médicale), inaugurated in 1974 at the National Institute of Health and Medical Research (Institut National de la Santé et de la Recherche Médicale, INSERM) by physician Constant Burg, the Institute's general director. The Committee, which consisted of eight members (four research physicians, two research biologists, one physician administrator, and one specialist in medical law) began to function in 1976. When mathematician-epidemiologist Philippe Lazar succeeded Burg as INSERM's general director in 1982, he was confronted with the fact that the Medical Ethics Committee was receiving a veritable flood of requests for advice from outside of the Institute as well as from within it. It was this situation that precipitated the decision to move the Ethics Committee out of INSERM, and its transformation into the National Consultative Ethics Committee on Life Sciences and Health (CCNE) that Mitterand's 1983 decree effected.

France was "the first country in the world to create [such a] *permanent* national commission on biomedical ethics issues" (Minot 2000: 426, author's italics). In this respect, it differed from the series of congressionally and presidentially established bioethical commissions in the United States, with their specified, relatively short terms, which began in 1976 with the National Commission for the Protection of Human Subjects of Biomedical and Behavioral Research. The stated mission of the CCNE, which was defined as "an independent authority," was to "give its opinion on moral problems raised by research in the domain of biology, medicine and health, whether these problems concerned human persons ("*l'homme*"), social groups or the whole society."[3] It also was expected to organize annual conferences through which important bioethical questions could be debated publicly. In the 2004 revised version of the so-called "bioethics laws" passed by the French Parliament in 1994, the mission of the Committee was slightly rephrased. Its charge, this legal text stated, was to "give advice on ethical problems and questions of society raised by the progress of knowledge in the domains of biology, medicine and health."[4] The Committee is subsidized by funds from the budget of the general services of the prime minister, and the annual report of its activities that it is required to prepare is submitted to the president of the Republic and the Parliament, and also made public.

At its inauguration, the CCNE was composed of 40 members, 5 of whom were appointed by the President of the Republic. Another 19 individuals were chosen for their "competence, and interest in ethical problems,"[5] and the remaining 16 members were selected from the research sector of the society. Members serve for a four-year term that can be renewed once, with the exception of the president of the Committee, who is named by the President of the Republic for a renewable two-year term.

The formality with which bioethics was publicly introduced in France exemplifies some of its characteristic features: "a politically initiated, sort of top-down, strongly institutionalized, norm-producing framework, with the purpose of organizing and controlling the discussion of controversial bioethical issues, and counseling government on appropriate action" (Bateman, personal communication, Sept. 23, 2005). In several additional respects, the CCNE represents and embodies other distinguishing attributes of bioethics in France.

Components and Characteristics of Bioethics in France

The Professional and Public Authority of French Physicians

The composition of the CCNE is indicative of the professional and public authority of physicians in France, and the considerable control that they exercise over the national bioethics agenda and debate. Three of the four persons who have served as the CCNE's president have been physicians, and many of its members, including those named for competence in ethics, are also medical doctors. This is congruent with the significant number of physicians who have been members of the French Parliament. In 2005, a total of 42 physicians[6] were deputies in the National Assembly (the lower house of the French Parliament), which constitutes an overrepresentation of members of the medical profession in relation to their number in the country's population (Isabelle Baszanger, personal communication, May 28, 2005).

As sociologist of medicine Claudine Herzlich has pointed out, physicians have "long been active in public affairs" in France:

Several doctors played major parts in the French Revolution and during the events in 1848. In the late 19th century, there was a very tight alliance between the medical profession and politicians with regard to public health issues. Several doctors sat in Parliament, very often on the "center left"; they were the mainstays of the newly born Third Republic. In exchange, the government fully recognized their professional monopoly.... [T]he status of "doctor" has long served as a springboard for entering politics in France. Since the 19th century (at least), it bestows legitimacy on what doctors have to say about society; it authorizes them to diagnose crises and propose remedies. (Herzlich 1995: 1617–1618)[7]

The high esteem accorded to physicians in France, their public voice, and the influence they wield are also associated with the fact that some of their prominent members belong to the socially elite French intelligentsia to whom a special "collective conscience" kind of role is attributed. "Since the Dreyfus Affair in the 19th century," Herzlich maintains, French intellectuals have been "expected to make value choices and defend them. Whenever they do not do so, the press often expresses its surprise about 'the silence of the intellectuals'" (Herzlich 1995: 1619). In this regard, for example, it is not gratuitous that Jean Bernard, the first president of the CCNE, was a recognized writer and member of the august Académie Française, as well as a physician, an internationally renowned hematologist, and a university professor of medicine.

The dominion of physicians over the sphere of bioethics in France is reinforced by an indwelling procedural pattern: namely, the traditional political process of seeking advice about normative issues and their resolution primarily, even exclusively, "from individuals with technical competence in the involved domain" (Novaes [Bateman] 1992: 161). Bateman cites the so-called Lenoir report (Lenoir 1991), which deals with "medically assisted procreation" practices as a "representative example of this approach":

[The report] compares the present situation of medical practices and French law with the measures taken by other countries; but there is not a real analysis of the ethical problems posed by the practices or of possible solutions, legal or otherwise, that could be brought to bear on them. Rather, the argument is based on a position that is defined as what is appropriately French.... The term public debate seems to be used in a very restricted fashion: it is limited to the consultation of public authorities with experts—most of whom are physicians and biologists—and to parliamentary debate. As to the solutions envisaged for the regulation of these practices, the mediation of the institution of medicine seems to go without saying. (Novaes [Bateman] 1992: 161)

The Scope of What Are Called Bioethical Issues

The issues on which the CCNE has been asked to give an opinion represent the scope of questions addressed by bioethics in France. Their range is narrower than those with which U.S. bioethics has grappled since its inception. It is also notable that the use of the term "bioethics" is more restricted in France than in the United States. It is most likely to appear in the promulgation of certain laws, and in public debate. But there is reluctance to extend its usage beyond this, partly because of French resistance to recognizing bioethics as a de novo, specialized field.

French bioethics has been heavily focused on questions that concern research on human subjects: medically assisted procreation; prenatal diagnosis; the gift, preservation, and use of human organs, tissues, cells, and gametes (ova and sperm); the use of gene therapy or xenogenic cellular therapy; research on the embryo; and embryonic stem cell research. As will be seen, it was not until the early years of the 21st century that end-of-life issues received national bioethical attention in France.[8]

Bioethics, the Polity, and the Law

The processes by which the CCNE was established and through which its members are appointed, and the nature of its mandate, are indicative of some of the interconnections between French bioethics, the polity, and the law. All the ministers of the national government, as well as the president and prime minister participated in naming its initial members. The president has the special prerogative of appointing the Committee's president and five of its members. In this context, the French Revolution-inherited "republican" tradition of separation of church and state legally obliges the president to distribute his appointment of Committee members equally between the country's "principal philosophical and spiritual families." Generally, the president has selected representatives of Catholicism, Protestantism, Judaism, and Islam, and a fifth member who represents those who have no religious affiliation.[9]

Because of the nature of French law, Parliament has the major responsibility for any legislative action pertaining to bioethical issues. Changing the legal status of a practice in France, particularly those that are politically and morally charged, requires an act of Parliament—the passage of legislation—rather than the decision of a French magistrate or court. It thus differs from the American system in which the law evolves primarily through changes in jurisprudence, on a case-by-case, court-mediated basis. This accounts in part for the fact that France has been more inclined than the United States, and also more than numerous other European countries, to promulgate national laws on bioethics.

In addition, French laws pertinent to bioethical issues contain certain specifications that extend beyond the orbit of legislation in the United States. The legislation regulating organ transplantation in France is an illustrative example. France has always been ethically reluctant to use live organ donors, on the grounds that it entails "violating " the body of a healthy person. Nevertheless, the procedure was legally authorized in 1976 (Law no. 76–1181 of Dec. 22, 1976—the so-called Caillavet Law—"relative to the removal of organs"). However, after 1994, live donor transplants were rendered basically illegal by the passage of Law no. 94–653 of July 29, 1994 (Article 16–3), "relative to respect for the human body," which forbade "undermining the integrity of the human body except in the case of a therapeutic necessity for the person," and only with his or her consent. In order to restore the legality of live donor transplants, an exception to this rule also was passed on July 29 (Article L. 671–3 of Law no. 94–654), which stated that "the removal of organs from a living person, who makes a gift of them, can only be carried out in the direct therapeutic interest of a recipient." The law specified that "the recipient must be the father or the mother, the son or the daughter, the brother or the sister of the donor...[except] "in the case of emergency, [when] the donor could be the spouse." Until recently, most of the transplants performed in France have been transplantations of cadaver organs. But the difficulty in procuring a sufficient number of these organs to meet the escalating performance of transplants and demand for them has led to the loosening of restrictions on live organ donations. On August 2004, still another law was passed, revising the law of 1994, by expanding the list of persons deemed eligible to be live donors to include first cousins, uncles and aunts, spouses, the spouse of a father or a mother, and anyone who could provide proof of having cohabitated with a prospective organ recipient for at least two years (Gateau, Soubrane, and Fagot-Largeault 2005: 25).

The tendency to make recourse to parliamentary legislation, which is strongly entrenched attitudinally as well as institutionally in the French system, has evoked admonitory statements about some of the negative consequences that can ensue from relying too greatly on trying to clarify and resolve complex bioethical issues in this manner. It can lead to a "false sense of security" through the oversimplification of the lived reality of the problems and questions involved that, Simone Bateman has suggested, "nourish the illusory hope that the codification in law of a certain number of rules...can eliminate the need for further interrogation about the best way to act"; "short-circuit" motivation to challenge and break through "habitual and familiar...ways of thinking"; and "dim capacity for ethical reflection and intervention" (Bateman Novaes 1997: 31–32). A more exhortative, moralistic statement to the same effect was made in the concluding paragraph of the report on end-of-life questions, published by the parliamentary Mission of Information established in October 2003 by the president of the National Assembly to deliberate on these issues:

It would be wrong to think that all the problems of a society can be solved solely by law ("*le droit*"), and inside the law, by the passage of laws ["*par la loi*"]. Because all situations cannot be apprehended by the law, it is also necessary to be capable of accepting doubt. A society that always demands more security and assurance forgets that progress and the general interest have more to gain from a confrontation with questions about knowledge than from the artificial maintenance of certitudes. (Leonetti 2004: 1:264)

The most fundamental legislation relevant to bioethics that has been enacted in France consists of the following laws:

- Law no. 88–1138 of December 20, 1988, concerning the protection of the human subjects of biomedical research (often referred to as the "*loi Huriet*"). This law (which was not implemented until 1990) brought into existence "consultative committees for the protection of persons who undergo biomedical research." Their powers extend beyond consultation, since the law made it obligatory that all public and private projects involving research with human subjects submit their protocols to these committees for review and approval, and require the committees to inform the national Ministry of Health of any unfavorable opinions they have about the research project. One of the side effects of this legal formalization and centralization of the ethical evaluation of research with human subjects, which some commentators deplore, has been the diminution of the number of local hospital ethics committees that previously existed (Minot 2000: 426–428; Leonetti 2004: 2:228–229). However, enough of them continue to function to have warranted the creation of a small, informal association of the presidents of such committees. Certain aspects of the Huriet law were revised in 1994 (Law no. 94–630), and in 2004 (Law no. 2004–800).

- The passage of a set of three laws that are usually referred to as the "bioethics laws": Law no. 94–548 of July 1, 1994, concerning the confidentiality of medical data; Law no. 94–653 of July 29, 1994, "relative to respect for the human body"; and Law no. 94–654 of July 19, 1994, "relative to the gift and utilization of parts and products of the human body, medical assistance to procreation, and prenatal diagnosis."
- Law No. 2002–303 of March 4, 2002, "relative to the rights of patients and the quality of the system of health." Although this tome-like law, composed of 125 articles, is not directly concerned with bioethics, it has significant bearing on many issues that arise in this sphere, because it clarifies and gives higher legal status to questions about the doctor-patient relationship that are addressed by decree in the medical professional code.

All of these laws specify the ways in which the different legal codes of the country—its civil code, public health code, and penal code—will be modified. And all of them have been revised by the passage of still another law "relative to bioethics"—Law no. 2004–800 of August 6, 2004.[10]

Despite the penchant of the French system to approach bioethical issues through national parliamentary action, the passage of the first bioethical laws, based on the advisory opinions of the CCNE, involved a protracted process that "fed" what the French press described as "an intense cacophony in the government" (Nau 1992). The prolonged time and the maneuvers that it took to arrive at a political consensus that unblocked the legislative path to bioethics laws was characterized by one journalist as "the tiresome hesitation waltz" ("*la pénible valse-hésitation*") (Nau 1993).[11]

Training in Bioethics

Organizationally and institutionally, bioethics in France is a more ambiguous and diffuse entity than it is in the United States. It is not located in centers, institutes, or departments that carry the name "bioethics." Rather, it consists of a general area that might be called "ethics, science, medicine, society," in which academic intellectuals with different affiliations, and from a variety of backgrounds, including medicine, philosophy, law, and social science, participate. Nevertheless, and in spite of the fact that the French are averse to preparing people for a role called "ethicist," there is some specialized training in bioethics.

In 1984, the Université Catholique de Lille founded the Centre d'Éthique Médicale, one of the first centers for the study of medical ethics in the country. Its three-pronged program involves teaching, research, and activities in the sphere of clinical ethics. A number of training programs in bioethics for which academic diplomas are awarded have also been created. One of the earliest of these was the DEA (Diplôme d'Études Approfondies/Diploma of Detailed Study) program in "Medical and Biological Ethics" that was established in 1992 in the Laboratory of Medical Ethics and Legal Medicine at the Faculty of Medicine of Necker-Enfants Malades, by the esteemed professor of psychiatry Yves Pélicier. (In 1998, two years after his death, Pélicier was honored by an international congress dedicated to him and to his interest in psychological, biological, social, ethical, and metaphysical aspects of personhood.) The DEA program that he founded was inaugurated by the professor of medicine and humanist Jean Bernard, who was then president of the CCNE. This "laboratory" (which has been renamed the Laboratory of Medical Ethics, Public Health, and Legal Medicine) became part of the new Faculty of Medicine of the Université René Descartes (Paris V),[12] and is now directed by another physician, Professor Christian Hervé, who has been associated with it since its inception. The DEA curriculum has consisted primarily of a series of lectures on an array of bioethical topics, given by specialists in medicine, law, philosophy, and social science. Physicians and biologists have been most preponderant in its student body, which has also included nurses, social workers, and some lawyers. In 2003, the DEA curriculum was transmuted into a master's program of "Research in Ethics, Medicine and Society," in the new French academic system that standardizes the diplomas given in European universities. This master's program entails two years of course work as a point of departure for the development of ethical reflection.

Another, comparable master's program called "Ethics, Science, Health, and Society" has been launched in the Faculty of Medicine of the Université de la Méditerranée, Aix-Marseille II. It is codirected by professors Jean-Robert Harlé and Jean-François Mattei, and it grew out of the teaching in medical ethics that was organized in the mid-1990s by Mattei, who is a physician, a deputy in the French Parliament, a former Minister of Health, and the author of one of the many reports written in preparation for the Bioethics Laws of 1994. At the beginning of the 2005–2006 academic year, the Aix-Marseille II program announced that henceforth, under the terms of a joint agreement, it would be collaborating with the Paris V program, and also with the master's program in "Ethics, Science, Health and Society" that was being started in the Department of Research in Ethics at the University of Paris-Sud XI, under the auspices of "Espace Éthique, Assistance Publique Hôpitaux de Paris," directed by Professor Emmanuel Hirsch, a philosopher and a former journalist at *France Culture*. This program, like the other two, takes an interdisciplinary approach to the ethics of health and medical practice, care, scientific research, and research in ethics, but it is more philosophically based.

The so-called "Espace Éthique" for bioethical reflection of which the latter program is a part was initiated by the Parisian hospital system in 1995, and has been extended into a network throughout France. The term "space" (*"espace"*) has two meanings in this context: a physical locale and a symbolic place where bioethical thought can occur in a way that extends beyond the media, and scientific, political, or ecclesiastical institutions. In liaison with university hospital centers, these "spaces of reflection" are intended to constitute places of training, documentation, meeting, and interdisciplinary exchange on ethical questions concerning health and medicine. They also function as regional or interregional "observatories" of medical practice from an ethical point of view, and participate in the organization of public debates with the aim of providing information and consultation for citizens about ethical questions. The rules of their constitution, composition, and functioning are defined by the decree of the Minister of Health, with the advice of the National Consultative Committee of Ethics (http:www.espace-éthique-org/fr/acceuil.php).

There is another master's of research in ethics program, entitled "Life, Norms, and Societies," which was in an early stage of development in 2005 at the three universities of Strasbourg: Louis Pasteur, Marc Bloch, and Robert Schuman. Its founders are physicians who are also theologians (Protestant and Catholic). The foci of its curriculum are listed as medical ethics and bioethics, human rights, ethics and society, and ethics and religions. The program's description gives some of the distinctive features of its orientation: the historical and geographic situation of Strasbourg, which predisposes its universities to have a European and international outlook and to collaborate with other European universities; its involvement in human rights issues in this connection; and its interest in the place of religion—particularly Christianity—in ethical discernment (http://www.éthique-alsace.com).

Two other master's degree programs relevant to bioethics complete the list of those that currently exist in France: the program in Law, Health and Ethics, founded at the University of Rennes 1 by Professor of Law Brigitte Le Mintier, and the master's in life science, developed at the University of Toulouse by geneticist Cambon Thomsen.

In May 2002, the first (and still only) Center for Clinical Ethics in France was created at the Cochin Hospital in Paris by a physician, cardiologist Véronique Fourier. She had previously been involved in the medical humanitarian organization

Médecins Sans Frontières (MSF)/Doctors Without Borders—and had served in the cabinet of Bernard Kouchner, one of the founders of MSF, when he was the national Minister of Health, and the Socialist party was in power. During that time, she played a significant role in writing the law on the rights of patients, which was passed in March 2002. She made preparations to open a French version of the MacLean Center for Clinical Medical Ethics at the University of Chicago,[13] and enrolled in MacLean's training program for that purpose. What she envisioned was progressively training French participants in clinical ethics so that eventually they could open similar centers in other parts of France. According to the Center's self-description, drawing on a "pluridisciplinary" team (psychologists, sociologists, philosophers, theologians, jurists, nurses, and physicians) affiliated with numerous institutions, it offers help in the face of ethically difficult medical decisions. Its consultant advice is based on the premise that "ethics belongs to everyone and merits a collegial and multidisciplinary discussion" that can be initiated by patients and their families, as well as by health professionals.[14] The notions of ethics consulting and of training for it on which the Center for Clinical Ethics is founded run counter to the persistent, mainstream idea in France that, by virtue of their technical competence and professional ethics, physicians are moral authorities in the sphere of medicine, who do not need instruction in bioethics, consultation with bioethicists, or input from laypersons to help them make moral decisions (Bateman 2004).

Bioethics and the Reemergence of "Moral Sociology"

It appears to be more than accidental that the inauguration of bioethics in France coincided in time with initial attempts to reestablish what sociologist Patrick Pharo terms a *"sociologie morale"* ("moral sociology") in the realm of French social science. In his opinion, "The emergence of the ethics 'theme' in public debate, and in particular biomedical ethics, certainly shaped [the] reappearance of moral sociology in France" (Pharo 2004: 17). The effort to relegitimate and revitalize the study of the moral dimensions of social life (including norms, values, beliefs, symbols, rituals, and meaning) that had occupied a central place in the oeuvre of the great French sociologist Émile Durkheim was spearheaded by contemporary sociologists François-André Isambert, Paul Ladrière, and Jean-Paul Terrenoire— all three of whom had roots in the sociology of religion. In 1978, they published a path-making coauthored article in which they presented their commentary on why "moral life," as part of "social life," had ceased to be explicitly dealt with in French sociology, and set forth their argument for what they called a "sociology of ethics" (a term that they preferred to Durkheim's *"sociologie morale"* appellation, because they regarded the word *éthique* as more neutral and less moralistic than the word *moral*). In this same article, they also announced their creation of a research team devoted to "ethical sociology and symbolic practices"—L'Équipe de Sociologie Éthique et Pratiques Symboliques (Isambert, Ladrière, and Terrenoire 1978). Subsequently, in 1994 when, after Isambert's death and Ladrière's retirement, Pharo assumed its directorship, the research team was renamed the Center of Research on Meaning, Ethics, and Society (Centre de Recherche, Sens, Éthique, Société—CERSES).

The first topics that the team on ethical sociology and symbolic practices tackled were the morally and politically sensitive questions surrounding contraception and abortion, which had become public issues well before bioethics appeared on the French scene. These topics subsequently fell outside the orbit of French bioethical deliberation when they were legislatively resolved by Parliament with the passage of the Neuwirth Law on contraception (Law No. 67–1175) in December 1967, and the Veil Law on abortion (Law No. 75–18) in January 1975.[15]

Particularly during the early years of its existence, the team devoted a considerable amount of its empirical work to ethical questions connected with biomedicine, especially to some of the phenomena around which the nascent French variant of bioethics was crystallizing—notably, assisted conception and prenatal diagnosis, in which the sociological research of Simone Bateman figured prominently (Isambert and Ladrière 1979; Isambert 1980; Isambert et al. 1980; Isambert 1982; Bateman Novaes 1979, 1982, 1992).

The research and reflections of Isambert, Ladrière, and their colleagues were implicitly structured around a cluster of historical, social, and institutional queries about the projection of ethical questions into the public sphere of a society, and the cultural meaning both of their appearance and their nonappearance in this domain:

Why and when do certain moral questions become the subject of public debate?...What means does the society create to manage these questions?...How are they discussed and by whom?...Who in the context of these debates acquires ethical competence?...What accounts for the fact that certain questions are not publicly debated in certain societies while they are the subject of intense debate in a "neighboring society"? (Bateman Novaes 1998: 7)

During 1984, the year following the French government's creation of the CCNE, as Isambert wrote in a letter to Renée Fox, he and his colleagues were kept very busy by the work that the National Committee asked them to do, which included helping to carry out a national survey on the functioning of ethics committees in France, preparing a report on the survey, and also drafting a report on a poll concerning the public's opinion of the CCNE. In addition, the Ministry of Justice asked Isambert to organize a colloquium on surrogate mothers. These activities, Isambert wrote, were accompanied by an "arousal" of public interest in problems of "biomedical ethics," which took the form of "one colloquium after another" in which he and his associates were involved—meetings that lasted for as long as two days, in auditoriums that could accommodate as many as 800 persons, and were always full. "I believe that there is the beginning of an understanding of the interest there would be in developing research in the social sciences around questions of biomedical ethics," he ventured (F. A. Isambert, personal communication to R. Fox, Dec. 18, 1984).

Nevertheless, the Center that Isambert, Ladrière, and Terrenoire founded has always been uneasy about being identified as an institute with a narrow normative agenda that is confined to bioethics. Furthermore, it has never had some of the institutional characteristics of other entities in France that are involved in bioethical issues: it was not politically initiated; there are no physicians on its staff, although it collaborates, formally and informally, with physicians on the Faculty of Medicine of Université Paris V; and it is not oriented to working toward changes in policy. "Our legitimacy," Simone Bateman, its current director asserts, "is based on the quality of the research done in full-fledged disciplines such as sociology and philosophy, with a central focus on ethics. This is a more general agenda than that of bioethics and...it keeps us out of trouble...in the politically charged context surrounding bioethics" (Bateman, personal communication, Aug. 2, 2005).[16]

End-of-Life Issues

Perhaps the greatest change in the focus of bioethics in France occurred during the years 2003–2005, when "end-of-life" and "death-with-dignity" issues, which had been overshadowed by a pervasive preoccupation with beginning-of-life phenomena and questions, were catapulted into the arena of intense and continual public debate. Until then, as sociologist Isabelle Baszanger and physician Michèle Salamagne put it, discussion about these issues had been much more "muffled" (*"feutré"*) than in the "Anglo-Saxon" countries of England and the United States, despite the attention paid to them at various times during the late 20th century by certain governmental and nongovernmental groups.[17] A consideration of how this shift in bioethical attention came about, the questions and values that it brought to the surface, and how it has been dealt with institutionally illustrate some of the patterns in French bioethics that we identify in this chapter.

In 1991, CCNE issued the first of three successive *"avis"* (opinion papers) that addressed the question of whether the description of euthanasia in French law as willful homicide, murder, or failure to assist a person in danger ought to be modified. In this document, CCNE expressed its disapproval of "legislation or regulations that legitimize the act of taking the life of a patient" (CCNE 1991). Seven years later, in 1998, in a report titled "Informed Consent of and Information Provided to Persons Accepting Care or Research Procedures," CCNE declared itself in favor of a "serene public discussion" on the problem of end-of-life care, including euthanasia, and emphasized the importance of "collective reflection" on the "circumstances before death" (CCNE 1998). This was followed in 2000 by another text in which CCNE went further, this time advocating "a position based on commitment and solidarity" in the face of the difficult and painful issues of "the end of life and the ending of life," which recognizes that the question of euthanasia "cannot be isolated from the broader context of dying today in a world profoundly marked by medical technicality and its obvious advantages, but also its limitations." This challenge facing society, CCNE stated, could best be met by "resolutely implementing a policy of palliative care, care for the dying, and the rejection of "*l'archarnement thérapeutique*," defined as "*obstination déraisonnable*"—that is, aggressive and futile treatment that stubbornly refuses to recognize that a person is dying and cannot be cured.[18] Although such a policy should reduce requests for euthanasia, it could not be expected to eliminate this issue. Regardless of what the circumstances and justification may be, the CCNE *avis* concludes, willfully inflicting death is a "transgression." However, terminating life-sustaining treatment—which should never become routine—may lead to accepting "the paradox of transgressing what is considered untransgressible" (CCNE 2000).

The evolving statements issued by CCNE over the course of ten years may have laid some groundwork for the public discussion of these issues that it recommended, and for legislative notice to be paid to them. But it was not until 2003 that they erupted on the national scene. Two events that received prominent and widespread media attention were precipitating factors in the escalated attention that the French public and polity and French bioethics now fixed on end-of-life issues.

One of these catalytic events was the death of numerous elderly people in Paris during an unusual heat wave in the summer of 2003. What this revealed to the public, through the accounts of their deaths by the media, was how many of these individuals were frail older persons who were residents of understaffed, underequipped retirement homes, or who were living alone in sweltering rooms or apartments, with no caring family or friends to watch over them and ensure that they did not suffer from life-threatening dehydration. This tragedy also raised collective awareness of the significance that the demographic aging of the French population had for nationwide end of life issues.

But it was above all the "case of Vincent Humbert" that played a cardinal role in triggering public debate and action about death and dying issues. Humbert, a young fireman who had become mute, practically blind, and quadriplegic as the result of an automobile accident in 2000, but who retained all of his intellectual faculties, made an impassioned plea for euthanasia to be legalized in France. He did so in two ways. He wrote a letter to President Chirac that was carried by the press in which he demanded from him "the right to die," to which Chirac personally responded, "I cannot bring to pass for you what you expect." Humbert also published a book entitled *I Ask the Right to Die*, which he wrote "by counting out letters of the alphabet with his thumb and head" (Smith 2005). In September 2003, his mother, Marie Humbert, tried to end his suffering by injecting him with a toxic dose of barbiturates that plunged him into a deep coma. Two days later, the medical team caring for Humbert disconnected him from an artificial respirator and caused his death by injecting him with potassium chloride. For the acts that they had performed, his mother was potentially subject to five years in prison "for the administration of toxic substances," and his chief physician, Dr. Frédéric Chaussoy, to life imprisonment for "poisoning with premeditation" (Nodé-Langlois 2004: 5).

Parliamentary Mission of Information on "End of Life"

An outpouring of sympathy for Humbert, his mother, and his physician ensued. Two deputies in the National Assembly—Nadine Moran, whose father had languished in a state of hemiplegia, aphasia, and depression for four years after a grave stroke, and Gaëtan Gorce, whose father had died in a state of severe pain from lung cancer—held a press conference to demand that a commission of inquiry be organized or, failing that, a parliamentary Mission of Information (Blanchard 2004: 8). On October 15, 2003, at the demand of the president of the National Assembly, such a Mission of Information on "accompaniment of the end of life" was established. Jean Leonetti, a deputy in the National Assembly, a cardiologist, and a member of the UMP (Union pour un mouvement populaire/Union for a Popular Movement)—the political party then in power in France, made up of a coalition of parties of the center and the right—was named its president and rapporteur.

The Mission had 31 members, representative of the entire French political spectrum. Over a period of 8 months, they heard 81 invited presentations, made by historians, philosophers, sociologists, members of various heath professions and health care institutions, jurists, political officials, and, in keeping with the "neutrality" of the French secular Republic in treating all religions and philosophies equally, authoritative spokespersons for Catholicism, Protestantism, Judaism, Islam, and the Masonic Lodges.[19] A verbatim transcript of the hearings was published in 2004, as volume 2 of the Mission's final report, *Respecter la vie, Accepter la mort* (*Respect Life, Accept Death*) (Leonetti 2004). In addition to its hearings, the Mission organized three round table discussions that were attended by the press. The members made a collective visit to a palliative care unit in Paris, and traveled to Belgium and to Holland to discuss in situ the laws those countries had passed to legalize euthanasia.

The Mission approached the issues with which they were asked to deal as a "national representation," within the framework of an explicitly French societal perspective. It organized its final report around three major questions: "What is the point of view of our society on death? What are the expectations of our society? What are the possible responses to the expectations of our society?" (Leonetti 2004: 1:12). One of its orienting goals became that of identifying the way of "approaching death while respecting life" that was best adapted to the French medical and social context.

Part 1 of the Mission's report discusses and analyzes the tendency to "repress," and even "deny" death in present-day France; the progressive degree to which it has become less "familiar," and more "individualized" and "solitary" than in the past; its "rationalization" and "medicalization"; and its "deritualization" and "secularization" (Leonetti 2004: 1:13–103). Detailed attention is given to "personal and social dignity" as a moral quality inherent to all persons, and as a principle of national and international law that is related to "freedom" and to "the autonomy of each individual [as] one of the forms of freedom." How the conditions of freedom and dignity can be reconciled through a "medical pact" between the caretaker and the person being cared for is considered. The concept of dignity, the report points out, is invoked as a premise by two very different "normative ideologies" and models of "dying well" without undue suffering: on the one hand, "voluntary euthanasia," based on the notion of a "right to die" and, on the other, the philosophy and practices of palliative care.

Part 2 of the report addresses the second question on which the Mission's reflection was centered: What are the expectations of French society regarding the conditions under which its members would wish to end their lives if suffering from an incurable illness? Based on the testimony that they heard, and the relevant studies reported to them, the Mission concluded that:

Everybody wishes for him/herself and for their relatives an end of life without pain, wishes not to suffer possible physical, medical or moral degradation, or to be maintained in life through artificial means dependent on machines, and aspires to have a peaceful old age. Since this is the case, it is not surprising that our fellow citizens reject pain and degeneration, and that they want to see the rights of patients more affirmed,[20] and the care of elderly persons better guaranteed. (Leonetti 2004: 1:105)

The last section of part 2 of the report discusses the expectations of physicians and other health professionals who increasingly care for dying persons in hospitals and "retirement homes." In these settings, they are called upon to allay their patients' suffering, and to try not to prolong their "mortal agony" through the use of unduly "efficacious" treatments. With regard to the questions and pressures that physicians face under these circumstances, the report indicates, they "wish to have certain of their practices that they consider legitimate better understood and recognized, to have precise definitions and recommendations frame certain of their prescriptions, and to see the health system improved in a number of ways" (Leonetti 2004: 1:138–139). The terms, concepts, and practices that they would like to have clarified, distinguished from one another, and better understood include euthanasia; assisted suicide; morphine treatment; sedation; treatment with a "double effect"; forgoing, limiting, or stopping treatment that is "useless," "futile," or has "become inhumane"; and palliative care. They want to be better protected legally when they prescribe morphine for the relief of pain, a sedative, or the cessation of treatment, and they would like to see palliative care better developed in France. What is important to note in this connection is that in the French system, the clarification of the situation of physicians delivering requested end-of-life care must be effected through legislation.

Finally, in part 2 of the report, the Mission deals with its third question: How the expectations of French society regarding end-of-life treatment could be appropriately and optimally met? From the hearings, the members of the Mission concluded, several alternative responses had emerged: maintaining the status quo; "depenalizing" euthanasia, drawing upon the examples of the legislation that Holland and Belgium have passed; or a "third way," responsive and adapted to the French milieu. It was the "third way" that the mission adopted and recommended (Leonetti 2004: 1: 171, 191).

In the words of the then-Minister of Health and Social Protection Philippe Douste-Blazy,[21] the "original French vision of the question" that the Mission proposed maintained a distinction between "letting die" ("*laissez mourir*"), and "making die" ("*faire mourir*"), by taking a stand against changing the penal code to legalize euthanasia, while at the same time advocating that certain important legislative modifications be made in the public health code and in the code of professional medical ethics.[22]

Legislation "Relative to the Rights of Patients and the End of Life"

In November 2004, the National Assembly of Parliament passed the recommendations of the Leonetti Mission. And on April 13, 2005, they were passed by its Senate as well, after a stormy last effort of Socialist and Communist senators to amend the law so that physicians could be permitted to "actively help" patients to die was defeated by the senators affiliated with the center-right wing of UMP, the party that held a majority in Parliament at that time. On April 22, 2005, the recommendations became a law "relative to the rights of patients and the end of life."

In October 2005, the case of Vincent Humbert resurfaced in the French press, as the judicial investigation that had been initiated after his death drew to a close, and the dossier of evidence that had been gathered by the judge in charge of the inquiry was about to be transmitted to the public prosecutor's office. At this level of the French court system, a judge would then decide if no infraction had taken place (a "*non-lieu*"); whether a violation had occurred that was a minor one (a "*délit*"), which would then be judged in a correctional tribunal; or whether a crime had been committed that would have to come before the court of "*assises*."

On February 6, 2006, the law "relative to the rights of patients and the end of life" passed in April 2005 was completed by two decrees (No. 2006–119 and No. 2006–120) that were issued by the Ministry of Health and Social Protection.

The first of these decrees specifies how adult persons can legitimately and effectively express their wishes about the end of their lives through a written "advanced directives" document. The second decree, which in effect constitutes an alteration in the code of medical ethics, enjoins the physician to "try hard to relieve the suffering of the patient through means appropriate to his state and to assist him morally." The physician "must abstain from all unreasonable obstinacy in investigations or therapy," the decree states, and "can cease to undertake or to continue treatments that appear to be useless, disproportionate, or that have no purpose or effect other than the artificial maintenance of life."[23]

Closure of the Case of Vincent Humbert by the Courts

The "*affaire* Vincent Humbert" was juridically closed on February 27, 2006, when the *juge d'instruction*, Anne Morvant, issued an order of *non-lieu* that exonerated both his mother, Marie Humbert, and his physician, Frédéric Chaussoy from "'all penal responsibility'" for the "'administration of harmful substances'" and '"poisoning with premeditation.'" In the case of Marie Humbert, the judge ruled that Vincent's mother had been under a "'double constraint'": the '"internal'" constraint of the "'invasion of her sentiments, of her duty of loyalty to her son,'" and the "'external'" constraint of the publication of Vincent Humbert's book, his appeal to the Chief of State, and the repercussions of public opinion. A "'sort of affective blackmail'" was involved through which Marie Humbert was "'pushed'" by Vincent to commit a definitive act that was '"the expression of the choice of her son…a gesture carried out for him as an ultimate act of love.'"

Dr. Chaussoy's act of injecting potassium chloride, the judge opined, was carried out "'under the constraint of seeing his patient returning to a prior, even worse state, in spite of his repeated demands, of extreme compassion for his mother, and under the constraint of the media, resulting in the absence of the possibility of serene reflection within a reasonable period of time.'" Under these circumstances, the judge held that "'a criminal intention ("*intention dolosive*") cannot be attributed to him.'" Furthermore, she added, a "'juridical vacuum'" had existed at the time that he acted. It was not until the law of April 22, 2005, "relative to the rights of patients and the end of life" that this "'domain'" was legally addressed (Blanchard 2006a).[24]

Marie Humbert reacted to this *non-lieu* decision by stating to the press that she was "'very disappointed.'" "'It signifies,'" she declared, that "'they are going to bury the history as if my son had not existed, as if his combat had not existed.'" She announced that she would go on fighting for a "'Vincent Humbert Law'" that would allow euthanasia to take place in certain cases (Sabéran 2006).

Dr. Chaussoy initially expressed "relief" with the decision, and gratification that he had played a part in the "collective reflection" that had led to the passage of a law on the end of life. But in an article that he subsequently published in

Le Monde, he wrote that now that he could speak freely once again he felt compelled to state as a physician that "we all have the duty to listen to and hear what our human brothers [in Vincent Humbert's "exceptional situation"] demand." "We have the duty to help them," and the end of life law that has been passed "would have had no utility for Vincent" (Chaussoy 2006).

Apparently, the deliberations of Parliament, the passage of national end-of-life legislation, and the judicial decision reached in the case of Vincent Humbert have not definitively resolved the issue of euthanasia in France, or stilled emotional debate about it. In the opinion of Jean Léonetti, "no law can resolve all, no end of life case resembles another" (Blanchard 2006b).

Value-Emphases of French Bioethics

In contrast to what French public health physician Jean-Christophe Mino describes as "the concepts of individual autonomy and self-determination…dominant in American bioethics" (Minot 2000: 426), French laws, bioethics, and the nexus that they form emphasize the value precepts of "human dignity," "human rights," "respect for the human body," its "inviolability" and "integrity" (Mattei, Laboire, and Novaes 1995: in passim), "social solidarity," and fidelity to "Frenchness" and a certain model of French society.

The idea of "social solidarity" has roots in the heritage of the French Revolution, with its emphasis on *fraternité* as well as liberty and equality, and in both European Christian (primarily Catholic) and Socialist thought, and their political expression in French and other European parties of Christian Democratic, Social Christian, Social Democratic, and Socialist orientation. It is integrally related to France's strong tradition of "public service" that affects many areas in the society, including transportation, energy, and mail, as well as health care. It underlies the country's national "social security" system. *Solidarité* is also a concept of pivotal importance in French sociology—one that is analytically central to the works of Émile Durkheim and his intellectual heirs.

The notion of solidarity stresses the interdependence of persons: their mutual interests, needs, and responsibilities for one another's well-being, their reliance on one another and on the groups that they form for support, a sense of identity, unity, and meaning, and for the coherence and integration of their lives together within the larger society to which they mutually belong. On a more macro-level, it refers to the common good, expressed in and through the good society—its ethos and moral foundations—with particular emphasis on social justice and concern for the welfare of all its citizens. In this regard, when French commentators refer to "Anglo-Saxon" bioethics, they usually contrast it with their own solidarity-based bioethics—depicting the former as more individualistically rights-oriented than French bioethics, and therefore less mindful of the kind of society that one wants to achieve and uphold. The at-once utopian and monolithic vision of French society that is both implicitly and explicitly invoked here is that of a republican, unified, lay (secular) society, committed to the "worldly care" of its citizens, who are endowed with equal rights and who inhabit a "level public sphere" (Asad 2005: 2, 5).

The significance that French bioethics attaches to the idea of solidarity contrasts sharply with its conspicuous absence in the predominant framework of American bioethics. Even more striking is the criticism to which the concept of "human dignity" that is so salient in French bioethics has been subjected by some American bioethicists (Macklin 2003; Childress 2003: 16–17). Ruth Macklin has been the most vehement of its American critics. Although she acknowledges that the concept of "the 'dignity' of the human being" is "prominent in the Kantian tradition in continental philosophy," that it "has gained currency in much discourse of European bioethics" ("but not among UK and US bioethicists," she adds), and that it "is expressed in numerous United Nations human rights instruments," she contends that it is "so vague [that] it is nearly devoid of meaning without further elucidation." " 'Respect for human dignity' has in some contexts become a mere slogan," she claims (Macklin 2004a: 196–197). "Why, then, do so many articles and reports appeal to [the] useless concept" of human dignity, "as if it means something over and above respect for persons and their autonomy?" she asks rhetorically (Macklin 2003: 1419).

Some Concluding Questions

Our attempt to identify and reflect on some of the characteristics and components of bioethics in France that we believe merit attention and empirical study leaves us with at least two sets of questions—one relevant to the cultural and societal wellsprings of French bioethics, the other to French and American bioethics seen in relationship to each other.

The French Republic is founded on the official premise of a strict separation between religion and state, inherited from the French Revolution. As part of this separation, it upholds the political principle of "*laïcité*" that "forbids the display of religious identities and symbols in what is considered to be public space" (Fredrickson 2005: 91; Asad 2005: in passim). Furthermore, in common with other European countries, France has supposedly become a pervasively secular society with regard to its citizens' practice of religion and their professed faith. Nevertheless, France is singular in having once borne the honorific title of "*la fille aînée*" (the eldest daughter) of the Roman Catholic Church. And institutionally, "although the Republic is secular, the Church of Rome" has had a "special position in it" since the beginning of the twentieth century:

The modus vivendi put in place from 1922 to 1924 between France and the Holy See allows the Republic to recognize "diocesan associations" within the framework of the 1905 law. These autonomous associations are territorially defined, and they have complicated

financial rights and obligations in relation to the state. Today they are the bodies representing the Catholic Church in official dealings with the Republic. (Asad 2005: 5)[25]

It seems to us that there are signs that the Catholic heritage of France may have
a continuing latent influence on the thematic foci of French bioethics. The major
place that matters pertaining to the beginning of life occupied in bioethics throughout its first decades of existence in France, and the prominence that questions about
the end of life assumed once they took their place alongside of them in the early
years of the 21st century appear to us to be two such indicators. These human condition concerns about our "coming in" and our "going out" and about our human
identity and essence are as religiously resonant as they are ethical. And they are
doctrinally and politically as well as spiritually of central importance to the Catholic
Church. A culturally Catholic perspective may also have contributed to the fact that
the French Parliament took a resolute stand against legalizing euthanasia, deem-
ing it not to be the "French way," while espousing palliative care as a desired and
desirable means to fulfill "the right to die with dignity," to which each is entitled.[26]
What is more, the concept of "dignity" invoked here, and also that of "solidarity,"
both of which are of central significance in French bioethics, have important, albeit
not exclusive, connections to Catholic, especially European Catholic, thought. In
addition, the importance that French bioethics accords to the "inviolability" and
"integrity" of the human body may be implicitly influenced by the Catholic-Chris-
tian metaphysical assumption that "the spirit is indivisible from, and in some fashion sanctifies, the body"—an assumption that lawyer-bioethicist R. Alta Charo has
claimed shaped the approach of the CCNE to the status of the human body when it
was under the leadership of Jean Bernard (Charo 1995: 492).

What kind of empirical evidence does one need to rule in (or rule out) our
hypothesis that French Catholicism has an inherent cultural influence on the roster, ethos, and outlook of French bioethics? This is neither an easy question to
answer nor to investigate. For, it exemplifies how complex it is to sociologically
study "religion" in ways other than simply counting such things as how many
people attend church services, or profess to believe in God, and also how subtle
and challenging it is to analyze social and cultural phenomena that are "latent."
In the case of medicine, biomedical research, and bioethics in France, it is made
all the more complex by such paradoxical phenomena as the fact that the founder
of the first semen banks in France, Georges David, a physician and biologist, and
a practicing Catholic, created this network of centers with the consultant help of
a professor of moral theology at the Institut Catholique de Paris (Father René
Simon), despite the Catholic Church's official disapproval of donor insemination,
other medically assisted procreation practices, and prenatal diagnosis (Bateman
2002). Nor has the stance of the Church deterred the many other French physicians who are practicing Catholics from working in these areas (Bateman, personal communication, Aug. 2, 2005). Another kind of fact that needs to be taken

into account in assessing what sort of influence Catholicism may or may not have on French bioethics is that unlike France, Belgium, a neighboring European society, which traditionally is also a Catholic country, passed a national law in 2002 that legalized euthanasia.[27]

Our second question concerns why American bioethicists have been disinclined to systematically consider whether there are elements in the framework of bioethics in other countries that might fruitfully be incorporated into the structure of U.S. bioethics in a way that would enlarge and enrich it. In this chapter, we have reflected on the case of France. But, as James Childress has pointed out, the precepts of human dignity, human rights, and solidarity that we have found are basic components in the purview of French bioethics, and occupy a significant place in European bioethics more generally.[28] American bioethics has "neglected other moral frameworks" such as these, Childress said in his presentation at the symposium held at the Medical College of Wisconsin in May 2004 to celebrate the 25th anniversary of the Belmont Report.[29] He made this statement in a tone of voice that implied it was an oversight that ought to be remedied. We agree.

Notes

1. Through face-to-face meetings, correspondence, and the exchange of publications, Fox has had continual intellectual contact with French physicians, medical scientists, sociologists and historians of medicine, anthropologists, and journalists since 1959, when she did exploratory research for what became her long-term study of social, cultural, and historical factors affecting medical research in a continental European country. Although Belgium became the focus of that study, she spent prolonged periods in France every time that she made field trips to Belgium. During the month of June 1989, she was a Directeur d'Études Associé at the École des Hautes Études en Sciences Sociales in Paris, and she has had a number of articles published in French journals. Since 1994, she has been returning to Paris periodically in connection with her current research on Médecins Sans Frontières. It is in these contexts that she has known sociologist Simone Bateman for many years. Bateman, who is now a Directeur de Recherche in the Centre National de la Recherche Scientifique, and Directeur of the Centre de Recherche Sens, Éthique, Société (Center for Research on Meaning, Ethics, and Society), was our chief informant for this chapter on bioethics in France. The wealth of pertinent documents that Bateman made available to us, and the pages of informative and perceptive commentary on successive drafts of our chapter that we received from her were indispensable.

   We are also indebted to French sociologist Isabelle Baszanger and economist Martine Bungener for the valuable data and insights that they provided, and for their helpfully critical reading of this chapter. Baszanger and Bungener are both directeurs de recherche in the Centre National de la Recherche Scientifique, and members of the Centre de Recherche, Médecine, Sciences, Santé et Société (Center of Research on Medicine, Science, Health and Society/CERMES), of which Bungener is the director.

2. In her earlier publications Simone Bateman used the name Simone Bateman Novaes. At present, she publishes under the name of Simone Bateman.

3. Renée Fox translated all the quoted French words and passages in this chapter into English.

4. Loi no. 2004–800 du 6 août 2004 relative à la bioéthique, titre 1, article 1, chapitre 2, art. L.1412–1.

5. Among these members were a deputy and a senator designated by the presidents of their assemblies; a member of the Council of the State chosen by the vice president of the Council; an advisor at the Court of Appeals named by the first president of this court; one person designated by the prime minister and one by the Guardian of the Seals of the Ministry of Justice; two persons designated by the minister of research; and one person each designated by the ministers of industry, social affairs, education, work, health, communication, family, and the rights of women.

6. In their listing of deputies by "socio-professional categories," the National Assembly distinguishes between "médecins" (physicians) and "chirurgiens" (surgeons). There were 31 "médecins" and 11 "chirurgiens" among the deputies in 2005.

7. Herzlich comments on the fact that French physicians "have often actively taken sides in politics. During the 1930s, several doctors and medical students stood in the front ranks of the xenophobic far right, which would later support the Vichy government. This government would fulfill the wishes of the most reactionary factions in the medical profession by creating the Ordre des Médecins. On the side of the Resistance in WWII, a group of doctors led by Robert Debré supported plans for setting up national health insurance and drew up a reform [the Reforme Debré] for creating the modern hospital system in France." [Debré's son became President Charles De Gaulle's prime minister in 1958] (Herzlich 1995: 1617–1618).

8. Professor of medicine Didier Sicard, the former chief of the internal medicine service of the Hôpital Cochin of Paris, who is the current president of the National Consultive Ethics Committee (CCNE), has publicly expressed his consternation over the narrow skew of the agenda of bioethics in France, and in Western societies more generally. In a book that he authored entitled *L'alibi éthique*, published in 2006, Sicard wrote at length about what he considers to be the unacceptable degree to which bioethics and bioethicists, with the support of the media, are engaged in debates about reproductive cloning, stem cells, the embryo, and the end of life, while virtually ignoring essential questions such as the numbers of persons who are excluded from health care in an advanced modern society like France, or the even more dramatic and deplorable lack of access to health care in poor, developing societies. In Sicard's view, bioethics should above all manifest a "felt and reasonable sense of responsibility" for those who are "the weakest, the most deprived, the sickest, the most desperate, the most naked, the most shut up, the smallest, the poorest, the most unconscious, the most different, the most silent, the most invisible…." And yet, he goes on to say, "Never have the most poor been more solidly excluded. Never has the patient felt more abandoned or deprived by all-powerful medicine. Maybe bioethics only exists for bioethicists!" (Sicard 2006: 118, 136).

9. President François Mitterand appointed Lucien Sève, a Marxist philosopher, to represent those with no religious affiliation. He was a highly esteemed member of the CCNE for many years.

10. In December 2006, according to a note in *Science*, a parliamentary committee adopted a report "that advocates loosening France's 2004 bioethics law, which includes restrictive rules for research with human embryos." The report also advocates that France end its ban on therapeutic cloning, suggests a series of ethical guidelines for egg donation, and recommends that the 2004 law be reviewed in 2007 rather than its scheduled review date in 2009 (Enserink 2006).

11. For a fuller account of the 10-year-long process, the issues, and the maneuvers that the passage of the bioethics laws entailed, see Charo 1995: 486–490.

12. There are several faculties of medicine in Paris, belonging to the different Parisian universities. The Université René Descartes (Paris V) had more than one teaching hospital. Two of these hospitals—Necker and Cochin—are renowned institutions. Despite the fact that their relationship over the years had been a rivalrous one, in 2004, along with the various other teaching hospitals of Paris V, they both became part of the one large "Faculté de Médecine de Paris V."

13. The MacLean Center, founded in 1984, was the first program in the United States devoted to clinical medical ethics. Physician Mark Siegler, whose original, primary intent was to train physicians in bioethics, heads it.

14. Information about the Center can be found at http://www.éthique-clinique.com/intro v2.htm.

15. The Veil Law was voted for a probationary period of five years, and was reaffirmed on Jan. 1, 1980.

16. There are other centers of research in France oriented to "moral sociology," notable among which is Le Groupe de Sociologie Morale et Politique. Furthermore, there are interdisciplinary centers—for example, the Centre de recherche, médecine, sciences, santé et société (CERMES)—and also centers specializing in law, which are conducting some research relevant to bioethics.

17. Among nongovernmental groups, the ADMD (Association pour le Droit de Mourir dans la Dignité [Association for the Right to Die with Dignity]), which was founded in 1980, is the oldest, best known, and most active (http://www.admd.net). It was modeled on the Euthanasia Educational Council in the United States, later renamed Concern for Dying.

    During the 1970s the Ministry of Health had issued a report on problems of death, and various colloquiums on topics such as the evolution of death in contemporary society, the physician facing death, and "the right to death" were held. In the 1980s, a French branch of the World Federation of Associations for the Right to Die with Dignity was organized and began to campaign for the "depenalization" of euthanasia and for the legalization of assisted suicide; and during the 1990s, a French Society for Palliative Care was created with which more than 145 voluntary associations affiliated themselves, and Parliament passed a law guaranteeing the right of access to palliative care for all. By 2002, there were 91 hospital-based palliative care units in France, 291 palliative care mobile teams, and 46 "*ville-hôpital*" ("city-hospital") networks organized around palliative care, which were financed by the "Agences régionales d'hospitalisation" (Regional Agencies of Hospitalization) (Baszanger and Salamagne 2004).

18. There is no precise English equivalent for the term "*l'archarnement thérapeutique*, which is a vital part of the vocabulary currently used in France to discuss end-of-life issues, although it is a notion that does not exist in French law. Without the adjective "thérapeutique" attached to it, and outside of a specifically medical context, "*archarnement*" means "fierceness," "relentlessness," "fury," and "obstinacy." The word *futile* does exist in French, but its meaning is too superficial to be applied to the solemn contexts of death and dying. The French phrase "*obstination déraisonnable*" ("unreasonable obstinacy") is invoked to refer to continuing strenuously to treat patients in what in English would be called "futile" situations.

19. The persons invited to give testimony at the parliamentary hearings included the representatives of Free Mason Lodges: the Grand Loge de France, the Grande Loge féminine de France, the Grande Loge nationale française, and the Ordre de Grand Orient de France.

Freemasons are organized, governed, and linked together in local units called lodges. Freemasonry—the beliefs and practices of Freemasons—has historical origins in organizations formed in the Middle Ages by craftsmen who built and worked with stone. In the 18th century, its membership ceased to consist only of Masons, and the term "Masonry" became symbolic. During the 1730s and 1740s, it began its extensive geographical spread from England to the rest of Europe, North America, and Asia.

What could be called the religio-philosophical outlook of Freemasonry is based on the premise that "there exists a moral law to be apprehended by human reason and binding upon all men alike. Men from all walks of life meet together in their adherence to a moral code whose principles are largely conveyed through symbols and allegories connected with the art of building, emphasizing benevolence." The rituals and certain other matters of Freemasonry are secret.

In France, under the "ancien régime" and restored Bourbons, the theological faculty in Paris declared Freemason rituals to be blasphemous. Freemasonry was condemned in bulls by popes Clement XII and Benedict XIV in 1737 and 1751, respectively, and it was "only barely tolerated" under Louis XVII and Charles X. As a result, Freemasons grew hostile to both ecclesiastical and secular authorities. The French Grand Orient Lodge "became so anticlerical as to abolish what English Freemasons regarded as a fundamental condition of membership, the requirement to believe in the Great Architect of the Universe. For that reason, the English grand lodge in 1878 severed relations with it and thereafter refused to recognize any variety of Freemasonry erring in the same way" ("Freemasonry" 1958, 9:732, 735).

Freemasonry retains an anti-ecclesiastical, anticlerical orientation to this day in France. In 2005, French Freemasonry consisted of 135,000 members—the largest membership in its history. It has had considerable political influence in the country. According to a 2005 article published in the French newspaper *Libération*, "[I]t is estimated that under the Third Republic two-thirds of the members of Parliament were Masons." However, the political influence of Freemasonry has sharply declined since then, and today there are fewer than a hundred Masons in the two parliamentary chambers combined (Lecadre 2005: 38).

The history, evolution, and organizational structure of Freemasonry in the United States are very different from those in France, and also from those in all the other countries in the world where it exists.

20. The patients' rights that the report identifies—the right to information, to refuse treatment, to stop all treatment (including artificial feeding), to make one's last wishes known through advance directives and/or "a person of confidence," to be cared for and die at home, and to be supported and accompanied in the process of dying by family members, as the Mission acknowledges, are all recognized by a law enacted in 2002, "relative to the rights of patients and to the quality of the system of health," and in the French public health code. But if they were stated more precisely, the report opines, they might be better applied.

21. Philippe Douste-Blazy is a physician who is a specialist in cardiology. On June 2, 2005, in the wake of the French public's rejection of the European Union's proposed constitution, and the shuffling of his cabinet that President Jacques Chirac effected in response to it, Douste-Blazy, a Chirac loyalist, was named Minister of Foreign Affairs. Prior to becoming Minister of Health and Social Protection, he served as Delegate Minister of Health (1993–1995) and Minister of Culture (1995–1997). In the latter post he fought hard to protect the French language against the encroachment of American English. He has also been a member of the French Parliament, general secretary of the UMP, a min-

ister of the European Parliament, and the mayor of Lourdes and of Toulouse (Sciolino 2005).

22. These modifications include stating that medical treatment does not have to be pursued with "unreasonable obstinacy when there is no hope for improvement in the state of a patient, and the treatment involves the artificial prolongation of life"; that when a person is in an advanced or terminal phase of an ailment...decides to limit or stop treatment, the physician must respect his/her wish"; and that if such a gravely and incurably ill person is unconscious or unable to express his/her wishes, the opinion of a "person of confidence" whom he/she has chosen should "prevail over all other non-medical opinions with regard to decisions about investigations, interventions or treatment by the physician."

23. The first decree also specifies how the directives must be composed, signed, and dated, or attested to by two witnesses as constituting an expression of the individual's "free and clear-minded wishes," if the person to whom it pertains is unable to write or sign the document. In addition, it states that the advanced directives can be modified at any time; that they are valid for three years, and renewable by "simple decision or confirmation" signed by their author or by the witnesses; and that they should be kept in a place "easily accessible to the physician called upon to take a decision to limit or stop treatment," who will be expected to consult the directive.

    The second decree explicates the conditions under which physicians can decide to limit or stop treatment. It is a decision that must be made by the physician in charge of the patient, in collaboration with the medical care team if it exists, taking into account the "justified" ("*motivé*") advice of at least one physician called in as a consultant, and with the advice of a second consultant if one of the physicians deems it useful. The decision is also expected to consider the wishes the patient has previously expressed, particularly in the form of advanced directives if they have been drafted. In the case of a decision concerning a minor, the physician should seek the advice of "the holders of parental authority," "save in those situations where an emergency makes this impossible." "The advice gathered, the nature and sense of the consultations that took place within the medical care team, as well as the motives for the decision are to be recorded in the patient's dossier," the decree concludes.

24. The judge stated that even though the injection of potassium chloride that Dr. Chaussoy administered "contradicted Article 38 of the code of medical ethics," and "a physician does not have the right to deliberately cause death," he "did not have the intention of bringing about his [patient's] death in the penal sense of the term, but rather to preserve the dignity of Vincent Humbert and his family."

25. The Protestants, Jews, and Muslims of France also have bodies that are their official representatives to the State: the Fédération Protestante de France, created in 1905, which groups under its aegis most of the Protestant churches and associations in France; the Conseil représentatif des institutions juives de France (C.R.I.F.) that was initiated in 1943 during the German occupation of France, as a clandestine organization to assist threatened and persecuted Jews; and the much more recently established Conseil Français de Culte Musulman (CFCM), founded in 1999, representing all Muslims in France.

26. Isabelle Baszanger and Michèle Salamagne (2004, 1062–1063) have ventured the opinion that a major source of support that palliative care has received in France is attributable to the fact that it is considered to be a "rampart against euthanasia."

27. However, Catholic hospitals in Belgium have elected not to comply with the law, and they are not legally obliged to do so.

28. Childress does not mention the other value-constellation that we found to have an important place in the ethos of French bioethics—namely, respect for the human body, its inviolability and integrity. We do not know whether these concepts are important constituents of the framework of bioethics in other European countries as well, or if they are distinctive to French bioethics and, if so, to what in French society and culture the weight accorded to them might be attributed.

29. We transcribed Childress's remarks from the videotapes of the *Belmont Report*'s 25th Anniversary Symposium hosted by the Medical College of Wisconsin, May 14, 2004.

10

The Development of Bioethics in the Islamic Republic of Pakistan

As we have observed in our previous two chapters, knowledge about bioethics in countries other than the United States is sparse, and cross-cultural understanding of how and why bioethics may differ from one society to another is superficial. Especially notable is the dearth of information about the circumstances surrounding the origins of bioethics in non-Western societies, the cultural outlooks and traditions within which the field has developed in those localities, and the issues with which participants in bioethics in these settings are dealing.

In this chapter, drawing principally on the rich documentary material that pediatric surgeon and bioethicist Farhat Moazam has made accessible to us in the form of papers, lectures, and personal correspondence,[1] we present a narrative overview of the trajectory of bioethics in the Islamic Republic of Pakistan. As was the case with our presentation of bioethics in France, our rather vicarious scholarly and empirical knowledge of Pakistani society and culture only qualifies us to suggest what a more authoritative, analytic account of bioethics in this Islamic, South Asian republic might include, and what its implications for furthering the internationalization of bioethics might be.

The Pakistan Context

Pakistan came into being as an independent Islamic republic in 1947, as a consequence of a partition of the Indian subcontinent between Hindus and Muslims. About 95 percent of its population of some 160 million people are Muslims, of whom approximately 80 percent are Sunni, and 20 percent Shi'i. The country is predominantly rural, with a few large cities such as Karachi. According to government figures, the average per capita income in 2004–2005 was $492, and "the overall literacy rate is low—estimated to be no more than 41.5%—and even lower for women in many areas" (www.infopak.gov.pk/public/govt/basic_facts; Moazam and Jafarey 2005: 249). The country has a complex culture, with numerous ethnic and tribal groups and socioeconomic strata. Its society is hierarchically structured and ordered "in both public and private domains," and its population is characteristically "religious and family-centered" (Moazam and Jafarey 2005: 249).

In the sphere of medicine and health care, the country is experiencing "an increase in high-tech tertiary-level medicine." Pakistan does not have a national health insurance system or third-party payers, and only a few health insurance plans in the private sector. Care is provided free of charge by government-run clinics and hospitals, "but these institutions are generally understaffed, overcrowded, and inefficient;… many have a reputation for providing substandard care"; and patients are usually required to pay for medications and special tests or investigations. Although private fee-for-service health care institutions have been developing, especially in the larger cities of Pakistan, "due to existing poverty and an absence of national health coverage or health insurance schemes," for the most part, they are "beyond the reach of the majority of the population" (Moazam and Jafarey 2005: 249).

The Aga Khan University and the Beginning of Bioethics

Bioethics in Pakistan had its inception in 1984 at the Aga Khan University (AKU) in Karachi, which began with a nursing school and a medical college and was the first private university to be established in the country. It was chartered in 1983, with an initial endowment by the Aga Khan, who is the temporal and spiritual head of the Ismaili, an offshoot of the Shiite branch of Islam.[2] The University, which was built on land that was a gift from the Pakistani government, defines itself as a private, nondenominational, self-governing, and international institution. It is part of the Aga Khan Development Network, a group of private agencies "working to improve living conditions and opportunities in the developing world through social, economic, and cultural development." The Network has teaching and research programs in Kenya, Tanzania, Uganda, Afghanistan, Syria, and the United Kingdom, as well as in Pakistan.

At first, AKU's Pakistani faculty consisted largely of physicians who had received their training in the United States or the United Kingdom. More recently, a significant number of faculty members have been drawn from graduates of AKU's residency programs, and AKU medical school graduates who trained abroad before returning to assume their university posts. Over the two decades of this elite university's existence, its curriculum has expanded from the undergraduate training of nurses and physicians to include 25 medical residency programs, master's degree programs in nursing, epidemiology and biostatistics, health policy and management, and a PhD program in health sciences. The University has its own hospital that is primarily run on a fee-for-service basis, with a budget for the treatment of indigent persons.

When AKU introduced bioethics into the curriculum of its initial class of medical students in 1984, it was the first university in Pakistan to do so. Since then, bioethics has progressively been integrated into all of the university's academic programs and into its clinical and research activities. Bioethics was launched at AKU by an American public health physician, Dr. Jack Bryant, at that time chairman of the Department of Community Health Sciences, whose background included extensive prior work in developing countries, close involvement with the World Health Organization, and recognition as one of the drafters of the International Ethical Guidelines for Biomedical Research issued by the Council for International Organizations of Medical Sciences (CIOMS). At this initial stage, the bioethics teaching consisted of a series of lectures based on the American paradigm of the "four principles," with respectful reference to the first edition of Tom Beauchamp and James Childress's *Principles of Biomedical Ethics.*

Several years after Bryant began bioethics lectures at AKU, when the university's first medical students had reached the clinical phase of their training, he invited pediatric surgeon Farhat Moazam to bring actual cases of local patients into the bioethics seminar for discussion in the light of the principles. As is suggested by Bryant's work at AKU, and his recruitment of Moazam, it was health care professionals, primarily physicians, who took the lead in initiating bioethics and setting its agenda. "This is an important difference that cannot be overemphasized" between "the birth of bioethics" in the United States and in Pakistan, Moazam has observed.[3]

Both in Pakistani and in American medical academic milieus, Moazam was recognized as an outstanding teacher and educational leader as well as an excellent surgeon. After receiving her medical degree from Dow Medical College in Karachi in 1967, she had been a rotating intern at Flushing Hospital and Medical Center in New York, where she continued on to do a residency in general surgery during 1970–1974. In 1975, she accepted a position as a fellow in pediatric surgery at the University of Florida in Gainesville, moving up the academic ladder over the course of the next decade to be named a clinical professor in the Department of Surgery in 1985. In that same year, she was recruited by Aga Khan University to become the founding chairperson of its Department of Surgery, the Quaid-e-Azam Professor of Surgery, and chief of Pediatric Surgery. Her colleagues at the University of Florida insisted that she maintain an honorary clinical professorship in the Department of Surgery, which she did until 2000. By the early 1990s, Moazam had begun bioethics meetings with residents, fellows, and students who rotated with her in pediatric surgery. In 1995, she assumed the post of associate dean of AKU's new Department of Postgraduate Medical Education, created by the then-dean of AKU, Dr. John Dirks, a professor of nephrology from the University of Toronto. In that position she made attendance at ethics lectures and workshops a requirement for all AKU physicians in residency training, focusing them on morally troubling cases that these young physicians were encountering in their delivery of care. The following year, she instituted annual conferences with international speakers, for students, residents, and faculty of AKU and other Pakistani medical institutions, at which at least one featured session dealt with bioethics. Another milestone in the development of bioethics at AKU was the formation of the Bioethics Group in 1997, founded and chaired by Moazam, which drew its voluntary membership from faculty in departments throughout the medical and nursing schools and a wide gamut of hospital staff (Jafarey 2002). The Group met regularly around case presentations and discussion, launched a newsletter, organized bioethics grand rounds, set up a system of ethics consults, and began to advise the university on problematic ethical matters that were brought to their attention.

"Death with Dignity" was the topic of the first Bioethics Grand Rounds that were held in March 2002. The titles of the rounds that followed included "The Critically Ill Neonate: A Right to Live"; "The Patient with Cancer: To Disclose or Not"; "Kidney for Sale"; "Whose Rights? Confidentiality vs. The Right to Know"; "Down's Dilemma"; "Whose Life Is It Anyway?"; "Between the Devil and the Deep Blue Sea"; "Research in the Developing World"; "Consent: How Informed Is Informed?"; and "Doctor, Please Don't Tell My Mother She Has Cancer! The Right to Know vs. The Right to Say No" (Jafarey 2002: 165–166).

What the Bioethics Group established has not only endured at AKU, but has become a resource for other institutions in Karachi with which it has formed links. For example, it has organized combined Grand Rounds with Ziauddin Medical University and Patel Hospital in Karachi, and has collaboratively worked with colleagues there to help them develop institutional guidelines for ethical research (Jafarey 2002).

Aga Khan University has had a hospital-based Human Subjects Protection Committee for all research involving human experimentation since 1987, which was reconstituted as a University Ethical Review Committee (ERC) in 1999. In the same year, AKU established a Hospital Ethics Committee (HEC) whose objective, according to Jafarey, is to "facilitate the establishment of a community of health care professionals at the Aga Khan University who are sensitive to issues of ethics in health care," and that "provides a round-the-clock ethics consultative service" that is unique in Pakistan. Some of the members of the Bioethics Group, he noted, sit on the ERC and HEC.[4]

Although approval by an institutional review board such as the ERC is not yet required for obtaining funding from Pakistani sources, their establishment is seen as a vital element in the country's becoming involved in international research. "[T]here is a dawning realization in the medical community," according to Moazam and Jafarey, "that this step is now essential in order to attract and participate in collaborative research with institutions in the United States, [the] European Union, and international organizations such as [the] World Health Organization…, and a requirement for any publication in international indexed journals" (Moazam and Jafarey 2005: 250). However, they have pointed out, as of 2004, formal ethical review bodies for research or clinical practice "[were] still a rarity in Pakistan." At that juncture, aside from AKU, only two other private universities in Karachi—Ziauddin Medical University and the Liaquat National Hospital and Postgraduate Institute—had begun to set up committees to review research proposals. and the AKU hospital was the only institution in Pakistan with a formal ethics consultation service (Moazam and Jafarey 2005: 250, 255n6).[5]

In 2002, AKU received a two-year grant for 2003–2005 from the Fogarty International Center of the U.S. National Institutes of Health, to develop a training program in bioethics for local researchers and Ethical Review Committee members, through which three faculty obtained a master's degrees from the University of Toronto. The University has set up a Web site that gives details about the various bioethics activities taking place at AKU. A "module-based" educational program "for professionals from a variety of fields who have a direct or indirect role to play in heath care, and who desire an in-depth knowledge of bioethics," was launched in November 2005; another plan, to start a master's program in bioethics, was on hold because it had not received funding as of the end of 2005. "At present [2003]," Jafarey wrote, "bioethics is a part of all the syllabi at AKU and the institution has in place all the ethics-related processes that any developed world institution has to offer."[6]

The paramountcy of bioethics in the ethos and organization of this Pakistani medical university, the protean ways in which it has unfolded there, and its perceived status-enhancing association with high-quality medicine and medical education in advanced societies, are striking features of its presence at AKU. So is the fact that its discourse in this setting continues to be heavily influenced by American bioethics—especially by the principles of autonomy, beneficence, nonmaleficence, and justice elucidated in Beauchamp and Childress's text. What is less manifest, but highly significant nonetheless, are the unease and discontent that are often felt about the "non-fit" of the individualistic, rights-oriented, secular aspects of this ethical paradigm, and the cultural and religious values and beliefs that pervade the experiences and meaning of everyday life in Pakistan, and the statuses, roles, and relationships around which these lived realities (including health, illness, and the doctor-patient relationship) are structured.[7]

In 2002, the Aga Khan University Institute for the Study of Muslim Civilization (AKU-ISMC) was established in London. As the Institute's brochure states, its overall goal is to "strengthen research and teaching on the heritage of Muslim societies in all its historic diversity" through the study of "systems of moral and ethical thought, structures of governance and public life, and artistic and creative experiences in all forms." The Institute is committed to do this in ways that further "the adoption and techniques of modern scholarship without losing sight of the 'lived' and historical experience of Muslim struggles to resolve contemporary challenges," that avoid the "faults" of transmitting knowledge about Islam that is "oblivious to the deep changes brought about by modernization," and that eschew "a reductionist approach to religious traditions found in some Western institutions."

In 2004, the "theme of bioethics" was chosen as a focus for an AKU-ISMC fellowship, "not only because of its importance in current intellectual debates, including among Muslims," the announcement of the fellowship stated, "but also because of its relevance to the work of other components of AKU, especially the Faculty of Health Sciences." The description of the fellowship went on to say that it would center on "discourses about bioethics in religious communities,… a comparative approach that is preferred because many of the concerns faced by Muslims in this area are shared among religious communities as they emerge from epistemological assumptions and worldviews common to all religions." Candidates eligible to apply for the fellowship were expected to have a doctorate in medicine, philosophy, sociology, law, or "other relevant fields"; to have "reading and writing abilities in English, as well as Arabic and/or Persian," with additional languages considered to be "an asset"; and to have a demonstrable interest in the field of bioethics ("through appropriate publications, for example") (Jafarey, personal communication, Nov. 7, 2004).

Governmental Recognition and Support

On a governmental level, two important steps were taken in 2002 and 2004 that advanced the formal, national recognition of bioethics, and its state-supported institutionalization. In 2002, the Pakistan Medical and Dental Council (PMDC), the government regulatory body that registers all graduates from medical and dental colleges in the country, published a revised code of ethics for practitioners that included a recommendation that education in bioethics be incorporated into medical and dental curricula. The second measure was the approval given by the Pakistani government in January 2004 for the establishment of a 20- or 21-member National Bioethics Committee (NBC). The Committee, under the auspices of the Pakistan Medical and Research Council (PMRC), was envisioned as an "umbrella body linked with the ethical review bodies in organizations and institutions like the Pakistan Medical and Dental Council, the Medical Training and Teaching Institutions and the…Good Clinical Practices committee of the Ministry of Health's Drug Division." As described by Moazam and Jafarey (2005), the NBC's "patrons" are the Minister of Health of the Secretary of Health, and its chairman, the Director General of Health in the Ministry of Health, and the Committee will be "chaired by the Director General of Health in the Ministry of Health, with the [PMRC] acting as its secretariat."[8] The NBC's mandate involves acting as an advisory body dealing "with all aspects of bioethics in the health care sector in the country," and, working through subcommittees on medical ethics and research ethics, to "promote and facilitate ethical health services delivery and health research." As of summer 2007, however, the Committee had yet to be activated (Moazam, personal communications, Nov. 16, 2005; July 3, 2007).

Centre of Biomedical Ethics and Culture (CBEC)

Another significant development that marked the growing recognition and institutionalization of bioethics in Pakistan took place on October 8, 2004, when the Centre of Biomedical Ethics and Culture (CBEC) of the Sindh Institute of Urology and Transplantation (SIUT) in Karachi was ceremonially launched. The inaugural talk was delivered by Professor Atta-ur-Rahman, an internationally known biochemist who is Pakistan's Federal Minister for Education, Science and Technology who is chairman of the Higher Education Commission; and advisor to both the president and the prime minister of the country. He publicly endorsed CBEC, and told the audience that plans were also being set in motion to create an International Centre of Bioethics of Pakistan, connected to the University of Karachi, that would undertake bioethically relevant research and educational activities on national, regional, and international levels. The person who played the chief catalytic role in bringing these events to pass was Farhat Moazam, who was named chairperson of CBEC.

In fall 2000, Moazam had resigned from all her positions on the faculty of AKU in order to undertake full-time study for a PhD in the Department of Religious Studies at the University of Virginia in Charlottesville, chaired by James Childress. Her entwined goals were to advance her scholarly knowledge and understanding of the philosophical background of bioethics, and of Muslim moral and ethical values and their roots in the Qur'an, and the writings of Muslim *ulema* (scholars), jurists, philosophers, and physicians; to achieve fluency in Arabic; and to further her training in anthropology and sociology. Underlying her decision to pursue these studies was her desire to learn more about what she characterized as the "intellectual tradition informed by Anglo-European philosophical thought dating back to the 16th century" that presently "dominates" bioethics, in relationship to "foundational ethical concepts in Islam," and their potential relevance to "contemporary discourse in bioethics," and her conviction about the important role of "cultural and religious values in shaping the understanding of ethics and morality in a society."[9] In this latter regard, her comparative experiences as a practicing physician in Pakistan and the United States had convinced Moazam that the prevailing Western secular and rational principles on which the predominant outlook of bioethics is based, especially its conception of individualism and its emphasis upon it, did not fit what she termed the "relational morality" that prevails in Pakistani society and culture. This is a morality, she has written, that "rests on a strong sense of mutual responsibilities and obligations in life,[10] where people are comprehended as interdependent beings with different levels of power, wisdom and privilege":

The family is the fundamental unit of society in Pakistan, a country [in which] 95 percent of the citizens are Muslims.... For Muslims, religion defines the role of the individual, the family, and the physician in life passages including birth, illness, and death.... The "doctor sahib" (*sahib* has an Arabic root meaning "lord") remains the authority in matters relating to disease and medical interventions...and is expected to direct rather than just facilitate medical management. In the final analysis, however, God, not man, controls life and death....

[In Pakistan] people have longstanding cultural traditions and religious beliefs that place the family at the center of one's existence. Lives are spent within extended families in which power structures are clearly delineated. Familial structures are not merely horizontal but also vertical across three or more generations....

The physician in particular is often adopted into the family unit by being referred to as mother, father, or older sibling... Aunty or Doctor Aunty. Male physicians are referred to as uncles.... I believe that awarding physicians an adoptive kinship reflects a collectivistic culture (as opposed to one that is individualistic) that experiences life primarily as a mosaic of interdependent family relationships that extend from the cradle to the grave....

Whereas in the States, I was expected to *facilitate* patients, in Pakistan, I was expected to *direct* patients *and* their families ...frequently...to play the role of an "elder" who could provide "a solution" for what needed to be done.

In Pakistan, the physician is held in high esteem by a society that respects authority and condones hierarchical systems.... The privileged position of physicians is derived through a historical understanding of the healer as an instrument of divine mercy.... One of the Arabic words for a physician is *Hakim*. It means one who has knowledge and wisdom and is a name for God. (Moazam 2000: 28–31, author's italics)

Moazam's PhD dissertation, which was published as a book in 2007, was based on a firsthand ethnographic study of the ethical issues surrounding live, related renal transplantation that she conducted at the SIUT, part of a large public hospital in Karachi, and the only site in the country that offers dialysis and renal transplants free of charge. This experience provided her with rich, often poignant knowledge of how distinctive attributes of Pakistani Muslim culture not only shaped the giving and receiving of kidneys in this context, but also the motives of families to donate organs to kin, and why they were reluctant to do so. In addition, her research also documented the extended kinship-like community formed by the doctors and nurses of the Institute's staff, their hierarchy, ethos of duties and obligations, and interactions with patients, and the ways in which they influenced and manipulated as well as reacted to family decisions about who would donate a kidney (Moazam 2007).

Throughout the duration of her field research Moazam had the strong support of Dr. Syed Adibul Hasan Rizvi, the surgeon-director of SIUT, and had many opportunities to discuss with him the kinds of ethical challenges and dilemmas that he and his staff faced in trying to give care to the hundreds of mainly poor kidney patients who came to SIUT from all over Pakistan, and to offer hemodialysis and renal transplants to those who were in the end-stage of their disease. In the face of limited financial resources, the nonlegitimation of cadaveric organ transplants in Pakistan, and complex, culturally imprinted questions about who in the kinship system could, should, and would donate a kidney to a family member for a live transplant, the SIUT medical staff continually faced massive problems of how to live up to its "motto"—"We cannot let anyone die because he (she) cannot afford to live" (quoted in Atta inaugurates Centre of Biomedical Ethics and Culture 2004).

What gradually emerged from Moazam's and Rizvi's conversations was the idea of founding a center of biomedical ethics that could deliberate on such issues, locating it at SIUT, and appointing Moazam as professor of surgery and the new center's chairperson. Plans for the development of such a center moved forward rapidly. By October 8, 2004, when the inauguration of the Centre of Biomedical Ethics and Culture (CBEC) took place on its new premises—at the Sindh Institute of Urology and Transplantation, in the Dewan Farooq Medical Complex—its conception had become more far reaching than had been initially envisioned. As Moazam explained in the introductory address that she delivered on this occasion:

What Pakistan lacks…is a recognized, indigenous center in the public or private sector devoted specifically to research and education in all aspects of bioethics and particularly those relevant to the needs of the country. The Centre of Biomedical Ethics and Culture (CBEC)…is the first step Pakistan will take in correcting this deficiency.…

The location of CBEC in the public sector gives it the added advantage of accessibility to healthcare professionals and researchers, a large number of whom still work within public institutions.

The primary goal of CBEC is to serve as an academic and intellectual source for Pakistan and eventually the region. Its aim will be to foster an understanding of contemporary bioethics, and to explore the influence of cultural and religious values in shaping the understanding of ethics and morality in a society.

Besides undertaking educational and research programs such as workshops, courses and seminars on various aspects of bioethics, and organizing national and international conferences, CBEC will assist in enhancing existing bioethical activities within the public and private sectors in Pakistan.

As a national entity, CBEC will establish links and collaborations with international bioethics centers and organizations, and will be in a position to contribute a unique cultural perspective to enrich international bioethics discourse and activities that are at present largely secular and philosophical in nature.[11]

"Accordingly," Moazam added in the brochure prepared for circulation at the Center's inauguration, "another important function CBEC will undertake is to explore the role of cultural, societal and religious norms in shaping indigenous value systems that are seminal components of human moral comprehension." One aspect of such an indigenous value system, she pointed out in a later talk, is "[t]he importance of excellence of character [that] lies at the heart of ethics and morality in Islam.... This is evident in the ethico-religious concepts repeated again and again in the verses of the Qur'an."[12]

The inauguration was a stellar event, which included three invited speakers: the "chief guest," Atta-ur-Rahman, Pakistan's Federal Minister for Education, Science and Technology and chairman of the country's Higher Education Commission; Luc Noël, coordinator of Clinical Procedures and Essential Health Technologies of the World Health Organization; and Paul Lombardo, director of the Program in Law and Medicine in the Center for Biomedical Ethics at the University of Virginia. Lombardo delivered the guest lecture on the origin and evolution of eugenics and its impact on American society and culture. But it was the address by the chief guest, Federal Minister Atta-ur-Rahman, that had the most political import. He stated that Pakistan's wealth and resources are controlled by 20 percent of its 150 million population, and that only 2.9 percent of its youth have access to higher education. He declared that "we need to improve primary education, science and technology for striving towards a balanced development," and reported that under an initiative aimed at reversing the brain drain, the government had succeeded in attracting back to Pakistan 43 academics who were working in well-known institutions abroad. He then informed the audience that, in addition to lending its support to CBEC, the Higher Education Commission that he headed would be creating an International Centre of Bioethics at Karachi University, where he is a professor and heads a scientific research center (Atta Inaugurates Centre of Biomedical Ethics and Culture 2004; Biomedical ethics, culture centre at SIUT 2004). What he did not say publicly at this time was that he had invited Moazam to organize and launch this international center, or that he had personally told her that he hoped that this offer would be an added inducement for her to return to Pakistan from the University of Virginia. Among the factors contributing to his desire to have such a center in Karachi was that the 58 Muslim countries of the Organization of Islamic Conferences (OIC), of which he is an influential member, had seriously discussed the need for this sort of institution.

Some 300 invitees attended the inauguration of CBEC. It was accompanied by great fanfare and ritual, such as the ceremonial unveiling of the Centre's plaque, and it also received prominent press and television coverage and highly positive responses from other sources. For example, the announcement of a seminar and intensive course on "Foundations of Moral Thought: From the Greeks to Contemporary Bioethics" to be offered by CBEC in April 2005, which was distributed during the inauguration and also communicated via Internet, elicited an unexpectedly enthusiastic response from many persons who were eager to register for it immediately. This seminar and intensive course was described as aiming to examine "the diverse secular and religious influences on the shaping of moral thought from the times of the Greeks to the birth of contemporary bioethics in the 20th century." "Although the role of Anglo-European and American thinkers is well documented," the statement of objectives went on to say, "there has been insufficient acknowledgement of the contributions made by Muslim scholars to this process. A distinctive feature of this course will be special emphasis on the historical contributions of Muslim philosophers, theologians, jurists, and *ulema* [scholars] who made a significant, and enduring impact on fashioning the chain of moral thought that stretches from antiquity to modern times."

Moazam went back to the University of Virginia soon after the inauguration to prepare for her departure from the United States in February 2005 in order to assume her responsibilities as professor and chair at CBEC/SIUT. About a month before she returned to Pakistan, another development in the burgeoning of bioethics was the formation of the Karachi Bioethics Group (Moazam, personal communication, July 26, 2005). The Group's creation was spearheaded by Moazam's younger colleague, surgeon Aamir M. Jafarey, who has been her chief associate in developing the Centre's local, national, and international activities.

To Moazam's surprise, because as she commented to us, "the movement in the public sector in Pakistan is generally more like that of molasses," plans for the International Centre of Bioethics proceeded so rapidly that by October 21, the proposal for its establishment was completed—including its staffing, details of a building to be constructed on a two-acre plot, the formation of a "planning group" from North American universities and WHO that would meet for two to three days in April 2005 during the period when CBEC would hold its "Foundations of Moral Thought" course, and a requested commitment of approximately $485,000 in U.S. dollars to finance the first year of the center's operation. The proposal, accompanied by supporting letters solicited from U.S. academic centers and faculty[13] to "strengthen" it, was submitted for approval to the appropriate government offices in Islamabad at the end of October, and was given final approval in November 2005.[14]

The five-day seminar and intensive course on "Foundations of Moral Thought: From the Greeks to Contemporary Bioethics" took place as planned on April 4–9, 2005, with an international faculty.[15] CBEC's chairperson launched the course with a spirited and, in certain respects, provocative introductory talk. "It has become fashionable now to talk of ethics," Moazam said:

In the last two decades, the terms *bioethics* and *biomedical ethics*, coined in the West, have become household words in our part of the world. In Pakistan it is now difficult to find a conference or seminar that does not include some talks or a session or two on bioethics.... But what do we in this part of the world understand by bioethics and biomedical ethics, and what do we mean when we use these words? Perhaps more importantly, how are we educating ourselves and imparting education in this discipline?

I learned of a recent seminar in this country, which was constructed around four lectures: one lecture was on autonomy, another on beneficence, the third on non-maleficence, and the last on justice. In actuality, these are...four philosophical principles that were taken straight out of a very influential book, *The Principles of Biomedical Ethics*, written by two U.S. philosophers, James Childress and Tom Beauchamp....

A few words about these four ethical principles—we seem to believe that if we can recite them and teach them to our students we understand what bioethics is all about. What we forget, however, is that Beauchamp and Childress wrote this book within the context of the existing legal and value systems and socioeconomic realities of the United States. It is these that are reflected in their discussions on how these principles are to serve as guides for moral dilemmas. The central values in the United States include a belief that the rights of an autonomous individual take precedence, and must remain central in any discussion on biomedical ethics. It is the individual who is the legal and social unit, not the family. In addition, the authors subscribe to the view that knowledge of right and wrong must be derived from human reason alone, and that religious beliefs and values are not necessary as guides to lead an ethical public and professional life.

This particular view of contemporary bioethics, "Principlism" as it is called, is rooted in Anglo-European and American history and its philosophical traditions. But it has become the dominant language and methodology of almost all international discourse on bioethics. And we, the English-speaking professionals of this country and the region, have learned to speak this language and use words that often do not have equivalent terms in Urdu, the language understood and spoken by a majority of those we serve in our professions.

It is this language, this essence, and this methodology of "doing" ethics that is being "globalized." It is being globalized to countries that have strong and longstanding religious and cultural ethical values, a sense of morality that differs in significant ways from those in which bioethics was founded. In my opinion, we imported from the West science, medicine, and biomedical technology in the last century; in this century we are doing the same with bioethics. As a nation, so far we have largely been passive conduits and receptacles rather than informed and critical contributors to the international dialogue and bioethics.

The title of the course, Moazam explained to the attendees, was meant to draw their attention to the fact that contemporary bioethics was only "one small link in a long train of Western moral thought that extends from antiquity to modern times," and that it was not "the final link in this chain, nor a link that is capable of providing specific answers to every ethical problem everywhere in the world.... All of us, whether from the East or West, traditional or modern, secular or religious, can contribute to this process through cool, thoughtful discourse." In this connection, she stated, one of the important objectives of the course was to "explore the historical contributions of Muslim scholars and Muslim values to human understanding of morals and ethical conduct," with the hope that the participants in the course would leave at the end of its five days' duration "curious to learn more about contemporary bioethics and Islamic moral traditions, and how our own indigenous norms and value systems impinge on our struggle to arrive at ethical decisions."

Moazam concluded her talk by inviting the assemblage to "gaze at contemporary bioethics through...constructively critical eyes," while "turn[ing] an equally critical eye on our own cultural and religious practices." "We do our religion and our tradition a great disservice," she declared, "when we approach them with blind, *taqlidee* eyes that cannot see beyond the veils of rituals."[16]

The response to the course and seminar surpassed its organizers' expectations. The morning talks, which were open to all applicants, were attended by some 100 people each day, and on the two days devoted to Muslim moral thought, the attendance increased to 140 persons. There was difficulty in trying to limit the afternoon seminars to 30 participants. In the end, 38 individuals were enrolled for these daily, four one-hour-long sessions. The applicants and participants came from Iran, the United Arab Emirates, Turkey, and Egypt, as well as from different regions of Pakistan. Moazam described them as "superbly interactive." In the 90-minute debriefing that was held with the participants at the end of the seminar "one of the common remarks was that this was the first time in Pakistan" that they had been involved in "such a course, that the instructors were 'teachers and not preachers', that more, similar courses were needed, that 'we now know how little we know about Islam,' and thanks, and more thanks." The only "weakness" a few people pointed out was "insufficient 'practical' scenarios...related to Pakistan, and guidance about how to deal with them—the concrete approach of many physicians." Once again, as had been the case in the inauguration of CBEC in October 2004, what was billed by the local press as "an international seminar and course" received extensive media coverage. In fact, there were so many newspaper and TV journalists present at the certificate-giving ceremony at the end of the course who were eager to interview its organizers, faculty, and enrollees, that the teaching on the final day was shortened somewhat to make time for them to do so (Moazam, personal communication, Apr. 11, 2005).

Despite the enthusiasm with which this first major CBEC educational undertaking was received, it was not devoid of tension. These strains centered around some of the issues that were considered by its participants to be among the most important: how Islam and Muslim values differ from "secular" principles, and why and how it is necessary to look at Muslim history and values as guidance in life. They surfaced during the discussion that took place in response to the talk given in eloquent Urdu by Jawaid Ghamadi, a Sunni scholar from Lahore, educated in the classical Muslim tradition, who is well known and respected in Pakistan. Moazam had asked him to speak on the difference between *Sharia* ("God-given") and *fiqh* (derived from *Sharia* and a part of it, but "man-made" and thus open to change). His talk was very well received. But in the course of the afternoon discussions about it, controversy arose about some of the opinions he expressed:

The [question] was raised about why Muslims were in the abject condition they were in today. Reference was made to Iraq and the Palestinian issue, including suicide bombers. [Ghamadi] was asked about how Muslims could handle these issues.... [He], who is a severe critic of American policies, nevertheless made several points—that violence at this time was counterproductive for Muslims and would never succeed; that historically (he quoted specific instances in Muslim history), Muslims, too, when in power had done wrong things to other civilizations; that if Muslims united nobody (U.S. and Israel included) could touch them. He then gave his opinion that in the late seventh century, Imam Hassan, one of the grandsons of the Prophet, declined to take up arms against rival groups to avoid a breakdown of Muslim unity. However, when his brother, Imam Hussain (who is respected by Sunnis as the grandson of the Prophet, but whom Shias revere as their unblemished imam-leader) went to war against Muwayyia (a Sunni leader) and was martyred, he laid the grounds for a schism between Muslims.... [T]his did not go over very well with some of the participants...[who later complained] that in effect Ghamadi had "destroyed" Muslim heroes. (Moazam, personal communication, Apr. 11, 2005)

This incident made a strong impression on Moazam. She regarded it as an instructive though daunting contribution to her "education" about "how sensitive it can be to begin to talk about these issues in Pakistan, which is currently torn by politically motivated sectarianism, and where there is little tradition of objective analysis and discourse" (Moazam, personal communication, Apr. 12, 2005). In addition, in the form of a letter that they received from a more fundamentalist Muslim scholar of East African and American origins after the seminar and course were over, Moazam and her colleagues were confronted with the indignant opinion that CBEC had "embarked on a secular bioethics which will in the long run set a wrong paradigm in Pakistan." It is not "the right kind of program for a society that is informed by religious values at its core," he insisted (Moazam, personal communication, Apr. 11, 2005).

As a consequence of the energetic initiatives of CBEC and the ripple effects of their first undertakings, the Centre and Moazam were plunged into a cascade of activities.[17] During 2005–2006, for example, CBEC created a monthly newsletter (*Bioethics Links*), launched its first biannual national bioethics seminar, established a one-year-long postgraduate diploma course in biomedical ethics for midcareer professionals, conducted workshops on how to establish a research ethics committee, and was involved in planning and participating in the 7th Global Forum for Research Ethics that was held in Karachi and sponsored by AKU. On the international plane, Moazam was an invited participant in numerous meetings, including one held in Kuwait in June 2005 by the Islamic Organization for Muslim Studies, whose purpose was to design a course in ethics for countries in what WHO designates as the Eastern Mediterranean Region, and in August 2006, the 8th World Congress of the International Bioethics Association in Beijing.

In some of her presentations Moazam emphasized how important she thought it was for bioethicists to be aware of the attempts being made in areas with substantial Muslim populations "to find directions and ethical resolutions that reflect indigenous cultural and religious values." In others, particularly in her talk at the Global Forum for Research Ethics, she took note of what she rather acerbically referred to as the "intriguing priority" that has been accorded to research ethics in Pakistan over the past decade. Although she made positive statements about the importance of medical research that "will help improve the health and lives of the citizens of this country," and of conducting such research "in an ethical manner," she was sharply critical of what she termed "this almost exclusionary pursuit of research ethics." In a country like Pakistan, she declared, in which "patients bleed to death as they lie unattended in emergency rooms, seriously ill patients are denied hospital admission because of the inability to provide cash deposits, and physicians ostracize patients with HIV/AIDS and STD [sexually transmitted disease]," top priority should be given to "our unethical clinical practices."[18]

Violence, Electricity Breakdown, and the Earthquake

Religious Violence. In the midst of all these fruitful and far-reaching activities of the CBEC and Moazam, an event occurred that cast a shadow over its early days. Although it was an ephemeral happening, it was nonetheless a sobering reminder of the adverse effects that the religious strife in Pakistan between Sunni and Shiite groups and the violence accompanying it might have on the pursuit of bioethics in this setting. On May 30, 2005, at the beginning of evening prayers at a Shiite mosque in Karachi, a suicide bomber "believed to belong to a Sunni extremist group linked to Al Qaeda, blew himself up inside the mosque compound. Minutes later, a mob, believed to be led by outraged Shiites, stormed a Kentucky Fried Chicken restaurant...an American symbol." They set it on fire with gasoline, and blocked the entry of rescue workers. Six hours later, six bodies of restaurant employees were retrieved. "Four had been burned. Two had frozen to death in the walk-in freezer.... [They] were all local men in their mid-20s." "It is no secret that symbols of American commercial might are lightning rods for anti-American sentiment," *New York Times* correspondent Somini Sengupta commented. "But the deadly strike on this fast-food restaurant on a hot summer night in Pakistan's most populous city, revealed something much more potent: It showed how existing strains—in this case a deep sectarian divide that is roiling this city—can tap a well of anti-American fury to create an explosion of violence" (Sengupta 2005).

These events set off a rampage in the city. The high tension and sporadic disturbances continued throughout the next day. On June 1, the opposition political parties declared a complete "*hartal*" (strike) that stopped all transportation, closed all shops, and kept most of the city's population at home and off the streets. In the light of these developments, CBEC regretfully decided to postpone its second "Ethics and Culture Hour," which was scheduled for 8:15 A.M. on June 1. It was to have been a talk, entitled "Physicians Sans Frontières," about contributions that physicians have made "beyond medicine," to "literature, philosophy, music and adventure," delivered by Iftikhar Salahuddin, an otolaryngologist and head and neck surgeon, and an outstanding photographer. Since the talk had been advertised in the local newspaper, and was open to the general public, the CBEC staff had to quickly find ways to widely communicate the change in plans.

At the end of the day, after the personnel of CBEC had been sent home early because of the lingering threat of more violence or rioting, Farhat Moazam sat alone in her office, "angry and sad about what is going on in the world, especially in this region—Pakistan, Afghanistan, Iraq, and Palestine." "There are some days (not all by any means) when I wonder about establishing an entity such as CBEC, [about] its usefulness and relevance in a world gone stark, raving mad around me," she wrote in an e-mail to us before shutting down her computer for the night. She was experiencing, she said, what she had come to call one of her "transient bouts of existential moroseness." Nonetheless, demonstrating her commitment to the work she had returned to Pakistan to undertake, she energetically resumed her activities at CBEC the next day.

Electricity Breakdown. On a relatively less serious front, the subject of a communication we received from Moazam on June 30, 2005, read, "Hello from a technology challenged country." "Summer," she wrote, "brings with it…problems of 'first world' technology installed in 'third world' countries such as Pakistan, including daily breakdowns of electricity." "This will by necessity be a (relatively) brief email," she told us, because "we are having 'technological' problems with the internet in Pakistan. Apparently, earlier this week the major internet cable that connects us with the rest of the world…blew up in a section that lies in the depths of the Indian Ocean." The loss of the Internet cable took many days to fix. "Am sending this email on a wing and a prayer, as they say," she wrote on July 5. "Our problems with the internet access continues…[but] suddenly my old fashioned dial-up [at home] seems to be working (no idea why)—it is the fast speed systems (the kind we have in CBEC) which are still mostly kaput in the country." With rueful humor, she commented that "by stretching the analogy it is almost akin to our importation of modern bioethics into Pakistan and then struggling [with] how to apply/use it in a totally different world."

The October 2005 Earthquake. The successful completion of CBEC's international conference on fundamentals of research ethics at the end of November brought no respite in their activities, or in Moazam's escalating commitments. She was racing against a deadline to review the page proofs of her dissertation-based book for the University of Indiana Press (Moazam 2007). Of far deeper professional and personal meaning for her were the preparations that she was making to travel to Islamabad and outlying villages in northern Pakistan, to render medical care to the victims of the devastating earthquake in the mountainous terrain of the Hindu Kush that had occurred in October. Farhat flew north in December, accompanied by a physician friend. Two days after her return to Karachi, we received an e-mail from her recounting some of what she had encountered:

We saw a world turned upside down. There are no words in my vocabulary that can capture what we saw or communicate what we heard from the quake victims…. Massive swaths of white streaks gouged down the face of towering mountain sides, the insides exposed as though scraped off with a huge knife, entire villages leveled to the ground with an occasional building standing seemingly untouched, incongruously pushing its head out of the surrounding rubble. A sea of tents everywhere, some sturdy others merely flimsy white cloth with plastic sheets thrown over them to retain heat inside. In them thousands of the displaced survivors huddle in the cold of winter. We heard stories of how mothers buried their children pulled out dead from the rubble, extended families that lost as many as 18 members in the quake. It is estimated that besides the 100,000 or so killed about 5 million people have been permanently displaced.

[We] would get in the van we were provided by the Pakistan Medical Association (PMA) which was very helpful in arranging our visit, fill it with cartons of medicine (some available in the small hospital that served as our base, others we had carted from Karachi and more that we bought locally when we ran out of these), and try to identify those tent *bastis* villages (by stopping and asking if they had) been visited by any physician. We would then set up a makeshift clinic in a tent which the camp refugees would gratefully provide, placing 2 chairs or a *charpoy* (a kind of bed) in it. One of these makeshift clinics was in one half of a tent the other half of which was a "school" set up by the immensely large hearted citizens of Mansehra many of whom were themselves quake victims, and in which 65 children were sitting on a mat on the floor. That day we looked at over 100 patients in the background of the laughter of little children aged 2–12 reciting the alphabet. The flap on our side of the tent opened onto a small dusty enclosure in which half a dozen cows were tethered, some which had been salvaged from the quake affected villages.

Word…would spread that there were doctors in the camp and people would begin to stream in. On some days we saw as many as 120 patients, mostly women and children, with common ailments such as flu, coughs, severe anemia, occasional diarrhea, scabies, intestinal worms, ringworm infections and on and on. Children with faces chapped by the cold, many shoeless, 30 year old women pregnant with their 10th child, some who had buried their children killed in the collapse of their houses, others who had lost husbands and parents…. It is the women and children who have suffered the most; [we] felt that it is the women and not the men who were struggling to continue their lives with some semblance of normality. We saw them cooking in the open (basic rations are provided by NGOs and the government), washing clothes and laying them out on the tents to dry in the sun. And yet despite all their misery, when we had seen the last patient in the camp, women would come up and insist that we have tea with them, or that they had just cooked *chapatee* (local bread) and would we please join them for lunch.

Our last morning spent in a PMA hospital…was especially upsetting—rows of women with one or more extremities in plasters and surgery done for broken bones, amputees, some still with open wounds, all supposedly in a "hospital" but getting little…care.

The people of Pakistan have opened their hearts and emptied out their pockets for the quake victims but the scale of the disaster, the number of the dead and the displaced, is so unbelievably horrible that it is impossible to wrap one's mind around it. Whatever we did, in my opinion, counts for no more than a very tiny drop of what will be needed to attend to this ocean of misery that Pakistan is now awash in. (Moazam, personal communication, Dec. 13, 2005)

Vending Kidneys

Ever since Farhat Moazam became intensively involved in the complex, often tragic realities of the conditions surrounding kidney transplantation in Pakistan through her ethnographic study at the Sindh Institute of Urology and Transplantation—the parent institution of CBEC—she has grown more morally disturbed and indignant about the extensive practice of vending human kidneys for this purpose that exists in the country, and the circumstances under which it takes place. Payment for organs was not illegal in Pakistan. Certain physicians and hospitals as well as members of the government reportedly have been complicit in organizing and perpetuating the practice; and all signs point to the fact that those who vend their kidneys are individuals and families who belong to the most disadvantaged members of Pakistani society.

In 2007, Moazam and her CBEC associates decided to enter the struggle to control and if possible abolish this commerce in organs by undertaking a "psychosocial, ethnographic study" of kidney vending in some of the villages in Punjab whose inhabitants provide kidneys to hospitals in Pindi and Lahore. In June, they made their initial three-day visit to a medium-size town in Punjab, in an area that constitutes the main pool from which a particular hospital draws its vendors. "It was an incredible, very disturbing experience," Moazam wrote to us upon her return to Karachi:

We interviewed 20 vendors (2 women) in detail in different *deras*, and also the wives of two of them.... *Deras* is the term for small groups—2 or more—of mostly mud, single room dwellings occupied by farm workers, many in proximity of brick residences of *zamindars*, i.e., landowners for whom they work.... We found 100% illiteracy and a level of poverty one does not often come across. There was one family in which 6 out of 7 brothers have sold their kidneys within the last 2 years, and they still remain in debt. Another family—the wife, her second son, and husband have sold kidneys, and the oldest son is thinking of doing the same.

Of the 20 we interviewed, one was hypertensive, and 2 had traces of blood in their urine. And there is absolutely no follow-up, no place for them to go, and no money to get anywhere. Using a WHO approved assessment form, [we] found 7 who were depressed enough (one who had made a suicide attempt) to need referral for further evaluation and possible medication.... All, no exceptions, said they would not suggest to anyone that they sell a kidney....

If what we found is not a form of slavery...then I do not know what is. I went into the study with an obvious bias against kidney vending. I have returned with it reinforced (and my anger increased at the dirtball physicians and hospitals who benefit from the practice), but also upset as I can begin to understand why vendors sell their kidneys. I do not see how these people can break out of shackles (unending debts) that are passed down the generations. (Moazam, personal communication, June 9, 2007)

Moazam envisions this study as a long-term CBEC project. It is fueled by the burning commitment that she expressed in a letter she wrote to an American physician who is a transplantation nephrologist:

In my opinion, this form of brutalizing our fellow human beings, where the only option left to them to raise money for their needs is to sell a part of their body, is or should be a source of deep shame for any society. We are and must remain advocates for our patients of course, but we also owe responsibilities towards the larger ills that beset societies we live in. (personal communication, June 23, 2007; forwarded to us by F. Moazam)[19]

The Case of Bioethics in Pakistan: An Overview

The central figure and galvanic force in the field of bioethics in Pakistan manifestly has been Farhat Moazam. She has brought to the bioethical mission that she has undertaken her training, experience, and influence as a surgeon and medical educator in both the United States and Pakistan; her thorough grounding in U.S. bioethics, and her at-once appreciative and thoughtfully critical perspective on it; and her determination to implement her conviction that, with the spread of bioethics around the globe, it has become more imperative than ever for the field to take cognizance of the cultures (including the religious traditions) of the different societies in which it has been developing. Working from the baseline of Pakistani society, she feels, gives her both the obligation and opportunity to foster the integration of Islamic thought, values, and beliefs into the conceptual framework of the field, to disseminate knowledge about the development of bioethics in the Muslim world, and thereby to help make bioethics more genuinely international. At the same time, she considers it both intellectually and morally imperative to maintain a sharply critical attitude toward some of the cultural and religious practices in Pakistani society and, above all, toward what she refers to as "the larger ills that beset" the society, which underlie the bioethical issues to which CBEC is actively responding.

Although as of 2007, in a country of 160 million people, there were only a very few formally trained bioethicists in Pakistan, all located in Karachi at AKU or CBEC, the enthusiasm that bioethics and Moazam's conception of it has elicited, and the alacrity with which institutional structures for it were provided, surpassed her expectations. Why this much medical professional, political, and public interest in bioethics exists in Pakistan is an important question to consider. It does not have a simple, self-obvious explanation. Contributing to it seems to be a diffuse appreciation of the great advances in biomedical research, science, and technology of the 20th and now the 21st century, and of the clinical achievements resulting from them—to which modern Western societies and civilization have been foremost contributors. Coupled with this is awareness of the international recognition and prestige that accompanies being associated with these scientific and clinical developments. In Pakistani academic medical circles, there is also keen awareness of the raised ethical consciousness about the moral dilemmas, the risks, and the inadvertent harm, as well as the benefits of this progress that has developed and is being professionally and publicly displayed in the West in the form of bioethics, most notably in the United States. As Moazam has observed, there has been a tendency in these Pakistani milieus to "import" bioethics from the West, in a manner comparable to the importation of modern science, medicine, and biotechnology.

Nevertheless, the groundswell of interest in the heritage of Islam that currently exists in Pakistan, in medical as well as other settings, has quickened the development of bioethics. What some refer to as this "general Islamic revival" is not confined to Pakistan. It is being broadly expressed in and through phenomena such as plans to create a Centre of Biomedical Ethics and Religion in Kuwait, which is the headquarters for the Islamic Organization of Medical Sciences (IOMS), established in the late 1970s. The IOMS also has undertaken, as a major project, the formulation of an Islamic code of medical ethics, derived from Islamic Sharia. The code will address "the newer medical research and discoveries…emerging at a fast pace," often involving the use of human subjects, as well as the situation of medical practice.

Within this larger context in Pakistan, there has been a growing sense of the points of disjunction between the religiously rooted conception of "relational morality" that predominates in the society, and the resolutely secular notion of individual autonomy around which Western, and especially American, bioethics is structured, which has kindled a search to discover whether and how Muslim values and beliefs can be integrated into the outlook and discourse of present-day bioethics. "It is time for us to move from serving as passive receptacles of contemporary bioethics to active participants in its evolution," Moazam declared in 2006 at the close of her talk for the 7th Global Forum for Research Ethics. "What is needed," she stated, "is a collective, systematic effort to bring contemporary bioethics and Muslim values together [in Pakistan]. It is necessary for us to evolve bioethics in a coherent way in this country, give it a form that resonates with our values. Otherwise, bioethics in Pakistan will remain an academic exercise…irrelevant to the needs of the population.… [B]y shouldering this task we also enrich the dry, rights-based, legalistic discourse of contemporary bioethics."[20]

Bioethics has the prospect of simultaneously associating Pakistan and its medical profession with modern medical science and clinical care, and enlightened contemporary thought about their ethical complexity on the one hand and, on the other, with the venerable intellectual, medical, moral, and religious tradition of virtue ethics that is intrinsic to Muslim tradition. For this reason, the national, regional, and international connection of the Islamic Republic of Pakistan with bioethics has potential political and symbolic importance. As such it could make a powerful statement about the virtues of Islam and of Pakistan that contravenes the stereotypical "terrorist" and "fundamentalist" characteristics too often attributed to them in the West in the "post-9/11" era. The case of Pakistan will be an interesting and important one to follow, as it further develops its proliferating bioethical activities, and strives to enrich, broaden, and deepen bioethical thought and action, locally, nationally, and internationally.[21]

Notes

1. Farhat Moazam has provided us with the great majority of our information about bioethics in Pakistan. We first met her in 1999, when we made joint presentations about our research on organ replacement and our perspective on bioethics at the University

of Virginia where she was then enrolled in the master's degree program in Religious Studies and Bioethics. After Dr. Moazam returned to Pakistan, and to her positions as professor and chair of Surgery, and dean of Postgraduate Education at Aga Khan University in Karachi, she invited Fox to participate in a postgraduate medical educa-tion conference that she organized there in May 2000. When she subsequently resumed graduate study at the University of Virginia, with the assent of her doctoral degree director, philosopher-bioethicist James Childress, Fox became Moazam's major tutor-from-a-distance in the sociology of medicine, and especially in ethnographic methods of social research, and was closely involved in supervising Moazam's fieldwork for her PhD dissertation. Swazey's colleagueship with Moazam quickened during 2004, and both she and Fox have had a lively, regular exchange of ideas via correspondence with her that turns around her activities associated with the Centre for Biomedical Ethics and Culture (CBEC) in Karachi.

We are also indebted to Dr. Aamir M. Jafarey, a surgeon with training in bioethics, a lecturer in the Department of Surgery of the Aga Khan University, and an assistant professor at CBEC, who is Moazam's close junior colleague, and who has provided us with valuable documents and information, including several of his publications.

2. Partly because of the relationship to the United States that the Aga Khan developed through his years as a student in the States, Americans have been prominent members of AKU's board of trustees. In addition, until 2003, some of the deans of the Faculty of Health Sciences, and top hospital administrators, as well as the chair of the Department of Community Health Services, have been North Americans (Canadian and American). And for brief tenures, Canadians have served as chairs of Medicine and of Obstetrics and Gynecology.

3. F. Moazam, Making a case for "indigenizing" bioethics. Plenary talk, 7th Global Forum for Research Ethics, Karachi, Pakistan, Feb., 17, 2006. Unpublished paper sent to us by Moazam.

4. A. Jafarey, Bioethics at the Aga Khan University. 2003. Unpublished document sent to us by Jafarey.

5. In their paper, Moazam and Jafarey report that in 2004, the U.S. Office of Human Research Protections (OHRP) listed eight approved ethics review committees in Pakistan, three of which were university-based and five were nongovernmental organizations (Moazam and Jafarey 2005: 255n6).

6. A. Jafarey, Bioethics at the Aga Khan University. 2003. Unpublished document sent to us by Jafarey.

7. One example of the ways that Pakistani culture affects the interactions between phy-sicians and patients in both medical care and clinical research is the nature of the informed consent transaction. As Jafarey and Farooqui (2005) describe in their paper on an "informal qualitative study" of how physicians obtain consent at AKU Hospital, the decision-making process "is often done by family members or is left up to the attending physician."

8. The Committee's proposed membership is an eclectic, nationwide one, with five ex-officio representatives (from the PMDC, CSPP [the College of Surgeons and Physi-cians of Pakistan], PMRC, WHO, and a lawyer), two each from the categories of biosci-entists, academics, and universities/medical colleges, and one representative each from general practitioners, nurses, journalists (identified in the membership list as the man-aging editor of the *Pakistan Journal of Medicine* and Chief Executive of Professional Medical Publications), social scientists, religious scholars, industry, and the Human Rights Commission, as well as a nominee of the Surgeon General of the Pakistan Army

and two "co-opted members"—the latter apparently referring to two nominees from departments of health (www.pmrc.org.pk/nbcmain).

9. F. Moazam, Foundational ethical concepts in Islam: The Qur'an, Imam al-Ghazali, and Muslim physicians. Plenary speech, Aga Khan University symposium on clinical ethics. October 8, 2004. Unpublished paper sent to us by Moazam.

10. In a personal communication (Nov. 8, 2002), Moazam pointed out that in Urdu, the major language of Pakistan, the word *rights* is generally translated as *haquaq*, the plural form of *haq*, a word with Arabic roots. *Haquaq* is difficult to translate into English, she explains, because rather than sharply distinguishing between rights and obligations, it expresses an inextricable relationship between them—the intertwining of one's "due," and of one's "duty," with special emphasis on the "distribution of obligations."

11. F. Moazam. Foundational ethical concepts in Islam.

12. F. Moazam, Making a case for "indigenizing" bioethics.

13. Among the letters of support requested and sent were those written by James Childress and Jonathan Moreno of the University of Virginia, and by Renée Fox.

14. As of Summer 2007, the establishment of the International Bioethics Centre was still in a preliminary stage. Funds had been released to Karachi University in 2006 to begin construction at a site on the University campus, and architects were working on a design for the building (Moazam, personal communication, July 3, 2007).

15. In addition to Moazam and Jafarey, the faculty consisted of Manzoor Ahmed, a moral philosopher and professor and dean at the Usmania Institute of Technology in Karachi; Jawaid Ghamadi, a Muslim scholar and president of Al-Mawrid Institute of Islamic Sciences in Lahore, Pakistan; M. Haytham Al-Khayat from Cairo, Egypt, another Muslim scholar and senior policy advisor to the Eastern Mediterranean Regional Office (EMRO) of the World Health Organization; Jonathan Moreno, professor and director of the Center for Biomedical Ethics at the University of Virginia; and Abdul Aziz Sachedina, professor in the Department of Religious Studies at the University of Virginia. We had planned to serve as faculty for the course, but at the last minute, because of the terminal illness and death of one of our closest colleagues and friends, Willy De Craemer, an emeritus faculty member in the Department of Sociology at the University of Pennsylvania, we were obliged to cancel our trip to Karachi. However, we prepared three lectures for the occasion to be delivered as a "team of two," videotaped them, and sent them via Federal Express to Karachi in time for them to be presented to those attending the course. The topics of our lectures, selected by Dr. Moazam out of a list of possible subjects that we had proposed to her were: (1) "American Bioethics," in which we focused on areas of concern and controversy about the current state of the field, and some of the ways in which we feel U.S. bioethics needs to be reshaped; (2) "Organ Transplantation: Giving and Receiving a 'Gift of Life'"; (3) "Bioethics Circles the Globe," with emphasis on how although bioethics has become more international, in our view, there are important ways in which it is not necessarily becoming more "internationalized."

16. These passages were excerpted from a copy of the text of her introductory talk that Moazam sent us.

17. This roster of activities was compiled from e-mails to us from Farhat Moazam and from calendars of events and announcements issued by CBEC, and from Jafarey 2005.

18. Moazam proposed several reasons for the priority that bioethics in Pakistan has placed on research ethics. These include the challenge of research, its ability to "widen our intellectual and scientific horizons," and its potential to "improve health and human life." Research, she said, also is "seductive because of the many personal gains it offers

to researchers." Two additional factors that she cited are the fellowships in research ethics, not clinical ethics, hosted by developed countries for professionals from developing countries, and the "phenomenal increase in the 'outsourcing' [to developing countries] of drug studies and trials funded by the multinational pharmaceutical industry, (F. Moazam, Making a case for "indigenizing" bioethics.")

19. After more than a decade of failed efforts to proscribe the buying and selling of organs, in September 2007 a presidential ordinance was passed making commercial dealings in human organs and tissues illegal. Farhat Moazam was instrumental in pushing through this law, which she and others hope will reduce if not completely halt kidney vending.

20. F. Moazam, ibid.

21. On Dec. 27, 2007 Benazir Bhutto, two-time former prime minister of Pakistan and lifetime head of the Pakistan People's Party, one of the country's two main opposition parties, was assassinated. In the midst of this tragedy and the turmoil that ensued, the activities of CBEC continued. On Dec. 29, two days after the assassination, the Centre held the debriefing and concluding teaching session for the diploma students in its Class of 2007.

IV

TAKING STOCK OF
BIOETHICS IN THE
UNITED STATES

11

The Coming of the Culture Wars to American Bioethics

In various of the chapters composing this book, we have contended that the significance of U.S. bioethics is not confined to intellectual or to biomedically associated ethical issues. Rather, we have characterized this field as a hybrid phenomenon that has roots and repercussions in the public square[1], the academy, biomedical research, and health care, and that is deeply related to pervasive questions of values and beliefs with which American society is collectively grappling. While this relationship has been true of bioethics since the field's emergence, it has become especially apparent in a worrisome way since the early 1990s, as the polarizing issues and divisive atmosphere of the so-called "culture wars" between "liberals" and "conservatives" occurring on the national scene have progressively penetrated U.S. bioethics. Increasingly, within bioethical circles, the terms "liberal" and "conservative" have become recriminatory labels, rather than nonpolemical descriptors of differences in political philosophy and perspective. They have taken on what Daniel Callahan describes as "the strongly ideological, often nasty emotive twist" of the societal culture wars, in ways that not only "call into question…the arguments on each side of a debate but also the moral character and shady, hidden agenda of the contending parties" (Callahan 2005: 428).

Arthur Caplan has associated the involvement of U.S. bioethics in the culture wars with the increased extent to which the field has become more influential as well as enmeshed in the polity of the public square. Caplan interprets and embraces the "ideological disputes in bioethics" as an indicator of bioethics' "success." "Bioethics has become a field. It has made a difference. It has matured into a position of power in American society," he has proclaimed. "No power exists in a political vacuum. Bioethics finds itself in a new world—the public arena, a stormy, unpredictable, and even dangerous place.[2] The key to navigating it is to admit these facts" (Caplan 2005: 12–13). In sharp contrast, Callahan contends that bioethics had a stronger influence on health and medical policy in the 1970s than it has had during the past decade (personal communication, July 31, 2006). Furthermore, he regards the kind of divisiveness that bioethics is currently displaying as an ominous threat to the field's integrity and survival. "[I]f bioethics is to retain its vitality and be taken seriously," he has forcibly stated, "it will have to find a way to extricate itself from the culture wars":

Bioethics harms itself if it turns into a moral crusade, either for the values of the left or the right. A healthy bioethics will be one where conservatives and liberals understand that they have a common cause, one best pursued in lively dialogue rather than as opposing armies.... A field that aspires to serious ethical thinking and analysis, that aims to speak to everyone, not just those of a certain ideological stripe, and that wants to be taken seriously even by those who disagree with many of those within it cannot long flourish under the present emerging conditions. (Callahan 2005: 430–431)

Callahan is joined in this view by Jonathan Moreno, who has expressed the opinion that "[w]hether and how we can keep talking to each other during the next years may define the outcome of what may justly be characterized as a crisis of identity and perhaps the survival of bioethics as we know it" (Moreno 2005: 15).

We share Callahan's and Moreno's concern about the infiltration of the animus of the American culture wars into bioethics, and what it portends for the field. We have gone on record to say that it is "our strong conviction" that U.S. bioethics will be "seriously jeopardized" unless it is pervaded by the sort of colloquy that journalist-religionist Peter Steinfels has called for—"an honest discussion of the moral stances dividing Americans [with] each side (and there may be more than two) addressing the contending arguments at their best and not at their worst" (Fox and Swazey 2005: 369–371; Steinfels 2004).

Caplan implies that it is only when bioethics had "matured" and acquired "power" that it was catapulted into the "public arena" (Caplan 2005: 12–13). Callahan views the involvement of bioethics in "larger cultural and political struggles going on in American society" as a more gradual, cumulative process—one that developed "over a couple of decades" as bioethics "moved outside an academic context into the world of public and health policy," was "increasingly called upon by the media," and as the "latent activism" that the first generation of bioethicists brought with them into the field from the civil rights and antiwar activities in which many of them had engaged during the 1960s and 1970s in their college, graduate school, and/or professional school years, was rekindled (Callahan 2005: 414: 426). It is our view, however, as we have stated in previous chapters, that from the beginning of its institutionalization a "defining feature of American bioethics—one that distinguish[ed] it from more strictly academic, scholarly fields—[was] its public status" (Messikomer, Fox, and Swazey 2001: 486). More than 20 years ago, Renée Fox wrote an unpublished paper entitled "American Bioethics Goes to Washington (with Apologies to Mr. Smith)," in which she observed that "the phenomena and problems…referred to as 'bioethics' [have been] public issues in American society…in the media and the polity, and in the nexus between them" since early in the field's inception. "The entrance of bioethical issues into the polity began in the late 1960s, and has developed at an exponential rate ever since":

> Political display of these questions, deliberations upon them, and measures to resolve them have taken multiple forms. Cases that involve bioethical issues fill our courts. They have appeared and been heard on every level of the judicial system, from the lower courts to the United States Supreme Court…. The legislative bodies of our society—city, state and national—are also deeply and extensively involved in dealing with such matters. State legislatures, and to a greater degree the United States Congress, have held hearings, inquiries, and commissioned studies, and published reports on many bioethical topics and questions. Numerous of these have been highly publicized, and some of them have resulted in the drafting, proposing, and/or passage of legislation…. [T]wo, consecutive [federal] commissions [have been created] to study and report on a number of bioethical issues, and to offer guidelines and recommendations for decision-making and public policy that bear upon them [the National Commission, 1974–1978, and the President's Commission, 1978–1983]…. As the appointment of a presidential commission in this area indicates, along with the courts and the legislatures, the executive branch of the government actively participates in bioethical issues.

And ever since the 1960s, the questions with which American bioethics has dealt have been "continually, extensively, and prominently covered by the media" (R. C. Fox 1983).

In an addendum to that same paper, Fox expressed concern over the fact that by and large, bioethicists were not being reflective about the implications and some of the possible pitfalls of the projection of bioethics into the public arena in these ways, and about their own involvements and responsibilities in the process. Partly as a consequence, she stated, bioethicists might be contributing "passively, if not actively [to the] politicization" of the field in certain respects. She pointed especially to the fact that "some of the most powerful and persistent bioethical themes and concerns" that were being "played out…in the polity" were "structured around questions of life and death, identity and meaning, and ultimate values and beliefs that [were] essentially religious. Their presence in the polity posed the dilemma-ridden question of whether it was legitimate, or even wise for government…to take authoritative positions and binding decisions on such matters on behalf of the whole society. For, American society is not only founded on the precept of governance under law, but also on the sacredly secular principles of the separation of church and state, and the freedom and pluralism of belief."

Fox cited two troubling examples of how, in the early 1980s, President Ronald Reagan and his administration actively intervened in religiously toned, life-and-death, bioethically important matters. In response to a memorandum written by Reagan, the Department of Health and Human Services (DHHS) issued a so-called "Baby Doe" rule concerning the care and treatment of newborns in hospitals receiving federal funds.[3] As a condition for federal funding, the rule required hospitals to place large notices in every delivery, maternity, and pediatric ward, and intensive-care nursery stating that "discriminatory failure to feed and care for handicapped infants in this facility is prohibited by federal law." The notices provided a 24-hour-a-day, toll-free "handicapped infant hotline"—a Washington, D.C. number—which "any person having knowledge that a handicapped infant [was] being denied food or customary medical care" was urged to use; and the DHHS created what it termed a "Special Assignment Baby Doe Squad" to act on these calls.

Reagan also used his office to help families find donor organs and the means to pay for them. This entailed an "unusual series of federal interventions on behalf of families, including pressurizing private health insurers, state Medicaid directors, and the DHHS to pay for organ transplants; making arrangements with the Air Force to ferry organs and patients;...assisting in local fundraising efforts to pay for the operation" (Iglehart 1983: 126); and assigning an aide from the White House Office of Public Liaison to continually intercede in this sphere. Bioethicists made "virtually no comment" about any of these actions emanating from the executive branch of the federal government, Fox pointed out at the time, or about the danger of "the politicization of bioethics more generally."

Our reason for reviewing these observations made over two decades ago about the relationship between American bioethics and bioethicists, religiously resonant questions, the polity, politicization, and the media is that they are key components in the culture wars that began to flare up in U.S. bioethics in the 1990s, became progressively more pronounced in the field at the time of the presidential election of 2004, and have continued in its aftermath. We agree with Jonathan Moreno's contention that "the ideological struggle" that currently besets bioethics "has been latent in the field from the very beginning," and that among the issues around which largely quiescent tensions existed were questions that pertained to "the origins of human life," and to "reshaping the human" (Moreno 2005).

Callahan identifies "the matter of religion" as another long-standing "quiet issue" in U.S. bioethics. "Earlier, as President of the Hastings Center," he has recalled, "I had considerable trouble persuading my philosophical colleagues that theologians and religious leaders should be represented in our meeting and research projects." However, he recollects, before the 1990s, the indwelling strains in the field regarding the compatibility of religion and religious belief with "acceptable rational [philosophical] analysis" and liberal thought were "muttered about here and there but rarely surface[ed] as anything more than inside gossip" (Callahan 2005: 427). For example, he has recounted, "theologian Paul Ramsey [who] was part of our starting group...[was] understood to be conservative. But this was just of interest. It was not important in the discussion. We argued with each other, we disagreed, and we had a very interesting time" (Center for American Progress 2006: panel 1).

A third set of questions cited by Callahan that bioethicists discussed in a non-adversarial way during the early, preculture wars period of American bioethics concerned "what ought to be [bioethics'] general stance toward medical progress and technological innovation? Enthusiastic support? Neutrality? Skepticism?" (Callahan 2005: 429). He describes the 1960s as a time when bioethicists, along with many scientists, "felt free to speak out about some of the dangers of science, and some of the horrible possibilities of the biological revolution." He associates the atmosphere surrounding these issues "in the early days of bioethics" with the fact that this was the era of the United States' involvement in the war in Vietnam, when "there was a sense that technology was part of the problem" of that war, and "the shadow of nuclear weapons [was] still hanging over everything." And he contrasts this ambience with what he portrays as the "shift away from a wariness of technology in bioethics to an embrace [of it]," which "by the late 1990s" had reached a point where "if one raised too many questions" about it one was in danger of "being called a Luddite," or even "being labeled a right-wing religious nut...standing in the way of progress" (Center for American Progress 2006: panel 1).

In Moreno's view, the potentialities for overt "ideological struggle" in the field erupted with the ending of what he calls "the Great Bioethics Compromise" that had previously prevailed within it—a compromise that consisted of an "implicit agreement" based on a "consensus philosophy" that "allowed deep divisions about certain issues...to be courteously ignored" (Moreno 2005: 14). This breach occurred concomitantly with the outbreak of culture wars inside of bioethics, and "the incorporation of [U.S.] bioethics into the national culture wars" (Callahan 2005: 427). In our examination of the internal and external manifestations of American bioethics' enmeshment in the culture wars—their foci and consequences—we will consider an array of factors that have accompanied the erosion of what Albert Jonsen has rather idyllically portrayed as the relatively "irenic" intellectual atmosphere that previously characterized the field (Jonsen 1996: 4). We see some common elements in the pacifically silent, muted, or tangential ways that bioethicists previously dealt with potentially charged ideological and political issues that arose in their midst or in the public arenas on which their field abutted, and in the vocal discord about such issues in which they have escalatingly engaged since the 1990s. By and large, in both instances, American bioethicists have been disinclined to recognize the ideological nature of some of the convictions that underlie and sustain how they view and intellectually analyze ethical questions. And although they have been active participants in consultant, advisory, and policy-formation roles in a variety of political and quasi-political spheres in which bioethical issues are dealt with publicly in the United States, they have not been disposed to train their professional powers of reflection onto the process into which they have been continually drawn, and its implications for the integrity and comity of the field that they represent.

A noteworthy exception to these patterns is present in the flow of some of the oral and published admonitions that Daniel Callahan has addressed to his fellow bioethicists over the course of the past decade. In a talk that he gave on the occasion of his retirement as president of the Hastings Center in 1996 (which was subsequently published in *The Hastings Center Report*), he said:

> [W]hile it would be naïve to expect that bioethics could or should be ethically neutral, it should aim to respect the different positions in the debates that break out.... [O]f late there has been an increasing embrace of strong advocacy as a proper role for those in bioethics. To be sure, one's moral convictions should be pursued and advocated.... But this needs to be done in a way that takes the enterprise of bioethics seriously: fairly and carefully stating opposing positions...and...be[ing] acutely aware of one's own ideological bias, lying like a snake in the grass below one's arguments and supposedly rational convictions. (Callahan 1996: 4)

"[S]tep on that snake sometimes," he exhorted. He also expressed foreboding about the fact that "with the trappings of the culture around them," U.S. bioethics and its practitioners might be in the process of becoming "accommodating handmaiden[s]," serving mainly to add "the imprimatur of ethical expertise" to the research that "somebody or other wants to do." For, he warned, "[i]n this country those who would legitimate morally controverted scientific research long ago learned how to put together commissions and panels to include sympathetic and progress-affirming ethicists" (Callahan 1996: 3, 4).[4]

In two subsequent articles (published in 2003 and 2005), Callahan observed that "in recent years," bioethics had "taken on a liberal cast." The "reigning values espoused in the field [have become] those of liberal individualism," he stated. In this constellation, "autonomy"—coupled with "a strong antipathy to comprehensive notions of the common good"—is "the reigning moral principle," he continued. It is "closely followed by justice." A high value is accorded to "biomedical progress with few constraints." The "convergence of the liberal value of maximizing individual choice in matters bioethical and of the libertarian commitment to the market" is detectable, he stated. Although, Callahan cautioned, for bioethics to have a "liberal cast" was "not, in and of itself, sufficient to equate it with the culture wars," what he deemed "the almost complete triumph of liberal individualism" had, in his view, also "led to a systematic marginalization of religious and conservative perspectives, often treated with disdain and hostility" (Callahan 2003a: 498; Callahan 2005: 427–428). "I call this [liberal individualism] an ideology rather than a moral theory," he explained, "because it is a set of essentially political and social values brought into bioethics not as formal theory but as a vital background constellation of values.... [I]t is clearly present and pervasive as a litmus test of the acceptability of certain ideas and ways of framing issues" (Callahan 2003a: 498).

In 2006, Callahan returned to the theme of how insidiously ideological factors, that fall outside the awareness and self-knowledge of bioethicists, might be interwoven in their reason-based thought, irrespective of whether they considered themselves to be liberals or conservatives:

Below the surface of debates on, say, utilitarianism versus deontology, lie broader but more inchoate ways of looking at the world and society, influential in the other debates. Arguments about the niceties of the familiar moral theories, conducted in the needlework style of careful, wholly "rational" analysis, serve to mask the lower ideological forces at work, which are usually a jumbled mixture of reason and emotion.... The main problem with ideology, usually well below the surface, is that it invites self-deception: we can have trouble understanding our own deepest motivations, whether in judging our own commitments and predilections or appraising those of others. My problem with both true blue liberals and hard core conservatives [in bioethics] is that they seem to know their own convictions far better than they know themselves. (Callahan 2006: 3)

For Callahan, the issues surrounding the relationship between "bioethics and ideology" were now of sufficient import and gravity, as well as interest, to "propose that, for those interested in ethical theory, a new category be added to the agenda, to be called "ideological theory," and that along with "social science inquiry," it should become "the fare of serious self-analysis among those in bioethics" (Callahan 2006).[5]

Characteristics and Foci of the "Cultural Divide" in U.S. Bioethics

It is unclear at what precise juncture it "became common for bioethicists to be identified as liberals or conservatives by each other" (Callahan 2005: 428), for those terms to be used in pugnacious, accusatory ways, or which group sparked the belligerence. A number of liberally inclined bioethicists, such as philosopher Ruth Faden, associate what they call this "politicization" of bioethics with "the maturing and the expanding of the American conservative movement," and the "rise of interest among American conservatives" in the kinds of "social questions [and] issues" with which bioethics deals (Center for American Progress 2006: panel 1). Irrespective of who initiated them, the animosity-accompanied divisions that now rend the field rapidly became reciprocal.[6]

The entire gamut of issues around which the culture wars on the national scene have ignited has not been transposed into the arena of bioethics. For example, those surrounding feminism, homosexuality, gay rights and nontraditional marriages, evolution and "intelligent design," political litmus tests for appointments to federal advisory committees, and environmental issues such as climate change have fallen outside the orbit of the "conservative" vs. "liberal" confrontations that have been occurring between bioethicists. As might be expected, culture wars-infused bioethical disputes have focused on biomedical and biotechnological modalities. The most salient and heated controversies have been those that concern the use of human embryos in research, particularly stem cell research that involves destruction of embryos; therapeutic and reproductive cloning; in vitro fertilization and other assisted reproduction technologies; biomedical means intended to enhance appearance, or physical or mental capacities—especially genetic enhancement; and life-sustaining and life-extending technologies. The degree to which the most acute conflicts between so-called "liberal" and "conservative" bioethicists are concentrated around such a narrow range of biomedical instrumentalities, all of which are associated with the beginning or the end of human life, and with fundamental questions about human identity, is striking.

Cross-cutting these conflicts are deep differences in perspective on the individual and collective good that can come from advances in biomedical knowledge and technology, on the unanticipated and unintended harm and suffering that their deployment can also bring in their wake, and on the question of whether, for pragmatic and moral reasons, committed belief in biomedical progress ought to be accompanied and tempered by vigilance and the setting of limits. Lawyer-bioethicist R. Alto Charo considers what she calls this "cultural divide" that exists "between those who celebrate the transformative power of science and those who fear it," to be "profound." She regards it as "a divide that reflects competing fears, with one group [conservatives] most fearful of the social change wrought by technology and the other [liberals] most fearful of the oppressive overreaching of a government bent on controlling those changes." It opens onto a debate that "has been brewing for years…in the bioethics world," she writes, which has now been more explicitly joined: "a debate over political philosophy and the role of the government in morals regulation" that, in Charo's view, is as much or more about "the ethics of governance" as "about the ethics of biology or medicine" (Charo 2004: 311–312).

It is not just sharply differing attitudes toward the implications of certain biomedical developments, scientific and technological progress more generally, and what the place of government should (or should not) be in regulating medical science and technology that are focal to the cultural split in U.S. bioethics. Even more sensitively problematic are the existential questions associated with the biomedical developments that preoccupy American bioethicists, and the fact that these questions are persistently present in the legislatures, courthouses, and executive offices of the country's state and national governments: "What is life? What is death? When does a life begin? When does it end? What is a person…. How vigorously should we intervene in the human condition to repair and improve ourselves? And when should we cease and desist?" (R. C. Fox 2000: 422).

A dramatically revealing manifestation of how deeply and seriously ideologized and politicized the cultural divide in the United States has become over these life and death questions was the case of Terri Schiavo, which was played out on political, legislative, legal, religious, and bioethical fronts over several years in the 1990s.[7] When her case began to receive virtually unprecedented, nonstop electronic and print media coverage of the events during the two weeks preceding her death on March 31, 2005, she had been in a persistent vegetative state for 15 years, receiving artificial feeding and hydration and care at a hospice in Florida, with no written advance directives stating how she would want to be treated in such circumstances. Her husband and legal guardian, Michael Schiavo, and her parents, Mr. and Mrs. Robert Schindler, had been locked in a moral and legal battle with each other since 1989 over removal of the feeding tube: her husband strongly believed his wife would not have chosen to be kept alive; her parents held, with equal certitude, that Terri would not want the tube removed if she could make her wishes known, and also refused to accept the neurological determination of persistent vegetative coma with no hope of recovery.

A series of court rulings between 2001 and 2003,[8] and a bill passed by the Florida legislature's lower house known as "Terri's Law," which authorized Florida Governor Jeb Bush to order her physicians to provide artificial feeding and hydration had, in a revolving-door fashion, variously upheld the feeding tube's removal or ordered its reinsertion. The denoument of the back-and-forth decisions about whether Terri Schiavo should or should not be maintained by artificial feeding began on March 16, when a Florida appellate court refused to stay its discontinuance, and set March 18 as the date for the feeding tube's removal. That decision triggered further court appeals by the Schindlers and a series of political efforts by the U.S. Congress and Governor Bush to once again block removal of the feeding tube,[9] and affirmations by President Bush and the Vatican that they were unswervingly committed to what Pope John Paul II had termed "the culture of life."[10] These legal and political maneuverings and religious affirmations took place in the glare of intensive, nationwide media coverage, which included innumerable live interviews with Terri Schiavo's husband and parents, other family members, and advocates for both sides of the increasingly bitter dispute, and televised coverage of public protests and vigils by religiously based "right to life groups," some of which were held in front of the hospice.

Terri Schiavo died on March 31, 2005, 13 days after her feeding tube was removed as ordered by an appellate court judge in Florida. Beyond the at-once florid and tragic way that the decision making about whether her life should continue to be sustained by artificial means illuminated the depth of the culture wars, it starkly framed another, deeper question for us. That question, we wrote soon after her death, is "how, in a secular but nonetheless religiously resonant society under law rather than under men like the United States, such ultimate questions of life and death that are intrinsically religious can be resolved in the name of all its citizens—or even whether this is possible" (Fox and Swazey 2005: 370).

We have long maintained and frequently commented on the fact that such meta-questions concerning human personhood, mortality, and finitude, which are "as religious and metaphysical as they are medical and moral" (R. C. Fox 2000: 422), are integrally related to what are defined and delineated as ethical questions in American bioethics. As such, they constitute potential points of tension within the predominantly rational secular outlook and mode of thought of the field. By and large, even bioethicists trained in theology or religious studies have felt compelled to comply with the strong intellectual and normative pressure exerted by the field to "ethicize" religious questions by addressing them in a secular philosophical vocabulary, particularly in the realm of public policy (Messikomer, Fox, and Swazey 2001: 490).[11] And with awareness of the American constitutional principle of the separation of church and state, and the religious diversity and pluralism of U.S. society that are constraining factors in how, and to what extent religious identity, symbols, and beliefs are expected and permitted to be expressed or displayed in the public square, American bioethicists have been "characteristically circumspect about the place [they] have accorded to religion in [their] public policy activities and deliberations." They have exhibited "a complex mix of prudence and reluctance about making religion too central, explicit, or conspicuous in this domain" (Messikomer, Fox, and Swazey 2001: 498). However, these managed strains have been exacerbated by the contentious atmosphere that has flared up in the wake of what numerous so-called "mainstream" bioethicists[12] regard as "a new conservative movement in bioethics." That movement, mainstream protagonists charge, is attacking "the assumedly 'liberal' tradition" of the field, and is aligned (if not allied) with "the most conservative wing of the Republican party in American politics" (Macklin 2006: 34), the activism of the Christian right on the American political scene, and their "open[ness] to an increased permeation of religious values" into government, political life, and public policy (Charo 2004: 311).

Bioethics and Human Dignity. The liberal/conservative divisions in bioethics have also involved strongly felt differences in the use of particular concepts, terms, and modes of reasoning, and in styles of rhetoric. The concept of "human dignity" is a flashpoint in this regard. It occupies a place of central importance in the thinking and writing about bioethical issues by persons who are conservatively oriented, for whom it is "ontological": intrinsic to "what it means to have a human life and to be a human person...regardless of size, age, wealth, stage of development, cognitive powers, or level of dependence on others" (Cohen 2006a: 47). It is a concept that is frequently invoked by more conservatively inclined bioethicists in connection with their convictions about the biological and moral status of human embryos, and their disquietude about how certain developments in genetics or reproductive technology—most notably human cloning (for biomedical research, as well as for reproduction)—may be violating the "dignity" of prenatal human life. It also appears in their discussions of end-of-life issues, in contexts where they are contending that the foregoing or withdrawing of life-sustaining treatment, or engaging in physician-assisted suicide, profanely abrogates doing everything possible to save a life, and ensure a dignified "natural" death.

As we mentioned in chapter 9 ("Bioethics in France"), the most vociferous critic of the way that appeals to human dignity are made by certain bioethicists, particularly those of conservative suasion, has been Ruth Macklin, who has vehemently declared herself to be "a liberal, humanitarian bioethicist" (Macklin 2006: 42). "Dignity is a useless concept in medical ethics and can be eliminated without any loss of content," she wrote in a blistering editorial published in the *British Medical Journal* (Macklin 2003: 1420). She based this statement primarily on the grounds that, to her, it is used in an unanalytic, unreasoned, unspecified way, particularly when it is deployed by conservative bioethicists such as Leon Kass, the former chair of the President's Council on Bioethics:

The US President's Council on Bioethics appointed by President George W. Bush issued its first report in July 2002. Its title, *Human Cloning and Human Dignity*, illustrates the prominent place the concept of dignity occupies in the committee's discussions. In one of many references the report says that a begotten child comes into the world just as its parents once did, and is therefore their equal in dignity and humanity. The report contains no analysis of dignity, or how it relates to ethical principles such as respect for persons. In the absence of criteria that can enable us to know just when dignity is violated, the concept remains hopelessly vague. Although there are many persuasive arguments against human reproductive cloning, to invoke the concept of dignity without identifying its meaning is to use a mere slogan.... The president's council is equally concerned about existing modes of assisted reproduction. Draft documents specify scientific experiments that the committee would like the US Congress to prohibit in a law to be called the "Dignity of Human Procreation Act." One can readily identify procreative acts between two human beings that are abusive or degrading. But it is a mystery how modes of in vitro fertilization can have or lack dignity. (Macklin 2003)

In another publication, Macklin links "Kass's appeals to...what is 'dignified'" to the way in which his references to "what is 'natural,'" and "what is distinctively 'human'" pervade his writings without any apparent need to analyze such terms or to justify their use." This is "a style of writing," she says, "alien to that found in mainstream bioethics" (Macklin 2006: 39). Here she ties the invocation of "dignity" to her disapproval of what she depicts as some of the characteristics of the writings of conservatives more generally—namely, "the use of metaphor and other poetic language...designed to appeal to readers' emotions or intuitions...as substitutes for empirical evidence and reasoned arguments; patently offensive analogies; [and] deliberately misleading terminology" (Macklin 2006: 38). Some of the language that she finds most objectionable includes phrases like Kass's allusions to "'the wisdom of repugnance,'" which she characterizes as "the emotion of revulsion (his own) as sufficient grounds for rejecting any public policy short of total prohibition" (Macklin 2006: 38); the "poetic" and "mystical" nature" of Yural Levin's statement of the mission of conservative bioethics: "to prevent our transformation into a culture without awe filled with people without souls" (Y. Levin 2003: 65);[13] and the way that "the new conservatives in bioethics" apply the term "artificial" to "all sorts of interventions," such as "artificial reproduction, artificial life extension, artificial intelligence and artificial life," in a manner that implies that "artificial" is bad, and "natural" is good (Macklin 2006: 35). Although Macklin considers "terminology, including metaphors," used by religious scholars that come from "the moral beliefs [of] a religious tradition" and are "accepted by their coreligionists" to be "justified," she takes exception to the use of language with religious connotations, such as Levin's phraseology, or the invocation of "natural" versus "artificial" distinctions, when they are not explicitly associated with "an intended literal truth of theology" (Macklin 2006: 38).

Macklin's critique of conservative bioethicists' appeal to human dignity[14] is only one emanation of her overall opposition to their "style of writing" and "methodology." Her greatest overall objection is that in her view, their approach originates in their "rejection of clear and explicit rational arguments." For an ardent analytic philosopher like Macklin, fervently committed to rational thought and rhetoric, who declares herself to be a dedicatedly liberal bioethicist, this is unacceptable. It does not mean, she contends, that she denigrates the role of feeling in moral life, or dichotomizes emotions and reason. Quite to the contrary, she insists, "There is no inconsistency in holding deep moral sentiments and formulating rational arguments in their defense. Indeed [she avers], rational arguments can often be mounted in a 'passionate' defense of a position" (Macklin 2006: 39). But for Macklin, rationality is the sine qua non and guarantor of objective, ideology-free bioethical analysis. In this respect she differs from Daniel Callahan—whose "breadth of writings in the field" she admiringly characterizes as making it impossible to "shoehorn him into a neat [liberal or conservative] category" (Macklin 2006: 35). It "makes no sense" to Callahan to draw too "sharp a distinction between reason and emotion." He regards them as forming "a continuum, rather than discrete categories." In his view, the "problem is to know how to use reason to evaluate emotion and no less to know how to pay attention to our emotions when they challenge our reasoning" (Callahan 2001: 6). He considers rationality to be among the important "intellectual skills" that "will enable [the] leading questions [in bioethics] to be approached in the richest and deepest way possible," and believes that "[r]eason can, on occasion, cut through to some truths not reducible to the passions." Nonetheless, he warns that it is not "easy for any of us to see how our tacit political and social ideologies, lurking just below the surface [might be] pulling the strings of our 'rational' thought," and that "[b]eing right and being rational are not necessarily synonymous" (Callahan 2003a: 501).

Like Macklin, R. Alta Charo, who defines herself as a liberal bioethicist, deplores the way in which the notion of human dignity has been woven into the "worldview" of what she terms "neoconservative" bioethicists. She alleges that they have made human dignity dependent on "eschewing technology or adhering to a set of arbitrary rules...[and] moral absolutes." She is more sanguine than Macklin about the potentialities of the "adoption" of a "richer understanding" of the concept of human dignity by "a progressive bioethics" that would include within it "the presence of the necessities of life ensured to all, including access to food and education and healthcare as an entitlement and not as a privilege" (Charo 2004: 311; Charo at Center for American Progress 2005). Macklin is no less ardent in her commitment to these values. "As a liberal, humanitarian bioethicist," she has written, "I acknowledge that my chief concerns lie in striving for greater social justice, within and among societies, and reducing disparities in health, wealth, and other resources among populations in the world" (Macklin 2006: 42). However, she is disinclined to believe that an enlarged and enriched notion of human dignity is an appropriate way to conceptually formulate and express these aspirations.

Bioethics and the Pharmaceutical Industry. Still another dimension of the divisions that now exist between what are labeled "conservative vs. liberal" stances within U.S. bioethics involves the relationship of the field, its individual members, and the organizations of which they are a part to the pharmaceutical industry. Some of the issues that are at stake in this polemicized arena include questions of human progress and betterment, and social justice and equity, as well as those that pertain to a market-driven health care system, various motivations and behaviors of the pharmaceutical industry, and the ethical propriety of bioethicists collaborating with drug firms. The content and tone of the controversy that swirls around these matters is epitomized by the contentious debate between Arthur Caplan and Carl Elliott:

Elliott: Those of us who worry about medical enhancement are usually less worried about the technologies themselves than about the larger social effects of embracing them too enthusiastically.... Let's look at three of the most commercially successful medical enhancements of recent years: selective serotonin reuptake inhibitors, hormone replacement therapy, and the diet drug fenfluramine-phentermine (Fen-Phen). What can we learn from these interventions?

First, the manufacturers of enhancement technologies will usually exploit the blurry line between enhancement and treatment to sell drugs.... Second, an alarming number of supposedly risk-free enhancements have lately been associated with unanticipated side-effects, some of them deadly.... Third, the most successful enhancement technologies have been backed by tremendously influential public relations campaigns....

The pharmaceutical industry can buy politicians to pass industry-friendly legislation; it can buy academic scientists to publish favorable journal articles; it can buy professional societies and patient support groups to spread the word on the newly medicalized disorders that its interventions are developed to treat. It can even buy bioethicists to dispense with any moral concerns....

Caplan: Elliott...gravely warns us that you and I do not really decide a direction when it comes to matters of enhancement. It is—listen carefully for the Darth Vader-esque hissing—drug companies!

The rest of Elliott's viewpoint amounts to what is his increasingly familiar harangue against the pharmaceutical industry. The drug companies sucker us into buying enhancement by getting us hooked on pseudotherapies. The drug companies rob us of our will to fend off their siren-like messages of better living through chemistry. And the drug companies get us feeling so bad about ourselves that we empty our wallets on their latest overpriced geegaws....

When Elliott eagerly dons his hair shirt to bemoan Big Pharma he finds so much sin to revel in that he forgets a reason, any reason, why enhancement is, in itself, immoral.... Okay, so let's take Big Pharma out of the picture. If we left the encouragement of enhancement to the government, the military, schools, foundations, doctors, or parents, would this be more morally acceptable?

Elliott: Caplan does not defend medical enhancement so much as attack its critics. Or rather, he attacks a small group of conservative critics who want to preserve "human nature."... My worry is that we will ignore important human needs at the expense of frivolous human desires; that dominant social norms will crowd out those of the minority; the self-improvement agenda will be set not by individuals, but by powerful corporate interests, and that in the pursuit of betterment, we will actually make ourselves worse off.

We live in a country where 46 million uninsured people cannot get basic medical care, while the rest of us spend a billion dollars a year on baldness remedies. It is not just the inequity here that is so impressive. It is the fact that we have gotten so accustomed to the inequity that we do not see it as obscene. (Caplan and Elliott 2004)

Classifying Liberals and Conservatives. This exchange between Caplan and Elliott illustrates another, rather curious characteristic of the way that the culture wars are being played out in the milieu of bioethics. In spite of the intense, emotion-laden differences that exist between "liberal" and "conservative" perspectives in the field, it "may be difficult to determine which advocates [of which positions] are 'liberals' and which 'conservatives'" (Macklin 2006: 35). Caplan associates Elliott's outlook on medical enhancement with what he terms the "anti-meliorism" of conservative bioethicists who have "a static vision of human nature," and who "fear that in applying new biomedical knowledge to improve human beings, something essential about humanity will be lost" (Caplan and Elliott 2004). However, Elliott's outlook on the motivation and behavior of drug firms, access to health care, and economic and social injustice has more in common with left-of-center liberal convictions than with conservative thought. And even though in Elliott's view, Caplan is an ally of free-market conservatives who are defenders of the "medical industrial complex" that includes drug firms, Caplan nevertheless shares the concerns of liberals about the gaping disparities in wealth, health, and health care that exist between advantaged and disadvantaged people in American society.

Further complicating the discernment of who and what are "liberal" or "conservative" in bioethics is an emerging pattern in the field that Callahan has identified, and that he considers "unfortunate": what he has described as the coming together of "the liberal individualism on the left which has been very powerful in bioethics...and market conservatism on the right." These "two streams," he has commented, "are thought to be different because they have a different set of actors." But they "both love choice." And "they end up in much the same place, which is, let's leave it up to individual choice in the market" (Center for American Progress 2006: panel 1).

For Macklin, Callahan personifies some of the ambiguities of what the categories of "liberal" and "conservative" mean in bioethical contexts. "Back in 1973, when Daniel Callahan began his three-decade critique of runaway science and technology, arguing for the need for limits in the use of technology," she writes, "he did not identify himself as a 'conservative' or label the position he criticized as 'liberal' ":

Today, the conservative bioethicists could consider Callahan one of them, as he has opposed the use of embryos in research, is critical of developing life-extending technologies, and has questioned the reigning paradigm of autonomy in bioethics. Yet Callahan's views on social justice in health care and the breadth of his writings in the field make it impossible to shoehorn him into a neat category.... Indeed, liberals could also count Callahan as one of their own since he is in favor of universal health care, has been pro-choice on abortion since before *Roe vs. Wade*, and has been an outspoken critic of the pharmaceutical industry. (Macklin 2006: 35)

"I would like to declare myself an independent," Callahan has affirmed, "and I would hope that those of us in the field will always be somewhat unpredictable" (Center for American Progress 2006: panel 1).

However, there is one prominent figure in bioethics—physician-biochemist-humanist Leon R. Kass—who has not only been regarded by numerous self-defined "mainstream" bioethicists of "liberal" suasion as someone "whose views could uncontroversially be characterized as conservative," but also as "the chief public spokesperson for conservative bioethicists in the United States" (Macklin 2006: 35). This attribution, along with the ad hominem hostility that has been directed toward Kass by liberal critics, emanates as much from his appointment and role as chair of the President's Council on Bioethics from 2002 through 2005, as it does from his reputedly conservative values and opinions, the larger framework of reflection in which he has embedded them, and the language he has used to express them.

President Bush, His Council on Bioethics, and Leon Kass

On August 9, 2001, speaking from his ranch in Crawford, Texas, George W. Bush delivered his first nationally televised speech as President of the United States (White House 2001). Those who heard or read about his statement might well have thought that his topic was an unusual one for such an occasion: He used his presidential forum to announce and explain his decision regarding federal funding for research with human embryonic stem cells. Until the terrorist attacks on

September 11, 2001, however, stem cells had been the defining issue of his presidency, and an important "hot-button" issue in the 2000 campaign leading to his election. Since winning the election, Mr. Bush had been under intense pressure from various constituencies to decide whether he would allow federal funding for research with stem cells derived from human embryos. He was on the horns of a political dilemma, which was the subject of widespread media attention. If he refused to provide federal funding, he would face strong opposition from the scientific community, from patient organizations for conditions that might be treated by stem-cell transplants, and from many members of Congress. On the other hand, if he decided to permit federal funding, he would anger powerful religious constituencies, including the Roman Catholic Church and a variety of fundamentalistically and evangelically oriented Protestant religious groups, and the socially conservative political right. During his campaign, Bush had repeatedly pledged to oppose funding for research with stem cells that are obtained by "destroying living human embryos." In addition to political considerations, the president had voiced his personal, religiously grounded conviction that abortion is morally wrong.

Bush's decision about federal funding sought what he hoped would be a principled middle ground that would partially satisfy both the proponents and opponents of embryonic stem cell research, and his own questions about the best course of action. "As I thought through the issue," the president said:

I kept returning to two fundamental questions: First, are these frozen embryos human life, and therefore, something precious to be protected? And second, if they're going to be destroyed anyway, shouldn't they be used for a greater good, for research that has the potential to save and improve other lives?... I have given this issue a great deal of thought, prayer, and reflection. And I have found widespread disagreement [among those I have talked with].

...Embryonic stem cell research offers both great promise and great peril. So I have decided we must proceed with great care.

As a result of private research, more than 60 genetically diverse stem cell lines already exist. They were created from embryos that have already been destroyed, and they have the ability to regenerate themselves indefinitely, creating ongoing opportunities for research. I have concluded that we should allow federal funds to be used for research on these existing stem cell lines, where the life and death decision has already been made.

In reaching his decision, the president said, he had consulted with many people, including scholars, religious leaders, researchers, members of Congress, his cabinet, and friends. Three prominent bioethicists with whom he spoke were Daniel Callahan, founder of the Hastings Center; LeRoy Walters, director of the Kennedy Institute for Ethics; and Leon Kass, the Addie Clark Harding Professor in The College and the Committee on Social Thought at the University of Chicago.

Mr. Bush concluded his televised address by announcing that "I will also name a President's Council to monitor stem cell research, to recommend appropriate guidelines and regulations, and to consider all of the medical and ethical ramifications of biomedical innovation. This council will consist of leading scientists, doctors, ethicists, lawyers, theologians and others, and will be chaired by Dr. Leon Kass, a leading biomedical ethicist from the University of Chicago." "This council," the president continued, "will keep us apprised of new developments and give our nation a forum to discuss and evaluate these important issues."

The president issued an Executive Order creating his Council on Bioethics on November 28, 2001, and the White House released the names of its 17 members—in addition to Kass—on January 16, 2002, the day before its first meeting (Bush 2001; White House 2002).[15] From the outset, the Council was viewed by many liberal bioethicists as being stacked with conservative and neoconservative members and staff, who were "hostile to stem cell research and other icons of biomedical progress" (Callahan 2005: 428), and whose intent was to endorse the conservative political views, pro-life moral convictions, and born-again Christian religious beliefs of George Bush and some of his staunchest supporters. Caplan scathingly referred to it as a "council of clones," and predicted that it would "do nothing to jostle any of the president's already espoused positions condemning stem cell research, cloning, and the creation of human embryos for research" (Hall 2002: 322). And Kass was derisively characterized by some as the White House's "official standard-bearer for the neoconservative agenda in bioethics" (L. Vogel 2006: 43). In contradiction to these charges, Kass holds that "there were no litmus tests for appointment. As many as 8 or 9 of the original 18 members did not vote for President Bush.... More to the point, the President wanted the group to be able to argue out the important competing positions, and he produced a membership guaranteed to this. To facilitate this process we were explicitly released from the obligation to seek consensus" (personal communication, Aug. 22, 2006).

In the political climate surrounding the Council, the fact that its membership included two theologians—William May and Gilbert Meilander—and that it made itself open to insights from religious traditions (albeit on what Kass describes as "the plane of public reason") may have contributed to its becoming a target of attack for some mainstream bioethicists who had especially strong feelings about the urgency of separating ethics from religion. According to Kass, however, "no one on the Council ever made a specifically religious argument," and "no more than one or two members from the religious right" were ever invited as witnesses or presenters (personal communication, Aug. 22, 2006).

The politically partisan and accusatory reaction to the composition and presumed orientation of the President's Council contrasted markedly with the climate that had surrounded three previous national bioethics commissions—the National Commission, the President's Commission, and the National Bioethics Advisory Commission (NBAC), created, respectively, in the 1970s, 1980s, and 1990s.[16] Although all those commissions were "chaired by liberals, staffed by liberals, [and had] overwhelmingly liberal...members," Daniel Callahan has observed, they "received hardly any criticism at all" for this fact (Callahan 2005: 428). Both inside and outside these prior commissions, it was assumed, without turbulence, that their creation was an inherently political act. As Eric Meslin, the former executive director of NBAC put it, "[T]he mere existence of...[such] a public advisory body is an exercise in political action." This is all the more true, he went on to say, because since the passage of the Federal Advisory Committee Act in 1972, such committees are required by law "to do their work in public, to meet in public,... to make the public aware of what they're doing, to give the public the opportunity to speak and really to engage in a process of public conversation.... Inside the tent of commissions [then], there is a public politicization that occurs by the mere fact that commissions exist and the public has access to them; and there are the *real-politik*, influential political activities that occur by those who stand to gain or lose by those activities" (Center for American Progress 2006: panel 1). Patricia King, who has served on numerous federal commissions concerned with bioethics, agrees with Meslin's portrayal of the sense in which such bodies are generically political.[17] She recalls that nevertheless, in contrast to the "divisive" environment in which the President's Council for Bioethics has had to function, the National Commission for the Protection of Human Subjects, for example, was very "consensus-focused," as well as "procedurally" and "process-focused" in a way that was neither enmeshed in, nor buffeted by, ideologically driven, factional politics (Center for American Progress 2006, luncheon presentation).

During Kass's term as chairman of the President's Council, the range of ethical issues that it discussed included cloning, assisted reproduction, reproductive genetics, in vitro fertilization, preimplantation genetic diagnosis, sex selection, inheritable genetic modification, life span extension, organ transplantation, treatment of the aged, and the long-term care of patients with dementia. The Council issued seven publications: five reports (on human cloning, on enhancement uses of biotechnology, on stem cell research, on regulating new reproductive biotechnologies, and on caregiving of the aged), a white paper on alternative sources of human stem cells, and an anthology of readings on "Being Human" (President's Council 2002, 2003a, 2003b, 2004a, 2004b, 2005a, 2005b).

The Council, Stem Cell Research, and Human Cloning

Independently of the Council's composition and of its stewardship by Leon Kass, the political climate in which it was convoked, and the subject matter of its initial work were highly conducive to its deliberations and recommendations being surrounded by intense controversy. To begin with, the Council's creation in 2001 flowed from the plethora of issues raised by the cloning of Dolly the sheep in 1997 (see chapter 4), and from Bush's publicly stated, religiously grounded opposition to human cloning and to the destruction of human embryos in the context of stem cell research. Thus, although the Executive Order establishing the Council did not include a specific list of topics to be addressed, the first two tasks it undertook, not surprisingly, were to examine the interrelated subjects of human cloning and why and how embryonic stem cell research should be monitored.

Stem cell research, primarily for so-called therapeutic cloning, but linked as well with the possibility that it might lead to human reproductive cloning, has aptly been characterized by British nurse-sociologists Stephen Wainwright and Clare Williams as "one of the most highly contested…of contemporary biomedical science," involving the manipulation of what they call "morally difficult materials" in "ethically sensitive" ways (Wainwright, Williams, and Michael, et al. 2007). Stem cell research emerged as a controversial, hotly debated issue in the Bush vs. Gore presidential campaign, and by the time of the bitterly contested 2000 election, it had become "a defining and central issue in American politics" (Cohen 2006b: 164), and arguably "bioethics issue number one" (Kass, personal communication, Oct. 6, 2005). "Not by choice—and certainly not mine," Kass stated at the last meeting of the Council that he chaired, " '[T]he council was born smack in the middle of 'embryoville,' and it has never been able to leave this highly political field' " (quoted in Vergano 2005: 2D). And he referred to "the embryo question" as among the "truly intractable" issues that, "like Solomon's baby…cannot be split down the middle" (Kass 2005: 248). Because stem cell research is a topic that raises questions about the biological, moral, and existential status of the human embryo, it opened onto issues associated with the continuing national abortion debate. In addition, as Kass has pointed out, it ignited arguments that centered on what he termed "the life principle"—"the principle that calls for protecting, preserving, and saving human life." As posed in this connection, he stated:

[I]t appears as an argument between two sorts of "vitalists" who differ only with respect to whose life matters most: the lives of sick children and adults facing risk of decay and premature death, or the lives of human embryos who must be directly destroyed in the process of harvesting their stem cells for research.… These are surely…*crucially*…important concerns.… But… I wish to suggest that concern for "life"…is not the only important good relevant to our deliberations. We are concerned also with human dignity, human freedom, and the vast array of human activities and institutions that keep human life human.… [T]he "life principle" cannot continue to be the sole consideration in public bioethical discourse. Some efforts to prolong life may come at the price of its degradation, the unintended consequences of success at life-saving interventions…while the battle against death itself—as if it were just one more disease—could undermine the belief that it matters less how long one lives than how well one lives. (Kass 2005: 248–249, author's emphasis)

The fact that Kass was known to have forcibly argued for a ban on human cloning prior to his appointment as head of the President's Council exacerbated the barrage of criticism emanating from liberally oriented mainstream bioethicists to which he and the Council were subject throughout his term as its chair. Kass's most prominent and evocative statements about why he thought human cloning should be banned had been made in two articles—"The Wisdom of Repugnance"

(1997), and "Preventing a Brave New World" (2001)—both of which had been published in *The New Republic*, and to which he had referred when he testified in favor of the Human Cloning Prohibition Act on June 20, 2001, at hearings on human cloning held by the U.S. House of Representatives Committee on Energy and Commerce. In these presentations of his ideas and convictions, Kass used the kinds of imagistic, metaphoric, emotive, and religiously suggestive language that liberal bioethicists most fervidly committed to "reasoned" arguments and analysis found objectionable, and equated with the rhetoric of conservatives and neoconservatives. What aroused their greatest discomfort and indignation was Kass's invocation of "the wisdom of repugnance" (a term that he coined): his contention that the "revulsion" that many or most people feel about human reproductive cloning is an intuitive, "emotional expression of deep wisdom, beyond reason's power fully to articulate it" (Kass 1997: 20). This "deep wisdom," he held, apprehends the intrinsic immorality of human cloning, of the gravely dehumanizing harm it could do to identity and individuality, and is attuned to the most profound, teleological meanings of human sexuality, of having children, and of the parent-child relationship.

Another source of liberal bioethicists' unease and disapproval about Kass's anti-human cloning stance was his association of the prospect of reproductive cloning with the specter of the "Brave New World" depicted in Aldous Huxley's dystopian novel, where the failure to exercise some control over the enthusiastically unrestrained pursuit of biomedical and biotechnological advance had resulted in a "humanly debased" individual and collective condition. An avowedly liberal bioethicist such as Arthur Caplan has characterized Kass as "[p]erhaps the most outspoken and influential critic of the utilitarian justification" for biomedical research, and the benefits to be gained from it. "Kass has long been concerned about the ways in which biotechnology undermines or shifts our understanding of the family, marriage, sexual relations, aging and parenting," Caplan has written. "Recent developments in cloning, stem cells, genetic testing, pharmacology, anti-aging research, and the neurosciences have only intensified his concerns." Caplan has firmly rejected what he refers to as the "moral worries" of Kass and other like-minded thinkers that biology, biomedicine, and biotechnology may be taking us toward the alteration of human nature, the commodification and objectification of human life, and "a loss of authenticity and meaning in human experience." "When the stakes are enormous—continued premature death, disability, chronic suffering," Caplan has asserted, "then much more is required of those who would challenge the wisdom of the aggressive pursuit of biomedical knowledge that is the only hope of solving these terrible problems" (Caplan 2004a).

"[A] funny thing happened to this [allegedly] 'stacked' council on its way to a supposedly foregone conclusion" regarding human cloning, *Science* magazine reported. "The intellectual arguments were spirited and profound and, in public at least, the stridency of Kass's written views did not influence his public stewardship of the conversation. He proved to be a nimble and fair-minded moderator, giving all points of view their due and egging on all participants to better articulate and defend their position" (Hall 2002: 323). "The chair of the Council on this (and other) issues did not see it as a primary goal of the Council to achieve unanimity," theologian and religious ethicist William F. May, a Council member, attested. "That goal would require either stacking the membership of the Council to guarantee unanimity or drafting a common denominator document, perhaps acceptable to diverse Council members, but so vacant and vapid as to be unhelpful. Instead, the chair hoped that the staff and Council might draft a report on cloning that all Council members could sign, because it stated as fairly and reflectively as possible the arguments on *both* sides of various issues (May 2005: 231, author's emphasis). Council members easily reached unanimous agreement about recommending a ban on cloning to produce children, but they were deeply divided in their opinions about cloning for biomedical research. After 18 months of deliberation they arrived at a compromise position: the recommendation that a four-year moratorium on federally funded cloning for biomedical research be established; and that there be a "federal review of current and projected practices of human embryo research, pre-implantation genetic diagnosis, genetic modification of human embryos and gametes, and related matters" (President's Council on Bioethics 2002: xxxvi; Mahowald 2005: 166–167). A majority of 10 members voted for the moratorium, while a minority of seven voted to permit such research, accompanied by firm regulations applicable to both federally and privately funded work. "A majority of council members [had] expressed support in principle for research cloning, and the moratorium option became the majority opinion only after two members [of this group] changed their publicly stated opinions" following the Council's June 2002 meeting (Hall 2002: 322). On July 11, 2002, the Council delivered its recommendations for a ban on reproductive cloning and a moratorium on cloning for biomedical research to President Bush in its report entitled *Human Cloning and Human Dignity*. Although Kass regarded this outcome as a "principled compromise" (Hall 2002: 324), several Council members who strongly supported research cloning were disturbed by the result and how it had been reached; and "[p]olitical camps on both sides of the issue immediately sought to capitalize on the…recommendations" through the media (Hall 2002: 322)—including liberal and conservative individuals and subgroups within bioethics.

The depiction of Kass as an even-handed chairman did not stem the accusatory criticism about his ideological partisanship that emanated from liberal bioethical circles. If anything, it escalated as the work of the Council proceeded under his direction. For example, when William May and cell biologist Elizabeth Blackburn were rotated off the Council as it began its second two-year term, prominent liberal bioethicists drafted a petition to President Bush condemning this act as a membership "purge." The petition implied that, with Kass's complicity, Blackburn and May had been replaced because of the positions they had taken on cloning for biomedical research. Blackburn had firmly supported research cloning, and opposed a moratorium on it; and May had voted to recommend cloning for medical research, but with strong arguments for its regulation and for the just distribution of its benefits (Blackburn 2005: 173–176; May 2005: 238–239). In a March 2004 article in the *Washington Post*, entitled "We Don't Play Politics with Science," Kass responded to the petition's insinuations. "Unfortunately," he commented, "these membership changes were met with unfounded and false charges of political 'stacking' of the council. Such charges are as bogus today as they were when the council was formed.[18] We shall continue to honor the diversities of our views, confident that the reports we write will contribute to public understanding and earn the respect of fair-minded readers" (Kass 2004: A27). Later that year, just before the November 2004 national presidential election, when Kass gave a plenary lecture at the 2004 annual meeting of the American Society for Bioethics and Humanities (ASBH), devoted to his thoughts on what it was like to be doing public bioethics "from the trenches" of the President's Council, he was rebuffed by some of the liberal bioethicists in the audience, who stood and turned their backs on him as he spoke.[19] In contrast, at another ASBH session, a speaker who attacked the Council's work received a standing ovation from roughly half the assemblage.

A Richer Public Bioethics

Complex biological and moral questions regarding human fertilization, reproduction, cloning, stem cell research, and the status of the embryo were central to three of the reports that the President's Council produced—*Human Cloning and Human Dignity*, *Monitoring Stem Cell Research*, and *Reproduction and Responsibility*. The reports also dealt with what has been termed "the biotechnological imperative," which figures as well in its report *Beyond Therapy: Biotechnology and the Pursuit of Happiness* (President's Council on Bioethics 2003b). The Council's treatment of these matters, which are foci of some of the deep differences between liberals and conservatives both inside and outside of bioethics, significantly contributed to the accusatory way in which the label of "conservative" was applied to Kass and the Council by liberal bioethicists. Equally important in their adverse reactions to the orientation of the Council, and perhaps more fundamental in certain respects, was the conception of what Kass called "a richer bioethics" that shaped its work, and that in his view distinguished the Council from previous bioethics commissions.

At the final meeting of the Council that Kass chaired, he invited its members to engage in a "taking stock" process, looking back at what they had done together over the course of four years, and ahead to what they might undertake in the future. As part of his own appraisal, he presented his overview of "a richer bioethics," which he defined as one of the major "purposes" that had "guided" the Council:

The first purpose has been to pursue what we've been calling a richer bioethics. That is to say, to consider not just the technologies or the way in which they have given rise to questions familiar to either clinical medical ethics or to general sorts of common concerns of a liberal democratic society, but also to see how these things which impinge on our humanity…touch our personal aspirations, our human longings, our duties,…the way we actually live life every day in deep and serious ways. We've tried to think about what it means to suffer, what it means to welcome a child into the world, what it means to perform with excellence, what it means to respect life, what it means to age well and care always, and almost everything we've done has been informed by attention to these anthropological and not merely ethical matters. And I don't think that this Council would have been satisfied with the view that all that bioethics can say is that everyone should make informed choices for themselves. As a public bioethics body respecting…the pluralisms of the society, we've been asked to offer as the charge this Council had, the results of serious inquiry into the human and moral significance of these advances, and that we've tried to do…. (President's Council on Bioethics 2005b)

In an excerpt from his article "Reflections on Public Bioethics: A View from the Trenches" that Kass distributed to Council members at this session, he elaborated further on the "larger vision of the purpose of bioethics," which he said had been core to their work, and that he hoped would "also be [their] lasting legacy to the field":

In the age of biotechnology, bioethics must do more than take up various technologies, and measure them to see if they might run afoul of beneficence, respect [for autonomy] and justice, and then move along…. Bioethics…must do us all the service of leaning against our modern inclinations and correcting for our excesses. This means that it must do much more than enforce a checklist of liberal shibboleths that need guarding. And it must offer more than an exchange of sanctimonious permission slips for unrestrained scientific freedom and technological innovation.

A proper bioethics must lead public reflection on the ways in which new biotechnologies may affect those things that matter most regarding how human lives are lived—things like family, and friendship, childhood and parenthood, youth and old age, pride and humility, excellence and charitable love, and countless other crucial human intangibles that stand to be profoundly altered by new biotechnical powers. This means beginning by reflecting upon the highest human goods and understanding the latest technological advances in this light. It means practicing a truly humanistic bioethics enriched by the wisdom of the ages, suitably vitalized to inform the judgment of our democracy in an age of very complicated choices. (Kass 2005: 246)

In reflecting on his experiences as a member of the Council, William May associated its "best work" with its "aspir[ation] to move toward what Kass called 'a richer bioethics,'" and its "educational goal" of not only contributing to public policy, but also to "public culture." And in "wrestl[ing]" with questions like cloning, stem cell research, and the genetic enhancement of human beings, he continued, it enabled the Council to "stand back from the immediate tactical struggle over federal policies and reflect on the human condition—the whence and whither of being human, the mysteries of mating and parenting, and the human drives that underlie scientific inquiry." For May, the anthology of writings that the Council published under the title *Being Human* epitomized such an enriched, deeper bioethics. It "offer[ed] a...treasury of work by novelists, poets, playwrights, and artists" who through their "exploration of image, metaphor, and symbol...freshen[ed] language and perception" in ways that "broaden[ed] sensibilities beyond the narrow urgencies of legislative and court dockets," took "soundings on the human condition," and "contribut[ed] thereby to a public culture upon which the resiliency of our common life and our politics depends" (May 2005: 229, 239).[20]

In a number of respects, this "richer" bioethical perspective calls into question some of the premises and emphases, the mode of thought, and the style of discourse espoused by liberal bioethics. It does not restrict itself or cleave to the principles-based analytic philosophical approach that underpins the predominant theoretical framework of mainstream bioethics, or strictly abide by the importance that this approach attaches to "clear conceptual definitions, distinctions, and theoretical parsimony" (Jennings 2006: 45). Political philosopher-bioethicist Bruce Jennings describes "the moral landscape" in which the Council's report on "ethical caregiving in our aging society" is cast, for example, as one that the report terms "prudence"—a "classical and early modern humanistic term that...[it] tries to rejuvenate. Prudence refers here to the moral imagination of taking particularity, relationship, context, and difference seriously" (Jennings 2006: 46).

The notion of "a richer bioethics" also includes in its sphere fundamental human experiences and yearnings, sources of angst and fulfillment, human duties and virtues, and problems of meaning intrinsic to the human condition. For some of the more outspoken liberal bioethicists, the importance that it accords to a humanistically centered, existentially attuned bioethics conceived in this manner, blurs the boundaries between ethics and religion—which they find objectionable. Additionally, although it attaches value to lucidity, such an "enriched" bioethics, unlike analytic philosophy, does not elevate rational argumentation to the status of the sine qua non of valid ethical thought and insight. Nor does it confine itself to austere, logical language. It includes images, metaphors, and symbols in its vocabulary, and it views them as wellsprings and enhancers of moral sensibility and understanding.

In Callahan's perspective and parlance, these attributes of the conception of bioethics that framed the work of the President's Council under Kass's direction allied it with "an ethics of ends." That is to say, it placed heavy emphasis on trying to address "fundamental questions, goals and purposes." This "ethics of ends" orientation, he contends, characterized the outlook of the first two decades of American bioethics.[21] However, in his view, by the 1980s this framework was gradually shifting toward what he calls "the ethics of means" that came to dominate the field, with its stress on "the principles of autonomy and choice as...the most profound values," and an overriding interest in "regulation," which gave greater priority to devising "rules and regulations" that would ensure that such activities as human subjects research, end-of-life care, and genetic screening were conducted "in an ethical fashion," than to "asking where the medical and biological trajectory was taking us." Callahan maintains that the fact that Leon Kass "went back to an ethics of ends"—which had been his orientation when he became associated with the Hastings Center as a young scholar—was a major source of the antagonism that his "richer" bioethics evoked from mainstream, liberal bioethicists (Center for American Progress 2006: panel 1).

So, too, was the kind of agenda for public bioethics that Kass envisioned: one that was not pragmatically limited to the relatively narrow list of concrete issues around which the field of bioethics has turned since its inception, and to being useful to those who have the responsibility of formulating and enacting public policy. Rather, as May has stated, its purview was also "educational" and "cultural" on a societal scale (May 2005: 239). This aspiration elicited acerbic comments from prominent liberal bioethicists like Moreno, Charo, and Caplan:

If the president wants a council that serves as a public seminar in moral philosophy, indeed, that is what he got. (Moreno, quoted in Vergano 2005: 2D)

...I wish the President's Council [Charo has declared] had...pa[id] attention to the fact that it is not merely a group of individuals who are attempting in a platonic tradition to engage in a public debate in which they exercise moral leadership for the rest of us, producing volumes of readings for us to use in our classrooms because we are too feebleminded to imagine how to teach ourselves, but instead would recognize that they've been given a public trust, and part of that public trust is understanding that their role is to set public policy.... (Charo at Center for American Progress 2005)

...[T]he council [Caplan has declared] has abrogated its public responsibilities. It has become more of a national seminar or teach-in about certain issues.... [T]here is a need to examine problems in equity and fairness around healthcare access.... To me,...that is the core issue...the major challenge.... (Caplan at Center for American Progress 2005)

Two Anomalies

We have been struck by what seems to us to be at least two rather anomalous characteristics of the continual criticism by liberal bioethicists of the President's Council and of Leon Kass during the four years that he presided over it. One of these is their faulting of the Council for its failure to take up questions pertaining to access to health, health care, and health insurance in American society, with the implication both that this oversight was attributable to the conservatism of the Council, and that previous, more liberally disposed bioethics commissions had paid serious attention to them. In fact, it was only the President's Commission that issued a report on this subject (President's Commission for the Study of Ethical Problems in Medicine and Biomedical and Behavioral Research. *Securing Access* 1983), and as we described in chapter 7, the members of that Commission not only initially expressed considerable reluctance to deal with this topic, but the report about it that they published was not one of their strongest. Impugning the President's Council for neglecting these issues also carried with it the more general connotation that, in contrast to conservative bioethics, liberal bioethics has been highly attentive to such ethically important matters. Ruth Macklin has made one of the most strongly felt invidious comparisons between liberal and conservative bioethicists in this regard:

> So-called liberals in bioethics have been paying increasing attention to matters of justice in access to health care and the gap in health status between rich and poor, as well as broader issues of global justice in medical research and health disparities between industrialized and developing countries. These concerns appear to be completely absent from the conservatives' "project," to borrow their term....
>
> As a liberal, humanitarian bioethicist, I acknowledge that my chief concern is in striving for greater social justice within and among societies, and reducing disparities in health, wealth, and other resources among populations in the world. Unless the conservative bioethicists begin to address these topics, I for one will not find common cause with their main worries about where we are headed. (Macklin 2006: 42)

Macklin's moral indignation about these health-related conditions of inequality and injustice, and her dedication to using the analytic abilities of an ethicist to identify and help to ameliorate them, is one of her bedrock commitments. But as we discussed at some length in chapter 6, there are relatively few other American bioethicists, whether liberal or conservative, who have accorded such a high degree of saliency and weight to these issues in their work—Macklin's allegation that liberal bioethicists are increasingly paying attention to them notwithstanding.

The second anomaly that we have noted is the dramatic difference that exists between the respected and respectful way that Leon Kass's ideas were received during the early years of bioethics, and the derisive reactions that they presently evoke from liberal bioethicists. What makes this difference all the more striking is that the ideas that Kass has set forth in his recent publications, and as chair of the President's Council, are essentially the same as those that are integral to his previous thought and published work. Callahan has testified that Kass, who "helped me to get the [Hastings] center going," was "understood to be conservative," but that in those "apolitical...early days" of bioethics, it was "not important," and "there was very little castigation of people as individuals" for the views that they held (Center for American Progress 2006: panel 1). And philosopher Lawrence Vogel has conceded that "we would be mistaken, I think, to dismiss Kass as a Republican ideologue who tailored his ideas to please the powers-that-be so that he could break out of the ivory tower and into the halls of power. His views germinated during thirty years of teaching." (Vogel 2006: 40).

The fact that the opprobrium of liberal bioethicists to which Kass has been subject is so tightly associated with his appointment by George W. Bush to the chairmanship of the Council, and with their belief that the composition of the

Council and their choice of topics were collusively connected with a national, conservative power elite, is indicative of the extent to which the societal culture wars have penetrated the American bioethics community, altering its mood and normative behavior, and of how politicized U.S. bioethics has become.

Reactions to Edmund Pellegrino's Becoming Chair of the President's Council

In September 2005, President Bush appointed Edmund Pellegrino to succeed Leon Kass as chair of the President's Council.[22] Kass had asked to be replaced when his four-year term as chair ended on October 1 (Weiss 2005a). Pellegrino's appointment was not only accompanied by tributes to his "virtues" on the part of both liberal and conservative bioethicists but also by appeals like that of Tom Beauchamp to refrain from "labeling" Pellegrino as conservative, or attacking him on those grounds:

The appointment of Edmund Pellegrino...deserves support from all quarters of American bioethics. Ed is a trustworthy and diplomatic leader. His virtues are many, his vices are few.... It is unlikely that he will take orders from, or otherwise fall in line with preferences of the White House.... Similarly, despite certain conservatism in matters ecclesiastical and political, including his strong commitment to Roman Catholic beliefs, he will not be an ideological presence on the Council.

Pellegrino will probably not, in upcoming months, escape criticism from significant voices in bioethics on grounds that he is unduly conservative or that he brings a religious viewpoint to public bioethics. I hope that members of the bioethics community will be both constrained and conscientious if they determine to serve up such criticism....

I have debated bioethics endlessly with Ed Pellegrino. As is no secret, he usually reaches very different conclusions than I do—so different that, in the current environment of bioethics, the label "conservative" dogs him, much as "liberal" follows me. I would caution against structuring the world in this way, especially if the language implies a defect in Pellegrino. (Beauchamp 2005b: W21)[23]

Pellegrino introduced himself to the Council at the final meeting chaired by Kass, in September 2005, and quietly assumed the reins as chair at the next meeting, on December 8–9. The change in leadership was greeted with a number of expectations. One was that Kass, although he remained a member of the Council, would no longer be a major player in conservative bioethics. At the symposium titled "Bioethics and Politics" held by the Progressive Bioethics Initiative in April 2006, for example, liberal bioethicist Kathryn Hinsch remarked that "I heard a scholar tell me last night, 'Well, we don't need to worry about Leon Kass anymore; he's over.' " "All right. Great," she went on to say, but warned that "the type of coalitions that he has put in place are not over and they're moving ahead and... we ignore them at our own peril" (Center for American Progress 2006: panel 2). Another forecast made was that, in the words of *Science* magazine reporter Constance Holden, the Council "might be slipping out of the limelight," absent

Kass as its chair. She quoted Daniel Perry, head of the Coalition for Medical Research, as stating that " 'I wouldn't be surprised if the council recedes into the background from now on...Pellegrino is not the lightning rod that Leon was.' " Similarly, Kathy Hudson, director of Johns Hopkins's Genetic and Public Policy Center, remarked that " 'Leon defined this council." Pellegrino, Holden wrote, is "renowned for his diplomatic skills," and on that basis, Hudson said that she expects that the new chairman will " 'rein in the council's recent activist tendencies' " and " 'boost public confidence in the importance of this important body' " (Holden 2005).

It remains to be seen whether Kass's influence will in fact diminish, and whether the Council and its new chairman will receive less attention in Washington and in the media, and less critical scrutiny by liberal bioethicists. It does seem safe to say, however, that those on the liberal side of the bioethical divide should not expect the Council to have a notably different perspective on bioethical issues, and how they should be approached, than under Kass's tenure. Pellegrino's writing over the years, grounded in his deeply held, in part religiously rooted values and moral convictions, and in the roles he has played such as establishing and directing the Institute on Human Values in Medicine, which trained a generation of young scholars to become teachers of the medical humanities (see chapter 1), is focused, like his predecessor, on considering and weighing "the ethics of ends" rather than of "means." Like Kass, he is inclined to invoke concepts such as human dignity, and to draw on a wide array of resources including more-than-biomedical and philosophical literature, in his reflections and deliberations. Another indicator of Pellegrino's orientation is the status he maintains as a senior fellow of the Center for Bioethics and Human Dignity, an organization formed in 1974 by a group of leading Christian bioethicists.[24] Not surprisingly, then, four sessions of the first two Council meetings that he chaired were devoted to bioethics and the concept of human dignity, including discussion of a staff working paper on that topic.[25]

Quo Vadis?

The bioethical questions that have found their way into the civic consciousness of the public have entered the polity, where they have become political issues whose significance extends beyond the realm of technical, administrative, and regulatory matters, and scientific, medical, and bioethical expertise.[26] They are crucial and complex issues, which involve values, beliefs, and ends that are inherently difficult to resolve, especially on a total society basis. They are also inherently divisive and generative of deep disagreements. Nonetheless, once they have been taken up in the political process, it calls into play—even necessitates—making concrete policy and judicial decisions that bear on such big, disputed questions as those that pertain to the beginning and end of life.

At this juncture, it is not clear whether American bioethicists will demonstrate the concerted will to searchingly examine the origins, manifestations, and consequences of the impact that the culture wars have had on the field, or whether they will have the committed capacity to extricate the field from the "politicization and polarization" (Kahn 2006: 10) that have accompanied the cultural strife. When we wrote this in summer 2006, the signals were mixed. While partisan and polemical divisiveness have not abated on the U.S. bioethics scene, concerns about their implications for the intellectual and moral integrity of bioethics, its professional and public credibility, and its long-term viability had become more vocal and organized. Thus far, however, as illustrated by the Progressive Bioethics Initiative launched by Jonathan Moreno in his role as a fellow with the Center for American Progress, located in Washington, D.C., in October 2005, these concerns have largely been manifest within the partisan camps. Moreno inaugurated the Center by convening a small group of liberal bioethicists—Arthur Caplan, R. Alta Charo, and Vanessa Gamble—to discuss with him "challenges for progressive bioethics"[27] and to formulate the key tactics the Initiative group needed to employ to counter the influence of conservative bioethics.[28]

The overall mission of the Progressive Bioethics Initiative was described in the following way:

As the pace of scientific innovation continues to accelerate exponentially, the Center for American Progress wants to ensure that these advances are shaped by our shared...timeless, progressive values of justice, equity, dignity and critical optimism.... Moving beyond the narrow concerns and ideological conflicts that have plagued contemporary bioethics, the Progressive Bioethics Initiative provides a voice for the millions of Americans who do not see their views or concerns represented in current bioethics debates....

Rather than decry progress as inherently dangerous, the Progressive Bioethics Initiative embraces the promise of science to improve our lives with a critical optimism that understands that science must be guided by our values....

We believe in the potential of medical science to improve the lives of all people, shaped by our shared values and addressing the causes of human suffering while advancing the creative spirit. Society and government must work to nurture this science, ensuring that it continues to develop ethically and engaging in the new complexities that arise from our burgeoning technology.

We will work with progressive thinkers, policymakers and organizations to address both longstanding and emerging bioethics issues in the light of our principles and develop positions and plans that will help ensure that science and medicine are a continuing source of intelligence in the service of humanity.[29]

The second event held by the Center for American Progress took place on April 21, 2006, in the form of a day-long symposium on "Bioethics and Politics: Past, Present and Future." The meeting's stated intent was to "discuss both the history and future of progressive bioethics," within the context of the fact that "over the last 35 years, [as] bioethics has evolved from an obscure academic field to one on the cutting edge of America's consciousness,... [it] has entered the public realm

[and]…also become more politicized." The major questions around which the symposium was structured were: "[H]ow has bioethics evolved to this point in the current political climate? And what opportunities are there for progressives to advance a bioethics vision that expresses and helps to implement their values?"

The symposium consisted of a morning panel that centered on the theme of "The Emergence of Politicized Bioethics," and an afternoon panel that considered "The Future of Progressive Bioethics." A keynote luncheon talk was given by lawyer-bioethicist Patricia King, who made it clear at the outset that she did not think of herself as "being either liberal, or conservative…or progressive, or whatever." She brought her own vast and varied experience on federal commissions concerned with bioethics[30] to bear on her discussion of the increasingly "divisive and more ideologically focused" characteristics of bioethics. Although she was critical of this development, she stated that it did not "surprise" her, since she assumed that "bioethics would have evolved in the same way that our society and culture have evolved."[31]

One attempt to bring individuals from each side of the bioethical divide together to develop a genuine, face-to-face civil dialogue has been made by Daniel Callahan. He has convoked small, what he sometimes calls "ecumenical," meetings of liberal and conservative bioethicists, at which, in a spirit of amity, they can hear, discuss, and learn about each other's ideas and points of view. Despite the need for such an effort to bridge the partisan divides, however, within the larger context of the ideological, moral, and political conflict that is occurring nationwide, the possibility that bioethics might formally split apart into separate liberal/conservative, left/right, Democratic/Progressive/Republican, scholarly/advocacy entities is being mentioned for the first time, accompanied by questions about whether, if this comes to pass, the whole enterprise known as bioethics may self-destruct.

The May–June 2006 issue of *The Hastings Center Report*, for example, contained a one-page "Policy and Politics" commentary entitled "What Happens When Politics Discovers Bioethics?" by philosopher-bioethicist Jeffrey Kahn, who directs the Center for Bioethics at the University of Minnesota. It is essentially a statement of alarm about bioethics' current "participation in politics," and what "costs to the field" this state of affairs may incur. In his view, bioethics is facing a "field-changing moment," because it finds itself "in the midst of…the rough and tumble…of heated political debates" (Kahn 2006). "We must "mak[e] sure that policy and politics don't become one and the same," he cautions:

One way to assure this outcome is to treat the two as distinct areas…. Bioethics scholars should feel free to engage in political bioethics, of course, but it should be clear when they are "doing" politics versus scholarship. It is difficult to imagine a more important time for political advocacy, but confusing advocacy with scholarly efforts serves to undermine both. (Kahn 2006)

Kahn's emphasis on the importance of separating "political bioethics" from "scholarly" bioethics overlaps with the recommendation that John Evans made at the "Bioethics and Politics" symposium held by the Center for American Progress in 2006. "I'm sympathetic to Dan Callahan's lament for what has been lost in bioethics in this divide," Evans said on this occasion. "However, I think it's time to strategically cut the losses":

...I think I would divide bioethics into two levels. The first level is debate among academics and public intellectuals about these deep...foundational questions: the ends that we should pursue. It was a debate that existed 20, 30 years ago.... This [foundational] debate would have liberals and conservatives.... [G]iven its distance from actual policymaking [and the fact that its] stakes would be lower, it would be more calm...I envision a unified discussion at level one.... [A]t the second level,...I envision at least two groups.... At this level, people and their different communities have decided the ends they will pursue and there's no reason to debate it further.... You're never going to be able to convert people to your side.... (Center for American Progress 2006: panel 1)

A second manifestation of the increased disquietude about the fractured state of the field was the American Society for Bioethics and Humanities (ASBH) summer conference on "Bioethics and Politics: The Future of Bioethics in a Divided Democracy," which was held in Albany, New York, in 2006. It was organized by the Alden March Bioethics Institute of Albany Medical College, in collaboration with the ASBH, the Nelson Rockefeller Institute of Government, the Stanford University Center for Biomedical Ethics, the University of Pennsylvania Department of Medical Ethics, the University of Virginia Center for Bioethics, and the *American Journal of Bioethics*. "Bioethics has always fueled contentious debates in politics about matters such as abortion, civil rights and the allocation of scarce resources," the conference announcement stated. "Yet many in the field see themselves as scholars, stunned when their work hits center stage in politics and the media":

Has a new kind of bioethics emerged, one that is more political than scholarly?
Or is bioethics finally correcting a long-standing liberal bias? Can bioethics scholars of strong conviction work together, or will there be "two bioethics," one for the right, and one for the left?
  Bioethics itself is at stake. (Emphasis in the announcement)

The conference program included a keynote speech titled "Bioethics and Politics: Why We Must Repair the Rift," delivered by Edmund Pellegrino; a luncheon lecture given by R. Alta Charo on "My View: Bioethics and Politics"; and sessions entitled "Bioethics, Politics, and Religion in America: Bioethics Began in Religion, But Where Is Religion Now?"; "Thinking, Writing about and Disseminating: How Has Politics Affected How We Do Bioethics"; and "Can We Talk and Can We Listen: Making Peace and Finding Common Ground in Bioethics." Among the striking characteristics of the conference were how many bioethics groups it collaboratively involved; how centered it was on the schism in bioethics, and on whether and how it can be defused and bridged; and the amount of attention it paid to the relationship between bioethics and religion. Another of its notable features was its "ecumenical" inclusion of prominent conservative figures such as Eric Cohen, editor of *The New Atlantis*; Richard Doerflinger, deputy director of the Secretariat for Pro-Life Activities of the United States Conference of Catholic Bishops; and Wesley Smith, a senior fellow at the Discovery Institute and attorney at the International Task Force on Euthanasia and Assisted Suicide,[32] in the roster of faculty-participants, alongside mainstream liberal bioethicists.[33]

Seen in relation to one another, these events suggest that awareness and concern are mounting among American bioethicists about how the future of their field may be imperiled by the degree to which it has allowed itself to be torn apart by the same ideological, moral, and political conflict that is occurring nationwide. The possibility that bioethics might be formally split apart into separate liberal/conservative, left/right, "red"/"blue," Democratic/Progressive/Republican, religious/secular, scholarly/advocacy entities is being mentioned for the first time, accompanied by questions about whether, if this comes to pass, the whole enterprise known as bioethics may self-destruct.

In the paper based on his lecture to the ASBH conference on "Bioethics and Politics," Edmund Pellegrino exhorted the "bioethics community [to] assume leadership in recovering" what he termed "the art of civilized dialectics. This does not mean that bioethicists must abandon their personal views," he stated, "only that they present themselves in a civil as well as rigorous manner":

> The bioethicist's purpose should be to provide the basis for the kind of moral considerations upon which good policy rests. In the political arena, partisanship is inevitable, and indeed necessary, but it should not be the fate of important issues to be decided by polemic or sophistry. The public deserves more than that.... Partisan politics, for good or bad, is established as a mechanism in democratic societies by which citizens can exert influence on established institutions of government. But for bioethicists particularly, this means that ethics must drive partisanship, not partisanship drive ethics. (Pellegrino 2006)

It will be a daunting challenge to depoliticize U.S. bioethics' presence and participation in the public square, and to develop intellectual and moral bases of unity, while at the same time fostering dynamic debate about differences. It appears that American bioethicists are beginning to comprehend the importance and urgency of this needed work. We consider it imperative for the probity, productivity, and effectiveness of U.S. bioethics—indeed, for its continued existence—that American bioethicists collectively undertake this task with lucid understanding of what is at stake.

Notes

1. One recent indicator of the nexus that has existed between bioethics and the public sphere since the field's inception, and of the increasing recognition and formal institutionalization of this interrelationship, is the $2.1 million grant that the Hastings Center received in 2007 from the Ford Foundation for a three-year initiative on "Bioethics

and the Public Interest." According to the announcement issued on March 8, 2007 by Hastings, the grant, which represents a substantial broadening of its founding scholarly research mission, "will enable the Center…to expand its capacity to help policy makers, journalists, and opinion leaders better understand the ethical dimensions of end-of-life care, public health priorities, and new medical technologies, among other bioethical issues." The first step in this program that Hastings plans to take is to create a "communications department" that will be headed by a "permanent, senior-level director of public affairs/communications" (Hastings Center 2007).

2. In our view, the assertion that bioethics has "matured into a position of power in American society" is one that needs further elaboration if it is to be accepted, or refuted. For example, in what areas has bioethics attained "power," and according to what criteria or evidence? With respect to the influence of bioethics on federal policies, for instance, the claim of power needs to be supported by a careful documentation of a direct causal relationship between the various bioethics committees and commissions' recommendations, and the enactment of new policies or regulations. In this connection, we note one such indicator of powerful influence—namely, that the legislation establishing the National Commission contained a unique provision for such a body: rather than issuing only advisory recommendations, the Secretary of DHEW was required to respond to the Commission's recommendations regarding the protection of human research subjects within a given period of time, either by issuing regulations or explaining why the agency would not do so.

3. "Baby Doe," born on April 15, 1982 in Bloomington, Indiana, was an infant with Down syndrome and a surgically repairable tracheoesophageal fistula that made it impossible for her to eat. The parents elected not a have the defect repaired, and following a court-approved decision upholding the parents' decision, the baby was medicated with phenobarbital and morphine and died of starvation when she was six days old. The aftermath of Baby Doe's death began a month later, when the DHHS Secretary issued a letter notifying hospitals receiving federal financial assistance that it is "unlawful" under the 1973 federal Rehabilitation Act regulations to withhold nutrition or a surgically or medically indicated treatment to correct a life-threatening condition on the grounds that an infant is handicapped. Some 10 months later, the "Who Should Survive" film about the death of the Down syndrome baby at Johns Hopkins who was not surgically treated for duodenal atresia—which, as we noted in chapter 3, had featured prominently in the inaugural conference of the Kennedy Institute of Ethics—aired on public television. That same week, President Reagan, who reportedly had seen the film, directed DHHS to issue a more forceful follow-up to its May 1982 notice. In response, DHHS issued an "interim final rule" requiring every intensive-care nursery, nursery, and maternity ward to conspicuously display a poster with the gist of the May 1982 notice, including the toll-free 24-hour-a-day "hotline" number; DHHS officials also were authorized to take "immediate remedial action" to protect an infant reported to the hotline, and hospitals were required to give Department investigators access to a facility and its records.

On March 18, 1983, four days before the interim final rule was due to become effective, a suit was filed against DHHS by four medical organizations seeking to enjoin the interim final rule. United States District Court Judge Gerhard Gesell granted an expedited review of the suit and scheduled a hearing on April 8, following submission of written documents and arguments. After the hearing, Gesell concluded, in part, that because the interim rule had no definition of "customary care," it was "virtually without meaning beyond its intrinsic *in terrorem* effect." He further ruled that the regulations were invalid, calling them "arbitrary and capricious," because DHHS had not followed the Administrative Procedure Act's requirement that a proposed rule must allow at least 30 days for comments by interested parties before it becomes a final rule. At the behest of the White House, however, DHHS reissued regulations in July 1983, which attempted to deal with the procedural issues raised by Gesell's ruling. The legal validity of the 1983 regulations then wended its way to the U.S. Supreme Court, which in 1986 held that its four mandatory provisions were not authorized under the applicable section of the Rehabilitation Act of 1973. (This summary of the Baby Doe case is drawn from Annas 1988: 126–142; and Annas, Law, Rosenblatt, and Wing 1990: 663–666.)

4. In his oral presentation at the meeting of the Hastings Center marking Callahan's retirement as president, and in the short essay he based upon it ("Bioethics, Whose Crowd, and What Ideology?"), Albert Jonsen spiritedly disagreed with what he termed the "provocative statement" that Callahan had made. "As one who long ago sat on the first two commissions," Jonsen declared, "the National Commission…and the President's Commission…, I deny that my colleagues and I 'legitimated' anything, much less any 'morally controverted research.'" "I do not fear that our crowd has been seduced by partisan ideologies," he went on to say. "I do worry that the partisans will either ignore us or breed up their own 'ethicists' who have little tolerance for moral ambiguity or for democratic solutions that permit us to live tolerably well amidst the puzzles that beset us" (Jonsen 1996: 4–5).

5. Defining an ideology is not a simple matter. Even in the social science literature, where one would expect to find edification about the attributes of ideology, there is disagreement about its characteristics, components, and perspectives. Anthropologist Clifford Geertz has gone so far as to say that in certain respects, "the term 'ideology' has become…ideologized" in that literature (Geertz 1973: 193). His ironic critique is principally addressed to what he considers to be the excessive, pejorative emphasis that numerous social scientists place on the propensity for "distortion" and "unduly selective" ideas in ideological thought.

   However, some consensus does exist among social scientists about the nature and functions of an ideology, and the tensions associated with it. In this view, an ideology consists of a system of ideas in which cognitive and moral beliefs, social values, cultural symbols, empirical facts, and some nonempirical referents are constituent elements. The body of ideas pertains to a collectivity and the larger society of which it is a part—the definition and membership of the collectivity, the structure of the situation in which it is placed, and the shared goals and course of action to which its members are committed. Ideologies, which to a significant degree are responses to social, cultural, and psychological strains, provide a framework for collective attempts to make social situations more meaningful, and to act purposefully within, and upon them. Nevertheless, Talcott Parsons observed, "It is likely that ideologies will become the symbolic background of some of the principal elements of tension and conflict within a social system. In the nature of the case, there would seem to be an inherent tendency to polarization, [and] to the development of vicious circles.…" (Parsons 1951: 358). For additional analyses of ideology, see also Johnson 1968 and Shils 1968.

   This social science outlook on ideology seems to be roughly congruent with the way that Daniel Callahan uses the term, and with some of the features of the "culture war."

6. Callahan has suggested that "it was conservative commentators who began the fight, particularly in the pages of *Commentary*, *The Weekly Standard*, *The Public Interest*, and *First Things*" (Callahan 2005: 428).

7. This synopsis of the Schiavo case is drawn from Fox and Swazey 2005: 369–371, 373n36.

8. Court rulings included an appeal to the U.S. Supreme Court by the parents to overturn a lower court decision ordering removal of the feeding tube. In April 2001, the U.S. Supreme Court held that it would not intervene in that decision, which led to the feeding tube's removal, followed by another lower court order to have the tube reinserted. Yet another lower court decision in October 2003 led to the tube's removal, but it was then reinserted after Florida's lower house passed "Terri's Law." In September 2004, the Florida Supreme Court struck down Terri's Law, upholding the lower court decision that it was unconstitutional and a violation of the right to privacy. In January 2005, the U.S. Supreme Court refused to hear an appeal by Governor Bush to change the Florida ruling, and the case was remanded to the Florida courts.

9. These events included the following: On March 17, the Schindlers filed another emergency appeal with the U.S. Supreme Court, arguing that the lower courts needed to review their daughter's case again on the grounds that religious freedom and due process rights had been violated. The Court once more declined to hear their appeal. The next day, March 18, the U.S. Congress moved to block the tube's removal; this effort was rejected by the appellate judge who had ordered its removal on that day, and the tube was removed. Then, on March 20 and 21, the U.S. House and Senate passed, and President Bush immediately signed into law, special emergency legislation for a federal court review of the case. Between March 20–27, a series of state courts rejected further emergency appeals by the Schindlers, as well as a petition by Governor Bush to be named as Terri Schiavo's legal guardian, and refused to order reinsertion of the feeding tube. The Florida rulings were rapidly upheld by a federal appellate court, and the U.S. Supreme Court twice more refused emergency appeals to intervene in the case.

10. Pope John Paul II reportedly first used the term *the culture of life*, during a tour of the United States in 1993, in the context of denouncing abortion and euthanasia. He evoked this phrase again in 1995 in his encyclical *Evangelium Vitae* (Gospel of Life), stating that "[I]n our present social context, marked by a dramatic struggle between the culture of life and the culture of death, there is a need to develop a deep critical sense capable of discerning true values and authentic needs." After *Evangelium Vitae* was issued in April 1995, The Culture of Life Foundation and Institute was established in the United States to promote the encyclical's concepts; the foundation was recognized and blessed by the pope in 1997. The appeal to upholding the culture of life entered into U.S. politics in October 2000, when, during a debate between presidential candidates George W. Bush and Al Gore, Bush voiced his concern that a new contraceptive pill would increase the incidence of abortions, and stated that his goal was to "promote a culture of life" that, among other things, would markedly decrease abortions (Wikipedia, "Culture of life," http://en.wikipedia.org/wiki/Culture_of_Life).

    The pope had also used the term *culture of death* during his Christmas message from the Vatican on December 25, 2000, referring to his deep concerns about matters such as the upsurge of secular and religiously based international violence and " 'the endless stream of exiles and refugees,' " as well as "the 'shadows of death' that are 'especially menacing at (life's) earliest beginning and its natural end.' " The pope warned that the world is "confronted by " 'alarming signs of the culture of death which pose a serious threat for the future' " (Pope Warns over 'Culture of Death,' Dec. 25, 2000, http://archives.cnn.com/2000/WORLD/europe/12/25/pope.christmas/.

11. Robert Veatch also made this point at the Acadia Institute Project's advisory committee meeting on Sept. 8, 2000. We have noted that in response to the pressures of the field, many of the religiously trained thinkers in bioethics shed "the dictates of bioethics' secular philosophical vocabulary and canon when they [write] about bioethically

related matters for religious journals and magazines" (Messikomer, Fox, and Swazey 2001: 490).

12. Ruth Macklin uses the term *mainstream bioethics* to refer to "the field whose more prominent members are nationally and internationally recognized as contributors to the literature, or as educators and consultants. These include physicians, other health professionals, biological scientists, philosophers, lawyers, social scientists, theologians, scholars in religious studies, political scientists, health economists, and any others who may not fall into these categories" (Macklin 2006: 42, reference 1). In our view, *mainstream* and *liberal* bioethics are essentially synonymous terms, which often are used interchangeably.

13. Yural Levin is one of the senior editors of *The New Atlantis*, a conservative journal, launched in 2003, which is principally concerned with "technology and society," but has devoted a significant amount of space to bioethics in articles that are often critical of the positions taken by persons considered to be "mainstream" contributors to the field. Levin is a former congressional staffer who served as acting executive director of the President's Council on Bioethics when Kass was its chair, and since early 2005 has been a member of the White House domestic policy staff.

   The New Atlantis was founded by Eric Cohen, who is its editor-in-chief, and the director of the Bioethics and American Democracy Program at the Ethics and Public Policy Center. He also served as a senior consultant to the President's Council on Bioethics when Kass headed it. In 2005, the United Nations Educational, Scientific, and Cultural Organization (UNESCO) selected the Ethics and Public Policy Center as a Chair in Bioethics, with its activities as one of UNESCO's chairs directed by Cohen (http://portal.unesco.org/education).

   The following statement about the title and focus of the journal appears on the masthead of the page listing its editors; information about its editorial, subscription, advertising, and submission offices; and its quarterly publishing schedule:

   > *The New Atlantis* (1627) was the title Francis Bacon selected for his fable of a society living with the benefits and challenges of advanced science and technology. Bacon, a founder and champion of modern science, sought not only to highlight the potential of technology to improve human life, but also to foresee some of the social, moral, and political difficulties that confront a society shaped by the great scientific enterprise. His book offers no obvious answers; perhaps it seduces more than it warns. But the tale also hints at some of the dilemmas that arise with the ability to remake and reconfigure the natural world: governing science, so that it might flourish freely without destroying or dehumanizing us, and understanding the effect of technology on human life, human aspiration, and the human good. To a great extent, we live in the world that Bacon imagined, and now we must find a way to live well with both its burdens and its blessings. This very challenge, which now confronts our own society most forcefully, is the focus of this journal.

14. Macklin's perspective on appeals to human dignity is not as adamantly fixed or as belligerent as it may have appeared to some of the readers of her "Dignity Is a Useless Concept" editorial in the *British Medical Journal*. For example, in a personal communication to us on January 6, 2004, she wrote: "Of course, I am unalterably opposed to the forms of behavior that are alleged to violate human dignity, conduct that demeans, humiliates, or degrades people; arrogance and dismissive behavior, etc. What I was arguing against is the use of the term 'dignity' as a conversation stopper in arguments of all sorts where the concept remains unanalyzed. Interesting how one's intentions can be so misread!"

The invited reflections that she presented at, and about, a symposium titled "Human Dignity, Narrative Inquiry, and Ethical Decision Making at the End of Life" that took place in June 2004 in St. John's, Newfoundland, and Labrador, Canada, are interesting in this regard. A large number of the attendees at the symposium were academicians and/or clinicians involved in palliative care, whose "basic tenets...including symptom control, psychological and spiritual well-being, and care of the family, are frequently subsumed under the goal of helping patients to die with dignity" (Chochinov, Hack, and Hassard et al. 2004: 134). Macklin's editorial had been published five months prior to this symposium and had been read by many of the participants in it with considerable indignation because, as Harvey Max Chochinov in the Department of Psychiatry at the University of Manitoba, the Manitoba Palliative Care Research Unit, and the Department of Psychosocial Oncology remarked, "Like others who have entered into the dignity fray, she [Macklin] learned that the topic is not passion-neutral and, in fact, is often perceived as a sacred terrain [in the field of palliative care]." As he humorously put it, upon meeting and hearing Ruth Macklin at the symposium, he was pleased to discover that "she is not a moral monster.... She bears no horns, has no witch's cackle; rather she is a bright and articulate person," one whose primary concern is "dignity's lack of definitional specificity" (Chochinov 2004).

In her remarks on the symposium, which she subtitled, "Is Dignity a Useless Concept?" Macklin stated, "Apparently, dignity is *not* a useless concept because people use it in all sorts of ways" (author's italics). The authors of the symposium papers, she said, had "identified a great variety of circumstances in which people hold the concept of dignity to be valuable, important, indispensable, and relevant to law, human rights, and treatment at the end of life." At the same time, she continued, "it is evident that disagreements remain: whether there exists a universal concept of dignity, or whether it must always be understood and applied in specific contexts; whether autonomy and maintaining control of one's self and one's environment are essential elements in dignity, or whether diminished autonomy and extreme dependence on others are consistent with maintaining dignity; whether the concept of dignity properly applies only to living human beings, or whether it can be meaningfully applied to embryos, non-human animals, and dead bodies." Although these disagreements would "not go away," she concluded, that is "no case for despair." Rather, what is needed is more discussion and debate to "clarify the various meanings that people have in mind when they invoke the concept of dignity. Only then can appeals to dignity become more than mere slogans, or a device for closing off debate or controversy" (Macklin 2004b: 212, 216).

15. The 17 "leading scientists, doctors, ethicists, social scientists, lawyers, and theologians" named by Bush as members of the Council for its first two-year term, in addition to its chair, Leon Kass, were: Elizabeth H. Blackburn (cell biology), Stephen Carter (law), Rebecca S. Dresser (law and bioethics), Daniel W. Foster (internal medicine), Francis Fukuyama (political science), Michael S. Gazzaniga (neuroscience), Robert P. George (law), Mary Ann Glendon (law), Alfonso Gomez-Lobo (metaphysics and moral philosophy), William B. Hurlbut (medicine and neuroscience, with formal training in theology and medical ethics), Charles Krauthammer (psychiatry and journalism), William F. May (religious ethics), Paul McHugh (psychiatry), Gilbert C. Meilaender Jr. (religious [Christian] ethics), Janet D. Rowley (molecular genetics), Michael J. Sandel (political philosophy), and James Q. Wilson (political science).

16. The President's Council was not the first time that the effects of the politicization of bioethical issues with respect to federal-level commissions manifested themselves. An earlier and largely forgotten instance, which took place between the end of the

President's Commission and the creation of NBAC, was the stillborn attempt by Congress to establish the Bioethics Advisory Commission (BEAC) and its oversight body, the Bioethics Ethics Board (BEB), which was modeled on the Technology Assessment Board that oversees Congress's Office of Technology Assessment. Congress established BEAC in May 1985 (Public Law 99–158), with three mandated topics: gene therapy, fetal research, and the use of artificial feeding and hydration for dying patients. It took almost a year for the House and Senate to appoint six members each to BEB, who in turn were responsible for appointing BEAC's 14 members. Barbara Mishkin, who had been deputy director of the President's Commission, had been approached to serve as director of BEAC (which she declined). She recalled that BEAC's "first order of business was going to be to revisit research with the human fetus," which would plunge the group into the volatile issue of abortion, as would stem cell research almost two decades later. "It was obvious to many of us that [BEAC] was going to be dead in the water," Mishkin said. "There was so much manipulation, trying to stack the Commission with people who would be sympathetic to one view or the other, it was just so politically embroiled [that] it never got off the ground" (Mishkin, interview, 1998: see appendix). BEAC did, indeed, prove to be "dead in the water": it took two and one-half years for the commission members to be appointed, and their first meeting took place less than one week before the commission was slated to expire. With a deadline extension, BEAC held a second meeting in February 1989. "Shortly thereafter, however, Senate BEB members deadlocked on choosing a chairman along partisan, prochoice-anti-abortion lines. BEAC's proposed budget…was cut and spending made contingent on a fully constituted BEAC. BEAC expired in September 1989 having issued no reports" (U.S. Congress 1993: 12–13, 82–83).

17. In a commentary published in *Nature*, George Annas and Sherman Elias state that not all the blame for the political character of the President's Council can be placed on President George W. Bush. Rather, they contend, any bioethics panel established by any American president would be embroiled in politics. Therefore, they recommend that in the future such bioethical bodies should be "independent, not 'presidential'" (Annas and Elias 2004).

18. In his *Washington Post* article, Kass stated that William May, "having recently entered retirement, indicated his interest in stepping down at the end of the two years he had agreed to serve," and that he had "happily agreed to serve as a senior consultant for the council's new work on aging and the care of the elderly" (Kass 2004).

    The three new persons who were named to replace May, Elizabeth Blackburn, and Stephen Cutter (a professor of law who had left the Council in 2002) were surgeon Benjamin Carter, chair of pediatric surgery at Johns Hopkins Medical Center; Peter Lawler, a political philosopher; and Diana Schaub, a political scientist.

19. The October 2004 meeting of the ASBH took place in Philadelphia. Kass's plenary lecture became the basis for his article "Reflections on Public Bioethics: A View from the Trenches" (Kass 2005).

20. *Being Human* epitomizes one focus of criticism about the Council's work during Kass's chairmanship by a number of liberal bioethicists: its attention to educating the public about social, cultural, and ethical aspects of the issues the Council was dealing with rather than focusing on what these critics saw as the Council's primary task: "setting public policy" (see the statements by Moreno, Caplan, and Charo on p. 309 *supra*). Such an educative role, however, was part of the Council's mandate in Bush's Executive Order, whereas "setting" rather than advising on public policy was not its charge. Moreover, when we talked informally with Kass in the early months of the Council's work, he

commented that he did not expect the Council's products "to have a policy influence." Rather, he said, his "main hope for the Council's having some impact lies in developing educational materials," such as a reader with stories and other materials that probe "sociocultural issues, not strictly 'bioethics.'" The audience for such materials, he hoped, would include students at the high school level (J. Swazey and C. Messikomer, conversation with Leon Kass during meeting of the President's Council, Apr. 25–26, 2000).

An initial furor about Kass's use of literature was created when he assigned Council members to read Nathaniel Hawthorne's short story "The Birthmark," "a literary exploration of mankind's apparent aspiration to root out his own imperfections," as a springboard to open the discussion at the group's first meeting (Russo 2002; see also Groopman 2002; Safire 2002). In our view, Kass's giving his colleagues on the Council such a homework assignment, as well as producing *Being Human* and his conception of a "richer bioethics" were not surprising: they reflect his vocation as a teacher, his long-standing concerns about "the ethics of ends," and, akin to many people working in the medical humanities, the use of literature to educate students of all ages about the ramifications of science and medicine.

21. As we discuss in chapter 8, "Bioethics Circles the Globe," the complex of attitudes, beliefs, and values that form a focus on "the ethics of ends" is similar in many respects to that of the lay and professional "techno-skeptics" in Germany who are apprehensive about what they see as unbridled biomedicine and technology, and have been engaged in a public and political bioethical debate with "techno-optimists" about matters such as preimplantation genetic diagnosis, reproductive and therapeutic cloning, and end-of-life decision making. The apprehension of the "techno-skeptics" has roots in Germans' historical memory of the Nazi medical war crimes committed during World War II (Braun 2005; Krones 2006).

22. Pellegrino is the professor emeritus of medicine and medical ethics at the Center for Clinical Medical Ethics at Georgetown University Medical Center. He was previously the John Carroll Professor of Medicine and Medical Ethics, the head of the Kennedy Institute of Ethics, and the director of the Center for Advanced Study of Ethics, and of the Center of Clinical Bioethics at Georgetown University; president of Catholic University; president and chairman of Yale-New Haven Medical Center; vice president of health affairs at the University of Tennessee; founding chairman of the Department of Medicine at the University of Kentucky; dean of the School of Medicine at the State University of New York, Stony Brook, and founder of the Health Sciences Center there.

According to philosopher Tom Beauchamp, Pellegrino is "perhaps best known [in American bioethics] for his views on the virtues of the physician and the ends of medicine, especially for his relentless pressing of the thesis that '[i]n the real world of clinical medicine, there are no absolute moral principles, except the injunction to act in the patient's best interest'" (Beauchamp 2005b).

23. This is not the first time that Tom Beauchamp has publicly expressed his concern about the gravity of the partisan divisions in bioethics, and the importance of bridging them. He also did so in his acceptance speech, when he, along with James Childress, received a Lifetime Achievement Award at the October 2005 annual meeting of the American Society for Bioethics and Humanities.

24. For more information about the Center, see its Web site at http://www.cbhd.org.

25. The Council's December 8–9 meeting included a session with presentations on "human dignity as a bioethical concept" by Paul Weithman, Chair, Department of

Philosophy, University of Notre Dame, and by James Childress, and a session discussing the staff working paper. The February 2–3, 2006 meeting began with two sessions on the concept of human dignity, with presentations by Patricia Churchland, Professor and Chair, Department of Philosophy, University of California at San Diego, and by Daniel P. Sulmasy, Chair, John J. Conley Department of Medical Ethics, St. Vincent's Hospital and Medical Center, New York. (Sulmasy is a Franciscan priest, as well as a physician.)Transcripts of these sessions are available on the Council's Web site (http://www.bioethics.gov).

26. With respect to the place of bioethical "expertise" in developing public policies, sociologist John Evans has examined the origins, nature, and consequences of what he terms "public bioethics." In its "dominant forms," he holds, public bioethics "has been legitimated by reference to [liberal] academic philosophical norms"—particularly the common morality tenets of analytic philosophy—"and not the norms of the public sphere that it operates in." Because common morality theories are "portrayed as having a fact-like status," Evans argues, they "aspire to technocratic legitimacy, which would give bioethicists the same kind of legitimacy that nuclear physicists have when they discuss how nuclear power works." However, he finds, "as claims to technocratic authority go, bioethics is in an incredibly weak position, which partly explains why it has never gained the degree of public legitimacy that other technocracies have attained" (Evans 2006: 1, 2, 9).

27. The daylong discussion of "challenges for progressive bioethics" also was convened to mark the release of a new book by Moreno, *Is There an Ethicist in the House?*

28. As Ericka Check observed in a news story about the meeting published in *Nature*, the panelists at the progressive bioethics meeting "define[d] themselves partly by what they oppose: the conservative stance embraced by Republican political leaders, by right-leaning think-tanks, and by the President's Council on Bioethics." Quoting Arthur Caplan as declaring that " '[i]t is important for progressive bioethics to enter the political fray,' " she reported that "the progressive group hopes to emulate the conservatives' success in influencing public policy," and, referring specifically to the Terri Schiavo case, that "the group hopes to avoid the political missteps that have sometimes resulted from conservative approaches" (Check 2005: 932).

29. This undated statement of the Initiative's "Progressive Values in Bioethics" was included in the resource materials for the April 2006 symposium (www.americanprogress.org/at/cf/bioethics_initiative_summary.pdf).

30. The numerous federal bioethics commissions on which Patricia King has served include the National Commission, the DHEW Recombinant DNA Advisory Committee, the Advisory Committee on Human Radiation Experiments, and the ethical, legal, and social issues working group of the Human Genome Project. She was appointed to the President's Commission, but resigned from it at the outset because of her many other commitments.

31. In addition to Moreno and King, the other speakers in the symposium were bioethicists Daniel Callahan, Ruth Faden, Glen McGee, Eric Meslin, and Virginia Ashley Sharpe; Kathryn Hinsch, founding director of the Women's Bioethics Project; sociologist of religion and bioethics John Evans, at the University of California, San Diego; and James Fossett, an expert on health policy, urban politics, and intergovernmental relations, who teaches in the Graduate School of Public Affairs at the State University of New York in Albany.

32. Wesley Smith, JD, to our knowledge, is one of the few neoconservatives who has been actively involved both in bioethics, particularly in the area of death and dying

(W. J. Smith 2000, 2001), and in the scientific-religious controversy over evolution vs. creationism. The Discovery Institute, of which he is a senior fellow, is a nonprofit organization whose main focus is intelligent design.

33. Other faculty-participants listed in the conference announcement were: Nigel M. de Cameron, president, Institute on Biotechnology and the Human Future; Arthur Caplan, director, Center for Bioethics, and chair, Department of Medical Ethics, University of Pennsylvania; James Fossett, codirector, Program on States Federalism Bioethics, Rockefeller Institute of Government and Alden March Bioethics Institute, Albany; Jeffrey Kahn, director, Center for Bioethics, University of Minnesota; David Magnus, director, Stanford Center for Biomedical Ethics; William May, Department of Religious Studies, University of Virginia Health System; Chris Mooney, Washington correspondent, *The Seed* magazine; Jonathan Moreno, director, Center for Biomedical Ethics, University of Virginia; John Robertson, Vinson and Elkins Chair at Law, University of Texas Law School; Brian Salter, professor of biopolitics, Global Research Group, University of East Anglia, United Kingdom; Bonnie Steinbock, director, Doctoral Program, Alden March Bioethics Institute, Albany Medical School; Rabbi Gerald Wolpe, senior fellow emeritus, Center for Bioethics, University of Pennsylvania; Paul Root Wolpe, senior fellow, Center for Bioethics, University of Pennsylvania, and president-elect, ASBH; Laurie Zoloth, director, Center for Bioethics, Science, and Society, and professor of medical humanities, bioethics, religion, and Jewish studies, Northwestern University.

Afterword
The View from Khayelitsha and La Mancha

Renée C. Fox

The highway along which one drives to Khayelitsha is splendidly paved.... Nothing prepares you for the world you enter when your car crosses an overpass and turns into the streets of the township. The fact that these labyrinth streets, like the highway, are smoothly paved seems incongruous—even ironic—in this crowded, poverty-stricken universe of improvised shacks. Nevertheless, Khayelitsha pulsates with vigorous activity. During the daylight hours, an unending procession of women, men, and children move swiftly and gracefully through its streets.... [O]n Saturdays the streets are filled with funeral processions, predominantly organized around commemorating, mourning, and burying those who have died from HIV/AIDS.
— Renée C. Fox, "Khayelitsha Journal," 2005a

Our basic principles remain those expressed in the Charter and Chantilly documents. These principles should be referred to when taking and reviewing decisions, with the acknowledgement that every decision is a singular act and not made by the mechanical application of principles.... [S]uch documents have limits. They are not substitutes for strategic thinking. Defending the principles is not an end in itself. We should be ready to revisit and change them.
— "La Mancha" Meeting of Médecins Sans Frontières (MSF), Luxembourg, March 8–10, 2006

Ideology and ideological wording are banned in MSF, as it is supposed to be neither a leftist nor a rightist movement. This sort of depoliticization is to accommodate all tendencies [since] humanitarian beliefs are supposed to transcend political ideology. The second reason is…linked to political neutrality in the movement which is very cautious not be associated with any political party or tendency, either in headquarter countries or mission countries.

—Eric Goemaere, MD, Mission Head, MSF South Africa,
personal communication, May 25, 2006

Since 1996, and throughout the time that we have been absorbed in writing this book, I have been conducting firsthand research on Médecins Sans Frontières (MSF)—also known as Doctors Without Borders—which has centered on the moral dilemmas encountered by MSF, its members, and its staff in carrying out their medical humanitarian, witnessing, and advocacy action (R. C. Fox 1995, 2005b). I have been a solo investigator in this undertaking, but Judith Swazey and I have continually discussed it as it has unfolded, and she entered the field with me on one of my trips to Khayelitsha, the primary site of MSF's HIV/AIDS program in Cape Town, South Africa. As a consequence, my involvement with MSF has had a notable impact on how she, as well as I, regard some of the characteristics of American bioethics that we have identified, described, and analyzed in the body of our book. Although this afterword is written in my first-person voice, it represents our shared perspective, and expresses our common views.

It is clearly beyond the capacity of any sociological researcher to directly observe the 365 projects, in some 77 countries in which MSF is currently engaged, or even to spend sustained time in the headquarters of every one of its 19 sections. But my inquiry has brought me into prolonged contact with certain MSF programs and several of its chief operational sections, and it has also given me access to a number of the annual meetings that bring members of MSF together, nationally and internationally, for debate and decision making. The MSF program in Khayelitsha, on the periphery of Cape Town, South Africa, which provides antiretroviral (ARV) treatment for residents of that Black township who have HIV/AIDS, is a project to which I have made three consecutive field trips—the most recent, in October–November 2005, was the one on which I was accompanied by Judith Swazey. And in 2006, I traveled to Luxembourg, where I was the only non-MSF person invited to attend the so-called "La Mancha" conference of MSF on March 8–10. This meeting was a culminating point in the process that MSF's International Council had launched in November 2004, with the aim of reevaluating the operating framework of the organization, and revisiting its foundational principles in the light of what was referred to as "the external challenges and internal changes" that had had a profound impact on MSF and its functioning since 1995, when the last such organization-wide process of self-examination and debate had taken place in Chantilly, France. Experiencing and reflecting on some of the attributes of MSF that are embodied in Khayelitsha and "La Mancha," in relationship to those of American bioethics, has heightened our critical awareness of certain traits of U.S. bioethics that we have consistently found troubling.

Making comparisons between MSF and U.S. bioethics may seem incongruous, far-fetched or, at best, a juxtaposition that results solely from the simultaneity of my relationship with both of them. But, in fact, as I have written elsewhere, they have corresponding origins, and certain features in common:

[B]ioethics emerged in the United States and MSF originated in France in the late 1960s and early 1970s during a time of reverberating social protest in both societies, spearheaded by the…"student revolution," and a cascade of "liberation" and "rights" movements, including women's, antiwar, and human rights movements, [and] the civil rights movement in the United States, and in Europe, especially in France, [by what historian Tony Judt terms] "tiers-mondisme," or "third-world-ism" (Judt 1992: 284–286), precipitated by the widespread occurrence of anticolonialist movements in Africa, Asia, and Latin America. A significant number of the founder-leaders and the first-generation members of MSF and American bioethics had been intensively involved in these movements. (R. C. Fox 2005b: 301)

They brought to the new realms of humanitarian and bioethical activity that they initiated their fervid commitment to some of the values on which their previous engagements were based. Foremost among these shared values is their mutual espousal of the precept of "universalism." MSF's very name—"sans frontières," "without borders"—expresses the transnational, transsocietal, and transcultural vision of universalism on which it was founded. U.S. bioethics' universalistic outlook is articulated in the conception of "the common morality" to which many bioethicists, including some of its most prominent figures, subscribe. Both U.S. bioethics and MSF express their basic values in the form of principles.[1] Both are confronted with the challenge of conceptually and empirically reconciling their universalism with recognition of the particularistic social and cultural differences that exist within and between societies. And both are centrally involved with medicine and medical care—albeit in different ways—and with associated moral issues that are matters of high public interest and media attention, and of major policy and political concern.

The Significance of Khayelitsha for American Bioethics

In an article that I coauthored with Dr. Eric Goemaere, the physician who is the head of mission for MSF programs in South Africa, we described the social and medical situation in Khayelitsha in the following way:

Khayelitsha is an enclave of some 500,000 inhabitants, most of whom live in corrugated-iron shacks, without running water or electricity. Unemployment is extremely high; crime and violence (including robbery, domestic violence, rape, and murder) are rampant. The general prevalence of HIV/AIDS is 26%, measured among pregnant women. The tuberculosis rate is one of the world's highest for open-space sites (1,380/100,000). Unsurprisingly,

TB/HIV coinfection is very high too: 63% of those with TB are also infected with HIV. (R. C. Fox and Goemaere 2006: 302)

These data not only reflect in microcosm the epidemic proportions of HIV/AIDS in South Africa where, out of a national population of some 45.5 million people, as many as 5.2 million are currently HIV-positive—more than in any other country in the world. Viewed in a global framework, they represent what has become "the most serious…threat to the health of humankind": "the eruption and spread of a multitude of 'old' and 'new' infectious diseases…among which the HIV/AIDS pandemic has had the most catastrophic consequences,"[2] but which also includes the "return" of tuberculosis and of malaria, often in multi-resistant forms, and sporadic outbreaks of epidemics of diseases such as cholera, measles, and polio (S. H. Benatar and R. C. Fox 2005: 345).

In Khayelitsha, the "emergence and re-emergence" of infectious diseases, and their relationship to adverse historical, social, economic, and political factors is not a remote, public health abstraction. It is intrinsic to the throbbing, everyday life of the township. It has thousands of human faces. It is accompanied by pervasive suffering, and by valiant individual and group efforts to overcome the stigma of HIV/AIDS, to survive the ravages of disease, poverty, and violence, to have access to needed health care, and to attain a sufficient modicum of human support and of well-being to be able to affirm, in the words of the Xhosa language, "I feel strong!" (R. C. Fox 2005a: 73–74). It also entails a constant, dilemma-ridden struggle on the part of health professionals to provide ARV treatment to as many persons with HIV/AIDS as possible, in a way that is fair and just, and that maximizes its medical benefits, while minimizing its harm (R. C. Fox and Goemaere 2006).

Our exposure to these realities of Khayelitsha has intensified the moral disquietude that we have always felt about what we regard as the restricted and skewed range of medical developments and problems on which U.S. bioethics has concentrated. As we discussed at some length in several of the preceding chapters, American bioethicists have devoted a great deal of attention to issues associated with advances in "high-tech" medicine, such as modalities of life support and intensive care, organ transplantation, assisted reproduction technologies, gene therapy and other forms of genetic engineering, and the prospect of human cloning. This has overshadowed bioethicists' consideration of ethical questions raised by inequalities in health and in access to health care in American society; and it has overridden engagement in serious ethical reflection on the global implications of the growing disparities in life expectancy and health between societies, to which the rise and spread of communicable diseases are major contributors. In fact, with some notable exceptions, U.S. bioethics is narrowly "American-ocentric."[3]

The preoccupation of American bioethics with issues that are located in the United States, and with the way that they present themselves and are played out in this society, is nationally understandable and culturally appropriate in certain respects; and it is not surprising that its outlook reflects the limitations, along with the strengths, of a predominantly American perspective. We would contend, however, that in the globally connected world of which the United States is a powerful and affluent part, it is not only in the self-interest of this country but also one of its special responsibilities to be highly attuned and responsive to the threats, the tragic human concomitants, and the catastrophic societal consequences of HIV/ AIDS and other infectious diseases, wherever in the world they are occurring (S. H. Benatar and R. C. Fox 2005).[4] Our visits to the township of Khayelitsha have reinforced our conviction that this enlarged state of awareness and sense of responsibility ought to occupy an important place in U.S. bioethics; that the scope of its intellectual geography, and the outreach of its moral agenda, should extend beyond its own national boundaries; and that it should be more centrally and deeply involved with the kinds of suffering and the issues of social justice of which Khayelitsha is a living and death-fraught emanation.

There is another phenomenon in Khayelitsha that has pertinence for U.S. bioethics: the kind of relationship to the pharmaceutical industry that MSF has established, which has contributed to the capacity of the Khayelitsha HIV/AIDS program to continually expand the number of patients it enrolls for ARV treatment. A dearth of ARV drugs, or of sufficient funds to purchase them, is no longer a major deterrent for the project.[5] This is partly a consequence of MSF's catalytic leadership in raising public awareness of the fact that life-saving medicines are not available and affordable to people in many of the countries in which they work. Using the money that MSF received in 1999 when it was awarded the Nobel Peace Prize, it launched an ongoing campaign for access to essential medicines:

A key focus of their advocacy has entailed demonstrating and speaking out about the part that drug companies have played in this "lack of access" through their profit-oriented, exorbitant pricing of drugs; their blockage of the distribution of less expensive generic drugs by the self-protective maintenance of patents on drugs that they manufacture;…their reluctance to produce, sell, or try to develop effective drugs for diseases…that primarily affect the poor and are the most common killers in developing countries; [and their] emphasis on tapping into more lucrative…markets by developing drugs for conditions such as heart disease, obesity, and impotence. MSF also organized and convened the Drugs for Neglected Diseases Initiative, a framework for experts around the world to tackle these matters. The working group's analysis not only held the pharmaceutical industry responsible for the access to essential medicines, neglected diseases, and "orphan drug" problems, but also the public sector for failing to set up "solidarity mechanisms" to counter this [state of affairs]. (R. C. Fox 2005b: 302)

Both locally and internationally, MSF has played an important and effective role in the reduction of the prices of ARV drugs and in the suspension of patents on them that previously impeded the development, manufacture, importation, and sale of their much less expensive generic equivalents in countries such as South Africa.[6] The advocacy by MSF has been a significant part of this accomplishment, which it has helped to bring about without soft-pedaling its criticism of drug firms, demonizing, or totally alienating them, while at the same time remaining faithful to its principles and steadfast in its commitments. In contrast, as we have recounted in chapter 11, U.S. bioethics has an inwardly embattled relationship to the pharmaceutical industry that divides its "liberal" and "conservative" members into polemicized confrontations over who among them is allied with drug firms, and who is not, with what ethical implications; and it is a relationship that appears to have had little effect on the policies and conduct of the industry. It seems to us that there is much of value that American bioethicists could learn from MSF and Khayelitsha in this regard.

MSF's work in Khayelitsha has also involved collaboration with the Treatment Action Campaign (TAC), a South African civic organization that developed from the anti-apartheid movement. Since its founding in 1998, "through the courts, the media, the Internet, widely publicized acts of civil disobedience, grassroots HIV/AIDS awareness campaigns conducted in clinics, schools, factories, community centers, and churches, ... door-to-door visits in black African townships; and by networking with other national and international civic organizations," TAC has led a powerful struggle to:

raise consciousness about the HIV/AIDS epidemic; promote openness about it; reduce the stigma associated with it; implement educational programs to lower its incidence, prevent its transmission, and foster "treatment literacy"; lobby the pharmaceutical industry to provide cheap anti-retroviral (ARV) drugs…; persuade the South African government to allow generic drugs to be imported and to be produced locally…; and, above all, pressure the government to enact a national HIV/AIDS prevention and treatment program that includes ARV therapy for every inhabitant of the country who needs it. (R. C. Fox 2005a: 70)

Médecins Sans Frontières has participated with TAC in some of their activist endeavors. But it has been aware that without thoughtful self-monitoring, its engagement with TAC could lead to the sort of politicization of its HIV/AIDS program, and its presence in South Africa, that would violate one of its cardinal principles—what it describes in its so-called "Chantilly document" as its "independence of spirit":

The independence of MSF is characterized above all by an independence of spirit which is a condition for independent analysis and action, namely the freedom of choice in its operations, and the duration and means of carrying them out. This independence is displayed at both the level of the organization and of each volunteer.

MSF strives for strict independence from all structures or powers, whether political, religious, economic, or other. MSF refuses to serve or be used as an instrument by any government.

The concern for independence is also financial. MSF endeavors to ensure a maximum of private resources, to diversify its institutional donors, and, sometimes, to refuse financing that may affect its independence.

From their side, MSF volunteers are expected to be discreet and will abstain from linking or implicating MSF politically, institutionally or otherwise through personal acts or opinions.

The commitment of MSF members to making a continuous individual and organizational effort to remain "independent" in "thought and action" differentiates it sharply from the partisan entanglements in political ideology and politics that characterize U.S. bioethics in its present state, rent by the culture wars. This effort also calls into question the assertion made by Caplan that the political enmeshment of American bioethics is an understandable, unavoidable, and perhaps even desirable concomitant of the fact that the field has "matured into a position of power" (Caplan 2005). Médecins Sans Frontières has become a multinational association worth approximately €500 million, and employs more than 24,000 people in the field. It is developing assistance operations in some 70 countries, provides care for millions of patients in health centers, vaccinates hundreds of thousands of others against meningitis or measles, and undertakes more than 43,000 major surgical operations and 73,000 obstetrical deliveries a year. This organization, which receives support for 78 percent of its resources from more than 3 million donors and has been recognized with a Nobel Peace Prize, is indisputably more "powerful" than U.S. bioethics. Nevertheless, it is unwavering in its resolve to maintain "political neutrality," to "transcend political ideology," and to "not be associated with any political party or tendency, either in headquarter countries or mission countries" (Eric Goemaere, personal communication, May 25, 2006). And it has developed social control processes to fortify and implement this resolve. "[P]aradoxically, whilst the solicitations [for its] opinion…on issues…multiply, … MSF has become much less hasty…[and] more prudent…in the formulation of political recommendations and solutions" (Buissonnière 2006: 2).

"La Mancha," U.S. Bioethics, Self-Questioning, and "Principles"

The March 2006 "La Mancha" conference in Luxembourg, and the preparatory interaction, discussion, and communication that preceded it, which began in November 2004, exemplify MSF's self-scrutiny, self-criticism, and what James Orbinski, former president of MSF's International Council (1998–2001), has termed its "culture of debate" (J. Orbiniski, personal communication, April 11, 2002). "The belly of MSF is open," was the surgical image that Rowan Gillies (president of MSF's International Council at the time of the meeting) used in his introductory statement to the assemblage.

"La Mancha"—the name that MSF gave to the conference and to the process leading up to it—encapsulates other, related attributes of MSF. It intentionally connects the organization and its members with the chivalrous escapades and battles (including those with windmills) of Don Quixote, the hero of Miguel de Cervantes's romance. In this metaphoric way, it expresses both the ardor of MSF's dedication to humanitarian ideals, and its self-directed, ironic wit about the exalted nature of those ideals, its supposed nobility in pursuing them, and its hope that through its actions (in the words of the theme song from the musical play "The Man From La Mancha"), it can "right the unrightable wrong."[7] Throughout the conference, MSF's capacity for self-examination and self-mockery was on display in the flow of the captioned cartoons, drawn extemporaneously by the organization's official cartoonist, which were projected onto a publicly viewed screen in synchrony with the unfolding of the meeting. They provided a satirical running commentary on major themes of the conference, and on key utterances as they occurred.

Nothing quite like this complex of elements characterizes U.S. bioethics—that is, MSF's combination of seriousness of purpose and its comedic sense of itself, its foibles, limitations, and mistakes; its great diversity of opinions and passionate, ongoing internal debate; its "spirit of independence" and yet (to use MSF's terminology) the "coherence," and the degree of "cohesion" that, with considerable struggle, it has attained. In comparison, mainstream American bioethics seems disinclined to be self-questioning, entrenched in its conviction about the "rightness" of its perspective and predominant conceptual framework (particularly in relationship to "conservative" and "neoconservative" thinkers), overly impressed with its importance and influence, and unduly solemn.

It is also illuminating to comparatively examine the differences in the way that the La Mancha conference approached a reconsideration of MSF's core principles articulated in its Charter and Chantilly document, and how American bioethicists "revisited" the fundamental "Belmont principles" on the 20th and 25th anniversaries of their issuance. As we described in chapter 5, the various meetings that were organized around *Belmont* celebrated the historical import of this triad of bioethical principles (respect for persons, beneficence, and justice). Tributes were paid to them because of their enduring significance as precepts underlying ethically conducted research involving human subjects, and their impact on practice, public policy, and federal regulations. In addition, their relationship to Tom Beauchamp's and James Childress's four principles of biomedical ethics (autonomy, nonmaleficence, beneficence, and justice), which became cornerstones of the chief conceptual framework of U.S. bioethics, was recognized. The atmosphere surrounding these meetings sometimes bordered on veneration for the principles.

The most intellectually searching of these events was the "*Belmont* Revisited" conference held in 1999. One of its intents was to have a "conversation" about whether, with the passage of 20 years since the principles were formulated, some alterations in them might be warranted. Each of the presenters made suggestions about modifications that converged on a consideration of the possibility of narrowing the range of the principle of respect for persons, expanding the scope of the principle of justice, and adding a new principle—"respect for community"—that would respond to "concerns about relationships," and about the heavy weight attached to individualism by the principle of respect for persons. And in the epilogue that he wrote in the published volume of papers that grew out of the presentations made at the *Belmont* conference, James Childress affirmed: "We can learn much from various efforts to apply, modify, expand, restrict, supplement, and reinterpret these principles as we seek to determine the best framework for analyzing and directing biomedical research and practice" (Childress 2005: 251). However, in the end, allegiance to the *Belmont* principles in their unaltered, original form, and something akin to pride in their essential "correctness" and in their more than local or temporary validity, prevailed over whatever impetus existed to modify them.

A premise of the La Mancha conference was that the "basic principles" of MSF "remain those expressed in the Charter and Chantilly documents," and that "[t]hese principles should be referred to when taking and reviewing decisions."[8] Thus, it was predicated on the same kind of respect for basic principles as the *Belmont* anniversary meetings. However, in contradistinction to *Belmont*, it was also assumed from the outset that because of the magnitude of the changes that had taken place "in the contextual reality" in which MSF was functioning, serious attention would have to be given to "adjustments" or alterations that might need to be given to the principles. The changes that they thought would have to be taken into account included the great growth that MSF had undergone, the new projects and commitments on which it had embarked—especially the creation of programs to prevent and treat the "life-long" pandemic disease, AIDS—and the momentous medical, economic, political, cultural, and religious events that had occurred globally, which had affected the conditions surrounding the humanitarian action in which it was engaged.[9] "The Chantilly texts will be revised, fortunately," one of the participants in the Luxembourg meeting declared:

Chantilly was about clarifying the Charter and adapting it to the contexts we were working in at the time. I think we do things completely differently now. We work on diseases, on AIDS; refugees have virtually disappeared [from our programs].... If we want a text that reflects our reality, we have to seriously reconsider the Chantilly document. (Eric Goemaere, quoted in Delafortrie 2006: 8)

No comparable reference was made in the Belmont gathering to the ways that ethical principles might have to address and be responsive to the empirical world in which conduct takes place—especially in the face of major changes that may have occurred in what MSF terms "contextual reality."

What could be described as the "anti-reverential" attitude toward the Charter and Chantilly principles that was endorsed, and even encouraged at the "La Mancha" conference is another way in which it differed strikingly from "Belmont." At various points during the Luxembourg meeting, admonitions were voiced about the drawbacks of "defending the principles [as] an end in itself," "mechanically" applying them, or treating them as "sacrosanct." The latter has "a religious tone," someone disapprovingly commented, eliciting sympathetic, generalized laughter from the participants when he declared that "[w]e should have the right to violate every principle!" "We had better be violating the principles all the time," someone else responded. "They are not vehicles for purity."

The "La Mancha Agreement" that emerged from the Luxembourg meeting, the president of MSF's International Council explained, "should not be seen as a replacement of the 'Chantilly Principles,' but as building on the principles in the Charter and Chantilly, and should be read in conjunction with these documents." "There was recognition at the conference," he went on to say, "that there is a need to pursue a new description of these principles; however that is another process":

It was recognized that the "La Mancha Agreement" should not be prescriptive, and could never be comprehensive, but should describe our current approaches, provide an opportunity to learn from our successes and failures, reaffirm what we value, and provide an impetus and framework to help us move forward. (Gillies 2006: 1)

As the foregoing indicates, MSF is as intellectually and morally committed to its set of principles as U.S. bioethics is to theirs. It could even be said that MSF's commitment is the greater, because it strives to implement its principles in and through its humanitarian action, which entails interventions that carry with them considerable risk. Its independent and innovational spirit does not extend to capriciously changing the founding precepts of its Charter, or their elaboration in the Chantilly document. It was anticipated at the Luxembourg meeting that whatever alterations might eventually be made in these principles would require more long-term, thoughtful work that would have to continue after the La Mancha conference ended. I cannot predict whether big changes in MSF's principles will be forthcoming. But at this juncture (Summer 2007), it appears that the organization has moved in the direction of "considering the applicability of its existing principles" through ongoing informal discussion, rather than engaging in the formal process of drafting a new text. In any case, as one of its long-term, influential members affirmed, MSF does "not take [the Charter and Chantilly documents] as 'bibles,' but simply as guides, whose interpretations have to be permanently re-discussed."

It seems to me that the "diversity of opinions and ongoing internal debate," which characterize MSF, and which it regards as among its major strengths, in combination with its responsiveness to its lived experiences in the field, and to the larger historical context of which they are a part, dispose it more than American bioethics to questioningly reviewing its principles, and seriously contemplating modifying them. In this respect, American bioethics appears more rigidly and statically sealed into itself, more self-confirming, and more absolutist.

Judith Swazey and I have always been surprised by these attributes of U.S. bioethics. This is partly because we had expected a field that is intellectually grounded in philosophy to be self-searching a quality that we not only esteem, but one that we consider an essential component of both objectivity and perspicacity. It is rather startling, and in a way paradoxical, to have discovered that a group like MSF, which is continuously immersed in front-lines action, is more argumentatively thoughtful and self-critical than philosophically oriented American bioethics appears to be.

A Final Comment

This afterword was written neither with the intention of idealizing MSF, nor of demeaning bioethics. In keeping with their value system, members of MSF would chide me, in their distinctively humorous way—as they have—for exaggerating their virtues, or being too tolerant of their shortcomings. This is illustrated by an e-mail exchange that I had with the president of one of MSF's sections. He had written to tell me that he would be interested in my "perception" of what had transpired at the La Mancha conference. When he received my response, he thanked me for my "thoughts on the Luxembourg meeting," which he deemed "very interesting" because they constituted "an outsider, and at the same time... insider point of view." "I will try to comment on it," he wrote; but "first of all, I am not sure that you are so impartial when you look at us.... I feel sometimes you are very (too?) indulgent with us.... But of course I cannot blame you for that!" It is hard to imagine being reproached in a comparable manner by American bioethicists for not being sufficiently critical of them.

Furthermore, my attendance at the Luxembourg meeting brought me face-to-face with the extent to which MSF feels that it has violated its "sans-frontières" principles of impartiality and non-discrimination, "diversity and inclusion," and "associative participation" through the way that it has been treating its so-called "national" staff—personnel described in the "La Mancha Agreement" document as "our colleagues who live and work in the countries of intervention," and who perform the "majority [of the] individual humanitarian acts [that are] central to the work of MSF."[10] "We have not tried to understand who they are and the nature of their relationship with MSF," it was admitted; and they have been excluded from "involvement in decision-making and access to the associative life of MSF." Strong feelings of shock and indignation about this were openly voiced in plenary sessions; and it was decided that the "issue must be urgently and concretely addressed," and remedied. Thus, the candor with which MSF discusses what it regards as its "failures" has given me access to knowledge about some of its deficiencies.

As for our perspective on U.S. bioethics, although we have implied that some bioethicists have exhibited a tendency to overestimate its influence, the criticisms of the field that we have expressed here, and in numerous other connections throughout this book, are indicative of the fact that we take it seriously, and consider its existence to be a phenomenon of considerable sociological significance on the American scene. If, as we wrote more than two decades ago, U.S. bioethics is "an indicator of the general state of American ideas, values, and beliefs, of our collective self-knowledge, and our understanding of other societies and cultures" (Fox and Swazey 1984: 360), then, in our opinion, it is not only important that it be appreciatively recognized. It is also socially and morally crucial for U.S. bioethics to be closely and critically examined—and self-examined.

Notes

1. The principles of MSF are set forth in its founding Charter, and in what it calls its Chantilly document. The MSF Charter, the Chantilly document, and also the text of the La Mancha Agreement, which is discussed in this afterword, are all public documents. The text of the Charter is available on the Web sites of MSF in the various countries in which it has offices. The Web site of MSF in the United States is www.doctorswithout borders.org. The Chantilly document and the La Mancha Agreement are available upon request from Doctors Without Borders/Médicins Sans Frontières, 333 Seventh Ave. 2nd floor, New York, NY 10001, USA.
2. An estimated 25 or more new infectious diseases have made their appearance during the past 27 years, of which HIV/AIDS has been the most devastating.
3. Daniel Callahan, Norman Daniels, Ruth Macklin, Patricia Marshall, and Angela Wasunna are among the American bioethicists whose thought and writing encompass HIV/AIDS, infectious diseases, developing societies, and global health.

   Through his example as a physician-anthropologist caring for poor patients in Haiti, Peru, Rwanda, and Russia, as well as in Boston, and in his writing, Paul Farmer has made some of the most impassioned statements about the gravity of the fact that, in his opinion, U.S. bioethics has had "almost nothing to say" about the injustice and the ravaging human consequences of the growth of medical, scientific, economic, and social inequality on a global scale (Farmer 2003: 196–212).

   In sharp contrast to his American colleagues, the bioethicist who has written the most consistently and fervently about moral, particularly social-justice issues associated with global health, infectious disease, the HIV/AIDS pandemic, and the delivery of health care to the poor and the vulnerable—especially in developing countries—is the South African physician Solomon R. Benatar.
4. "I believe with great wealth comes great responsibility—the responsibility to give back to society and make sure those resources are given back in the best possible way, to those in need" is the statement that Bill Gates, chairman and cofounder of Microsoft, made in announcing the fact that he will be stepping down from his day-to-day role with the company by July 2008, in order to work full time for the Bill and Melinda Gates Foundation that he founded with his wife, which focuses on global health and education (Amanda Cantrell, CNNMoney.com, June 16, 2006). Gates's personal statement is relevant to why we think the United States, which is the wealthiest society in the world, and its institutionalized form of bioethics, have a special responsibility to be attentively and responsively concerned about disparities in health and health care within, among, and between populations and societies the world over.
5. Initially, the Khayelitsha program was mainly supported by private funds from different MSF sections, Belgian and Danish Cooperation funds, the Letten Foundation in Nor-

way, and public funds from the provincial government of the Western Cape of South Africa. At present, 80 percent of its funding comes from this provincial government.

It is shortage of staff rather than restrictions in funding that now limits the number of patients who are enrolled for treatment. This shortage is due in part to the fact that many South African physicians and nurses have migrated to the United Kingdom, Canada, Australia, and the United States, where they have been able to find professional positions for which they can earn a higher income than would be possible in South Africa. This flow of African doctors and nurses to Europe, North America, and Australia is a problematic phenomenon that exists throughout the continent of Africa. In addition, the HIV virus is also contributing to the scarcity of available health professionals, many of whom have been infected with AIDS.

6. Originally, the three drugs that compose the ARV treatment used in Khayelitsha were mainly imported from a state-controlled Brazilian company. Subsequently, they were chiefly supplied by Indian companies. Most recently, this first-line, three-drug regimen "has been offered to public services for US $15 per month by Aspen Pharmacare of South Africa. Aspen, based in Johannesburg, is the largest drug company in Africa. It has the permission of GlaxoSmith Kline and Boehringer-Ingleheim to produce generic versions of AIDS drugs with valid patents for the South African market" (R. C. Fox and Goemaere 2006: 312).

7. All the persons who attended the La Mancha conference received T-shirts with the full text of this song "The Impossible Dream," printed on their backs.

8. The major principles of MSF are rooted in its conception of itself as "an organization based on volunteerism," which operates as a "solidarity"-based "association" dedicated to contributing to "the protection of life and the alleviation of suffering out of respect for human dignity." "Linked to the idea of volunteerism, the associative character of MSF permits an openness towards our societies and a capacity for questioning ourselves." "MSF brings care to people in precarious situations," its principles state, and "consists of providing curative and preventive care to people wherever they may be," and whatever the cause of their suffering and need be it warfare within or between nation-states, epidemics, poverty, disenfranchisement, oppression, persecution, terror, exile, exodus, or natural disasters such as earthquakes, floods, hurricanes, and droughts. The principle of "impartiality is fundamental to the mission of MSF and is inextricably linked to [its principle of] "independence of action." "Impartiality is defined by the principles of non-discrimination and proportionality"—"non-discrimination in regard to politics, race, religion, sex or other similar criteria"; and "proportionality of assistance as it relates to the degree of needs—those in the most serious and immediate danger will receive priority." "MSF does not take sides in armed conflicts and in this sense adheres to the principle of neutrality. However, in extreme cases where volunteers are witness to mass violations of Human Rights, MSF may resort to denunciation as a last available means in helping the populations it assists." "Witnessing" ("*témoignage*") is another "integral" MSF principle. The intention of witnessing is to "improve the situation for populations in danger. It is expressed through the presence of volunteers with people in danger as they provide medical care which implies being near and witnessing; a duty to raise public awareness about these people; [and] the possibility to openly criticize or denounce breaches of international conventions." (The latter is considered to be "a last resort used when MSF volunteers witness mass violations of human rights, including forced displacements of populations, *refoulement* [repression] or forced return of refugees, genocide, crimes against humanity and war crimes.") "Médecins Sans Frontières subscribes to the principles of Human Rights and

International Humanitarian Law. This includes the recognition of: the duty to respect the fundamental rights and freedoms of each individual, including the right to physical and mental integrity and the freedom of thought and movement, as outlined in the 1949 Universal Declaration of Human Rights; the right of victims to receive assistance, as well as the rights of humanitarian organizations to provide assistance." "Faced with populations in distress, MSF has an obligation to mobilize and develop its resources in a manner that fulfills the principles of 'accountability' and 'transparency.' Aiming at maximum quality and effectiveness, MSF is committed to optimizing its means and abilities, to directly controlling its aid, and to regularly evaluating its effects. In a clear and open manner, MSF assumes the responsibility to account for its actions to its beneficiaries as well as to its donors."

The quoted phrases and sentences in the foregoing statement of MSF's chief principles come from its Chantilly document.

9. Among the changes and revisions in the principles that were considered at the La Mancha conference were:
   - The possibility of adding a principle of "humanity" to them.
   - More strongly affirming that an "inextricable link" exists between the "medical and humanitarian" bases of MSF's action, and its principle of *témoignage.*"
   - A principles-based statement about the "inherent risk" that MSF incurs in carrying out its work, its commitment to reducing the risk, chiefly "by promoting the acceptance of [its] presence and action as an impartial humanitarian organization," and about the fact that "MSF will not encourage individuals to take more risk than the organization is prepared to assume."
   - Now that most of the persons who work for and with MSF receive remuneration, a modification of the Chantilly statement that MSF is an organization of volunteers, who have made a "nonlucrative commitment" to "people in precarious situations" and to the "associative life" of the organization, which will assert nonetheless that "a volunteer spirit" is still a basic principle.

10. "National" staff, indigenous to the array of countries in which MSF has projects, consist of some 22,640 persons who fill nearly 92 percent of all field positions, as compared with only 2,026 of so-called "expatriate" or "international" staff, who occupy 8.2 percent of these positions.

Appendix
The Acadia Institute Bioethics Project:
Interviews and Advisory Committee Members

Our initial proposal to the National Science Foundation (NSF) for the project entitled "Bioethics in American Society," as we realized when it was submitted, was ambitious both in terms of its scope and in the number of interviews we planned to conduct as one of our sources of primary data and for archival deposition. Following the recommendations of the proposal's reviewers and our program officer at the NSF, we "downsized" the scope of the study and the number of interviews, bringing them more in line with the length of the project and funding for personnel and travel. As the reviewers also suggested, we formed a small advisory committee, whose members agreed, when requested, to review and comment on various aspects of our work as the study progressed. Near the end of the project, we convened the committee for a one-day meeting to discuss some of the major themes and findings that had emerged from our research, which we had articulated in short papers that we had prepared for this purpose and circulated in advance.

The interviews that we conducted constituted a type of social science research covered by the federal regulations for the protection of human research subjects, which required the review of our interview protocol and consent form by an institutional review board (IRB). Because the Acadia Institute, as a small free-standing research organization, did not have an IRB or an affiliation with an institutional IRB, we received permission to have the protocol and consent form reviewed by Dr. Robert J. Levine at Yale University School of Medicine, one of the country's leading authorities on human subjects research and IRBs. Dr. Levine recommended, and we adopted, several changes in the protocol and consent form, which in turn were approved by the NSF. When we later received a publication support grant from the National Library of Medicine, after the interviews had been completed, the National Institutes of Health stipulated that funding was contingent on a review by a full IRB of the interview protocol, consent form, and use of interview materials in a book or other publications. At the principal investigator's request, that review was undertaken by the IRB at Eastern Maine Medical Center, which unanimously approved these materials.

We conducted a total of 45 face-to-face interviews, which ranged in length from 2 to over 10 hours. Prospective interviewees were sent an introductory letter about the project and the nature and purposes of the interviews, and a consent form, which they were asked to return if they were willing to meet with us. We took detailed field notes during the interviews, and all but two were tape-recorded and transcribed. After initial editing by project staff, the interviewees were sent a copy of their transcript for review and further editing and corrections, both for our use and for archival deposition. Those attending the day-long advisory committee meeting in September 2000 also were given the option of reviewing the edited transcript prepared by project staff, which most declined to do.

Project Interviewees and Advisory Committee Members

Judith Andre, PhD, Department of Philosophy and Center for Ethics and Humanities in the Life Sciences, Michigan State University
    Date of interview: 9/15/98
    Interviewer: Judith P. Swazey
George Annas, JD, MPH, Department of Health Law, Boston University School of Public Health*[1]
    Date of interview:12/16/97
    Interviewer: Judith P. Swazey
Margaret Battin, PhD, Department of Philosophy, University of Utah and Adjunct Professor, Division of Medical Ethics, University of Utah School of Medicine*
    Date of interview: 6/23/98
    Interviewer: Judith P. Swazey
Tom Beauchamp, PhD, Kennedy Institute of Ethics, Georgetown University*
    Date of interview: 3/10/00
    Interviewer: Judith P. Swazey
Baruch Brody, PhD, Center for Medical Ethics and Health Policy, Baylor University*
    Date of interview: 11/19/98
    Interviewer: Judith P. Swazey
Howard Brody, MD, PhD, Center for Ethics and Humanities in the Life Sciences, Michigan State University*
    Date of interview: 9/14/98
    Interviewer: Judith P. Swazey

Daniel Callahan, PhD, The Hastings Center*
    Date of interview: 5/11/00
    Interviewer: Judith P. Swazey
Arthur Caplan, PhD, Center for Bioethics, University of Pennsylvania*
    Dates of interviews: 10/15/97; 11/21/97; 1/16/98; 3/2/98; 5/24/99
    Interviewers: Renée C. Fox and Judith P. Swazey; Renée C. Fox, Carla
    M. Messikomer, and Judith P. Swazey; Renée C. Fox and Carla M. Mes-
    sikomer; Renée C. Fox and Carla M. Messikomer; Renée C. Fox and Carla
    M. Messikomer
Alexander M. Capron, LLB, Henry W. Bruce University Professor of Law and
    Medicine, The Law School, University of Southern California*
    Date of interview: 6/17 and 6/18/98
    Interviewer: Judith P. Swazey
Ronald Carson, PhD, Institute for Medical Humanities, University of Texas
    Galveston*
    Date of interview: 11/18/98 and 6/15/99
    Interviewers: Judith P. Swazey; Renée C. Fox and Judith P. Swazey
James Childress, PhD, Department of Religious Studies, University of Virginia*
    Date of interview: 3/29/99
    Interviewers: Renée C. Fox and Judith P. Swazey
K. Danner Clouser, PhD, Professor of Medical Humanities Emeritus, Hershey
    Medical School*
    Date of interview: 12/17/98
    Interviewers: Carla M. Messikomer and Judith P. Swazey
Bette Crigger, PhD, The Hastings Center*
    Date of interview: 5/12/00
    Interviewers: Carla M. Messikomer and Judith P. Swazey
Norman Daniels, PhD, Department of Philosophy, Tufts University*
    Date of interview: 5/14/99
    Interviewer: Judith P. Swazey
Elliot N. Dorff, PhD, Professor of Philosophy, University of Judaism*
    Date of interview: 6/15/98
    Interviewer: Judith P. Swazey
H. Tristram Engelhardt, MD, PhD, Center for Medical Ethics and Health Policy,
    Baylor University*
    Date of interview: 6/14/99
    Interviewers: Renée C. Fox and Judith P. Swazey
Ruth Faden, MPH, PhD, The Bioethics Institute, Johns Hopkins University*
    Date of interview: 3/11/99
    Interviewer: Judith P. Swazey
John Fletcher, PhD, Clinical Bioethics Program, University of Virginia*
    Date of interview: 3/22/99
    Interviewers: Renée C. Fox and Judith P. Swazey

Norman Fost, MD, Program in Medical Ethics, University of Wisconsin School of Medicine*
Date of interview: 6/13/00
Interviewer: Judith P. Swazey

Leonard H. Glantz, JD, Associate Dean and Professor of Health Law, Boston University School of Public Health*
Date of interview: 12/15/97
Interviewer: Judith P. Swazey

James Gustafson, PhD, Woodruff Professor of Comparative Studies and Religion, Emeritus, Emory University
Date of interview: 6/17 and 6/18/99
Interviewer: Renée C. Fox and Judith P. Swazey

Albert R. Jonsen, STM, PhD, Department of Medical History and Ethics, University of Washington*
Date of interview: 6/19 and 6/22/98
Interviewer: Judith P. Swazey

Eric Juengst, PhD, Center for Biomedical Ethics, Case Western Reserve University*
Date of interview: 9/16/98
Interviewers: Carla M. Messikomer and Judith P. Swazey

Leon Kass, MD, PhD, Committee on Social Thought, University of Chicago*
Date of interview: 6/16/00
Interviewer: Judith P. Swazey

Patricia King, JD, The Law Center, Georgetown University*
Date of interview: 11/11/99
Interviewer: Judith P. Swazey

Ruth Macklin, PhD, Department of Epidemiology and Social Medicine, Albert Einstein College of Medicine*
Date of interview: 5/17/99
Interviewers: Renée C. Fox and Carla M. Messikomer

Patricia Marshall, PhD, Department of Medical Humanities, Loyola University*
Date of interview: 6/20/00
Interviewers: Carla M. Messikomer and Judith P. Swazey

Martin Marty, PhD, Fairfax M. Cone Distinguished Service Professor, University of Chicago*
Date of interview: 6/21/00
Interviewers: Carla M. Messikomer and Judith P. Swazey

Charles McCarthy, PhD, Office for Protection from Research Risks, NIH (Ret.), Richmond, Virginia*
Date of interview: 11/9/99
Interviewer: Judith P. Swazey

Glenn McGee, PhD, Center for Bioethics, University of Pennsylvania*
Date of interview: 11/18/97
Interviewers: Renée C. Fox, Carla M. Messikomer, and Judith P. Swazey

Eric Meslin, PhD, National Bioethics Advisory Committee, Rockville, Md.*
  Date of interviews: 3/19/98; 3/10/00
  Interviewers: Carla M. Messikomer and Judith P. Swazey; Judith P. Swazey
Barbara Mishkin, JD, Hogan and Hartson, Washington, D.C.*
  Date of interview: 3/18/98
  Interviewers: Carla M. Messikomer and Judith P. Swazey
Thomas Murray, PhD, Center for Biomedical Ethics, Case Western Reserve University*
  Date of interview: 11/20/98
  Interviewer: Judith P. Swazey
Laurence O'Connell, PhD, STD, Park Ridge Center for the Study of Health, Faith,
  and Ethics*
  Date of interview: 6/20/00
  Interviewers: Carla M. Messikomer and Judith P. Swazey
Edmund Pellegrino, MD, Center for Clinical Bioethics, Georgetown University
  Medical Center
  Date of interview: 3/25/99
  Interviewers: Renée C. Fox and Judith P. Swazey
Warren Reich, STD, Georgetown University School of Medicine*
  Date of interview: 3/29/00
  Interviewer: Judith P. Swazey
Hon. Paul Rogers, JD, Hogan and Hartson, Washington, D.C.
  Date of interview: 3/18/98
  Interviewers: Carla M. Messikomer and Judith P. Swazey
Mark Siegler, MD, McClean Center for Clinical Ethics, University of Chicago
  Hospitals*
  Date of interview: 6/15/00
  Interviewer: Judith P. Swazey
Rob Streiffer, PhD, Program in Medical Ethics and Department of Philosophy,
  University of Wisconsin Madison*
  Date of interview: 6/13/00
  Interviewer: Judith P. Swazey
William Stubing, MDiv, The Greenwall Foundation
  Date of interview: 5/10/99
  Interviewers: Renée C. Fox and Carla M. Messikomer
Robert Veatch, PhD, Kennedy Institute of Ethics, Georgetown University*
  Date of interviews: 3/26/99; 11/8/99
  Interviewers: Renée C. Fox and Judith P. Swazey; Judith P. Swazey
LeRoy Walters, PhD, Kennedy Institute of Ethics, Georgetown University*
  Date of interview: 3/13/00
  Interviewer: Judith P. Swazey
Alan Weisbard, JD, Program in Medical Ethics, University of Wisconsin
  Date of interview: 5/5/00
  Interviewer: Judith P. Swazey

James Wind, PhD, The Alban Institute, Bethesda, Md.*
  Date of interview: 11/9/99
  Interviewer: Judith P. Swazey
Stuart Youngner, MD, Center for Biomedical Ethics, Case Western Reserve
  University*
  Date of interview: 9/17/98
  Interviewers: Carla M. Messikomer and Judith P. Swazey

Project Advisory Committee, September 8, 2000, Meeting Transcript

Participants

Daniel Callahan, The Hastings Center
Arthur Caplan, Center for Bioethics, University of Pennsylvania
Howard Kaye, PhD, Franklin and Marshall College
Victor Lidz, PhD, MCP-Hahnemann School of Medicine
Ruth Macklin, PhD, Albert Einstein College of Medicine
Robert Veatch, PhD, Kennedy Institute of Ethics, Georgetown University

Project Investigators

Renée C. Fox, PhD, Annenberg Professor of the Social Sciences Emerita, University of Pennsylvania
Carla M. Messikomer, PhD, The Acadia Institute
Judith P. Swazey, PhD, The Acadia Institute

Guest

Rachelle Hollander, PhD, Program Director, Societal Dimensions of Engineering,
  Science, and Technology, National Science Foundation

Notes

1. Transcripts of interviews marked with an *, and the transcript of the advisory committee meeting, are deposited at the National Reference Center for Bioethics Literature/Kennedy Institute of Ethics Library. Six interviews were not deposited, for the following reasons: two were not taped due to a malfunction of the recording equipment, although detailed written field notes were taken; two individuals requested that their interviews not be deposited; one, in our judgment, did not have sufficient content to warrant deposition; and one person did not review his transcript.

References

Agence France Presse. 1997. Scottish researchers produce first clone from adult animal. February 23.

Alexander, L. 1949. Medical science under dictatorship. *New England Journal of Medicine* 241 (July 14): 39–47.

Alexander, S. 1962. They decide who lives, who dies: Medical miracle puts a moral burden on a small community. *Life* 53 (Nov. 9): 102 ff.

———.1993. Thirty years ago. *The Hastings Center Report* 23 (6): S5.

Annas, G. J. 1988. *Judging Medicine*. Clifton, N.J.: Humana.

———. 1993. *Standard of care: The law of American bioethics*. New York: Oxford University Press.

———. 1997. Cloning: Crossing nature's boundaries. *Boston Globe* (March 2): D1–2.

———. 2004. American bioethics and human rights: The end of all our exploring. *Journal of Law, Medicine & Ethics* (Winter): 658–663.

———. 2005a. *American bioethics: Crossing human rights and health law boundaries*. New York: Oxford University Press.

———. 2005b. American bioethics after Nuremberg: Pragmatism, politics, and human rights. Lecture presented at Boston University, November 10.

Annas, G. J., S. Elias. 2004. Politics, morals and embryos: Can bioethics in the United States rise above politics? Commentary. *Nature* 431 (September): 19–20.

Annas, G. J., L. H. Glantz, and B. F. Katz. 1977. *Informed consent to human experimentation: The subject's dilemma*. Cambridge, MA: Ballinger Press.

Annas, G. J., and M. A. Grodin, eds. 1992. *The Nazi doctors and the Nuremberg code: Human rights in human experimentation*. New York: Oxford University Press.

Annas, G. J., S. A. Law, R. E. Rosenblatt, and K. R. Wing. 1990. *American health law*. Boston: Little, Brown and Company.

Appiah, K. A. 2006. *Cosmopolitanism: Ethics in a world of strangers.* New York: Norton.

Arras, J. 1991. Getting down to cases: The revival of casuistry in bioethics. *Journal of Medicine and Philosophy* 16:29–51.

Asad, T. 2005. Reflections on laicité and the public sphere. *Items and Issues* (Social Science Research Council) 5 (3): 1–12.

Associated Press. 1997a. Clinton proposes human cloning ban, more study. *Los Angeles Times* (June 10): 15.

———. 1997b. Clinton seeks to ban human cloning but not all experiments. *New York Times* 1997 (June 10): C4.

Atta Inaugurates Centre of Biomedical Ethics and Culture. 2004. *The News* (Karachi), Oct. 9.

Auerbach, S. 1971a. Bedeviling question: Who will play God? *Washington Post* (Oct. 17): A6.

———. 1971b. GU to study medicine's life and death decisions. *Washington Post* (Oct. 2): A1, 6.

Baker, R., ed. 1995. *The codification of medical morality: Historical and philosophical studies of the formalization of Western medical morality in the eighteenth and nineteenth centuries,* vol. 2. Dordrecht: Kluwer Academic Publishers.

———. 1998a. A theory of international bioethics: Multiculturalism, postmodernism, and the bankruptcy of fundamentalism. *Kennedy Institute of Ethics Journal* 8 (3): 201–232.

———. 1998b. A theory of international bioethics: The negotiable and non-negotiable. *Kennedy Institute of Ethics Journal* 8 (3): 233–274.

———. 2002. On being a bioethicist: A review of John H. Evans *Playing God?: Human genetic engineering and the rationalization of public bioethics debate.* University of Chicago Press. *American Journal of Bioethics* 2 (2): 65–99.

Baker, R., D. Porter, and R. Porter, eds. 1993. *The codification of medical morality: Historical and philosophical studies of the formalization of Western medical morality in the eighteenth and nineteenth centuries,* vol. 1. Dordrecht: Kluwer Academic Publishers.

Balance on the cloning issue: Clinton legislation offers some sensible middle ground. 1997. *Los Angeles Times* (June 12): 8.

Barker, V. L. 1987. *Health and human values: A ministry of theological inquiry and moral discourse.* Dallas, TX: United Ministries in Education.

Baszanger, I., and M. H. Salamagne. 2004. Soins palliatifs. In *Dictionnaire de la Pensée Médicale,* ed. D. Lecourt, 1058–1063. Paris: Presses Universitaires de France.

Bateman, S. 2002. Moraliser l'artifice: Religion et procréation assistée. Le cas du modèle CECOS. In *Religion et Sexualité,* ed. J. Maître and G. Michelat, 79–94. Paris: L'Harmattan.

———. 2004. L'expérience morale comme objet sociologique. *L'Année Sociologique* 54 (2): 389–412.

Bateman Novaes, S. 1979. La demande d'avortement. Paris: EHESS (Thèse de troisième cycle).

———. 1982. Les récidivistes. Numéro special sur la Libéralisation de l'avortement, dirigé par Paul Ladrière. *Revue française de sociologie.* 23 (3): 473–485.

———. 1992. Éthique et débat publique: De la responsibilité médicale en matière de procréation assistée. In *Pouvoir et légitimité: figures de l'espace publique,* vol. 3, dir. A. Cottereau and P. Ladrière, 155–176. Paris: Éditions de l'EHESS.

———. 1997. De la thérapeutique comme norme. *La Pensée* 312 (Oct.–Dec.): 21–32.

———. 1998. La bioéthique comme objet sociologique. *Cahiers Internationaux de Sociologie* 104:5–32.

Beauchamp, T. L. 2003. A defense of the common morality. Is there a common morality?, special issue. *Kennedy Institute of Ethics Journal* 13 (3): 259–274.

———. 2004. Does ethical theory have a future in bioethics? *Journal of Law, Medicine & Ethics* 32:209–217.

———. 2005a. The origins and evolution of the Belmont Report. In *Belmont Revisited: Ethical principles for research with human subjects*, ed. J. F. Childress, E. M. Meslin, and H. T. Shapiro, 12–25. Washington D.C.: Georgetown University Press.

———. 2005b. Reflections on the appointment of Edmund Pellegrino to the President's Council on Bioethics. *American Journal of Bioethics* 5 (5): W21.

Beauchamp, T. L., and J. F. Childress. 1994. *Principles of biomedical ethics*, 4th ed. New York: Oxford University Press.

———. 2001. Principles of biomedical ethics, 5th ed. New York: Oxford University Press.

Beecher, H. K. 1959a. Experimentation in man. *Journal of the American Medical Association* 169:461–478.

———. 1959b. *Experimentation in man*. Springfield IL: Thomas Press.

———. 1966. Ethics and clinical research. *New England Journal of Medicine* 274 (24): 1354–1360 (Comments NEJM 275 [14]: 790–791; 275 [15]: 852).

Begley, S. 1997. Little lamb, who made thee? *Newsweek* (March 10): 53–59.

Bellah, R. N. 1967. Civil religion in America. *Daedalus* 96 (1): 1–21.

Bellah, R. N., R. Madsen, and W. M. Sullivan et al. 1985. *Habits of the heart: Individualism and commitment in American life*. Berkeley and Los Angeles: University of California Press.

The Belmont Report: Ethical guidelines for the protection of human subjects of research. 1978. Washington, DC: DHEW Publication (OS) 78–0012. Appendix I, DHEW Publication (OS) 78–0013; Apendix II, DHEW Publication (OS) 78–0014.

Benatar, D. 2006. Bioethics and health and human rights: A critical view. *Journal of Medical Ethics* 32:17–20.

Benatar, S. R. 1998. Global disparities in health and human rights: A critical commentary. *American Journal of Public Health* 88:295–300.

———. 2004. Rationally defensible standards for research in developing countries. Review of R. Macklin, *Double standards in medical research in developing countries*. Cambridge: Cambridge University Press, 2004. *Health and Human Rights* 8 (1):197–203.

———. 2005. Explaining the failure of Roll Back Malaria and 3 by 5. (Unpublished paper.)

Benatar, S. R., and R. C. Fox. 2005. Meeting threats to global health: A call for American leadership. *Perspectives in Biology and Medicine* 49 (3): 344–361.

Berlin, I. 2004. A letter on human nature. *New York Review of Books* (Sept. 23): 26.

Berlinger, N. 2006. "Just act normally": How culture gives birth to policy. Review of R. DeVries, *A pleasing birth: Midwives and maternity care in the Netherlands* [Philadelphia: Temple University Press, 2005]. *The Hastings Center Report* 36 (4): 46–47.

Bevilacqua, A. 1997. Restrict cloning before it goes any further. We are all aware of things that we can do but, for the sake of morality, ought not to do. Cloning is one of them. *Philadelphia Inquirer* (March 3): A07.

Biomedical ethics, culture centre at SIUT. 2004. *Dawn Metropolitan* (Karachi) (Oct. 9): 17, 19.

Blackburn, E. 2005. Thoughts of a former council member. *Perspectives in Biology and Medicine* 48 (Spring): 172–180.

Blackhall, L. J., S. Murphy, G. Frank, et al. 1995. Ethnicity and attitudes toward patient autonomy. *Journal of the American Medical Association* 274 (10) (Sept. 13): 820–825.

Blanchard, S. 2004. Fin de vie: Une loi va permettre de "laisser mourir." *Le Monde* 26 (November): 8.

———. 2006a. Non-lieu général dans l'affaire du tétraplégique Vincent Humbert. *Le Monde* 1 (March): 1, 10.

———. 2006b. Un mari poursuivi pour l'euthanasie de sa femme est acquitté à Angers. *Le Monde* 26 (June): 12.

Blustein, J., and A. R. Fleischman. 2004. Urban bioethics: Adapting bioethics to the urban context. *Academic Medicine* 79 (Dec. 12): 1198–1202.

Bourdieu, P. 2001. Uniting to better dominate. *Items and Issues* (Social Science Research Council) 2 (3–4): 1–6.

Brand-Ballard, J. 2003. Consistency, common morality, and reflective equilibrium. *Kennedy Institute of Ethics Journal* 13 (3): 231–258.

Braun, K. 2005. Not just for experts: The public debate about reprogenetics in Germany. *The Hastings Center Report* 35 (3): 42–49.

Broad, W. 1981. Court affirms: boy clone saga is a hoax. *Science* 213 (July 3): 118–119.

———. 1982. Publisher settles suit, says clone book is a fake. *Science* 216 (Apr. 23): 391.

Brock, D. W. 2000. Broadening the bioethics agenda. *Kennedy Institute of Ethics Journal* 10 (1): 21–38.

———. 2001. Priority to the worst off in health care resource prioritization. In *Health care and social justice*, ed. M. Battin, R. Rhodes, and A. Silvers. New York: Oxford University Press.

Brown, R. G. 1995. Clones, chimeras, and the image of God: Lessons from Barthian bioethics. In *Bioethics and the future of medicine: A Christian appraisal*, ed. J. E. Kilner, N. M. de S. Cameron, and D. L. Schiedermayer, 238–249. Grand Rapids, Mich.: Eerdmans.

Buissonnière, M. 2006. La Mancha, here we come! *La Mancha Gazette* (MSF Internal newsletter) (May): 2–3.

Bush, G. W. 2001. Executive order 13237. Creation of the President's Council on Bioethics. Nov. 28, www.whitehouse.gov/news/releases/2001/11/print/20011128-13html.

Callahan, D. 1973. Bioethics as a discipline. *Hastings Center Studies* 1 (1): 66–73.

———. 1984. Autonomy: A moral good, not a moral obsession. *The Hastings Center Report* 14 (5): 40–42.

———.1990. Religion and the secularization of bioethics. Theology, religious traditions, and bioethics, special supplement. *The Hastings Center Report* 20 (4): 18–20.

———. 1992. When self-determination runs amok. *The Hastings Center Report* 22 (2): 52–55.

———. 1996. Bioethics, our crowd, and ideology. *The Hastings Center Report* 26 (6): 3–4.

———. 1997a. The cloning debate: Engineering life pulls wool over scientists' eyes. *Daily News of Los Angeles* (March 2): V4.

———. 1997b. A step too far: What if parents take reproduction literally? *New York Times* (Feb. 26): 23.

———. 1998. Cloning: Then and now. *Cambridge Quarterly of Healthcare Ethics* 7:141–144.

———. 1999a. The Hastings Center and the early years of bioethics. *Kennedy Institute of Ethics Journal* 9 (1): 53–71.

———. 1999b. The social sciences and the task of bioethics. *Daedalus* 128 (4): 275–294.

———. 2000. Universalism and particularism: Fighting to a draw. *The Hastings Center Report* 30 (1): 37–44.

———. 2001. Dialogue: Reason and repugnance. *Medical Ethics* (newsletter published by Lahey Clinic in collaboration with Dartmouth-Hitchcock Medical Center) (Fall): 6–7.

———. 2003a. Individual good and common good: A communitarian approach to bioethics. *Perspectives in Biology and Medicine* 46 (4): 496–507.

———. 2003b. *What price better health? Hazards of the research imperative.* Los Angeles and Berkeley: University of California Press.

———. 2005. Bioethics and the culture wars. *Cambridge Quarterly of Healthcare Ethics* 4 (4): 424–431.

———. 2006b. Bioethics and ideology. *The Hastings Center Report* 36 (1): 3.

Callahan, D., and C. S. Campbell. 1990. Theology, religious traditions, and bioethics, special supplement. *The Hastings Center Report* 20 (4): S1–S24.

Campbell, C. S. 1997. Religious perspectives on human cloning. In *Cloning Human Beings,* vol. 2. National Bioethics Advisory Commission. Commissioned papers. Rockville, Md.: NBAC.

Campbell, C. S., and J. Woolfrey. 1998. Norms and narratives: Religious reflections on the human cloning controversy. *Journal of Biolaw & Business* 1 (3): 8–20.

Caplan, A. L. 2002. Review of M. L. Tina Stevens, *Bioethics in America: Origins and cultural politics.* Baltimore: Johns Hopkins University Press, 2002. *Isis* 93 (4): 757–758.

———. 2003. Media bungled clone claim coverage. News outlets failed dismally in reporting on Clonaid. Jan. 3, http://www.msnbc.com.

———. 2004a. Is biomedical research too dangerous to pursue? *Science* 303 (Feb. 20): 1142.

———. 2004b. Power failure—how the President's Council on Bioethics lost its credibility and what this means for the future of ethical debate in America and Europe about advances in biomedicine. [English translation provided by Caplan]. *Die Zeit,* May 6.

———. 2005. "Who lost China?" A foreshadowing of today's ideological disputes in bioethics. *The Hastings Center Report* 35 (3): 12–13.

Caplan, A. L., and C. Elliott. 2004. Is it ethical to use enhancement technologies to make us better than well? *PLoS Medicine* 1: (3) December 28: at www.plos-medicine.org.

Capron. A. M. 1997. Inside the beltway again: A sheep of a different feather. *Kennedy Institute of Ethics Journal* 7 (2): 171–179.

———. 1999. What contributions have social science and the law made to the development of policy on bioethics? *Daedalus* 128 (4): 295–325.

Capron. A. M. 2005. The dog in the night-time: Or, the curious relationship of the *Belmont Report* and the President's Commission. In *Belmont revisited: Ethical principles for research with human subjects,* ed. J. F. Childress, E. M. Meslin, and H. T. Shapiro, 29–40. Washington, D.C.: Georgetown University Press.

Carrese, J. A., and L. A. Rhodes. 1955. Western bioethics on the Navajo reservation. *Journal of the American Medical Association* 274 (10): 826–829.

CCNE (Comité Consultatif National d'Éthique pour les Sciences de la Vie et de la Santé). 1991. Avis concernant la proposition de resolution sur l'assistance aux mourants, adoptée le 25 Avril au Parlement européen par la Commission de l'environnement, de la santé publique et de la protection des consommateurs. No. 26, June 24. Paris.

———. 1998. Rapport et recommedations sur le consentement éclairé et information des personnes qui se prêtent à des actes de soin ou de recherche. No. 58, June 24, Paris.

———. 2000. Fin de vie, arrêt de vie, euthanasie No. 63, January 27, Paris.

Center for American Progress. 2005. Is there an ethicist in the House? Challenges for a progressive bioethics. (Unpaginated transcript of October 3 symposium, http://www.americanprogress.org.)

———. 2006. Bioethics and politics: Past, present, and future. Panel 1: The emergence of politicized bioethics; Luncheon discussion: Patricia King; Panel 2: The future of progressive bioethics. (Unpaginated transcript of April 21 symposium, http://www.americanprogress.org.)

Chambers, T. 1998. Retrodiction and the histories of bioethics. *Medical Humanities Review* 12 (1): 9–22.

———. 2000. Centering bioethics. *The Hastings Center Report* 30 (1): 22–29.

Charo, R. A. 1995. "La Pénible Valse Hésitation": Fetal tissue research review and the use of bioethics commissions in France and the United States. In *Society's choices: Social and ethical decision making in biomedicine*, ed. R. E. Bulger, E. M. Bobby, and H. V. Fineberg, 477–500. Washington, D.C.: National Academy Press.

———. 2004. Passing on the right: Conservative bioethics is closer than it appears. *Journal of Law, Medicine & Ethics* 32:307–314.

Chaussoy, F. 2006. Je suis du côté de la vie. *Le Monde* (March 16): 20.

Check, E. 2005. U.S. progressives fight for a voice in bioethics. *Nature* 473 (13 Oct.): 932–933.

Childress, J. F. 1990. The place of autonomy in bioethics. *The Hastings Center Report* 20 (1): 12–17.

———.1994. Principles-oriented bioethics: An analysis and assessment from within. In *A Matter of Principles? Ferment in U.S. Bioethics*, ed. E. R. DuBose, R. Hamel, and L. J. O'Connell, 72–98. Valley Forge, Pa.: Trinity Press International.

———.1999. Religion, morality, and public policy: The controversy about human cloning. In *Notes from a narrow ridge: Religion and bioethics*, ed. D. S. Davis and L. Zoloth, 65–85. Hagerstown, Md.: University Publishing Group.

———. 2003. Human cloning and human dignity: The report of the President's Council on Bioethics. *The Hastings Center Report* 33 (3): 15–18.

———. 2005. Epilogue: Looking back to look forward. In *Belmont revisited: Ethical principles for research with human subjects*, ed. J. F. Childress, E. M. Meslin, and H. T. Shapiro, 244–251. Washington, D.C.: Georgetown University Press.

Childress, J. F., E. M. Meslin, and H. T. Shapiro, eds. 2005. *Belmont revisited: Ethical principles for research with human subjects*. Washington, D.C.: Georgetown University Press.

Chochinov, H. M. 2004. Afterthoughts. *Journal of Palliative Care* 20 (3): 141–142.

Chochinov, H. M., T. Hack, T. Hassard et al. 2004. Dignity and psychotherapeutic considerations in end-of-life care. *Journal of Palliative Care* 20 (3): 134–141.

Choices on our conscience. 1971. IDOC North America. Documents (Nov. 11): 52–56.

Christakis, N. C. 1992. Ethics are local: Engaging cross-cultural variations in ethics for clinical research. *Social Science and Medicine* 35:1079–1091.

Churchill, L. 1994. Rejecting principlism, affirming principles: A philosopher reflects on the ferment in U.S. bioethics. In *A matter of principles? Ferment in U.S. bioethics*, ed. E. R. DuBose, R. Hamel, and L. J. O'Connell, 321–331. Valley Forge, Pa.: Trinity Press International.

————. 2005. Toward a more robust autonomy: Revising the *Belmont Report*. In *Belmont revisited: Ethical principles for research with human subjects*, ed. J. F. Childress, E. M. Meslin, and H. T. Shapiro, 111–124. Washington D.C.: Georgetown University Press.

Cimons, M., and J. Peterson. 1997. "No" to human cloning. Use of federal funds barred. *Denver Post* (March 5: A01.

Clark, David. 2002. *Cicely Saunders—founder of the hospice movement: Selected letters 1959–1999*. Oxford, UK: Oxford University Press.

Clinton bans U.S. funds for human cloning research. Science: He urges private sector to refrain from such experiments, warns of new ethical burdens. The federal agency that provides money doesn't support any projects. 1997 *Los Angeles Times* (Mar. 5) : 1.

Clinton, W. J. 1997a. Letter to H. Shapiro, Feb. 24. In *Cloning Human Beings*, vol. 1. Report and recommendations. Rockville, Md.: National Bioethics Advisory Committee.

————. 1997b. Memorandum for the heads of Executive Departments and Agencies. Subject: Prohibition on federal funding for cloning human beings, March 4.

————. 1997c. President Clinton's apology for the Tuskegee Syphilis Study. Washington, D.C.: The White House, Office of the Press Secretary, May 16.

Clouser, K. D. 1978. Bioethics. In *Encyclopedia of Bioethics*, vol. 1, ed. W. T. Reich, 115–127. New York & London: Free Press.

————. 1993. Bioethics and philosophy. The birth of bioethics, ed. A. R. Jonsen, special supplement. *The Hastings Center Report* 23: (6): S10–S11.

Clouser, K. D., and B. Gert. 1990. A critique of principlism. *Journal of Medicine and Philosophy* 15 (2): 219–236.

Cohen, E. 2006a. Conservative bioethics and the search for wisdom. *The Hastings Center Report* 36 (1): 44–56.

————. 2006b. Life, death and stem cells. In *The Fulbright brainstorms on bioethics—Bioethics: Frontiers and new challenges* ed. P. Z. e Melo, 162–169. Lisbon: Principia.

Cooke, R. 1997. Monkeys too: Cloning creates identical primates helpful in research. *Newsday* (New York) (Mar. 3): A05.

Cooke, R., and T. Maier. 1997. Rules on cloning: Clinton blocks federal support for research on humans: The President's order. *Newsday* (New York) (Mar. 5): A05.

Crigger, B-J. 1996. In search of the good society: The work of Daniel Callahan. Special issue, *The Hastings Center Report* 26 (6): 2.

Curran, W. J. 1970. Governmental regulation of the use of human subjects in medical research: The approaches of two federal agencies. In *Experimentation with Human Subjects*, ed P. A. Freund, 402–454. New York: George Braziller.

Daniels, N. 1986. Why saying no to patients in the United States is so hard: Cost containment, justice, and provider autonomy. *New England Journal of Medicine* 314 (May 22): 1380–1383.

————. 2006. Equity and population health: Toward a broader bioethics agenda. *The Hastings Center Report* 36 (4): 22–35.

Daniels, N., B. Kennedy, and I. Kawachi. 1999. Why justice is good for our health: The social determinants of health inequalities. *Daedalus* 128 (4): 215–251.

Daniels, N., B. Kennedy, and I. Kawachi. 2000. *Is Inequality Bad for Our Health?* Boston: Beacon Press.

Daniels, N., D. W. Light, and R. L. Caplan. 1996. *Benchmarks of fairness for health care reform*. New York: Oxford University Press.

Daniels, N., and J. E. Sabin. 2002. *Setting limits fairly: Can we learn to share medical resources?* New York: Oxford University Press.

Daniels, N., and D. I. Walker. 1985. *Just Health Care*. New York: Cambridge University Press.

Davis, D. S., and L. Zoloth, eds. 1999. *Notes from a narrow ridge: Religion and bioethics.* Hagerstown, Md.: University Publishing Group.

Davis, J. R., R. De Vries, and J. Evans. 2005. The intersection of sociology and bioethics. *Footnotes* (American Sociological Association) (May/June): 21.

De Craemer, W. 1983. A cross-cultural perspective on personhood. *Milbank Memorial Fund Quarterly/Health and Society* 61 (1): 19–34.

De Grazia, D. 2003. Common morality, coherence, and principles of biomedical ethics. *Kennedy Institute of Ethics Journal* 13 (3): 145–160.

A definition of irreversible coma: Report of the ad hoc committee of the Harvard Medical School to examine the definition of brain death. 1968. *Journal of the American Medical Association* 205 (6): 337–340.

Delafortrie, A. 2006. From a monastery to an abbey: MSF, the last of the Mohicans? *La Mancha Gazette* (MSF Internal Newsletter) (May): 7–9.

Delbanco, A. 1999. *The real American dream.* Cambridge: Harvard University Press.

De Tocqueville, A. 1835. 1969 edition, ed. J. P. Mayer, trans. George Lawrence. *Democracy in America.* New York: Harper & Row.

De Vries, R. 2003. How can we help? From "sociology in" to "sociology of" bioethics. *Journal of Law, Medicine & Ethics* 32 (2): 279–292.

———. 2005. *A pleasing birth: Midwives and maternity care in the Netherlands.* Philadelphia: Temple University Press.

De Vries, R., L. Turner, C. Orfali, and C. Bosk. 2006. Social science and bioethics: The way forward. *Sociology of Health & Illness* 28 (6): 665–677.

Dorff, E. 1998. *Matters of life and death: A Jewish approach to modern medical ethics.* Philadelphia: Jewish Publication Society.

Dubose, E. R., R. P. Hamel, and L. J. O'Connell, eds. 1994. *A matter of principles? Ferment in U.S. bioethics.* Valley Forge, Pa.: Trinity Press International.

Duff, N. J. 1997a. Clone with caution: Don't take playing God lightly. *Washington Post* (March 2): C01.

———. 1997b. Playing God? Moral insight ought to accompany science. *Houston Chronicle* (March 9): 1.

Eisenberg, L. 1976. The outcome as cause: Predestination and human cloning. *Journal of Medicine and Philosophy* 1 (4): 318–331.

Elliott, C. 1999. *A philosophical disease: Bioethics, culture, and identity.* New York: Routledge.

———. 2003. *Better than well: American medicine meets the American dream.* New York: Norton.

Emanuel, E. J. 1991. *The ends of human life.* Cambridge, Mass.: Harvard University Press.

Emanuel, E. J., C. Weijer. 2005. Protecting communities in research: From a new principle to rational protections. In *Belmont revisited: Ethical principles for research with human subjects,* ed. J. F. Childress, E. M. Meslin, and H. T. Shapiro, 165–183. Washington, D.C.: Georgetown University Press.

Enda, J., and S. Vedantam. 1997. Clinton asks Congress to ban human cloning. *Houston Chronicle* (June 10): 9.

Engelhardt, H. T. Jr. 1980. Bioethics in the People's Republic of China. *The Hastings Center Report* 10 (2): 7–10.

———. 1986. *The Foundations of Bioethics.* 1st ed (2nd ed. 1996). New York: Oxford University Press.

———. 1999. Bioethics in the third millennium: Some critical anticipations. *Kennedy Institute of Ethics Journal* 9 (3): 225–243.

————. 2006. Global bioethics: An introduction to the collapse of consensus. In *Global bioethics: The collapse of consensus*, ed. H. T. Engelhardt Jr. Salem, Mass.: Scrivener, 1–17.

Enserink, M. 2006. French vote with their Euros. *Science* 314 (5806): 1669.

Evans, J. H. 2002. *Human genetic engineering and the rationalization of public bioethical debate*. Chicago: University of Chicago Press.

————. 2006. Between technology and democratic legitimation: A proposed compromise position for common morality public bioethics. *Journal of Medicine and Philosophy* 31:1–22.

Faden, R. R., A. C. Mastroianni, and J. P. Kahn. 2005. Beyond Belmont: Trust, openness, and the work of the advisory commission on human radiation experiments. In *Belmont revisited: Ethical principles for research with human subjects*, ed. J. F. Childress, E. M. Meslin, and H. T. Shapiro, 41–54. Washington, D.C.: Georgetown University Press.

Farmer, P. 1995. On suffering and structural violence: A view from below. *Daedalus* 125:261–283.

————. 2003. *Pathologies of power: Health, human rights, and the new war on the poor*. Berkeley and Los Angeles: University of California Press.

Farmer, P., and N. Campos. 2004. Rethinking medical ethics: A view from below. *Development of World Bioethics* 4 (1): 17–41.

Fleischer, T. 2002. Review of *Principles of Biomedical Ethics* by T. L. Beauchamp and J. Childress. *Journal of the American Medical Association* 287 (12): 1582–1583.

Fletcher, J. ed., 1954. *Morals and medicine*. Boston: Beacon Press.

————. 1966. *Situation ethics*. Philadelphia: Westminster.

————. 1971. Ethical aspects of genetic controls. *New England Journal of Medicine* 285:776–783.

————. 1974. *Ethics of genetic control: Ending reproductive roulette*. New York: Anchor/Doubleday.

Fox, D. M. 1993. Three views of history: View the second. *The Hastings Center Report* 23 (6): S12–S13.

Fox, R. C. 1957. Training for uncertainty. In *The student-physician*, ed. R. K. Merton, G. Reader, and P. L. Kendall, 207–241. Cambridge, Mass.: Harvard University Press. (Reprinted in Fox, R. C. 1988. *Essays in medical sociology: Journeys into the field*. 2nd ed. New Brunswick, N.J.: Transaction Publishers, 19–50.)

————. 1959. *Experiment perilous: Physicians and patients facing the unknown*. Glencoe, Ill: Free Press (1974, Philadelphia: University of Pennsylvania Press; 1997, Transaction Publishers, with a new epilogue by the author.)

————. 1974. Ethical and existential developments in contemporaneous American medicine: Their implications for culture and society. *Milbank Memorial Quarterly/ Health and Society* 52 (Fall): 445–483.

————. 1976. Advanced medical technology—social and ethical implications. *Annual Review of Sociology* 2:231–268.

————. 1983. American bioethics goes to Washington (with apologies to Mr. Smith). (Unpublished paper, presented at OHPE Retreat Sept. 16; and Wellesley College, Sept. 22.)

————. 1984. "It's the same, but different": A sociological perspective on the case of the Utah artificial heart. In *After Barney Clark: Reflections on the Utah artificial heart program*, ed. M. W. Shaw, 68–90. Austin: University of Texas Press.

————. 1985. Reflections and opportunities in the sociology of medicine. *Journal of Health and Social Behavior* 36 (1) (March): 6–14.

————. 1988. The autopsy: Its place in the attitude-learning of second-year medical students. In *Essays in medical sociology: Journeys into the field*, 2nd ed., 51–77. New Brunswick, N.J.: Transaction.

————. 1989. *The sociology of medicine: A participant observer's view*. Englewood Cliffs, N.J.: Prentice Hall.

————. 1990. The evolution of American bioethics: A sociological perspective. In *Social science perspectives on medical ethics*, ed. G. Weisz, 201–220. Philadelphia: University of Pennsylvania Press.

————. 1994. The entry of U.S. bioethics into the 1990s: A sociological analysis. In *A matter of principles? Ferment in U. S. bioethics*, ed. E. R. DuBose, R. Hamel, and L. J. O'Connell, 21–71. Valley Forge, Pa.: Trinity Press International.

————. 1995. Medical humanitarianism and human rights: Reflections on Doctors Without Borders and Doctors of the World. *Social Science & Medicine* 41 (12): 1607–1626.

————. 1999. Is medical education asking too much of bioethics? Teaching the "nonbiomedical" aspects of medicine: The perennial pattern. *Daedalus* 128 (4): 1–25.

————. 2000. Medical uncertainty revisited. In *The handbook of social studies in health and medicine*, ed. G. L. Albrecht, R. Fitzpatrick, and S. C. Scrimshaw, 409–425. London: Sage.

————. 2003. The transplant surgeon, the sociologist, and the historian: A conversation with Thomas E. Starzl. In *Society and Medicine: Essays in Honor of Renée C. Fox*, ed. C. M. Messikomer, J. P. Swazey, and A. Glicksman, 145–159. New Brunswick, N.J.: Transaction Publishers.

————. 2004. Observations of a perpetual fieldworker. *Annals of Political and Social Science* 595 (September): 309–326.

————. 2005a. Khayelitsha Journal. *Society* 42 (4) (May/June): 70–76.

————. 2005b. What do American bioethics and Médecins Sans Frontières have in common? The relevance of Talcott Parsons's theory of universalism, particularism, and modernity. In *After Parsons: A theory of social action for the twenty-first century*, ed. R. C. Fox, V. M. Lidz, and H. J. Bershady, 289–307. New York: Russell Sage Foundation.

Fox, R. C., and E. Goemaere. 2006. They call it "patient selection" in Khayelitsha: The experience of Médecins Sans Frontières-South Africa in enrolling patients to receive antiretroviral treatment for HIV/AIDS. *Cambridge Quarterly of Healthcare Ethics* 15 (3) (Summer): 302–312.

Fox, R. C., and J. P. Swazey. 1973. Chronicle of a cadaver transplant. *The Hastings Center Report* 3:1–3.

————. 1974. *The courage to fail: A social view of organ transplants and dialysis*. Chicago: University of Chicago Press (2002, 2nd ed. with new introduction by the authors. New Brunswick, NJ: Transaction Publishers).

————. 1982. Critical care at Tianjin's First Central Hospital and the fourth modernization. *Science* 217 (Aug. 20): 700–705.

————. 1984. Medical morality is not bioethics—medical ethics in China and the United States. *Perspectives in Biology and Medicine* 27 (Spring): 336–360.

————. 1992a. Leaving the field. *The Hastings Center Report* 22 (3): 9–15.

————. 1992b. *Spare parts: Organ replacement in American society*. New York: Oxford University Press.

————. 2005. Examining American bioethics: Its problems and prospects. Quo vadis? Mapping the future of bioethics, special section. *Cambridge Quarterly of Health Care Ethics* 14:361–373.

Framing the news: The triggers, frames, and messages in newspaper coverage. 1997. Project for excellence in journalism. Columbia University Graduate School of Journalism.

Francis, L. P., M. P. Battin, J. A. Jacobson, and C. B. Smith. 2006. The patient as victim and vector: The significance of contagious infectious disease for bioethics. *ASBH Exchange* 9 (1): 1, 4–5.

Fredrickson, G. M. 2005. Diverse republics: French and American response to racial pluralism. *Daedalus* 134 (Winter): 88–101.

Freemasonry. 1958. *Encyclopedia Britannica*, vol. 9. Chicago, London, and Toronto: Encyclopedia Britannica.

Freund, P. A., ed. 1970. *Experimentation with Human Subjects.* New York: George Braziller.

Friedman, S., K. Villamil, A. Suriano, and B. Egolf. 1996. Alar and apples: Newspapers, risk, and media responsibility. *Public Understanding of Science* 5 (1): 1–19.

Gallagher, E. B., P. Schlomann, R. B. Sloan, et al. 1998. To enrich bioethics: Add one part social to one part clinical. In *Bioethics and Society: Constructing the Ethical Enterprise*, ed. R. DeVries and J. Subedi, 166–191. Upper Saddle River, N.J.: Prentice Hall.

Gateau, V., O. Soubrane, and A. Fagot-Largeault. 2005. Les aléas du don d'organe entre vivants. *Le Monde* (June 19): 25.

Geertz, C. 1965. The impact of the concept of culture on the conception of man. In *New views of the nature of man*, ed. J. R. Platt, 93–118. Chicago and London: University of Chicago Press (reprinted in C. Geertz, *The Interpretation of Cultures: Selected Essays*. New York: Basic Books, 1973).

———. 1973. *The Interpretation of cultures: Selected essays.* New York: Basic Books.

———. 2000. *Available light: Anthropological reflections on philosophical topics.* Princeton, N.J.: Princeton University Press.

Gellman, M. 1991. On Immanuel Jakobovitz: Bringing the ancient world to the modern world. *Second Opinion* 17 (1): 97–117.

Gellner, E. 1968. *Language and solitude: Wittgenstein, Malinowski and the Hapsburg dilemma.* Cambridge: Cambridge University Press.

Genesis the sequel. Cover Editorial. 1997. *Newsday* (New York) (Mar. 9): G01.

Gert, B., C. M. Culver, and K. D. Clouser. 1997. *Bioethics: A return to fundamentals.* New York: Oxford University Press.

Gillies, R. 2006. From here to the La Mancha Agreement. *La Mancha Gazette* (MSF Internal newsletter) (May): 1–2.

Goodfield, J. 1981. *Reflections on science and the media.* Washington, D.C.: American Association for the Advancement of Science.

Gorovitz, S. 1986. Baiting bioethics. *Ethics* 96 (January): 356–374.

Gorovitz, S., R. Macklin, A. Jameton, J. M. O'Connor, et al., eds. 1976. *Moral problems in medicine.* Englewood Cliffs, N.J.: Prentice Hall. (2nd ed., 1983).

Gracia, D. 2001. History of medical ethics. In *Bioethics in a European perspective*, ed. H. ten Have and B. Gordijn, 17–50. Dordrecht: Kluwer Academic Publishers.

Gray, B. H. 1995. Bioethics commissions: What can we learn from past successes and failures? In *Society's choices: Social and ethical decision making in biomedicine*, ed. R. E. Bulger, E. M. Bobby, and H. V. Fineberg, 261–306. Washington, D.C.: National Academy Press.

Gray, H. T. 1997. Sheep and monkeys, yes…but not us? Ethicists, theologians and clergy urge caution in development of cloning. *Kansas City Star* (Mar. 8): E1.

Gray, J. 2006. The case for decency. Review of I. Berlin, *Political ideas in the Romantic Age: Their rise and influence on modern thought*, ed. H. Hardy. Princeton, N. J.: Princeton University Press. *New York Review of Books*, July 31:20–22.

Groopman, J. 2002. Science fiction. *The New Yorker* (February): 4:23–24.

Gudorf, C. E. 1994. A feminist critique of biomedical principlism. In *A matter of principles? Ferment in U.S. Bioethics*, ed. E. R. DuBose, R. Hamel, and L. J. O'Connell. Valley Forge, Pa.: Trinity Press International.

Gurmankin, A. D., D. Sisti, and A. L. Caplan. 2004. Embryo disposal practices in IVF clinics in the United States. *Politics and the Life Sciences* 22 (2): 2–6.

Gustafson, J. M. 1970. Basic ethical issues in the bio-medical fields. *Soundings* 53:151–180.

———. 1975. *Can ethics be Christian?* Chicago: University of Chicago.

———. 1978. Technology confronts technology and the life sciences. *Commonweal* 105 (June 16): 386–392.

———. 1990. Moral discourse about medicine: A variety of forms. *Journal of Medicine and Philosophy* 15 (2): 125–142.

———. 1991. Ethics: An American growth industry. *Key Reporter* (of Phi Beta Kappa) 56 (Spring): 1–5.

———. 1995. Explaining and valuing: An exchange between theology and the human sciences. *Zygon* 3 (2) (June): 159–175.

———. 1996. *Intersections: Science, theology and ethics*. Cleveland: Pilgrim.

———. 2004. *An examined faith: The grace of self-doubt*. Minneapolis: Fortress.

Guttentag, O. E. 1953. The problem of experimentation on human beings—the physician's point of view. *Science* 117 (Feb. 27): 207–210.

Hall, S. S. 2002. President's Bioethics Council delivers. *Science* 297 (5580): 322–324.

Harris, J. F. 1997. Clinton advocates ban on cloning of humans: Research involving animals, genes would be allowed. *Washington Post* (June 10): A02.

Hastings Center. 2001. *Annual Report*. Garrison, N.Y.: Hastings Center.

Havel, V. 1994. Text of address on receiving the Liberty Medal, July 4, Independence Hall, Philadelphia.

Hearts of the city: Navigating the real world. 1997. *Los Angeles Times* (Feb. 26): 2.

Hebert, H. J. 1995. Radiation victims get an apology. *New Standard*, Oct. 4, http://archive.southcoasttoday.com/daily/10-95-10-04-95/1004radiatio.html.

Hedgecoe, A. M. 2004. Critical bioethics: Beyond the social science critique of applied ethics. *Bioethics* 18 (2): 120–143.

———. 2007. Medical sociology and the redundancy of empirical ethics. In *The principles of health care ethics*, 2nd ed., ed R. E. Ashcroft, A. Dawson, H. Draper, and J. McMillan, 167–175. New York: Wiley.

Heller, J. 1972. Syphilis victims in U.S. study went untreated for 40 years. *New York Times* (July 26): A1, A8.

Herzlich, C. 1995. Professionals, intellectuals, visible practitioners? The case of medical humanitarianism. *Social Science and Medicine* 41 (12): 1617–1619.

Hilts, P. J. 1982. Publisher settles in clone book case. *Washington Post* (Apr. 8): A5.

Hoffmaster, B. 1990. Morality and the social sciences. In *Social Science Perspectives on Medical Ethics*, ed. G. Weisz, 241–260. Dordrecht: Kluwer Academic Publishers.

———. 1992. Can ethnography save the life of medical ethics? *Social Science & Medicine* 35:1421–1436.

Holden, C. 2005. Pellegrino to succeed Kass on U.S. panel. *Science* 309 (5742): 1800.

Holmes, H. B., and L. Purdy, eds. 1992. *Feminist perspectives in medical ethics*. Bloomington: Indiana University Press.

Hopkins, P. D. 1998. Bad copies: How popular media represent cloning as an ethical problem. *The Hastings Center Report* 28 (2): 6–13.

Human cloning and Catholic teaching. 1994. *Medical-Moral Newsletter* 31 (1): 1–2.

Huxley, A. 1932. *Brave new world*. London: Chatto and Winders.

Iglehart, J. K. 1983. Transplantation: The problem of limited resources. *New England Journal of Medicine* 309 (2): 123–128.

Institute of Medicine. 2002. *Unequal treatment: Confronting racial and ethnic disparities in health care*. Washington, D.C.: National Academy Press.

Isambert, F-A. 1980. Éthique et génetique. De l'utopie eugénique au contrôle des malformations congénitales. *Revue Française de Sociologie* 21 (3): 331–354.

Isambert, F-A. 1982. Une sociologie de l'avortement est-elle possible? Numéro spécial sur la Libéralisation de l'avortement. *Revue Française de Sociologie* 23 (3): 359–381.

Isambert, F-A. et al. 1980. L'amniocentèse et les médicins: Le diagnostic prénatale des malformations congénitales. *Cahier no. 1 de l'Equipe de Sociologie Éthique et Pratiques Symboliques*.

Isambert, F-A., and P. Ladrière. 1979. *Contraception et avortement: Dix ans de débat dans la presse (1965–1974)*. Paris: CNRS.

Isambert, F-A, P. Ladrière, and J-P. Terrenoire. 1978. Pour une sociologie de l'éthique. *Revue Française de Sociologie* 19 (3): 323–339.

Jafarey, A. M. 2002. The bioethics group of the Aga Khan University, Karachi. *Issues in Medical Ethics* 10 (1) (January–March): 165–166.

———. 2003. Bioethics at the Aga Khan University. (Unpublished document).

———. 2005. Sixth global forum for bioethics research. *Bioethics Links* 1 (1) (April): 4.

Jafarey, A. M., and A. Farooqui. 2005. Informed consent in the Pakistani milieu: The physician's perspective. *Journal of Medical Ethics* 31:93–96.

Jakobovits, I. 1959. *Jewish Medical Ethics*. New York: Bloch.

Jennings, B. 1990. Ethics and ethnography in neonatal care. In *Social science perspectives on medical ethics*, ed. G. Weisz, 261–271. Dordrecht: Kluwer Academic Publishers.

———. 1998. Autonomy and difference: The travails of liberalism in bioethics. In *Bioethics and society: Constructing the ethical enterprise*, ed. R. DeVries and J. Subedi, 258–269. Upper Saddle River, N.J.: Prentice Hall.

———. 2006. The President's Council calls for prudence. *The Hastings Center Report* 36 (3): 45–46.

Johnson, H. M. 1968. Ideology and the social system. In *The international encyclopedia of the social sciences*, ed. D. L. Sills, 7:76–85. New York: Macmillan and Free Press.

Jonas, H. 1974. *Philosophical essays: From ancient creed to technological man*. Englewood Cliffs, NJ: Prentice Hall.

Jones, J. H. 1981. *Bad blood: The Tuskegee Syphilis Experiment*. New York: Free Press (rev. ed. 1993).

Jonsen, A. R. 1993. The birth of bioethics, special supplement. *The Hastings Center Report* 23 (6): S1–S16.

———. 1994. Foreword. In *A matter of principles? Ferment in U.S. bioethics*, ed. E. R. DuBose, R. Hamel, and L. J. O'Connell, ix–xvii. Valley Forge, Pa.: Trinity Press International.

———. 1996. Bioethics, whose crowd, and what ideology? *The Hastings Center Report* 26 (6): 4–5.

———. 1998. *The birth of bioethics*. New York: Oxford University Press.

———. 2005. On the origins and future of the Belmont Report. In *Belmont revisited: Ethical principles for research with human subjects*, ed. J. F. Childress, E. M. Meslin, and H. T. Shapiro, 1–11. Washington, D.C.: Georgetown University Press.

Jonsen, A. R., and S. Toulmin. 1988. *The abuse of casuistry: A history of moral reasoning.* New York: Oxford University Press.

Jonsen, A. R., R. M. Veatch, and L. B. Walters, eds. 1998. *Source book in bioethics: A documentary history.* Washington, D.C.: Georgetown University Press.

Judt, T. 1992. *Past imperfect: French intellectuals, 1944–1956.* Berkeley and Los Angeles: University of California Press.

Kahn, J. P. 2006. What happens when politics discovers bioethics? *The Hastings Center Report* 36 (3): 10.

Kass, L. R. 1972. Making babies—the new biology and the old morality. *Public Interest* (26) (Winter): 18–56.

———. 1990. Practicing ethics: Where's the action? *The Hastings Center Report* 20 (1): 5–12.

———. 1997. The wisdom of repugnance. *The New Republic* (June 2): 17–26. (Reprinted in L. R. Kass and J. Q. Wilson, *The ethics of human cloning.* Washington, DC: AEI, 1998, 3–59.)

———. 2001. Preventing a brave new world: Why we should ban human cloning now. *The New Republic* (May 21): 30–39.

———. 2004. We don't play politics with science. *Washington Post.* March 3: A27.

———. 2005. Reflections on public bioethics: A view from the trenches. *Kennedy Institute of Ethics Journal* 15 (3) (September): 221–250.

Katz, J. 1972. *Experimentation with human beings.* New York: Russell Sage Foundation.

———. 1984. *The silent world of doctor and patient.* New York: Freeman. (Reissued in 1992 with a new introduction by Alexander Morgan Capron. Baltimore: Johns Hopkins University Press.)

———. 1992. The consent principle of the Nuremberg Code: Its significance then and now. In *The Nazi doctors and the Nuremberg Code: Human rights in human experimentation,* ed. G. J. Annas and M. A. Grodin, 227–239. New York: Oxford University Press.

———. 1993. Ethics and clinical research revisited. *The Hastings Center Report* 23 (5): 31–39.

Katz, J., and A. M. Capron. 1975. *Catastrophic diseases: Who decides what?* New York: Russell Sage Foundation.

Kaye, H. 1998. Anxiety and genetic manipulation: A sociological view. *Perspectives in Biology and Medicine* 41:483–490.

Kendall, P. 1997. Cloning of Scottish lamb sparks debate on ethics. *Pittsburgh Post-Gazette.* Feb. 24: A10.

Kenen, J. 1997. Cloning question now has a human face. *Pittsburgh Post-Gazette.* Feb. 25: A8.

Kennedy, D. 2006. Editorial retraction. *Science* 311 (Jan. 20): 335.

Kerr, K. 1997a. Commission says ban cloning of humans. *Newsday* (New York) (June 8): A43.

———. 1997b. Panel to seek limit on embryo cloning. *Newsday* (New York) (June 5): A17.

Kevles, D. J. 1997. Dialogue. Study cloning, don't ban it. Society finds ways to resolve problems posed by science. *New York Times.* Feb. 26: A23.

King, P. A. 2005. Justice beyond *Belmont.* In *Belmont revisited: Ethical principles for research with human subjects,* ed. J. F. Childress, E. M. Meslin, and H. T. Shapiro, 136–147. Washington, D.C.: Georgetown University Press.

Kloehn, S., and P. Salopek. 1997. Humanity still at heart, soul of cloning issue: Scientists and theologians agree we are our own persons. *Chicago Tribune.* Mar. 2: 1.

Kolata, G. 1997a. Adult mammal cloned in historic breakthrough. *Denver Post*. Feb. 23: A–01.
———. 1997b. An adult mammal is cloned in first. Scottish scientists copy sheep: Humans next? *Pittsburgh Post-Gazette*. Feb. 23: A3.
———. 1997c. Commission on cloning: Ready-made controversy. *New York Times*. June 9: A12.
———. 1997d. Ethics panel recommends a ban on human cloning. *New York Times*. June 8: 22.
———. 1997e. Iconoclastic genius of cloning. *New York Times*. June 3: C1, 7.
———. 1997f. Scientist reports first cloning ever of adult mammal. *New York Times*. Feb. 23: 1.
———. 1997g. With cloning of a sheep, the ethical ground shifts. *New York Times*. Feb. 24: A1, 15.
———. 1998. *Clone: The road to Dolly, and the path ahead*. New York: Morrow.
———. 2003. First mammal clone dies: Dolly made science history. *New York Times* Feb. 15: 15, www.nytimes.com/2003/02/15/science.
Kotulak, R. 1997a. First mammal is cloned: Breakthrough could make it possible to duplicate humans. *Chicago Tribune*. Feb. 23: 1.
———. 1997b. Researchers successfully clone sheep: Creating copies of humans could be possible. *Seattle Times*. Feb. 23: A4.
Krones, T. 2006. The scope of the recent bioethics debate in Germany: Kant, crisis, and no confidence in society. *Cambridge Quarterly of Healthcare Ethics* 15:273–281.
Kübler-Ross, E. 1969. *On death and dying*. New York: Macmillan.
Ladimer, I., and R. W. Newman, eds. 1963. *Clinical investigation in medicine*. Boston: Boston University Law-Medicine Research Institute.
LaFleur, W. R. 2004. Ancestors/ourselves/descendants: Watsuji Tetsur and Hans Jonas on the ethics of human continuity. (Unpublished paper.)
Lammers, S. E. 1996. The marginalization of religious voices in bioethics. In *Religion and medical ethics: Looking back, looking forward*, ed. A. Verhey, 19–43. Grand Rapids, Mich.: Eerdmans.
Lebacqz, K. 2005. We sure are older but are we wiser? In *Belmont revisited: Ethical principles for research with human subjects*, ed. J. F. Childress, E. M. Meslin, and H. T. Shapiro, 99–110. Washington, D.C.: Georgetown University Press.
Lecadre, R. 2005. Quand la maçonnerie s'effondre. *Libération* (Sept. 22): 38–39.
Lederberg, J. 1966. Experimental genetics and human evolution. *The American Naturalist* 100: 519–531.
Lederer, S. E. 1995. *Subjected to science: Human experimentation in America before the Second World War*. Baltimore: Johns Hopkins University Press.
The Legacy of Hans Jonas. 1995. Special issue, *The Hastings Center Report* 25 (7).
Lenoir, N. (with the collaboration of B. Sturlese). 1991. *Une éthique biomédicale à la française*, vol. 1; *Paroles d'éthique*, vol. 2. Paris: La Documentation Française.
Leonetti, M. J. 2004. Respecter la Vie. Accepter la Mort. Rapport Fait au nom de la Mission d'Information sur l'accompagnement de la Fin de Vie. XIIᵉ Legislateur Assemblie Nationale. Documents de'information. Rapport no. 1708. Tome 1, Rapport; Tome 2, Auditions. Paris.
Levin, I. 1976. *The boys from Brazil*. New York: Random House.
Levin, Y. 2003. The paradox of conservative bioethics. *The New Atlantis* 1 (Spring): 53–65.
Levine, R. J. 1986. *The ethics and regulation of clinical research*. 2nd ed. Baltimore, MD: Urban & Schwarzenberg.

————. 2005. The National Commission's ethical principles, with special attention to beneficence. In *Belmont revisited: Ethical principles for research with human subjects*, ed. J. F. Childress, E. M. Meslin, and H. T. Shapiro, 126–135. Washington, D.C.: Georgetown University Press.

Lewontin, R. C. 1997. The confusion over cloning. *New York Review of Books* 44 (16) (Oct. 23): 18–23.

Long, K. R. 1997a. Ban urged on cloning of humans: Concerns about safety dominate discussion by ethics commission. *Cleveland Plain Dealer*, June 1: 1A.

————. Scientists urge care on outlawing cloning. *Cleveland Plain Dealer*, Mar. 6: 1A.

Macer, D. 2003. Geographical issues in IAB membership and board representation. *IAB News* 14 (January): 11–15.

Macklin, R. 1997. Human cloning? Don't just say no. *U.S. News and World Report* (Mar. 10): 64.

————. 1998. Ethical relativism in a multicultural society. *Kennedy Institute of Ethics Journal* 8 (1): 1–22.

————. 1999. *Against relativism: Cultural diversity and the search for ethical universals in medicine*. New York: Oxford University Press.

————. 2003. Dignity is a useless concept. Editorial. *British Medical Journal* 20 (327) (December): 1419–1420.

————. 2004a. *Double Standards in Medical Research in Developing Countries*. Cambridge: Cambridge University Press.

————. 2004b. Reflections on the human dignity symposium: Is dignity a useful concept? *Journal of Palliative Care* [A thematic issue: Dignity and the End of Life] 20 (3): 212–216.

————. 2006. The new conservatives in bioethics: Who are they and what do they seek? *The Hastings Center Report* 36 (1): 34–43.

Mahowald, M. B. 2005. The President's Council on Bioethics, 2002–2004: An overview. *Perspectives in Biology and Medicine* 48: (2) (Spring): 159–171.

Marshall, P. A. 1992. Anthropology and bioethics. *Medical Anthropology Quarterly* 6:49–73.

Marshall, P. A., and B. A. Koenig. 1996. Anthropology and bioethics: Perspectives on culture, medicine, and morality. In *Medical anthropology: Contemporary theory and methods*, 2nd ed. Westport, Conn.: Praeger.

Marshall, P. A., and B.A. Koenig. 2004a. Accounting for culture in a globalized bioethics. *Journal of Law, Medicine & Ethics* 32 (2): 252–256.

Marshall, P. A., and B. A. Koenig. 2004b. Anthropology and bioethics. In *Encyclopedia of Bioethics*, 3rd ed., ed. S. G. Post. New York: Gale Group/Macmillan, 1:215–225.

Martin, W. 1986. *Recent theories of narrative*. Ithaca, N.Y.: Cornell University Press.

Marty, M. E. 1992. Medical ethics and theology: The accounting of the generations. *Second Opinion* 17 (April): 70–82.

————. 1997a. Cloning: The ultimate human-potential movement. Faith: What about the exalted individual? *Los Angeles Times*. Mar 2: 1.

————. 1997b. If humans were cloned…what makes human beings individuals? *Philadelphia Inquirer*. Mar. 8: A09.

————. 1997c. Will our distinctiveness survive? *Newsday* (New York) (Mar. 7): A45.

Mastroianni A. C. and J. P. Kahn, guest editors. 1996. Advisory committee on human radiation experiments. Kennedy Institute of Ethics Journals 6(3) (special issue).

Mattei, J-F, F. Laboire, and S. Novaes. 1995. Dilemmes de la procréation assistée. Rencontre entre un médecin parlementaire et deux sociologues: Jean-Francois Mattei, Françoise Laboire, Simone Novaes. *Nature-Sciences-Société* 3 (3): 236–245.

Matthews, R., and J. Thornton. 1997. The sheep that man made. *Sunday Telegraph* (London) (Feb. 23): 1.

Maugh, T. H. 1997a. After sheep cloning, ethics debate looms: The feat theoretically opens the door to cloning humans, a possibility fraught with moral ambiguities. *Philadelphia Inquirer*, Feb. 24: A01.

———. 1997b. Science file: Brave new world. Last weekend, Scottish researchers announced that they had cloned an adult mammal—Dolly, a 7-month-old ewe. What is cloning? Why did past efforts fail? Can it be done with humans? And what does the success of the procedure portend? *Los Angeles Times*, Feb. 27: 2.1997c.

———. 1997c. Scientists report cloning adult mammal. *Los Angeles Times* Feb. 23: A1.

May, W. F. 2005. The President's Council on Bioethics: My take on some of its deliberations. *Perspectives in Biology and Medicine* 48 (2) (Spring): 229–240.

McCormick, R. A. 1993. Should we clone humans? *Christian Century* 110 (33): 1148–1149.

McElhinney, T. K., and E. D. Pellegrino. 2001. The Institute on Human Values in Medicine: Its role and influence in the conception and evolution of bioethics. *Theoretical Medicine* 22:291–317.

Mckie, R. 1997. Scientists clone adult sheep. *The (London) Observer*: 1.

Medical College of Wisconsin. 2004. The Belmont Report's 25th anniversary symposium & webcast. Milwaukee, May 14.

Meisel, A. 1997. The cloning conundrum. *Pittsburgh Post-Gazette* (Mar. 2): E1.

Mendelsohn, E., J. P. Swazey, and I. Taviss, eds. 1971. *Human aspects of biomedical innovation*. Cambridge, Mass.: Harvard University Press.

Merton, R. K. 1957. Priorities in scientific discovery. *American Sociological Review* 22 (6): 635–659.

Messikomer, C. M, R. C. Fox, and J. P. Swazey. 2001. The presence and influence of religion in American bioethics. *Perspectives in Biology and Medicine* 44 (4): 485–508.

Miles, S. 2002. Does American bioethics have a soul? *Bioethics Examiner* 6 (2): 1, 2, 5.

Miles, S. H. 2004. Medical ethicists, human curiosities, and the new media midway. *American Journal of Bioethics* 4 (3): 39–43.

Minot, J-C. 2000. Hospital ethics committees in Paris. *Cambridge Quarterly of Healthcare Ethics* 9:424–428.

Moazam, F. 2000. Families, patients, and physicians in medical decisionmaking: A Pakistani perspective. *The Hastings Center Report* 30 (6): 28–37.

———. 2004. "Foundational ethical concepts in Islam: The Qur'an, Imam al-Ghazali, and Muslim physicians." Plenary speech, Aga Kahn University Symposium on Clinical Ethics, Oct. 8. (Unpublished manuscript.)

———. 2007. *Bioethics and organ transplantation in a Muslim society: A study in culture, ethnography, and religion.* Bloomington: Indiana University Press.

Moazam, F., and A. Jafarey. 2005. Pakistan and biomedical ethics: Report from a Muslim country. *Cambridge Quarterly of Healthcare Ethics* 14:249–255.

Monmaney, T. 1997. Prospect of human cloning gives birth to volatile issues. Ethics: Twins scoff at notion of creating duplicate personalities, but possibilities are troublesome to many. *Los Angeles Times*. Mar. 2: 1.

Moreno, J. D. 2004. Bioethics and the National Security State. *Journal of Law, Medicine, & Ethics* 32 (2): 198–208.

———. 2005. The end of the great bioethics compromise. *The Hastings Center Report* 35 (1): 14–15.

Moreno, J. D., and S. R. Lederer. 1996. Revisiting the history of cold war research ethics. *Kennedy Institute of Ethics Journal* 6 (3): 223–238.

Morison, R. S. 1984. The biological limits on autonomy. *The Hastings Center Report* 14 (5): 43–49.

Murray, T. H. 1997. Who's afraid of the big bad clone? Parent-child relationship, not appearance, is issue. *Cleveland Plain Dealer*, (Mar. 1): 6E.

National Research Council and Institute of Medicine. Committee on the Biological and Biomedical Applications of Stem Cell Research. 2002. *Stem cells and the future of regenerative medicine*. Washington, DC: National Academy Press.

National Bioethics Advisory Commission. 1997a. *Cloning human beings*. Executive summary. Report and recommendations of the National Bioethics Advisory Commission. Rockville, Md.: NBAC.

———. 1997b. *Cloning human beings*, vols. I and II. Report and recommendations of the National Bioethics Advisory Commission. Rockville, Md.: NBAC.

———. 1999a. *Ethical issues in human stem cell research*. Executive summary. Rockville, Md.: NBAC.

———. 1999b. *Ethical issues in human stem cell research,* vol. I. Report and recommendations of the National Bioethics Advisory Commission. Rockville, Md.: NBAC.

———. 1998. 1996–1997 Annual Report. Rockville, Md.: NBAC.

National Society for Medical Research. 1959. *Report on the national conference on the legal environment of medical science*. Chicago: National Society for Medical Research and University of Chicago.

Nau, J-Y. 1992. Régards sur la legislature bioéthique: Une pénible valse-hésitation. *Le Monde*, March 19.

———. 1993. L'Assemblée Nationale examine trois projets de loi sur la bioéthique: Les gardes-fous de la science. *Le Monde*, November 20.

Neikirk, W. 1997. No U.S. funds for human cloning: Clinton also asks private-sector labs to shelve research. *Chicago Tribune* (Mar. 5): 3.

Nelkin, D. 1984. *Science in the streets*. Background paper. Report of the twentieth century fund task force on the communication of scientific risk. New York: Priority Press.

———. 1987. *Selling science: How the press covers science and technology*. New York: Freeman.

———. 1989. Communicating technological risk: The social construction of risk perception. *Annual Review of Public Health* 10:95–113.

Nelkin, D., and S. Lindee. 1995. *The DNA mystique: The gene as a cultural icon*. New York: Freeman.

———. 1998. Cloning in the popular imagination. *Cambridge Quarterly of Healthcare Ethics* 7:145–149.

Next, really prolific cows: Scientists clone a sheep, but we needn't fret the doomsday scenarios. Editorial. 1997. *Los Angeles Times* (Feb. 25): 6.

NHLI (National Heart and Lung Institute). 1973. The totally implantable artificial heart: Legal, social, ethical, medical, economic, and psychological implications. Report by the Artificial Heart Assessment Panel. DHEW publication no. (NIH) 74–191.

Nodé-Langlois, F. 2004. Fin de vie: Le droit de mourir dans la dignité. *Le Figaro* (Aug. 27): 1, 5.

Norton, C. 1997. Sheep clone raises alarm over humans. London *Sunday Times*, Feb. 23.

Novaes, S. 1992. Éthique et débat publique. Raisons Pratiques 3, Pouvoir et légitimite, 155–176.

Numbers, R. L., and D. W. Amundsen, eds. 1986. *Caring and curing: Health and medicine in the Western religious traditions*. New York: Macmillan.

Nussbaum, M. C. 1996. Patriotism and cosmopolitanism. In *For love of country: Debating the limits of patriotism*, ed. M. C. Nussbaum and J. Cohen, 2–16. Boston: Beacon Press.

O'Neill, O. 2002a. *Autonomy and trust in bioethics*. Cambridge: Cambridge University Press.

———. 2002b. Reason and passion in bioethics. Review of L. Kass *Life, liberty, and the defense of dignity. The challenge for bioethics* [San Francisco: Encounter, 2002]. *Science* 298 (Dec. 20): 2335.

Oransky, I. 2005. First dog cloned. *The Scientist*, Aug. 3, http://www.the-scientist.com/news/20050803/01.

Parsons, T. 1951. *The social system*. Glencoe, Ill.: Free Press.

Pellegrino, E. D. 2006. Bioethics and politics: "Doing ethics" in the public square. (Draft paper, Oct. 2, 2006, to be published in *Journal of Medicine and Philosophy*, based on "Bioethics and politics: Why we must repair the rift," First John Balint Lecture, Alden March Bioethics Institute, Albany, NY, July 13, 2006.)

Pellegrino, E. D., and D. C. Thomasma. 1993. *The virtues in medical practice*. New York: Oxford University Press.

Pennisi E. 1997. Breakthrough of the year: The lamb that roared. A lamb cloned from a single cell of an adult sheep demonstrated the power of cloning technology, surprising both researchers and the public, and igniting a fierce debate about ethics. *Science* 278 (5346): 2038–2039.

Pharo, P. 2004. *Morale et Sociologie: Le Sens et les Valeurs Entre Nature et Culture*. Paris: Galliard.

Potter, V. R. 1970. Bioethics: The science of survival. *Perspectives in biology and medicine* 14:120–153.

———. 1971. *Bioethics: Bridge to the future*. Englewood Cliffs, N.J.: Prentice Hall.

President's Advisory Committee on Human Radiation Experiments. 1996. *The human radiation experiments*. Final report of the President's Advisory Committee. New York: Oxford University Press.

President's Commission for the Study of Ethical Problems in Medicine and Biomedical and Behavioral Research. 1983. *Deciding to forego life-sustaining treatment*. Washington, D.C.: U.S. Government Printing Office.

———. 1983. *Securing access to health care: The ethical implications of differences in the availability of services* (vol. 1, Report; vol. 2, Appendices: Sociocultural and philosophical studies; vol. 3, Appendices: Empirical, legal, and conceptual studies). Washington, D.C.: U.S. Government Printing Office.

President's Council on Bioethics. 2002. *Human cloning and human dignity: An ethical inquiry*. Washington, D.C.

———. 2003a. *Being human: Readings from the President's Council on Bioethics*. Washington, D.C.

———. 2003b. *Beyond therapy: Biotechnology and the pursuit of happiness*. Washington, D.C.

President's Council on Bioethics. 2004a. *Monitoring stem cell research*. Washington, D.C.

———. 2004b. *Reproduction and responsibility: The regulation of new biotechnologies*. Washington, D.C.

———. 2005a. *Taking care: Ethical caregiving in our aging society*. Washington, D.C.

———. 2005b. Taking stock: looking back, looking ahead. September 9 meeting, session 5. (Unpaginated transcript, http://www.bioethics.gov.)

Proctor, R. N. 2000. Nazi science and Nazi medical ethics: Some myths and misconceptions. *Perspectives in Biology and Medicine* 43 (3): 335–346.

The quest for justice and community in health care: A quarter century of bioethics. 1994. *The Hastings Center Report* (25th anniversary issue) 24 (3): 5–41.

Quinn, J. 1997. Scientists pledge: No production line cloning. *Press Association Limited* (Pennsylvania News, Feb. 23).

Ramsey, P. 1970a. *Fabricated man: The ethics of genetic control.* New Haven, Conn.: Yale University Press.

———. 1970b. *The patient as person.* New Haven, Conn.: Yale University Press.

Recer, P. 1997a. Panel: Ban human cloning. But commission says laws should allow research using human cells. *Pittsburgh Post-Gazette* (June 8): A16.

———. 1997b. Panel wants ban on human cloning. *Cleveland Plain Dealer* (June 9): 4A.

Reich, W. T., editor-in-chief. 1978. *Encyclopedia of Bioethics* (2nd ed. 1995). New York and London: Free Press and Collier Macmillan.

———. 1993. How bioethics got its name. *The Hastings Center Report* 23 (6): S6–S7.

———. 1995. The word "bioethics": Its birth and the legacies of those who shaped it. *Kennedy Institute of Ethics Journal* 5 (1): 19–34.

———. 1996. Revisiting the launching of the Kennedy Institute: Re-visioning the origins of bioethics. *Kennedy Institute of Ethics Journal* 6 (4): 323–327.

———. 1999. The "wider view": André Hellegers' passionate, integrating intellect and the creation of bioethics. *Kennedy Institute of Ethics Journal* 9 (1): 25–51.

Reinhardt, U. 2004. Health care in the service of science? *Science* 303 (Mar. 12): 1613–1614.

Reuters. 1997. Scientists produce clone of adult animal: The procedure was a first. *Philadelphia Inquirer* (Feb. 23): A2.

Reverby, S. M., ed. 2000. *Tuskegee's Truths: Rethinking the Tuskegee Syphilis Study.* Chapel Hill: University of North Carolina Press.

Ribadeneira, D. 1997. Reconciling "Dolly" and divinity. *Boston Globe* (Mar. 6): A10.

Richardson, H. S. 1990. Specifying norms as a way to resolve concrete ethical problems. *Philosophy and Public Affairs* 19:279–310

———. 2005. Specifying, balancing, and interpreting bioethical principles. In *Belmont Revisited: Ethical principles for research with human subjects*, ed. J. F. Childress, E. M. Meslin, and H. T. Shapiro, 205–227. Washington, D.C.: Georgetown University Press.

Ritter, M. (and Associated Press). 1997. Researchers clone adult mammal: Lamb named Dolly was born in July. *Cleveland Plain Dealer* (Feb. 24): 1A.

Rodgers-Melnick, A. 1997. Cloning a difficult issue for churches. *Pittsburgh Post-Gazette* (Mar. 1): A1.

Rorvik, D. 1978. *In his image: The cloning of a man.* Philadelphia: Lippincott.

Rosenfeld, A. 1969. *The second Genesis: The coming control of life.* Englewood Cliffs, N.J.: Prentice Hall.

Ross, E. 2003. Cloning pioneer Dolly the sheep put to death due to progressive lung disease. Associated Press. *Bangor Daily News* (Feb. 15): A1.

Ross, S. 1997. Clinton bars human clone funds: No federal money now involved; Let's keep it that way. *Pittsburgh Post-Gazette* (Mar. 5): A3.

Rothman, D. J. 1987. Ethics and human experimentation: Henry Beecher revisited. *New England Journal of Medicine* 317 (19): 1195–1199.

———. 1991. *Strangers at the bedside: A history of how law and bioethics transformed medicine decision making.* New York: Basic Books.

Rothman, D. J., and S. M. Rothman. 1984. *The Willowbrook wars: Bringing the mentally disabled into the community.* New York: Harper & Row.

Ruse, M., and A. Sheppard, eds. 2000. *Cloning: Responsible science or technomadness?* Amherst, N.Y.: Prometheus.

Russo, E. 2002. Advice fit for a president. *The Scientist* 16 (4) (Feb. 18): 22.

Sabéran, H. 2006. Affaire Humbert: Le non-lieu ravit le médecin, désole la mere. *Libération*, February 28: 14.

Safire, W. 2002. The crimson birthmark. Opinion. *New York Times*, Jan. 21, http://www.nytimes.com/2002/01.21/opinion21SAFI.html.

Savage, D. G. 1997. 3- to 5-year ban on any human cloning is urged. *Los Angeles Times* (June 8): 1.

Sciolino, E. 2005. After a fall in popularity, Chirac shifts cabinet posts. *New York Times*, June 3: A10.

Seelye, K. Q. 1997. Clinton bans federal money for efforts to clone humans. *New York Times*, Mar. 5): A13.

Selgelid, M. J. 2005. Ethics and infectious disease. *Bioethics* 19 (3): 272–289.

Send in the clones. 1997. *Scottish Sunday Mail*, Feb. 23.

Sengupta, S. 2005. Colonel Sanders finds himself under fiery siege in Pakistan. *New York Times*, June 8: A1, 4.

Seoul National University 2006. Investigation Committee Report, Jan. 10. (A summary of the Final Report on Professor Wook Suk Hwang's Research Allegations was published in *New York Times*, Jan. 9, 2006, http://www.nytimes.com/2006/01/09/science/text-clonereport).

Shapiro, H. T. 1999. Ethical considerations and public policy—a ninety day exercise in practical and professional ethics: Cloning human beings. *Science and Engineering Ethics* 5 (1): 3–16.

Shapiro, H. T., and E. Meslin. 2005. Relating to history: The influence of the National Commission and its *Belmont Report* on The National Bioethics Advisory Commission. In *Belmont Revisited: Ethical principles for research with human subjects*, ed. J. F. Childress, E. M. Meslin, and H. T. Shapiro, 55–75. Washington, D.C.: Georgetown University Press.

Shaw, M. W., ed. 1984. *After Barney Clark: Reflections on the Utah artificial heart program*. Austin: University of Texas Press.

Sheep cloning. CNN Evening News for Feb. 27, 1997. Vanderbilt University Television News Archive.

Sherwin, S. 1992. *No longer patient: Feminist ethics and health care*. Philadelphia: Temple University Press.

———. 2005. *Belmont* revisited through a feminist lens. In *Belmont revisited: Ethical principles for research with human subjects*, ed. J. F. Childress, E. M. Meslin, and H. T. Shapiro, 148–164. Washington, D.C.: Georgetown University Press.

Shils, E. 1968. The concept and function of ideology. In *The international encyclopedia of the social sciences*, ed. D. L. Sills, 7:66–76. New York: Macmillan and Free Press.

Sicard, D. 2006. *L'alibi Éthique*. Paris: Plon.

Silver, L. M. 1997. *Remaking Eden: Cloning and beyond in a brave new world*. New York: Avon.

Singer, M. 1955. The cultural pattern of Indian civilization. *Far Eastern Quarterly* 15:23–26.

Smelser, N. J. 2003. Sociology: Spanning two centuries. *The American Sociologist* 34 (3): 5–19.

Smith, C. S. 2005. France lets terminally ill refuse care, but still bans euthanasia. *New York Times* (Apr. 14): A13.

Smith, D. H. 1996. Religion and the roots of the bioethics movement. In *Religion and medical ethics: Looking back, looking forward*, ed. A. Verhey, 9–18. Grand Rapids, Mich.: Eerdmans.

Smith, W. J. 2000. Is bioethics ethical? *Weekly Standard* 5 (28): 26–30.

————. 2001. *Culture of death: The assault on medical ethics in America*. San Francisco: Press.

Solomon, D. 2006. Domestic disarray and imperial ambitions: Contemporary applied ethics and the prospect for global bioethics. In *Global bioethics: The collapse of consensus*, ed. H. T. Engelhardt Jr., 335–361. Salem, Mass: Scrivener.

Spotts, P. 1997. Anatomy of a decision: Ethics panel's wooly work. *Christian Science Monitor* (June 13): 4.

Spotts, P., and R. Marquand. 1997. A lamb ignites a debate on the ethics of cloning. *Christian Science Monitor* (Feb. 26): 3.

Steinfels, P. 1997. When it comes to cloning, for some, any hint of a limit on scientific inquiry is an affront akin to blasphemy. Where and when can lines be drawn? *New York Times*, Mar. 8, 29.

————. 2004. Voters say values matter, but it's important to find out what reality is behind this convenient catchall. *New York Times*, Nov. 6, A15.

Stevens, M. L. T. 2000. *Bioethics in America: Origins and cultural politics*. Baltimore: Johns Hopkins University Press.

Stevens, M. L. T., and R. Baker. 2002. Correspondence. *Journal of the History of Medicine and Allied Health* 57:345–348.

Successful cloning raises unsettling ethical issues. 1997. *Saint Louis Post-Dispatch*, Feb. 25, 1A.

Sugarman, J., and D. P. Sulmasy. 2001. *Methods in medical ethics*. Washington, D.C.: Georgetown University Press.

Swazey, J. P. 1975. Forging a neuroscience community: A brief history of the Neurosciences Research Program. In *The neurosciences: Paths of discovery*, ed. F. G. Worden, J. P. Swazey, and G. Adelman, 529–546. Cambridge, Mass.: MIT Press.

————. 1978. Protecting the "animal of necessity": Limits to inquiry in clinical investigation. *Daedalus* 107 (2): 129–145.

————. 1993. But was it bioethics? *The Hastings Center Report* 23 (6): S5–S6.

Taylor, G. 1968. *The biological time bomb*. Cleveland: World.

ten Have, H. 1994. Principlism: A Western European appraisal. In *A matter of principles? Ferment in U.S. bioethics*, ed. E. R. DuBose, R. Hamel, and L. J. O'Connell, 101–120. Valley Forge, Pa.: Trinity Press International.

ten Have, H., and B. Gordijn, eds. 2001. *Bioethics in a European perspective*. Dordrecht: Kluwer Academic Publishers.

Thomas, L. 1974. The technology of medicine. In *The lives of a snail: Notes of a biology watcher*, 31–36. New York: Viking.

————. 1979. *The Medusa and the snail: More notes of a biology watcher*. New York: Viking.

Toulmin, S. 1982. How medicine saved the life of ethics. *Perspectives in Biology and Medicine* 25 (4): 736–750.

Turner, L. 1997. The media and the ethics of cloning. *Chronicle of Higher Education* (Sept. 26): B4–B5.

————. 2003. Zones of consensus and zones of conflict: Questioning the "common morality" presumption in bioethics. *Kennedy Institute of Ethics Journal* 13 (3): 193–218.

Tuskegee University. News coverage of the presidential apology, http://www.tuskegee.edu/Global/story.asp?S=1211608 (downloaded April 15, 2006).

Twenty years after: The legacy of the Tuskegee Syphilis Study, special section. 1992. *The Hastings Center Report* 22 (6).

Tye, L. 1997. Mass. scientists aim to match cloning feat: Medical, ethical questions posed. *Boston Globe*, Feb. 25, A1.

UNESCO. Division of Cultural Policies and Intercultural Dialogue. 2002. *UNESCO universal declaration on cultural diversity: A vision, a conceptual platform, a pool of ideas for implementation, a new paradigm.* Cultural Diversity Series no. 1, http://unesdoc.unesco.org/images/0012/001271/127162e.pdf.

United Press International (UPI). 1997. Researchers clone lamb from adult sheep. Feb. 23.

U.S. Congress. Office of Technology Assessment. 1993. Biomedical ethics in U.S. public policy—background paper. OTA–BP–BBS–105. Washington, D.C.: U.S. Government Printing Office.

U.S. DHEW. Office of the Secretary. 1979. Protection of human subjects. Notice of report for public comment. Belmont Report: Ethical principles and guidelines for the protection of human subjects of biomedical and behavioral research. *Federal Register*, part4 (April) 18:23192–23197.

U.S. DHEW. Public Health Service. 1973. Final report of the Tuskegee Syphilis Study, ad hoc advisory panel. Atlanta: U.S. Centers for Disease Control.

U.S. Senate Subcommittee on Government Research. Committee on Government Operations. 1968. Hearings on S. J. Resolution 145, 90th Congress, 2nd Session, March 8–9, 21–22, 27–28, April 2.

U.S. Senate Subcommittee on Health. Committee on Labor and Public Welfare. 1973. Quality of health care—human experimentation. Washington, D.C.: U.S. Government Printing Office.

Vaux, K. 1970. *Who Shall Live?* Philadelphia: Fortress.

Veatch, R. M. 1976. *Death, dying, and the biological revolution.* New Haven, Conn.: Yale University Press.

———. 1981. *A theory of medical ethics.* New York: Basic Books.

———. 1984. Autonomy's temporary triumph. *The Hastings Center Report* 14 (5): 38–40.

———. 1993. From forgoing life support to aid-in-dying. *The Hastings Center Report* 23 (6): S7–S8.

———. 2002. The birth of bioethics: Autobiographical reflections of a patient person. *Cambridge Quarterly of Healthcare Ethics* 11:344–352.

———. 2003. Is there a common morality? *Kennedy Institute of Ethics Journal* 13 (3): 189–192.

———. 2005. Ranking, balancing, or simultaneity: Resolving conflicts among the Belmont principles. In *Belmont revisited: Ethical principles for research with human subjects*, ed. J. F. Childress, E. M. Meslin, and H. T. Shapiro, 184–204. Washington, D.C.: Georgetown University Press.

Veatch, R. M., and W. Gaylin. 1972. Teaching medical ethics: An experimental program. *Journal of Medical Education* 47 (10): 779–785.

Veatch, R. M., W. Gaylin, and C. Morgan, eds. 1973. *The teaching of medical ethics.* Hastings-on-Hudson, N.Y.: Institute of Society, Ethics and Life Sciences.

Vedantam, S. 1997a. Big question—should humans be cloned? *Houston Chronicle*, Feb. 24, 6.

———. 1997b. Experts suggest ban on human-cloning. *Seattle Times*, June 2, A4.

———. 1997c. A few rise to support the cloning of humans. *Seattle Times*, Mar. 10, A1.

———. 1997d. Maybe Solomon himself could be cloned: Theologians join scientists in a widening and difficult debate. *Philadelphia Inquirer*, Mar. 16, E03.

———. 1997e. Theologians diverge on human cloning. Catholics and Protestants said it was wrong. Jewish and Islamic scholars saw a use for infertile couples. *Philadelphia Inquirer*, March 15, A04.

———. 1997f. To clone or not to clone? Theologians offer diverse opinions to panel. *Houston Chronicle*, Mar. 15, 8.

Vergano, D. 2005. Bioethics hits a crossroads: Critics of president's council hope for more "practical" focus. *USA Today*, Sept. 29, 1D–2D.

Verhey, A. D. 1994. Cloning: Revisiting an old debate. *Kennedy Institute of Ethics Journal* 4 (3): 227–234.

Verhey, A., ed. 1996. *Religion and medical ethics: Looking back, looking forward*. Grand Rapids, Mich.: Eerdmans.

Verhey, A., and S. E. Lammers, eds. 1993. *Theological voices in medical ethics*. Grand Rapids, Mich.: Eerdmans.

Vogel, G. 2005. Korean team speeds up creation of cloned human stem cells. *Science* 308 (May 20): 1096–1097.

Vogel, L. 2006. Natural law Judaism? The genesis of bioethics in Hans Jonas, Leo Strauss, and Leon Kass. *The Hastings Center Report* 36 (3): 32–44.

Vovelle, M. 1980. The rediscovery of death since 1960. The social meaning of death, ed. R. C. Fox, special issue. *Annals of the American Academy of Political and Social Science* 447 (January): 89–99.

Wainwright, S. P., C. Williams, A. Cribb, et al. 2006. Ethical boundary-work in the stem cell laboratory. The view from here: Bioethics and the social sciences, ed. R. de Vries et al., special issue. *Sociology of Heath and Illness* 28:732–748.

Wainwright, S. P., C. Williams, M. Michael, et al. 2006. From bench to bedside? Biomedical scientists' expectations of stem cell science as a future therapy for diabetes. *Social Science & Medicine* 63:2052–2064.

———. 2007. Remaking the body? Scientists' genetic discourses and practices as examples of changing expectations on embryonic stem cell therapy for diabetes. *New Genetics & Society* (in press).

Walter, J. K., and E. P. Klein, eds. 2003. *The story of bioethics: From seminal works to contemporary explorations*. Washington, D.C.: Georgetown University Press.

Walters, L. 1985. Religion and the renaissance of medical ethics in the United States: 1965–1975. In *Theology and bioethics: Exploring the foundations and frontiers*, ed. E. E. Shep, 3–16. Dordrecht/Boston: Reidel.

Walters, L., T. J. Kahn, and D. M. Goldstein, eds. 2005. *Bibliography of Bioethics*, vol. 31. Washington, D.C.: Kennedy Institute of Ethics, Georgetown University.

Watson, J. D. 1971. The future of asexual reproduction. *Intellectual Digest* (October): 69–74.

———. 1973. Children from the laboratory. *Prism* 1 (2): 10–11 ff.

Weiss, R. 1997. Panel backs some human clone work: Board would ban implanting embryos. *Washington Post*, June 4, A01.

———. 2005a. Bioethics council head to step down. *Washington Post*, Sept. 29, A06.

———. 2005b. Stem cell advance is fully refuted. *Washington Post*, Dec. 30, A01.

———. 2006. U.S. stem cell researcher rebuked. *Washington Post*, Feb. 11, A08.

Whitcomb, M. E. 2004. Urban health: An important issue for academic health centers. *Academic Medicine* 79 (12) (December): 1129.

The White House. 2001. President discusses stem cell research. The Bush ranch. Crawford, Texas. Office of the Press Secretary, Aug 9, www.whitehouse.gov/news/releases/2001/08/print/20010809-2.html.

The White House. 2002. President names members of Bioethics Council. Statement by Press Secretary, January 16, www.whitehouse.gov/news/releases/2002/20020116-9.html.

Whong-Barr, M. 2003. Clinical ethics teaching in Britain: A history of the London Medical Group. *New Review of Bioethics* 1 (1): 73–84.

Wildes, K. 2006. Global and particular bioethics. In *Global bioethics: The collapse of consensus*, ed. H. T. Engelhardt Jr., 362–379. Salem, Mass.: Scrivener.

Wilkie, T., and E. Graham. 1998. Power without responsibility: Media portrayals of Dolly and science. *Cambridge Quarterly of Healthcare Ethics* 7:150–159.

Wilmut, I., A. E. Schnieke, J. McWhir, et al. 1997. Viable offspring derived from fetal and adult mammalian cells. *Nature* 385:810–813.

Winsten, J. A. 1985. Science and the media: The boundaries of truth. *Health Affairs* 4 (1): 5–23.

Wohn, Y. 2006. Seoul National University dismisses Hwang. *Science* 311 (Mar. 24): 1695.

Wolf, S. M. 1998. Facing assisted suicide and euthanasia in children and adolescents. In *Regulating how we die: The ethical, medical, and legal issues surrounding physician-assisted suicide*, ed. L. L. Emanuel. Cambridge: Harvard University Press.

Index

APR 2009

R 724 .F62 2008

Fox, Renée C.
Observing bioethics /

Middlesex County College
Library
Edison, NJ 08818